Footprint

Costa Rica

The travel guide

Handbook

Peter Hutchison

*"On the trail of discovery followed by all the
long line of our predecessors in the forests
and on the cerros of Costa Rica, can we truly
believe that man is so foolish as to completely
destroy this special world?"*

L.D. Gómez and J.M.Savage, *Searchers on that
Rich Coast: Costa Rican field biology 1400-1980*
from *Costa Rican Natural History* (ed. Daniel H
Janzen)

Costa Rica Handbook
First edition
© Footprint Handbooks Ltd 2001

Published by Footprint Handbooks
6 Riverside Court
Lower Bristol Road
Bath BA2 3DZ. England
T +44 (0)1225 469141
F +44 (0)1225 469461
Email discover@footprintbooks.com
Web www.footprintbooks.com

ISBN 1 903471 06 0
CIP DATA: A catalogue record for this
book is available from the British Library

Distributed in the USA by
Publishers Group West

Credits

Series editors
Patrick Dawson and Rachel Fielding

Editorial
Editor: Sarah Thorowgood
Maps: Sarah Sorensen

Production
Typesetting: Emma Bryers, Leona Bailey,
Davina Rungasamy and Jo Morgan
Maps: Robert Lunn, Claire Benison and
Angus Dawson
Colour maps: Kevin Feeney

Cover: Camilla Ford

Design
Mytton Williams

Photography
Front cover: gettyone Stone
Back cover: Image Bank
Inside colour section: Getty Images,
Robert Harding Picture Library, South
American Pictures, Jeff Booth.

Print
Manufactured in Italy by LEGOPRINT

Every effort has been made to ensure
that the facts in this Handbook are
accurate. However, travellers should still
obtain advice from consulates, airlines
etc about current travel and visa
requirements before travelling. The
authors and publishers cannot accept
responsibility for any loss, injury or
inconvenience however caused.

Costa Rica

Caribbean Sea

NICARAGUA

PANAMA

Pacific Ocean

PUERTO LIMON

LIMON

Tortuguero

Siquirres

CARTAGO

CARTAGO

HEREDIA

HEREDIA

SAN JOSE

SAN JOSE

Puerto Viejo
de Sarapiquí

Cordillera Central

Punta
Caliente

Cordillera de Talamanca

San Isidro
de El General

Dominical

Parrita

Quepos

Jacó

Paso Real

Palmar
Norte

Rincón

Golfito

Puerto
Jiménez

Península de Osa

*Península
de Burica*

PUNTARENAS

PUNTARENAS

ALAJUELA

ALAJUELA

Tanque

Fortuna

Cordillera de Tilarán

Esparza

Cóbano

PUNTARENAS

Golfo de Nicoya

Isla Chira

Península Nicoya

Tilarán

Cañas

Laguna de Arenal

Los Chiles

Upala

Guayabo

La Cruz

Lago de Nicaragua

Cordillera de Guanacaste

GUANACASTE

LIBERIA

Nicoya

Salinas

Tamarindo

N

0 km   20
0 miles 20

Contents

1

3   **A foot in the door**
11 **Wildlife**

2

17 **Essentials**
19 Planning your trip
29 Before you travel
32 Money
33 Getting there
39 Touching down
43 Where to stay
46 Getting around
52 Keeping in touch
54 Food and drink
55 Shopping
57 Holidays and festivals
58 Special interest travel
69 Responsible travel
71 Health
80 Further reading

3

83   **San José**
86   Ins and outs
90   History
92   Sights
100 Essentials
134 Escazú and Western
        suburbs

4

139 **Central highlands**
143 Alajuela
155 Heredia
165 Cartago
173 Turrialba

5

179 **The northern region**
182 The Puerto Viejo Loop
189 San José to Fortuna

190 Fortuna
197 Fortuna to Tilarán
203 North of Fortuna
206 Reserva Biológica
        Bosque Nuboso
        Monteverde and
        Santa Elena

6

219 **Guanacaste**
223 Cañas
227 Liberia
237 La Cruz
239 Peñas Blancas and the
        border with Nicaragua

7

241 **The Nicoya Peninsula**
245 Northern beaches
249 Northwestern beaches
        and inland
262 Western beaches
269 Southern peninsula

8

277 **Central Pacific**
280 Puntarenas
289 Jacó
295 Quepos
300 Manuel Antonio

9

315 **The southern region**
318 Southern Pan-American
        Highway
322 San Isidro de El General
326 San Gerardo de Rivas
327 Parque Nacional Chirripó
331 Palmar Norte and Palmar
        Sur
333 Ciudad Neily
335 Valle de Coto Brus

10

339 **Golfito and the Osa
        Peninsula**
347 Puerto Jiménez
352 Parque Nacional
        Corcovado
354 Golfito
358 Beaches north of Golfito
359 South of Golfito

11

363 **Caribbean lowlands**
366 Highway 32 to Puerto
        Limón
370 Puerto Limón
375 North Caribbean
376 Parque Nacional
        Tortuguero
385 South Caribbean

12

401 **Background**
403 History
413 Government and the
        modern country
417 Culture
420 Land and environment
423 Wildlife of Costa Rica

13

443 **Footnotes**
445 Basic Spanish
448 Index
452 Shorts
453 Map Index
453 Advertisers
457 Colour maps

Inside front cover
Hotel and restaurant price guide
Exchange rates
Dialling codes

Inside back cover
Map symbols

A foot in the door

Below and right: "If you don't change direction you'll end up where you're heading" – this bus stops at Cartago, which will take you to the pilrimage site of the Basílica de Nuestra Señora de Los Angeles (below).

Above: harmless dust plumes by day, red hot lava by night – Volcán Arenal.
Right: oxen cart – getting there is half the fun.

Highlights

You've got to hand it to Columbus – he had a talent for being ahead of the game. While the rest of Europe was struggling to accept a world that was no longer flat, Columbus had disembarked from his fourth voyage down Central America's eastern coast, explored a little and declared this new and abundantly blessed land to be *costa rica* – a rich coast. While you can rely on a mariner to be aquatically biased, *tierra rica* would never have worked – Columbus got it right.

Natural worlds collide

Costa Rica's rise to the status of natural goldmine occurred long before Columbus's arrival. The Central American isthmus became a hotbed of natural activity as the continents of North and South America collided some five million years ago. Huge pressures forced mountains upwards, the friction of grinding continental plates creating volcanoes and earthquakes, while rain-laden winds of the Caribbean and Pacific soaked the ever-changing landscape. Such dramatic changes demanded an impressive response – the gauntlet was thrown down and nature rose to the challenge.

Packing it in

The richness that is Costa Rica today, the wealth that inspired Columbus is the outcome of millions of years of life, death and dynamic evolution. Diversity in Costa Rica truly boggles the mind. With just 0.03% of the planet's surface area, the country manages to play host to 6% of the earth's species. Costa Rica – almost half the size of the state of Kentucky or slightly larger than the Netherlands – has 870 species of birds. Birds and mammals in the USA total 996. Making allowances for size, inch for inch, mile for mile, Costa Rica knocks spots off countries like Colombia, Brazil and Indonesia, all renowned for their wildlife. In short, here you will travel far less to see much more.

Peace prevails

The *Tico* way of life stands in stark contrast to the harsh realities of the natural world. Personally, publicly and internationally neutral, the Costa Rican version of road rage has two drivers stuck at a junction gesturing madly, "after you!" By fortune or disinterest, Costa Ricans have never really got the hang of conflict. As far back as the 1930s some commentator blessed with ironic wit named Costa Rica the 'Switzerland of Central America', a title which this most democratic of Central American nations wears proudly on its sleeve.

Too big a choice?

But despite being the smallest Central American nation, having access to both the Caribbean and the Pacific, means there is almost too much to see and nature documentaries the world over flaunt the beauty of this most spectacular of destinations. You can visit lush tropical rainforest and still be relaxing in the comfort of your hotel by sunset. You can carefully explore volcanic slopes that smoke, bubble, hiss and explode. Drift through inland waterways of the northern lowlands and enjoy the simple excitement of not knowing what may happen round the next meander.

...or not enough time?

With so much on offer, it's tempting to pack it in. But life is too short to rush around trying to fit everything in. Pick a few salient spots, a few magic morsels and leave enough time at the end to relax on at least one of the country's spectacular beaches. As any Costa Rican will tell you, life should be untainted, life should be relaxed, life should be *pura vida*.

Tierra Rica

So Columbus only saw the coast's riches, but there's no reason why shouldn't adventure further inland. In stark contrast to the rest of the country, San José, although rarely charming, is at the very heart of the central highlands. And it's just a short trip from impressive volcanic peaks, national parks swathed in rainforest and lovingly maintained botanical gardens and waterfall paths.

On to new heights More explosive in impact are the volcanic peaks of the Central, Tilarán and Guanacaste mountain ranges which divide the Caribbean and Pacific. This spine has half a dozen active volcanoes including one of Central America's most active, Arenal, which spews a constant flow of lava. More genteel activity at Rincón de la Vieja and Tenorio National Parks create mud baths and thermal pools to wallow in. The Talamancas, the country's highest mountain range, mark the continental divide south of San José. Mountain streams carve steep-sided valleys, each with a slightly varied ecology profile, providing dramatic scenery stretching from the ominously named Cerro de la Muerte (Hill of Death) south to the distant border with Panama.

Jungle joy If you're looking for the twisted lianas and vines of rainforest, with the occasional forest giant towering above a dense canopy of green, head for the Osa Peninsula – the most southerly appendage of Costa Rica's Pacific coast. One of the most cut-off parts of the country, the isolation has preserved the rich diversity of the rainforest in Corcovado National Park. Whether setting out on a challenging trek through the park, skirting the edges travelling along the coast or just enjoying the comforts of one of the many nearby lodges you cannot fail to be impressed by a rainforest teems with life, bombarding the senses on all sides with shades of green and cacophonous noise.

Beach life The Nicoya Peninsula to the north is a more serene delight. Rainfall levels drop considerably and the skies are cloudless from December to April. Beautiful beaches hide in quiet secluded coves, separated by rocky outcrops and fringed by jauntily angled palms rustling in the coastal breeze. There are quiet deserted spots for peaceful relaxation, or smaller resorts with a bit more life. The Central Pacific coast ups the pace marginally with the laid-back hang-out of Jacó and the unmistakable beauty and golden sand beaches of Manuel Antonio National Park.

Keep it natural In the far northwest, Guanacaste has the largest remaining area of dry forest in Central America. Protected as a UNESCO Natural World Heritage Site, the region has seen a steady shift away from its cultural heritage, based on ranching, towards conservation. Over 25% of Costa Rica is now protected in national parks, wildlife reserves or land of some other legally protected status. Few countries would, or even could, hand over such a large area to conservation but in Costa Rica it's an economic asset as well as a natural one. Contrary to widespread belief, it's not an easy option to take – more a tribute to a small but expanding band of passionate individuals and organizations.

Caribbean charms The Caribbean coastline marks a big change with its undeveloped comforts along beaches to the south. The coastal waterways of the north around Tortuguero are a teasing mix of natural wonder and hopeful expectation. If you're lucky, you may see a huge leatherback turtle lumber out of the ocean to lay soft-skinned leathery eggs in their sandy nests. On a good day you may catch the looping flight of a toucan, or the vivid luminescence of a morpho butterfly. If you're quiet and patient, you will see all manner of natural magical wonders.

Left: organized industry – a coffee plantation in the central highlands.

Above: Paquera on the Guanacaste coast, quiet, calm and peaceful…
Left: mysterious, magical, secretive cloudforest.

8

Right: life on the river channels of the rainforest in the northern lowlands.
Left: the calming and surreal crater of Volcán Poás.

Above: canopy tours on a rope bridge or why not try a zip wire both great ways of getting above the rainforest floor and pretending to be a bird.
Right: run the whitewater on Orosí river.

Natural born thrillers

The bottom line is that few people can truly relax on a beach, doze in a hammock, or chill out at the poolside for long. You have to do something. Costa Rica, at the cutting edge of natural diversity, has taken the world of activity to heart. In a fine display of mimicry, equally diverse activities and adventure have taken root. And before you say "not me", think, "why not?".

Wildlife watching

Low-key it may be, but sooner or later, every visitor to Costa Rica will get involved – maybe even hooked on wildlife watching. Birdlife is colourful for the generalist and hypnotic for the specialist. We all have a list of must-sees and wanna-sees. You won't forget your first sighting of a keel-billed toucan, with a beak looking like the palette of some frantic artist or the brief crimson flash of the resplendent quetzal's breast. The looks from a capuchin monkey, as curious about you as you are about it. Whatever your passion – whether it creeps, walks, swims or flies – you'll find it and probably see it in Costa Rica. Whether monkeys or motmots, jacanas or jaguars, turtles or tapirs, sloths or sharks, work out what you're looking for and take it from there.

Up & away

Why do so many birds flock to Costa Rica? Maybe it's to see the views. You can easily join them by attaching yourself to a taught steel cable, stretched out between a couple of trees, and whizz through the tree tops from forest giant to tree platform on a canopy tour, waving at the passing birds as you go. Too fast? Then take the pedestrian route of canopy tour over sturdy suspension bridges strung out across the rainforest. Still too energetic? Relax in the comfort of an aerial tram that moves you slowly and silently through the forest canopy or drift through the Central Valley in a hot air balloon, the ultimate in up-there relaxation. But for real speed, bungee jump off a bridge – although you're unlikely to see much wildlife.

These feet were made for walking

Trekkers and hikers will love Costa Rica. There are plenty of short hikes around the national parks, with trails lasting from 30 minutes, to several hours. But for the longer treks, head through the rainforest of Corcovado National Park, top-out on Cerro Chirripó Costa Rica's highest peak at 3820 m, or take on the gruelling trans-Talamanca challenge – 10 days, coast to coast, no frills.

Water water everywhere

With all these mountains and so much rainfall, rivers throw up a challenge. Whitewater rafting is always exhilarating … in Costa Rica it's spectacular. Between adrenaline pumping rapids, green carpeted valleys and dramatic canyons create images like the Garden of Eden. From the river-bank, the odd bit of wildlife indulges in some people watching. ("Mad homo sapiens".) Just as you're settling into the view, there's another stretch of boulders to navigate. Splash – oops, got it wrong! On coastal waters, you can ride tidal surf in kayaks. The balletically gifted can hop (or clamber) on surf boards to ride an *Endless Summer* of tubes and surges that line the coast. If wind is your preference, world class gales blow across Lake Arenal and the north Pacific shore. Above water – for you at least – pick up a rod and enjoy a spot of sports fishing. And under the surface, scuba divers can mingle with manta rays and sharks in a world of aquatic wonders.

Wheeling around

The freedom to explore is never better than with your own set of wheels. Renting a jeep is the most comfortable way to go, with a fine selection of unplanned adventures around every corner. Mountain biking has gripped Costa Rica, whether just touring for the day, or taking on an adventurous coast-to-coast challenge. Motorized tours are possible on Harley Davisons and of course there are quad-bikes for the truly insane.

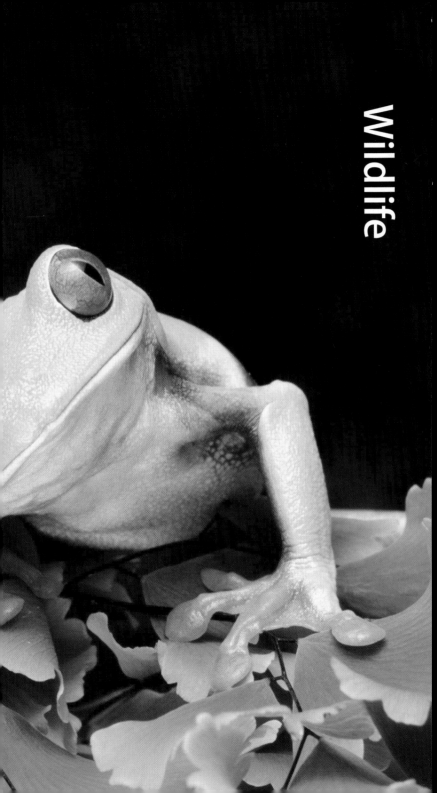

wildlife

Reptiles

Previous page: Costa Rica's natural, national emblem – a red-eyed tree frog (Agalychnis callidryas).
Right: the fairly easily seen spectacled caiman (Caiman crocodiles).
Below: a strawberry poison dart frog (Dendrobates pumilio) – a bitter and unadvisable taste experience.

Above: hypnotically alluring – an eyelash viper (Bothriechis schlegelii).
Right: a green turtle hatchling (Chelonia mydas) make a bid for freedom.

Mammals

Left: *Capuchin monkeys (Cebus capucinus) relaxing in a tree.*
Below: *the elusive and endangered jaguar (panthera onca).*

Above: *the unually nocturnal and therefore rarely spotted, Hoffman's two-toed sloth (Choloepus hoffmanni).*
Left: *The ocelot (F. Pardalis) is one of the smaller cats found in the Costa Rica.*

Birds

Right: the largest of the vultures found in Costa Rica – the King Vulture (Sarcoramphus papa).
Below: a courting magnificent frigatebird (Fregata magnificens) – these birds have spectacular aerial manoeuvrability.

Above: a turkey vulture (Cathartes aura) dries condensation from its wings in the morning sun.
Right: green-crowned brilliant hummingbird (Heliodoxa jacula), one of 50 species found in Costa Rica alone.

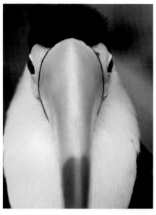

Clockwise from top left: *the wonderful colours of the Keel-Billed Toucan (*Ramphastos sulfuratus), *the ungainly Brown Pelican (*Pelecanus occidentalis)*, the Resplendent Quetzal (*Pharomachrus mocinno) *and a solitary roosting Scarlet Macaw (*Ara macao).

Next page: *Monteverde Cloud Forest Reserve – come in, enjoy and explore.*

Essentials

2

Essentials

19 Planning your trip

29 Before you travel

32 Money

33 Getting there

39 Touching down

43 Where to stay

46 Getting around

52 Keeping in touch

54 Food and drink

55 Shopping

57 Holidays and festivals

58 Special interest travel

69 Responsible travel

71 Health

80 Further reading

Planning your trip

Where to go

Choosing where to go in Costa Rica is tantamount to being a child in a huge sweet shop – the choice is daunting and you want to do it all...immediately. Once reality has beckoned, your precious vacation needs to be planned – not rigidly, but al least realistically. The longer you have the better, but even with just a few days, you can visit a couple of spots and still have time to relax on a beach before heading home.

Just one starting point: there are no 'must-sees' in Costa Rica that are universally appealing, although there are several front runners. Have a rough idea what you like – quiet natural settings or places with a few activities, secluded beaches, or lively resorts – and what sort of places you like to stay in. Below are a few suggested itineraries.

Most people arrive in **San José**, the capital, where you can spend a couple of days sightseeing. It's really the only place in the country with significant cultural attractions, so if you like museums, art galleries and cerebral fodder beyond the totally natural you should stop for a couple of days. Beyond the capital, the Central Highlands are a tidy mosaic of coffee plantations, and volcanic hills dotted with towns normally close to a national park. Typical **day trips from the capital** take in the craft town of Sarchí with a steady climb to the huge crater of Volcán Poás. A tour of the scenic Orosi valley, is easily followed by a steady climb to the steaming vents of Volcán Irazú. Or ride a ski lift through the rainforest canopy in Parque Nacional Braulio Carrillo, just 90 minutes from the capital.

North of San José, **Volcán Arenal** leaves onlookers trance-like as the glowing lava crashes down the mountainside. Nearby the world-famous cloudforests around **Monteverde** provide a brief insight to the magnificent diversity of the highlands.

Guanacaste to the northeast draws visitors to the volcanic landscape and bubbling mudpots of **Rincón de la Vieja**, the birder's wetland paradise of **Palo Verde** and the **Tempisque** river basin, the dry forests of **Santa Rosa** and the cultural landscape of the *sabanero* – Costa Rica's very own cowboy.

Beach lovers and **surfers** can pick almost any spot from the Nicoya Peninsula down to the Central Pacific coastline to find a personally tailored version of paradise with lively resorts and quiet hideaways covering all budgets and tastes.

Southern Costa Rica is generally a tougher option. Travelling overland down the mountainous spine of the country, **Chirripó Grande** is the country's highest peak and a challenge for the trekker, and to the south on the Osa Peninsula, the pristine **Parque Nacional Corcovado** is a moment of magic for the adventurer and wildlife lover.

The **Caribbean** divides neatly in two halves. North of Puerto Limón, the canals of **Tortuguero** provide a quiet moment of awe struck contemplation encountering the wildlife and vegetation of this aquatic inland waterworld, while on the coast turtles nest on the beaches as they have for millions of years. South of **Limón** – the carnival capital of Costa Rica – the discerning traveller can find a blend of comfortable, laid-back retreats offering personal service, sometimes at a price, and quiet undeveloped beaches – perfect for the budget traveller.

Getting a cross-section of Costa Rica in 10 days could be tough. Space it out, and it **10 days** could be ideal. After a day in **San José** or a nearby town of the Central Valley, it's a short trip north to **Fortuna** taking in the craft capital of **Sarchí**, and the topiary creations of **Zarcero** en route. A couple of days in Fortuna allows plenty of time to see the **Arenal** volcano and the nearby waterfall, and still have time for a day trip north to the wetlands of **Caño Negro Wildlife Reserve** close to the Nicaraguan border, before

Essentials

 **Top 10 national parks (according to international visitors)**

1 Parque Nacional Volcán Poás, scenery, volcano viewing
2 Parque Nacional Manuel Antonio, short hikes, wildlife viewing, beaches
3 Parque Nacional Volcán Irazú, scenery, volcano viewing
4 Parque Nacional Carara, short to medium length hikes, wildlife viewing
5 Parque Nacional Corcovado, short to long hikes, wildlife viewing
6 Parque Nacional Santa Rosa, short to long hikes, wildlife viewing

7 Parque Nacional Rincón de la Vieja, short to long hikes, wildlife viewing, volcanic features, activities
8 Parque Nacional Tortuguero, wildlife viewing, short hikes
9 Parque Nacional Isla del Caño, short hikes, diving
10 Parque Nacional Marino las Baulas de Guanacaste, wildlife viewing
NB A visit to Arenal volcano does not involve entering the park. If it did, Arenal would probably be in the top four.

---

heading round Lake Arenal to **Santa Elena** for a couple of days exploring the delights of the cloudforest in the **Monteverde** area.

Heading further north you could have a few days' adventure at one of the lodges close to **Rincón de la Vieja** hiking through the national park, or simply taking it easy.

With just a few days left, head out to the **Nicoya Peninsula** to a beach that takes your fancy. **Tamarindo** is a lively spot, **Sámara** and **Nosara** are quieter but pricier options. Get some genuine rest and relaxation with the odd locally organized excursion before heading home (a journey of about 40 minutes by plane or half-a-day overland.

10 active days Many options in Costa Rica have been packaged to create two, three or four day trips. By mixing and matching, you create the tailor-made trip that goes at the pace you want. Try two or three days **whitewater rafting** on the Pacuare or Reventazón rivers near Turrialba, take a flight down to Palmar Sur or Puerto Jiménez for a bit of **trekking** through Parque Nacional Corcovado before heading to Drake for some relaxing **diving**.

Two weeks A couple of weeks would allow you to tag on a trip to Parque Nacional **Tortuguero** on the Caribbean to the above itinerary.

Alternatively after visiting Arenal and Monteverde, you could head out to Parque Nacional Tortuguero before turning south to relax on the quieter beaches and at one of the secluded homely lodges.

Two weeks is long enough to consider doing a fly-drive option. Take the first week to acclimatize yourself to Costa Rica, seeing a couple of places that you can't reach in a private vehicle, and then head out on your own to explore a region with the pleasures of going left, right, straight on or backwards whenever you please.

Three weeks You are now moving into the realms of really being able to explore. After a brief foray through the **Central Valley** exploring the delights of the region, heading out to Arenal and Monteverde, take a slow journey south down the **Pan-American Highway** through **San Isidro de El General**. Hikers can stop off for a few days to knock off **Chirripó**, while others can explore the quieter options of this forgotten region. Continue south through the scenic **Coto Brus** valley to **San Vito** and finally to **Golfito**, where you can step out to explore the coast or tramp through the rainforest of **Parque Nacional Corcovado**.

Awe struck and amazed, head up the coastal road slowly taking in **Dominical**, **Jacó** or **Manuel Antonio** – depending on whether you like deserted, busy or hectic – for a bit of beach before heading back to San José.

When to go

If your trip is about beaches, clear blue skies and bare flesh go to the **north and central Pacific coast** between December and April – the high season. This clear and well defined season is based on a marked dry season in the Central Highlands and the Pacific regions where almost no rain falls from mid-December to April. Outside these months rains fall steadily, and is heaviest in September and October.

If you have special interests to pursue, see 'Special interest travel' on page 58 and take advice before travelling

On the **Caribbean** slope – everywhere east of the continental divide – rains fall more consistently throughout the year with the drier months being February to June, with a small summer (*veranillo*) in September and October.

Outside the high season, rainfall normally occurs in bursts lasting a couple of hours and travel is possible in the vast majority of places. This rainy season has been renamed the green season by some marketing wag at the Costa Rican Tourism Institute with good effect. The green season is an increasingly popular time to visit as the country tends to be quieter and discounts are often possible. A word of warning – some places do close for a break or remodelling and a few – very few – become inaccessible in normal green season conditions. Check before travelling.

How to go

Costa Rica has been seen as an exotic Central American destination for over a decade now. The options for visitors are genuinely as wide and varied as tourists come. At the top of the price bracket it is possible to fly in a chartered helicopter from exclusive hotel to exclusive jungle lodge, enjoying fantastic views, personalized service and what would certainly be a rare insight into a wonderful country. It is also equally possible to travel on a tight budget, using public transport – where there is a road there is normally a bus. Clearly this option leaves you to the vagaries of bus timetables, but there is an undoubted charm in travelling the way the vast majority of *Ticos* do. Whichever option you choose, Costa Rica is perfect for the independently minded traveller. You decide what you want to do and where you want to do it – and then sort it out.

Tours and tour operators

Costa Rica is sufficiently developed for tour operators to be able to provide complete packages, or just to sort out a couple of time-crucial events while you're in the country. If there is something you simply have to do, or somewhere you just have to stay, it is worth trying to make arrangements in advance.

See page 69 for information on eco-tourism and operators

Abercrombie & Kent, 1520 Kensington Road, Oak Brook, Illinois, 60523-2141, T1-800-323-7308, F630-954-3324, www.abercrombiekent.com Luxury tours based on nature, adventure or family vacations. *Costa Rica Experts*, 3166 N. Lincoln Avenue, Suite 424, Chicago, IL 60657, T1-800-827-9046, or T773-935-1009, F773-935-9252, www.costaricaexperts.com Endless variety for a bespoke holiday or one off-the-shelf. Very good prices without skimping on quality. *GAP Adventures*, 760 North Bedford Road. #246, Bedford Hills, New York, 10507, toll free on 1-800-692-5495, T914-666-4417, F914-666-4839, www.gap.ca Good tours at good prices. *Elderhostel*, 11 Avenue de Lafayette, Boston, MA 02111-1746, toll free on T1-877-426-8056, or F1-877-426-2166, from outside the US and Canada call T1-978-323-4141 or F1-617-426-0701, www.elderhostel.org Trips for the over 55s with gentle and useful pursuits like 'An Introduction to Birdwatching'. *Holbrook Travel*, 3540 NW 13th Street, Gainesville, FL 32609, toll free on 1-800-451-7111 or T352-377-7111, F352-371-3710, www.holbrooktravel.com Everything from a specialist nature tour to full-on adventure, also owners of the Selva Verde Lodge near Puerto Viejo de Sarapiquí. *Martinez*

Tour operators in North America

Essentials

Essentials

Associates, T1-800 327 6162, www.ladatco.com *Mila Tours*, T1-800 249 2111, www.milatours.com *Sunny Land Tours*, 166 Main Street Hackensack, NJ. 07601, toll free on 1-800-783-7839, T201-487-2150, F201-487-1546, www.sunnylandtours.com Build your own bespoke tour from start to finish or just pick a couple of trips from their itineraries. *Tara Tours*, 6595 NW 36th Street, Suite 306, Miami, Florida 33166, toll free on 1-800-327-0080, T305-871-1246, www.taratours.com One week trips. *Tico Travel*, toll free on T1-800-493- 8426, www.ticotravel.com Very cheap flights (US$280 Miami–San José return in the green season), and good deals on surf and fishing trips. *Wildland Adventures*, 3516 NE 155th Street, Seattle, WA, 98155, toll free on T1-800-345-4453, T206-365-0686, F206-363-6615, www.wildland.com Soft adventure trips, some family friendly, to Costa Rica.

Tour operators in the UK & Ireland

Condor Journeys and Adventures, 1 Valley Rise, Mill Bank, Sowerby Bridge HX6 3EG, T01422-822068, www.condorjourneys-adventures.com *Exodus Travels*, T020-8772 3822, sales@exodus.co.uk *Journey Latin America*, 12-13 Heathfield Terrace, Chiswick, London, W4 4JE, T020-8747-8315, F020-8742-1312, www.journeylatinamerica. co.uk Providing the best deal on flights from London with bespoke and adventure tours available. *Last Frontiers*, Fleet Marston Farm, Aylesbury, Buckinghamshire HP18 0QT, T01296-658650, www.lastfrontiers.co.uk *South American Experience*, 47 Causton Street, Pimlico, London, SW1P 4AT, T020-7976-5511, F020-7976-6908, www. southamericanexperience.co.uk Flights, pick'n'mix bespoke tour options and a couple of tours. *Reef & Rain Forest Tours*, T01803-866965, www.reefrainforest. co.uk *Sunvil Discovery*, Sunvil House, Upper Square, Old Isleworth, Middlesex, TW7 7BJ, T020-8758-4774, F020-8758-4711, www.sunvil.co.uk Fully supported trips for a week and 10 days, and fortnight or longer fly-drive options. *Trips Worldwide*, 9 Byron Place, Clifton, Bristol, BS8 1JT, T0117-311-4400, F0117-311-4401, www.tripsworldwide.co.uk Tailor-made trips to Costa Rica with over 10 years' experience.

Tour operators in Europe

France *Images du Monde*, 14 rue Lahire, 75013 Paris, T01-4424-8788, F01-4586-2773, www.imagenes- tropicales.com Flights and tailor-made trips to Costa Rica, with an agency in San José to ensure good support.

Germany *Die Reisegalerie*, Myliusstr 48, 60323 Frankfurt, T069-9720-6000, F069-9720-6002, www.reisegalerie.com Trips to Costa Rica or just the flight with LTU if you want to go alone. *MD-Tours*, Rathausstrasse 9, D-72810 Gomaringen, T070-7292-0270, F070-7292-0271, www.mdtours.net Specializing in individual flights and tours to Costa Rica – from 2 to a maximum of 8 people.

Holland *Thika Travel*, T03-624-2526, F03-624-2525, www.thika.nl Providing flights through Martinair and working with *Ecole Travel* in San José.

Switzerland *Kundert Travel*, Fähnlibrunnenstrasse 3, 8700 Küsnacht, Zurich, T01-910-9969, F01-910-5585, www.kundertravel.ch Will make arrangements or organize flights. *Helvetic Tours*, Neuengasse 26, 3001 Berne, T031-329-4242, F031-329-4272, www.helvetictours.ch Good for the last minute and the tour market.

The Adventure Travel Company can organize trips to Costa Rica and has a branch in Australia at PO Box 174, South Melbourne, VIC 3205, Australia, T1-800-238-368 or T03-9696-8400, F03-9696-8600, www.adventure-travel.com.au and in New Zealand at PO Box 2477, 60 Oxford Terrace, Christchurch, T03-379-7134, F03-379-9016, jillg@hot.co.nz The Costa Rica Tourist Board Japanese website is at www.costarica.co.jp

Tours & information in Australia, New Zealand & Japan

Flights can be booked through *STA* at one of 10 branches including Cape Town, 31 Riebeek Street, Cape Town, T021-418-6570, www.statravel.co.za

Flights from South Africa

Finding out more

The efficient and nationally important **Costa Rican Tourism Institute (Instituto Costarricense de Turismo or ICT)** has several offices in the US and Europe. There are various ways of getting in touch, the easiest is at www.tourism-costarica.com Alternatively you can contact them on T223-1733, F223-5452 or toll free from the US and Canada on T1-800-343-6332 or you can write to PO Box 777-1000, San José, Costa Rica, Central America.

Comprehensive sources of information can be found in libraries and in your national press. The country is a popular destination and articles are fairly common.

If you want more streetwise information look up the weekly English-language newspaper The *Tico Times* – they have an internet site at www.ticotimes.net You can also arrange a subscription, from US$34 for six months in the US, Apdo 4632, San José, Costa Rica, T258-1558, F233-6378, or in the US c/o The *Tico Times*-SJO 717, 1601 NW 97th Ave Unit C-101, PO Box 025216, Miami, Fl. 33102-5216.

Also look out for the bimonthly *Costa Rica Outdoors*, with good information on outdoor activities. T1-800-308-3394, in Costa Rica on T282-6260, or www.costaricaoutdoors.com

General maps of the country are available on arrival. Several companies provide very good maps of the country. *International Travel Maps*, published by ITMB in Canada (www.itmb.com), produce an excellent 1:500,000 travel map which is widely available in stores throughout the country, and internationally in good book stores.

Maps

The *Instituto Geográfico*, at the Ministry of Public Works and Transport (MOPT) in San José, sells good 1:50,000 topographical maps. See San José, page 117.

SINAC (Sistema Nacional de Areas de Conservación, Apdo 10104-1000, San José, Costa Rica, T234-0973, F283-7343, www.sinac.go.cr) administer the national park system. For information, write in advance or contact *Fundación de Parques Nacionales*, 300 m north and 150 m east of Santa Teresita Church, C 23, Av 15, Barrio Escalante, San José, T257-2239, F222-4732, open 0800-1200 and 1300-1700, Mon-Fri. In reality you can pay to enter most parks at entrance stations. *InBio Parques*, T244-4730, F244-4790, www.inbio.ac.cr, is also a good resource for national park information (see page 159).

National parks

Essentials

Language

Spanish is the official language. If you want to learn Spanish, there are **schools** in San José (see pages 60 and 132), up in the mountains of Monteverde and at several Pacific beach locations. A grasp of the basics will help greatly in showing willing to communicate even if you can't quite get the finer details sorted out. **English** is spoken well in many of the popular resorts and destinations, as well as the main services – vehicle hire, hotels and tour operators – that the visitor would normally encounter. In Limón a **creole** dialect derived from English is spoken, which is just about understandable to English speakers after a couple of beers. Several thousand also speak **Chinese** as a first language. Indigenous languages are still spoken with **Bribrí** and **Cabecar** in the southern Caribbean being the most widespread.

Women travellers

For the vast majority of women visiting Costa Rica is trouble-free and enjoyable. The status of women in society is classic post-feminist – for those seeking a professional career, education and opportunity is widely available. Certain sections of society acknowledge the desire to take gender out of business relations but don't be fooled. Across the country as a whole, the reality is that the domain of the woman is still that of wife and mother at home – even if the woman does go out to work.

As in any country, women, especially those travelling alone, should exercise a degree of caution. In general, Costa Rica is much safer (in terms of violent crime against women) than the USA or Europe, and rape and muggings are uncommon. However, there have been some well publicized incidents in which female tourists have been attacked and even killed, and you should exercise the normal caution you would anywhere in the world.

Women will be judged by the clothes they wear, and while skimpy tops and short shorts are acceptable around beach areas, you should be aware that white women attract more attention than a *Tica* in the same clothes. Regardless of where you are, you should always wear a bra. In towns and cities, you should avoid short skirts and shorts, and try to dress more as the locals do: you will notice they dress more formally away from home. You should bear in mind that machismo is a strong element in Costa Rican culture, and you should expect to be hissed or whistled at when you pass men. In general, these appreciative responses to your presence are best ignored – simply walk on and try not to let it bother you. If you are being seriously pestered, simply say, *"no me moleste por favor"*, or more strongly, *"dejéme en paz."*

You can greatly reduce the risk of getting into dangerous situations by avoiding getting drunk when you are out by yourself or with a group of girls, and by bearing in mind that most people who invite you for a stroll on the beach are not motivated by a desire to practice their English.

Student travellers

An *International Student Identity Card* (ISIC) is very useful in Costa Rica. You get discounts on entry to museums, cinemas, events and at some hotels. It's normally only a couple of dollars, but it adds up over a few weeks. You can obtain an ISIC from your college or university at home. Student status also entitles you to very good discounts on flights. The best student travel agent is *OTEC*, C 3, Av 1-3, T256-0633, www.otec.co.cr with stupendous discounts (up to 50%) off flights for students, teachers and others who can convince staff that you are in education. Almost enough to make you change career! The student discount agent *USIT* has an office out in Los Yoses on Paseo Ruben Dario (Av Central) on the corner with C 35. T280-5182, F225-9325, www.usitworld.com

Gay and lesbian travellers

A vibrant and lively gay scene exists in San José and various places throughout Costa Rica. Attitudes to gay and lesbian people fits in with the non-confrontational approach to life in general – live and let live. However, that said, public displays of affection should be avoided in the street – best left to the bars, clubs and meeting places that entertain the pink dollar. Information on the internet is available at *www.gaycostarica.com*

As a first point of contact in San José the *Joluva Guesthouse* is a gay-friendly hotel which will share information on the vibrant gay scene in San José and throughout the country. Several publications including *Gayness* (T280-4832, F253-7625, www.gaynesscr.com), *Gente 10* (T258-4561, F258-4025, www.1en10.com) and *Homogenio* have listings of hotels, restaurants, bars, clubs and events in the gay circuit. *Triángulo Rosa* and the *Rainbow Group* are both involved in raising awareness of HIV and other issues.

Disabled travellers

It would be fair to say that Costa Rica is opening up – rather – than open to the disabled traveller. Some hotels and restaurants have gone out of their way to include ramps, lifts and bathrooms for guests in wheelchairs and some popular sights are easily accessible. For the hearing and visually impaired, there is no reason to expect problems or difficulties if you can provide guidance as to any special requirements.

Vaya con Silla de Ruedas (*Go with Wheelchairs*) is a specialist organization that works primarily to provide day tours for passengers on cruise ships, but can also plan other trips, T391-5045, F454-2810, www.gowithwheelchairs.com *FAUNA* (*Fundacion para el Acceso Universal a la Naturaleza*, PO Box 217-8000, San Isidro de El General, Perez Zeledon, T/F771-7482, chabote@racsa.co.cr) helps organize trips for the physically disabled, providing information and evaluating services, as well as training for tourist industry workers and organizing accessible tours to Costa Rica.

Travelling with children

Food can be a problem if the children are not adaptable. It is easier to take biscuits, drinks, bread, etc with you on longer trips than to rely on meal stops where the food may not be to taste. Avocados are safe, easy to eat and nutritious; they can be fed to babies as young as six months and most older children like them. A small immersion heater and jug for making hot drinks is invaluable, but remember that electric current varies. Try and get a dual-voltage one (110v and 220v).

For health matters, see page 71

Remember that a lot of time can be spent waiting for public transport, so make sure you pack that favourite toy. Nothing beats a GameBoy, unless it's two GameBoys and a link cable. Also take reading material with you as it is difficult, and expensive, to find

Fares On long-distance buses children generally pay half or reduced fares. For shorter trips it is cheaper, if less comfortable, to seat small children on your knee. Often there are spare seats which children can occupy after tickets have been collected. In city and local excursion buses, small children do not generally pay a fare, but are not entitled to a seat when paying customers are standing. On sightseeing tours you should always bargain for a family rate – often children can go free. Note that a child travelling free on a long excursion is not always covered by the operator's travel insurance; it is advisable to pay a small premium to arrange cover.

All airlines charge a reduced price for children under 12 and less for children under two. Double check the child's baggage allowance – some are as low as 7 kg.

In hotels try to negotiate family rates. If charges are per person, always insist that two children will occupy one bed only, therefore counting as one tariff. If rates are per bed, the same applies. In either case you can almost always get a reduced rate at cheaper hotels. In the better hotels in more commercial resorts, it is quite common for

Essentials

UK-based organizations specializing in work abroad

Quest Overseas, T020-8673-3311,
www.questoverseas.org
Raleigh International, T020-7371-8585,
www.raleighinternaional.org
Project Trust, T01879-230444,
www.projecttrust.ork.uk
Students Partnership Worldwide,
T020-7222-0138, www.spw.org
Community Service Volunteers,
T0800-3749911, www.csv.org.uk

Voluntary Service Overseas,
T020-8780-7200, www.vso.org.uk
Gap Year Company, T020-8996-2999,
www.gapyear.com
Year Out Group, T07980395789,
www.yearoutgroup.com
Vacation Work, T01865-241978,
www.vacationwork.co.uk

children under 10 or 12 to be allowed to stay for no extra charge as long as they are sharing a room.

Travel with children can bring you into closer contact with Latin American families and generally presents no special problems – in fact the path is often smoother for family groups. Officials tend to be more amenable where children are concerned and they are pleased if your child knows a little Spanish. Moreover, even thieves and pickpockets seem to have some of the traditional respect for families, and may leave you alone because of it! Always carry a copy of your child's birth certificate and passport-size photos.

Working in the country

Working in Costa Rica is not a problem – getting paid for it could well be. With the right skills and qualifications it is possible to arrange a job after arriving in the country. The skills that are most in demand, and consequently the best paid, are for qualified English teachers – employed with a proper school you will get you the best pay. Alternatively you may be able to get work in the tourism industry where service and English is much appreciated – but don't expect to get paid much.

Technically you should get a work permit from immigration if you are planning to work. If the job is above board, you receive support from your employer in tackling the process which is long and drawn out, taking as much as four months. In reality, most people cross the border every three months to refresh their visa, or just pay the fine when leaving. One word of warning, however, government authorities have let it be known they intend to crack down on so-called permanent tourists.

Volunteering | Volunteering to help with environmental and conservation work is very popular in Costa Rica. If your idea of volunteering is turning up and showing willingness to help sometimes when you're not going to the beach then forget it. Volunteering in Costa Rica is well developed, organized and you normally have to pay for food and some-times lodgings. The workload and type varies enormously. You may be building and maintaining paths, recording information about plant and wildlife populations, clearing out animal cages or have general administration duties. What you do will depend partly on what you can do and what you're prepared to do.

Most volunteers organize a placement before arriving. The first stage is to success-fully complete the application process. The most popular places are often filled more than six months in advance. Once working you will normally work a shift pattern with two to four day breaks for travel.

One rather strange development in Costa Rican volunteering is that you pay. To me the normal idea of giving services and paying money contravenes the idea of volun-teering, but it would appear I'm in a minority. The charge varies from US$75 to

US$150 a week. In return for your time, energy (and money), you receive food and lodgings, often with a Costa Rican family.

Volunteering at national parks can be organized through *ASVO*, the *Asociación de Voluntarios para el Servicio de las Areas Protegidas*, T233-4533, F233-4989, asvi89@racsa.co.cr

You can also contact organizations direct. Look in the text for *Hacienda Barú* near Dominical (page 309), *Genesis II* (page 319) on the Pan-American Highway close to San Isidro de El General, *Zoo Ave* in the Central Highlands (page 148), *Caño Palma Biological Station* in Tortuguero (page 380), *Pacuare Nature Reserve* close to Limón (page 370), *Aviarios del Caribe* (page 386), *ANAI* (page 400) and the *Talamanca Dolphin Foundation* (page 399) on the south Caribbean coast close to Puerto Viejo de Talamanca, the *Children's Eternal Rainforest* in Monteverde (page 217) and the *Delfín Amor Eco Lodge* in Drake (page 344). This is not a comprehensive list – just a series of pointers.

It is also possible to organize volunteering through intermediary companies in your home country. The cost is higher but the degree of support is normally greater. In the US try *Global Services Corp*, 300 Broadway, Suite 28, San Francisco, CA 94133, T415-788-3666 ext 128, F415-788-7324, www.globalservicecorps.org In the UK *World Challenge Expeditions* provide a volunteer program, Black Arrow House, 2 Chandos Road, London, NW10 6NF, T020 8728-7200, www.world-challenge.co.uk Also try *i-to-i*, One Cottage Road, Headingley, Leeds, LS6 4DD, T0113-217-9800, www.i-to-i.com

Essentials

Before you travel

Citizens of Canada, the United States and Panama are allowed to enter the country with a tourist card and one other piece of identification such as a driver's licence, birth certificate and a passport. However, while you may be able to enter, several other transactions may prove difficult without a passport, so take one anyway.

Visas & immigration

Citizens holding valid passports from most Western European nations and Japan (and the US and Canada) are permitted to stay in Costa Rica for 90 days without a visa.

Citizens holding valid passports from Australia, New Zealand and South Africa are allowed to stay in Costa Rica for 30 days without a visa.

Citizens of all countries not listed above must obtain a visa from a Costa Rican embassy or consulate before travelling, at a cost of US$20.

Extensions – *a prorroga de turísmo* – can be obtained at *migración* in San José, on the road from the capital to the airport. For this you need four passport photos, an airline or bus ticket out of the country and proof of funds (for example travellers' cheques); you can apply for an extension of one or two months at a cost of 300 *colónes* per month. The paperwork can take up to three days but travel agents can arrange all extension and exit formalities for a small fee. Alternatively, you can leave the country for 72 hours and get a new 30 or 90 day visa when you re-enter. If entering overland an onward ticket is sometimes requested. A bus ticket can be bought close to the border immigration office which can then be refunded in San José if required.

Residency If planning on taking up residency, the process requires a degree of administration. There are a number of options for retired and investing individuals. Essentially you need to prove that you have a regular income or that you are going to invest over US$50,000 to create a regular income. Full details about requirements and the process can be obtained on the internet at www.rree.go.cr/Residency.html For assistance in understanding and tackling the process contact the *Association of Residents of Costa Rica*, Casa Canada, Av 4 and C 40, PO Box 1191-1007, Centro Colon, San José, Costa Rica, T506-233-8068, F506-233-1152, www.casacanada.net/arcr

Essentials

 ## Costa Rican embassies abroad

Embassy addresses are listed on www.rree.go.cr

Australia and New Zealand, 11th Floor, De la Sala House, 30 Clarence St, Sidney NSW 2000. Postal address: PO Box 2513, NSW 2001 Sydney, T2-9261-1177, F2-9261-2953, perezdls@ozemail.com.au

Canada, 325 Dalhousie St, Suite 407 Ottawa, Ontario K1N 5TA, T613-562-2855, F613-562-2582

Cuba, 5ta. Ave No.6604, e/66 y 66 Miramar, Havana, T7-246-938, F-246-937

France, 78 Avenue Emile Zola, 75015 Paris, T1-4578-9696, F1-4578-9966, embcr@wanadoo.fr

Germany, Dessauerstr. 28 -2, D-10963 Berlin, T30-2639-8990, F30-2655-7210

Israel, Reh ov Deskin 13 Apto.1 Jerusalem 91012, T2-566-197, F2-563-2591, emcri@netmedia.net.il

Italy, Vía Bartolomeo Eustachio 22, Interno 6, Rome 00161, T06-4424-0954, F06-4425-1048, misfao@tiscalinet.it

Japan, Kowa Building No.38 9F 901 4-12-24 Nishi-Azabu Minato-Ku Tokio, 106-0031, T3-3486-1812, F3-3486-1813, ecrj@tky3.3web.ne.jp

Netherlands, Laan Copes Van Cattenburg 46, 2585 GB Den Haag-La Haya, T70-354-0780, F70-358-4754, www.embacrica.demon.nl

Nicaragua, Embassy: Callejón Zelaya, 2 blocks and ½ block from the Montoya statue, T266-2404, F2-681479. Consular office: ½ a block from Montoya statue, 27 de mayo Managua, T/F266-5719.

Panama, C Samuel Lewis, Edificio Plaza Omega 3 piso, contiguo Santuario Nacional, Panama City, T264-2980. Consular services T264-2937, F264-4057, embarica@cwpanama.net

South Africa, PO Box 68140 Bryanston 2021, T11-705-3434, F11-705-1222, ricacost@netactive.co.za

Spain, Paseo de la Castellana 164, 17-A, 28046 Madrid, T91-345-9622, F91-353-3709.

Switzerland, Schwarztorstrasse 11, 3007 Berna, T31-372-7887, F31-372-7834, embajada.costa.rica@thenet.ch

United Kingdom, Flat 1, 14 Lancaster Gate London W2 3LH, T020-7706-8844, F020-7706-8655, www.embcrlon.demon.co.uk

USA, **Embassy**, 2114-S Street, NW, Washington, DC 20008, T202-234-2945/6/7, F202-265-4795, www.costarica-embassy.org

Consular offices: **Atlanta**, 1870 The Exchange, Suite 100 Atlanta, GA 30339, T770-951-7025, F770-951-7073. **Boston**, 672 Chesnut Hill, Brookline, MA 02146, T617-738-9709, F617-698-2170. **Chicago**, 203 N Wahash Ave Suite 1312, Chicago, IL 60601, T312-263-2772, F321-263-9123. **Denver**, South Xenia St, Denver, COSTA RICA 80231, T303-696-8211, F303-696-1110. **Houston**, 2901 Wilcrest Suite, Houston, TX 77042, T713-266-0484, F713-266-1527. **Los Angeles**, 1605 West Olympic Blvd, Suite 400, Los Angeles, CA 90015, T213-380-6031, F213-380-5639. **Miami**, 1101 Brickell Ave Suite 704-5, Miami, FL 33131, T305-871-7485, F305-871-0860. **New Orleans**, World Trade Center Building 2 Canal St Suite 2334 New Orleans, LO 70130, T504-581-6800, F504-581-6850. **New York**, 80 Wall St, Suite 718, New York, NY 10005, T212-509-3066, F212-509-3068. **San Francisco**, 870 Market Suite 647, San Francisco, CA 94102, T510-790-0785, F510-792-5249.

Insurance Travel insurance is essential. If you are cutting back on costs make sure that it at least covers medical accidents and emergency repatriation. Luggage, delay and theft should also be covered if possible. If you are taking items of high value (binoculars, cameras, videos or laptops) make sure they are covered – some policies do not cover goods over a certain value unless declared in advance. Insurance companies vary in their requirements relating to claims and payments. The bare minimum requirement is a police report – for more details you should read the small print in your policy. If you have had a theft and did not have travel insurance, it is possible that your house insurance provides cover.

Beyond ensuring that you have protection against tetanus and diphtheria, you should have a vaccination against hepatitis A and typhoid. If staying for an extended period or in a rural location rabies and hepatitis B should also be considered. Vaccination against tuberculosis should also be considered.

Vaccinations
*See also 'Health',
page 71*

Malaria is a risk in some areas and **dengue fever** should be tackled primarily by avoiding being bitten. Use insect repellent and cover up, particularly at dawn and dusk.

It is paramount that you take the latest advice before travelling. In the US contact the *Centre for Disease Control*, T1-877-394-8747, www.cdc.gov UK residents can contact *Nomad* on 09068-633-414 (calls 60p a minute), www.nomadtravel.co.uk Limited to internet users is the UK-based website *www.fitfortravel.scot.nhs.uk* which in addition to good, clear health advice encourages you to give blood before going abroad – because you can't for several months after your return. The *World Health Organisation* has a very detailed site on international health issues, www.who.int

What to take depends completely on how long you're staying and what you're doing. As far as **clothes** are concerned, it's simplest to think through what you'll be doing and work out what you would wear. Starting at the lower altitudes you'll need beachwear, your shades and a sun hat – which you'll probably need everywhere – and sun cream. When venturing on trails, shorts and a light shirt are ideal. If you're a bug magnet some of the lightweight long trousers available from outdoor supply stores are perfect – even better if you can find ones that unzip above the knee. The same lightweight approach works wonders for the Central Highlands with a light sweater or jacket for the evenings when there may be a slight chill in the air. At higher altitudes you'll need something a bit thicker. When preparing for rain it's tempting to take a raincoat – don't bother unless going on very long treks. Few *Ticos* possess a raincoat so take guidance from them – buy an umbrella locally and use that for critical short journeys or sit the rain out. Comfortable shoes appropriate to your chosen activity be it hiking, horseriding or pool siding, as well as a change if they get wet. Buying large shoes in Costa Rica is not impossible, but the choice will be restricted.

What to take

Invaluable **personal items** worth taking if you're travelling independently include: a penknife, torch (head torches as used by climbers are particularly useful), camera with film (it is generally available in Costa Rica but if you buy in advance you can be certain you have sufficient quantity and quality), wash bag (the smaller the better – with toothbrush, toothpaste, soap, shampoo, deodorant, tampons, shaving kit, small mirror and dental floss), alarm clock, strong cord, sewing kit, a water bottle, wet wipes (once only for wimps now almost an essential item), insect repellent and the eternally useful universal sink plug (it's amazing how few even mid-range hotels don't have plugs. Spectacle or contact lens wearers should take a spare pair or sufficient supplies to last the trip – although it is possible to get most items in Costa Rica.

If you have personal **medical** requirements make sure you enough to last your trip and seek medical advice before leaving home if you have any reason to be concerned.

As ever, specialists will want to take items particular to their speciality. A good pair of **binoculars** is useful. Birders and nature lovers will want to take field guides – they're available in some of the better lodges but it's better to have your own if possible. **Divers** and keen snorkellers may want to consider taking their own mask, and experienced **anglers** may want to travel with the lucky lure.

All this should be packed in a strong **bag**, the lighter the better, and ideally one that can be locked with a removable padlock that can be used on dodgy doors and lockers if the need arises in cheaper hotels. Most mid- and upper-range hotels have safe boxes.

Essentials

Duty free & customs The duty free allowance is 500 cigarettes and three litres of wine or spirits. No customs duties are charged on personal luggage, including items for personal and professional use as long as they are not in sufficient quantities that suggest commercial use. As with all immigration post, your bags may be searched on entering the country. In the case of families, one declaration can be filled out for the whole family.

Money

Currency
See inside front cover for exchange rate
The unit of currency is the *colón*, consisting of 100 *céntimos*. Golden coloured coins are minted for five, 10, 25, 50 and 100 *colónes*. Public telephones use older silver five, 10 and 20 *colón* coins. Notes in use: 50, 100, 500, 1,000, 2,000, 5,000 and 10,000 *colónes*.

Dollars cash are widely accepted but don't rely on it outside the most popular destinations. Always have a stash of *colónes* you can call on if required.

Cash, travellers' cheques or credit cards? All three is the easy answer. Each has weaknesses and strengths – the last thing you want is to be stranded without cash so it's worth spreading the risks if you can. Cash should be taken in dollars – it is by far the easiest currency to change. It is possible to change other currencies but the rate is normally reduced and you may have to walk around several banks. No banks have plans to accept Euros for January 2002.

Travellers' cheques have added security being replaceable if they are stolen or misplaced. Take dollar travellers' cheques and make sure they are a well known names like *American Express*, *Citibank* or *Thomas Cook*. Keep the original purchase receipt separate from the cheques – for added security make a photocopy.

Credit cards are widely accepted in hotels and restaurants in San José and the more established resorts, but may be difficult to use beyond these areas. Check with hotels in advance when making reservations. The real value of a credit card is for easy cash advances from Automated Teller Machines (ATMs) and banks. *Visa* and *MasterCard* are accepted with *Visa* probably having the edge. *American Express* and *Diners* are accepted in business hotels but shouldn't be relied upon outside the business setting.

Banks & changing money Getting some 'first day' money before departure can prove difficult, although you may be able to get some in Miami if are catching a connecting flight. There is a bank, just after customs, at the Juán Santamaría International Airport in San José which opens to meet arriving flights so you can change money immediately on arrival if you need to.

Banks are the easiest place to change money. Branches of the state banks **Banco Nacional** and **Banco de Costa Rica** are most common throughout the country. The core opening hours are from 0900-1500, Mon-Fri. However, some branches are opening for longer; occasionally extending to Sat morning. Service varies wildly – it can be incredibly slow or surprisingly fast. Be prepared to wait. Banks in areas where processing travellers' cheques and credit cards is a rare occurrence may take a little longer but even this isn't a golden rule.

Commission rates tend to be around 1%. Charges against credit cards vary – it may be as much as 5% when buying goods or tours. Check beforehand and avoid using a card if you have the option.

The black market in Costa Rica has largely disappeared, and the few street changers that hang around the central area are used for convenience as much as anything. In general it's best to avoid changing money on the street unless you are totally relaxed with the idea. Don't flash large amounts of money around. Know how much money to expect before asking. While you may show your dollars to the changer in advance, don't hand over the money until you have counted the money you are to receive.

Budgeting for a trip is always difficult and is clearly dependent on your tastes, styles and mode of travel. Income per head of population is around the US$3,600 mark, but this varies widely throughout the population. Basic rented accommodation starts at around US$250 a month and rises according to the level of comforts and services.

Cost of living & travelling

Planning for day to day travel is difficult. At the bottom end of the scale you could manage on US$20 to US$25 a day to cover accommodation, hotels and travel by bus. But this would leave very little for comforts, trips and tours. Comfortable travel is found in the US$40 to US$60 range. This will cover reasonable accommodation – allowing for regional differences – and pleasant meals based on preference rather than cheapest cost. Beyond US$60 things start to get comfortable with serious attention to service levels, design and décor.

The cost of a room for two people is normally only 25% higher than for a single. The cost of adding a third person is often only a small increase. This does bring the daily budget per person down considerably.

There are two extra costs that should be considered. Renting a vehicle will set you back around US$350 a week. This will bump up the cost considerably. Likewise, tours are an extra cost ranging in price from US$45 for a day trip up to US$250 for a two day all-inclusive whitewater rafting or Tortuguero wildlife trip.

As a very rough guideline, bus travel works out to be between US$1 to US$1.50 per hour of travel. The longest possible single journey in the country is eight hours, although three to five is more common.

Getting there

Air

Daily flights leave various locations in the United States and Canada for Costa Rica. There are direct daily flights from Atlanta, Dallas Fort Worth, Houston, Miami, Newark and New York with **American Airlines**, **Continental**, **Delta**, **Grupo Taca**, **Martinair** or **United Airlines**. *Grupo Taca* also provide a four times a week service from Orlando.

North America
See also 'Tour operators in North America', page 21 and discount flight agents box below

Indirect flights offer a broader range of departure points but normally stop in one or more Central American capital en route. Flights from Los Angeles, via Guatemala City, are provided by *Grupo Taca* and *United Airlines*. From New Orleans *Grupo Taca* have a flight via Cancun. From Chicago *United Airlines* have a flight via Mexico City.

Scheduled flights from Canada leave Montreal and Toronto going via Havana and San Salvador, before eventually arriving in San José.

There are charter flights to Daniel Oduber airport in the northwestern province of Guanacaste direct from Canada and increasingly from the US in the high season. Try **Canada 3000**, **Air Transat** or **North West**.

Flight **prices** vary but start from as little as US$318 from Miami. The full economy fare from Miami is around US$850

There are no direct flights to Costa Rica from the United Kingdom or Ireland. You will have to make at least one stopover. **American Airlines**, **Continental**, **Delta** and **United Airlines** connect through Miami, or any of their direct services from the US.

UK & Ireland
See 'Tour operators in UK & Ireland', page 24 and discount flight agents box below

Alternatively you can link through a European agency. *Iberia* flights connect through Madrid. *Martinair*, a low-cost subsidiary of KLM, connect through Amsterdam.

If you want a really long trip you can go via Bogotá, Colombia, with **Avianca**.

Prices vary from £479 return with *Martinair* in the low season, up to £799 with *Avianca* in the high season. The low season price corresponds roughly to the winter months in the northern hemisphere.

Essentials

Airlines and internet travel resources

Air Transat www.airtransat.com
American Airlines www.aa.com
Avianca www.avianca.com
British Airways www.british-airways.com
Canada 3000, www.canada3000.com
Continental Airlines
www.continental.com
Delta Airlines www.delta.com
Grupo Taca www.grupotaca.com
Iberia www.iberia.es
LTU www.ltu.com

Martinair www.martinair.com
North West www.nwa.com
United Airlines www.ualcostarica.com

Web resources
www.expedia.com
www.travelocity.com
www.orbitz.com
www.opodo.com
www.priceline.com
www.lastminute.com

Europe
See 'Tour operators in Europe' page 24 and discount flight agents box below

Direct options from Europe are encouraging but varied. *Iberia* have direct daily flights from Madrid. *Martinair* have direct flights from Amsterdam and *LTU* have flights six days a week from Dusseldorf. The frequency of the *Martinair* and *LTU* flights varies every year.

Australia, New Zealand & South Africa
See page 24 and discount flight agents box below

Routes from Australia and New Zealand go through Los Angeles and then south picking up one of the North American airlines to go south. Flying with *Quantas* to Los Angeles and connecting to *Grupo Taca* will cost around A$2500 return. Connecting with *United Airlines* is around A$2300, and with *American Airlines* expect to pay around US$2700.

Discount flight agents

North America

EXito, 1212 Broadway Suite 910, Oakland, CA 94612, T1-800-655-4053; worldwide T510-655-2154, www.exitotravel.com
Council Travel with over 80 locations throughout the USA or try the Customer Contact Center on T1-800-226-8645, F617-528-2091, www.counciltravel.com
STA, with offices throughout the country or call on T1-800-781-4040 www.statravel.com
Tico Travel, T1-800-493-8426, www.ticotravel.com digs out some very good deals on just flights.

United Kingdom

Journey Latin America, 12-13 Heathfield Terr, Chiswick, London, W4 4JE, T020-8747-8315, F020-8742-1312, www.journeylatinamerica.com

South American Experience, 47 Causton St, Pimlico, London, SW1P 5AT, T020-7976-5511, F020-7976-6908, www.southamericanexperience.co.uk
STA, 6 Wrights Lane, London W8 6TA, T08701-600-599, www.sta.co.uk
Trailfinders, 215 Kensington High St, London W8 6BD, T020-7937-5400, www.trailfinder.com

Australia, New Zealand, South Africa

STA Australia (T1300-360-960) and New Zealand (T0800-874-773) share the same website at www.statravel.com.au
Trailfinders Australia, 8 Spring St, Sydney, NSW 2000, T02-9247-7666, F02-9247-6566, www.trailfinders.com.au
STA South Africa, T021-418-6570, www.statravel.co.za

Essentials

From South Africa the situation is even worse with flights going via Europe and possibly the United States or Mexico before touching down in San José. With **British Airways** via London and Mexico return, the fare is R$7700

Regular daily flights are available from Panama and Nicaragua with **Grupo Taca**. Further afield there are daily connecting flights with every Latin American capital with *Grupo Taca*.

Latin America

Hard and fast rules are difficult to establish but a few general guidelines can be helpful. **1**. Fares vary **seasonally** and from destination to destination. If you have flexibility check with a local agent for the cheapest time to travel. The high (popular) season in Costa Rica (December-April) does not correspond with the high (expensive) season for airline tickets (July-September) from the northern hemisphere. The very busy seasons are 7 December-15 January and 10 July-10 September.

Prices & discounts

2. Flight choices

a. **Student** (or under 26) and **teacher** fares. Generous discounts for students, the young and, increasingly, teachers. Although not always the cheapest available flight it is possible to get some great deals. Contacting a specialist student agent is the quickest way of getting the best deal.

Confirm flight details in advance: 24 hrs is the minimum, 72 hrs is recommended

b. **Apex or excursion** (return) fares purchased a certain number of days in advance, these normally provide a healthy discount to the full economy fare. Flexibility is normally restricted but you can change details for a fee.

c. **Discounted** fares which come and go with the popularity of a particular flight are sold through discount companies or consolidators with the aim of filling up the plane, but restrictions normally apply. The internet offers opportunities to pick up a bargain with online auctions, but you do risk not being able to get a ticket at all.

d. **Yearly** fares are simply return tickets with a return date set to a year or several months from departure, or left open. You are required to fix the route in advance and are normally charged a fee to make changes.

Essentials

www.journeylatinamerica.co.uk  GO

JOURNEY LATIN AMERICA

BRITAIN'S FOREMOST LATIN AMERICAN SPECIALIST
20 YEARS
SINCE 1980

 Flights only

 Escorted Groups

 Tailor-made Tours

 Cruises

 Insurance

 Brochures

 **Active Adventures**

Search: Favourites ▶ ▲

Mexico City
Oaxaca
Yucatan
Belize Cayes
Tikal
Lake Atitlan
Copan
Masaya
Corcovado
Panama Canal ▼

Rafting
Hiking
Kayaking
Biking
Riding

Search: Regions ▶ ▲

Belize
Caribbean ▶
Costa Rica
Cuba
El Salvador
Guatemala
Honduras
Mexico
Nicaragua
Panama
Ruta Maya
South America ▶ ▼

FULLY
BONDED

AITO

ABTA

IATA

ATOL
2828

 JOURNEY LATIN AMERICA

12-13 Heathfield
Terrace, Chiswick
LONDON
W4 4JE
020 8747 8315
Fax 020 8742 1312

28-30 Barton Arcade
Deansgate
MANCHESTER
M3 2BH
0161 832 1441
Fax 0161 832 1551

Essentials

e. **Open jaw** tickets allow you to enter through one airport and leave through another; the best option if you want to travel overland across countries. A standard method of calculating miles travelled means this is much cheaper than it was several years ago.

f. The last time anyone paid the full fare was when the company was paying. It doesn't happen as a rule, but this is what you will pay if you approach the larger airlines direct.

g. Costa Rica is not an easy destination to include as part of a round the world package. There is a possibility that this will change with the growth of *Grupo Taco* – a Central American regional international airline – which may build alliances with other airlines.

Baggage allowance

There is always a weight limit for your baggage. With European carriers, this is generally two bags per person of checked luggage weighing up to 20 kg for economy class and 30 kg for first class. One piece of hand luggage is permitted and the weight limit is set at 7 kg. Some airlines permit greater allowances (ie *American Airlines*: each bag up to 32 kg). If you are travelling with specialist equipment, make enquiries about the cost of transport in advance. Excess luggage is permitted if your weight or size allowance is exceeded. The cost structure varies with each airline so make enquiries with the airline before purchasing the ticket if you intend taking a surf board, for example.

Land

Travelling overland to Costa Rica is possible and distinctly enjoyable from North America and all countries in Central America. Whether travelling by bus or private vehicle, you should allow plenty of time for the journey. Although you could do the journey in a manic week, taking a few weeks to travel slowly through Mexico, Guatemala, Honduras and Nicaragua would be a far more rewarding experience. Flying is both cheaper and quicker so wanting to see the region or transporting a vehicle would be part of the reason for choosing this way of travel. If so, the *Footprint Central America and Mexico Handbook 2002* (Peter Hutchison ed., published by Footprint Handbooks and updated annually) will take you every step of the journey, guiding you through the interesting sights of the region.

Changing money at border posts seems inherently risky, but it is rarely that bad. Try to get an idea of what your money is worth before asking a money changer. Given that you are in a buyer's market, you are unlikely to get the best deal, but at least you can avoid being totally ripped off.

By private vehicle

Travelling overland is fairly simple with a degree of advance planning and a vehicle that can make the journey. You will need vehicle registration documents, your

driver's licence and an international driver's licence, which although not essential can be useful, and insurance. Insurance can be arranged through **Sanborn's**, Travco Services Inc, 2009 S 10th Street, McAllen, TX 78503, T 956-686 3601, F956-686 0732, toll free 800-222-0158, www.sanbornsinsurance.com On entering Costa Rica you will be required to buy compulsory insurance (US$30 for three months) and road use tax (US$10 per month). Although there are no charges for entering any Central American country with a vehicle, it would be wise to check with embassies before setting out.

The journey itself is certain to be set with wildly varying experiences. Drive with caution: pot-holed roads, hazardous roads, animals – domestic and wild – and people are some of the many problems that may stop you in your tracks. Avoid driving at night unless totally essential and take utmost care when choosing when to pull up and where to park your car.

Naturally enough a good map is essential. An excellent series of maps covering the region and each country is published by **International Travel Maps** (ITM), 345 West Broadway, Vancouver BC, V5Y 1P8, Canada, T604-879-3621, F604-879-4521, www.itmb.com most compiled with historical notes by the late Kevin Healey.

By bus The bus journey is equally challenging. You can drift through the countries one by one using local buses or take an international bus and see the countries passing you by through the window – missed opportunities all over the place, but needs must when someone else drives. The most direct service is with **Ticabus** starting in Guatemala City (11 C 2-72, Zona 9, T502-331-4279, www.ticabus.com) at 1230 daily.

Border posts **Peñas Blancas – Nicaragua** On the western side of the isthmus, Peñas Blancas is the only road crossing between the two countries. It is simple and straightforward taking the traffic of the Pan-American Highway. There is a US$1 fee for entering the border crossing area, and a US$2 fee for having your passport checked. After completing formalities at the new immigration office on the Nicaraguan border (open 0600-2000, Mon-Fri, 0600-1800, Sat and Sun), head to the Costa Rican border post.

Pedestrians will need to purchase a *cruz roja*, fill out an immigration card and then get both stamped and checked. If travelling by international bus, the driver will wait for all passengers to go through immigration. If making your own way, buses going to **La Cruz**, **Liberia** and **San José** stop just outside the immigration offices.

If driving, once you have completed immigration and customs you will need to buy compulsory insurance and road use tax at the border if the car is not registered in Nicaragua or Costa Rica: US$30 a month. All cars are fumigated at a cost of US$4.

Services at the immigration post include an ICT-run tourist office which has maps of the country and can provide some advice and a small restaurant serving cheap snacks and drinks.

Bear in mind the last fuel stop in Nicaragua is in Rivas, 37 km from the border. The first fuel stop in Costa Rica is in La Cruz, 19 km from the border.

Los Chiles – Nicaragua Inland, to the southeast of Lake Nicaragua, there is a daily boat service along the Río Frío, from San Carlos to **Los Chiles**, US$5, 45 mins. Departure formalities must be completed in San Carlos, including payment of the US$2 departure tax.

Immigration in Los Chiles is open daily from 0800-1600, usually closing for lunch. The crossing post, which is actually 4 km north of Los Chiles, is reported to be less straightforward than Peñas Blancas due to the high number of Nicaraguans that use the border crossing. It is not possible to cross this border by vehicle.

San Juan del Norte, Nicaragua – Barra del Colorado, Costa Rica There is no immigration post on this route but, in theory at least, it is possible to cross the border from Nicaragua to Barra del Colorado in Costa Rica by taking a boat from San Carlos down the Río San Juan to San Carlos del Norte. From there you can catch a boat to Barra del Colorado and work down the coast to Limón. The cost of such a journey is likely to be prohibitive, and you should visit immigration as soon as possible in Limón – where you are likely to be treated with a degree of suspicion.

Paso Canoas – Panama On the western side of Costa Rica, *Paso Canoas* marks the frontier with Panama as the main road crossing and the route of the Pan-American Highway. Entering and departing the country is straightforward. Immigration and customs are open 24 hrs on the Panama side which is frustrating given that Costa Rica provides services 0600-2200.

Panama is 1 hr ahead of Costa Rica

Bus services on the Panamanian side take you to and from David, the nearest town of significance to the border, with connecting services further south.

On the Costa Rican side, there are plenty of cheap hotels, restaurants and buses heading inland to **Ciudad Neily**, **Golfito** and **San José**.

Río Sereno – Panama A short distance from San Vito, at the head of the Coto Brus valley, the crossing of Río Sereno is handy if you are heading to or from the Chiriquí Highlands in Panama, but the crossing is closed to vehicle traffic.

Sixaola – Panama At the far southeastern corner of Costa Rica, Sixaola has the frontier spirit that all borders should have. Either side of the creaking rail bridge that connects Panama and Costa Rica, the immigration posts check people crossing the border, and the odd vehicle that inches along the sleepers stands out a mile. It all seems very *ad hoc* but it works, with Costa Rican immigration open from 0700-1700, in Panama 0800-1800 – the same hours given the time difference.

All formalities are completed as with other borders but with a more gentle laid-back approach. It doesn't take long, but don't come this way if you're in hurry.

Boat

Cruise liners stop at **Puntarenas** on the Pacific coast and **Limón** on the Caribbean coast before passengers disembark for a whirlwind tour of a couple of places. A good way of seeing lots of different places, but not the best way to see Costa Rica unless you can arrange to leave the vessel.

Touching down

Airport information

Juan Santamaría International Airport is 16 km northwest of San José on the southern outskirts of the town of Alajuela. For arrivals the airport is simply laid out with immigration, baggage reclaim and customs following naturally one after the other.

After customs, but before leaving the customs hall, there is a tourist desk which can provide maps and information, as well as book hotel accommodation and transport to San José and other areas. In the same area is a branch of *Banco Nacional*, which opens to meet international flights, and a line of car rental desks where you can pick up or arrange vehicle hire.

Outside, the swarms of greeting taxis will compete for your business. US$12 is the standard fare to downtown San José but you may pay between US$10-15. If you're looking for something a little cheaper it's a short walk to the bus stop where buses leave every 10 mins for the 40-min, 100 *colónes* (US$0.40) trip. Head out to the main road following the short airport access road, and join the queue opposite the petrol station.

Essentials

Essentials

Touching down

Official time *GMT -6, equal to Central standard time. No daylight saving time.*
Official language *Spanish*
Country Code (IDD) *506*
Equal tones with long pauses means it is ringing. Equal tones with equal pauses indicates engaged
Directory inquiries *113*
Emergency *911*
National Park information *192*
Business Hours *Banks 0900-1500, Mon-Fri. Some banks open longer and on*
Sat morning. Government offices 0800-1600, Mon-Fri. Commercial offices 0800-1800, Mon-Fri, Shops 0800-1800 Mon-Sat. While the tendency to close for lunch is becoming a thing of the past, service is often reduced at lunchtimes.
Voltage *110 volt, 60 cycles AC with US flat-pin plugs.*
Weights and measures *For customs the metric system is compulsory. Traders use a variety of weights and measures including imperial and the old Spanish ones.*

Sleeping at the airport The closest hotel to the airport is **AL** *Hampton Inn*, T443-0043, F442-9523 (toll free within Costa Rica 800-426-7866), www.hamptonhotel.co.cr Handy if you want to get in or get out quickly with the minimum of fuss, made easier with a courtesy pick-up. The price includes continental breakfast, free local calls, free stay for kids and the third and fourth adult sharing the same room. Add the free form pool and complimentary transportation to and from the airport and this could be the starting or finishing post you're looking for.

Airport facilities
Information T441-0744 or T443-2622
Airport services close to check-in and the departure area include currency exchange, bank ATMs, a few small shops and a café and restaurant. Beyond passport control there are a couple of cafés, a newsagent and gift store, a well stocked perfumer and a poorly stocked drink store. Services will probably improve as the airport expands to fill the new space provided by redevelopment.

Airport departure tax Departure tax of US$20 is payable before checking in. The small booth on the entrance walkway is certain to have been replaced by the time you read this.

Daniel Oduber Quirós International Airport, in the northwest of the country 13 km from Liberia along Highway 21, is a much smaller airport. Reopened in 1995, renovation and expansion continues, but the modern terminal has full customs and immigration services, a small café and a branch of *Banco de Costa Rica* is planned soon. A good spot if you want to head straight for the beach. Transport from the airport is limited to readily available taxis – ask around to get the best price.

Tourist information

The *Costa Rican Tourist Board* (Instituto Costarricense de Turismo or ICT) has spent the last 10 years promoting Costa Rica as a destination. Tourism is now so important that the ICT can largely take a back seat as private industry works on all levels to promote various attractions, hotels and restaurants. Guides are readily available at nature attractions. If you are looking for a specialist guide you should book through a tour operator or travel agent in advance.

The efficient and helpful **tourist information office** is below the Plaza de la Cultura in San José. The staff can help with general information and maps, and assist with any specific inquiries and problems. ■ *Open 0900-0600, Mon-Fri. The ICT also has an official website www.tourism-costarica.com with extensive information about the country. The ICT also have a desk at the Juan Santamaría International Airport.*

Beyond the capital, ICT information offices are rare. Privately run tour operators that have developed a reputation for excellent service and regional knowledge are mentioned in the text.

Local customs and laws

At the cutting edge of social change, the broad tolerance that is Costa Rican society prevails. You can do more or less what your heart and body desires as long you're not harming someone or something else. The US State Department produce *Tips for Travelers to Central and South America* which can be obtained through the US Government Printing Office, Washington, DC 20402 or via the Bureau of Consular Affairs at travel.state.gov

Most Costa Ricans devote a great deal of care to their clothes and appearance. How **Clothing** you dress is how people will judge you, particularly in the business arena. Beyond business, smart, clean clothes are always appreciated. In beach communities, wear a sarong and a shirt when walking round town or if you're away from the beach.

Politeness and courtesy, even a little ceremoniousness, prevails in all situations – in **Conduct** fact, even the traffic police give tickets in a rather pleasant manner. Being flustered, rushed and hurried simply doesn't fit in with the way of doing things in Costa Rica – a common trait throughout Latin America. Equally common is the sometimes extended process of introductions – a good greeting invariably leads to a good meeting. Likewise when departing, take the time to say goodbye.

Drinking is a part of life, but drunkenness is fairly uncommon. Yes, walking through San **Drink & drugs** José, Limón or other cities and popular areas in the early hours of Saturday morning you will find a few individuals worse for wear, but nothing excessive.

Drugs too are frowned upon, although their presence is increasing as Costa Rica is used as a transhipment port for cocaine travelling up from South America. All drugs – hard or so-called recreational – are illegal in Costa Rica with a jail term being the likely penalty for possession.

Visitors should keep to time arrangements – or as it is known the *hora inglés*. With just a **Mañana** tinge of sadness, the mañana culture of tomorrow is taking a back-seat in many areas that affect the tourist. Tours leave on time, private bus services tend to leave promptly and restaurant reservations should be honoured accordingly.

Get involved with the government and bureaucracy and it's a different world. To be fair, governments and councils worldwide have their procedures and things take time, but sometimes the frustrations mount and the sheer amount of paperwork required is frightening. Keep a fair degree of patience and a healthy dose of tolerance to hand if dealing with officials.

Once a reward for exceptional service and attention to detail the tendency to tip at the **Tipping** drop of a hat is taking over in Costa Rica. In the better restaurants, a 13% sales tax and a 10% service charge is automatically added to your bill. You are welcome to contest paying the service charge if you wish. The general consensus is that bellboys and chambermaids do receive tips of between US$0.50 and US$2 per item or day. Taxi drivers are not tipped but if the service is exceptional then why not? Tour guides can be tipped as you see fit – again, it is recommended that the tip reflects the degree of personal service and attention rather than an assumed payment.

Essentials

Religion While 90% of Costa Ricans are nominally Roman Catholic, the number that actually attend church on a regular basis is far less. This should not be confused with a lack of respect for the church which is still very high.

Commercial sex workers Prostitution for women over 18 is legal in Costa Rica. Prostitutes are supposed to carry health cards which indicate when they last received a check-up. The line of tolerance has created a sex tourist industry which is easily accessed if you are interested, and equally easily avoided. The liberal approach to legalizing the world's oldest profession is normally followed by confusion and rumours. Tolerance has become confused with anything goes, and one area that has caused concern is the growth in child prostitution. This is illegal and government authorities have promised to come down heavily on offenders.

Safety

Emergency 911, Police 117 In general Costa Rica is an extremely safe country. While long term residents say crime has increased, it is still very low in comparison to most countries. The majority of crimes can be avoided by being aware of the risks – sadly the nefarious elements of society don't take the week off just because you're on vacation. Leave your stresses at home, not your brain. Government authorities have committed to increasing the police presence with the introduction of a Tourist Police Corp in many popular tourist centres.

Protecting money & valuables If you can trust your hotel, leaving your valuables at reception or in a safe box in your hotel is the safest way of protecting them. If you need to carry cash around, keep it in a safe place about your person, preferably somewhere under your clothing so it is concealed. Do not walk around with highly visible bumbags or fanny packs which might as well have, 'this is precious to me, please steal it', printed on the front. If you are carrying a camera, make sure you have your hand on it or the bag at all times. Avoid walking through dark areas on your own at night.

Dangerous places Bus stops are notoriously busy places where confusion and bewilderment are the main feelings for the first time visitor – perfect conditions for the bag-lifter to relieve you of your belongings. Remain calm at all times. Try not to appear unnecessarily rushed or lost. If you need to get your bearings, sit down, gather your bags and thoughts together. If you need to ask directions, avoid leaving one person in charge of more bags than they can physically hold.

The Coca Cola Terminal and surrounding area in San José has a reputation for crime. A police office has opened in the terminal area and some locals say that crime is now falling but nevertheless, take utmost care.

At the end of the day, if you've ever seen a well organized team work a crowd, you realize that you have no chance if you have been picked as a victim. Do what you can to avoid being a victim, don't bring anything so precious you can't afford to lose it and don't put yourself at risk.

Con tricks To say there is less creative theft in Costa Rica than in neighbouring countries is little consolation once you've had your pockets emptied. Be wary of various scams or tricks that attempt to distract you or take advantage of a lapsed moment of concentration. A common trick is to throw shampoo or mud on your person, a helper clears it off while a third relieves you of your possessions. Other tricks involve dropping money and asking if it is yours. In the ensuing conversation with your guard dropped, your pockets are pilfered.

Driving Rental cars are commonly the target of theft and normally rich pickings if you're carrying all your holiday gear. The tourist number plates that used to be on rental vehicles and stick out like a sore thumb have now gone. However, your vehicle will still obviously be a hire car. Do not park in the street – use hotel parking or find a nearby parking lot. Do not leaves valuables in the car at any time and if you have no choice, do your best to put them out of sight. Do not park on the roadside in popular quiet spots – your car will be seen by acquiring eyes. Regular letters to the *Tico Times* report the highly organized scams that operate close to the Crocodile Bridge, between Jacó and Orotina.

The risks for women travelling in Costa Rica is no different to the risks in your home country. Common sense should see you through most situations. Avoid alcohol and drugs if you are likely to be on your own. Avoid accepting alcohol and drugs from anyone that you can't trust 100%.

Women
See also page 26

If the last two years are anything to go by, violent crime with at times fatal consequences is on the increase, with three incidents in 2000 and 2001 resulting in four murders. It is extremely rare - if for any reason you are subject to violent crime do not put your life at risk in defence of your possessions.

Violent crime

The hypnotic beauty of some of Costa Rica's beaches hide the very real threat of rip-tides – currents which pull you out to sea. If you know what you are looking for, it is possible to see rip currents which have a noticeable difference in water colour, a gap in the breaking waves and foam or other objects floating out to sea. Naturally, it is sensible and best to avoid the problem if possible. Apart from Manuel Antonio, there are no lifesaving programmes in Costa Rica and you will often only have local advice if that. Dangerous beaches popular with tourists are Playa Jacó, Playa Esterillos, Playa Palma, Playa Espadilla, Playa Bonita and Playa Cahuita.

Swimming & rip tides

If you get caught in a rip tide the first advice is don't panic – 80% of ocean drownings occur in rip tides when people panic and try to fight the current. Swim at a manageable pace parallel to the shore until you are clear of the current – the waves at either side of the rip tide will take you back to the shore. If you cannot break free of the current, let it take you out beyond the breakers, then swim diagonally toward the shore. Trying to swim against the current will result in exhaustion and ultimately could prove fatal.

Where to stay

Accommodation options cover all styles and budgets. It is hardly surprising that in Costa Rica the variety and diversity is spectacular. Eccentric and purist designs perched on the hillside providing respite for mind and body, quiet hotels in secluded private reserves, beachfront properties and glorious romantic hideaways, down through steady steps of luxury, comforts and services to the simplest, basic rooms which find you searching your soul for inspiration.

The level of service varies fantastically. While some realize the value of service for its own sake, others budge, grunt and groan reluctantly into action. Price is a pretty good indicator of standards – service levels are a bit hit-and-miss.

The good hotels fill up in the high season (and some in the green season as well) and booking in advance is advisable. Mid- and upper-range hotels will require a deposit in advance. Lower budget hotels will also accept reservations and while you may not be able to secure the room, do what you can to check the booking is being honoured. If you plan to arrive late in the evening, let the hotel know.

While a few companies may have two or three hotels in the country, there are not really any chains as such beyond *Best Western*, which has six hotels throughout the country in the main tourist areas. A number of hotels have grouped together, one of

Accommodation price codes

LL US$150+	**C** US$21-30
L US$100-149	**D** US$ 16-20
AL US$66-99	**E** US$ 11-15
A US$46-65	**F** US$ 7-10
B US$31-45	**G** Under US$6

LL-L Hotels in these categories can be found throughout the country. They focus on providing exceptional service in natural surroundings and unique opportunities. They may have full comforts and services or they may make a virtue out of silence being golden. You will be pampered, spoilt, well tended and want for nothing.

AL-A This price bracket has slipped slightly from the 'exclusive' to the very comfortable. You should expect a wide range of services – many that you will probably never use including a pool, sauna, gym, Jacuzzi, restaurant, bar and safe box. There is often a casino, depending on the style and location of the place.

B Hotels in this category should provide more than standard facilities and a fair degree of comfort. Many include a good breakfast and offer extras such as a colour TV, minibar, a/c and a swimming pool. As a rule they accept credit cards, and in many cases children under the age of 12 are allowed to stay for free if they stay in the same room.

C-D Hotels in these categories range from very comfortable to functional and there are some real bargains to be had – although there is a tendency to drift towards floral bedspreads, plastic flowers and ornamental lighting. You should expect your own bathroom, constant hot water, a towel, soap and toilet paper. There is sometimes a restaurant and a communal sitting area. In tropical regions you may have the option of a/c but may have to pay extra.

E-F Hotels in these categories are often extremely simple with bedside or ceiling fans, shared bathrooms and little in the way of furniture. While rooms may not have been painted for quite a few years, standards of cleanliness are generally OK with some notably pleasant surprises around the country.

G In this category you'll get four walls and a bed – count yourself lucky.

particular note is the **Small Distinctive Hotels of Costa Rica**, T258-0150, F258-0153, www.distinctivehotels.com five hotels which are small, distinctive providing excellent service.

Taxes, discounts & children Hotels are subject to a 16.39% sales tax - an intriguing number to choose. The more expensive hotels tend not to include this in the quoted price, so make sure you know whether the price you are quoted includes tax or not. Tax is included in the prices quoted in this guide – see box for breakdown of what to expect in each category.

The high season generally runs from December to April. Outside of these months it is the green season. Discounts at this time are common and can be as much as 50%. They vary greatly from location to location – some places choose not to discount at all, others prefer to close rather than operate at a reduced capacity.

Many of the mid-range hotels and above allow children under 12 to stay for free or a fraction of the full adult rate. Ask when making reservations.

Food Many hotels provide food but at an extra cost. The typical cost of meals at an **AL** category hotel might be US$5 for breakfast, US$8 or US$8 for lunch and dinner. While this system is ideal if you want to move around and eat in different places, when you are stranded in an isolated place, meal costs can quickly mount up so be sure to budget accordingly.

In general, away from San José the better establishments are outside the main town, seeking the exclusivity of a natural setting while being close enough to a town or village to provide opportunities for excursions. These hotels and lodges tend to have their own restaurant or at least comfortable snack options. Services vary greatly as some aim for a pure ambience devoid of external influences, while others have options for all forms of sport, pampering and relaxation. Although not essential, it is often useful to have your own transport. **Out of town**

Cheaper accommodation tends to be in or close to the centre of town or at least easily accessible to public transport routes. Options range from very comfortable family run hotels with the cozy comforts of home to penny-pinching flea-pits. **In town**

Costa Rica has cottoned on to the opportunities for business travel and provides some of the best business hotels and conference facilities in Central America for capacities of up to 1,200 delegates. Service levels start at the very height of luxury down to more rustic settings, with nature as the backdrop. **Business hotels**

Setting out with a filling breakfast inside you is easily the best way to travel. The **Costa Rica Bed & Breakfast Group** is a network of small B&Bs offering smart and friendly sleeping options throughout the country. In addition to a reservation service, they also provide itinerary planning to get you between the 200+ inns and hotels in their directory. ■ *c/o Pat Bliss, Interlink 978, PO Box 025635, Miami, Florida 33152, T/F228-8726, www.catch22.com/~vudu/bliss2.html* **Bed & breakfast**

Long term rentals of rooms or apartments are popular for people staying in the country for a month or two. The discounts are considerable and it can be worthwhile if staying in the country for a while. Some places will even give a discount for stays of over three nights. If you're looking to have a base, ask about discounts when making a reservation. **Long term rentals**

Eleven hostels and lodgings are affiliated to the **International Youth Hostelling Federation** throughout Costa Rica. While they do not all offer discount for membership, you will find a clean bed and a friendly face. For information write to Recaj, PO Box 10227, 1000 San José or visit www.hostelling-costarica.com   Hostels are mentioned throughout the text. **Youth hostels**

At the rustic end of the scale **Cooprena** heads a network of co-operatively owned lodges and houses that provide accommodation throughout the country in rural settings. Conditions are normally basic, but are in excellent positions for experiencing rural Costa Rican home life and with opportunities for activities nearby. Close to the ideals of eco-tourism, the impact of visitors is minimal; sustainable use of the environment primary, and the money goes to the local community. ■ **Simbiosis Tours**, PO Box 6939-100, San José, T/F286-4203, www.agroecoturismo.net **Eco-tourism – Cooprena**

Camping is possible in Costa Rica but it does seem to be on the decline in all but the most out of the way places. Given the difficulties of getting to quiet secluded spots on public transport, it is probably better to camp in Costa Rica as a preferred style of sleeping rather than a way of saving money and getting to quiet hideaways. There are, of course, exceptions and these are **Santa Rosa** and **Corcovado National Parks** – most easily visited when you have your own tent. If you want to camp, normal rules apply to take all your rubbish with you – even if that is contrary to local habits. **Camping**

Getting around

Transport within Costa Rica is simple and straightforward by air or road, whether in a private or rented vehicle or on public buses. In an ideal world, judicious use of hotel-provided transport to get to out of the way places like Tortuguero or Corcovado National Park, combined with a rented vehicle, provide the freedom to explore a bit of the country going at your own pace.

If public buses are more in keeping with your budget or style, there is an efficient and generally effective network of buses to get you to all major destinations and most smaller towns. You may find that occasionally you have to go via one town to make a connection, but the extra time taken is rarely excessive.

Air

See also schedule on next page Two companies provide a scheduled service to destinations throughout the country. *Sansa*, T221-9414, F255-2176, info@flysansa.com and www.flysansa.com and *Travelair*, T220-3054, F220-0413, reservations@travelair-costarica.com and www.travelair-costarica.com

Sansa fly out of the domestic terminal at Juan Santamaría Airport near to Alajuela. Flights are in Cessna Caravans and have a reputation for being late, frequently cancelled and overbooked. Flights must be paid for when you make the reservation, which can be done online, and tickets are non-refundable. *Sansa* introduced an experimental **Costa Rica Airpass** offering unlimited air travel for one week for US$280, two weeks for US$320 and additional weeks at US$140. Check with them directly to see if they plan to continue the programme.

Travelair operates out of Tobías Bolaños airport, in Pavas, 5 km west of San José. They use 15-seater Lets and 7-seater Britten-Norman Islanders. Reservations can be made in advance and *Travelair* will work with *Adobe Rent a Car* to arrange for a rented

Domestic flight destinations

Domestic flights in Costa Rica – high season schedule

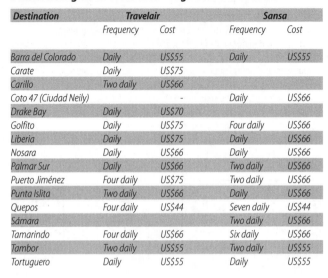

Destination	Travelair		Sansa	
	Frequency	Cost	Frequency	Cost
Barra del Colorado	Daily	US$55	Daily	US$55
Carate	Daily	US$75		
Carillo	Two daily	US$66		
Coto 47 (Ciudad Neily)		-	Daily	US$66
Drake Bay	Daily	US$70		
Golfito	Daily	US$75	Four daily	US$66
Liberia	Daily	US$75	Daily	US$66
Nosara	Daily	US$66	Daily	US$66
Palmar Sur	Daily	US$66	Two daily	US$66
Puerto Jiménez	Four daily	US$75	Two daily	US$66
Punta Islita	Two daily	US$66	Daily	US$66
Quepos	Four daily	US$44	Seven daily	US$44
Sámara			Two daily	US$66
Tamarindo	Four daily	US$66	Six daily	US$66
Tambor	Two daily	US$55	Two daily	US$55
Tortuguero	Daily	US$55	Daily	US$55

NB Not all flights are direct. Services are reduced in the low season.

Essentials

vehicle to be picked up or dropped off at the airport.

Children from under two years travel free, from two to 12, there is a 25% discount. Weight allowances are minimal at 12 kg (25 pounds) with a US$0.45 surcharge for every pound.

Aero Costa Sol has a fleet including twin engine Navajos, one Azteca and a Let operating out of Juan Santamaría Airport, T440-1444, F441-2671, www.costasol.co.cr Working out of Tobías Bolaños is *Alfa Romeo Aero Taxi*, T/F296-4344, operates mainly between the capital and the southwest but covers countrywide as well. *Pitts Aviation* do sky tours and an air charter service, T296-3600, F296-1429, www.pitts-aviation.com *Travelair* provide a charter service to all their scheduled destinations from Tobías Bolaños airport. You can also charter a helicopter with *Helisa*, T231-6867, F231-5885, helisa@sol.racsa.co.cr

Charter flights

Road

The road network throughout Costa Rica is generally very good with most destinations of interest accessible by paved road. As a whole the roads are better than most in Central America, but still liberally doused in potholes – not always big, but sometimes unbelievably deep. The majority of roads in the Central Highlands are paved, creating a warren-like network of poorly signposted confusion. Beyond the highlands, paved roads link most regions in the country, apart from the northeastern lowlands.

Moving between major destinations is easy but as soon as you want to deviate slightly, the roads deteriorate from well packed stony roads which allow a fair speed, if a somewhat juddering ride, to wash-board bone-shakers, loosely packed sandy shales which become quicksand in the rain or rocky roads more like dry-stream beds. You don't know the quality of a road when you start out, so the only solution is to take advice from locals – and do listen – and be flexible about your travel plans.

Essentials

Car rental   Renting a vehicle in Costa Rica is extremely popular and provides the freedom of movement that many enjoy at home. You choose when to start, stop, dally and deviate. What could be better than cruising along with the windows down, your favourite tunes playing?

Well consider a few of the possibilities: minor road accidents; mechanical breakdown; new road rules; speeding tickets. Even worse there's something about being behind a wheel in a foreign country that makes the impossible possible. You could end up with an empty fuel tank and a seasonally flooded river between you and the next gas station, or, worse still, be in a serious accident. However, the vast majority of people who rent a vehicle return it to the rental company without so much as a scratch or the slightest hiccup and if you've got the budget, and can face the new challenges it's definitely worth considering.

If you do rent, make sure you are going to use the vehicle. In some locations you won't need it and it is pointless to have the thing sitting around doing nothing. You

No motorized vehicles

Maximum width

No parking

Maximum speed

Taxi rank

No overtaking

Silence

Maximum speed

No U-turn

U-turn permitted

Stay to right

Parking limited to one hour

Yield

Stop

can get round this problem to a certain degree by arranging drop-offs and pick-ups from different locations around the country. There is normally a charge for this service but it works out cheaper than driving back to the original rental office.

Think about where you are likely to want to go – the general recommendation is to get a four-wheel drive with high clearance, but if you only intend to stay on good roads and visit the main areas then you'll be paying for more fuel and vehicle than you need. If you are thinking of travelling around the quieter areas of the Nicoya Peninsula, heading for Santa Elena/Monteverde or the Osa Peninsula, driving in the rainy (erm, green) season, or just striking out to see where a road goes then four-wheel drive is almost a must.

What vehicle?

Vehicles available for hire are normally Japanese: mainly Toyotas with some Suzukis and other makes, ranging from simple sedans like the Toyota *Tercel*, through mid-size four-wheel drives like the Suzuki *Sidekick* or Toyota *Rav 4*, up to the beefy Toyota *Land Cruisers*. Most cars will have a/c, a good radio and cassette and locking system.

To drive in Costa Rica you have to be over 21 (although some hire companies insist on your being over 23) have a full driving licence from your home country, your passport and be able to pay a deposit (normally put on a credit card, deductable) of up to US$1500 against any possible damage.

Prices vary from around US$30 a day for the cheapest cars. A Suzuki *Sidekick* is around US$55, a *Rav 4* US$60 and a Toyota *Land Cruiser* between US$80 and US$120. The weekly rate is normally priced at six days for the price of seven. The monthly rate is the week rate by 3.5. To this you need to add insurance which ranges from US$12 to US$25 a day. All fuel in Costa Rica is unleaded. As of June 2001, regular was 198 *colónes*/litre (US$0.60), super 204 *colónes* (US$0.62) and diesel 147 *colónes* (US$0.45). A few roads, mainly in the Central Highlands, have road tolls with minimal charges.

There are more than enough car hire firms in San José to choose from. The main international companies have offices in the city and at the airport, or you can go with a local company, or even companies that specialize in using not A-1 quality vehicles – reliable but not so precious. Beyond San José, there are few rental companies with maybe just one company in the popular Pacific Coast towns.

Car rental companies

Most companies are fair with you if you are fair with their vehicle. When checking the vehicle out, stay with the assistant and agree on paint chips, dents and damage. Check the amount of fuel in the tank. Likewise when returning it stay with the assistant and agree on any charges to be paid before you leave the office. Also make sure the fuel tank is filled to the agreed level – you will be charged heavily if the company has to fill the vehicle. If the car is exceptionally dirty, it may be worth getting it cleaned for a few dollars before returning it to the hire company.

It has been argued that Latin Americans are some of the best drivers in the world – how could they survive the road conditions with so few accidents if they weren't. Labelling Costa Rican driving as good or bad is unfair for obvious reasons. The only good rule is that *Tico* drivers are observant – which is the best advice for any prospective driver. Look out for other drivers, for pot holes, poorly sign-posted roads, be wary of unmarked speed restrictions and aspire to develop a sixth sense. Beyond that, here are a few tips.

Driving in Costa Rica

Signposting around the country is generally appalling. Most will start their journey in San José, and you could well end up driving round the city for a couple of hours before you've got anywhere. Instinct is useful, a compass is better, local knowledge is best.

Driving in the **rain** clearly has an added danger especially in torrential downpours. Be especially careful when roads are drying out. Overhanging trees mean roads dry out in patches – particularly in and approaching the Central Highlands where twisting roads making driving dangerous at the best of times. Moving **away from populated**

Essentials

Essentials

areas, be aware that some vehicles do not always have lights. Don't drive at night unless it is essential. **Gas stations** in parts of the country are few and far between. Fill up when you get the chance. Driving **off-road** creates new hazards, apart from the fact that your rental company may stipulate you are not allowed to drive off-road. If you've ended up in difficulty unintentionally, retrace your route and find another way through. If you come across a landslide, mudpools or a fjord, get out and walk the route first – if you can't walk through, round or over the obstacle it's unlikely the vehicle will make it in good condition.

Rules &
regulations
Naturally rules
and regulations
of the road have
to be obeyed!

Speed limits. On highways and secondary roads the speed limit is 80 kph. In urban areas the limit is 40 kph. Around schools, hospitals and clinics the limit is 25 kmph.

Driving under the influence of **alcohol** and/or **drugs** is strictly prohibited.

Wearing a **seatbelt** is a legal requirement.

You must **pull over** if requested to do so by a police officer.

Your personal **documents** and the vehicle registration are private property and may not be retained by a police officer for any reason. If the police officer insists on retaining your documents ask him to escort you to the nearest police station to clear up the problem. If you believe a police officer has acted inappropriately call T257-7798 ext 2506.

If you are involved in an **accident**, do not move your vehicle until a police officer has arrived and prepared a report. The accident can be reported on 911 or direct to the transport police on 117. You should also call the car rental company.

If you are fined for an **infringement** of the law, do not give money directly to the police. Pay the fine, which is subject to 30% tax, at the nearest *Banco Nacional*.

Driving on **beaches** is prohibited everywhere, except when there is no other path connecting two towns.

Motorbike
rental

For some, motorbikes are the only way to travel. You can rent good quality off-road bikes, Suzuki DR 250s and 350s, from *Wild Rider Motorcycles*, T/F258-4604, in San José for one-day guided tours or just head out on the open road. A one-day guided tour of Irazú, Cartago, the Orosi Valley and Ujarrás – roughly 180 km – will cost you US$79. If you want to travel out in a little more style, then *Rent-a-Harley* in San José, T289-5552, F289-5551, www.mariaalexandra.com is a service provided by *Apartotel Maria Alexandra*. Day and multi-day tours available. Rental starts at US$135 a day, all gear included.

Bus travel

Bus travel is by far the most popular mode of travel in Costa Rica – for Costa Ricans at least. You can get anywhere in the country by catching a bus or two. Buses range from comfortable cushioned and air conditioned highway cruisers to chicken buses that crawl along stopping every 10 m to pick up passengers.

San José is the main hub of the service with most buses starting or finishing in the capital with a few regional exceptions. Nationwide services are provided by a couple of dozen private companies which are dotted around the city in clusters. A few services have clustered together and the **Coca Cola Terminal** is the centre for central highland services with a few offices in surrounding streets and to the north providing many other services. All Caribbean destinations are neatly served from the **Gran Terminal del Caribe**.

Beyond the capital a few towns act as a point to change direction. To the west **Puntarenas** is a good stop-off point, negating the need to return to the highlands and linking to services down the Pacific coast and up to Santa Elena and Monteverde. Further north **Cañas** is the point to break from the Pan-American Highway and head inland to **Tilarán** and from there to **Fortuna** or **Monteverde**. **Liberia** offers similar, but lesser opportunities with links to the Nicoya Peninsula. Heading south, **San Isidro de El General** is a useful place to change buses, as is **Palmar Norte** where you can link with the southern section of the coastal road (*costanera*) and travel north to

Dominical, Quepos and Manuel Antonio. On the Caribbean, Limón is the main transport hub, but it is possible to get buses travelling all the way down the coast from San José so you don't have to change unless you're stopping over.

Buses tend to depart promptly so it is best to arrive on time, and the service tends to be reliable if the weather and conditions have been kind to the road. The cost of travel is cheap, working out at roughly between US$1 and US$1.50 an hour. The longest journey in the country is currently that between San José to Puerto Jiménez on the Osa Peninsula (eight hours), and will set you back US$6.30. Local buses exist in the larger towns but tend to be of limited use to the passing visitor outside San José.

There are alternatives to using public buses. The Fantasy Bus operated by *Grayline* **Private bus** (T220-2126 or T1-800-326-8279, www.graylinecostarica.com) have several daily services. Starting from San José, buses go to and through Arenal to Liberia, Tamarindo and Playa Hermosa. Heading south, buses go to Jacó and Manuel Antonio. Heading east, buses travel through Limón to Cahuita and Puerto Viejo de Talamana. Most buses start from the *Hotel Best Western Down Town*. Buses also leave Jacó linking to the northern destinations. Each journey costs US$19. *Interbus* (T283-5573, F283-7655, www.costaricapass.com) offer a similar service with daily routes from San José linking to: Arenal and Fortuna; Jacó, Quepos and Manuel Antonio; Limón, Cahuita and Puerto Viejo de Talamanca; Monteverde; Flamingo and Tamarindo. Charges are a little higher than the Fantasy Bus starting at US$17 rising to US$45 for San José to Monteverde.

If you are travelling in a group (up to six people), you could rent a bus from *Coach Costa Rica*, T229-4192, F292-5003, www.coachcostarica.com Rates are for destination on a daily basis, or for US$125 a day with chauffeur, if booked for more than three days.

Taxis are usually the easiest mode of transport in San José and many of the larger **Taxis** towns. They are a surprisingly affordable way of putting together your own tour if you are in a group of four. In San José taxis have a list of tariffs for long-distance journeys. Taxis can be hailed in the street or booked in advance – your hotel will have a number for a local firm.

Costa Rica is generally 'cyclist friendly', with less traffic than in neighbouring Central **Cycling** American countries. However, paving is thin and soon deteriorates, especially at the shoulders, so look out for cracks and potholes, which bring traffic to a crawl. The prevailing wind is from the northeast, so if making an extensive tour, travelling from Panama to Nicaragua is slightly easier. The Nicoya Peninsula is particularly bad for cyclists – a mountain bike is recommended for the terrain and the poor road state.

Recommended reading for all users: Bill Baker's *Essential Road Guide to Costa Rica* (1995), with detailed strip maps, kilometre by kilometre road logs, motoring information plus San José map and Bus Guide.

If you like hitch-hiking Costa Rica is as safe a place as any – with normal and sensible **Hitch-hiking** precautions you will undoubtedly have some of the most enjoyable, honest and open conversations while sharing a couple of hours with the temporary friend. The inverse traffic rule applies – where there is less traffic you're less likely to find a ride, but if a vehicle passes it will quite often pick you up. Likewise, busy roads tend to be far too anonymous – the Pan-American Highway is a particularly difficult place to catch a ride.

Sea

Ferry services are available to both the **Nicoya Peninsula** and the **Osa Peninsula**. Vehicle and passenger ferries are available between Puntarenas and Playa Naranjo and Paquera to the south and between Puerto Nispero and Puerto Moreno at the mouth of the Río Tempisque. The passenger only ferry service to the Osa Peninsula leaves from Golfito for Puerto Jiménez.

Train

The train line which once linked Puntarenas on the Pacific and Limón and the Atlantic have steadily fallen into disrepair and there are no passenger services. There is talk of a section of the Jungle Train running between Siquirres and Limón. The trip is provided by *HJ Tours*, T758-1369, or mobile on T392-2462, alanzer@sol.racsa.co.cr The only other service is the private cargo operation down the Caribbean coast.

Keeping in touch

Internet   Internet access is widely available in Costa Rica and by far the cheapest and easiest way to stay in touch. There are several internet cafés in San José, but fewer services in the smaller towns. However, enterprising individuals and organizations are setting up small offices in out of the way places like Puerto Viejo de Talamanca and Ciudad Neily. Prices vary, but expect to pay between US$2 and US$5 an hour, although some places will charge a fortune if they can get away with it. Connections are normally good.

If you intend to use email to keep in touch make sure you have web-based email such as Yahoo or Hotmail. Some internet companies provide this service already so you will not need to set up a new account. If you need to set up an account, most internet café owners will happily help. With Hotmail it is possible to make internet telephone calls to the US and Canada which are charged at the internet connection rate – a fraction of the price of a traditionally routed telephone call.

Post   The Costa Rican postal system (*correo*) is seen as dependably slow and unreliable. Parcels often go missing, whether being sent or received, so think twice before sending anything of value. Post takes about 10 days to North America, and two to three weeks to Europe. Sea mail, which is generally only used for large packages can take up to three months. Postal rates are affordable. If sending a package don't seal the bag before you go to the post office as it needs to be cleared by customs first. Packing materials are available at post offices in San José and Limón.

The post office is introducing *punta.com* a country-wide internet system that plans to make the internet available in every post office. In small towns this is certain to be a major benefit, but for the time being the roll-out of technology and training has created a few teething problems. Enquire at post offices for the service.

■ *Opening hours vary between cities and towns. In San José the post office is open 0730-1800, Mon-Fri, 0730-1200 Sat.*

Receiving mail   Post can be sent to the *Lista de Correos* of your local post office if you wish to receive mail. For San José, the address would be Your Name, Correo de Costa Rica, Lista de Correos, San José, Costa Rica, Central America. There is a nominal charge of US$0.15 for each item.

Courier services are also available from San José. *DHL*, Paseo Colón, C 30-32, T210-3838, F290-3000, www.dhl.com *Jet Ex* is the Federal Express agent, on Pavas road, T293-0505, F239-3658, www.jetex.co.cr *UPS*, Av 3, C 30-32, T290-2828, F232-8800, www.ups.com

Telephone   Costa Rica has the dubious honour of having the highest number of land and mobile telephone lines per head of population in Central America. Even the smallest towns and

Postal rates from Costa Rica

Region	Postcard	Letter	Package up to 2 kg
USA/Canada	55	70	3225
Europe	70	90	5400
Rest of the world	65	100	6750

NB Prices in colónes

For international operators in your home country call:

Belgium 00-800-3200-3200	**New Zealand** 0800-064-1064
Canada 0800-015-1161	**Spain** 0800-034-1034
France 0800-033-1033	**Switzerland** 00-800-2341-2341
Germany 00-800-0049-0049	**United Kingdom** 0800-044-1044
Israel 0800-972-1972	**United States** AT&T 0800-011-4114
Italy 0800-039-1039	MCI 0800-012-2222
Japan 0800-081-1081	Sprint 0800-013-0123
Netherlands 0800-031-1111	Worldcom 0800-014-4444

Essentials

villages have at least one phone line, and more lines are being installed. This is all very well if you have your own phone, but the majority of visitors will be subjected to hotel telephones, which attract a hefty surcharge, or public telephones, which double as municipal artwork – seeing as they rarely function as telephones. Public telephones that do work and that take cash, accept small change of five, 10 and 20 *colónes*. Simply dial the number and feed in the money. Rates are cheap but it's a good idea to have plenty of change handy. To get the **international operator** or to make collect calls dial 116.

The network is provided by the state-owned telecommunications company *RACSA*, with competing services provided by *ICE-tel*, a subsidiary of the national power company ICE which also happens to be the sole owner of RACSA.

Calling cards Phone or calling cards are very useful. There are three systems in operation in Costa Rica, the most useful is *Viajera Internacional 199* which permits national and international calls from any telephone. Available in values of 100, 200, 500, 1000 and 3000 *colónes*. After scratching off the security patch, dial 199 and then follow the instructions. It can get rather tedious tapping in the 20-digit security code – to make a follow-on call hit '#'. *Colibri 197* provides a similar national service but their permitted number of lines are often busy. The *CHIP* cards work from blue public phones.

Fax and credit card calls In San José you can send and receive faxes (US$0.30 receiving up to five pages) and make credit card calls from the *RACSA Telecommunications Centre* office at Av 1, C 5, T287-0087, F223-1709. They also have a (pricey) internet service. Many hotels, even at the cheaper end, have fax machines and may be happy for you to receive faxes for a charge.

Media

Of the six daily national newspapers the most popular and oldest is *La Nación* (www.nacion.co.cr) which tows – or creates – the establishment line. It also has the best arts and listings section. *La República* (www.larepublica.net) is the main competition, slightly slimmed down in content and style. Bringing up the from the rear – or the gutter – is *Al Día* which tends to have a more frivolous approach to events but good

Newspapers

sports coverage. *La Prensa Libre* (www.prensalibre.co.cr) is a good evening paper. *Rumbo* is the main weekly news magazine of the three which also include *Triunfo* and *Perfil*. *La Gaceta* is the official government weekly paper.

English language readers are treated to the *Tico Times* (www.ticotimes.net) with a gentle mix of national and international issues. They also publish the densely informative *Exploring Costa Rica* which stuffs everything you need to know about Costa Rica into a few hundred pages. *Costa Rica Today* is a free general interest weekly found in the better hotels and restaurants. Free regional magazines in Jacó (*Jacó News*), Quepos (*Quepolandía*) and Tamarindo (*The Howler*) provide local information.

Television   There are, at the last count, 13 local television channels which carry a mix of imported novellas, sport and news. The main station is *Channel 7*, which competes with the introduction of cable and satellite services importing a staggering array of programmes. If you time it right, you can watch the *Discovery Channel* documentary on Monteverde Cloudforest after walking through the area.

Radio   Over 100 radio stations are available on the FM band – a few of which broadcast in English. *107.5 FM* provides a heady mix of good driving music, and *Radio Dos* (Doze) on 99.5 FM plays an similar mix of hits. Once you've had enough of living the past, explore the wavelengths with the search button. You'll find Jazz on *Echo 95.9*. Outside the Central Highlands reception is patchy.

Food and drink

Few people return from Costa Rica raving about the national dish. The food is simple, relying heavily on the staples of rice and beans. Mixed with shredded beef, chicken or sometimes fish, served with a couple of warmed tortillas and hey presto you have the dish of *casado* that fuels the majority of the country's workers. Only you will know how long you can enjoy the pleasures of rice and beans day after day. One way of spicing up the food is with liberal helpings of *Salsa Lizano* which is always somewhere near the dinner table.

If you want to try national dishes the best place to head for is the central markets. While general advice is to avoid markets, fairly good food hygiene and food sold so quickly it barely has time to go off make most markets in Costa Rica a fairly safe bet. You can tell if the food is good by the number of people waiting. Ultimately you will have to decide but some of the best food encounters are to be had in the markets. The market is also a fairly good place to pick up fruit and salad if you want to prepare some food yourself. Naturally you will need to clean it, but the produce is often fresher than it is in supermarkets – and a fraction of the price.

Restaurants   Courtesy of the influx of nationalities from around the globe, dining in Costa Rica is tantamount to culinary globetrotting. You have the freedom to explore national delights one day, and more familiar dishes from around the globe the next.

Moving up slightly from the markets, restaurants cover a wide range of atmospheres. Local restaurants tend to do most of their business at lunch times when *comida típica* (typical food) is served at a cost of a few dollars. A salad starter, rice 'n' beans served with a lump of chicken or beef for the main course, and a rather strange looking desert – rarely attractive, but always filling.

More upmarket restaurants improve the level of service, atmosphere, food and, naturally, the price. You'll find almost anything your palette desires in San José – French, Italian, Asian, Pacific fusion, seafood – and in the more popular locations round the country. Further afield you can enjoy regional specialities and menu limitations.

Restaurant pricing

Expensive	over US$20	6000+ colónes
Mid-range	US$10-19	3000-5700 colónes
Cheap	US$4-9	1200-2700 colónes
Seriously cheap	less than US$4	less than 1200 colónes

Being a fairly conservative nation, Costa Ricans don't indulge heavily in drinking. On Friday and Saturday nights the streets are not filled with people struggling from one bar to another – but the bars are lively. Once you've tapped into the local happening bar, beer is the lubricant of choice with *Imperial* and *Pilsen* being the most popular lagers and *Bavaria* a darker malty option. **Drinking & bars**

The spirit of choice and convenience is *ron* – not a person, but the Spanish word for rum (a rather immature joke which is considerably more funny after several glasses readily mixed with coke or sprite). Other spirits and good wine find their way to the tables of bars and restaurants as the price rises. How much do you need a gin 'n' tonic?

The sugar-cane, falling-over juice found in dive-bars hidden down poorly lit alleys and best kept there is *Guaro* – guaranteed to provide a sore head and a night you won't forget, even if it is only for the headache the following day.

Café Rica is a caffeine-based liquor, true to the country's coffee origins.

Fruit *Cas* – bitter tasting straight from the fruit mixed with honey or sugar a great *refresco*. *Pejibaye* – almost unique to Costa Rica, it's popular fruit from palm with a soft spikey outside. Sold by the bag-load along the roadside, some people love it, for others it's more effort than it's worth. *Tamarindo* – a date-like fruit that is refreshing to the core when pulped and mixed with ice-cold water. **Food glossary**

Dishes *arroz* – rice. *arroz con… pollo* – rice with… chicken. *bocas* – small dishes for nibbling which may be meat, chicken, fish in various forms. *carne/bistek* - meat/steak. *casados* – standard national lunchtime dish of rice, beans with meat, chicken and fish and a bit of salad. *cerdo* – pork. *ceviche* – fish marinated in lemon, coriander and normally absolutely divine. *chicharrón* – deep fried pork skin cooked until crispy. *corvina* – sea bass. *empanadas* – deep fried tortilla stuffed with meat or chicken. *gallo pinto* – rice'n' (black) beans, which in the Caribbean has the distinctly pleasurable addition of coconut milk. *langosta* – lobster. *mariscos* – seafood. *patacones* – mashed plantain deep fried and normally served with beans. *pescado* - fish. *plátano* – plantains or savoury banana, often fried. *pollo* – chicken. *tamales* – a cornflour-based pastie mixed with chicken, meat or vegetables served in a plantain leaf. *tortillas* – cornflour pancake.

Sweets *cajetas* – a delightful, tooth-achingly sweet spread. *cajeta de leche* – thick, fudge-like milk pudding. *dulce de leche* – baked sweet milk, the gloopy stuff found at the bottom of banoffee pie. *helados* – ice cream. *miel de abeja* – glorious Costa Rican honey. *tres leches* – sponge cake soaked in sweet milk.

Shopping

If you're on an organized tour there will always be a souvenir-buying stop and there is certainly no shortage of things to buy. Items range from small collectables, fridge magnets, knick-knacks and T-shirts of the anthropomorphized gaudy-leaf frogs and "My Uncle went to Costa Rica and…" genre, to genuinely well made wooden furniture and

The fabulous four

If the truth be known, there is a lot of rubbish sold in the tourist market throughout the world and Costa Rica is no different. But there are some gift shops that stand out as offering exceptional choice. Here are the Fabulous Four.
Galería Namu, *in the heart of San José*

behind the Aurola Holiday Inn
Si Como No, *on the road between Quepos and Manuel Antonio*
Toad Hall, *on the northern shore of Lake Arenal*
Finca Cantaros, *south of San Vito close to the Panamanian border.*

---

decorative pieces. Bargaining is not entered into as a rule but you may find the occasional opportunity to flex your negotiating might.

Tips   If you want to buy a few gifts, it's worth having a look at some shops in San José early on in your trip – then as you travel round you'll know what is available at the last minute and can make an informed choice.

Don't buy any archaeological artefacts or items made from endangered species including turtles, animal skins and coral.

What to buy   With row upon row of carefully decorated gifts sitting in neat rows it's easy to think Costa Rica is only full of mass-produced items. Look a little closer and you'll see the quirky touch and character of the hand-painted items.

The main place to buy gifts – for some the only place – is **Sarchí** in the Central Highlands. The town has become the artisan centre of the country, churning out creations of colourful, hand-decorated *carretas* (ox-carts). Given that oxen are rarely used by visitors to Costa Rica, time has seen the carts evolve and shrink to become garden ornaments, drinks cabinets and jewellery boxes. Don't worry about getting them home – they can be flat-packed and shipped if required, as can the sturdy wood and leather rocking chairs sitting on porches and balconies throughout the country. You can relax even further laying back in a hammock.

But if you can't get to the densely packed one-stop shop that is Sarchí, don't worry. You can buy gifts throughout the country. **Wooden carvings** are popular with decorative and functional pieces including bowls, trays and carvings, as well recycled wood from coffee plants used to create figures and animals. Lightweight balsa is often carved into tropical wildlife creations.

Jewellery sets semi-precious jade in gold and silver, and jade, copper and bronze are used to create **precolumbian replicas**. Indigenous pieces are available in a few select places, including the deep red **ceramics** of the Chorotegas in Guaitil, the **masks** and **woven goods** of the Boruca, or the **carved gourds** or *jícara* of the Guaymi and Bribrí in the far south.

Textiles provide plenty of options beyond the simple T-shirt, with mats, table cloths and napkins evoking memories of Costa Rica when you're having a meal back home several months later. Although they're from Panama, vividly colourful *molas* (brightly coloured appliqués) are available in some parts of the south of the country.

Contemporary, traditional and religious **art** hangs off the walls of galleries dotted around San José and Escazú. A personal favourite is the vibrancy of Patricia Erickson – but look around, you'll find something you like. Ceramic creations are no more distinctive than in the colourful and slightly humourous pieces of Cecilia Figueres.

Music makes a good gift and brings back memories faster than a hypnotist in a clock factory. For folklore you won't get a broader swatch than *Costa Rica Pura Vida*, sold in market squares and record shops. Less manic on the *marimba* is the ambient jazz feel of *Editus* who, with Panamanian Rubén Blades, won a Grammy for their album *Tiempos*. Also look out for Costa Rica's very own boy band – the *Brillianticos*. (Those marketing people don't miss a beat.)

Finally fill any spare space in your bag with freshly roasted **coffee**, **liquors** or **paper** and **envelopes** recycled from banana leaves.

Costa Rica is photogenic beyond belief – but getting the animals of the rainforest on film requires patience, a good SLR camera, a zoom lens and a tripod to keep things steady. If you want to carry all the gear, your best choice of film is something reasonably fast (400 ASA) which can tolerate the poor lighting.

Photography

Beyond the specialist, a good quality point and shoot is very good at capturing the moment quickly, allowing you to enjoy the moment once you've taken the shot.

It is always best to take all the film supplies you need to avoid getting stuck with something you are not familiar or comfortable with. However, *Kodak* and *Fuji* (good for slides) have begun to open up air-conditioned stores all around the country. A 24 exposure 100 ASA film is US$6, 200 ASA US$12. For print it's 100 ASA for US$5, 200 ASA for US$6.

Essentials

Holidays and festivals

Bank holidays are normally a cause for celebration and Costa Rica is no different. Big festivals tend to go big on processions, costumes and traditional marching bands, but find a small town and you'll find horse-racing, bull-friendly bull fighting (where the lucky beast leaves the ring exhausted but alive) and a chance to rub shoulders with the townsfolk and any minor gathering.

The main holiday period of the year is Christmas and New Year, and Easter week when much of San José decants from the highlands to the beaches. Book well in advance.

On national holidays, banks, government offices and stores close down so make sure you have enough money. National holidays are listed here marked, regional and local festivals are listed in the relevant chapter.

January 1 – *New Year's Day*
March (second Sunday) – *National Oxcart Day* with colourful processions and music in Escazú. **March/April** – *Maundy Thursday* and *Good Friday*, Easter Week. **April 11** – *Juan Santamaría Day*, celebrating the victorious Battle of Rivas against William Walker in 1856.
May 1 – *Labour Day* which apparently heralds the President's State of the Nation address, cricket matches and a day off. Howzat.
July 25 – *Annexation of Guanacaste*, celebrating Guanacaste's decision to stay with Costa Rica over Nicaragua in 1824
August 2 – *Virgin Mary Queen of Angels*, Patron of Costa Rica celebrated with religious pilgrimages to the Basilica in Cartago. **August 15** – *Day of the Virgin Mary's Assumption to Heaven* and Mother's Day
September 15 – *Independence Day* with parades and marching bands through the streets of San José.
October 12 – *Spanish discovery of the New World* celebrated with particular energy and flair in Limón and the Caribbean.
November 2 – *All Soul's Day* or the Day of the Dead, showing respect to those who have passed on.
December 25 – *Christmas* celebrations build before and continue in the week after, particularly in San José but also at a smaller scale throughout much of the country.
December 31st, January 1st and 2nd – *La Danza de los Diablitos* a festival with traditional masks, costumes, music and dancing in the Indian village of Boruca.

Special interest travel

Evoking images of anoraks and a rather naff dress sense, special interest travel is not just the realm of the 'specialist' – Costa Rica is a great place to try out a new activity, spend more time on a new hobby and, of course, for the specialist to really focus on your chosen area.

While some activities make little demands on the physical body, some do involve obvious risks. In general, Costa Rican tour operators make every effort to ensure safety in all their activities. However, accidents do and can happen and there is no way of avoiding them all the time. Both the tour operator and the client have a responsibility to know and accept their limits. Seek assurances from tour operators that they have considered any risks and ultimately go with your own instincts. Any responsible company will be more than happy to discuss safety issues. Likewise if you feel something is unsafe or close to your personal limits, have the courage to speak out and stop. The Costa Rican Tourist Board has undertaken to introduce a licensing scheme which should ensure certain standards of operations.

Birdwatching
If visiting in the low season, make sure the lodges you are visiting have guides

With more birds than the whole of North America or Europe – 875 at the last count – Costa Rica is undoubtedly a birdwatcher's paradise. Thousands of birders visit Costa Rica every year, either travelling on their own or as part of a small group bird watching tour, to see some of the most magnificent birds in the Neotropics; the resplendent quetzal, three-wattled bellbird, bare-necked umbrellabird, violaceous trogon, scarlet macaw, chestnut-bellied heron, turquoise cotinga, sunbittern and hundreds more species.

Birdwatching is good all year round. Of course, rainforests need rain, but you'll seldom miss a day of birdwatching because of the weather. Most places have the highest rainfall during September to November. While Costa Rica's tourist high season is from December to April. If you've already seen many of the North American migrants, you'll be happy to visit Costa Rica later in the year to see the resident bird species. Birds are often easier to spot during the breeding season. Nesting reaches its peak from April to June according to locality and continues on a diminishing scale until August or September.

If you want to experience the **raptor migrations** between North and South America, then plan your birdwatching trip during March/April or September/October. *La Selva Biological Station* and *Selva Verde Lodge* along the route of the Río Sarapiquí, the Siquirres/Guácimo area along the route of the Reventazón, Pacuare and Parismina rivers and several spots down the southern Caribbean are good places to see migrations.

The **resplendent quetzal** is considered by many to be the most beautiful bird in the world. While Monteverde is famous for quetzals, you can easily see them less than two hours from San José in the Cerro de la Muerte highlands (guided walks can be arranged at *Finca Mirador de Quetzales* or *Savegre Mountain Lodge*).

Two of the best known birding spots are *La Selva Biological Station* in the Caribbean lowlands – which runs birdwatching courses – and the world famous **Monteverde cloudforest**. La Selva is part of the *Organisation for Tropical Studies* (www.ots.ac.cr). And check www.cloudforestalive.org for live views of the quetzal nesting or for more information on Monteverde.

Once out of the towns and cities of the Central Valley you'll find a tremendous diversity of habitats from the lush cloudforests of Monteverde, to the dry deciduous forests of **Guanacaste**, to the rainforests of the **Caribbean lowlands**. And even subalpine *páramo* in the **Cerro de la Muerte highlands**. During recent years many new private reserves with comfortable lodging have opened up throughout the country, some bordering national parks. A typical birdwatching trip might include *Villa Lapas* (bordering Parque Nacional Carara), *Tiskita Lodge* in the south pacific coast (near

Punta Banco), Monteverde Cloudforest, Tortuguero National Park on the Caribbean coast, and a visit to *La Selva Biological Station*.

When planning a birdwatching trip, while Costa Rica looks small on a map, it's very mountainous and what seems like a short journey might take several hours to drive. So always allow yourself at least 3 nights at each place to give you at least two full days to see the birds. Of course, serious birders will need the "bible"; *A Guide To The Birds Of Costa Rica* (by Gary Stiles and Alexander Skutch, published by Cornell University Press).

If you're seeking a birdwatching trip contact a specialist. *Birdwatch Costa Rica*, who supplied this information, arrange customized birdwatching trips of two weeks or more. **Birdwatch Costa Rica**, Apdo 7911, 1000 San José, Costa Rica, F228-1573, birdwatch@racsa.co.cr

The **Birding Club of Costa Rica** has monthly outings which you can join with a temporary membership of US$10, get details from crbirdingclub.tripod.com as well as a complete and up-to-date Costa Rica bird list.

More general tours can be arranged through tour operators in San José. From the United States you can organize tours with *Field Guides*, 9433 Bee Cave Road, Building 1, Suite 150, Austin, TX 78733, T800-728-4953 or T512-263-7295, F512-263-0117, www.fieldguides.com Also look at *Wings*, 1643 N.Alvernon, Suite 105, Tucson, AZ 85712, T888-293-6443 or T520-320-9868, F520-320-9373, www.wingsbirds.com or **Cheeseman's Ecology Safari Tours**, 20800 Kittredge Road, Saratoga, CA 95070, T800-527-5330 in the US or T408-867-1371, F408-741-0358, cheesemans@aol.com

You've had enough, it's all too much, time to jump off a bridge. Probably the biggest buzz in Costa Rica, *Tropical Bungee* will attach you to a big elastic band outside an inflatable raft and let you freefall to the Río Colorado some 80 m below. Since beginning in 1991, *Tropical Bungee* have had over 10,000 jumps to their name. They are based on the Pan-American Highway close to Grecia, T232-3956, F232-3961, www.bungee.co.cr

Bungee jumping

The rainforest canopy is where most of the wildlife action takes places and there are now a multitude of ways of getting you up there.

Canopy tours

The calmest is probably exploring on a suspension bridge, strung out along the trees where you are free to walk at leisure or with a guide in complete silence if you wish. The main suspension tours are in **Santa Elena**, close to Puerto Viejo de Sarapiquí, and **Rainmaker** near to Quepos.

An equally calm way through the canopy is on an aerial tour, using adapted ski lifts to carry you through the canopy. The most well known (and expensive) is on the eastern fringes of **Braulio Carrillo National Park** with another less impressive option in **Monteverde**.

The best high adrenaline option is the zip wire, which has hundreds of people whizzing down high-tension steel cables strung out between forest giants. You won't see much as you fly through the air, but it is good fun and you do get close to the forest canopy. It's a popular option and spreading like wildfire. But be wary, there have been several fatal accidents on zip wires in Costa Rica. If you do not receive sufficient reassurance of the safety of the equipment don't do the ride. The introduction of licencing should ensure that every operator has properly considered safety.

Finally there is the good old-fashioned option of climbing a tree – almost. A couple of places, in particular *Hacienda Barú*, let you use tree climbing grappling and ropes. Prices vary greatly starting at US$8, rising to around US$75. Such is the cost of tree climbing these days.

Essentials

Essentials

Diving

Costa Rica gets a bit of a hard time on the diving front primarily because of sporadic visibility which hangs around the 30-50 ft range in the wet season. Go when there is less rain and you can enjoy the warm waters

The northern Pacific coast around **Playa del Coco** is a local diving hotspot with trips out to nearby islands. Further south, **Drake**, on the northern coast of the peninsula, is a popular base to visit Isla del Caño where you're almost guaranteed sightings of sharks, ray and other pelagics. On the Caribbean side, the dive action is in the coral waters off the coast of **Cahuita National Park** and further south around **Gandoca-Manzanillo National Wildlife Refuge**. Each region has specialist dive shops that can arrange diving – although you might want to book Drake in advance if you're planning to visit.

The very best diving happens miles away, literally, in the clear waters of the **Cocos Islands**, over 500 km southwest of Costa Rica in the Pacific. Undisturbed corals and hammerhead and white-tipped sharks await visitors on the live-aboard dive boats sailing from Puntarenas.

The **cost** of diving starts at around US$35 for a beach dive on the south Caribbean, rising to around US$85 for a two tank dive. A *PADI* Open Water Course out of Playa del Coco is about US$285. Diving trips out to the Cocos Islands on live-aboard boats start at around US$2800 for a nine-day trip, with six full days diving.

Driving

See also page 48

The freedom to move around at will has seen a steady growth in the fly-drive option in Costa Rica – and it's difficult to beat. Take two weeks, the first planned for you, the second with a vehicle, a good map and a guide book. You move and stop when you like, and it is very popular – as proven by the large number of car hire firms in San José and other parts of the country.

But the fly-drive option is not just limited to cars. You can tour by motorbike (see page 50) or have someone else do the driving in exciting off-road adventures. For details contact *Aventuras 4x4 Costa Rica*, T289-9528, toll free from the US on 1-866-494-8687, www.aventuras4x4.com Tours start at US$200 a day.

Golf

Spoiling a good walk, as Mark Twain once described golf, is definitely on the up

In Costa Rica the Pacific Coast has seen a spate of 18-hole championship links courses come to fruition including **Los Sueños Marriott** in the Central Pacific. Further north close to Tamarindo and Playa Conchal are the **Garra de León** and **Royal Pacific**, or just south of Tamarindo is **Hacienda Pinilla**. In the Central Highlands you'll find the opportunity to swing your clubs at the **Melía Cariari** outside San José or a short distance west of Santa Ana at the **Valle del Sol**. Prices range from US$45 up to US$140 in some of the country clubs. All tee times and arrangements can be booked through *Costa Rica Golf Adventures*, T877-258-2688 toll free from North America, www.golfcr.com Bespoke tours combining nature tours and fishing can also be arranged.

Hot air ballooning

Take to the air and enjoy the view from above in a hot air balloon floating above the Central Highlands and around **Lake Arenal**. A truly unforgettable experience that can be organized through *Serendipity Adventures*, T558-1000, F558-1010, or in USA T800-635-2325, www.serendipityadventures.com Flights start at US$500 for two people from **Turrialba**, around Arenal the price is US$900 for up to five people.

Language schools

When learning a language, accept early on that you will have to make a fool of yourself at some point

There are over 40 language schools throughout Costa Rica providing a mix of Spanish courses. The majority are in San José and the surrounding Central Highlands. Classes normally last for four hours, given in the morning or afternoon (some people just can't study in the mornings), five days a week. Although one week is helpful, longer stays are encouraged for real progress. Conventional wisdom suggests that one-to-one classes create the optimum learning conditions, but some people don't like the intensive focus. More commonly, classes are in groups of two to six people. Good schools provide an activity programme with trips to attractions and national parks to complement classes, and some also provide academic credits.

If you're serious about learning Spanish, choosing a **homestay** is the best option because you avoid contact with English speakers. A homestay is literally staying in the

home of a *Tico* family. By taking classes and living with a Spanish speaking family you maximize the opportunities for learning and practising your new language skills. This so-called "immersion technique" can be pretty tough, but it does work.

Beyond San José there are schools in several parts of the country. You can hang out at the beach in Flamingo or down in Montezumo, take classes in the cloudforests of Montverde or relax in the Orosi Valley while you practice your verbs. No one ever said learning a language was easy, but it can be easier in a beautiful place.

Prices vary considerably. The **Centro Panamericano de Idiomas**, who have schools in Flamingo, Monteverde and Heredia, charge US$660 for two weeks of 4 hours a day. **Amerispan** offer classes at eight different locations, charging between US$625 and US$910. Contact *Amerispan* in the US on T800-879-6640, F215-751-1986, www. amerispan.com See San José (page 132) and other destinations' directories for schools in the capital and throughout the country.

Mountain biking

Pedal power has taken over in parts of Costa Rica. You can rent a bike for a couple of hours, a day or a couple of weeks. You can strike out on your own and just see where your instincts take you. If you're really into the idea of mountain biking, consider joining a tour. It's the best way to get to some of the off-road sites without leaving the whole thing down to chance.

Naturally the opportunities vary greatly. According to Brenda Kelly at *Coast to Coast*, **Guanacaste** is ideal for hugging the coastline, getting fantastic views and a challenging ride. Several two-day trips out of **San José** give you the chance to get seriously muddy, ending up in places like Manuel Antonio, or mixing the biking with paddling down whitewater. The ultimate adventure is a *Coast to Coast* ride which takes 14 days, lots of muscle and determination – there are some serious uphill sections – but it's ultimately rewarded with views from the continental divide and down the Orosi Valley. *Coast to Coast Adventures*, T280-8054, F225-6055, www. ctocadventures.com can provide bespoke biking tours, or you can fit in with their busy and often recommended schedule. They provide all the gear including bike, water bottle and helmet. Mountain bike rental from a general hire company works out at around US$5 an hour. A two-day trip with *Coast to Coast* is US$250 all inclusive. For serious adventure sports fans, *Coast to Coast* offer several trips that combine biking, hiking and rafting which work as ideal training for the various Eco Challenge events around the world.

National parks & nature tourism

Volunteering in the national park system can be arranged through ASVO, Av 8, C 25, San José, T222-5085, F233-4989, asvo89@racsa.co.cr

With so many national parks and protected areas, natural attractions are most of the appeal of Costa Rica. Turtle watching in Tortuguero and Las Baulas National Park, dolphin and whale spotting around the Osa Peninsula, birdwatching through the protected areas throughout the country.

The 25 national parks, biological reserves, wildlife refuges and other protected areas protect 25.4% of the national territory according to *MINAE* – the *Ministerio de Ambiente y Energía*, who have overall control of administering and managing the parks. For more detail on specific parks, see the relevant entry in the text and for more detail about the national park system see the Background chapter, page 401.

Entrance to all national parks costs US$6. Entrance times vary, while a handful (Manuel Antonio, Braulio Carrillo, Guayobo and Cabo Blanco) actually close for a day or two to relieve pressure on the areas and for maintenance.

Most parks can be visited easily and conveniently simply by turning up. If you have a specific enquiry or want to book in advance, contact the **Fundación de Parques Nacionales** in San José on 192 or visit them at C 23-25, Av 15, Barrio Escalante, T257-2239, F222-4732, azucena@ns.minae.go.cr or look at the website www.minae.go.cr which has information about some of the protected areas and is growing to encompass the whole network.

Sometimes the whole country feels like a botanical garden but areas of particular interest to botanists and orchidophiles will be the *Lankester Botanical Gardens*, a short trip southeast of San José which breaks into a riot of blooms between February and April. On the road to Puerto Viejo de Sarapiquí you will find *Isla de las Heliconias*, with over 70 examples of heliconias. Nearby *La Selva Biological Station* and *Rara Avis* are equally inspiring with incredible rainforest diversity on the Caribbean slopes. In the far south of the country, close to San Vito, *Wilson Botanical Gardens* is the treasured reward of 40 years of visionary planting, with over 5,000 tropical species.

Orchids, flowers & botanical gardens

Fishing just doesn't get any better than you will find in Costa Rica, with tarpon and snook on the Caribbean; marlin, sailfish, dorado, tuna and other species on the Pacific and trout, rainbow bass (guapote), bobo, machaca and more in inland lakes and rivers.

Sport fishing

Essentials

According to Jerry Ruhlow – who has been living, fishing and writing about fishing in Costa Rica since 1983 – it is essential to plan ahead. Peak fishing varies with the time of year and beach accommodations and the top boats are often hard to find when fishing is at its best, so book ahead. Jerry has kindly summarized the best seasons in the different parts of Costa Rica. Naturally they vary from year to year, depending on weather, water temperatures and other factors.

Pacific coast   On the southernmost Pacific coast, in the **Golfito**, **Puerto Jiménez** and **Drake Bay** region, **marlin** action is best from August to December. There are **sailfish** year round, but the peak is from late November to March. It may slow from April into June then pick up again in July. If **non-stop action** is your preference and you don't have to hang a billfish to be happy, the Golfito region is your best bet. More than 40 International Game Fish Association (IGFA) certified world records have been established here and the species you can expect to catch at almost any time of year include **tuna** (sometimes to 400 pounds), **wahoo**, **amberjack**, **jack crevalle**, **grouper**, **cubera**, **barracuda**, **big roosterfish**, **corbina** and **snook**.

Next major fishing area heading north is **Quepos** where December to end of April is the best season for **billfish** although some **marlin** and **sailfish** are taken year round. **Dorado** and football-size **tuna** are nearly always plentiful, and they often get giant yellowfin tuna as well.

Mid-December to April are the best months for boats based in **Playa Carrillo** and the **Sámara** region as the main body of fish continue moving north. They often get there earlier and stay longer, depending on water temperature and other factors. **Dorado** and **tuna** are also plentiful these months.

A northerly wind blows from December into May in the **northernmost region**, but once the calm has returned the fishing is little short of sensational from late May or June into early September, with **marlin** peaking in August and September. There are two major tournaments in July – a few years ago one of those tournaments posted a record 1,696 billfish in a four-day competition out of Flamingo Marina. Charter boats operate out of Tamarindo, Flamingo, Portrero, Ocotal and Playa de Coco. There's always plenty of **dorado** and **tuna** in the area, and anglers working the nearby Catalina and Murcielago (Bat) Islands also score **wahoo**, **amberjack**, **cubera**, **roosters** and other structure fish.

Caribbean Coast   On the northern Caribbean coast, **tarpon** and **snook** are around most of the year, with slumps from May to mid-July when the rains are at their heaviest. Peak season is from about September through April, although late July during the veranillo (little summer), when rains usually stop for two or three weeks, is also excellent most years. **Rainbow bass** (*guapote*) and other freshwater species can be caught here year round in the miles of rivers and backwater lagoons. Most consistent fishing is out of the lodges near the mouth of the **Río Colorado**, but some are also caught at

Tortuguero and **Parismina**. Northern Caribbean coast does not offer much in the way of sportfishing.

Inland waters For inland waters, **Lake Arenal** offers year-round fishing, but the quality will vary depending on wind and water level. It is a beautiful 22-mile long lake about 3½ hours' drive from San José. Guides are available locally with fully equipped boats complete with tackle. **Rainbow bass** (*guapote*) are the species most anglers go for. A beautiful fish in pastel shades of pink, rose, greens and blues, with feathered caudal and dorsal fins and a mean set of teeth, they are found only in Costa Rica and a few inland waters of southern Nicaragua. *IGFA* record is 12½ lbs, taken here. Rainbow bass, **bobo**, **machaca**, **tepemechin** and other tropical species are also found in rivers throughout the country, along with **rainbow trout** in some high mountain rivers.

Caño Negro Lagoon is a huge inland waterway that offers all of the above, plus **tarpon** and **snook**. Some waters are seasonal, and regulations often change from year to year, so check in advance.

Cost The cost of fishing varies considerably depending on the type of fishing, location, number of days and people, and accommodation requirements, to the extent that generalizing is difficult. Deep sea fishing starts at around US$600 for one day, inland waterways can start as little as US$250 for the day. For more specific information and updated fishing reports contact Jerry Ruhlow on T1-800-308-3394, info@costaricaoutdoors.com or at www.costaricaoutdoors.com Also look at lodges in the main fishing areas.

Surfing

The only drawback to surfing in this country can be the annoyance of jellyfish, sea lice and the odd crocodile! And remember, pack mosquito repellent

Costa Rica offers the travelling surfer world class waves in beautiful surroundings with air and water temperatures averaging in the high 20s! Personally, every attempt to get on a surfboard from Hawaii to California has resulted in spectacular and dismal failure. Fortunately Phil Miller, surfer and videographer knows a thing or two about the subject. Here's Phil's run-down of the surf spots in Costa Rica.

Most breaks work better at the end of the wet season, supposedly when the rivers have had time to form the sand bars properly. The tidal range for the Pacific coast is quite large, being up to 12 ft and this can obviously affect the size of the waves. If surfing on the Pacific coast, grab yourself a tide chart – freely available in most surf centres or printed in the free regional magazines. On the Caribbean coast the variation is not so much of a problem with daily fluctuations of around 1½ ft.

A four-wheel drive can be a necessity if travelling along much of the Costa Rican coast as many waves are only accessible along dirt tracks and even these can be inaccessible during the wet season. Check at a local surf shop before leaving for possible cut off breaks. Also a number of breaks are only accessible by boat. Once more, you may need to check on how to access these waves before leaving and being disappointed!

Pacific coast One of the towns most associated with surfing in Costa Rica is **Tamarindo**. Located about 450 km northwest of San José, Tamarindo is an excellent place from which to access the quality breaks which lie along the north Pacific coast. Best surfing conditions are from December through to June. Tamarindo itself has lots of good hotels and three good breaks; El Estero, a long right hander; Pico Pequeño; and Langosta, a strong quality point wave. Just north of Tamarindo lies **Potrero Grande**. Known as Oli's Point (supposedly after Oliver North who had a secret base nearby), Potrero Grande is a fast right-hand point breaking over a reef. A southerly swell can give a quality wave of up to 7 ft plus. Access is by boat. **Playa Grande** is the most westerly point of Costa Rica and as a result can get swells from north, south and west.

To the far north is **Santa Rosa National Park** and **Playa Naranjo**, home of Peña Bruja, mistakenly translated in the eighties as 'Witches Rock'. The name has now stuck and the beach provides a high quality and picturesque beach break with fast hollow waves. Access is by four-wheel drive during dry season (boat during the wet) and camping is available at the Park Ranger's Station.

South from Tamarindo around the coastline of the Nicoya Peninsula lie **Avellanas**, **Playa Negra**, **Callejones** and **Junquillal**. Avellanas is a quality beach break with a right point known as Little Hawaii. Playa Negra is 10 minutes south of Avellanas and a popular spot. This solid right hand point wave can be crowded and dangerously shallow at low tide. The spot holds up to 10 ft on a westerly swell. Some 600 m further south lies Callejones which can be much less crowded than Playa Negra. Further south still lies Junquillal which can offer beach break waves throughout the tidal range.

Towards the end of the Peninsula and the Cabo Blanco Reserve are a number of beautiful and uncrowded beach breaks, including **Nosara**, **Sámara** and **Punta Guiones**. After this spot, the waves become more of a challenge to get to, with many only accessible by four-wheel drive.

Boca Barranca, just north of Jacó, has a long, fast left hander that breaks over a sand bottom and into the river mouth. It needs a good-sized swell to get through reefs which can make for a smaller wave than further down the coast. The best time to surf here is early in the morning and on a good day it can hold up to 10 ft. The river is supposedly free of crocodiles but it's worth keeping a wary eye out!

Essentials

Surf sites

N

0 km   30
0 miles   30

	4 Playa Tamarindo	15 Playa Escondida	26 Drake Bay
	5 Langosta	16 Playa Jacó	27 Matapalo
	6 Avellanas	17 Roca Loca	28 Pavones
	7 Playa Negra	18 Playa Hermosa	29 Punta Burica
	8 Nosara	19 West Esterillos	30 Manzanillo
	9 Playa Coyote	20 East Esterillos	31 Puerto Viejo
	10 Malpaís	21 Boca Damas	32 Black Beach, Cahuita
1 Potrero Grande	11 Cabuya	22 Quepos	33 Westfalia
2 Playa Naranjo	12 Boca Barranca	23 Playa Espadilla	34 Uvita Island
(Witch's Rock)	13 Caldera Port	24 Playa El Roy	35 Playa Bonita
3 Playa Grande	14 Tivives Beach & Valor	25 Playa Dominical	

South of Boca Barranca towards Jacó is **Puerto Caldera**, a popular left-hander best surfed on the incoming tide. Further south off the Costanera Highway lie **Tivives** and **Valor**. Tivives is a beach break that offers lefts and rights and also a hollow left breaking into the river-mouth. Access to Valor is by paddling across the river. Both can sometimes be polluted.

Playa Escondida lies at the mouth of the Gulf of Nicoya and is accessible only by boat. Situated just to the north of Jacó, this beach offers both lefts and rights and is best between mid and high tide. **Jacó**, as well as being a lively spot to stay for the travelling surfer and a useful base for exploring the area, is the closest beach resort to San José and so can become quite crowded. However, there are a number of quality breaks located close to the town. **Roca Loca** is five minutes' south of Jacó and is accessible only by climbing down the cliff then across the rocks – a good quality wave that is not for the faint hearted. Ten minutes south of Jacó lies **Playa Hermosa**, a high quality break with a hollow peak that could be compared to Puerto Escondido in Mexico. The peak tends to shift around and can become crowded.

On the journey south towards Quepos is **Esterillos**, located some 40 minutes drive from Jacó. It is a quiet, uncrowded beach break with entertainment provided by the nearby town. Between Esterillos and Quepos lies the town of **Parrita**, offering both reef and beach breaks, and **Playa El Rey**, which is accessed via a palm tree plantation and has waves similar to Playa Hermosa. Just north of Quepos lies **Boca Damas**. Located next to the mouth of the Damas River, this spot that can hold a sizeable swell. **Quepos** itself offers a choice of accommodation and a lively nightlife with a beach break with strong lefts. **Playa Espidilla** in Manuel Antonio, just south of Quepos, needs a good size swell to work but can offer both lefts and rights.

Further south again is the town of **Dominical**. This surf town is basic but offers some of the best beach breaks in Costa Rica. It also has a left and right reef break and the area is often frequented by pods of dolphins. Working better at the end of the wet season, the waves can be very hollow.

The South Pacific coastline is dominated by the Osa Peninsula. At the north end close to the mainland is **Bahía Drake**. Only accessible by boat, Drake is a beautiful spot for surfing or just simply enjoying if the surf is flat. At the southern tip of the Peninsula is **Matapalo**, which can be reached by car from Puerto Jiménez or by boat from Pavones, just across the mouth of the Golfo Dulce. The best waves are a 15 to 20 minute walk through jungle teeming with native fauna. The three spots worth checking out in the area are **Back Wash**, a slow right hander which works best on a big swell, **Pan Dulce**, a small white sand bay with a hollow right that works well on a mid to large swell, and **Matapalo**, a powerful right hander which can hold a sizeable swell.

Across the Gulf lies **Pavones**, the longest ride in Costa Rica. On a large swell the left hander can give a ride for approximately 800 m as the different sections connect together. Pavones is a 5-hour drive from south of Dominical, or a short boat taxi from Golfito, but it's quality can lead to a crowded line up. However, as luck would have it, there are a number of other left handers around the point and also a beach break which can be bigger than the point itself.

Towards the border with Panama lies **Punta Banco**, a left and right breaking over a coral reef. Located 3 km south of Pavones, a good place to check if the waves there are too small or crowded. **Punta Burica** is the last beach on the Costa Rican Pacific coast before Panama, which shares this headland with Costa Rica. This beach is only accessible by boat.

Caribbean Coast Storms in the Caribbean Sea produce swells which can become quite sizeable depending on direction, and which break on the coral reefs close to the Costa Rican coast. The best waves are found November to March. The coastline is much shorter than the Pacific coast with Limón at the centre with most of the breaks to the south of the town.

The three quality breaks in **Limón** worth checking out are **Playa Bonita**, a strong left breaking over a coral reef which can be a challenging drop, **Portete**, which is a hollow right hander breaking over coral, and **Isla Uvita**, only accessible by a dawn boat out of Limón, with a wave that breaks in three sections over a shallow coral reef. On a good day this can produce a powerful wave of up to 10 ft.

South from Limón towards the Panamanian border lies **Cahuita**, a beautiful National Park with great beaches and waves. Further south still is **Puerto Viejo**. Known as '*Salsa brava*', Puerto Viejo is an extremely powerful wave breaking over coral – you may need to pack a spare board for this one. Ten minutes further down the coast is the fun beach break of **Playa Cocles**, which can have strong currents, and **Manzanillo**, which has good quality, uncrowded waves.

Tour operators You can rent a board or even take classes in the fine art of surfing at many of the more popular destinations, and get water taxis to some of the more secluded spots. If you want someone to do the organizing of a one-day tour or a fortnight trip try *Alacran Surf Tours*, 100 m north of Banco Interfin in San José, T/F232-9297, toll free on 1-866-252-2726, www.alacransurf.com who are also a full service travel agents. You can also try *Tico Travel*, toll free on T1-800-493-8426, www.ticotravel.com with very cheap flights and good deals on surfing trips.

Short treks ranging from 20 minutes through to multi-day trips can be found throughout the country, but with so many competing activities, hiking and trekking often takes a bit of a back seat. But beyond the dashing between nature reserves and short guided walks lasting a few hours there are some very good hiking opportunities. Just look at a topographical map and let your mind get carried away.

The most popular hike has to be up **Cerro Chirripó**, the country's highest peak at 3,820 m. The shortest route is a steady trudge up and down, but there are many variations on that theme that add to the two- or three-day hike. Second on the list is hiking through the tropical wet forest of **Corcovado National Park** on the Osa Peninsula. Hot, sweaty, hard work and very rewarding.

Less common walks head from the cloudforests of Monteverde down the Caribbean slope to Arenal, and further north trails lead through the national parks of **Rincón de la Vieja** and **Tenorio**.

The ultimate trek has to be **crossing the continental divide** following ancient indigenous trails from Puerto Viejo de Talamanca heading west to the Pacific. Ten tough days, carrying all your own gear, through an altitude gain of over 3,000 m – scenic, arduous and oh so satisfying.

Tour operators Most treks can be organized by *Ocarina Expeditions* in San José contact them on T221-5322, F221-5031, www.ocarinaexpeditions.com Fully supported day treks start at around US$60-US$85. A four-day trip to Chirripó is roughly US$450 per person. The tough coast to coast trip is provided by *ATEC* based down in Puerto Viejo de Talamanca on T750-0398 or T/F750-0191, greencoast.com/atec.htm US$400 per person no frills.

Whoever created this sport deserves a medal. In Costa Rica rafting takes you through some of the most spectacular scenery in the country. One moment you're drifting through valleys that merge the highlights of the Hanging Gardens of Babylon with the Garden of Eden, the next you're fighting for dear life as your adrenaline-pumped body is forced head-first through a wall of water. It isn't everyone's cup of tea, but it is mighty refreshing.

Whitewater rafting needs mountains (or at least hills) and water. "Costa Rica has an abundance of water," according to Michael Mayfield and Rafael Gallo in *The Rivers of Costa Rica: A canoeing, kayaking and rafting guide*. It is this surfeit of water that fills the

Trekking & hiking

Rafting

Essentials

Essentials

River ratings

Class I *Easy. Moving water a few ripples and small waves.*
Class II *Novice. Easy rapids with waves up to three feet, and wide, clear channels that are obvious without scouting.*
Class III *Intermediate. Rapids with high, irregular waves often capable of swamping an open canoe.*
Class IV *Advanced. Long, difficult rapids*

with constricted passages that often require precise manoeuvring in very turbulent waters.
Class V *Expert. Extremely difficult, long and very violent rapids with highly congested routes that nearly always have to be scouted from shore.*
Class VI *Extreme difficulties of Class V carried to the extreme of navigability.*

channels of the **Reventazón**, **Pacuare** and **Sarapiquí** on the Caribbean slope, and the **General** and **Corobicí** on the Pacific creating a fantastic array of aquadventure.

Whitewater rafting in Costa Rica started in the early 1980s. From early pioneer days of struggling with equipment to hidden put-ins the most popular rivers and routes are now well established with fairly easy access.

Most trips in Costa Rica start from San José and head out to the chosen river. The all-inclusive nature of trips removes the need to think about food and refreshment. You will need a change of clothes for the night if you are on a two or three day trip, and some clothes for the end of the trip.

As with all adventure sports safety is paramount – fatal accidents have occurred in Costa Rica. Good commercial outfitters like *Costa Rica Expeditions* or *Rios Tropicales* will assess your experience and suitability before taking your booking. You receive a complete safety briefing before beginning rafting and if you're not up to standard you will be asked to leave. Likewise, if you are not satisfied with the level of safety seek reassurance and if still not reassured, ask to leave.

You don't have to be an adrenaline junky for whitewater rafting, or even incredibly fit. Rafting assesses rivers in terms of difficulty. A simple trip or float down parts of the Corobicí or Sarapiquí is a Class I or II – gentle and relaxing, it's a great way to see wildlife. Class III marks the beginning of whitewater rafting, with Classes IV and above requiring previous experience. The most popular Class III and IV rivers are sections of the Pacuare and Reventazón, near Turrialba, the Sarapiquí and General. Class V requires experience and specialist knowledge.

You can raft all year round although conditions vary. If you want to go down a particular river it is worth planning in advance with a specialist tour operator. Costs vary considerably depending on the number of days, with a one-day trip starting at around US$75, with a couple of days costing US$250 and three days US$300, including all meals and transport to and from San José.

Tour operators *Costa Rica Expeditions*, Av 3, C Central-2, T257-0766, F257-1655, www.costaricaexpeditions.com are the longest running kayak operation in Costa Rica, and highly respected as are ***Ríos Tropicales***, C 38, between Paseo Colón and Av 2, 50 m south of Subway, T233-6455, F255-4354, www.riostropicales.com who have a lodge on the Pacuare. For other operators see San José.

Westerly trade winds blow across northern Costa Rica between December and April. Reluctantly the air is pushed up and over obstacles eventually being forced through the corridor that is Lake Arenal. The most reliable winds in the northern hemisphere provide the western end of the lake, and Bahia Salinas on the Pacific to the north, with world-class windsurfing destinations.

Windsurfing

Opportunities for novices and experts exist. Beginner courses are provided by a couple of lodges in the area, with boards, wetsuits and even money-back guarantees provided. For the experts, if you fancy a change you can try out the latest watersport developments including kite-surfing.

Tilawa, T695-5050, F695-5766, www.hotel-tilawa.com provides windsurfing, kitesurfing, wakeboarding and a windsurfing school at their hotel. *Ticowind*, T1-800-433-2423, www.ticowind.com

By this point you will have realised that the options are wide and varied in Costa Rica. A top personal tip is to try and do nothing for a while. Tough it's true, but give it a shot. Pick up a book, open the covers, read it even…

Doing nothing

Spectator sports

The national sport in Costa Rica is football and it's a great experience to join the migrating colours to a Sunday morning match. In all honesty, the quality is not fantastic but football lovers already know that the beautiful game is not all fine touches and wizardry, but more about loyalty. And in Costa Rica of that there is no doubt.

Football
For information on fixtures and league tables look in the local press or on the net at www.intnet.co.cr/ sports/sports.html

The 12 teams that make up the national league play on Sunday mornings, and occasionally mid-week on Wednesday, and tickets are rarely sold out. The two dominant sides are Saprissa, who play in Tibas north of San José, and La Liga in Alajuela. By all accounts the country went mad in 1990 when the national squad qualified for the World Cup, and everytime Paulo Wanchope touches the ball for Manchester City in the UK, Costa Rican newspapers plaster the sports pages with reports.

Responsible travel

Costa Rica has undergone a phenomenal change in recent decades from the slash and burn deforestation to being one of the planet's leading exponents of nature tourism and what is currently called 'ecotourism'.

Costa Rica is indisputably one of the world's most popular nature destinations and tourism, which attracts over one million visitors to the country every year, is the country's leading foreign exchange earner. But while there are clearly benefits from international travel for both the host country and travellers – employment and cultural exchange – there can also be a downside. Where visitor pressure is high and poorly regulated, adverse impacts on society and the natural environment may be apparent. In Costa Rica environmentalists have criticized several tourism projects including the huge Papagayo project on the north Nicoya Peninsula and the Barcelo Tambor to the

Essentials

 **How big is your footprint?**

- *Where possible choose a tour operator or hotel with a proven ethical and environmental commitment - if in doubt ask.*
- *Consider staying in local accommodation rather than foreign-owned hotels – the economic benefits for host communities are far greater – and there are far more opportunities to learn about local culture.*
- *Spend money on locally produced (rather than imported) goods and services and use common sense when bargaining – your few dollars saved may be a week's salary to others.*
- *Use water and electricity carefully – travellers may receive a preferential supply while the needs of local communities are overlooked.*
- *Learn about local etiquette and culture – consider local norms, behaviour and dress appropriately for local cultures and situations.*
- *Protect wildlife and other natural resources – don't buy souvenirs or goods made from wildlife unless they are clearly sustainably produced and are not protected under CITES legislation (CITES controls trade in endangered species).*
- *Always ask before taking photographs or videos of people.*

south of the peninsula for infringing and destroying sensitive ecosystems.

The supposedly "smokeless" travel industry has profound and detrimental impacts on the environment which can seem remote and unrelated to an individual trip or holiday. Air travel is clearly implicated in global warming and damage to the ozone layer, resort location and construction can destroy natural habitats and restrict traditional rights and activities. With this in mind, individual choice and awareness can make a difference in many instances (see box), and collectively, travellers are having a significant effect in shaping a more responsible and sustainable industry.

Of course travel can have beneficial impacts and this is something to which every traveller can contribute – many national parks are partly funded by receipts from visitors. Similarly, travellers can promote patronage and protection of important archaeological sites and heritage through their interest and contributions via entrance and performance fees. They can also support small-scale enterprises by staying in locally run hotels and hostels, eating in local restaurants and by purchasing local goods, supplies and arts and crafts.

Increasingly, visitors are keen to be involved in eco-tourism – tourism that promotes and supports the conservation of natural environments and is also fair and equitable to local communities. The problem lies in deciding where you draw the line between what conserves the environment and what does not.

The **Costa Rican Tourist Board** (ICT) has undertaken to introduce an environmentally based classification system which could help travellers a lot when choosing between hotels. However, the ICT is certain to have some problems deciding which hotels have environmental considerations at the heart of their management system.

In essence, it comes down to the individual to make choices and informed decisions. In the US contact the **International Ecotourism Society**, PO Box 668, Burlington, VT 05402, T802-651-9818, F802-651-9819, for a comprehensive breakdown of the issues. The *International Ecotourism Society* has links with several Costa Rican organizations that share an interest in promoting eco-tourism including: **Costa Rica Expeditions**, **Horizontes Nature Tours** and **Holbrook Travel** and **Lapa Rios** resort on the Osa Peninsula.

Organizations like **Conservation International** (in the US on T1-202-429-5660, www.ecotour.org) and **Tourism Concern** (in the UK on T020-7753-3330, www.tourismconcern.org.uk) have begun to develop and promote eco-tourism projects and destinations. Additionally, organizations such as *Earthwatch* (US and Canada on T1-800-776-0188, in the UK on T01865-311601, www.earthwatch.org) offer opportunities to participate directly in scientific research and development projects.

While the authenticity of some eco-tourism operators' claims need to be interpreted with care, there is clearly both a huge demand for this type of activity and also significant opportunities to support worthwhile conservation and social development initiatives.

Health

Staying healthy in Costa Rica is straightforward. With the following advice and precautions you should keep as healthy as you do at home. Most visitors return home having experienced no problems at all beyond an upset stomach. However, the health risks are different from those encountered in Europe or the USA. Your health also depends on how you travel, and where. There are clear differences between the risks for the business traveller, who stays in international-class hotels, the backpacker, and the tourist who heads for the beach. There are no hard and fast rules to follow: you will often have to make your own judgement on the healthiness or otherwise of your surroundings. There are English (or other foreign language) speaking doctors in most cities who have particular experience in dealing with locally occurring diseases. Your embassy representative will often be able to give you the name of local reputable doctors and most of the better hotels have a doctor on standby. If you do fall ill and cannot find a recommended doctor, try the Outpatient Department of a hospital – private hospitals are usually less crowded and offer a more acceptable standard of care. It is worth remembering that, apart from mosquitoes, the most dangerous animals are men, be they bandits or behind steering wheels. Think carefully about violent confrontations and wear a seat belt if you are lucky enough to have one available to you.

Before travelling

Take out medical insurance. Make sure it covers all eventualities especially evacuation to your home country by a medically equipped plane. You should have a dental check-up, obtain a spare glasses prescription, a spare oral contraceptive prescription (or enough pills to last) and, if you suffer from a chronic illness (such as diabetes, high blood pressure, ear or sinus troubles, cardio-pulmonary disease or nervous disorder), you should arrange for a check-up with your doctor. He will be able at the same time to provide you with a letter explaining the details of your disability in English and if possible Spanish. Check the current practice for malaria prophylaxis (prevention). If you are on regular medication, make sure you have enough to cover the period of your travel.

More preparation is probably necessary for babies and children than for an adult, and perhaps a little more care should be taken when travelling to remote areas where health services are primitive. This is because children often become ill more rapidly than adults (although, on the other hand, they often recover more quickly). Diarrhoea and vomiting are the most common problems, so take the usual precautions, but more intensively. Breastfeeding is best and most convenient for babies, but powdered milk and baby foods area available in Costa Rica. Papaya, bananas and avocados are all nutritious and can be cleanly prepared. The treatment of diarrhoea is the same as it is for adults, except that it should start earlier and be continued with more persistence. Children get dehydrated very quickly in hot countries and can become drowsy and uncooperative unless cajoled to drink water or juice plus salts. Upper respiratory infections, such as colds, Children

Essentials

catarrh and middle ear infections are also common and if your child suffers from these normally, take some antibiotics against the possibility. Outer ear infections after swimming are also common and antibiotic ear drops will help. Wet wipes are always useful and sometimes difficult to find, as, in some places, are disposable nappies.

Medicines & what to take

There is very little control on the sale of drugs and medicines in Costa Rica. You may be able to buy any and every drug in pharmacies without a prescription. Be wary of this because pharmacists can be poorly trained and might sell you drugs that are unsuitable, dangerous or old. Many drugs and medicines are manufactured under licence from American or European companies, so the trade names may be familiar to you. This means you do not have to carry a whole chest of medicines with you, but remember that the shelf-life of some items, especially vaccines and antibiotics, is markedly reduced in hot conditions. Buy your supplies at the better outlets where there are more refrigerators, even though they are more expensive, and check the expiry date of all preparations you buy. Immigration officials occasionally confiscate scheduled drugs (Lomotil is an example) if they are not accompanied by a doctor's prescription. Self-medication may be forced on you by circumstances so the information given here contains the names of drugs and medicines which you may find useful in an emergency or in out-of-the-way places. You should, however, always seek medical advice, if at all possible.

Medical kit check list

Sunglasses, a type designed for intense sunlight; **earplugs**, for sleeping on aeroplanes and in noisy hotels; **sun screen** with a high protection factor; **insect repellent** containing DET; **mosquito net**, lightweight, permethrin-impregnated; **travel sickness tablets**; **tampons**, can be expensive in some countries in Latin America; **condoms**; **contraceptives**; **water sterilizing tablets**; **anti malarial tablets**; **anti-infective ointment**, eg Cetrimide; **dusting powder for feet, etc**, containing fungicide; **antacid tablets**, for indigestion; **sachets of rehydration salts plus anti-diarrhoea preparations**; **painkillers**, such as paracetamol or aspirin; **antibiotics** for diarrhoea, etc; **first aid kit**, small pack containing a few sterile syringes and needles and disposable gloves (the risk of catching hepatitis, etc from a dirty needle used for injection is now negligible in Costa Rica, but you may feel safer carrying your own supplies – available from camping shops and at airports).

Vaccination

Smallpox vaccination is no longer required anywhere in the world and cholera vaccination is no longer recognized as necessary or effective for international travel by the *World Health Organisation*. Nevertheless, some immigration officials are still demanding proof of vaccination against cholera, following the outbreak of the disease which originated in Peru in 1990-91 and subsequently affected most surrounding countries. Although it is very unlikely to affect visitors to Costa Rica, the cholera epidemic continues to make its greatest impact in poor areas where water supplies are polluted and food hygiene practices are insanitary.

Vaccination against the following diseases is recommended:
Yellow Fever This is a live vaccination not to be given to children under nine months or persons allergic to eggs. Immunity lasts for 10 years, an International Certificate of Yellow Fever Vaccination will be given and should be kept because it is sometimes asked for. Yellow fever is very rare in Costa Rica, but the vaccination is practically without side effects and almost totally protective.

Typhoid A number of new vaccines against this condition are now available; the older TAB and monovalent typhoid vaccines are being phased out. The newer, for example Typhim Vi, cause less side effects, but are more expensive. For those who do not like injections, there are now oral vaccines.

Poliomyelitis Despite its decline, this remains a serious disease if caught but is easy to protect against. There are live oral vaccines and in some countries injected vaccines. Whichever one you choose it is a good idea to have a booster every 3-5 years if visiting developing countries regularly.

Tetanus & other routine vaccinations One dose should be given with a booster at six weeks and another at six months and 10 yearly boosters thereafter are recommended. Children should already be properly protected against diphtheria, poliomyelitis and pertussis (whooping cough), measles and HIB, all of which can be more serious infections in Latin America than at home. Measles, mumps and rubella vaccines are also given to children throughout the world, but those teenage girls who have not had rubella (German measles) should be tested and vaccinated. Hepatitis B vaccination for babies is now routine in some countries. Consult your doctor for advice on tuberculosis inoculation: the disease is still widespread in Latin America.

Infectious Hepatitis This is less of a problem for travellers than it used to be because of the development of two extremely effective vaccines against the A and B form of the disease. It remains common, however, in Latin America. A combined hepatitis A & B vaccine is now licenced and has been available since 1997 – one jab covers both diseases.

Other vaccinations These might be considered in the case of epidemics for example meningitis. There is an effective vaccination against rabies, which should be considered by all travellers, especially those going through remote areas or if there is a particular occupational risk, for example for zoologists or veterinarians.

Further information on health risks abroad, vaccinations, etc may be available from a local travel clinic. If you wish to take specific drugs with you such as antibiotics these are best prescribed by your own doctor. Be aware, however, that not all doctors are experts on the health problems of remote countries. More detailed or more up-to-date information than some local GPs can provide is available from various sources. In the UK there are hospital departments specializing in tropical diseases in London, Liverpool, Birmingham and Glasgow and the Malaria Reference Laboratory at the *London School of Hygiene and Tropical Medicine* provides advice about malaria, T0891-600350. In the USA the local Public Health Services can give such information and information is available centrally from the *Centre for Disease Control* (CDC) in Atlanta, T404-332-4559, www.cdc.gov In Canada contact *IAMAT*, 40 Regal Rd, Guelph, Ontario, N1K 1B5, www.sentex.net/~iamat/index.html

There are in addition computerized databases which can be accessed for destination-specific, up-to-the-minute information. The *Scottish Centre for Infection and Environmental Health* have a website database providing information for travellers at www.fitfortravel.scot.nhs.uk Other information on medical problems overseas can be obtained from the book by Dr Richard Dawood (Editor) – *Travellers' Health, How to Stay Healthy Abroad* (Oxford University Press 1992 £7.99). We strongly recommend the new, revised and updated edition, especially to the intrepid traveller heading for the more out of the way places. General advice is also available in the UK in *Health Information for Overseas Travel* (Department of Health) available from HMSO and *International Travel and Health* (WHO). Handbooks on first aid are produced by the British & American Red Cross and by St John's Ambulance (UK).

Further information

On the way

For most travellers a trip to Costa Rica means a long flight. If this crosses time zones then jetlag can also be a problem. The main symptoms are tiredness and sleepiness at

Essentials

Essentials

inconvenient times and, conversely, a tendency to wake up in the middle of the night feeling like you want your breakfast. Most find that the problem is worse when flying in an easterly direction. The best way to get over jetlag is to try to force yourself into the new time zone as strictly as possible. This may involve, on a westward flight, trying to stay awake until your normal bedtime and on an eastward flight, forgetting that you have lost some sleep on the way out and going to bed relatively early but near your normal time on the evening after you arrive. The symptoms of jetlag may be helped by keeping up your fluid intake on the journey (not with alcohol!). The hormone melatonin seems to reduce the symptoms of jetlag but is not presently licensed in most of Europe although it can be obtained from health food stores in the USA.

On long-haul flights it is also important to stretch your legs at least every hour to prevent slowing of the circulation and the possible development of blood clots. Drinking plenty of non-alcoholic fluids also helps.

If travelling by boat sea sickness can be a problem – this is dealt with in the usual way by taking anti motion-sickness pills.

Staying healthy on arrival

Intestinal upsets The thought of catching a stomach bug worries visitors to Latin America but there have been great improvements in food hygiene and most such infections are preventable. Travellers' diarrhoea and vomiting is due, most of the time, to food poisoning, usually passed on by the insanitary habits of food handlers, however, in Costa Rica this is rarely the case. But, as a general rule the cleaner your surroundings and the smarter the restaurant, the less likely you are to suffer.

Foods to avoid: uncooked, undercooked, partially cooked or reheated meat, fish, eggs, raw vegetables and salads, especially when they have been left out and exposed to flies. Stick to fresh food that has been cooked from raw just before eating and make sure you peel fruit yourself. Wash and dry your hands before eating – disposable wet-wipe tissues are useful for this.

Shellfish eaten raw are risky and at certain times of the year some fish and shellfish concentrate toxins from their environment and cause various kinds of food poisoning. The local authorities notify the public not to eat these foods. Do not ignore the warning. Heat treated milk (UHT) pasteurized or sterilized is becoming more available in Costa Rica, as is pasteurized cheese. On the whole matured or processed cheeses are safer than the fresh varieties. Fresh unpasteurized milk can be a source of food poisoning germs, tuberculosis and brucellosis. This applies equally to ice cream, yoghurt and cheese made from unpasteurized milk, so avoid these home-made products – the factory-made ones are probably safer.

Tap water is rarely safe outside the major cities, especially in the rainy season. Stream water, if you are in the countryside, is often contaminated by communities living up-stream. Filtered or bottled water is usually available and safe, although you must make sure that somebody is not filling bottles from the tap and hammering on a new crown cap. If your hotel has a central hot water supply, this water is safe to drink after cooling. Ice for drinks should be made from boiled water, but it rarely is, so stand your glass on the ice cubes, rather than putting them in the drink. The better hotels have water purifying systems.

Travellers' diarrhoea This is usually caused by eating food which has been contaminated by food poisoning germs. Drinking water is rarely the culprit. Sea water or river water is more likely to be contaminated by sewage and so swimming in such dilute effluent can also be a cause.

Infection with various organisms can give rise to travellers' diarrhoea. They may be viruses, bacteria, for example escherichia coli (probably the most common cause worldwide), protozoa (such as amoeba and giardia), salmonella and cholera. The diarrhoea may come on suddenly or rather slowly. It may be accompanied by vomiting or by severe abdominal pain, and the passage of blood or mucus is a sign of dysentery.

Diagnosis and treatment If you can time the onset of the diarrhoea to the minute ('acute') then it is probably due to a virus or a bacterium and/or the onset of dysentery. The treatment, in addition to rehydration, is an antibiotic such as ciprofloxacin 500 mg every 12 hours; the drug is now widely available and there are many similar ones.

If the diarrhoea comes on slowly or intermittently ('sub-acute') then it is more likely to be protozoal, that is caused by an amoeba or giardia. Antibiotics such as ciprofloxacin will have little effect. These cases are best treated by a doctor as is any outbreak of diarrhoea continuing for more than three days. Sometimes blood is passed in amoebic dysentery and for this you should certainly seek medical help. If this is not available then the best treatment is probably tinidazole (Fasigyn) one tablet four times a day for three days. If there are severe stomach cramps, the following drugs may help but are not very useful in the management of acute diarrhoea: loperamide (Imodium) and diphenoxylate with atropine (Lomotil). They should not be given to children.

Any kind of diarrhoea, whether or not accompanied by vomiting, responds well to the replacement of water and salts, taken as frequent sips of some kind of rehydration solution. There are proprietary preparations consisting of sachets of powder which you dissolve in boiled water, or you can make your own by adding half a teaspoonful of salt (3½ g) and four tablespoonful of sugar (40 g) to a litre of boiled water.

Thus the linchpins of treatment for diarrhoea are rest, fluid and salt replacement, antibiotics such as ciprofloxacin for the bacterial types and special diagnostic tests and medical treatment for the amoeba and giardia infections. Salmonella infections and cholera, although rare, can be devastating diseases and it would be wise to get to a hospital as soon as possible if these are suspected.

Fasting, peculiar diets and the consumption of large quantities of yoghurt have not been found useful in calming travellers' diarrhoea or in rehabilitating inflamed bowels. Oral rehydration has on the other hand, especially in children, been a life saving technique and should always be practised, whatever other treatment you use. As there is some evidence that alcohol and milk might prolong diarrhoea they should be avoided during and immediately after an attack. So should chillies!

Diarrhoea occurring day after day for long periods of time (chronic diarrhoea) is notoriously resistant to amateur attempts at treatment and again warrants proper diagnostic tests (most towns with reasonable sized hospitals have laboratories for stool samples). There are ways of preventing travellers' diarrhoea for short periods of time by taking antibiotics, but this is not a foolproof technique and should not be used other than in exceptional circumstances. Doxycycline is possibly the best drug. Some preventatives such as Enterovioform can have serious side effects if taken for long periods.

Paradoxically, constipation is also common, probably induced by dietary change, inadequate fluid intake in hot places and long bus journeys. Simple laxatives are useful in the short-term and bulky foods such as maize, beans and plenty of fruit are also useful.

There are a number of ways of purifying water in order to make it safe to drink. Dirty **Water** water should first be strained through a filter bag (camping shops) and then boiled or **purification** treated. Bringing water to a rolling boil at sea level is sufficient to make the water safe for drinking, but at higher altitudes you have to boil the water for a few minutes longer to ensure that all the microbes are killed.

There are sterilizing methods that can be used and there are proprietary preparations containing chlorine (for example Puritabs) or iodine (for example Pota Aqua) compounds. Chlorine compounds generally do not kill protozoa (for example Giardia).

There are a number of water filters now on the market available in personal and expedition size. They work either on mechanical or chemical principles, or may do both. Make sure you take the spare parts or spare chemicals with you and do not believe everything the manufacturers say.

High altitude Spending time at high altitude in Central America, especially in the tropics, is usually a pleasure – it is not so hot, there are no insects and the air is clear and spring-like. However, high altitude can cause medical problems, all of which can be prevented if you are careful.

On reaching heights above about 3,000 m, heart pounding and shortness of breath, especially on exertion, are a normal response to the lack of oxygen in the air. A condition called acute mountain sickness can also affect visitors. It is more likely to affect those who ascend rapidly. This takes a few hours or days to come on and its symptoms are: a bad headache; extreme tiredness; sometimes dizziness; loss of appetite and frequently nausea and vomiting. Insomnia is common and is often associated with a suffocating feeling when lying in bed. Keen observers may note that their breathing rate tends to wax and wane at night and that their face tends to be puffy in the mornings – this is all part of the syndrome. Anyone can get this condition and past experience is not always a good guide.

The treatment of acute mountain sickness is simple – rest, painkillers (preferably not aspirin based) for the headache and anti-sickness pills for vomiting. Oxygen is actually not much help, except at very high altitude. Various local panaceas – Coramina glucosada, Effortil, Micoren are popular.

To prevent the condition: on arrival at places over 3,000 m have a few hours' rest in a chair and avoid alcohol, cigarettes and heavy food. If the symptoms are severe and prolonged, it is best to descend to a lower altitude and to reascend slowly or in stages. If this is impossible because of shortage of time, or if you are going so high that acute mountain sickness is very likely, then the drug acetazolamide (Diamox) can be used as a preventative and continued during the ascent. There is good evidence of the value of this drug in the prevention of *soroche*, but some people do experience peculiar side effects. The usual dose is 500 mg of the slow release preparation each night, starting the night before ascending above 3,000 m.

Watch out for sunburn at high altitude. The ultraviolet rays are extremely powerful. The air is also excessively dry at high altitude and you might find that your skin dries out and the inside of your nose becomes crusted. Use a moisturizer for the skin and some vaseline wiped into the nostrils. Some people find contact lenses irritating because of the dry air. It is unwise to ascend to high altitude if you are pregnant, especially in the first three months, or if you have a history of heart, lung or blood disease, including sickle cell anaemia.

A more unusual condition can affect mountaineers who ascend rapidly to high altitude – acute pulmonary oedema. Residents at altitude sometimes experience this when returning to the mountains from time spent at the coast. This condition is often preceded by acute mountain sickness and comes on quite rapidly with severe breathlessness, noisy breathing, cough, blueness of the lips and frothing at the mouth. Anybody who develops this must be brought down as soon as possible, given oxygen and taken to hospital.

A rapid descent from high places will make sinus problems and middle ear infections worse and might make your teeth ache. Lastly, don't fly to altitude within 24 hours of scuba diving. You might suffer from 'the bends'.

Heat & cold Full acclimatization to high temperatures takes about two weeks. During this period it is normal to feel a bit apathetic, especially if the relative humidity is high. Drink plenty of water (up to 15 litres a day are required when working physically hard in the tropics), use salt on your food and avoid extreme exertion. Tepid showers are more cooling than hot or cold ones. Large hats do not cool you down, but do prevent sunburn. Remember that, especially in the highlands, there can be a large and sudden drop in temperature between sun and shade and between night and day, so dress accordingly. Warm jackets or woollens are essential after dark at high altitude. Loose cotton is still the best material when the weather is hot.

Insects These are mostly more of a nuisance than a serious hazard and with a bit of preparation, you can prevent being bitten entirely. Some, such as mosquitoes, are of course carriers of potentially serious diseases so it is sensible to avoid being bitten. Sleep off the ground and use an insecticide-impregnated mosquito net or some kind of insecticide. Preparations containing pyrethrum or synthetic pyrethroids are safe. They are available as aerosols or pumps and the best way to use these is to spray the room thoroughly in all areas (follow the instructions rather than the insects) and then shut the door for a while, re-entering when the smell has dispersed. Mosquito coils release insecticide as they burn slowly. They are widely available and useful out of doors. Tablets of insecticide which are placed on a heated mat plugged into a wall socket are probably the most effective. They fill the room with insecticidal fumes in the same way as aerosols or coils.

You can also use insect repellents, most of which are effective against a wide range of pests. The most common and effective is diethyl metatoluamide (DET). DET liquid is best for arms and face (take care around eyes and with spectacles – DET dissolves plastic). Aerosol spray is good for clothes and ankles and liquid DET can be dissolved in water and used to impregnate cotton clothes and mosquito nets. Some repellents now contain DET and permethrin, an insecticide. Impregnated wrist and ankle bands can also be useful.

If you are bitten or stung, itching may be relieved by cool baths, antihistamine tablets (care with alcohol or driving) or mild corticosteriod creams, for example hydrocortisone (great care should be exercised: never use if there is any hint of infection). Calamine lotion and cream have limited effectiveness and antihistamine creams are not generally recommended – they can cause allergies themselves. Bites which become infected should be treated with a local antiseptic or antibiotic cream such as Cetrimide, as should any infected sores or scratches.

When living rough, infestations of the skin with body lice (crabs) and scabies are easy to pick up. Use whatever local commercial preparation is recommended for lice and scabies. Crotamiton cream (Eurax) alleviates itching and also kills a number of skin parasites. Malathion lotion 5% (Prioderm) kills lice effectively, but avoid the use of the toxic agricultural preparation of malathion, more often used to commit suicide.

Ticks Ticks usually attach themselves to the lower parts of the body often after walking in areas where cattle have grazed. They take a while to attach themselves strongly, but swell up as they start to suck blood. The important thing is to remove them gently, so that they do not leave their head parts in your skin because this can cause infections or an allergic reaction some days later. Do not use petrol, vaseline, lighted cigarettes, etc, to remove the tick, but, with a pair of tweezers, remove the beast gently by gripping it at the attached (head) end and rock it out in very much the same way that a tooth is extracted. Certain tropical flies which lay their eggs under the skin of sheep and cattle also occasionally do the same thing to humans with the unpleasant result that a maggot grows under the skin and pops up as a boil or pimple. The best way to remove these is to cover the boil with oil, vaseline or nail varnish, thereby stopping the maggot from breathing, and then to squeeze it out gently the next day.

Essentials

Other animal bites & stings	It is a very rare event indeed for travellers, but if you are unlucky (or careless) enough to be bitten by a venomous snake, spider, scorpion or sea creature, try to identify the creature, without putting yourself in further danger. Snake bites in particular are very frightening, but in fact rarely poisonous – even venomous snakes bite without injecting venom. What you might expect if bitten are: fright, swelling, pain and bruising around the bite and soreness of the regional lymph glands, perhaps nausea, vomiting and a fever. The following would be symptoms of serious poisoning: numbness and tingling of the face, muscular spasms, convulsions, shortness of breath or a failure of the blood to clot, causing generalized bleeding. Victims should be taken to a hospital or a doctor without delay. Commercial snake bite and scorpion kits are available, but are usually only useful for the specific types of snake or scorpion. Most serum has to be given intravenously so it is not much good equipping yourself with it unless you are used to making injections into veins. It is best to rely on local practice in these cases, because the particular creatures will be known about locally and appropriate treatment can be given.

Treatment of snake bite   Reassure and comfort the victim frequently. Immobilize the limb with a bandage or a splint or by getting the person to lie still. Do not slash the bite area and try to suck out the poison – this sort of heroism does more harm than good. If you know how to use a tourniquet in these circumstances, you will not need advice. If you are not experienced, do not apply a tourniquet.

Precautions   Avoid walking in snake territory in bare feet or sandals – wear proper shoes or boots. If you encounter a snake, stay put until it slithers away, and do not investigate a wounded snake. Spiders and scorpions may be found in the more basic hotels. If bitten or stung, rest, take plenty of fluids and call a doctor. The best precaution is to keep beds away from the walls and look inside your shoes and under the toilet seat every morning.

Marine bites & stings   Certain tropical sea fish when trodden upon inject venom into bathers' feet. This can be exceptionally painful. Wear plastic shoes when you go bathing if such creatures are reported. The pain can be relieved by immersing the foot in extremely hot water for as long as the pain persists.

Sunburn   The burning power of the tropical sun, especially at high altitude, is phenomenal. Always wear a wide-brimmed hat and use some form of suncream or lotion on untanned skin. Normal temperate zone sun screen lotions (protection factor up to seven) are not much good; you need to use the types designed specifically for the tropics or for mountaineers or skiers with protection factors of 15 or above. These are sometimes not available outside tourist areas. Glare from the sun can cause conjunctivitis, so wear sunglasses especially on tropical beaches, where high protection factor sunscreen should also be used.

AIDS   In Latin America AIDS – called SIDA – is increasing and is not wholly confined to the well known high-risk sections of the population, that is homosexual men, intravenous drug users and children of infected mothers. Heterosexual transmission is now the dominant mode and so the main risk to travellers is from casual sex. Of 33.6 million adults and children affected by HIV worldwide, an estimated 1.7 million live in Latin America and the Caribbean. The same precautions should be taken as with any sexually transmitted disease. The AIDS virus (HIV) can be passed by unsterilized needles which have been previously used to inject an HIV-positive patient, but the risk of this is negligible. It would, however, be sensible to check that needles have been properly sterilized or disposable needles have been used. If you wish to take your own disposable needles, be prepared to explain what they are for. The risk of receiving a blood transfusion with blood infected with HIV is greater than from dirty needles because of the amount of fluid exchanged. Supplies of blood for transfusion should now be screened for HIV in all reputable hospitals, so again the risk is very small indeed. Catching the AIDS virus does not always produce an illness in itself (although it may do). The only way to be sure if you feel you have been put at risk is to have a blood test for HIV antibodies on your return to a place where there are reliable laboratory facilities. The test does not become positive for some weeks.

Malaria is theoretically confined to coastal and jungle zones, and is now on the increase again. Mosquitoes do not thrive above 2,500 m, so you are safe at altitude. There are different varieties of malaria, some resistant to the normal drugs. Make local enquiries if you intend to visit possibly infected zones and use a prophylactic regime. Start taking the tablets a few days before exposure and continue to take them for six weeks after leaving the malarial zone. Remember to give the drugs to babies and children as well. Opinion varies on the precise drugs and dosage to be used for protection. All the drugs may have some side effects and it is important to balance the risk of catching the disease against the (albeit rare) side effects. The increasing complexity of the situation is such that as the malarial parasite becomes immune to the new generation of drugs, concentration on the physical prevention of being bitten by mosquitoes has increased. This involves the use of long-sleeved shirts or blouses and long trousers, repellents and nets. Clothes are now available, impregnated with the insecticide permethrin or deltamethrin, or it is possible to impregnate the clothes yourself. Wide meshed nets impregnated with permethrin are also available, are lighter to carry and less claustrophobic to sleep in. | Malaria

Prophylaxis and treatment If your itinerary takes you into a malarial area, seek expert advice before you go on a suitable prophylactic regime. This is especially true for pregnant women who are particularly prone to catching malaria. You can still catch the disease even when sticking to a proper regime, although it is unlikely. If you do develop symptoms (high fever, shivering, headache, sometimes diarrhoea), seek medical advice immediately. If this is not possible and there is a great likelihood of malaria, the treatment is:

If the local strain is likely to be sensitive to it, then the treatment is Chloroquine: a single dose of four tablets (600 mg) followed by two tablets (300 mg) six hours later and 300 mg each day following.

If it is falciparum malaria or the type is in doubt, take local advice. Various combinations of drugs are being used such as Quinine, Tetracycline or Halofantrine. If falciparum malaria is definitely diagnosed, it is wise to get to a good hospital as treatment can be complex and the illness very serious.

The main symptoms are pains in the stomach, lack of appetite, lassitude and yellowness of the eyes and skin. Medically speaking there are two main types. The less serious, but more common is hepatitis A, for which the best protection is the careful preparation of food, the avoidance of contaminated drinking water and scrupulous attention to toilet hygiene. The other, more serious, version is hepatitis B which is acquired usually as a sexually transmitted disease or by blood transfusion. It is less commonly transmitted by injections with unclean needles and possibly by insect bites. The symptoms are the same as for hepatitis A. The incubation period is much longer (up to six months compared with six weeks) and there are more likely to be complications. | Infectious hepatitis (jaundice)

Hepatitis A can be protected against with gamma globulin. It should be obtained from a reputable source and is certainly useful for travellers who intend to live rough.

You should have a shot before leaving and have it repeated every six months. The dose of gamma globulin depends on the concentration of the particular preparation used, so the manufacturer's advice should be taken. The injection should be given as close as possible to your departure and, as the dose depends on the time you are likely to spend in potentially affected areas, the manufacturer's instructions should be followed. Gamma globulin has really been superseded now by a proper vaccination against hepatitis A (Havrix), which gives immunity lasting up to 10 years. After that boosters are required. Havrix monodose is now widely available as is junior Havrix. The vaccination has negligible side effects and is extremely effective. Gamma globulin injections can be a bit painful, but it is cheaper than Havrix and may be more available in some places.

Hepatitis B can be effectively prevented by a specific vaccine (Engerix) – three shots over six months before travelling. If you have had jaundice in the past it would be worthwhile having a blood test to see if you are immune to either of these two types, because this might avoid the necessity and costs of vaccination or gamma globulin. There are other kinds of viral hepatitis (C, E, G etc) which are fairly similar to A and B, but vaccines are not available as yet.

Other afflictions **Athlete's foot** This and other fungal skin infections are best treated with tolnaftate or clotrimazole.

Chagas' disease (South American trypanosomiasis) This is a chronic disease, very rarely caught by travellers and difficult to treat. It is transmitted by the simultaneous biting and excreting of the reduvid bug, also known as the vinchuca or barbeiro. Somewhat resembling a small cockroach, this nocturnal bug lives in poor adobe houses with dirt floors often frequented by opossums. If you cannot avoid such accommodation, sleep off the floor with a candle lit, use a mosquito net, keep as much of your skin covered as possible, and use DET repellent or a spray insecticide. If you are bitten overnight (the bites are painless) do not scratch them, but wash thoroughly with soap and water.

Further reading

Natural history Beletsky, Les *Costa Rica: The Ecotravellers Wildlife Guide* (1998, Academic Press). A fine overview of the natural health and heritage of the country, with colour drawings covering all wildlife – a good all-in-one choice.

Boza, Mario *Costa Rica National Parks* (1999, Incafo). Take the small, handy option, or the glossy coffee table one – both filled with good information and pictures compiled by the founder of the national park system.

Carr, Archie *The Windward Road: Adventures of Naturalist on Remote Caribbean Shores* (1979). Tales of Archie Carr's experiences on the north Caribbean shore and the turtle nesting beaches of Tortuguero.

Janzen, Daniel *Costa Rica Natural History* (1983, University of Chicago Press). A glorious weighty book, packed with highly accessible information edited by the "grandfather" of Guanacaste National Park.

Kricher, John *A Neotropical Companion* (1997, Princeton University Press). A detailed guide through the grey area between academic study and keen interest – now available in paperback.

Stiles, Gary and Skutch, Alexander *A Guide to the Birds of Costa Rica* (1989, Cornell University). *The* guide to the birdlife of Costa Rica – accept no imitations.

No romance please

Budget travellers have been known to sweat blood in search of a good book swap, only to discover the shelves littered with the mulchy love-smultz of romance novels. Steele and Collins beware – your cards are marked. You pick your novels as you fancy but in Costa Rica an increasing number of book swaps are getting wise to the problems of trying to swap romance and refusing to accept them. Is this censorship – who cares? Just leave the romance at home.

Baker, Bill *The Essential Road Guide to Costa Rica*, Baker, Apartado 1185-01011, San José, T/F220-1415. Detailed strip maps, kilometre by kilometre road logs, motoring information plus San José map and bus guide. Travel guides

Gallo, Rafael and Mayfield, Michael *The Rivers of Costa Rica: A canoeing, kayaking and rafting guide* (1988, Menasha Ridge Press, Alabama). A punchy little guide to the rivers of Costa Rica.

Tico Times, *Exploring Costa Rica*, updated annually. Produced and published by the staff of the Tico Times, Costa Rica's English language newspaper.

Ras, Barbara *Costa Rica: A Traveler's Literary Companion*, (1994, Whereabouts Press). A much loved collection of 26 stories drawn from across the country. Fiction

Edelman, Mark and Kenen, Joanne *The Costa Rica Reader* (1989, Grove Atlantic). A good historical overview of the country, although out of print so difficult to find. History

Daling, Tjabel *Costa Rica: A Guide to the People, Politics and Culture* (1998, Latin America Bureau). A pocket history and overview of the country, picking up on the main themes that make up modern Costa Rica.

Molina, Iván and Palmer, Steven *The History of Costa Rica* (1998, University of Costa Rica). A brief, up-to-date and illustrated history of Costa Rica in a highly manageable little package.

Palmer, Pauline *What Happen: A Folk History of Costa Rica's Talamanca Coast* (1977, Ecodesarollos). The hardships of life in Costa Rica's southern Caribbean. (NB 'Happen' is Creole.)

Costa Rica on the net

The presence of Costa Rica on the internet is positively daunting. Most hotels and organizations can be contacted by email, many have their own website. Despite the vagaries of the economy the use of the internet is the same as ever - if the site is up-to-date it serves its purpose.

www.tourism-costarica.com is the official *Costa Rican Tourist Board*. It's as good a place as any to start your surfing. Government & conservation

www.tourism.co.cr is the *Costa Rican Chamber of Tourism* site, with good hotel and background information.

www.ticotimes.net is the *Tico Times* website, very useful for catching up on the latest.

www.costarica-embassy.org – the *Costa Rican embassy site in Washington*, useful information and links.

usembassy.or.cr – the *US Embassy* site in Costa Rica with good travel information, and some interesting background on projects.

www.embcrlon.demon.co.uk – the *Costa Rican embassy site in London*. Good information and up-to-date links.

www.rree.go.cr – the *Costa Rican Ministry of Foreign Affairs* website with all the information you could need on visas, embassies, residency and so on.

www.minae.go.cr – the *Ministry for the Environment and Energy* which has overall control for *SINAC*, the national park programme, and energy development. Strange bedfellows and clearly uncomfortable on the same website.

www.sinac.go.cr – the *Sistema Nacional de Areas de Conservacion* website

www.inbio.ac.cr – the *INBioparques* site, with access to the conservation organization's databases.

General information | **www.yellowweb.co.cr** – is a good overall site with good information and links although not always up to date.

www.infocostarica.com – is another good general site.

www.costaricabybus.net – good sight for budget travel options and advice.

www.costaricaoutdoors.com – good general information and packed with snippets of background information and stories.

www.centralamerica.com/cr – is also a good base to start looking around.

www.costaricaexpeditions.com – the website of one of Costa Rica's best tour operators, but with up to date news, information and weather which isn't just trying to get you to spend more money.

San José and around

3

San José and around

86 Ins and outs

90 History

92 Sights

100 Essentials

134 Escazú and Western suburbs

Few visitors to Costa Rica return home with gasp-inducing tales of the beauty of San José. The reasons are simple enough: it is not particularly beautiful and any sharp intake of breath, will probably have more to do with an attempt to avoid the pollution. By day the city streets are packed with traffic as heavy buses barely moving beyond second gear crawl through the streets and keen-eyed kamikaze taxis look for the raised arm hailing business. At street level the general theme of clutter and chaos prevails with vendors selling fruit, cigarettes and other daily necessities as an endless stream of immaculately dressed Ticos scurry to, from and between work. By night, streets lit by the rhythmic flash and glow of neon slowly empty as the Joséfinos scurry home or out to bars, restaurants and clubs.

After almost two hundred years as capital, the city seems unwilling to take the lead. Attractions and activities awaiting the visitor come across as reluctant suggestions rather than vibrant 'must-sees'. With San José you may have to put in a little more effort and imagination than many cities, but if you know what you like there is something for everyone in San José. Love at first sight does happen and some are certain to become infatuated with the city, but San José's charm is more likely to grow on you after a couple of days exploring the capital's understated secrets.

Ins and outs

Getting there

Air
Colour map ref;
Population:
Officially 344,349,
wider metropolitan
area 1,100,000;
Altitude: 1,150 m

San José's recently renovated **Juan Santamaría International Airport** is 16 km north-west of the city centre on the outskirts of the town of Alajuela. The airport has international and domestic connections. Information T441-0744 or T443-2622.

After baggage reclaim and customs a tourist desk has supplies of basic maps and a selection of brochures. The desk can book accommodation and arrange transport to the city if required. There is also a small bank that can change currency and traveller's cheques and several car rental agencies.

Transport for the 30-min journey to San José downtown is easiest with one of the red taxis that greet international flights (US$12-15). A cheaper option is to take one of the regular local buses from the main road outside the terminal building. The 40-min journey is 100 *colones* (US$0.40). Buses leave every 10 mins through the day and slightly less frequently through the night. If you don't know exactly where your hotel is or if you arrive at night the simplest and safest option is to get a taxi. If travelling on your own, look for other travellers who may be happy to double up and share the cost.

Airport services close to check-in and the departure area include currency exchange, bank ATMs, a few small shops and a café and restaurant. Beyond passport control there are a couple of cafés, a newsagents and gift store, a well stocked perfumer and a poorly stocked drink store.

Bus
See also page 123

San José has very good local, national and international bus connections. National buses provide connections throughout the country serving most popular destinations with direct buses. International buses link the whole of Central America from Panama to Mexico. The standard of buses varies greatly ranging from the shell of a bus with plastic seats to a comfortable air-conditioned luxury 'liner', sometimes fitted with TV and video. If your destination is off the main routes, expect to travel in a beaten up old vehicle.

Car
See also page 125

Arriving by car the capital is served by roads on all sides that twist and turn round precipitous drops affording driver and passengers spectacular views and equally dramatic opportunities for accidents. Approaching San José from the west, traffic is channelled down Paseo Colón – the city's main thoroughfare which leads to Av Central. From the east, the route follows the potentially dangerous road through Parque Nacional Braulio Carrillo, complete with natural distractions, guiding you to the city from the north. From the south the Pan-American Highway, in southern Costa Rica called Highway 2, travels through the Talamanca Mountains descending quickly to skim west of Cartago approaching the capital from the southeast. *Ticos* believe that of the three routes, the last is the most dangerous due to large amounts of heavy goods traffic, but in reality there is little difference.

Getting around

Central San José conforms to the extended grid system building outwards from 2 main streets that cross in the centre of the city – Avenida Central and Calle Central. Avenues run west to east, with the odd numbers (Av 1, Av 3, etc) north of Calle Central and even numbers (Av 2, Av 4, etc) to the south. Likewise, the streets or *calles* are numbered odd to the east of the city and even to the west.

On foot
Central San José is easy to explore on foot – most places of interest are close to the centre. Joining the general mêlée, you can bump and grind your way through the chaos or

24 hours in the city

Given 24 hours in the city, what would you do? What could you do? Here's an outline you can take or leave. One word of warning, if your 24 hours is a Monday, you'll have to improvise with the museums.

If you want to see the city wake up, you'll have to be ready by 6am. There's a crisp chill in the air most days so take a jumper. Head for the **Mercado Central** where the collective rubbing of eyebrows happens under a flurry of activity and occasional song. You can breakfast on empanadas or tortillas and coffee at one of the many stand-up bars, or take a more leisurely sit-down option. You'll have to be early to catch the butchers and fishmongers stocking up.

After breakfast, take a stroll north to the **Centro Costarricense de Ciencias y Cultura** and then continue by foot or taxi out to the **Spirogyra** butterfly farm. Grab a coffee in the café here or at El Pueblo across the road. You can do a bit of shopping if places are opening, but don't worry, you'll be coming back later tonight.

Get a taxi (approximately 500 colónes) to the **Alianza Francesa** building on the corner of Av 7 and C 5 and from here explore the colonial splendour of Barrio Amón before walking down to the Plaza de la Cultura where you can lunch on the streetside café of the Hotel Gran Costa Rica.

Refreshed and revived, take in the attractions of the Plaza de la Cultura with the eloquence of the **Teatro Nacional**, contain your avarice at the underground **Museo de Oro** and transport some temporary patriotism east along Av Central to the **Museo Nacional**.

Close to exhaustion, return to base for a refreshing nap in preparation for the evening ahead which takes you out to **El Pueblo** to enjoy a meal – there are several options to suit all tastes and wallets. After dinner, walk off the meal exploring the small alleys, streets and stalls of the village. Have a few beers and dance 'till dawn or maybe you'll prefer to taxi back to town for a remarkably public statement of your love in front of the mariachis of **La Esmeralda**, before retiring, either through exhaustion or lack of money – having lost what is left in your wallet at the **casino** in the Hotel Gran Costa Rica.

stroll at leisure, stopping at will for caffeine fixes and nibbles. With the simplicity of the street layout, if you're lost just head back towards the lower numbered streets and you end up in the centre.

But hazards do exist. The streets of capital cities are rarely paved with gold, but in parts of San José they are barely paved at all. This is not a warning to watch out for the occasional raised or cracked paving slab, it is serious advice to look where you are walking. Slabs stick up at shin-cracking angles and in some places they're missing completely, revealing precipitous drops to the drainage system below. Keep your eyes down while walking – stop when you want to look around.

A second hazard, not that peculiar to San José, is the traffic. Crossing the roads is safest at pedestrian crossings which conform to the standard green man code. Arguably *Tico* drivers are no less jumpy than any other Latin nation, which means you'll be pushing your luck if you leave the kerb on anything but green. A complicated one-way system adds to the confusion, so when crossing roads the simple rule is to watch the vehicles. While courtesy does exist, few drivers at the lights hang around unnecessarily.

Bus An extensive service covers the surrounding districts and suburbs of the city. While buses can be a handy way of travelling longer distances around the city, snail-like paces are common, especially at rush hour. Once you get the hang of a few basic routes, judicious use of buses can be very convenient, but as a general rule unless weighed down with luggage, or late for an appointment (in which case consider a taxi), it's probably worth walking any distance up to twenty blocks or so.

San José and around

One benefit of travelling by bus is to share the experience of commuting – San José style in the raw. All but the very wealthiest travel by bus and you'll be elbow-to-elbow with a broad cross-section of *Joséfinos*. As ever, warnings related to busy places hold true. Pickpockets and bagsnatchers love cramped settings so take care.

Taxi
See also page 124

With over 7,000 cabs cruising the streets, taxis are a quick and efficient way of moving around the city. Official red cabs are marked with a yellow triangle on the side and equipped with meters or *marías* that should be used for all journeys within the metropolitan district. Although meters are generally used if you're travelling with a *Tico*, visitors often find them 'broken' which does little to enhance the universal suspicion that taxi drivers rip you off given half the chance. But the other universal truth holds true, taxi drivers know their patch and once you've made friends, they're an invaluable asset. On the whole, drivers are fair but get a rough idea of the cost before setting off. The meter starts at 165 *colónes* and advances 10 *colónes* every 100 m or so. A cross-town journey will be in the region of 500-600 *colónes*.

Driving
See also pages 48 and 125

Few would advise driving in San José as a way of seeing the city, but given that most car rental journeys will start and end in the capital you may find yourself behind the wheel in the city at some point. The combination of an unfamiliar vehicle, new road layouts, street signs and traffic flow systems, and uncertainty about where you may be going and how to get there make driving a potential disaster. Add heavy traffic loads and the urgency found in capitals throughout the world, and the best advice is simply to be cautious. One-way systems are poorly signposted, lane discipline is non-existent and pedestrians appear from nowhere. Keep your eyes peeled and a helpful passenger can be a godsend. Parking in the day is not that difficult with several *parqueos* dotted around the city. 24-hour parking is available but may be more difficult to find. If you are planning an early start make sure access is also 24-hour. One specific word of warning. Most car rental firms are located along Paseo Colón, one of the busiest and fastest stretches of San José, and it is a test to start you driving career in the city here. Added to that, traffic flows change at rush hour when the road becomes one-way. Eastbound, heading into the centre of town, on weekdays between 0630 and 0830.

Greater San José

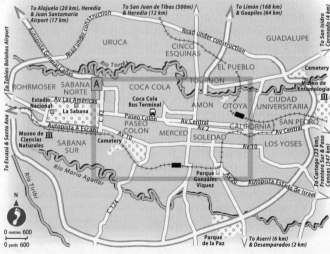

Related map
A San José Centre,
page 90

The fine art of umbrella dipping

Famous to a level approaching disbelief, the legendary Tico friendliness deserves a bit of healthy scepticism, a bit of testing and a bit of in-depth analysis. And what better place to test it out than amidst the stress of the city at rush hour?

In the capital's green season (May-November), clear blue morning skies are quickly sketched in with grey clouds which by early afternoon reliably douse the city with large quantities of warm tropical rain. As defence against the deluge, umbrellas of a thousand different designs miraculously appear: business types with knobbly cane handles; sporty Ticos shelter under vast golfing umbrellas;

cunning contraptions unfold out of ladies' handbags; and youngsters use Pokemon to ward off the horrible rain. In most cities an umbrella is a guarantee of pedestrian hold-ups, collisions and crashes, general misunderstandings, angst and certainly a drip or two down the neck. Costa Rica's peaceful contribution to the world is the umbrella dip.

With absolute certainty Ticos nimbly navigate the streets raising, lowering and dipping umbrellas to avoid collisions. Quiet observation reveals a guaranteed collision course, but at the final moment a deft twist of the wrist averts certain disaster and the umbrellas glide past.

Centred on the **Plaza de la Cultura**, San José has little by way of geography or history to help the newcomer set their bearings. The most useful locator by way of navigation is **Avenida Central** which for the course of its length draws a neat horizontal line through the city map. En route it guides you by, or pretty close to, the majority of the city's attractions from the streetwise banter of the **Mercado Central** in the west to the formal governmental chaos of the **National Assembly** to the east.

Orientation & information

A little further afield, the districts of **Barrio Amón** and **Otoya** to the northeast transform you to a world built on coffee wealth where once-common colonial splendour now stands more as a monument to grand living and architectural extravagance.

The **ICT (Instituto Costarricense de Turismo)** has an efficient and helpful tourist office below the **Plaza de la Cultura**. The staff can help with general information and maps, and assist with specific inquiries and problems. ■ *Open 0900-0600, Mon-Fri. The ICT also has a good website www.tourism-costarica.com and an information desk at Juan Santamaría International Airport.*

Other good sources of information are the numerous tour operators dotted throughout the city. While some may give you the hard sell, others are happy to provide the latest information on availability and accessibility.

The best time to visit San José is from December to April when guaranteed clear skies and very little rain remove the necessity of avid weather forecast watching from your day. At other times of year, trips out to the surrounding volcanoes may be more eerie because the peaks are often completely covered if you don't make an early start. The capital enjoys a comfortable climate throughout the year with temperatures fluctuating around the 20ºC (68ºF) mark by just a few degrees. The mildest time of year is January and February with a range of 15ºC (59ºF) to 23ºC (73ºF). By May the hottest weather is on its way but the temperatures have tweaked only slightly higher to 18ºC (64ºF) to 26ºC (79ºF). In essence you may want a jumper for early mornings, evenings and late nights, but by day a shirt is ideal.

When to visit

Rainfall, however, changes the situation dramatically. Almost dry from December to April, rainfall becomes a regular occurrence from May to November. The rainfall is rarely permanent, and tends towards intense, torrential downpours that last a few hours. *Joséfinos* prefer the umbrella to the raincoat as protection.

San José and around

San José and around

Festivals and celebrations are held throughout the year in the Plaza de la Cultura but perhaps the single greatest festival in the capital is Sep 15th, Independence Day, when costumed parades move down the street, marching bands mark time and crowds block the streets. Orchid lovers will enjoy a trip to the Central Valley in March when the annual National Orchid Show can be linked with trips to Lankester Gardens.

History

For much of its colonial history Costa Rica, with Cartago as its capital, was on the fringes of the New World. Most of the isthmus was governed by the

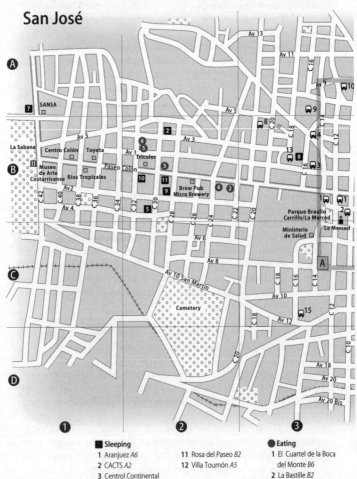

San José

N

0 metres (approx) 300
0 yards (approx) 300

■ **Sleeping**
1 Aranjuez *A6*
2 CACTS *A2*
3 Centrol Continental & Ritz *C4*
4 D'Raya Vida *A6*
5 Grano de Oro *B2*
6 La Mansión *C5*
7 Meliá Confort Corobicí *A1*
8 Musoc *B3*
9 Petit Victoria *B2*
10 Ritmo del Caribe *B2*
11 Rosa del Paseo *B2*
12 Villa Tournón *A5*

● **Eating**
1 El Cuartel de la Boca del Monte *B6*
2 La Bastille *B2*
3 Le Croissant *B2*
4 Lobster Inn *B2*
5 Machu Picchu *B2*
6 Peruveana *B2*

Audiencia de Guatemala which, ruling from southern Mexico in the north down to modern day Costa Rica in the south, barely mustered interest in the distant trading outpost. To the south Panama much preferred wealthy trade with the riches of South America.

Left alone with little colonial meddling, a slow and sometimes painful growth saw a string of communities build up in the central highlands among them San José (1737), Heredia (1706) and Alajuela (1782). In the mid-18th century San José was a ramshackle collection of barely 400 farms. By the end of the century, a monopoly in tobacco trade had given the city a slight prominence over the other towns of the region, fuelling the development of an urban economy and early signs of civic pride. When news of Guatemala's

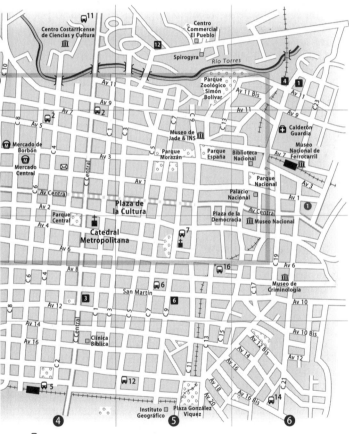

🚌 **Buses**
1 Alajuela & Airport Buses *B3*
2 Heredia Buses *B3/B4*
3 Liberia Buses *B3*
4 Panaline Bus *B3*
5 San Isidro Buses *D4*
6 Sirca Bus *C5*
7 Ticabus *C5*
8 Transnica Bus *B3*
9 Terminal Alfaro *A3*
10 Terminal Atlántico Norte *A3*
11 Terminal Caribe (Sixaola) *A4*
12 Terminal Cartago *D5*
13 Terminal Coca Cola *B3*
14 Terminal Los Santos *D6*
15 Terminal Puntarenas *C3*
16 Terminal Turrialba *C5*

independence from Spain in 1821 finally reached Costa Rica - information that is believed to have taken over one month to arrive - the citizens of San José, with the shoots of a promising coffee industry beginning to appear, were confident of their position and wealth and San José was ready to assume the status of capital.

The emerging agricultural élite combined with the entrepreneurial spirit of the time created a conflict between the emerging towns of the Central Valley, pitting the youthful energetic cities of San José and Alajuela against the more traditional forces of Cartago and Heredia who favoured annexation to a Central America Federation. The dispute was settled in 1823 at the Battle of Ochomongo but skirmishes continued for a further twenty years as the four towns fought for ascendancy of the Central Valley.

The victorious outcome for San José set a path for the nation's growth. Forced by necessity to enter the world economy, a flurry of activity promoted trade in mining and lumber, but it was coffee from the Central Valley that provided a stable and reliable market. As growth of the golden bean was promoted, *cafetaleros* (merchant classes) developed to take advantage of new opportunities. They controlled the export and processing of coffee as well as the credit going to family farms, getting rich in the process and quickly becoming the most influential players in the early development of the young republic.

The wealth of a coffee élite which sold directly to Europe quickly brought return trade in European tastes to the capital. Infrastructure improved with two-storey buildings, street lamps and cabs. The cultural landscape shifted with the introduction of language classes, Shakespeare, operetta and cockfighting. The University of Santo Tomás opened in 1843 and by 1897 the Teatro Nacional (National Theatre), financed by a coffee tax, stood at the centre of the capital as monument to the extravagant wealth, style and tastes that now dominated the lives of rich *Joséfinos*.

Although coffee cultivation spread throughout the Central Valley, the strength of the coffee oligarchy ensured San José remained in control. But the city depended on a strong economy and the air of opulence was considerably dampened by the depression of the 1930s. As the country spent a couple of decades drifting through depression, economic and social reform and civil war, the capital's stylish extravagance became a distant memory.

However, when economic growth stimulated expansion in the late 1950s, industrial development fuelled new prosperity in the capital and San José grew at the expense of the surrounding rural communities as people flocked to its bright lights. The rapid growth of the city, in the absence of urban planning, quickly destroyed its European charm, replacing it instead with blocked streets and increasing pollution.

Today *Joséfinos* are broadly indifferent about their capital. But like a close family member, the San José of today may have its weaknesses, but that's not an area for public discussion – certainly not by foreigners.

Sights

Few come to San José to see the sights, in fact there is a long tradition that comments on the absence of sights of interest in San José. But there is something about Costa Rica that encourages diversity and the capital is no different. In amongst the chaos of the streets, you can find somewhere to sit and wonder about the madness of it all. Between unimaginative high-rise blocks – some of which are exceptionally ugly – odd, solitary gestures to architectural style

Churches

San José has a good variety of churches drawing inspiration from many sources. But lovers of ecclesiastic architecture will most likely leave San José a little disappointed.

Frustration knocks with locked doors. Churches often only open their doors on service days and then possibly only for a few hours. In Barrio Mexico, northeast of the centre, the large dome of a church stands high above the surrounding buildings. The fine masonry work and detail would be suited to a city cathedral but in this quiet rundown corner of town north of the Coca-Cola terminal the church remains locked, bolted and beyond the eyes of visitors and worshippers alike.

Throughout the Central Valley spectacular churches dominate central plazas not only by sheer size but with attention to detail. These churches stand as monument to more than just the faith of the region. Many of the churches are way beyond the means of the small villages. It is difficult to imagine that not only wealth and faith drove the construction of these magnificent buildings, but also a fair amount of community rivalry. For the lover of fine architecture, churches in particular, you'll probably have more joy renting a car and drifting through the towns of the Central Valley – take a journey out to San Ramón, San Rafael de Heredia, San Isidro or head south to the Route of the Saints.

San José and around

stand out. The numerous parks and plazas dotted around the city, are often so cluttered with monuments and benches, winding paths and flower beds that few people pass through them, leaving them strangely empty and peaceful even at the busiest times of day.

On the museum front San José has its fair share. Compact and numerous, the museums are not daunting even if coverage is a little patchy. While they may leave the specialist wanting, if you just want a brief insight into Costa Rican culture and history you'll be more than happy. Of the many options available, if you only have limited time, the underground **Museo de Oro Precolumbiano** (Precolumbian Gold Museum) is impressive in content and presentation and the **Museo de Jade** (Jade Museum), with the largest collection of jade in the Americas, is a source of pride for all *Joséfinos*. The **Museo Nacional** (National Museum) now occupying Bellavista Fortress stands monument to the changing fortunes of the city and country. ■ *Most museums are closed on Sun and Mon. Check in advance before travelling to outer lying museums.*

While there may be no such thing as a normal city, San José seems less normal than most. Without the romantic legacy of Paris, the classical weight of Rome or the frightening chaos of some of the larger Latin cities, San José is manageable and, approached without too much expectation, almost refreshing.

The sights of the city are broken down into regions that link together in a fairly logical order. You can pick the odd bits you want to visit, or take in a few of the districts back to back.

Central San José

At the heart of the city **Plaza de la Cultura** is a vibrant hub of pedestrian activity on Avenida Central and Calle 3-5. The Plaza itself holds little of interest but for a few uncomfortable benches, clusters of telephones and queues of frustrated *Joséfinos* patiently waiting for access to one of the few that work. But people and a few hundred pigeons gather around to watch the constant flow of people from all walks of life. Where perfect people-watching conditions prevail you can usually find a street café and sure enough the **Hotel Gran**

Around the Plaza de la Cultura

Costa Rica offers a perfect vantage point for the urban anthropologist. In the drier months, the Plaza de la Cultura is the focus of evening performances of anything from classical orchestras to jazz, blues and cultural events often with international artists.

Buried like hidden treasure below the Plaza, through a rather daunting gated entrance on the eastern side is the **Museo de Oro Precolombiano** (Precolumbian Gold Museum). Delicate figurines of frogs, spiders, raptors and other creatures, glisten in the museum sponsored by the Banco Nacional. Plotting the development of metallurgical techniques in the Diquis region of southwest Costa Rica, the pieces demonstrate a fine degree of skill and crafts-manship. Gold work grew steadily from around 500 AD, marking a move away from the Maya influences of the north which preferred jade, to the southern influences of Panama and Colombia which placed greater impor-tance on gold. ■ *Tue-Sun, 1000-1600. US$5, students US$1. T223-0528, F257-0651, museoro@sol.racsa.co.cr Bags must be stored when visiting, secure cloakroom service provided. C5, Av Central-2. There is an audio guide to the room that can be rented from the cloakroom.*

Within the same three-storey underground complex the small **Museo Numismática** (Numismatic Museum) displays a selection of bills, coins and *boletos de café* reflecting Costa Rican history from the 16th century to the pres-ent day. An open area is used for temporary exhibitions displaying part of the Banco Nacional's large collection of fine arts and archaeological exhibitions. While you're here, you can pop into the **ICT Tourist Office** and pick up any extra information you may want.

Back at ground level, on the southern side of the plaza is the neoclassical **Teatro Nacional** (National Theatre) – one of the most impressive buildings in the city, and a source of considerable pride. Funded by a coffee tax in the late 19th century when the country's social élite realized the city was lacking a thea-tre suitable for world-class performances, construction of the theatre called on the skills of European artisans including Belgian architects and Italian artists to create this national treasure. The colonnades of the exterior are complemented by a lavish interior with a balance of extravagance and detail in the mahogany furniture, crystal chandeliers, gold-leaf murals and paintings including the well known image of *Marielitos* smiling out of the dockside scene *Alegoría a Las Exportaciones*. The stylish café is fitting tribute to the paymasters of the theatre and definitely worth a visit. ■ *Mon-Sat, 0900-1700, US$3, T221-5341. Guided tours are available. See La Nación or Tico Times for performances. Av 2, C 3. For the Coffee Culture Tour (US$39 – high season only) contact a tour operator or Café Britt direct on T260-2748, F260-1456, www.cafebritt.com*

Around Plaza de la Democracía Head east down Avenida Central from Plaza de la Cultura for half a dozen blocks and you reach **Plaza de la Democracía**. Created in 1989 to celebrate the centenary of Costa Rican democracy, the bare plaza looks rather like a vast tiered waterfall without the water. The bronze statue of **José Figueres** does lit-tle to lift the ambience of the quiet plaza which has a few benches for resting. A small craft market selling hammocks, pictures and wood items lines the west-ern side of the plaza.

Lining the plaza's eastern flank is the **Museo Nacional** (National Museum) now housed in the converted barracks of the Bellavista Fortress which still shows the bullet scars of battle from the 1948 civil war. A mixed bag of displays looks at Indian life pre-colonization and the introduction of Catholicism in Costa Rica, with a few rooms given over to lifestyle in the colonial era and art. Downstairs, a small exhibition leads through the quarters and prison cells of the fortress explaining events leading up to the civil war. Signs are mainly in Spanish and exhibits are changed from time to time. The exhibition rooms border a pleasant courtyard overlooking the city and the Plaza de la Democracía below. ■ *Tue-Sat, 0830-1630, Sun and holidays 0900-1630. US$4. T257-1433. C 17, Av Central-2. Entrance on plaza is often locked.*

One block north is the **Palacio Nacional** where the Legislative Assembly sits. Catch up on government business and brush up your Spanish at the same time, listening in on sessions. ■ *Mon-Fri from 1600. C 17, Av Central-2.*

The **Parque Nacional** covers a couple of blocks one block north of the Palacio Nacional. An extensive parkland densely packed with trees and palms where secretive couples hide in the shade and anyone with a bit of time to kill can be found adding to the laid-back atmosphere. Overseeing all the activity, the **Monumento Nacional** with a grandiloquent statue representing the five Central American republics ousting the North American filibuster William Walker, and the abolition of slavery in Central America. A statue of national hero **Juan Santamaría** donated by the Sandinista Government of Nicaragua stands in the southwest corner of the park.

On the north side of the park, the **Biblioteca Nacional** (National Library) hides behind a starkly modern exterior. In addition to several current periodicals, the archives hold national newspapers dating back to 1833. ■ *Mon-Fri, 0800-1830. Open to non-nationals with ID. Av 3, C 15.* At the northwestern corner of the park in the old liquor factory is the **Museo de Arte y Diseño Contemporaneo** (Museum of Contemporary Art and Design) along with the offices of the Ministry of Culture. There are changing displays with works by national artists. ■ *Tue-Sat, 1000-1700, closed Sun and Mon. US$1. T257-9370, Av 3, C 15, www.madc.co.cr*

Around Parque Nacional
In late 2000 the park was closed for extensive renovations and to clear some of the overgrown and dangerous trees

San José and around

If you like trains head for the **Museo Nacional de Ferrocarril** (National Railway Museum) in the old Atlantic Railway station behind the library. The station was the final stop of the San José to Limón line that linked the Central Valley to the Caribbean lowlands. When the trains stopped running in 1990, the station quickly fell into disrepair. The museum is reported to have a photographic history of the train line along with memorabilia. Unfortunately the museum has been closed for a few years and there are no suggestions that it will open again soon. But you can poke around the outside, imagine past glories and ask around if anyone has a key. ■ *Av 3, C 21.*

Northeast of Parque Nacional

A little further out of town **Museo Dr Rafael Angel Calderón Guardia** has displays on the life of the reformist president who laid the foundations for the Costa Rican welfare state in the early 1940s. Set in the old Calderón mansion, there are also temporary art exhibitions and a small library. ■ *Mon-Sat, 0900-1700. US$0.50. T222-6392, Av 11, C 25.*

From Parque Nacional heading west down Avenida 3 back towards the centre is the southern side of **Parque España**, a refreshingly verdant square with an air of calm. On Sunday there is normally an outdoor market in the square. Directly north of the square is the INS or Instituto Nacional de Seguros which houses on the top floor the **Museo de Jade Fidel Tristan**. In addition to the largest collection of jade carvings in the Americas with literally hundreds of smoothly fashioned pieces, there are displays of precolumbian art, pottery and sculpture. Renovated in late 2000, the museum also provides an excellent view over the city. ■ *Mon-Fri, 0830-1630. Closed weekends. US$3. T287-6034, Av 7, C 9-11.*

Around Parque España & Parque Morazán

From Parque España you can clearly see the ornate **Casa Amarilla** to the northeast which holds Costa Rica's Ministry of Foreign Affairs and, reportedly, a piece of the Berlin Wall. The building is not, however, open to the public. To the west, the simple yet bizarre structure of the **Edificio Metálico**, designed in Belgium and shipped from France, is a school today as it was in the 1890s when first welded together. Over and above the sheer cost and effort that went into producing the building, the overwhelming feeling on seeing it is, "so?".

Crossing Calle 9 leads west to **Parque Morazán** overshadowed by the 17 or so stories of the *Aurola Holiday Inn* (with excellent views from the top floor casino). The park's namesake General Francisco Morazán briefly tried to reunite Central America using Costa Rica as the military base in 1842 – the General was executed shortly after in the Parque Central. The largest of the green spots in the centre, the park is remarkably quiet for most of the day and an ideal spot to rest and meet up after exploring the relatively uninspiring gift shops on the south and west side of the park.

Behind the two parks the historic districts or *barrios* of **Amón** and **Otoya** lead to the north. This was once the residential district of the coffee élite and wealthier classes and single storey architecture of the colonial period with low slung eaves shading broad balconies abounds. Today the tiled courtyards, lush private gardens and patios are enjoyed by guests, diners and employees of hotels, restaurants and some of the more style-conscious embassies who stepped in with renovation plans just in time to stop the complete destruction of the district. Some of the most accessible examples are the **Alianza Francesa** building on the corner of Avenida 7 and Calle 5, which has a fine exterior. **Hotel Britannia** on Calle 3 and Avenida 11 and the beautifully restored **Hotel Alóki** on Calle 13, Avenida 9-11 both welcome non-resident diners. Other treasures can be found in the area, including **El Castillo** on Avenida 11 and Calle 3 where the defensive turrets and religious themes merge in the home of a former bishop. Along Avenida 9 between Calle 3 and 7 the walls lining the street are decorated with colourful ceramic tiles depicting rural scenes.

At the limit of comfortable walking distances is the **Parque Zoológico Simón Bolívar** where you can see many of Costa Rica's mammals, including monkeys, big cats and tapirs as well as caiman and several species of birds. The zoo is popular especially at weekends with young *Josefino* families. Zoos tend to turn people one way or the other, and while the zoo is not the best kept place in the world, as part of Costa Rica's overall conservation and awareness strategy it plays an important role. Conditions are improving slowly. ■ *Mon-Fri, 0800-1600, Sat-Sun, 0800-1600. US$2, donations welcome. Av 11, C 7. Go north on C 7 until you reach Av 11.*

Heading back towards town along Calle 9 or 11 until Avenida 1, pop in and visit the **Serpentarium** where many of the bright, colourful and legendarily dangerous creatures of Costa Rican wildlife can be found, including eye-lash vipers, poison arrow frogs, caimans and boa constrictors. There is even a piranha (just one!) to complete the life-threatening set. With labels in Spanish and English, this is an impressive collection of creepy, crawly, slimy things. Given the location on the second floor of a run-down office block you can't help thinking that the animals are simply biding their time until the great escape happens and the world will be theirs. ■ *Mon-Fri, 0900-1800, Sat-Sun, 1000-1700. US$4. T255-4210. Av 1, C 9-11, 2nd floor of an office block.*

Around Parque Central **Parque Central** is a couple of blocks west of the Plaza de la Cultura and distinctive for the huge bandstand in the centre bordered by Avenida 2 and Calle Central. Grandiose and imposing, the effect is one of instant repulsion for what is surely one of the most ugly metropolitan monuments anywhere. Add to this the serious need of a lick of paint and uneven steps that invite you to fall up or down, and there is a very little to endear you to the plaza. However, the Parque is a major thoroughfare of the city, and makes for good people watching. Even if there is no street café you can normally pick up an ice cream. At weekends, Sundays in particular, this is a popular spot with *Ticos* who seem to slow down to saunter and meander through any temporary stalls and general happenings that may be occurring. To the east is the slightly cramped **Catedrál Metropolitana** visited by Pope John Paul II in 1983 on his first visit to Central America. Recently renovated, the lines are clean and crisp if a little uninspiring. Gone are the polluting sooty candles replaced instead with a neat line of electric ones – 25 *centavos* will light your bulb for a few minutes, 50 *centavos* and you can brighten two.

North of the plaza on Avenida 2 is the **Teatro Melico Salazar** which after the Teatro Nacional is Costa Rica's most important theatre. Performances and shows at the Melico have a broader appeal ranging from pop and jazz concerts through to ballet and orchestral works. ■ *See press for details or call T221-4952.*

Within the boundaries of the central walking district, the pedestrianized Avenida Central heads west for a few blocks towards the **Banco Central**. Most banks have a branch close to the area and there are several ATMs nearby. Bustling with the busy chaos of people rushing around, the shops, banks and department stores make this one of the main arteries of the city. Three blocks west of the Plaza Cultura, a right up Calle 2 leads to the elegant façade of the **Correo Central** (Central Post Office). Understated and often overlooked, the building seems perfectly balanced in proportion and setting. Inside, the halls of postboxes are a bit daunting, but upstairs is the interesting **Museo Postal** (Post Museum), Telegráfico Filatélico de Costa Rica. ■ *Mon-Fri, 0800-1630. Free. T223-9766. C 2, Av 1-3.* The **Café del Correo** is a splendid café that retains some period pieces and serves excellent coffee and cakes.

A few blocks further west along Avenida 1 is the **Mercado Central** taking up a whole block bordered by Avenida Central-1 and Calle 6-8. The covered market is a noisy, colourful and in places rather smelly affair that also happens to sell things. In fact everything from cheese, spices, fruit, vegetables, dried and fresh flowers through to leather sandals, saddles, bridles and simple tourist gifts. The honey is particularly recommended and if you're looking to set up in business you can buy one of the small boxes used by the boot boys to hold their polish and brushes. Restaurants and juice bars serve good, cheap food and drinks which is generally cleanly prepared with a turnover so quick it doesn't have time to go off.

Parque Braulio Carrillo also known as *Parque La Merced* borders Avenida 2 sharing Calle 12 with **La Merced Church**. Eclectic-Gothic in style the church looks tired, weary and confused but there is enough detail to keep the eye amused for a few minutes. On the roof, ornate ironwork decoration contrasts disappointingly with iron panelling of the corrugated variety. Entering from the north, the nave appears fresh and airy, yet from the west the church seems cramped and cluttered. Built and rebuilt over a period of 80 years that ended in 1894, the church is Gothic and certainly eclectic. On the western side of the Parque is San Juan de Dios Hospital.

West of town the six-lane Paseo Colón feeds and drains the city centre of traffic. The pavements are dotted with offices, car rental companies, garages, restaurants, fast food outlets and the odd hotel and supermarket. It's a chaotic

Western Central

Paseo Colón & west of the centre

road that is daunting to the pedestrian and motorist alike but you will probably travel along it at least once while in San José. If you need to walk, there are several pedestrian bridges spanning the road.

At the western end of Paseo Colón is **Parque Sábana**. Until the middle of the 20th century the area was the city's airport but the transformation has created a vast parkland of trees and greenery just 30 minutes' walk or a short bus ride from central San José. On the western side is the **Estadio Nacional** (National Stadium) where the national football team plays in front of capacity crowds of 20,000, and valiantly attempts to qualify for the next World Cup for the second time in its history. There's a running track, sports centre with a swimming pool and a lake but most will travel out this far for the **Museo de Arte Costarricense** (Museum of Costa Rican Art) in the old terminal building. A small but good collection of 19th and 20th century art and sculpture by national and international artists with changing exhibitions to keep you going back. ■ *Tue-Sun, 1000-1600. US$2, US$1 for students, free on Sun. T222-7155. C 42, Paseo Colón and Av 2. Walk west down Paseo Colón for a 30-min walk. Buses for Sábana Cementerio leave from Av 2.*

At the southwestern corner the **Museo de Ciencias Naturales** in the Colegio La Salle has a huge collection of mounted, stuffed and stored animals which should help you recognize animals when you're out in the wild. ■ *Mon-Sat 0800-1630, Sun 0900-1700, US$2, T232-1306. Buses marked Sábana Estadio run close to the museum. Ask the driver where to get out for Colegio La Salle.*

Outside the centre

A few places of interest exist just beyond the realm of a comfortable walk. If you like to walk then striking out is not a problem, but otherwise taking a cab will leave you with enough energy to explore.

North of centre The Disneyesque façade of the **Centro Costarricense de Ciencias y Cultura** (Costa Rican Centre of Science and Culture) at the northern end of Calle 4 beyond Avenida 9 hides a fascinating mix of art, history, study and fun. Turrets and fluttering banners entice you towards the cells, wings and corridors of the former penitentiary. Photographs show the extent of the restoration work that began in 1992. The **Museo de Niños** (Children's Museum) is, judging by the amount of noise at least, a lot of fun with games and activities using up a couple of wings. The **Galería Nacional** (National Gallery) uses the vaulted ceilings and stark spaces to display a mix of permanent and temporary exhibitions. Leading to the **Biblioteca Carlos Luiz Saénz** (Carlos Luiz Saénz Library) a few cells and prisoner accounts report conditions of life in the prison. Completing the eclectic mix, the **Auditorio Nacional** (National Auditorium) is a performance venue with plays, occasional orchestral performances and other events. Lots to do and explore in a carefully restored building, and if the weather is good, you can sit outside on the lawns. The transformation from what was presumably a thoroughly unpleasant place to a site of learning, education and fun is impressive even if the contents don't overwhelm. ■ *Tue-Fri 0800-1500, Sat-Sun 1000-1600. US$2, US$1.30 children. T258-4929. Simply join C 4 and head north, or catch a cab. See local press for performances and exhibits.*

In **Barrio Tournón**, north of the River Torres, is the **Centro Commercial El Pueblo** shopping centre. A warren of paths and alleyways set out like a small colonial village comes alive at night. A wide variety of souvenir shops sells everything from colonial art, delicate wood carvings, fine ceramics and T-shirts. Although prices overall are higher than shops in the downtown area, you won't find so many shops in the same place elsewhere. As night falls, cafés, restaurants and bars open and the nightlife and finery of San José decants to El Pueblo and the place comes alive. As with the shops, some of the best restaurants in the city are in El Pueblo, but you can also just take a snack or a drink. Nightclubs will keep the dawnraiders going until the early hours. ■ *Some shops and restaurants open from mid-morning, most from mid-afternoon. Nightclubs stay open until early morning. You can walk to El Pueblo some 20 mins from the centre. A taxi will cost around US$2 from central San José – agree fare beforehand. Strongly advised at nighttime.*

Also in Barrio Tournón, one block east and south of El Pueblo, is **Spirogyra** a butterfly farm some 20 minutes' walk from central San José in one of the last truly natural green areas of the city. Tours consist of a short video followed by a 45-minute guided tour of the exuberant botanical garden that is home to the 20 or so species of butterfly bred for export. Several species of hummingbird visit the gardens. After the tour, you are welcome to stay as long as you like poking around looking under leaves for hatching larvae and watching the butterflies feed. There is a small café at the garden. ■ *Mon-Sun, 0800-1600 (last tour around 1500), US$6 adults, US$3 children, T/F222-2937, parcar@sol.racsa.co.cr Walking, head north out of the city along C 3, turning right at Highway 108 passing Hotel Villa Tournón, turn right at the main road opposite El Pueblo. A taxi from downtown San José is around US$2.*

If visiting in the green season, arrive early. Butterflies stop flying in the rain, preferring to take shelter instead

South of centre

Close to the centre, but not easily included within a walking route is the delightful **Iglesia Soledad** (Soledad Church). Often overlooked, the yellow church sits slightly elevated above the traffic, enjoying a rare spot of calm and solitude. A few blocks east the **Museo de Criminología** (Criminology Museum) hopes to point out that crime doesn't pay with displays of gruesome acts and various grisly exhibits representing the history of crime in Costa Rica. ■ *Mon-Fri 0700-1630. Free – crime doesn't pay and neither do you. T295-3850. C 17, Av 6-8.*

Eastern districts & San Pedro

Beyond the Museo Nacional, Avenida Central heads east through the residential districts of **Los Yoses** and **La California** to **San Pedro** and the vast campus of the **University of Costa Rica**.

Los Yoses and La California achieve the magical act of being calm residential areas just a few blocks from the city centre. Hardly surprising then that this home for some of the wealthier residents of the city, and a place with a few comfortable hotels, stylish restaurants and a few embassies.

Crossing the city's ring road leads to San Pedro, and the **University of Costa Rica (UCR)**. As you'd expect it's lively with student life, cafés, bookstores and a general feel of vitality. While younger visitors may simply enjoy joining the student scene, others can travel out to the campus to visit the **Museo de Entomología** (Insect Museum). Located, rather bizarrely, in the basement of the **Artes Musicales** (School of Music) there are hundreds of insects to gaze and gawp at so you'll be familiar with the thing climbing up your arm on the jungle treks. ■ *Mon-Fri,1300-1700, US$3, T207-5647. If closed, ask around. Buses travel from Av 2 out to San Pedro. Ask the driver to drop you at the C Central in San Pedro from where you can walk north a couple of blocks. A taxi out to San Pedro will cost around US$3.*

San José and around

Essentials

Sleeping

■ on maps pages 90 and 102 Price codes: see inside front cover

Accommodation in San José is as wide and varied as you would expect in the capital, with a surprising number of options in the middle price bracket indicating greater levels of development than found in many Central American capitals. For the visitor this means there is a wide – sometimes daunting – choice. Hotels range in size and style from the chains of Holiday Inn and Best Western, large business hotels which merge services and presentation to more stylish affairs that build on the history or architecture of a building or district. Lower down the price range there are many good choices before things start to creak a little at the edges.

You can find hotels of all ranges within the central district of the city – handy for a day or two at the beginning of your stay. However, the city is small enough to enjoy some of the very memorable hotels that can be found along and off Paseo Colón to the west of the city and northwest of the city in Barrios Amón and Otoya. Many expatriates living in Costa Rica prefer to stay in the quiet western suburb of Escazú or Alajuela close to the airport if catching a flight the next day instead of tackling the congestion of the capital.

Cheaper rooms tend to be a compromise. You either get a room on the road, which although well lit, is subject to early morning noise, or you get a room on the inside of the building which although quiet, probably has a window view of a wall and limited light. Ask to see a room first if you have the time or inclination.

Budget travellers and backpackers will find a concentration of hotels and accommodation around the Mercado Central area and the infamous Coca-Cola Bus Terminal. Both areas are lively and enjoyable but locals will tell you not to venture out at night. Safety can be a problem in these areas and there have been reports of muggings. Police are aware of the issue and while security has been stepped up, visitors choosing to stay in these areas should take appropriate precautions, including avoiding going out at night alone – both men and women.

Central **LL-L** *Aurola*, Av 5, C 5-7, T222-2424, F255-1171, auroven@racsa.co.cr Some 200 comfortable rooms varying in size with all the services expected of a Holiday Inn. The 17-storey building is a San José landmark with a spectacular view from the top floor casino. **L-AL** *del Rey*, Av 1, C 9, Apdo 6241-1000, T257-7800, F221-0096, www.hoteldelrey.com Standing proud on a busy corner in a fine blaze of pink and white the *del Rey* is almost part of San José legend, looking as it does like an iced cake. As the advert on Radio 107.5 FM says, "you don't have to stay at the *del Rey*, to play at the *del Rey*". The large rooms are a bit shabby given the pristine exterior of the building. What draws the crowds is the lively casino downstairs and the sports bar, a renowned hang-out for

- -

5 best budget hotels

D *Principe* – nothing special, but reliable and safe
E *Casa Ridgeway* – the comforts of home
F *Centro Continental* – mid-range service at budget prices
F *Gran Imperial* – the backpacker's favourite
G *España* – excellent value for the price, but just in the red light district

5 best for character

LL-AL *Grano de Oro* – Effortless style, abject luxury
A *Alóki* – Beautiful hotel and homely Tico charm
A-B *Kekoldi* – refreshingly original
B *La Mansion* – understated grace and charm, a quirky favourite
B *Petit Victoria* – Beautiful old home that keeps all the character of its Victorian heritage

professional sex workers. Join the queues like moths to the flame, or avoid at all costs.

AL *Balmoral*, Av Central, C 7, T222-5022, F221-7826, www.balmoral.co.cr 100 rooms with full services. Classic décor, in well appointed rooms with congenial service. Currently being refurbished and a casino is on the way. **AL** *Gran Hotel Costa Rica*, Av 2, C Central, T221-4000, F221-3501, granhcr@sol.racsa.co.cr Cable TV, fan, telephone, security box, laundry and room service. Mid-range restaurant and 24-hour street café open to non-guests. Casino and conference services. A great San José landmark, it is one of the oldest purpose-built hotels in the capital and lives up to the Grand name without being too ostentatious. Used by John F Kennedy on his visit to Costa Rica in 1963. **AL** *Presidente*, Av Central, C 7, T222-3022, F221-1205, www.hotel-presidente.com 96 rooms with cable TV, a/c, telephone, room service, safe box, laundry, business centre, sauna and Jacuzzi, the popular *News* bar decked with international newspapers, café and restaurant (mid-range), travel agency, parking and casino. Great sense of style to the place, comfortable without being overbearing. Good central location. **A** *Best Western – Downtown*, Av 7, C 6, T255-4766, toll free in the USA 1-800-526-1234, F255-4613, www.bestwestern.co.cr Private bathroom, TV, a/c, telephone, email, safe boxes, only hotel pool in downtown San José, free breakfast and coffee, parking and free airport transfers, email services. Makes good use of a small space with airy rooms, poolside restaurant and helpful staff. An oasis in the city. **A** *Europa*, 5 Av, C Central, T222-1222, F221-3976, europa@racsa.co.cr Almost 80 rooms, fully equipped with TV, telephone, fan and a/c, safe box, bathroom, minibar, tiled bathrooms with bath tub and room service. Crisp décor in spacious rooms in a relaxed and professional hotel. The international restaurant is expensive, but the hotel is excellent value. **A** *Talamanca*, Av 2, C 8-10, T233-5033, F233-5420, talamanca@racsa.co.cr Private baths, hot water, a/c or ceiling fan, cable TV, telephone, minibar, restaurant with balcony, fine bar with excellent views on the 9th floor. Quite small rooms but good service. Stylish décor throughout, the reception is decorated with replicas of precolumbian Huetares ceramics.

A-B *Costa Rica Morazán*, C 7, Av 1, T222-4622, F233-3329, www.hotels.co.cr/ morazan.html Rooms vary but all have private bathrooms, colour TV and telephone. The central location and casino make it popular. Parking and airport shuttle service. **A-B** *Doral*, Av 4, C 6-8, T233-0665, F233-4827, hdoral@sol.racsa.co.cr Private bathroom, TV, telephone, ceiling fans, safe box, laundry, restaurant and drinks service. Nice big rooms with strange colour combinations, some with balconies, although some on the inside are quite dark. Cheaper without breakfast. **B** *del Bulevar*, Av Central, C Central, T257-0022. Private bath with tub, telephone, TV, a/c, room service, restaurant and bar. Big rooms, some spacious enough for 4. Friendly and central, with bar overlooking the lively C Central – good place to stop for a couple of quiet drinks. Perched on the southwest corner of Parque Morazán is **B** *Diana's Inn*, Av 3, C 5, T223-6542, F233-0495. There's a friendly family feel in this central B&B. Former home of a Costa Rica president, it has 7 rooms with TV, private bathroom and hot water. **B** *Internet Hotel Rey Amón*, Av 7, C 7-9, T/F233-1769, reamon@yeess.com Private bathroom, hot water, cable TV, safe box, ample free parking, breakfast included, laundry service, luggage storage, travel services and internet access. Big rooms, spacious and airy, nice communal area that has a small bar. Very friendly and helpful new Polish owners. **B** *Park*, Av 4, C 2-4, T221-6944, F233-7602. Popular with those seeking a smarter room for 1 night or even just a couple of hours. Clean rooms with hot water. **B** *Plaza*, Av Central, C 2-4, T257-1896, F222-2641, hotplaza@sol.racsa.co.cr TV, radio, telephone, private bath, room service, laundry services, safeboxes and parking. Central location with pleasant friendly staff who will help with organizing tours and car rental. Some rooms a bit cramped, and the bathrooms could do with a refurb.

San José and around

B-C *Pensión de la Cuesta*, Av 1, C 11-15, T256-7946, F255-2896, www. suntoursandfun.com A little piece of eccentricity always brightens the day as does the lurid pink canopy over the entrance to the hotel. But inside, this old colonial home has smart and clean rooms and apartments. Shared bath and use of the kitchen. Can also arrange a package with *Hermosa Beach Apartments* and have a Rent-a-Van option complete with water sports equipment. **C** *Diplomat*, C6, Av Central, T221-8133, F233-7474. Not much to shout about apart from being very central and reasonably

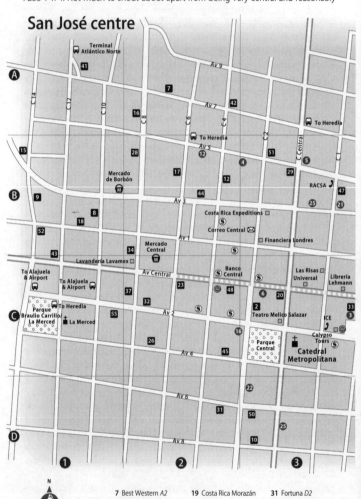

San José centre

Terminal Atlántico Norte
41

7
42

16
Av 7

To Heredia

15
Av 5
28
12
51
C Central
5
17
4
29
Mercado de Borbón
12
RACSA
47

9
Av 3
44
25
21
8
Costa Rica Expeditions
18
Correo Central
52
Av 1
Financiera Londres
43
34
Mercado Central
Lavandería Lavamex
Av Central
Banco Central
Las Risas
Librería Lehmann
To Alajuela & Airport
Universal
To Alajuela & Airport
37
23
48
6
20
To Heredia
32
2
33
Parque Braulio Carrillo La Merced
55
Av 2
Teatro Melico Salazar
3
La Merced
26
16
Calypso Tours
45
Parque Central
Catedral Metropolitana
Av 4
22
Av 6
31
50
25
Av 8
10

1
2
3

N

0 metres 100
0 yards 100

■ **Sleeping**
1 Aloki *A5*
2 Americana *C3*
3 Astoria *B5*
4 Aurola *B4*
5 Balmoral *C4*
6 Barceló Amón Plaza *A4*

7 Best Western *A2*
8 Bienvenido *B1*
9 Boruca *B1*
10 Boston *D3*
11 Britannia *A4*
12 Capital *B2*
13 Casa Ridgeway *D6*
14 Cinco Hormigas Rojas *A6*
15 Cocori *B1*
16 Colón *A2*
17 Compostela *B2*
18 Corobicí *B1*

19 Costa Rica Morazán *C4*
20 Del Bulevar *C3*
21 Del Rey *C5*
22 Diana's Inn *B4*
23 Diplomat *C2*
24 Don Carlos *A5*
25 Doña Inés *D5*
26 Doral *C2*
27 Edelweiss *B6*
28 España *B2*
29 Europa *B3*
30 Fleur de Lys *D5*

31 Fortuna *D2*
32 Gran Hotel Centroamericano *C2*
33 Gran Hotel Costa Rica *C3*
34 Gran Imperial *B2*
35 Hemingway Inn *A5*
36 Internet Hotel Rey Amón *B5*
37 Johnson *C2*
38 Joluva Guesthouse *A4*
39 Kekoldi *A4*
40 La Casa Verde Inn *A5*

priced. 29 rooms with private bath and hot water. **C Fortuna**, Av 6, C 2-4, T223-5344, F221-2466, hfortuna@infoweb.co.cr TV, telephone, internet service available, credit cards accepted. Simple rooms and tired décor in a very functional atmosphere. **C Gran Hotel Centroamericano**, Av 2, C 6-8, T221-3362, F221-3714. 45 rooms with private bath, self-service restaurant, telephone and laundry. Clean small rooms, although some a little dark, very helpful. **C Nuevo Alameda**, Av Central, C 12, T233-3551, F233-3551. Private bathrooms, some shared, some with TV, a/c which sometimes

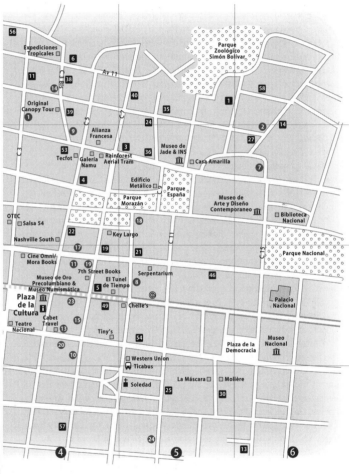

San José and around

41 La Posada de Don Tobías *A1*	52 Roma *B1*	4 China Bonita *B3*	15 La Hacienda Steak House *C4*
42 Marlyn *A2*	53 Santo Tomás *B4*	5 Choza del Sabor *B5*	16 La Perla *C2*
43 Nuevo Alameda *B1*	54 Segunda & Washington *C5*	6 Churrería Manolo *C3*	17 Lung Mun *C4*
44 Nuevo Central *B2*	55 Talamanca *C1*	7 Don Sol *B6*	18 Morazán *B5*
45 Park *C2*	56 Taylor's Inn *A4*	8 El Balcón de Europa *C5*	19 Pasta Factory *C4*
46 Pensión de la Cuesta *C5*	57 Tica Linda *D4*	9 El Museo *B4*	20 Pizza Metro *C4*
47 Pensión Otoya *B3*	58 Vesuvio *A6*	10 Fu Lu Su *C4*	21 Pollo a la Leña *B3*
48 Plaza *C2*		11 Goya *C4*	22 Soda El Parque *D3*
49 Presidente *C4*	● **Eating**	12 Gran Diamente *B2*	23 Spoon *C4*
50 Príncipe *D3*	1 Al Andalus *A4*	13 La Esmeralda *C4*	24 Tin Jo *D5*
51 Rialto *B3*	2 Café Mundo *B6*	14 La Esquina del Café *A4*	25 Vishnu *B3/D3*
	3 Café Parisienne *C3*		

works. Good spacious rooms at the front, a few cheaper rooms available but you'll have to ask. *Los Potrillos* restaurant serves a good selection of meals in a clean, pleasant dining room. Popular. **C** *Ritz*, Av 8-10, C Central, T222-4103, F222-8849, ritzcr@sol.racsa.co.cr Private bath, cheaper without, TV lounge, storage boxes, credit cards accepted. *Ritz Eco-Tourismo* travel agency downstairs. Smallish rooms but popular with friendly service and congenial atmosphere. Discounts available in the green season. Good choice and recommended.

D *Bienvenido*, C 10, Av 1-3, T233-2161, F221-1872, www.geocities.com/hotel_bienvenidocr One of the best hotels near Coca-Cola bus station. Clean, hot showers, good restaurant, near centre and airport bus. **D** *Boston*, Av 8, C Central-2, T221-0563, F257-5063. TV, private bath, hot water, laundry service, telephone in reception. Friendly service, but nothing makes it stand out. Several cheapies nearby if you're having no luck. **D** *Capital*, Av 3-5, C 4, T221-8497, F221-8583, yasser@sol.racsa.co.cr Private bath, hot water, fan, cable TV, laundry service. Pleasant clean rooms, ask for one facing the street for more light. Beautiful selection of 1920s railroad photographs in reception. **D** *Compostela*, Av 3-5, C 6, T257-1514. Hot water, most rooms with private bath. Rooms a little dark. Nice crocodile in reception. **D** *Cocori*, Av 5, C 16, T233-0081, F255-1058. Private bathroom, very clean, high standards and helpful owner. Ideal for early buses and just 100 m from Coca-Cola bus terminal. **D** *Johnson*, Av Central y 2, C 8, T223-7633, F222-3683. Private bathrooms, telephones in rooms, bar/restaurant. Friendly and helpful staff. Good value for the price, but get a room with a window. Popular with those seeking a break from the grunge of western San José. Recommended. **D** *La Posada de Don Tobías*, Av 7-9, C 12, T258-3162, F233-8754, hguapile@sol.racsa.co.cr Private bath, hot water. Clean, smart with well-lit rooms. Not the best location in San José but ideal for an early morning bus. **D** *Nuevo Central*, Av 3, C 4-6, T222-3509, F222-3231. Telephone, private bath, hot water, credit cards accepted. Good, efficient and friendly service, but rooms a little on the dark side. **D** *Rialto*, Av 5, C 2, T221-7456. Basic rooms close to the centre of town, a bit tatty, but some rooms well lit and spotlessly clean. **D** *Principe*, Av 6, C Central -2, T222-7983, F223-1589. Basic rooms, but good for the price especially on the top floor. Most rooms with private bath and hot water. Simple bar and café on 2nd floor open in high season. Safe, secure and friendly. Recommended.

E *Astoria*, Av 7, C 7-9, T221-2174. Shared bathroom, hot water. Basic. Singles **F** per person. **E** *Marlyn*, C 4, Av 7-9, T233-3212. Rooms are small and a little dark. Hot showers, good security, will store luggage, parking for motorcycles (just). Some rooms with private bath. **E** *Musoc*, Av 1-3, C 16, big pink building at the eastern entrance to the Coca-Cola terminal, T222-9437. Private bath, hot water, well maintained. Well run even if the rooms are a little cramped. Perfect for early morning buses, or if you arrive in the city late. **E** *Roma*, Av Central – 1, C 14, T223-2179. Basic, quiet and friendly with scruffy reception area. **E-F** *Pensión Otoya*, C 1, Av 3-5, T221-3925. Close to the centre, clean, friendly and quite popular. Hot water throughout and some rooms with private bath. Luggage store, telephone use, internet access and English spoken. Recommended.

F *Americana*, C 2, Av 2, T221-9799. Rooms are large, basic, with shared bath and mixed reports. Friendly, with luggage store and laundry facilities. **F** *Centro Continental*, Av 8-10, C Central, T222-4103, F222-8849, ritzcr@racsa.co.cr Simple basic rooms with access to the TV room and breakfast services of the *Hotel Ritz* (**C**) upstairs. A good deal considering the add-ons. Credit cards accepted. Recommended. **F** *Colón*, Av 5 y 7, C 8, T223-5277. Private bath, hot water, open 24 hrs. Another bargain that suffers from being in a bad area. **F** *Corobicí*, Av 1, C 10-12, T233-0564. Shared bath, sponge mattresses. Basic and a bit tatty, but would do at a push. **F** *Gran Imperial*, Av 1-Central, C 8, T222-8463, F256-9650, granhimp@sol.racsa.co.cr Basic rooms some with private bath, some without, hot water sometimes, restaurant. Mixed reports, small rooms, thin walls, getting grubby, sometimes noisy, good prices at restaurant, very popular with backpackers so probably the best place to meet other travellers. Balcony overlooking the street and central market is a great spot for relaxing. Reserve in advance if you can, locked luggage store. **G** *España*, Av 3 y 5, C 8, T221-1092. Simple rooms, shared bathrooms, cold water. Basic but very clean, excellent value for this price but just in the danger zone. **G** *Boruca*, Av 1-3, C 14, T223-0016. Basic. Simple all shared bathroom, rooms a bit dark, owner friendly and helpful. What else can you expect for these prices?

L *Barceló Amón Plaza*, Av 11, C 3 bis, T257-0191, F257-0284, www.barcelo.com A large 90-room hotel with all the comforts for the modern business traveller in the stylish district of *barrio* Amón. A 24-hr bar, ballroom, conference centre, gym and sauna. Lavish in the extreme. You could be anywhere – it just so happens you're in San José. **L-AL** *D'Raya Vida*, Av 11, C 15, T223-4168, F223-4157, www.rayavida.com An upmarket B&B option with 4 fine rooms individually decorated. A house has several moods, and includes a lounge with a baby grand piano and a small patio complete with fountain and pewter reliefs, all finished off with original artwork. Discounts for longer stays. **AL** *Britannia*, Av 11, C 3, T223-6667, F223-6411, US toll free T1-800-263-2618, britania@sol.racsa.co.cr An historic landmark, in a mansion dating back to the days of the coffee boom. After careful restoration the hotel keeps its former character while providing first-class service. Rooms offer all expected comforts with ceiling fans and large tiled bathrooms. The traditional courtyard reception continues downstairs to the converted wine cellar, now a restaurant. **AL** *La Casa Verde Inn*, C 7, Av 9, Barrio Amón, T/F223-0969, www.zurqui.com/crinfocus/verde/cverde.html A treasure of colonial architecture built in 1910. The renovation has produced a selection of deluxe rooms and suites which are luxurious in every detail, some with king-size canopy beds. All rooms have a private bath as you would expect and many have a patio. Recommended. **AL** *Villa Tournón*, on Highway 108, 150 m west of El Pueblo shopping village, T233-6622, F222-5211, hvilla@sol.racsa.co.cr Wheelchair access and all the normal treats. *Eclipse Tours* travel agency has an office in the hotel. A spacious and modern hotel with excellent service. **AL-A** *Santo Tomás*, Av 7, C 3-5, T255-0448, F222-3950, www.hotelsantomas.com In a district of good quality hotels, the cavernous rooms of this turn-of-the-century coffee plantation home stand out. Relaxed and professional service in a homely atmosphere, each of the 20 rooms has queen-size beds, private bath, cable TV and telephone. The garden patio is relaxing and a charming spot for your tropical breakfast, and for evening drinks and cocktails.

A *Alóki*, C 13, Av 9-11, T222-6702, F221-2533, www.traveltocostarica.com The courtyard restaurant of this early 20th-century house is a perfect combination of intimacy and formal service. Rattan chairs and table surround a small fountain, with just 6 rooms, each decorated with antique furniture and fittings. The restaurant serves local and international food and there is a small bar with live music in the evenings. **A** *Don Carlos*, C 9, Av 7-9, T221-6707, F255-0828, www.doncarlos.co.cr A family run hotel with 33 big rooms each with private bath, cable TV, room safes and secure parking and all possible services. Littered with art throughout, the precolumbian restaurant and cocktail lounge is overlooked by masks and sculptures. By the jacuzzi a couple of bronze characters muse over the day's events, and the older parts of the expanding hotel have an air of austerity with décor to match. The best piece is the exquisite 272 hand-painted tile mural of San José in the early 1900s created by Mario Arroyabe. **A** *Dunn Inn*, Av 11, C 5, T222-3232, F221-4596, www.hotel-sanjose.com Rooms and suites use wood panelling in some rooms to retain a sense of atmosphere in this late 19th-century house, with wall-to-wall carpets, cable TV, private bath, ceiling fan and telephone keep the comfort in the rooms. **A** *Edelweiss*, Av 9, C 13-5, T221-9702, F222-1241, www.edelweisshotel.com Hidden behind a rather austere looking exterior is a quaint

Barrios Amón, Otoya & Tournón

This region is home to historic houses and comfortable hotels – prices reflect the quality of hotels and the history of the barrio

San José and around

hotel of 25 rooms with hardwood floors and a stylish tropical garden patio bar. All rooms have private bath, ceiling fans and television. English, German and Spanish spoken, and continental breakfast included. **A** *Hemingway Inn*, Av 9, C 9, T/F221-1804, www.geocities.com/hemingwayinn No great surprise that the house is filled with photographs and references to the author. 17 simply decorated rooms named after the literati in a house full of twisting corridors and character. Rooms vary greatly in size so ask for a big one. Each room has private bath, cable TV. There is small patio restaurant and access to a kitchen if you want to prepare a meal yourself. Discounts for weekly and monthly rates, and paying in cash or TCs. English spoken. **A** *Taylor's Inn B&B Hotel*, Av 13, C 3-5, T257-4333, F221-1475, www.catours.co.cr Cable TV, telephone, fan, private bath with hot water. Old house beautifully restored keeping many of the original features. Very friendly and accommodating, with family atmosphere and professional service. Use of kitchen if not too busy. Small garden with hummingbird feeders that are also visited by bats at night. Part of *CA Tours* agency and travel operator who also own the *Cloudforest Lodge* in Monteverde. **A-B** *Kekoldi*, Av 9, C 3 bis, T223-3244, F257-5476, www.kekoldi.com An absolutely delightful hotel designed and elaborately decorated by the English artist Helen Eltis with fresh, breezy use of pastels. Drapes and windows painted in corners and on walls, in a style that continues throughout the 14 rooms each with private bathroom and telephone. German management, also English and Spanish spoken.

B *Cinco Hormigas Rojas*, C15, Av 9-11, T/F257-8581, crtimes.com/tourism/cincohormigasrojas/maincinco.htm – no www. A bed and breakfast in the heart of Otoya with 6 comfortable rooms filled with charm, serenity and even pictures by the artist owner Mayra Guell. **B** *Vesuvio*, Av 11, C 13-15, T/F221-7586, www.hotelvesuvio.com Clean, efficient, no great frills for the area, but good, helpful service. Simple rooms with TV, private bath, hot water and ceiling fan. Good mid-range Italian, seafood and international restaurant. Management overflowing with commercial savvy with discounts for booking on the internet, a 20% discount with the *Costa Rica Handbook* and discount agreements with car rental firms. **B-C** *Aranjuez*, C 19, Av 11-13, T256-1825, F223-3528, www.hotelaranjuez.com One of the cheaper options up in Barrio Aranjuez, but still filled with style in this 1930s house with a pleasant garden. Shared or private bathroom with hair dryers, splendid breakfast and free coffee all day. Friendly English speaking staff, clean, well kept, bag store, recommended. Visa Accepted. **B-C** *Joluva Guesthouse*, Av 9-11, C 3 bis, T223-7961, F257-7668, in the US call 1-800-298-2418, www.joluva.com A relaxing and welcoming gay-friendly hotel. Rooms vary greatly in size but all are clean and well looked after with cable TV and many with private bathroom. Continental breakfast, served on a quiet patio, included. Exclusive tours and information available for guests.

**Paseo Colón &
La Sábana
(west of
Central)**
*The business end
of town, handy
for getting out
of town quickly*

LL *Meliá Confort Corobicí*, Sábana Norte, T232-8122, F231-5834, www.solmelia.es Difficult to miss this vast hotel overlooking the northeastern corner of Parque Sábana. The 203 spacious rooms have all the comforts of a modern hotel, with tennis courts, a pool, gym and large, recommended casino. Popular with business travellers and vacationers alike. **LL-AL** *Grano de Oro*, C 30, Av 2-4, T255-3322, F221-2782, www.hotelgranodeoro.com Exquisite, lavish and warmly welcoming, this hotel enjoys the finest colonial architecture of an early 20th-century stately mansion with absolute luxury in a wide range of rooms. 30 rooms and 3 suites all provide complete comfort each uniquely decorated. The wrought ironwork beds set off rooms with the expected comforts of cable TV, television, Jacuzzi or sundeck spa, mini bar and ceiling fan. A luxuriant garden patio is decorated throughout with heliconias, orchids and palms. The excellent restaurant offers differing moods in the dining room, the sunroom or out on the tropical patio where the quiet murmur of conversation continues amidst top-class, attentive service.

A *Apartotel La Sábana*, Sábana Norte, T220-2422, F231-7386, www.crica.com/hotels/lasabana.html Just off the northern limits of Parque Sábana, 32 rooms and studio apartments with a/c, cable TV and a pool, sauna and parking. Apartments range in size sleeping between 2 and 4. All have fully equipped kitchens and the prices includes breakfast. **A** *Rosa del Paseo*, Paseo Colón, C 28-30, T257-3225, F223-2776, www.online.co.cr/rosa Private bath with bath tub, cable TV, price includes tropical breakfast. A Victorian colonial home until 1992, the refurbished 104-year old house has beautifully restored the original features while extending the hotel to include a small and quiet landscaped courtyard.

B *CACTS*, C 28-30, Av 3 bis #2845, T221-2928, F221-8616, www.tourism.co.cr/hotels/cacts/cacts.html A major refurbishment in late-2000 makes what is already a very good hotel even better. Nothing terribly original about the décor but has 32 spotlessly clean, bright rooms equipped with private bath, ceiling fans, telephone and cable TV. A little out from the centre of town, the hotel is very quiet and safe, has a sun deck with pool and Jacuzzi. The staff want to help you get the most out of your stay and will arrange tours and airport pick-ups. Discounts for students, families and groups. Internet access, free luggage storage, German, English and Spanish spoken. All this with breakfast included. **B** *Petit Victoria*, Av 2, C 28, 100 m south from Pizza Hut on Paseo Colón, T/F233-5193. Private bath, cable TV, parking, laundry service, car rental, bar and restaurant, room service, includes breakfast. Colonial, now fully restored, with all the charm you'd expect of a 120-year-old house. Ornate lattice carvings decorate the spacious reception. Rooms are smartly decorated to provide service without spoiling the atmosphere. The covered patio restaurant serves traditional food, and welcomes non-guests for *almuerzo* for under US$2. Steeped with tradition, the Petit Victoria was the former family home of Oscar Arias Sánchez, former President and Nobel Peace price winner and was used as campaign headquarters for his victorious presidential elections in the 1980s. Italian management, English, French and Spanish spoken. The best in its class. **B-C** *Ritmo del Caribe*, Paseo Colón, C 32 opposite Kentucky, T/F256-1636, www.ritmo-del-caribe.com Run by Tomas and Patricia, a German/Tica couple, the atmosphere in this hotel is comfortable and perfectly settling if you want to be able to relax but meet other people. 14 rooms, some with private bath and hot water, others shared in an old family home. Price includes breakfast and pick-up from the airport can be arranged in advance. Tomas also runs *Wild Rider Motorcycles*, a motorbike tour and rental agency – see below.

A *Fleur de Lys*, C 13, Av 2-6, T222-4391, F257-3637, www.hotelfleurdelys.com This **South of town** restored Victorian mansion is absolutely delightful with 32 uniquely decorated rooms, each named after a native Costa Rican flower. Each elegant room has a private bathroom, hair dryer, telephone and cable TV. A French restaurant and a bar will mean the only reason you have to leave the hotel is to visit the Museo Nacional one block away. Round the back of Iglesia de Soledad is **A** *Doña Inés*, C 11, Av 2-6, T222-7443, F223-5426, notadea@sol.racsa.co.cr A peaceful courtyard makes for a calming influence in this quiet Italian-run hotel. Rooms have TV, private bath and telephone. The hotel is quiet, safe and if you're driving there is parking and 24-hr security.

B *La Mansion*, Av 10, C 9, T222-0423, F222-7947, mansion@sol.racsa.co.cr The listed building is crammed with a collection of fine original paintings covering all types of styles enjoyed from the comfort of finely crafted antiques – the hotel is worth a visit in itself. All rooms have private bath and hot water. With attention to detail, friendly personal service and an intimate restaurant downstairs this place would be double the price in *barrio* Amón or Otoya, for the price, it is the best south of town.

A big drop in comforts to the old favourite of **E** *Casa Ridgeway*, C 15, Av 6 bis (between Av 6-8), T/F233-6168, friends@sol.racsa.co.cr A friendly and quiet spotting fitting for a small guest house operated by the *Friends Peace Center* . Private and dormitory rooms, along with a communal kitchen and patio-dining area add to the sense of calm relaxation. Exceptional value for money as well as being a pleasant place to stay. **E** *Segunda*, Av 2, #913, C 9-11, T222-0260, F257-4996, acebrisa@ sol.racsa.co.cr Basic accommodation east of the main plaza. Clean and safe, rooms upstairs slightly better but without bathroom. Pretty grubby overall. **E-F** *Washington*, Av 2, C 9 -11, T221-9332. Basic accommodation, next to *Segunda* and slightly better than its neighbour.

G *Tica Linda*, Av 6 -8, C 7, T/F222-8432. Dormitory accommodation, use of kitchen, hot water and laundry, TV in communal area. Will store luggage, popular with travellers. No sign, just a notice on the front, currently yellow door. Not the Hilton, but perfectly OK for the price and in an OK part of town.

Eastern suburbs
The hotels in these last sections are covered on any of our maps of the city

L-AL *Boutique Hotel Jade*, Paseo Ruben Dario, C 41, 275 m north of Autos Subarú, Los Yoses, T224-2455, F224-2166, amehotel@sol.racsa.co.cr Queen-size beds, cable TV, minibar, telephone, internet connection, safebox, room service, gym, parking, laundry, car rental, Jurgen's restaurant. A very comfortable hotel east of downtown San José that makes an ideal setting for business or pleasure visits. **AL** *Don Fadrique*, Los Yoses, C 37, Av 8, T224-7583, F224-9746, toll free in the US and Canada on 1-800-276-7501, www.centralamerica.com/cr/hotel/fadrique.htm A stylish and family-run hotel with one of the country's finest private collections of artwork adorning the walls, combines the amenities and services of a big hotel with the intimacy and personal attention of a traditional Spanish inn. 20 rooms, each with private bathroom and hot water, all with views over the garden or the peaks of the Central Valley.

A *Ara Macao*, Barrio California, 50 m south of Pizza Hut, C 25 bis, Av Central-2, Barrio California, T233-2742, F257-6228, www.hotels.co.cr/aramacao.html A small, quiet hotel with 8 smartly decorated rooms. Private bathroom, cable TV and fans in all rooms, with a small patio for relaxing. **A-B** *D'Galah*, north of the university campus in San Pedro, T/F234-1743, dgalah@sol.racsa.co.cr Handy for the university if that's where your business takes you. 21 rooms with private bath, hot water and TV. Also a pool, sauna, spa and jacuzzi. **B** *Apartamentos Scotland*, C 29, Av 1, T223-0033, F257-5317, www.goin2travel.com/a525.htm Weekly (from US$275) or monthly (from US$650) for furnished apartments. Comfortable, full-service apartments with kitchenettes. Apartments sleep up to 3.

E *Toruma Youth Hostel*, T234-8186, F224-4085, Av Central, C 29-31, www.hostelling -costarica.com 95 beds, restaurant open until 1400, clean, hot water, crowded but safe, lockable compartments in each room, safe deposit box, price per person including breakfast, slightly more for those who do not hold ISIC or YHA membership, credit cards accepted. Free bag storage for guests. A good place for meeting other travellers to arrange group travel. Relaxed atmosphere with big, airy lobby doubling as a TV lounge.

At the airport

AL *Hampton Inn*, T443-0043, F442-9523 (toll free within Costa Rica 800-426-7866), www.hamptonhotel.co.cr Closest hotel to the airport, handy if you want to get in or get out quickly with the minimum of fuss, made easier with a courtesy pick-up to both terminals (see Alajuela 'Sleeping' for more details).

San José – Airport Highway (Autopista General Cañas)

LL-L *Costa Rica Marriott*, 10 mins from Juan Santamaría airport, San Antonio de Belén, T298-0000, F298-0011, (US and Canada T1-800-228-9290), www.marriotthotels.com/ SJOCR More an experience than a hotel. Built in the style of a coffee plantation inside and out, every detail of this divine hotel is a joy. Heavy wooden beams, and tiled floors lit with ironwork chandeliers fill the reception and set the tone throughout. 276 fully equipped rooms and suites are spacious and most have balcony views. 6 restaurants offer the very best in cuisine with settings from formal dining to poolside snacks. A couple of pools, a 9-hole golf course and full health club. A good choice in the luxury end and you'll be in good company with a guest list that included the 260-person party of President Bill Clinton in 1997 – work out that bill to the US tax payer. **LL-L** *Meliá Cariari*, on Autopista General Cañas 10 mins from the airport, T239-0022, F239-2803, (US and Canada call 1-800-33-MELIA), www.solmelia.com An impressive hotel by any standard with 220 oversized rooms and every service imaginable for guests. In addition to full business services, the *Cariari* has 3 swimming pools, a gym, 11 tennis courts, and San José's only 18-hole golf course. A number of conference rooms accommodating up to 800 people this is very much a business hotel. **LL** *Herradura Golf Resort and Conference Center*, 10 mins from the airport, T239-0033, F293-2713, www.hotelherradura.com The 234 elegantly furnished rooms have a/c, cable TV, tele-phones and the full range of business services. 3 restaurants offer traditional and café-style dining as well as the authentic Sakura Japanese restaurant (also open to non-guests). High-tech conference spaces accommodating up to 2,000 people.

AL *Best Western Irazú*, La Uruca, next to San José 2000 shopping centre, T232-4811, F231-6485, www.bestwestern.co.cr After a large renovation, the modern and dependable *Best Western* on the outskirts of San José is ideally situated along the Autopista General Cañas. 325 rooms with private bathroom all have a/c, cable TV and telephone, and most with balcony overlooking the pool. Children under 12 are free. Full service tour operator in the hotel. There are a couple of restaurants including a 24-hr *Denny's* service, a large casino, and an exercise room and sauna.

AL-B *Apartotel El Sesteo*, 200 m south of *McDonald's*, Sábana Sur, T296-1805, F296-1865, www.sesteo.com Some double apartments with kitchenettes and living rooms, some simple rooms with ceiling fans, private bath, cable TV and telephone. There is a tropical garden, swimming pool and secure parking. Residents also get access to the nearby Costa Rica Tennis Club. **A** *Apartotel Don Carlos*, just north of the centre of town, T221-6707, F255-0828, www.doncarlos.co.cr Run by the top quality *Hotel Don Carlos*, there are 8 fully equipped apartments with kitchenettes only available for weekly (US$410) monthly (US$1050) stays. Apartments also have full maid service 6 days a week. **B** *San José*, Av 2, C 17-19, T256-2191, F221-6684, www.hotel-sanjose.com Just 50 m east of the Museo Nacional, the hotel is close enough to the centre for good access, but far enough out to be quiet. Rooms are simple, with private bathrooms, hot water and cable TV, but comfortable. English spoken, parking, 24-hr security and weekly discounts make this a good spot. **B-E** Studio apartments from US$100 to US$300 a week, 1 week minimum, through *Cabet Travel*, Av 2, C5-7, T257-8920, F256-1554, cabet1@sol.racsa.co.cr Apartments are in Los Yoses, 1 week minimum, ideal for language students, business trips and others seeking a secure spot with a sense of home. Apartments range from a basic and simple room, to comfortable studio flats with TV, telephone, kitchen and dining room.

Apartments
Apartotels provide the comforts of living at home with the services of a hotel – generally for people staying a week or so

Eating

Dining in San José takes on myriad forms, with inspiration coming from across the world. Traditional dishes, feasting on a steady supply of rice'n'beans, tend to be a little on the heavy side but definitely worth trying. Beyond *Tico* food, inspiration comes from as wide a source as the capital's citizens. Italian, French and Chinese restaurants are many but there are more national dishes to be found.

Fine restaurants tend to be in or near good hotels with one or two notable excep-tions. Consequently the best restaurants can be found west of Downtown on or around Paseo Colón and Parque Sábana, or to the north in the districts of Amón, Otoya and further east in the residential suburbs of Los Yoses. Escazú also has some memora-ble dining options, see page 136. Many of the good hotels also have exceptional res-taurants open to non-guests.

● *on maps pages 90 and 102*
Price codes: see inside front cover The more upmarket restaurants add a 10% service charge and a 13% tax. Tips over and above this occasionally shocking pair of surcharges are only expected if the service is exceptional

San José and around

A few local dining habits peculiar to San José and Costa Rica include the omnipresent *soda* which is the national version of a fast food outlet found on many street corners. Varying greatly in style, you can have a bite to eat with a hearty midday *plato del día* or *casado* which start at around US$2. The markets also provide a good choice of simple dishes and turnover of food is so fast the health risks are minimal and hygiene in food preparation is surprisingly conscientious.

The city also has a good number of cafés and bakeries where you can stop for a bite to eat and get coffee or refreshment before heading out to walk the streets again.

Breakfast tends to be a non-starter in the city so head for one of the markets or grab some fruit if your hotel doesn't provide breakfast. Lunch is the main meal of the day when *Joséfinos* stream from office blocks and pack the tables and chairs of the more affordable sodas and restaurants. For the end of the day, dinner options are as wide and varied as your tastes and budget.

Expensive **Paseo Colón** *Grano de Oro*, in the hotel of the same name, T255-3322, is as elegant and stylish as the hotel. Dining inside or out on the garden patio, the ambience is intimate and warm. Inspiration for the menu draws on national and French dishes. *La Bastille*, Paseo Colón, C 22, T255-4994. Stylish French food served in elegant surrounds. Closed Sun. *Lobster Inn*, T223-8594, is a popular seafood restaurant with a good selection on Paseo Colón and C 24.

The restaurants in this section are not covered by our maps

Los Yoses *Buenos Aires Tango*, Paseo Ruben Dario, C 29, Barrio la California, from the Nicaraguan embassy 200 m east and 75 m north, T233-9729, F233-9954. Argentine fare in a vaguely Mediterranean atmosphere in a Bavarian house – we're talking international here. Despite the eclectic mix, the authentic Argentine *parrillada* with a wide range of international dishes a la carte, make this a perfect spot to dine with friends indoors or outside in the large garden. *Euro Café (Romulo and Remo)*, Paseo Ruben Dario and C 41, T289-5206, rickyruiz@hotmail.com Chic, crisp décor, with service to match. Grecian urns provide stylish backdrop in a restaurant where you can choose to eat on the garden patio or dine in the pure white dining room laid with crisp linen tablecloths. *Jurgen's*, C 41 and Paseo Ruben Dario, 275 m north of Auto Subarú, Los Yoses, T224-2455, F224-2166. First class service, excellent international menu in a sophisticated atmosphere. Recommended. *Le Chandelier*, T225-3980, 100 m south and 100 m west of the ICE building in Los Yoses, is one of the best French restaurants in town.

North of town Considered by many to serve the best *Tico* food in the capital is *La Cocina de Leña*, T223-3704, in El Pueblo Commercial centre to the north. A rustic ambience with all sorts of homely paraphernalia hanging on the walls. The excellent menu has tasty and filling national dishes like *tamales* and creole stew, and a couple of seafood and vegetarian options. The service is perfect – good, but laid-back. Recommended. The best Japanese restaurant is *Sakura*, T239-0033, in the *Herradura Hotel* out on the road to the airport. It isn't cheap but it is popular and worth the trip out of town.

Mid-range *El Museo*, C 3 bis, Av 7-9, T223-9552, was formerly an antique store. It still is to a degree as you dine amongst fine pieces of furniture, art and ceramics. If while enjoying the intimate atmosphere you see a piece that takes your fancy, you're more than welcome to make an offer. With a rough and ready feel *La Hacienda Steak House* on C 7, Av Central-2, T222-5992 is good for a stock-up on meat. A little overpriced, upstairs is a good Mexican *taquería* with an all-you-can-eat buffet at weekends, 1200-1500, US$4. Not sure how long that will last.

On the north side of Parque Sábana are *Los Ranchos*, near *Hotel Corobicí*, T232-7757, and *El Chicote*, 400 m west of the ICE building, T232-3777, a couple of popular steak houses.

The chic, smart and suave will be seen at the **Café Mundo** on Av 9, C 13-15, opposite *Hotel Edelweiss*. The old mansion has been tastefully restored with great use of colours and space. Good salads, great pasta and bread to die for.

Al Andalus, C 3, Av 7 y 9, T257-6556, Spanish, Costa Rican and international blend with a pleasant atmosphere. **El Balcón de Europa** on C 9 and Av Central-1, is a well known Italian near the centre of town. Great atmosphere makes it popular, but some dishes rather small and tasteless. **Goya**, Av 1, C 5-7, T221-3887, Spanish food. **Pizza Metro** is at Av 2 and C 5-7, good Italian, small and cosy with pizza and pasta. Not that cheap but recommended.

Part of the scenery in San José, **La Esmeralda** at Av 2 and C 5-7, T221-0530, is reasonably priced with good local dishes. But you don't come here for the food, it's the wandering talents of the countless bands of *mariachis* – often outnumbering diners – that creates the atmosphere and vitality. Some will love it, others will crawl under the nearest napkin. North of the Coca-Cola district in Paso de la Vaca is **Mexico Bar** which although dead by day comes out at night with a flurry of music and good Mexican food, and the occasional *mariachi* band that has wondered up from La Esmeralda.

A couple of recommended Peruvian restaurants are **Machu Picchu**, C 32, Av 1-3, and nearby is **Peruveana**, C 32, Av 1-3, both with reasonable prices.

Tin Jo, C 11, Av 6-8, T221-7605, makes a refreshing change from rice and beans with Asian influences from several countries. It's popular, the atmosphere has enough authenticity without overflowing into the realm of tack and the food's great.

Cheap
See also 'Sodas'

Antojitos is a Mexican chain with branches on Paseo Colón, Pavas Highway west of Sábana and in Centro Comercial Cocorí. Excellent food at moderate prices. **El Cuartel de la Boca del Monte**, on Av 1 and C 21-23, doubles up serving good food that is popular with locals in the day before the musicians tune up and play to equally packed rooms in the evening. **Morazán**, C 9, Av 3, facing Parque Morazán, not touristy, in fact a bit of a dump really, but it is popular with locals and has a genuine character lacking from many busier places. Friendly with excellent breakfast and, reportedly, delicious blackberry juice. **Pasta Factory**, Av 1, C 7, is a low-key, but excellent Italian which has been recommended. Open Mon-Sat,1100-1430, 1730-2230. If you're looking for something to fill you up, a stroll down the 5 will take you past several cheap Chinese restaurants, including **Gran Diamente**, Av 5, C 4-6, with a "lively kitchen" where you can watch the food being prepared. Another cheap Chinese place worth trying is **Lung Mun** at Av 1, C 5-7, and the Korean food at **Fu Lu Su** at C 7, Av 2.

Seriously cheap

The fewer numbers of seriously cheap places do not indicate the absence of cheap eateries – more the lack of need to list them all. Reliable favourites are the Mercado Central, places around the Coca-Cola bus terminal and the area to the southwest of Parque Central. Places worth recommending are **Comedor**, beneath 'Dorado' sign, C 8, Av 4-6, very cheap. **Pollo a la Leña**, C 1, Av 3-5, which has seriously cheap chicken, popular with the locals. **Choza del Sabor**, on the corner of C Central and Av 5, has good, local *comida* with a couple of gestures to décor but the *menu del día* is a good and tasty bargain. Following the Chinese theme, one of the cheapest is **China Bonita** at Av 5, C 2-4.

Cafés & snack

Bagelman, Paseo Ruben Dario (Av Central), C 33, just east of Hostal Toruma. Smart and tasty fast food bagel heaven. **Café del Teatro**, Av 2, C 3, in foyer of National Theatre. Bit pricey but worth it for the sheer style and sophistication of the *belle époque* interior. Popular meeting place for poets and writers, pleasant for a snack and always busy. Open Mon-Sat. **Café Parisienne** on the Plaza de la Cultura, the street café of the *Gran Hotel Costa Rica*. As sure as night follows day, you will at some point take a meal, snack or at least a drink at this street café. Food is a little overpriced and the taste is hardly over the moon but that is not the point. Take a coffee and watch the world go by

San José and around

 **Modern day Mariachis**

Mariachis are a strange thing. Steeped in tradition that harks back to Mexico, and since hijacked by Hollywood, they border on the comical. But imagine if you will the days when you waited for your tune at the juke box, which somehow failed to play in the order requested. Not so with mariachis. There's a strict rota system, and like all the best journeys, it's nervously alien first time around but grows on you with familiarity.

It's the shapes and patterns that grate. Numbering at least four, but here in San José six seems the norm, the double bass guitaron trips out a steady beat, the smaller bihuela picks up the pace and the singer sets out. None of these guys to a man - and they all are - would claim to be good-looking, despite their Latin origins. A

bizarre mix of shapes and sizes. Vocalists lack size and depth, the bass struggles with height conversely against weight, hardly surprising given the size of his instrument, and the horn players toot out a harmonious tune.

While not built for speed, these guys are meant to be mobile, which must be why they have phones and pagers. And while the portly accordion player rests his minuscule instrument on his winter fuel, the trumpeter puffs on a cigarette between blows. Dressed in tailor-made suits by a Mexican tailor who had the good sense to head south and take up the slack, these fake cowboys squeeze into undersized garments reminiscent of the Wild West.

whether it glides in graceful steps or shuffles in a thoroughly unpleasant imitation of humanity. Tucked away up in Barrio Amón is *La Esquina del Café*, Av 9, C 3b, a speciality coffee roasters with beans from 6 different regions to taste, but also a good restaurant with a souvenir shop. Live music twice a month. Daily 0900-2200. *Ruiseñor*, Paseo Rubin Dario and C 41-43, Los Yoses. The smart place to take coffee and snacks out east. Be seen on the stylish patio even if it does overlook a busy road. *Spoon* has a central bakery at Av Central, C 5-7, where you can have good coffee and pastries to take-out or eat in. There are several others throughout the city. *Musmanni*, also has several outlets throughout the city serving bread and pastries which would double quite nicely as a door stop. Either I bought the wrong things or they really are committing a crime against bread. *Le Croissant*, Av Central, C 33, good French bakery with croissants and pâtisserie to die for.

Vegetarian   The best known vegetarian fast food is available at *Vishnu*, at #73 Av 3, C Central – 1, and Av 6-8, C Central with several branches in the city. Good quality, cheap, excellent *plato del día*, sells good wholemeal bread. Veggie burgers to gladden the heart of even the most carnivorous clients. Open daily, 0800-2000 – just about early enough for breakfast. *Don Sol*, Av 7b C 15, has an excellent 3 course lunch for US$2, run by integral yoga society (lunchtime only). *La Mazorca*, in San Pedro, near University of Costa Rica (Rodrigo Facio site), vegetarian and health foods. *La Nutrisoda*, Edif Las Arcadas, open 1100-1800, home-made natural ice cream. *Macrobiótica*, C 11, Av 6-8, is a health shop selling good bread. *Naturama Uno*, Av 1, C 3-5, opposite Omni Cinema building, cheap.

Ice cream parlours   Several good ice cream outlets to choose from. *Helados Boni*, C Central, Av 6-8, with home-made ice cream. *Helados Rena*, C 8, Av Central, excellent. *Pops*, near Banco Central, and other outlets, for ice cream (excellent). *Holanda*, Av Central, C Central and other outlets in San José, great ice cream.

Sodas   *Churrería Manolo*, Av Central, C Central-2 (new restaurant upstairs), and another branch on Av Central. Simple, quick food with takeaway options on the street, good sandwiches and hot chocolate. *La Vasconia*, Av 2, C 5, restaurant and soda bar has a good breakfast and is popular with locals. On Parque Central is *La Perla*. The food is OK, the service is poor, the waiters will stitch you up with a flurry of fingers over a calculator but it is open 24 hrs. *Soda El Parque*, C 2, Av 4-6, is also open 24 hrs and a popular spot for business people by day and relaxing entertainers by night. Just north of the centre is the cheap and cheerful *Soda Nini* at Av 3, C 2-4. East out towards Los Yoses is *Soda La Luz*, Av Central, C 33, good filling meals, cheap. *Soda Magaly* is a little closer to town at Av Central and C 23, near Youth Hostel, good, cheap.

Food bars in the Mercado Central (C 6-8) are good for a quick breakfast and lunch, but none of them are open in the evening, very clean. *Corona de Oro*, Av 3, C 2-4 (next to *Nini*) is excellent. Try *Soda Flor de Costa Rica*, northeastern entrance in the flower pavilion, very good and cheap meals, very clean, open 0700-1800; or the snack bars in the *Galería* complex, Av Central-2, C 5-7. Try *Chicharronera Nacional*, Av 1, C 10-12, very popular, or *Popular*, Av 3, C 6-8, good *casado*. *El Merendero*, Av 6, C 0-2, cheap local food, popular with Ticos.

Fast food

Autoservicios do not charge tax and service and represent best value

Bars and nightclubs

It is hardly surprising that a cosmopolitan city such as San José should have a wide and varied nightlife. If you know where to look you can find all sorts of nocturnal entertainment. There are plenty of simple bars where you can hunker down with a friend for a beer. Live music is also popular and a cover charge of around US$4 is charged. Music may be a head-thumping new rock band, a *Tico* Brillcream boy band such as the – are you ready for this – *Brillianticos*, or something a little more suave. In some bars the tendency is to just turn up and see what happens. Clubs too are popular and cover music from techno and garage, to reggae, jazz and salsa. Entrance is normally between US$2-US$6. If you want to look for a particular group look in the listings section of *La Nación* on a Thu, or in the *Tico Times*.

Joséfinos are almost always well dressed so it would be surprising if they didn't look smart when hitting the town. Smart jeans or a skirt, will get you in to most clubs, but locals will be dressed to impress

Below is a list of the permanent happening places but as is always the case, the fashionable joints change from day to day.

North of town in Barrio Tournón the *Centro Comercial El Pueblo* is a great place for exploring, dipping into a couple of bars and taking a meal. At certain times the queues of taxis and vehicles unloading *Ticas* exquisitely dressed in their finest and young suitors makes the place feel like one big film première. Once it has dawned on you why the downtown area of San José is almost dead, a gentle meander round the village and you'll stumble across a bar that suits your mood. One quiet spot to warm you up is *Los Balcones* which has live music, a small terrace and no cover charge.

Bars

In the **centre of town** *El Cuartel de la Boca del Monte* on Av 1, C 21-23, up towards Barrio California is where the young bohemians hang out – it's a lively spot in an understated way. There's a comfortably dark but not oppressive atmosphere to the place. Local up-and-coming bands often play live, the styles vary greatly and there is a cover charge of US$2. *Las Risas*, is as close to the centre of town as you can get at Av Central-1 and C 1. Spread over a couple of floors with a bar and a disco it is popular with young *Joséfinos*. If you can't sleep or simply don't want to, *Chelle's* on C 9 and Av Central, never closes. The bright lighting makes it stand out. The other dependable factor is the wonderful selection of drinkers that roll up, slightly more concerned with getting a drink than fussing over furnishings and delicate mood lighting.

At some point in your stay a visit to *La Esmeralda* is essential. Av 2, C5-7, T221-0530. As the *mariachi* Mecca for Costa Ricans, drinkers sip, diners eat and lovers coo as competing bands of portly musicians meander between tables offering a tune. The ambience and décor isn't up to much, the *bocas* are good but then why deflect too much attention away from the music. Open until about 4 am.

San José and around

You get a different perspective from the 17th-floor bar and casino of the *Hotel Aurora* on Parque Morazán. The drinks are pretty pricey but if you can get there for sunset and the weather is good, the view is spectacular. Not so high, but with a different prospect and without the gambling temptation is the 9th floor bar of the *Hotel Talamanca* on Av 2 and C 8-10. Both are open to non-guests.

You are unlikely to stumble across *Bar Mexico* on Av 13 and C 16-18, up in **Barrio Mexico**, but the trip may be worth it. *Mariachis* occasionally make it up this far and when they do the bar comes alive.

Out towards **San Pedro** and the university *La Villa* has a reputation as an academic watering hole – good to practice your Spanish. Also nearby are *Cocodrilo*, a typically loud, dark student bar, and *Río* which attracts the capital's wealthier youngsters doing their best to look cool. Live music at weekends.

There are several pubs and bars aimed at expats and tourists, many run by expats themselves, covering a few blocks to the east of **Plaza de la Cultura**. No great surprise that *Nashville South* on C 5, Av 1-3, takes inspiration from Country and Western. It's a gringo bar just off Parque Morazán where you can sit at the bar gazing at the TV, working your way along the optics as you talk with your new found friends. Good for food too. *Tiny's*, Av 2, C 7-9, also has a southern feel but as one of the few bars in the southern quarter of the downtown area it attracts a wide range of people, most just wanting a quiet drink. A little to the north is the *Beatle Bar* on Av Central and C 9. Also a popular spot with visitors where you can take a relatively quiet beer and exchange traveller's tales. *Blue Marlin Bar* is the very popular sports bar in the *Hotel del Rey*, Av 1, C 9. If you can keep you eye on the box, major sports events are shown on the TV, but for most the entertainment lies elsewhere. The bar is jam-packed with foreign visitors and courtesans hoping to make each other's acquaintance. Pop in for a drink for some most entertaining people watching. *Key Largo* around the corner on Av 7, C 3, has a very similar type of clientèle but is reported to be getting rougher.

If your tastes extend to real beer – or bitter as it is called in the UK – San José has the *Brew Pub Micro Brewery* on **Paseo Colón** between C 26-8, where a range of brewed beers onsite can be supped, considered and generally enjoyed. As many as 6 beers to try if you're lucky and most of them very good.

Nightclubs   As with bars, the greatest single concentration of clubs is in **El Pueblo**. In addition to the bars, *Cocoloco* is perhaps the liveliest one to hit with a young crowd that moves to a broad beat from the merengue and salsa of the new world to the latest sounds sweeping the world. Very hip. Early on in the evening, you can try out your karaoke. *Infinito*, gets a slightly older crowd and packs in 3 dance floors playing different styles so you can move from rock to reggae and finally romance before heading home. Outside the walls of El Pueblo is the slightly quieter and classier *La Plaza*. Still, the big dance floor does mean you can make a fool of yourself without crashing into other people.

El Tunel de Tiempo is close to the **centre** on Av Central and C 11-13, as is *Salsa 54* on C 3, Av 1-3. This is *the* place to go for salsa, although the mix includes a fair amount of Latin and rock music. If you're practising or simply expecting to see the best at work, you won't be disappointed.

South of town in the barrio of Desamparados in the Centro Commercial del Sur is *Dynasty* with distinctive Caribbean themes of soul and reggae.

Gay & lesbian   There are a few gay-friendly dance clubs playing a mix of techno and Latin themes
clubs   including *La Avispa*, on C 1 and Av 8-10, and *Déjà vu* on C 2, Av 14-16. *La Torre* on C 7, Av Central-Av 1, popular gay disco. None of these places are exclusively gay. A new place just opened is *Detour* – ask locally for directions.

¡Bailamos!

Not knowing your left foot from your right can be slightly daunting when you see two young latinos *gyrate past as if welded together at the hip by some invisible force. After visiting a club a few times you might feel the urge to learn a few steps and while the gifted may absorb moves by osmosis, the rest of us have to take classes. The steps are simple enough – until someone puts on a new*

record and changes the tempo. But a few sessions normally show good results and you'll have the basic skills to salsa, merengue and tango through the night. A few places worth checking out: **Danza Viva** *in San Pedro, T253-3110.* **Malecón** *at Av 2, C 17-19, T/F 222-324.* **Merecumbé** *has several centres in San Pedro, Escazú and the Central Valley, call San Pedro T224-3531.*

There are many 'gentlemen's clubs' in the city. **Josephine's**, Av 9, C 2-4, is one of the better known places, and certainly one of the classier and consequently more expensive places. The **Bikini Club** is at C 7, Av 0-1 – no prizes for guessing what the waitresses are wearing. Cheaper than Josephine's.

Strip clubs

Entertainment

As with most capital cities, San José has no shortage of cultural activities with a good range of permanent and changing events on the arts scene. The best single source of events is the listings (*Viva*) section of *La Nación* on Thursdays which you should be able to pick through with a minimum of Spanish or the *Tico Times* and look in the *Weekend* section.

Given the number of casinos around San José it would be reasonable to assume that gambling was a national sport. Given the absence of casinos in so many parts of Latin America, I'd wager the influence came from the north. Any takers?

Casinos

Better odds are available at the posher hotels, although the odds are reported to be lower than in North American casinos. If you fancy being fleeced the most popular casinos are at the *Hotel Costa Rica Morazán*, *Hotel del Rey*, *Hotel Gran Costa Rica* and the top floor of the *Hotel Aurora*. Out of town the *Meliá Confort Corobicí* near Parque Sábana and the *Best Western Irazú*, *Hotel Herradura* and the *Meliá Cariari* are popular casinos.

There are many excellent modern cinemas showing the latest releases and a couple of art movie theatres that look a little further back reminiscing in occasional glories of the past. Most films are in English with Spanish subtitles which can be useful if you're trying to improve you're language skills – it can also be incredibly amusing. Most theatres have comfortable seating and have a/c. As with all listings, *Viva* in *La Nación* on Thu will tell you what is showing. **Bellavista**, Av Central, C 17-19, T221-0909. **Capri 1 and 2**, Av Central, C 9, T223-0264. **Cariari 1-6**, Real Mall, Cariari, T293-3300. **Cinema Colón 1-2**, Paseo Colón, C 38-40, T221-4517. **Cinemateca** at the University of Costa Rica's Abelardo Bonilla auditorium, San Pedro, shows good films at 1700 and 1900 daily. **Cine Omni**, Av 1, C 3-5, T221-7903. **Cine Variedades**, C 5, Av Central-1, T222-6108. **Sala Garbo**, Av 2, C 28, T222-1034. Art-house movies.

Cinemas

A vibrant dance and theatre scene exists and you'll find everything from classy productions of opera and ballet at the *Teatro Nacional* to innovative creations like *The Full Monty*. Almost all productions will be in Spanish with the exception of those produced by the *Little Theatre Group* – call T228-0998 for details or look in listings. Other theatres often have workshops, especially for children. Orchestral works, jazz, concerts and dance are also common. Prices vary greatly but start from around US$5 rising up to

Theatres
Discounts for students at most performances. Look in press listing for two for one specials, often on Wed

San José and around

US$20-plus for international performers. Seasons for the *Teatro Nacional, Teatro Melico Salazar* and many others start in Mar.

Auditorio Nacional, in the Centro Costarricense de Ciencias y Cultura, set to become an increasingly popular venue. *Giratables*, Paseo Ruben Dario, C 33, Los Yoses, T253-6001. Popular and lively works often comical, and with occasional performances and workshops for children. *La Mascara*, Av 1, C 13, T222-4574. Adult theatre. *Molière*, Av 1, C 13, T255-2694. Innovative theatre group with recent productions including *The Full Monty*. *Skene*, Paseo Ruben Dario, C 33, Los Yoses, T283-9700. *Teatro de la Aduana*, C 25, Av 3-5, T257-8305, www.intnet.co.cr/cnt/cnt.html home to the National Theatre Company. *Teatro del Angel*, Central, C 13-15, T222-8258. Comedy, spoof and dance. *Teatro Arlequín*, C 13, Av Central-2, T221-4585. *Teatro Chaplin*, Av 12, C 11-13, T223-2919. Specialists in mime. *Teatro de la Comedía*, Central, C 13-15, T255-3255. Self explanatory. *Teatro Eugene O'Neill*, part of the Costa Rican- North American Cultural Centre, Central, C 37, Los Yoses, T207-7554, F224-1480, www.cccncr.com/TEO/index.htm Open to all performing arts including cinema, dance, music (popular, chamber, experimental, etc.) and theatre (children's, bilingual, etc). *Teatro Laurence Olivier*, Av 2, C 28, T222-1034. Comedies. *Teatro Melico Salazar*, Av 2, C Central-2, T221-4952, www.intnet.co.cr/culture/melico/melico.html One of the most popular venues in San José with regular performances of dance, music, theatre and orchestra, including the popular *Fantasía Folkorico* every Tue. *Teatro Nacional*, Av 2, C 3, T221-1329, www.intnet.co.cr/tn/tn San José's largest theatre and the main venue for classical performances – sometimes scoops to jazz, but whatever you see will be excellent.

Festivals

While all national holidays hold true in the capital, there are a few festivals in or close to the city that are worth looking out for if you happen to be in town at the time. Unlike many Latin American festivals which revolve heavily around drink, those in San José tend to be far more salubrious.

Mar *Día del Boyero* celebrates Day of the Oxcart Driver on the 2nd Sun of the month in San Antonio de Escazú. Once you've seen the Oxcarts you'll realize it is only natural for the driver to be carried into legend. Parades of ox-drawn carts, with music, dancing and blessings from the priesthood. *International Festival of Culture* 2nd week of the month, when musicians from throughout Central America assemble in a week of open air performances in the Plaza de Cultura and other venues throughout the city. *Día de San José* (St Joseph's Day) on 19th Mar, honours the patron saint of the capital. **Mar/Apr** *Semana Santa* or Holy Week. Parades during Easter week through the streets.

Aug *Virgin de Los Angeles* on 2nd of the month honours the patron saint of Costa Rica with a pilgrimage starting in San José and going to the basilica in Cartago.

Sep *Independence Day*, celebrating independence on 15 Sep 1821, when bands and dance troupes take to the streets. Things start to kick off the night before.

Nov *All Soul's Day* or Day of the Dead on the 2nd when, as throughout Latin America, families visit cemeteries and graveyards to remember the deceased.

Dec *El Tope*, the annual horse parade which starts at noon on the 26th and travels along the principal avenues of San José. A carnival starts next day at about 1700 in the same area. Fairs, firework displays and bull running (anyone can take part!) at El Zapote south of the city.

Shopping

Options for the shopaholic are many but only in a few cases exceptional. General produce markets sell the usual selection of fruit and vegetables as well as meat, poultry and fish. But if you're just looking for a fruit snack – and you're not reading this before you've arrived in Costa Rica – you have probably already stumbled into one of the fruit stalls found on almost every street corner.

Books & maps *Casa de la Revisita*, C5, Av 1-3, T256-5092. Good selection of maps and some books. *Librería Francesa*, C 5 y 7, Av Central-1, T223-7979, French, Spanish and English books, and also sells some good maps. *Librería Internacional*, Barrio Dent, 400 m west of *Taco Bell* in San Pedro, T283-6965, and Multiplaza Shopping Centre, T201-8320. English, German and Spanish titles at about 20% of US prices, special order service. *Librería Lehmann*, Av Central, C 1 y 3, T223-1212, F233-0713, has a large selection of Spanish books, some English books and magazines. They also stock several maps including the 1:50,000 topographical maps produced by the Instituto Geográfico Nacional de Costa Rica (IGN). *Mora Books*, Av 1, C 3-5, T/F255-4136, in Omni building above *Pizza Hut*, large selection of used books, reasonable prices. *Periódicos Americanos*, in the Yaohan Shopping Centre, Sábana Norte, T221-4664, best selection of magazines and some books. *Punto y Seguido*, San Pedro Mall, T280-9023, magazines in English and Spanish. *7th Street Books*, C 7, Av Central 1, T256-8251, marroca@sol.racsa.co.cr A wide range of new and used books, maps and brochures covering nature, national parks, history and culture on many topics of interest to visitors to Costa Rica. Good range of country guides, including Footprint Handbooks. Open 0900-1800 daily. *Staufer*, near Centro Cultural, Los Yoses, also in Centro Comercial San José 2000 and Plaza del Sol shopping mall in Curridabat, English and German books. *Universal*, Av Central, C Central-1, T222-2222, F222-2992, for Spanish books and maps, although there are a few titles in English. The *Instituto Geográfico*, Av 20, C 9-11 at Ministry of Public Works and Transport (MOPT), supplies good 1:50,000 topographical maps for walkers, 0730-1200, US$2. Topographical maps also available at *Lehmann* on Av Central, C 1-3.

Markets Of the several covered markets dotted around San José the largest is the *Mercado Central* at C 6 y 8, Av Central, which sells everything from leather sandals, horse saddles and bridles and simple tourist gifts through to cheese, spices, fruit, vegetables dried and fresh flowers. The honey is particularly recommended and if you're looking to set up in business you can buy one of the small boxes used by the boot boys to hold their polish and brushes. Restaurants and juice bars serve a wide variety of food and drinks at very good prices. Recently cleared off the streets, the *Vegetable Market* on Av 7, C6-8, is frighteningly clean and has a couple of good restaurants.

West of the **Plaza de la Cultura**, a small street market borders the Plaza de la Democracía selling a broad range of goods including hammocks, woven bags, wooden carvings and painted feathers.

Moravia Some 8 km northeast of San José *Moravia* is a popular spot for souvenir hunters often included in day trips from the capital. *El Caballo Blanco*, T235-6797, is a well established store that stocks leather goods harking back to its origins as well as other goods. *HHH* are good for leatherwork. The leather rocking chairs (which dismantle for export) found in some *artesanía* shops are sometimes cheaper in Sarchí. The largest one-stop shop is the *Mercado de Artesanías Las Garzas* with its countless stalls to tempt and tease with all manner of colourful goods and banter.

Photography There are several photographic supply shops throughout the city stocking print and slide film including *Kodak* and *Fuji*. *Fuji* offices in the centre and out in Los Yoses stock slide film including Sensia and Provia. Developing for print and slide is widely available but you may prefer to wait until you are at home rather than take the risk. One-hr developing is available but if you really want to see the pictures, try IFSA (Kodak) at Av 2, C 3-5, or Universal (Fuji).

San José and around

For camera repairs try *Tecfot*, Av 7, C Central, T221-1438 who repair all types of cameras, providing a good service at reasonable rates. They also have some second hand cameras in stock if you need a replacement. *Taller de Equipos Fotográficos*, 120 m east of kiosk Parque Morazán, Av 3, C 3-5, T223-1146, is an authorized *Canon* repairer.

Souvenirs The *Mercado Central* on Av Central and C 6-8 is filled with life, noise and a general chaos. Behind all the daily commerce and greetings, you'll find a few typical items for sale such as leather goods and wooden items – many without the price increases found in stores catering for tourists. You may have to rummage around a bit, but with a bit of luck, you'll find a truly memorable souvenir of your trip. Several craft cooperatives exist including *Mercado Nacional de Artesanía*, C 11, Av 4, T221-5012, www.asstcard.co.cr/mercarte.htm Mon-Fri 0900-1800, Sat 0900-1700, which has a good selection of items at reasonable prices. *Canapi* on C 11 and Av 1, is a co-operative and cheaper than most. *La Casona* C Central and Av Central-1, open daily from 0900-1900, is a market of small *artesanía* shops with lots of interesting stalls to sift through. There is also a selection of stalls on the west side of Plaza de la Democracía, which sells the full range of desirables including hammocks, paintings, wood carvings and T-shirts.

As a walking tour of shopping opportunities, head for **Parque Morazán**. The south and west side of the park is non-stop shops with many selling the same things, but the odd nugget can be found. Impromptu stalls sprout up around the **Plaza de la Cultura** along the Av Central, and you will always find a couple of wandering salespeople around *Café Parisienne* selling cigars, humidors and other souvenirs.

Galería Namu, opposite the Alianza Francesa building on Av 7 and C 5-7, T256-3412, www.galerianamu.com is the best one-stop shop for homegrown art. Indigenous art and crafts would be the traditional phrase, but Namu has blended conventional themes of rugs, throws, textiles and mask carvings, with many more contemporary developments. Not that these are their words, but to keep indigenous art alive it has to be living. The result is some inspired pieces. Any pieces bought come with an information sheet so you can spread the story behind the work. If San José is at the start and end of your trip, pop in on the first day, think about what you want to buy while you travel, and then visit again to buy it all just before you leave. If you're just passing, take your credit card and give yourself more than a ½ hr.

One of the best stops for coffee is *La Esquina del Café* on Av 9, C 3 bis, T257-9868, F258-2983, with a wide range of different blends of gourmet coffee from throughout Costa Rica which you can taste in the café-cum-restaurant out the back. You can also pick up several other mainstream souvenirs, but nothing tacky.

Boutique Annemarie is the souvenir and gift shop in the main lobby of the *Hotel Don Carlos* at C 9 and Av 7-9, open 365 days a year from 0900-1900. They guarantee the largest selection and the best prices in Costa Rica with over 100,000 handcrafted items and pieces of art on display.

El Pueblo, north of town in barrio Tournón, has several good shops, although prices vary greatly so shop around.

For more general stores you will find most of what you want down **Av Central** along the pedestrian area. *Universal* on Av Central and C Central-2, is a general department store serving as a handy one-stop shop with a broad range of practical items such as stationary and film. And of course there are big shopping plazas dotted around town including *San Pedro*, on the eastern ring road, and the *Multiplaza Mall*, near Camino Real, Escazú, both of which have excellent shops.

Sport

Parque Sábana is the place to stretch your legs for a **run in the park**. There's also a *swimming* pool in the park if you fancy a dip. If you're looking for a one-day *hike* go to Escazú and tackle some of the smaller hills, or head out to Volcán Barva and explore some of the higher trails. A good day's **mountain biking** starts at the Tara Spa Resort Hotel in Escazú. The Pico Blanco Plunge drops 4,000 ft over 17 miles and ends at the Butterfly Farm in La Gúacima. All equipment provided. Call the Tara Spa on T228-6992.

If you're staying in San José for a while, a steady trawl through the Calendar pages of the Tico Times reveals fascinating amusements like Hash House Harriers, badminton, and for the really hyperactive – darts!

For those that like to spoil a good walk, you can play 18 holes of golf at the Meliá Cariari (T232-8122) on the road out to the airport, or try the recently expanded Valle del Sol (T282-9222) out in Santa Ana.

Watching sport there is only one game that counts – football. Saprissa home games take place on Sun mornings. Catch a local bus heading north and you can buy a ticket on the gate. International games occasionally take place in the Stadio Nacional in Parque Sábana. Watch the local press for details, you may be able to get a ticket if you turn up in good time.

San José and around

Tour operators

Service levels across the board tend to be very high. Trips and tours are sold through a number of companies but many use the same operator to provide the service so a San José city tour is likely to be the same irrespective of who you book through. Trips will vary if the package involves an overnight stay, in which case you will want to check the standard of the hotel. Special interest groups will also want to be assured that any guides have appropriate experience and knowledge the planned trip.

For special interest travel see Essentials page 58. For rafting also see Turrialba page 175

What follows is a list of some of the main tour operators in San José and a few specialist providers.

Costa Rica Expeditions, Av 3, C Central-2, T257-0766, F257-1655, www.costaricaexpeditions.com Upmarket wildlife adventures taking you to popular but out of the way places in comfort and style. Very good and knowledgeable guides. Options include whitewater rafting (US$89 for 1-day trip on Río Pacuare, including lunch and transport, and other rivers from US$69-85). Owners of *Tortuga Lodge* on the Caribbean coast, *Corcovado Lodge Tent Camp* on the Osa Peninsular and *Monteverde Lodge* near Santa Elena. Open daily 0530-2100, highly recommended.

Expediciones Tropicales, C 3, Av 11-13, T257-4171, F257-4124, www.costaricainfo.com The full range of 1- and 2-day tours. Staff are friendly, helpful and happy to talk through the options without pushing the hard sell. They operate the *Four in One* tour – see 'Short tours from San José'. Open daily 0600-2200.

Horizontes, C 28, Av 1-3, T222-2022, F255-4513, www.horizontes.com A wide range of services and high standards from one of Costa Rica's most respected tour operators from basics, including car rentals, hotel reservations through to specialist trips focusing on natural history, conservation, birdwatching, photography, culture, agriculture and adventure. English, Spanish, Italian, German and French spoken. Open 0800-0530, Mon-Fri, 0900-1200, Sat from Dec to Apr, hours may change in green season.

Swiss Travel Service, one of the biggest operators with several branches around town in *Best Western Irazú, Barcelo Amón Plaza, Camino Real Inter-Continental, Herradura Hotel, Meliá Cariari Hotel, Meliá Confort Corobicí Hotel* and the *Radisson Europa*. T282-4898, F282-4890, www.swisstravelcr.com In addition to standard tours, arrange almost anything you can imagine. Provide a *Birdwatcher's Paradise* day trip for birders. Good guides, with a lot of cruise business – warmly recommended.

Tam Travel, 4 branches, 1 in *San José Palacio Hotel*, open 7 days a week, 24-hr answering service T256-0203, F222-1465, info@tamtravel.com or www.tamtravel.com Helpful and efficient.

Special interest & smaller operators
Look in text for regional tour specialists

Aguas Bravas, T292-2072, F229-4837, www.aguas-bravas.co.cr Whitewater rafting on various rivers throughout the country, with their own activity centre near Puerto Viejo de Sarapiquí. Can arrange a wide variety of adventure activities including kayaking, horse riding, mountain biking and tailor made trips.

Arakari Tours, C San Dimas y Av Castro Madriz, Apdo 1112-1011, San José, T227-1115, F226-3424, www.arakaritours.com A small *Tico* owned tour operator that started up in 1995 offering the full range of tours and a reservation service.

Armo Tours, C1, Av Central-1, T257-2620, F257-1389, armotours@racsa.co.cr and they're building a website at www.armotours.com Highly recommended for national tours, good service, German, English, French and Italian spoken.

Aventuras Naturales, Av Central, C 33-35, T225-3939, F253-6934, www.adventure costarica.com Well respected adventure tour operator, specialists in whitewater rafting with their own lodge on the Pacuare complete with canopy adventure tour.

Cabet Travel, Av 2, C 5-7, T257-8920, F256-1554, cabet1@sol.racsa.co.cr Low-key set-up, offering a wide range of ½-, 1- and 2-day trips throughout the country. Prices slightly cheaper than most others agencies. Helpful and useful information without heavy pressure to take a tour.

Calypso Tours, in the basement of Edificio Las Arcadas, next to the Gran Hotel Costa Rica, T256-8787, F256-8585, www.calypsotours.com The originators of the Pacific Island Cruise with an all-inclusive day trip from US$99 – a popular trip.

Central American Tours, Av 13, C3-5, T297-0343, F236-5270, www.catours.co.cr Will help with full trip planning service and day tours.

Costa Rica Sun Tours, Av 4, C 36, T255-3418, F255-4410, www.crsuntours.com Regular departures on many of the normal tours including Arenal, Monteverde, Corcovado, Tortuguero and Manuel Antonio. Tours can often be arranged at short notice, warmly recommended.

Ecole Travel, C 7, Av Central-Av 1, T223-2240, F223-4128, www.travelcostarica.net Chilean-Dutch owned agency that is consistently recommended for tours with cheaper options to Tortuguero, Corcovado and tailor-made excursions off the beaten track.

Green Tropical Tours, C El Rodeo, Coronado, 1 km north of the Catholic church, Apdo 675-2200 Coronado, Costa Rica, T229-4192, F292-5003, www.greentropical.com Specializing in tailor-made tours with many of the normal tours and some to less widely visited areas like Guayabo National Monument and Los Juncos Cloudforest.

The Original Canopy Tour, Av 9, C 3a, T257-5149, F256-7626, www.canopytour.com As the name suggests, the pioneers in Costa Rica with 7 different canopy tour dotted around the country including new installations at Drake and Tabacón. Rates from US$45 per person.

Ríos Tropicales, C 38, between Paseo Colón and Av 2, 50 m south of Subway, T233-6455, F255-4354, www.riostropicales.com Specialists in whitewater rafting with options on the Pacuare, Reventazón, Sarapiquí, General, Corobicí and sea kayaking with single day and multi-day trips. Good selection and careful to assess abilities, with excellent guides and good food. *Ríos Tropicales* is one of the longest running rafting operations in Costa Rica and is actively involved in conservation and reforestation projects. Several standard offerings, including 1-day trips from US$80, and US$250 for 2-day trip on Río Pacuare, waterfalls, rapids, including accommodation in the company's jungle lodge and excellent food. They can also organize special events and bespoke trips for the experienced.

Simbiosis Tours, Apdo 6939-1000 San José, Costa Rica, T/F286-4203, www.agroecoturismo.net The booking arm of Cooprena, a network of collectively owned community lodges and guesthouses in some secluded spots – probably the best shot at organized ecotourism in Costa Rica.

OTEC, C 3, Av 1-3, T256-0633, www.otec.co.cr A travel agent that provides stupendous discounts on flight for students, teachers and others who can convince staff that you are in education. Almost enough to make you go back to school!

Student travel agents

    USIT, student discount office, has an office out in Los Yoses on Paseo Ruben Dario (Av Central) on the corner with C 35. T280-5182, F225-9325, www.usitworld.com

Easy tours from San José

There are many tour operators in San José that offer all-inclusive trips in the city, in the surrounding area and throughout the country. Ranging in length from half a day to 2 or 3 days, here is a summary of the general offerings.

    Prices and details are intended to give an idea of cost and options, start times are approximate. It is possible to do most of the activities independently by public transport or using private vehicle. Few, however, are possible within the same time frames if travelling by public transport. As always with set tours, the disadvantage is a fairly strictly adhered to itinerary.

The aim is to give you an overview of the city moving around some of the urban areas, museums and architectural and historical sites of San José by bus but itineraries vary. Make sure that anything you want to see is included. The core elements normally include a drive through Sábana Park, a walking tour through the historic Teatro Nacional (National Theatre), a visit to the Museo Nacional (National Museum), the Corte Suprema (Supreme Court), and the Universidad de Costa Rica (University) in San Pedro. Tours often end with a stop in Moravia to pick up souvenirs from the many craft shops in the northeastern suburb. ■ *US$25, half day, am and pm, approx 4 hrs.*

San José city tour

A chance to appreciate the variety and history of Costa Rica all in one place. Pueblo Antiguo is not actually an old town, but a cultural amusement park which uses actors and architecture to recreate the customs and traditions found throughout Costa Rica. Both trips include shows, the night trip includes dinner. ■ *US$39, day or night tour, 0900 or 1700 start, approx. 3 hrs.*

Pueblo Antiguo

Trips climb to the windy and often cloudy summit of Irazú volcano for a view of the massive crater. On a clear day you can see both the Atlantic and Pacific oceans. After visiting the volcano, trips visit the old capital of Cartago stopping at the ruins of the old church and the pilgrimmage Basilica of the Virgen de los Angeles. ■ *US$35, 0830 start, approx 5 hrs. Take: sweater, binoculars and comfortable shoes.*

Irazú Volcano
See page 168

A trip heading southeast of San José to Lankester Botanical Gardens, followed by a ride through the understated beauty of the Orosi Valley, around the lake created by the Cachi Dam. Trip includes lunch at a lakeside restaurant, a visit to the country's oldest colonial church and to the carving workshop of the Dreamer's House. ■ *US$45 less without lunch, morning start, approx: 6 hrs. Take: sweater, binoculars, walking shoes and raincoat.*

Lankester Gardens & Orosi Valley
See page 169

Combines the Irazú Volcano and the Lankester Gardens & Orosi Valley tours. Makes for an impressive combination of scenery, history and botany all in one day. ■ *US$55, 0830 start, approx 9 hrs. Take: sweater, binoculars, comfortable shoes and raincoat.*

Irazú/Orosi/ Lankester Gardens

San José and around

Poás Volcano National Park
See page 149

Tours begin with a pleasant drive through the lush coffee plantations and flower farms of the northern Central Valley to Poás Volcano, one of the world's largest geysers. The volcano is active, but completely safe for viewing. Trips usually include a short hike in Poás National Park. ■ *US$35, 0830 start, approx 5hrs. Take: sweater, binoculars, comfortable shoes and raincoat.*

Grecia & Sarchí (Oxcart factory) Town
See page 150

Heading north, the trip drives through coffee and sugar cane plantations before arriving at Grecia, famous for its metal church, and then moving on to the craft factories of Sarchí where the colourful oxcarts that are almost a national symbol are built and decorated. ■ *US$30, 1100 start, approx. 5 hrs. Take: sweater, binoculars and comfortable shoes.*

Poás Volcano/ Grecia/Sarchí

Combines a trip to Poás Volcano National Park with a visit at Grecia and Sarchí. ■ *US$55, slightly less without lunch, start 0830, approx. 8 hrs. Take: sweater, comfortable walking shoes and raincoat.*

Carara National Park
See page 287

A short ride west for a couple of hours, the reserve is the best day trip to the rainforest from the capital. ■ *US$80, 0800 start, approx 9 hrs. Take: sun hat, suntan lotion, walking shoes, swimsuit and towel and binoculars.*

Braulio Carrillo National Park
See page 162

A trip over the continental divide and through the Zurquí Tunnel followed by a walk through the short trails of Braulio Carrillo National Park, one of many important rainforest reserves in Costa Rica. Some companies tag another ½-day activity on the end such as a river trip in Sarapiquí, or a ride on the aerial tram. ■ *US$35, 0715 start, approx, 4 hrs. Take: comfortable walking shoes, sweater, raincoat and binoculars.*

Rainforest aerial tram
See page 163

Ingenious in the extreme, the Rainforest aerial tram on the borders of Braulio Carrillo National Park has spawned many impersonations but this is the original. ■ *US$90, 0800 start, 6 hrs. Take: light clothing and shoes, raincoat, repellent and binoculars.*

Butterfly farm & coffee plantation tours

Visit two of Costa Rica's typical exports in one. Trips round coffee plantations are popular, and *Café Britt* has developed the experience into an art form. Butterfly farms, in particular Costa Rica's largest La Gúacima (see page 147), and the smaller but no less enjoyable Spirogyra both export butterflies throughout the world. The farms offer a fascinating insight into the life cycle of the butterflies. ■ *US$40 – US$80, 0800 start, 5-8 hrs. Take: comfortable walking outfit.*

The Best of Costa Rica (Four in One)

A pretty quick journey through a cross-section of Costa Rica, heading first for the vast crater of Poás Volcano, before going north to see La Paz waterfall with a drop of some 50 m. A couple of hours spent floating down the Río Sarapiquí and lunch before heading back to San José in a sweeping loop that brings you through Braulio Carrillo on the return to the capital. It is a lot to pack in one day but manageable. ■ *US$79, early morning start, approx. 11 hrs. Take: hat, light jacket, raingear, walking shoes, insect repellent and binoculars.*

Isla Tortuga – Pacific Island Cruise
See page 271

Take a boat trip on a luxury yacht visiting the pristine white sand beaches and crystal clear waters of Isla Tortuga off the southern Nicoya Peninsula. Meals include a seafood buffet served on the beach. Good opportunities for snorkelling and seeing marine life. ■ *US$89, 0630 start, approx: 11hrs. Take: sweater, binoculars, swimsuit, sunblock and towel.*

Whitewater rafting

If you've been whitewater rafting before you won't need convincing, if you haven't a one-day trip may be just right. 1-day trips up to Class III for beginners and beyond for experienced rafters are possible on the Río Sarapiquí, Reventazón and Pacuare. The scenery is unbelievable, and all equipment is provided. But it is better to go for longer if you can. ■ *US$ 75-95, 0600 start, approx 10 hrs. Take: sandals, sunscreen, towel and change of clothing.*

A tight 1-day trip but possible if tight for time. As one of the most active volcanoes (see page 196) in the Americas, the trip is subject to change depending on volcano activity. But expect to get a good view of lava flows and possibly to hear eruptions and the sound of the lava cascading down the volcano slopes. Later you visit thermal-heated springs, relaxing in the soothing warm waters of the beautifully kitsch baths of Tabacón resort (see page 198). Often includes dinner and stops along the way, possibly at Sarchi. ■ *US$75, 1035 start, approx: 11hrs. Take: swimsuit, towel, comfortable walking shoes, sweater, insect repellent and binoculars.*

Arenal Volcano by Night & Tabacón Hot Springs – 1- & 2-day options

2-day options are available incorporating a trip north to Caño Negro Lagoon travelling along the Río Frio by boat observing the wetland birdlife of the region (see page 194). Alternative second day trips incorporate horse riding, canopy tours or mountain biking. ■ *Prices from US$180 excluding overnight accommodation.*

Visiting Tortuguero National Park in 1 day is a long 13-hour trip, and it is far better to take 2 or even 3 days. Only take the 1-day option if time is really tight. On Costa Rica's north Caribbean coast, the turtle nesting beaches and the inland waterways are justifiably revered as a nature paradise. Transport to the area is by bus, then by boat through canals that lead through secondary and primary rainforest. After arriving, trips incorporate quiet trips by boat through the National Park before heading home. If staying overnight, trips include a beach night walk looking for nesting turtles and an early morning boat trip or hike. ■ *US$75–US$280, 0620 start. Take: raincoat, comfortable walking outfit, insect repellent and overnight bags if required.*

Tortuguero Canals – 1, 2 or 3 day
See page 376

Although logistically possible, a visit to Monteverde in 1 day is unlikely to be enjoyable. The road is unpaved, the journey tiring and you'll arrive at midday – not the best time to see birds. Some people and companies would like to see the road paved giving access to day-trippers. For the time being at least, however, this is not going to happen. Anyway, the place deserves more than just a cursory glance, so with luck Monteverde in a day will continue to be impossible for a long time to come.

Monteverde in a day?
See page 206

Transport

Buses The urban bus system is extensive and efficient enough allowing for traffic congestion. Buses run from around 0500 until 2300 or so at night. Urban buses cost 70 *colónes* (US$0.20) payable to the driver on bording, its a little more (100 *colónes*, US$0.30) for outer lying districts such as Escazú, Alajuela and Heredia. Buses get very crowded at rush hour, and luggage space is limited at the best of times.

Local

Bus destinations are marked on the front of the bus. Officially buses only stop for passengers to board and alight at official stops. Far from obvious, the cunningly disguised metal posts doubling up as stops are found through habit not design. Labelled on one side with the destination the bus stop blends in perfectly with the pavement furniture. The clearest indication is a neat line of people patiently queuing so join the end and wait.

A few general routes that may be of interest to visitors. Heading west towards **Parque Sábana** down **Paseo Colón** from the centre of town, buses leave from along Av 3. Returning from Parque Sábana buses travel down Paseo Colón before joining Av 2. With these 2 routes you can move through the heart of the city. A **cheap tour of San José** can be made on the bus marked *'periférico'* from Paseo Colón in front of the *Cine Colón*, a 45-min circle of the city. A smaller circle is made by the **'Sábana/Cementerio'**

San José and around

bus travelling along Paseo Colón out to Parque Sábana and then returning along Av 10. Pick it up on Av 2, at **Parque Morazán** or on Av 3.

A few starting points for stops and destinations: **Desmaparados**, Av 4, C 5-7; **Escazú**, Av Central-1, C 16; **Moravia**, Av 3, C 3-5; **Sábana Cementerio**, Av 2, C 8-10; **Sábana Estadio**, Av 2, C 2-4; **San Pedro**, Av Central, C 9-11.

Taxis With so many licenced cabs roaming the streets, a taxi is often the quickest and most efficient way around town locally. The basic fee of 165 *colónes* (US$0.60) plus 10 *colónes* (3 cents) for every 100 m or so, makes most cross-town journeys affordable and efficient. There are several taxi ranks throughout the city – the main one being on the north side of Parque Central – you can hail a cab in the street or get your hotel to book one by telephone. As with taxis worldwide they're everywhere on sunny days, but when it is raining or late at night you could end up waiting forever.

Motorcycles *Wild Rider Motorcycles*, Paseo Colón, C 32 diagonal Kentucky, T/F258-4604, www.ritmo-del-caribe Suzuki DR 250s and DR 350s available for rent from US$30 a day. Experience is essential not only to rent the bike, but also for your survival on the roads. San José and the surrounding area is not the place to learn to ride.

Long distance **Air** A good network of regional airports makes for quick and efficient travel around the country. Prices are reasonable and schedules are frequent enough to make it worth considering taking a flight if time is tight certainly to places like Puerto Jiménez, Tortuguero and Barra del Colorado.

The main domestic air services are provided by *SANSA* and *Travelair*. *SANSA*, Casa Blanca, La Sábana, San José, T221-9414, F255-2176, info@flysansa.com or www. flysansa.com operates out of the domestic terminal of Juan Santamaría International Airport to the northwest of the capital. *Travelair*, T220-3054, F220-0413, reservations@travelair-costarica.com or www.travelair-costarica.com flights leave from Tobías Bolaños airport (T232-2820), 5 km west of San José in the district of Pavas. See 'Essentials', page 47 for flight schedules. Tickets can be arranged direct or through most travel agents and tour operators.

Charter flights are also available and can be reasonably affordable if you are travelling in a group. Most charter companies work out of Tobías Bolaños airport. See Charter flights, in Essentials, page 47.

For the latest bus information you can contact the ICT office below the Plaza de la Cultura, or ask in your hotel

See also table on page 126

Buses cover the whole country and you can get between any 2 reasonably sized towns with just one bus journey. If there is not a direct service, you will be able to get a more local bus from a town near to your destination. The buses vary greatly in quality. Popular routes between cities are often serviced with luxury coaches with a/c as standard and occasionally TV and video. Moving off the well driven tarmac, the quality of bus matches the terrain perfectly: the rougher the road, the rougher the bus. Experienced global bus travellers will find the Costa Rican network pretty much a dream – first timers may have to learn the fine art of dozing while your head falls off.

Frequency also reflects the popularity of a destination. Buses to **Alajuela** and **Heredia** leave the capital every 5 mins. **Puerto Jiménez** down on the Osa Peninsula currently only has a couple of direct buses a day. Buses tend to leave on or close to the scheduled departure time, relatively uncommon in Latin America, so don't be late.

Prices vary greatly, but are not extortionate. By way of example, buses to **Limón** are around US$3 for the 2½-hr journey.

Bus **terminals** and **company offices** are spread through out the capital, with a general concentration on the **Coca-Cola** district. For several years the terminal has been notorious, providing rich pickings for thieves. While the police presence has increased in the last year, it isn't round-the-clock so keep your wits about you and don't leave bags unattended for a second. All destinations on the Caribbean coast are served by the new **Gran Terminal del Caribe** to the north of the city. For specific details of destinations and departure points see the table below. In recent years there has been a degree of consolidation in the long distance bus industry, and some companies now share offices and depots.

For most bus journeys buying **tickets** in advance, even by a couple of hours, is a good idea although not essential, so visit the terminal before departure to buy a ticket. At holiday times, Christmas, New Year and Easter in particular, advance booking is essential.

International buses Nicaragua and **Panama** are served by good international bus services. The buses are comfortable, the service is reliable and it is a good way of covering a lot of ground without the expense of a flight. Although it can hardly be called sightseeing, you will see a bit more than you would from an aeroplane. Several companies provide a service including: *Tica Bus*, Av 4, C 9-11, T221-8954, F223-8158, with a service covering the whole of Central America up to Guatemala. *Tica Bus* has a daily service to **Panama City**, departing at 2200, arriving at 1600 the following day, US$23 one way. For **Managua** buses leave at 0600 arriving at 1500, US$10 one-way. Moving on from Managua normally involves an overnight stay in Managua, but the *Tica Bus* terminal in Managua does have some basic accommodation. Other international bus companies include: *Sirca Express*, *Nicabus*, *Panaline* and *Tracopa*.

Car rental Paseo Colón is the home of the car rental firm. Every international and national car rental firm has an office and compound here. Most companies have an office at the airport as well so if you have booked in advance and want the vehicle immediately you will be able to arrange to pick it up at the airport. Most international companies have a presence in Costa Rica. Here is a selection of companies in San José. Office hours tend to be from 0800 until around 1800, while some companies are open until 2200. Check opening hours to ensure you don't miss the drop-off date and incur a penalty.

www.rentacar.co.cr lists most of the car hire companies and they can also take online bookings

Adobe, T221-5425, F221-9286, in North America T1-800-826-1134, adobecar@ sol.racsa.co.cr Japanese cars and 4-wheel drive, drop-off at the beach if you fly *Travelair* or *Sansa*, flexible insurance, drivers aged 18-21 accepted with US$1,500 on credit card. *Alamo*, in Costa Rica operated by *Ada*, Av 18, C 11-13, north side of Plaza Gonzalez Viquez, T233-7733, F233-5555, airport T440-0965, www.alamo costarica.com With 4 outlets in the capital and Liberia, Tamarindo, Quepos and Fortuna. *Avis*, Sábana Norte, T293-2222, airport T442-1321, F293-1111, www.avis.com Well known international name with offices in *Hotel Camino Real* and *Hotel Corobicí*. *Budget*, C 30, Paseo Colón, T223-3284, F255-4966, www.budget.co.cr Open Mon-Sat, 0800-1900, Sun, 0800-1800, also at international airport, T442-2495, open Mon-Sun, 0600-2100, and at *Hotel Meliá Conchal* at Playa Conchal. *Dollar*, Paseo Colón and C 32, T257-1585, F222-1765, airport office T/F443-2078, www.dollarcostarica.com Good rates. *Economy*, Paseo Colón, T231-5410, F232-7041, airport office, T442-8100, F440-0800, economy1@sol.racsa. co.cr Many branches throughout the country including Liberia, Flamingo, Tamarindo and Jacó Beach. *Elegante*, C 10 Av 13-15, Barrio Mexico, T257-0026, F221-5761, www.eleganterentacar.com Cars, jeeps, vans, minimum age 23, has branches throughout the country. *Europcar*, Paseo Colón, C 32-34, T257-1158. F255-4492, good cars, good prices and helpful staff. *Hertz*, C 38, Paseo Colón, T221-1818, F221-1949, airport T441-0097, www.hertzcostaricarentacar.com *Meir*, good rates for 4-wheel drive but check insurance, C 11, Av 14, T257-4666, F222-7447, meircr@racsa.co.cr *National*, C 36, Av 7, T290-8787, F290-0431, www.natcar.com Easy to get to on the *autopista* for Alajuela also with offices in Tamarindo, Heredia and Jaco. Open from 0600-2200 everyday. *Santos*, T441-3044, F223-4030, www.casantos.co.cr *Toyota*, Paseo Colón, T258-5797, F222-7875, call toll free from US and Canada on 1-800-894-6709,

San José and around

Buses from San José

Destination	Frequency	Duration	Cost
Alajuela (and airport)	Every 10 mins	30 mins	40 cents
Alajuela (and airport)	Every 10 mins, every 30 mins through the night	30 mins	40 cents
Arenal (see Fortuna)			
Braulio Carrillo NP (see Guapiles and Limón)			
Cahuita	3 daily	4 hrs	US$4.10
Caño Negro Wildlife Reserve (see Los Chiles)			
Cartago	Every 10 mins	45 mins	
Chirripo NP (see San Isidro de El General)			
Ciudad Neilly	1 direct at 1630	7 hrs	US$5.35
Ciudad Quesada (San Carlos)	Hourly	2½ hrs	US$2
Corcovado NP (see Puerto Jiminez)			
Dominical - buses via San Isidro de El General or Quepos			
Escazú	Every 10 mins	20 mins	30 cents
Fortuna	3 daily	3½ hrs	US$2.80
Golfito	0700, 1500	7 hrs	US$6
Guápiles	15 daily	2 hrs	US$1.70
Guayabo National Monument (see Turrialba)			
Heredia	Every 10 mins	30 mins	40 cents
Heredia	Every 20 mins	30 mins	40 cents
Irazú Volcano NP	1 Sat, 1 Sun 0800 in the morning		US$5
Jacó	3 daily	2 hrs 10 mins	US$2.40
La Cruz (see Peñas Blancas)			
Liberia	15 daily	4½ hrs	US$4.50
Limón	22 buses between 0500 and 2200	3 hrs, 2¾ hrs direct	US$3.50
Limón			
Los Chiles	2 daily	5 hrs	US$3.80
Manuel Antonio NP (see Quepos)			
Montezumo – buses going to Puntarenas and then ferry to Paquera			
Nicoya (by ferry)	2 daily	4 hrs	US$5.20
Nicoya (via Liberia)	5 daily	5 hrs	US$5.20
Nosara (by ferry)	1 at 0600	6 hrs	US$6
Palmar Norte/Sur	3 daily	6 hrs	US$4
Palmar Norte/Sur	1 daily	5 hrs	US$4
Paso Canoas	4 (1 direct at 1100)	7 hrs	US$8.20
Peñas Blancas	5, 10 at weekends	4 hrs	US$5.50
Playa del Coco	2 daily	5 hrs	US$5.20
Playa Flamingo	1 at 0800	5 hrs	US$5.60
Playa Panama	1 at 1530	4½ hrs	US$5.25

Company & terminal	Address	Telephone
Tuasa	*C 10, Av Central - 2*	*T222-5325*
Tuasa	*Av 2, C 10-12*	
Autotransportes Mepe, Gran Terminal del Caribe	*Barrio Tournon*	*T257-8129*
SACSA	*C 5, Av 18-20*	*T233-5350*
Tracopa	*Av 5 and C 14*	*T222-2666*
Autotransportes Ciudad Quesada, Atlantico Norte Terminal	*Av 9, C 12,*	*T256-8914*
Street stop	*C16, Av Central – 1*	
Atlantico Norte Terminal	*Av 9, C 12,*	*T256-8914*
Tracopa	*Av 5 and C 14*	*T222-2666*
Empresarios Guapileño, Gran Terminal del Caribe	*Barrio Tournon*	*T222-0610*
Street stop	*Av 2, C 10-12*	
Street stop	*Av 2, C 12-14*	
Buses Metropoli	*Av 2, C 1-3, in front of Gran Hotel Costa Rica*	*T272-0651*
Transportes Jacó, Coca-Cola Terminal		*T223-1109*
Pulmitan	*C 14, Av 1-3*	*T222-1650*
Autotransporte Mepe, Gran Terminal del Caribe	*Barrio Tournon*	*T257-8129*
Auto Transportes Caribeño		*T222-0610*
Autotransportes Ciudad Quesada, Atlantico Norte Terminal	*Av 9, C 12*	*T256-8914*
Empresa Alfaro	*Av 5 and C 14*	*T222-2666*
Empresa Alfaro	*Av 5 and C 14*	*T222-2666*
Empresa Alfaro	*Av 5 and C 14*	*T222-2666*
Tracopa	*Av 5 and C 14*	*T222-2666*
Autotransportes Blanco Lobo	*Av 9 y 11, C 12,*	*T257-4121*
Tracopa	*Av 5 and C 14*	*T222-2666*
Transportes Deldu	*Av 3, C 16*	*T256-9072*
	C 14, Av 1-3	*T222-1650*
	Av 3, C 18-20	*T221-7202*
	Av 3, C 18-20	*T221-7202*

San José and around

Buses from San José, continued

Destination	Frequency	Duration	Cost
Poás (from Alajuela)	1 at 0830	4 hrs	US$3.80
Puerto Jiménez	1 daily	8 hrs	US$6.30
Puerto Viejo de Talamanca	4 daily	4½ hrs	US$4.80
Puerto Viejo de Sarapiquí (por pista - through the Zurqui Tunnel)	8 daily	3 hrs	US$2.50
Puerto Viejo de Sarapiquí (via Varablanca)	3 daily	3½ hrs	US$2.50
Puntarenas	Hourly	2 hrs	
Quepos	8 daily, 2 direct	3½ or 4½ hrs	US$3.70 or US$4.30
Rio Frio	2 daily	2½ hrs	US$1.80
Sámara	1 at 1230	5 hrs	US$6
San Isidro de El General	18 daily	3 hrs	US$2.90
San Isidro de El General		3 hrs	US$2.90
San Isidro de El General		3 hrs	US$2.90
San Rafael de Guatasu	1 at 1545	4 hrs	US$3.50
San Ramón	Hourly	2 hrs	
San Vito	4 daily (1 direct at 1445)	6 hrs	US$6.70
Santa Cruz	8 daily	5 hrs	US$5.25
Santa Cruz (by ferry)	1 at 0800	5 hrs	US$5.25
Santa Cruz / Playa Flamingo	1 at 1530	5 hrs	US$5.25
Santa Elena / Monteverde	2 daily	4½ hrs	US$4.00
Santa Maria de Dota	13 daily	1½ hrs	
Sarchí	4 daily	1½ hrs	US$0.80
Siquirres	12 daily	2½ hrs	US$1.90
Sixaola – buses via Puerto Viejo	4 daily	6 hrs	US$5.80
Tamarindo	1 at 1600	6 hrs	US$6.40
Tamarindo (via Liberia)	1 at 1530	5 hrs	US$5.40
Tilarán (via Canas)	5 daily	5 hrs	US$2.80
Tortuguero - no direct service	Daily bus service (6 hrs) – bus to Puerto Caño Blanco and boat from there to Tortuguero		
Turrialba	15 daily	1½ hrs	
Upala	1 at 1500	4 hrs	US$4.30
Zarcero	8 daily	1½ hrs	US$1.40

Company & terminal	Address	Telephone
Tuasu	Av 2, C 12-14	T222-5325
Autotransportes Blanco Lobo	Av 9 y 11, C 12	T257-4121
Autotransporte Mepe, Gran Terminal del Caribe	Barrio Tournon	T257-8129
Autotransporte Sarapiquí, Gran Terminal del Caribe	Barrio Tournon	T222-0610
Autotransporte Sarapiquí, Gran Terminal del Caribe	Barrio Tournon	T222-0610
Empresario Unidos	C 16, Av 10-12	T222-0064
Transportes Morales, Coca-Cola Terminal		T223-5567
Autotransporte Sarapiqu, Gran Terminal del Caribe	Barrio Tournon	T222-0610
Empresa Alfaro	Av 5 and C 14	T222-2666
Autotransportes Blanco Lobo	Av 9 y 11, C 12	T257-4121
Vargas Rojas/Tuasar	C Central, Av 22-24	T222-9763
Transportes Musoc	C Central, Av 22-24	T222-2422
Transnorte de Upala	Av 3 y 5, C 10, 200m south of the old stop to Puntarenas	T221-9022
Empresario Unidos, C 16, Av 10-12	C 16, Av 10-12	T222-0064
Tracopa	Av 5 and C 14	T222-2666
Tralapa	Av 3, C 18-20	T221-7202
Empresa Alfaro	Av 5 and C 14	T222-2666
Tralapa	Av 3, C 18-20	T221-7202
Atlantico Norte Terminal	Av 9, C 12,	T258-5674
Autotransportes Los Santos Dota Coca-Cola Terminal	Av 16, C 19-21	T541-1326
Any bus going to the Caribbean (Lineares del Atlantico), Gran Terminal del Caribe	Barrio Tournon	T222-0610
Autotransporte Mepe, Gran Terminal del Caribe	Barrio Tournon	T257-8129
Tralapa	Av 3, C 18-20	T221-7202
Empresa Alfaro	Av 5 and C 14	T222-2666
Atlantico Norte Terminal	Av 9, C 12	T258-5674
Caño Blanco Marina	Edificio Las Arcadas, 2 piso, Local 11	T256-9444
Transtusa	C 13, Av 6-8	T556-0073
Transnorte de Upala	Av 3 y 5, C 10, 200m south of the old stop to Puntarenas,	T221-9022
Coca-Cola Terminal		

San José and around

www.toyotarent.com Good cars, very helpful staff, also have an office at airport and in Liberia. *Tricolor*, Paseo Colón, T257-4455, F233-4433, call toll free in the US and Canada on 1-800-949-0234, www.tricolorcarrental.com Good cars at competitive prices with friendly service and a good map.

Taxis Taxis offer alternative way of exploring the highlands. Talking with one taxi driver, he recounted a fine 1-day fare that took him out to Tamarindo and back, a mere US$150. More realistically, the recommended price for a trip in a cab to Volcán Irazú is 10,000 *colónes*, (US$32). With a group of 4, this becomes a remarkably affordable way to travel without the hassles of driving yourself. If taking a long distance ride, you may have to pay part of the fare in advance. Most red cab drivers have a list of recommended prices if you want to consider the options.

Directory

Airline offices *Aeroperlas*, see *SANSA* below. *Air France*, Condominio Vista Real, p 1, 100 m east of POP's, Curridabat, T280-0069, F280-9707, www.airfrance.com *Alitalia*, C 38, Av 3, T222-6138, F233-7137, www.alitalia.it *American Airlines*, opposite Hotel Corobicí, Av 5 bis, C 40-42, Sábana Este T257-1266, F222-5213, www.aa.com *Avianca*, Edif Centro Colón, p 2, Paseo Colón and C 38-40, T233-3066, F255-0940. *British Airways*, C 13, Av 11, T256-5264, F223-4863, www.british-airways.com *Continental*, Oficentro La Virgen, Edif #2, Pavas, T296-4911, F296-4920, www.continental.com *Copa*, Av 5, C 1, T222-6640, F221-6798, www.copaair.com *Delta*, 100 m east and 50 m south of Toyota, Paseo Colon, Ed Elizabeth, San José, T257-4141, F257-3344, www.delta.com *Grupo Taca*, see *SANSA* below. *Iberia*, Paseo Colón, C 40, T257-8266, F223-1055, www.iberia.com *Japan Airlines*, Paseo Colon, T257-4646, F258-3203, www.japanair.com *KLM*, behind Controlaría General Building, Sábana Sur, T220-4111, F220-3092, www.klm.com *LTU* (German charter airline), Condominio da Vinci, Oficina No 6, Barrio Dent, T234-9292. F234-8442, www.ltu.com *Martinair* (subsidiary of *KLM*) – Sábana Sur, behind Controlaría General Building, T220-4111, F220-3092, www.martinair.com *Mexicana*, C 5, Av 7-9, T257-6334, F257-6338, www.mexicana.com.mx *SANSA*, Casa Blanca, C 42 and Las Americas, La Sábana, T221-9414, F255-2176, www.flysansa.com *Travelair*, T220-3054, F220-0413, www.travelair-costarica.com *United Airlines*, Sábana Sur, behind Controlaría General Building, T220-2027, F220-4855, www.united.com

Banks Changing money in San José is not difficult. If you have a credit card, you can withdraw cash from ATMs dotted around the streets and found in the lobbies of some of the better hotels. Travellers' cheques (TCs) and dollars can be changed in many hotels and in banks where queues can be long and service slow – not particularly unique to Costa Rica but something to bare in mind. Opening hours are generally 0830-1530 with some opening a little later and on Saturdays.

Banco de Costa Rica, Av Central, C 6 y 4. 0800-1900. *Banco de Credito Agricola*, Av 4, C Central 1/2. 0800-1530. *Banco de San José*, Av 3 y 5, C Central, 0800-1900. MC ATMs. Cash advance against American Express, MC and Visa charging US$5 for up to US$1,500. 1% commission on TCs. *Banco Nacional*, Av 1-3, C 2 y 4. 0830-1900. 24-hr Visa ATMs, TCs and cash changed on the third floor, 1% commission. *Banco Popular*, Av 2, C 1. 0800-1500, Visa ATMs. *Financiera Londres*, Av 1, C Central, T258-3003, will take travellers' cheques and all major European currencies – no plans for the Euro. *OFINTERSA*, Casa de Cambio, Edificio Schyfter, 2nd floor, 20 m north of the junction of Av Central and C2. Will change TCs at 1% commission, no commission on cash. Open 0830-1700 can be quicker than the banks when they are busy. *Western Union*, Av 4, C 9-11, next to the *Tica Bus* office. Money transfer services, quicker than banks but you pay a price premium.

Internet *Cybercafé*, in the basement of Edificio Las Arcadas, next to the *Gran Hotel* **Communi-**
Costa Rica. Open 7 days a week, 0700-2300, very helpful staff, 250 colónes 10 mins, 600 **cations**
colónes 1 hr. Good machines, good atmosphere with a terrace café outside serving
excellent coffee and pizzas, newspapers. A rare thing indeed, a genuine internet café.
Internet Café, 4th floor, Av C, C4, open 0800-2400. A better way to spend less money at
just 500 colónes per hr and for each part of an hour, but scores a big zero on character
and where is the café? They do, however, have several branches around town includ-
ing 2nd floor, Av Central, C Los Estudiantes, open 0900-2100, at the western end of
Paseo Colón in Edifico Colón, C 38-40, and if you just have to tap all night there is a
24-hr café in San Pedro, close to *Banco Popular*. *Punta.com* shares the building of the
central post office at Av 1, C 2. Open 0900-2100 Mon-Fri, 1000-2100 Sat and 1000-1800
Sun. Still without character there is a ½ hr option costing 300 *colónes*, and 500 *colónes*
for the full hr. *RACSA* provide internet access at their offices at Av 1, C 5 charging US$3
for 1 hr, one of the more expensive internet providers.

The Central Post Office takes up much of a block with the entrance on C 2 between Av 1 **Post**
and 2, open 0730-1800, Mon-Fri, 0730-1200 Sat, closed Sun. If you are picking letters
up from the *Lista de Correos* you can read them in the traditionally decorated café
which serves excellent coffee and cakes in the post office building. The Museo de
Filateca may also take up a little of your time. There is a Visa ATM machine in the post
office, and parcel packing materials in a small store if required.

International courier services with *DHL*, Paseo Colón, C 30-32, T210-3838, F290-3000, **Couriers**
www.dhl.com *Jet Ex* (the Federal Express agent), on Pavas road, T293-0505, F239-3658,
www.jetex.co.cr *UPS*, Av 3, C 30-32, T290-2828, F232-8800, www.ups.com

The simplest way to make national and international telephone calls in San José is with **Telephone**
a phone card – the *Viajero Internacional* 199 cards are the most reliable to use. Avail- *There are lines of*
able in values of 100, 200, 500, 1000 and 3000 *colónes* from many of the small *tiendas*, *public telephones in*
you scratch off the security patch, enter 199 and then follow the instructions which *the Plaza de la Cultura*
include entering the rather long pin number on the back of the card. See Essentials, *and in Parque Central.*
page 52. If you want to use a credit card to pay for an international call, or to receive a *around the city*
fax, visit the *RACSA* (Radiografica Costarricense) office, Av 1, C 5, T287-0087. It also has
internet access.

Alianza Francesa, Av 7, C 5, T222-2283, F256-3360, French newspapers, French films **Cultural**
every Wed evening, friendly. *Centro Cultural Costarricense Norteamericano*, C 37, Av **centres**
1-5, Los Yoses, T207-7500, F290-2550, www.cccncr.com Good films, plays, art exhibi-
tions and English-language library, open until 1930. *Instituto Britanico*, 50 m south of
Automercado, Los Yoses, T234-9054. *Mexican Cultural Centre*, C 41, Av 10, T283-2333.

Belgium, Av 3, C 35-37, T225-6633, F225-0351, open 0800-1330. *Canada*, Building 5 **Embassies**
(3rd floor) of Oficentro Ejecutivo La Sábana, Sábana Sur, T296-4149, F296-4270, open
0800-1630, Fri until 1330. *France*, 200 m south, 25 m west of *Indoor Club*, Curridabat,
T234-4167, F225-7018, open 0830-1230. *Germany*, Rohrmoser, 200 m north and 75 m
east of the Casa de Oscar Arias, T232-5533, F231-6406, open 0900-1200. *Israel*, 11th
floor, Edificio Colon, Paseo Colón, C 38 y 40, T221-6444, F257-0867, open 0900-1230.
Italy, Av 10, C 33-35, Los Yoses, T234-2326, F225-8200, open 0900-1200. *Japan*, 3rd
floor, Edif #7, Oficentro La Sábana, Rohrmoser, T296-1650, F231-3140, open 0830-1200
and 1400-1700. *Mexico*, Av 7, C 13-15, T225-7284, F283-3867, open 0830-1230. *Neth-
erlands*, 3rd floor, Edif #3, Oficentro Ejecutivo La Sábana, T296-1490, F296-2933,
www.nethemb.or.cr open 0900-1200. *Nicaragua*, Av Central, C 25-27, opposite *Pizza
Hut*, T233-8747, F233-9225, open 0830-1130 and 1330-1500. *Panama*, C 38, Av 7

San José and around

San José and around

(275m north of Centro Colón building, Paseo Colón), T257-3241, F257-4864, open 0900-1400. *Spain*, C 32, Paseo Colón, T222-1933, F222-4180. *Switzerland*, 10th floor, Edif Colón, Paseo Colón, C 38, T221-4829, F255-2831, open 0900-1200. *United Kingdom*, 11th floor, Edif Colón, Paseo Colón, C 38, T258-2025, F233-9938, open 0800-1200. *United States*, opposite Centro Comericial, Pavas, T220-3939, F232-7944, usembassy.or.cr

Medical services The standard of medical facilities in Costa Rica, in San José in particular is very high with many doctors receiving additional training in North America and Europe. The best advice is to call your embassy and seek a recommendation. The clinic of choice for residents is *Clínica Bíblica*, C 1, Av 14, T257-5252, which also has an emergency service and a 24-hr pharmacy. *Hospital CIMA*, 1 km east of the Multiplaza on the Santa Ana road, T208-1000, is a modern hospital that opened in 2000. Fully equipped for 24-hr emergencies and pharmacy. Social Security Hospitals have good reputations (free to social security members), but few members of staff speak English: Dr Calderón Guardia (T222-4133), San Juan de Dios (T222-0166), México (T232-6122).

Readers have recommended the following should a problem arise: **Doctor**: Dr Jorge Quesada Vargas, Clinica Internacional, Av 14, C 3-5, speaks German. **Dentists**: Dra Fresia Hidalgo, Uned Building, San Pedro, 1400-1800, English spoken, reasonable prices, recommended, T234-2840. Fernando Baldioceda and Silvia Oreamuno, 225 m north of the Toyota intersection on Paseo Colón, both speak English. **Dermatologist**: Dr Elias Bonilla Dib, C Central, Av 7-9, T221-2025. Red Cross Ambulance, T221-5818. **Pharmacies** are widespread through the city, there are a couple on Av 2 close to the junction with C Central. There are also several close to Hospital San Juan on Paseo Colón.

Language schools The number of schools has increased rapidly in recent years. Listed below are a selection of schools that are widely respected or have been recommended by readers. *Academia Latinoamericana de Español*, Av 8, C 31-33, Apdo 1280-2050, San Pedro Montes de Oca, T224-9917, F225-8125, recajhi@sol.racsa.co.cr *Academia Tica*, out in San Isidro de Coronado, Apdo 1294, 2100 San José, T229-0013, F292-7136, www.academiatica.com *AmeriSpan*, PO Box 40007, Philadelphia, PA 19106-0007, T800-879-6640 (USA and Canada), T215-751-1100 (elsewhere), F215-751-1986, www.amerispan.com 8 affiliated schools in Escazú, Alajuela, Heredia and throughout the country. *Central American Institute for International Affairs*, Apdo 10302, 1000 San José, T233-8571, F221-5238, www.educaturs.com Conversation Spanish courses with accommodation with a Costa Rican family or in a small backpackers hotel. *Centro Linguistico Conversa*, Apdo 17, Centro Colón 1007, San José. T221-7649, toll free on T1-800-354-5036, F233-2418, www.conversa.co.cr A school in the centre of town and also out in Santa Ana. *Comunicare*, Apdo 1383-2050, San José, T/F224-4473, T1-800-367-7726, www.comunicare.co.cr Offering general language study and special interest courses covering medicine, environmental issues and Central American studies, and homestays, volunteer work and cultural activities. *Costa Rican Language Academy and Latin American Dance School*, Av Central, C 25-27, Apdo 336-2070, San José, T233-8914, F233-8670, www.learn-spanish.com With Latin American music and dancing on top of language study and local accommodation. *Costa Rica Spanish Institute*, in San Pedro district, Apdo 1366-2050, San Pedro, T234-1001, toll free on T1-800-771-5184, F253-2117, www.cosi.co.cr with a homestay in San José or the beach programme based in Manuel Antonio. The *Instituto Británico* in Los Yoses, Apdo 8184, 1000 San José, T225-0256, F253-1894, www.institutobritanico.co.cr with classes in English and Spanish. *Instituto de Español Costa Rica*, A 1, C Central – C 1, Apdo 1405-2100 Guadalupe, T280-6622, F283-4733, www.professionalspanish.com Close to the centre of San José, and complete with its own B&B (**C**). English, French and German spoken. Many special offers including 2 for 1, where the 2nd person receives the course for free. *Instituto Universal de Idiomas*, Av 2, C 9, Apdo 751-2150 Moravia, San José, T223-9662, F223-9917, www.universal-edu.com With the stress on conversational Spanish. *Intensa*, C 33, Av 1-3, Barrio Escalante, Apdo 8110-1000, T281-1818, F253-4337, www.intensa.com *Intercultura Language & Cultural Center*, Apdo 1952-3000, Heredia, T260-8480/260-9243, F260-9243, www.interculturacostarica.com

All but the very cheapest hotels will do laundry if requested. *Lavanderia Alemana*, C 19, Av 2-6, cheap, recommended. *Lavandería Costa Rica*, Av 3, C 19-21, US$5 for a large load. *Lavandería Lavamex*, Av Central y 1, C 8, in small shopping mall below *Gran Hotel Imperial*, T258-2303. US$6 wash and dry. Book swap, very popular with travellers. More than just a laundry, Karl and Patricia offer priceless travel advice on Costa Rica and can also help if you have problems. *Sixaola*, branches throughout San José, US$3.50 a load, 2-hr dry cleaning available, expensive. *Martinizing*, US franchise, at Curridabat, Sábana Oriente (by new ring road) and Escazú, recommended. **Laundry**

The *Biblioteca Nacional*, (National Library) Av 3 and C 15, is a useful reference resource for anyone looking to research Costa Rica with several current special interest periodicals, and copies of all national newspapers dating back to 1833. No lending facilities. Mon-Fri, 0800-1830, open to foreigners with identification. The *Centro Cultural Costarricense Norteamericano*, C 37, Av 1-5, has a good library. Also check out the *Universidad de Costa Rica* in San Pedro suburb, eastern of downtown San José. **Libraries**

Centro de los Amigo C 15, A 6 bis (between Av 6-8), T/F233-6168. *Escazú Christian Fellowship*, Country Day School campus, Sun 1730. *International Baptist Church*, San Pedro, T253-7911. *Roman Catholic*, services in English at the *Herradura Hotel*, 1600 every Sun. *Union Church*, Moravia, T235-6709, services at 1000, free bus service from downtown hotels. Also see the *Tico Times* for times and location. **Places of worship**

Immigration is on the airport highway, opposite *Hospital México*. You need to go here for exit visas, extensions, etc. If they are busy, you could queue all day. To get there, take bus 10 or 10A Uruca, marked 'México', then cross over highway at the bridge and walk 200 m along highway. Better to find a travel agent who can obtain what you need for a fee, say US$5. Make sure you get a receipt if you give up your passport. **Judiciary**, thefts should be reported in San José to Recepción de Denuncias, Organismo de Investigación Judicial (OIJ), C19, Av 6-8, T222-1365. The *Sistema Nacional de Areas de Conservación* (SINAC, Apdo 10104-1000, T234-0973, F283-7343) in San José administers the National Park system. For information and permits to visit and/or camp in the Parks apply to *Fundación de Parques Nacionales* (FPN), 300 m north and 150 m east of Santa Teresita Church, Barrio Escalante, C 23, 15, San José, T257-2239, F222-4732, open Mon-Fri 0800-1200, 1300-1700. Most permits can be obtained at park entrances, but **Useful addresses** *In emergencies dial 911*

San José and around

check in advance if your trip depends on gaining entrance. To contact park personnel by radio link or make accommodation reservations, T233-4160, but good Spanish is a help (bilingual operators at National Parks can be reached by dialing 192). If you make reservations at their San José office, make sure they have made them direct with the park and that you have clear references on the confirmation to avoid difficulties on arrival. If you want to work as a volunteer in the parks, contact *SINAC*. An alternative is to contact *ASVO*, 8, Calle 25, San José, T222-5085, F233-4989, asvo89@racsa.co.cr

Escazú and Western suburbs

Outside the boundaries of the city of San José, the fashionable suburb of Escazú made a break for independence several years ago. Away from the chaotic traffic and noise of the city centre, Escazú has the charm and feel of a small village which slowly creeps up the hills to the south.

Hotels and restaurants make the most of the setting on the lower slopes affording spectacular views across the Central Valley. Many expats living in Costa Rica would not dream of spending a night in the capital, choosing instead to stay in Escazú carrying out their business with a series of 20-min commutes by bus or taxi, keeping the capital's contamination to a bare minimum. First-time visitors to Costa Rica should spend at least some time in the capital. But if you're returning from previous visits, you'll know that Escazú has much to offer.

Getting there Buses leave the capital from C16, Av Central every 10 mins.

Sights Over and above the small-town feel Escazú has little in the way of sights. In keeping with the Central Valley way of things, the three smaller towns that make up the Escazú experience – San Rafael, San Miguel and further up the hill San Antonio – each has a church. Up in San Antonio de Escazú the bustle of the lower slopes has gone, and just enough adobe houses exist around the central plaza to create the effect of a village settlement. Facing the square the modest church of San Antonio de Escazú has a beautiful setting overlooking the valley of San José, even if the bright green of the church is a little painful on the eye against the rusty-browns and natural-greens of the village.

A couple of things draw Escazú out. **Día del Boyero** (Day of the Oxcart Driver), on the second Sunday of March, is one of the country's largest festivals. It fills the sleepy streets with colourful oxcarts parading through San Antonio de Escazú accompanied by music on *marimbas* (a kind of xylophone) and dancers in traditional dress. Another is the **wooden carvings** of Barry Biesanz, T228-1811, F228-6184, www.biesanz.com Using a mix of dark and light woods, Biesanz is one of the country's craftspeople who has created a distinctive style. The fine bowls are beautifully simple in shape and form with a lightness and fineness that seems almost unnatural. The boxes – be they humidors, jewellery boxes or simply what Barry calls for "small things" – are exquisite. You don't have to trek up to the workshop to buy a Biesanz piece, they are available in good souvenir shops in San José and in the *El Pueblo* commercial center.

A more mainstream shopping experience in Escazú includes, a number of modern shopping plazas on the main road running north to south. It seems a long way to come to walk through a shopping mall. But if that is where your interest lies, there are a couple along the main street of Calle Leon Cortes. To the north of town on Highway 27 you'll find Costa Rica's largest – the

Multiplaza. *E-Music* is in Multiplaza, T288-2000. Truly international music choice with Latin, Brazilian, African and Middle Eastern.

LL-L *Alta*, Escazú, T282-4160, F282-4162, in the US or Canada call 1-800-388-2582, **Sleeping** www.altatravelplanners.com Heading west out of Escazú on the old road to Santa Ana is this beautiful Mediterranean-style hotel with 23 rooms, each with a balcony overlooking the Central Valley, are fully-equipped with private bath, cable TV, a/c and telephone. Stylish hardwood furniture sits beautifully on the terracotta tiled floor contrasted against the maize-toned stucco walls. In the landscaped gardens is the glass-tiled pool and massage and reflexology is also available. Dining is at the stylish La Luz restaurant. **LL-L** *Camino Real* Próspero Fernández Highway, Multiplaza Mall, Escazú, T289-7000, F289-8930, www.interconti.com A mega-hotel which impresses from the moment you enter. Costa Rica's nature theme transfers to the rooms which have natural names as opposed to numbers. The rooms are fully equipped and suited for both business traveller and vacationer. 3 restaurants include the award-winning Mirage French restaurant, the international cuisine of Azulejos and the poolside Bananas Wet Bar & Grill. **LL-L** *Tara Resort Hotel*, San Antonio de Escazú, T228-6992, F228-9651, in the US, Canada and Mexico toll free on 1-800-405-5112, www.tararesort.com It's a long way up the hill to this beautiful plantation-style resort hotel, but the management probably don't give a damn. Once there, you're unlikely to leave. The former stately manor is now one of the most luxurious resort hotels in Costa Rica with 15 rooms, each decorated in a different style, reflecting the luxuries of the deep south. Many rooms have a spectacular view over the Central Valley, as does the Atlanta dining room. Outdoors there is a pool and a small garden lawn. And you're within walking distance of Pico Blanco mountain just to the south.

L-AL *San Gildar*, San Rafael de Escazú, 250 m west of Costa Rica Country Club, T289-8843, F228-6454, www.hotelsangildar.com Each of the 27 rooms overlooks the swimming pool surrounded by lush tropical gardens. The rooms have private bath, television and telephone. The *Terraza del Sol* restaurant overlooks the garden and pool, the service is excellent and the size of the hotel makes it a popular choice. **L-AL** *Posada El Quijote*, Bello Horizonte de Escazú, Apdo 1127-1250, T289-8401, F289-8729, toll free in the US and Canada on 1-800-570-6750, ext 8401, www.quijote.co.cr Renovated colonial house with modern art collection and fantastic view over the Central Valley. Private bathroom with hot water and cable TV. The breakfast is legendary and the garden patio relaxing. 10 mins from centre, 15 mins from airport. Airport pick-up available. **AL** *Pine Tree Inn*, San Rafael de Escazú, T289-7405, F228-2180, www.hotels.co.cr/pine.html 15 rooms each with private bath and cable TV. There is a pool and the price includes breakfast. **AL** *La Casa de las Tías*, 100 m south of Centro Comercial El Cruce, San Rafael de Escazú, T289-5517, F289-7353, www.hotels.co.cr/casatias.html 5 rooms in a large Victorian-style house, decorated with art from throughout Latin America. Price includes breakfast, each room has private bath and fan, airport pick-up available. **AL-A** *Amstel Escazú*, 300 m south of the Centro Comercial El Cruce, T228-1764, F282-0620, escazu@sol.racsa.co.cr The 14 rooms are pretty basic in terms of character and there are a couple of suites. There is also a pool and parking.

A *Pico Blanco Inn*, San Antonio de Escazú some 3 km up in the hills, T228-1908, F289-5189. All 20 rooms have balconies and great views of the Central Valley. Also a couple of self-contained cottages and a pool. English owner explaining the restaurant with English pub. Airport pick-up can be requested which will make finding the place easier. Price includes breakfast. Recommended. **A** *Villa Escazú B&B*, 1 km southwest of Escazú, T/F228-7971, www.hotels.co.cr/vescazu.html 6 comfortable rooms sharing 3 bathrooms in this Swiss-chalet style home rich in Costa Rican hardwoods. Good views from the garden patio, price includes breakfast. Ask for Inéz or Mary Ann who are

San José and around

appreciated as attentive and helpful hosts by guests. **A-B** *Costa Verde Inn*, 300 m south of the cemetery, T228-4080, F289-8591, www.hotelcostaverde.com A secluded and charming country home with 12 imaginatively-decorated rooms – a popular choice away from the centre of town. Tropical gardens surround a swimming pool, and in the evenings you can sit round the fireplace.

B *Tapezco Inn*, 25 m south west of San Miguel church, Escazú, T228-1084, F289-7026, info@tapezco-inn.co.cr Close to the main square, the simple rooms all have private bath with hot water. There's a jacuzzi, sauna and price includes breakfast.

Apartotels LL *Apartotel Villa de Río*, San Rafael de Escazú, 25 m before Costa Rica Country Club, T289-8833, F289-8835, www.villasdelrio.com 40 luxury apartments fully equipped with kitchenettes, including cable TV with VCR and smoke detectors. There is also a gymnasium, pool, sauna and transportation to city centre. Very secure and very smart. **L-AL** *Apartotel Maria Alexandra*, in San Rafael, T228-1507, F289-5192, www.mariaalexandra.com Comfortable apartments and town houses for 2 to 5 people, all with fully equipped kitchenette. The apartments have a laundry room, a/c, telephone and cable TV. There is also a swimming pool and a sauna. Discounts with longer stays.

Eating &
drinking
As with
accommodation,
eating out tends
to be in the higher
price brackets

Expensive *La Luz* in *Hotel Alta* on the road to Santa Ana, T282-4160, serves a California–Costa Rica fusion mix. Iron-work chandeliers and heavy wood beams set the atmosphere and the valley view is superb. In the restaurant's own words, "Dining at *La Luz* pushes every corner of the culinary envelope."! *Le Monastère* takes refuge in a restored monastery in the hills of Escazú. T289-4404. The international menu is served as "ritual, a celebration of life and a combination of mysticism." Add the twinkling lights in the valley below and this is memorable dining at its best. High on the lower slopes of the Pico Blanco hills, the *Atlanta* restaurant of the Tara Hotel is as sumptuous as the hotel. Wooden flooring and panelled walls warmed by the flickering flames of the fireplace set a tone of sheer elegance. Through the windows the night sky of San José and the Central Valley gently shimmers. The food is European continental and the experience is unforgettable.

Mid-range Rated by some as one of the best Italian restaurants in Costa Rica *Cerutti* T228-4511 is a smart restaurant in a 100-year old house in Escazú. Decorated with antiques and candles, the restaurant's speciality is "high Italian". Mid-range and upwards. *Chango* is on the outskirts of central Escazú, T228-1173, does a good trade with steaks and grills. *El Che*, T228-1598, is just to the south of San Rafael, and serves up a traditional Argentine *parillada* experience: meats grilled before your eyes.

In San Rafael the ever-popular *Il Capriccio*, T228-9332, serves good Italian. *El Exotico Oriente*, in front of *Scotiabank*, serves Indonesian and Thai dishes – the *padthai* is quite good and authentic. *Villa Rey*, on C Vieja toward Santa Ana, T289-5028. Chinese restaurant with traditional *cantones* dishes.

Not far from Autopista Prospero Fernandez is *La Cascada*, T228-0906, a long-time seafood and steak house favourite with *Ticos* and visitors alike. It's simple, popular and the food will fill you up. Nearby is *BBQ Los Anonos*, T228-0180, which serves meat dishes and is also popular. *María Alexandra* in the apartotel of the same name in San Rafael, T228-1507, is popular with a friendly atmosphere serving an international and European menu.

Saving the best almost until last, traditional fare is the order of the day at *Tiquicia*, south of Escazú, T289-5839. Quite an adventure to get here, the views are unbeatable day or night. Served in a positively rustic setting, Tiquicia is an institution and would be more so if the hours weren't so erratic. Mon-Fri 1700-midnight, Sat 1100-midnight, Sun 1100-1800, if they feel like it! Call first and check. Get a taxi or a 4-wheel drive if going after rain. Prices vary greatly but all in the expensive range.

There are several bars around San Rafael and San Antonio districts which are popular hang-outs with cool young *Ticos*, including **Fandango** in San Rafael.

About your only option on the cheap front here is the usual globally encompassing fast food chains. There are also several eateries in the various shopping malls where you can pick up a snack. See 'Cafés' below though. **Cheap**

Bagelman´s, Galerías San Rafael, T228 4460. Ten kings of bagel for 30 cents each. Open 0700-2200, Sun-Thu, 0700-2300, Fri-Sat. The **Deli Mundo**, Plaza Colonial, San Rafael de Escazú, serves light dishes of Jewish recipes, fresh juices and sells bagels. Across the way from *Bagelman's* is **La Chocolateria**, hand-made chocolate and cakes, quiet and elegant atmosphere, cozy. **Il Panino**, in Multicentro Paco 2 km west of Escazú on the old road to Santa Ana, is the best café in town. Smart, sharp and chic well dressed crowd, with Italian coffee or local brews. Surprisingly affordable, with great selection of Latin, Arabic, Italian and Turkish music. Sometimes shows classic old silent movies. Open until 2300 in the week, 0100 Fri and Sat. Next door is **Tre Fratelli**, a mid-range Italian with good pasta. **Cafés**

Cinema *Cine Colonial*, T289-9000, Plaza Colonia, San Rafael. A couple of theatres generally showing the latest international releases. *Cineplex* in the Multiplaza with US and European releases. **Entertainment**

Bowling *Metro Bowl*, next to the Multiplaza, open 1100-2400, Mon-Thu, until 0200 on Fri and Sat.

Art galleries *Galería Klaus Steinmetz Arte Contemporáneo* is right in the centre of Escazú, T289-5403. A couple of floors exhibiting and selling works from famous artists from all over Latin America. Definitely worth a look. *Café de Artistas*, T228-6045, exhibits only foreign painters and ceramics. Open Tue-Sat, 0730-1830. Closed Mon.

Language schools *Academia De Idiomas*, Escazú, Apdo 025216-SJO 491, Miami, Florida, 33102, T/F228-7736 or 385 4755, www.crspanish.com or *Ileri Instituto de Lenguas y Relaciones International*, Apdo 191, Escazú, San José, T289-4396, F228-1687.

Santa Ana

Growing quickly on the back of the popularity of Escazú, Santa Ana is a popular gringo hang-out and a place to stop over if heading out to the Pacific and looking for a place to stop for a while.

A *Hotel Posada Canal Grande*, T282-4089, F282-5733, www.novanet.co.cr/ canal Beautiful and elegant tropical paradise with wonderful views, designed and owned by friendly Mario from Turín (Italy). Sauna, small pool, rooms with cable TV and private bathrooms. Indonesian and Indian furniture, price includes breakfast. **Sleeping**

Las Carretas de Santa Ana, 200 m west of ICE Santa Ana, T282-5441. Delicious *arroz con pollo* or *camarones* served up in a colonial atmosphere. Recommended. **Restaurant Don Cipriano**, Montes de Santa Ana, T282-6308. Mexican restaurant with excellent tacos – open daily till 23:00. **Restaurant Hacienda** has typical Costa Rican dishes. *Santa Ana´s Tex Mex*, 75 m south of ICE, T282-6342. Popular expat hangout. **Eating**

Shopping Handcrafts are available at *Ceramica El Girasol*, 225 m east of Red Cross, T282-7886, and *Ceramica Valle Soleado*, 200 m east of the beach, T282-7816. Both sell beautiful ceramic cups, pots and dishes. You can fill up your vehicle at *Lubicentro JCHA*, and internet is available at *Café El Sol*, open from 0800-2200.

Transport Buses leave **San José** from the Coco-Cola terminal to Santa Ana Centro.

San José and around

Central highlands and the surrounding area

4

Central highlands and the surrounding area

142 Background

143 Alajuela and surrounding area

155 Heredia and surrounding area

165 Cartago and surrounding area

173 Turrialba and surrounding area

Bordered by mountains and looming volcanic peaks Costa Rica's Central Highlands are a curious mix of national parks, vibrant market towns and sleepy agricultural communities. And the nation's coffee heritage, evident in the neat lines of shimmering bushes that rise and fall with the contours of the lowland slopes, is very much alive and well.

Like the "golden bean", people flourish in the consistently temperate climate. Over two-thirds of the population live in these fertile valleys, home to the satellite towns of Alajuela, Heredia and Cartago which all once fought for domination of the region. Each now lives in the shadow of San José, with a feel that subtly betrays history and purpose; Alajuela's transience, the energy and creativity of Heredia and the shell-shocked wanderings and divine peregrinations of Cartago.

Heavenly inspiration and of coffee wealth created an impressive sense of civic pride. Even the smallest towns have churches of cathedral proportions. Equally unusual are the Dali-esque topiary creations of Zarcero and the frighteningly successful craft centre of Sarchí.

The volcanic national parks of Irazú and Poás, huff and fume, keeping everyone on their toes. Braulio Carrillo National Park, a vast area of primary rainforest, is ideal for guided walks, aerial tram rides and hiking up Volcán Barva. The calm of the Orosí Valley and the orchids of Lankester Gardens are worth a few hours of your time and the more adventurous can strike out through the rainforests of the Tapantí National Park, or get soaked rafting down the mighty Reventazón and Pacuare rivers.

Background

First impressions of the Central Highlands do little to inspire – the view of the Autopista General Cañas from a bus or cab running between the airport and San José might make it difficult to believe there is any nature out there. But beyond the urban landscape of the freeway, the fertility of the Central Highlands is the driving force behind modern Costa Rica. Colloquially called the *Meseta Central*; the literal translation means "central plateau". The volcanoes of Poás and Barva to the north, Irazú and Turrialba to the east and the northern limits of the Talamanca massif to the south create hundreds of rivers that have shaped and scarred the landscape. Only Turrialba sends all its rivers to one ocean the Caribbean, the rest preferring to share the rainfall between the Caribbean and Pacific.

After a brief foray through the region for easy pickings, colonization of Costa Rica was late in coming compared to its Central American neighbours. Although Columbus first landed in Limón in 1502, it was not until 1561 that the first permanent settlement of Garcimuñoz was founded in the western Central Highlands. The founding of Cartago in 1563 marks the beginning of the country's colonization proper, with cattle ranching, mule breeding and *cacao* farming sustaining the families of Cartago despite constant and ongoing uprisings from indigenous peoples protesting against the slave system of the *encomienda (see page 404)*. Fixed communities began to spring up across the fertile valley among them Heredia (1706), San José (1736) and later Alajuela (officially 1782).

Indifferent economic growth became prosperity with the introduction of coffee in the early 1800s and the region rapidly grew to produce and finally export sufficient quantities to fund the development of a vibrant middle-class. Comfortable temperatures ranging from 15°-23°C with rich volcanic soils and highland sun created perfect conditions for what became known as the "golden bean".

Despite the vagaries of the global coffee market, the wealth created from exports inspired and funded ecclesiastical architecture on an intensity of scale rarely seen. A spectacular trail of churches leads from one town to the next through the central highlands where ornate masonry and fine stained glasswork stand as monuments to priorities and wealth.

The rise of the banana in the tropical lowlands, the fall in coffee prices in the early 20th century, and greater access to education moved the focus away from coffee élites and the simple classification of the highlands ended. Today, the towns and cities have thrived or struggled depending on their respective histories. Agriculture has diversified beyond the golden bean. Economic necessity and the growth of communication has broken down the old barriers of time and distance. But instead of breaking down to become one large amalgamation of the central highlands many towns have held on to their differences, all the time watched over by the volcanic peaks that have created and shared the region's destiny.

Alajuela and surrounding area

Capital of the province of Alajuela, and just over 2 km from the international air- Colour map 2, grid B2
port, this once-quiet market town reflects the realities of modern living. Walking Population: 53,430
the streets, the atmosphere is one of latent energy, a feeling of nonchalance secure Altitude: 952 m
in the knowledge that if the townspeople tried, really tried, they could make a
world of difference. After all, the town and indeed the national hero Juan
Santamaría was born here and he, only a lad at the time, single-handedly saved
the country from foreign invasion in the battle of 1856.

The tempo picks up at weekends when farmers converge on the town from the
surrounding hills selling fruit, vegetables, flowers and dairy goods. It is difficult to
believe this is Costa Rica's third largest city – you won't be rushed off your feet. For
many Alajuela is an ideal spot to catch an early morning flight, to collapse after a
late-night arrival or as an alternative to staying in San José. It makes a good base
for exploring the craft centre of Sarchí, heading out to the Butterfly farm in La
Gúacima, the Zoo Ave bird sanctuary or up to the crater of Volcán Poás.

Ins and outs

Buses from San José run every 10 mins or so from C 10, Av Central - 2 and Av 2, C 10-12, **Getting**
with the latter location providing a half hourly service through the night between 2400 **there**
and 0500. Buses to San José leave from the main bus terminal and from Av 4 and C 2-4.
Take your pick, both cost 130 *colónes*. To get to the airport simply get on a bus going to
San José, from the airport, get a bus going to Alajuela. A taxi will cost about US$3.

Sights

Small enough to walk round, the town focuses on the **Central Plaza** shaded by
huge mango trees – a clear and obvious symbol giving lead to the town's mon-
iker as the 'city of mangoes'. When not craning your neck looking up in the
trees for the mythical sloths, join in the general mêlée of underactivity with the
townsfolk sitting on benches dotted through the plaza. There is an art to such
inactivity which requires practice.

An energetic meander of at most 100 m, will take you to the domed **Cathe-
dral** which was closed for renovation following earthquake damage in 1991.
Now reopened, the cathedral is one of several 19th- century buildings around
the plaza which suffer from general neglect. A more interesting church, in set-
ting as much as style, is **La Agonía** five blocks east of the plaza.

A monument to Juan Santamaría, the drummer boy who torched the
building in Rivas (Nicaragua) in which William Walker's filibusters were
entrenched in 1856 (see page 406), thus ending his plans for domination of
Central America, stands proud a couple of blocks south of the plaza. The
Museo Histórico Juan Santamaría, one block north of the plaza at Av 3 and
C 2, tells a somewhat confusing account of the war. A collection of paintings,
maps and descriptions mumble their way through events in Spanish. The
desire to improve the exhibitions and the centre is ongoing and expansion
plans include a Fosteresque glass conservatory in the central courtyard. How-
ever, with permission and funds lacking, the idea is certain to take several
years to get off the ground. ■ *Tue-Sun 1000-1800, closed Sun, US$2.*

On Saturday the **market** and surrounding areas can be a pleasantly chaotic
scene with the comings and goings of buyers and sellers and the oh-so-impor-
tant opportunity to catch up on social developments.

Central highlands & the surrounding area

Essentials

Sleeping
■ *on map*
Price codes:
see inside front cover

Without exception, no one knows street names and numbers. When looking for hotels, aim for the nearest landmark

In town A-C *Hotel 1915*, C 2, Av 5-7, 300 m north of Central Park, T/F441-0495. Beautiful old family home smartly refurbished with wooden furnishings and a stylish garden patio café. Very pleasant service. Rooms all have cable TV, mini fridge, telephone and price includes breakfast. Parking available. There are also several apartments just half a block away sleeping up to five people (**AL**). Best in town for the price and no prizes for guessing when the place was built.

B *Hotel Alajuela*, on corner across from Central Park at Av Central and C 2, T441-1241, F441-7912, alajuela@racsa.co.cr 50 generally good, although fairly standard rooms and apartments all with private bathroom. Exceptionally helpful staff and a garden patio and large restaurant. **B** *Charly's Place*, a couple of blocks north of the central park on Av 5, C Central-1, T/F441-0115, lilyhotel@latinmail.com Popular place, although slightly overpriced, with 14 rooms most with private bathrooms, **C** without, some with TV. Good source of information on activities and handy services for the newly arrived or just departing such as international calls and fax, laundry, use of kitchen and patio for relaxing. Breakfast in high season, parking available. Credit cards accepted. **B** *Islands B&B*, Av 1, C 7-9, 50 m west of La Agonía church, T442-0573, F442-2909, islandbb@racsa.co.cr A small family-run *Tico*-owned B&B with 8 comfortably decorated rooms. Rooms have cable TV, free local calls. Breakfast is served in a simple breakfast room spreading across to a small garden patio. Airport pick-up available, very secure and 24-hr parking.

C *Mango Verde Hostel*, Av 3, C 2-4, T441-6630, mangover@racsa.co.cr 6 clean rooms with private bath and hot water, and the courtyard and communal area create a relaxing atmosphere. Use of kitchen for guests, parking available and close to the centre of town. **C-D** *Pension Alajuela*, Av 9, C Central-2, opposite the court house,

Alajuela

To Buena Vista Hotel, Pura Vida B&B, Tuetal Lodge & Volcán Poas

	Sleeping				Eating
	1 1915	7 Mango Verde		●	1 Da Lucia
	2 Alajuela	8 Pensión Alajuela			2 El Cencerro
	3 Central Alajuela	9 Villa Real			3 Pizza Cayo
	4 Charly's Place				4 Pizza Hut
	5 Cortez Azul				5 Senor Gazpacho
	6 Islands B&B				6 Trigo Miel

0 metres 200
0 yards 200

T/F441-6251. Mixed bag of 10 simple rooms, some with private bath, some without. Each otherwise rather bare room has been painted with a nature scene. There's a small bar downstairs as well as a laundry and fax service. 24-hr parking lot next door.

D-E *Central Alajuela*, Av Central, C 8, close to the bus terminal, T443-8437. Under new administration, the rooms are pretty basic, the shared bathrooms have cold water but it is reasonably clean. Popular with *Ticos* arriving from out of town. **E** *Cortez Azul*, Av 3, C 2-4, 100 m west of Museo Juan Santamaría, T443-6145, corteazul@latinmail.com New place just opening up aimed at the backpacker. Still decorating late 2000 but looked promising. **E-F** *Villa Real*, Av 3, C 1, T441-4022. Claims of cleanliness are largely unjustified, but the place is popular with travellers and you can use the kitchen and wash clothes. Probably the cheapest place in town.

5 km north of Alajuela is **LL** *Villas Xandari*, T443-2020, F442-4847, toll free on 1-800-686-7879, www.xandari.com Formerly a coffee finca *Xandari* is an inspirational creation from the minds of Californian architect Sherrill Broudy and his wife Charlene. More a mind and body experience than a hotel. Overlooking the Central Valley with beautiful views and calming music from the restaurant balcony day and night, Xandari eschews conventions of room shape and design, drawing on Moorish origins. Each of the 16 excessively spacious private villas has a balcony, private bathrooms with all imaginable comforts. The restaurant revels in the organic produce of Xandari's gardens. If the calming serenity is not sufficient, you can wander through trails, dip in the pool or have a massage in the tropical garden. Without doubt, one of Costa Rica's most impressive hotels. **Around town**

AL *Las Orquídeas Inn*, further north on the road out to Grecía at the Alajuela, La Garita, San Pedro de Poás fork, T433-9346, F433-9740, www.hotels.co.cr/orquideas.html 12 spacious rooms with bath, 4 rooms shared bath, no children under 13 accepted, pick-ups from airport 10 mins away can be arranged. The Inn has a pool, and the restaurant are recommended.

A *Buena Vista*, 7 km north of Alajuela on the road to Volcán Poás, T442-8605, F442-8701, in the US and Canada 1-800-506-2304, www.arweb.com/buenavista/ 25 large rooms come with private bathroom and cable TV, many with balconies providing views of the Central Valley or Volcán Poás. Overlooking the Central Valley, this modern, tidy plantation-style hotel has an understated charm. Services include pool, well stocked gift shop, restaurant with a good mix of international dishes and wines and a quiet bar. Kids welcome. In the district of **Tuetal** to the northwest of Alajuela is **A-B** *Pura Vida B&B*, 2 km, T/F441-1157. Proprietor Katy Crawford runs a tight ship with 5 rooms and 3 bungalows equipped with kitchenettes. Well lit garden paths lead between gardens of tropical flowers and distant views of Volcán Poás. Katy knows Costa Rica well and can book rental cars, organize excursions and arrange airport pick-ups. **B** *Tuetal Lodge*, 3 km north of Alajuela, T442-1804,, www.islandnet.com/~tuetal/ Cabins in 5 acres of gardens, some with kitchenette, pool, restaurant, games room. Also has accommodation in the form of treehouses (**F**), a **camping** area (**F**) and plans to open a hostel. Very popular with 'young Americans'.

AL *Hampton Inn*, T443-0043, F442-9523 (toll free within Costa Rica 800-426-7866), www.hamptonhotel.co.cr Closest hotel to the airport, handy if you want to get in or get out quickly with the minimum of fuss, made easier with a courtesy pick-up. As with every Hampton Inn, the price includes continental breakfast, free local calls, free stay for kids and the 3rd and 4th adult sharing the same room. Add the free-form pool and complimentary transportation to and from the airport and this could be the final post you're looking for. **A** *La Rosa de America*, in Barrio San José on the road to Atenas, T433-2741. Pool, restaurant, fan, hot water. Recommended. **Close to the airport**

Central highlands & the surrounding area

B *Posada Aeropuerto B&B*, behind Juan Santamaría airport on road to Ojo de Agua, T/F441-7569, posada@sol.racsa.co.cr Free transport from airport, some rooms with private bath, useful for early flights.

Eating ● *on map*	Finding something to eat in Alajuela is not difficult, most restaurants and cafés are within a block or two of the Central Park. *El Cencerro* on Av Central facing the south side of Central Park, T441-4214. Crisp décor and clean restaurant specializing in grills and meat. Balcony overlooking the park which more than compensates for the mid-range price. *Las Concinas de Leña*, C 2, Av 6, is well established serving grills and seafood at mid-range prices. *Pizza Cayo*, C 1, Av 1-3, has a simple rustic charm, with good pizzas. *Restaurant da Lucia*, near Alajuela hotel on the corner of C 2 and Av 2, has good cheap Italian meals overlooking Parque Juan Santamaría. *Señor Gazpacho* on Av Central, C Central-1, is a popular dining spot serving Mexican dishes. Cheap. Several international fast food chains can be found on C Central leading south from Central Park.
Cafés, bars, nightclubs & entertainment	*Trigo Miel*, Av 2, C Central-2 is one of a couple of pâtisserie-style cafés in Alajuela serving divine snacks, good coffee topped off with a classy sense of style and finesse. There are a number of *sodas* dotted round the square and down C Central. Bars and nightclubs are limited in Alajuela with most people choosing to head into San José, but there are a couple overlooking the Central Park. *La Troja*, south of town, is always popular, but ask locally for the latest hotspots.
Festivals	**Juan Santamaría Day** on the *11th Apr* sees the town celebrate the life of the town's most famous son; commemorating the Battle of Rivas in 1856 with a week of general celebration, bands, concerts and dancing. *Mid-Jul* the fruitful heritage comes to the fore with a **Mango Festival** with parades, public concerts and an arts and crafts fair.
Shopping	Not much to splash cash on around Alajuela but *Llobet's*, Av Central-1, C 2-4, is a local institution and a rather amusing department store selling almost everything but rather strangely nothing you really want. *Fuji* have a store selling print and slide film on C Central, Av Central-2.
Sport	The local football team is Liga Deportiva Alajuelense or more simply *La Liga*, one of Costa Rica's best league teams. Games are normally on Sun but check locally for details, see local press or just watch for everyone heading to the stadium in the northeast corner of the town on match days. *Batik Rent a bike*, T443-0503, balibatik@hotmail.com offer bike rental but could well be a fly-by-night operation. Stop in at *Charly's Place* to get the latest information.
Tour operators	With so many tour operators in San José, Alajuela doesn't even bother trying to compete. *OTEC* have an office on C 2, Av Central-2, T442-4018, F442-7401, and although aimed at students and those in education, they should be able to help with most problems. *Faytur*, Av 3, C 2-4, T443-4171, F440-2230, faytur@racsa.co.cr Provides a wide range of services, primarily hotel bookings, car rentals and flights.
Transport	**Bus** Buses leave from the bus terminal or one of the many street stops nearby. Buses to **San José** leave from the main bus terminal and from the station at Av 4, C 2-4. The latter also provides a half-hourly service between 2400 and 0500. Take your pick, both charge 130 *colónes*. From **San José** buses leave from C 10, Av Central-2 and Av 2, C 10-12 with the latter providing the 24-hr service. Regular buses to **Heredia** leave from the terminal with the first at 0400 and the last at 2300. Buses to the **Butterfly Farm** at **La Guácima** marked "*La Guácima abajo*" leave from Av 2 between C 8-10. One block south of the terminal, buses depart from a muddy block to several small villages in the area, including **Laguna de Fraijanes** and **Volcán Poás**.

Banks Absolutely no shortage of banks to choose from and all within 3 blocks of each **Directory**
other. *Banco Nacional*, C 2, Av Central-1, is facing Central Park. *Banco Interfin* next
door has Visa and MasterCard ATMs. One block south of Central Park is *Banco Credito
Agricola de Cartago*, C 2, Av Central-2, and 2 blocks north is *Banco de Santa Cruz*, C 2,
Av 3, which is also the offices of *Credomatic*. **Communications** Internet: several
internet places around town but none firmly established. *Interplanet*, across from La
Agonía church on Av Central and C 9, stands out largely due to the fluorescent lighting.
Open every day 0830-2200. **Post office**: on the corner of Av 5 and C 1, Mon-Fri,
0730-1700. **Medical services** In emergency: T911. *San Rafael Hospital*, Av 9, C Cen-
tral-1, T440-1333, can help in a crisis. There are several pharmacies around town.

South and west of Alajuela

There are a couple of water parks within a few kilometres of Alajuela. *Ojo de* **Ojo de Agua**
Agua, T441-2808, is a spring-fed water park about 6 km south of town with a **& Water Land**
series of swimming pools including a children's pool, an Olympic pool for the
serious swimmer and a boating lake. There are areas for picnics, playing
games and generally having a good time and much of San José seems to
decamp here at weekends. ■ *Open until 1700 daily, US$1.20, children under 6
free, US$0.80 for parking. Direct bus from Av 1, C 20-22 in San José or take bus
to Alajuela and then on to San Antonio de Belén. Water Land*, formerly *Acua
Mania*, is an aquatic theme park just off the airport highway on the road to San
Antonio de Belén, which has pretty much every option going on the water
front. Water slides, a wave machine and underwater caves and miniature golf,
picnic areas and landscaped gardens for brief moments to dry out. It's a far
more upmarket affair than *Ojo de Agua*. ■ *Tue-Fri 0900-1700, Sat and Sun
members only. US$6.50 per person. T293-2891.*

The small town of La Guácima de Alajuela, some 20 km west of San José and **La Guácima**
7 km from Alajuela, would be a sleepy little backwater if it weren't for the **Butterfly Farm**
buses filled with visitors arriving to see the world's second largest exporter of
butterflies – the largest one is believed to be in Taiwan. The farm is a fascinat-
ing insight to the lifecycle of the butterfly. After a short introductory video, a
tour leads you through enclosed tropical gardens where the guide points out
some of the 120 native species at every stage of development explaining details
of habits and preferences.

Set up in 1984 by Joris Brinckerhoff, a former Peace Corp volunteer, the
Butterfly Farm was opened to the public in 1990. After visiting the laborato-
ries and completing the 90-minute tour you are free to wonder through the
fascinating gardens and enjoy the experience at a more leisurely pace. Visiting
in the morning, especially in the rainy season, is strongly recommended as the
butterflies tend to take shelter when it is raining or overcast.

■ *Daily 0830-1700, US$15 adults, US$9 students, US$7 children under
12, includes guided tour every 2 hrs, T438-0400, F438-0300,
www.butterflyfarm.co.cr Bus for La Guácima Mon-Sat from Av 1, C 20-22,
1100 and 1400, return 1515, 1 hr journey, US$0.40. At last stop walk 300 m
from school south to the butterfly sign. Also minibuses, US$5, From Alajuela
take bus marked "La Guácima abajo" from Av 2 between C 8-10, Pali Pacífico
75 m east, journey 40 mins, at 0830, 1030, 1230 and 1430, returning at 1110,
1310 1510, 1710. By car, turn east toward San Antonio de Belén from the air-
port highway (Autopista General Cañas) at the Herradura Hotel, and follow
The Butterfly Farm blue morpho road signs.*

Central highlands & the surrounding area

La Garita and west to Atenas

La Garita de Alajuela
Colour map 2, grid B2

Heading west towards Atenas the road drops slightly before arriving in La Garita de Alajuela, with a temperate climate perfect for **Zoo Ave**. Owned and operated by the *Nature Restoration Foundation*, this government recognized wildlife rescue centre is set in landscaped gardens. While visitors enjoy a relaxing day learning about the animals and plants, Zoo Ave educates visitors about the importance of Costa Rican wildlife through interactive exhibits and rehabilitation and release programs. Zoo Ave's breeding efforts are focused on threatened, endangered or otherwise sensitive species such as scarlet and green macaws, the green iguana and the squirrel monkey. Captive breeding programmes have successfully introduced 28 birds as part of the *Scarlet Macaw Restoration Program*.

While visiting you'll see over 100 species of native and exotic birds including toucans, parrots, black swans, eagles and the resplendent quetzal, as well as all four types of monkey, and other mammals and reptiles. ■ *T433-8989, F433-9140, www.zooave.org Open everyday from 0900- 1700. US$9. If driving, follow the signs to Zoo Ave from the Pan-American Highway heading west from Juan Santamaría International airport. Take a bus from Alajuela to La Garita. A cab to the zoo from Alajuela will cost around US$5.*

Sleeping and eating LL *Hotel Club Martino*, opposite Zoo Ave, T433-8382, F433-9052, toll free in the US on 1-800-368-4014, www.hotelmartino.com Luxurious and graceful elegance throughout the 34 rooms, excellent Italian restaurant and plantation-style family-run hotel. Large pool, gym, tennis courts and health spa. **AL-A** *Chatelle Country Resort*, T487-7781, F487-7095, www.hotelchatelle.com 15 rooms with bath, some with kitchenette and all with TV. Beautiful gardens, good restaurant, pool, weekly/monthly rates, airport pick-up available at no extra charge. Opposite is an orchid nursery with a marvelous variety of blooms, run as a hobby by an enthusiastic English-speaking optometrist, who will give you a guided tour for US$3.50.

If you're in the area and exploring by car, visit the *Fiesta del Maíz* soda/restaurant, which sells cheap products made only from maize, you can taste spoonfuls before you buy. Open weekends only, it's very busy as a stopping place for weekenders on their way to and from Jacó Beach. A second stopping point, almost as popular, is *Mi Quinta*.

Atenas
Colour map 2, grid B2
Population: 6,569

Next stop heading west from La Garita is Atenas, notorious for a consistency of climate that puts the temperatures between 17° to 32°C a fact that has become part of local legend. A second, less well known, local story is that both the church and the main plaza of this small town lie on an earthquake fault. Whether both either or neither are fact can be discussed while trying *toronja rellena* (local speciality: a sweet-filled grapefruit)

Sleeping and eating AL *El Cafetal Inn*, T446-5785, F446-7028, www.cafetal.com Out of town in St Eulalia, 4.7 km towards Grecia, beautiful private house set amongst fields of coffee bushes. Large pool, 10 rooms, all beautifully appointed, recommended. **B** *Ana's Place*, in Atenas, T446-5019. Includes breakfast, private bathroom, special weekly/monthly rates. **C** *Villa Tranquilidad*, T446-5460. 6 rooms, Canadian owned, quiet, welcoming, hard to find so phone ahead for reservations and directions.

Transport Buses to Atenas leave from the Coca-Cola bus terminal in San José departing every 30 mins. From Alajuela catch a bus from the bus terminal heading to La Garita. In Atenas the library on the plaza, also serves as the office for the bus company, *Cooptransatenas*, T446-5767.

Parque Nacional Volcán Poás

At a lofty 2,708 m this national park centres on the vast crater of Poás Volcano. *Colour map 2, grid B2*
Only 37 km north of Alajuela along gently winding roads which stop only a
few hundred metres from the summit, this is easily the most popular national *The best time of year*
park in the country. *for good views is*
between Dec and Apr.
The main draw is the vast crater, 1,320 m wide with it steeply sloping sides *Arrive early – clouds*
descending for a depth of 300 m. Currently filled with a simmering turquoise *often hang low over*
lake, in more active periods the crater dries out dowsing the surrounding *the crater after*
landscape with a sprinkling of sulphur. The most notorious eruption in the *1,000m obstructing*
20th century blew an ash cloud skyward some 8 km. The crater erupted *the view. But with*
between 1952 and 1954, with a couple of explosions in 1989 and again in 1994. *strong winds*
Today, volcanologists believe the magma chamber is just 4-500 m below the *throughout the year,*
lake's surface. Reassuringly for most visitors, the national park guards believe *gaps in the clouds*
it is a lot deeper. If there was any risk to visitors the park would be closed. *often provide brief*
glimpses
Beyond the drama of the volcano, 79 bird species, including quetzals and
several species of hummingbird, reside in the park's dwarf cloudforest and a
short trail of just over 1 km leads to a second crater now filled with the Botos
Lagoon. Last entry on the trail is at 1430. Free rambling around the park is not
permitted for fairly obvious safety reasons, so stick to the paths.

A good information centre is the final stop for visitors, from where it's a few
hundred metres uphill to the look-out post. In keeping with the popularity of
the park, there is road access almost to the summit for the disabled and those
unable to walk at this altitude. After visiting the information centre the *Café
Britt* coffee bar provides snacks and drinks.

■ *Daily 0800-1530, 1 hr later Fri-Sat from Dec-Apr. US$6. Plenty of parking
available. Tours to Poás are provided by many tour operators in San José. See
page 119. On a clear day with no wind you can wear shorts and T-shirts. When
the clouds come in and block the sun, the temperature plummets. Add a sprin-
kling of rain or just being drenched by clouds and you can quickly get cold so take a
rain jacket just in case.*

L-A *Poás Volcano Lodge*, PO Box 5723-1000, San José, 200 m from Vara Blanca junc- **Sleeping**
tion on road to Poasito approaching the volcano from the east. Sign on gate at El *You cannot camp in*
Cortijo farm where the farm road leads for 1 km to the house. 25 mins to volcano by car, *the park but there are*
1½ hrs from San José. T482-2194, F482-2513 or in UK T01420-549205, *a couple of good*
www.arweb.com/poas Merging English and Welsh farmhouse stonework from the *places listed here and*
owner's heritage and the openness of a ranch, this charismatic lodge has good views *several places*
of the volcano and gets a large amount of return clientèle and recommendations. The *advertising cabins*
9 rooms are spacious and accommodate couples and families equally well. There is a *leading up to Poás*
games room and mountain bikes are available for those with a bit more energy to *and in the*
burn. Price includes breakfast, good wholesome dinners cost between US$8-12. *surrounding area*
B *Alberque Ecológica La Providencia*, near Poás National Park up a steep and bumpy
road 2 km from green entrance gate to volcano, PO Box 319-1000, San José, T232-2498
and T380-6315, F231-2204. If you can get here and once you've found the place, the
quirky charm of the cabins defies conventional engineering theory. While the accom-
modation is rustic in the extreme and the food simple, the views of Poás when the
clouds have gone are excellent. Walking trails lead through primary dry, cloud and
dwarf forest making it an excellent spot for bird watching. Horse tours also available
from US$25. **D** *Lagunillas Lodge*, T448-5506. Simple farmhouse lodgings in a private
setting 3 km before the park entrance. Good views and horses available for hire.

Alajuela to Poás Travelling up to Poás, the road passes through good coffee country with gently undulating hills rising slowly towards the volcanic slopes of Poás. As you climb from the warmth of Alajuela, the temperature gives way to freshness and then a slight chill when in the shade.

There are two roads leading to Poás making for a pleasant circuit. One leads north from Alajuela towards **San Pedro de Poás**. En route the views are spectacular, shifting and changing with the light and the weather, a fact not wasted on *Casa del Café*, a roadside stop with a good viewing post overlooking the rows of fields. Beyond San Pedro the road continues to climb to the town of **Frajines** and the nearby resort of **Laguna de Fraijanes**, T/F482-2176/66. A natural lagoon is the focal point for a picnic and barbecue spot, and there are trails through 18 ha of forest, horses for rent, fishing and some basic cabins each sleeping three people (**D**).

An alternative route to Poás heads northeast of Alajuela toward Carrizal following the road to the lowland town of San Miguel, bearing left just before the town of Vara Blanca. Just beyond Vara Blanca the road crosses the saddle between the summits of Poás and Volcán Barva passing **Catarata La Paz** on the way. One of Costa Rica's most popular waterfalls, it is easily visited by private vehicle, or as part of a tour from San José. If trying to hitch, weekends are probably best. The recently opened La Paz Waterfall Garden is a nature park and wildlife refuge with 3.5 km of trails leading through forest to four other waterfalls upstream. There's also a butterfly garden and a full-service restaurant. ■ *Daily, 0830-1600, last admission 1530. US$24, children and students US$12. T482-2720, F482-2722, www.waterfallgardens.co.cr*

Towns northwest of Alajuela

Just like the flora and fauna of the country, the traditional communities of the central highlands have sought out the optimum place to live and farm the land. A neat line of villages and hamlets huddles round the lower western slopes of Poás Volcano sitting at an altitude of close to 1,500 m. Rivers have slowly carved the landscape, creating a mosaic of steep hills and deep valleys. But while this resulting countryside is scenic, it doesn't make for easy links between valleys. Before the advent of the car, each community developed almost in isolation, only coming together at market time and on special occasions.

Heading north west from Alajuela towards Ciudad Quesada (San Carlos) the road leads to **Grecia**, the craft centre of **Sarchí**, the transport hub of **Naranjo**, the topiary plaza fronting the church of **Zarcero** and further down the slopes to **San Ramón** and **Palmares**. None of these towns in their own right is an absolute 'must-see', but a quiet day spent meandering through the area is a good insight into the agricultural heartland of the highlands.

Grecia
Colour map 2, grid B2
Population: 17,173

A small town just over 18 km from Alajuela, Grecia adds the sweet delights of pineapple to the coffee produce of the region. A distinctive feature of the town is the all-metal red church dominating the leafy plaza and the Casa de la Cultura which houses the **Museo Regional de Grecia** – a range of small exhibits covering 200 years of history. ■ *Mon-Fri, 0900-1700, free.* A short distance before Grecia on the road to Alajuela is **El Mundo de los Serpientes**, a snake farm with over 50 species on display. ■ *0800-1600, US$11, reductions for biology students, information T/F494-3700, snakes@sol.racsa.co.cr*

Sleeping and eating A-B *Posada Mimosa*, Apdo 135-4100, Costa Rica, T/F494-5868, www.mimosa.co.cr Rooms, suites and a couple of cabins set in beautiful tropical gardens, with great views especially from the pool. All accommodation has private bath and hot water. Suites and cabins have a small kitchenette, ideal for longer stays. A few cheap options in town include **D** *Cabaña Los Cipreses*, and **G** *Pensión Quirós*.

Transport **Buses** to Grecia depart **San José** every 30 mins from the Coca-Cola terminal. Regular buses from **Alajuela** as well, with others travelling on to **Sarchí**.

Sarchí
Colour map 2, grid B2
Population: 10,772

Some might think Sarchí's charms somewhat lacking, but as a passing stop it's worth a visit. However, you can't fail to be hit by the blatant commercialism of the place. Not the once-popular advertising agency that threatened to take over the world before retiring in the Costa Rican highlands, but a craft village that owes its fame to the finely painted *carretas* (oxcarts) produced in the town. Originally distinctive to the area and still used by some farmers, the oxcarts are now seen throughout the country, their popularity elevating them almost to the status of national emblem. If you like them, you'll love the place.

Sarchí is actually two towns – Sarchí Sur and Sarchí Norte – separated by some 3 km, set amongst steep hills which afford impressive vistas across the valleys of coffee bushes. The heart of the town is to the north but there are *fábricas* (factories) in both parts. In Sarchí Norte, a gently tiered plaza leads to a birthday-cake church of bright lime green which positively glows at sunset. Inside, the vaulted wooden ceilings illustrate the creative individualism expressed in churches throughout the Central Valley.

The oxcarts and wooden furniture are mass-produced by hand in *fábricas* (factories) and *mueblarías* (furniture shops) and the town has done everything it can to help relieve you of your money, and why not? Visit the workshop of *Fábrica de Chaverri* (see below) and you can't help but be impressed by the craftsmanship of the artists. The brightly coloured floral and angular motifs are all hand-painted making each cart unique. A full-size cart costs between US$320 and US$360, but smaller options are available at a fraction of the price. If transport is a problem, worldwide flat-pack shipping can be arranged.

If your need for an oxcart is not great, don't worry – they double up as drinks trolleys and dressing tables. Problem solved, buy one

If you are still doubtful about spending your hard-earned cash the options are many. The colourful painting style is applied to benches and cluster tables. At some time in your stay in Costa Rica you will relax in one of the sturdy comfortable leather chairs rocking on balconies and patios throughout the country. You can buy them in Sarchí and again they can be flat-packed and shipped home. Other goods available include hammocks, salad bowls, walking sticks, wallets, vases and of course coffee.

Sights and shopping Approaching from the south you first come to **Fábrica de Carettas Chaverri**, T365-4448, F454-4944, oxcarts@sol.racsa.co.cr Established in 1903, the family-run operation has seen four generations of Chaverri's produce oxcarts in the area. Nearby is the **Plaza de la Artesanía**, a shopping complex with plenty of souvenir shops to explore. **Taller Lalo Alfaro**, the oldest workshop is in Sarchí Norte and worth a visit to get a more traditional line on production methods. Next to the Mercado de Artesanía in Sarchí Norte is **Valle de Mariposas**, a small butterfly garden where you can learn about the lifecycle of the butterfly with more than 40 species to see. ■ *0900-1700 daily, US$6.*

Sleeping and eating Just 800 m north of town in **San Juan de Valverde Vega** is **B** *Hotel Villa Sarchí*, T454-3029, 11 rooms with private bath, hot water, cable TV and pool. Difficult to find but the views are said to be good. In town, **D** *Cabinas Daniel Zamora*, T454-4596, has simple box-like rooms with private bath, fan, hot water and

 ## Jump off a bridge and fly with the birds

It happens all over the world so why not in Costa Rica? Jumping off bridges with nothing more than a huge cord of elastic attached to your ankles may not seem sensible, but if you like it, you like it! Costa Rica's only bungee operation, **Tropical Bungee**, drops people off an old iron bridge spanning the Río Colorado. A drop of around 80 m sends you flying with the birds in a way that no zip wire or canopy tour ever can. There is something unnatural about jumping off bridges – oh yes, that's it , the sense of impending death. While this adventure activity doesn't really involve sufficient skill to be called a sport, it does provide an awesome adrenaline rush. Operating since 1991 and with 10,000+ jumps to their name, Tropical Bungee has an unblemished safety record but, as ever, the risk is always yours. If bungee is not your style, you can also rappel down the Río Colorado and head up river for an exciting nature walk along the river gorge. ■ Open every day, but Sat is more popular. US$45 for 1st jump, US$25 for 2nd. Rappelling US$15. T232-3956, F232-3961, www.bungee.co.cr

extra blankets if the nights are cold. The rooms are bright and spotless, with parking available. **E** *Cabinas Sarchí*, T454-4425, with bath, opposite *Banco Nacional* above the hairdressers. Simple rooms but you may have to call in advance, often unattended.

Las Carretas, run by and next to *Fábrica de Chaverri* in Sarchí Sur, serves *comida típica*. In the north, the best restaurant is **Típico La Finca** serving authentic *Tico* cuisine in a pretty garden with good views. *Sodas* are dotted round the main shopping districts of both towns.

Transport **Bus**: travel to Sarchí from the Coca-Cola Terminal in San José four times a day, taking roughly 1½ hrs. Alternatively travel to Alajuela and get one of the half hourly buses to Sarchí. **Taxis** are readily available in Sarchí to make quick and frequent journeys between the two towns if you want to look around before buying.

Directory **Banks** *Banco Nacional* has branches in Sarchí Sur and Sarchí Norte. **Communications** **Post Office**: services are also found in both villages.

Parque Nacional Juan Castro Blanco & Bosque de Paz Rain- and Cloudforest Reserve
North of Sarchí and east of Zarcero, **Juan Castro Blanco National Park** (14,453 ha) protects the slopes and watersheds of **Volcán Porvenir** (2,267 m) and **Volcán Platanar** (2,183 m) the origin of many rivers that feed the northern lowlands. The national park has large areas of transitional rain and cloud forest, making it a perfect, albeit hidden-away, spot for birdwatchers.

Infrastructure in the park is virtually non-existent making the closest realistic visiting point **LL** *Bosque de Paz Rain/Cloudforest Private Biological Reserve*, T234-6676, F225-0203, www.bosquedepaz.com The lodge has 11 rooms set in the forest, each with two double beds, private bathroom and hot water. Pleasant touches like Costa Rican pottery are dotted round the hotel, and there is a reference library to explore in greater detail what you find on your forays into the cloudforest. The privately owned reserve with around 1,000 ha connects Juan Castro Blanco and Poás Volcano national parks acting as a biological corridor. A network of 28 km of trails winds through forest ranging in altitude from 1,400 m to 2,450 m. The bird list is currently up to 300 species with 324 orchid counted to date.

Transport The reserve is easiest to reach by heading north from Sarchí Sur, heading towards the town of **Bajos de Toro** in the saddle between the two national parks. An equally scenic alternative route leaves from east of **Zarcero** rising to the continental divide before falling again to arrive in Bajos de Toro. Contact the reserve in advance for precise directions. Pick-ups from the airport can be arranged.

Heading north along the Pan-American Highway from San José the River Colorado is at Km 37, the jumping off point for *Tropical Bungee*. After passing the Grecia turn, continue for 1 km over the river. Shortly after the river, looking to the right, you will see a large *Tropical Bungee* sign just off the road, take the next right. Follow the signs down to the bridge. If the office is not open, look for Carlos, the last house before the road descends. Even better, call in advance – see box.

The quiet agricultural town of Naranjo has an exquisite bright white church which is slowly being restored. To the side, a rather incongruous grotto leads to a small altar and behind is a small pond stocked with Koi carp. The main plaza has a shocking post-modern pyramidal structure which just tops off the feeling that despite being quiet, the desired gentle serenity of the place never quite materializes.

Naranjo
Colour map 2, grid B2
Population: 17,482

Sleeping If you end up staying the night, **F** *La Bambo*, down the hill by the football pitch may have mustered up enough energy to let you stay in one of their simple rooms. **Out of town**, travelling north on the Pan-American Highway 1 km past the Naranjo turn, a more enjoyable but expensive option, is **A** *Rancho Mirador*, T451-1302, F451-1301. It has 6 good value *cabañas*. The restaurant is well known for good local food and spectacular views of coffee *fincas* and San José in the distance. Owner Rick Vargas was formerly a stunt pilot in the USA. If you are looking for food in town there are several *sodas* around the bus stop, one block south and west of the church. Heading north to *Zarcero* is *Restaurante El Mirador* with great views over coffee *fincas* neatly leading down the slope to the Central Valley.

Transport *Transportes Naranjo*, T451-3655, have buses to and from **San José's** Coca Cola terminal every 20 mins. Buses also connect to other towns and villages in the area.

Directory Banks *Banco Nacional*, on north side of plaza, has ATMs taking Visa and MasterCard.

At the northern limit of the Central Valley, Zarcero enjoys a fresh mountain climate where the bean gives way to the beast. After climbing the gently meandering lower slopes the roads adopt an obsessive winding tendency scaling the last few kilometres. The views are scenic for the passenger, but drivers should keep their eyes on the road! Dairy cattle chewing the cud fuel the local economy. A local speciality is *palmito*, a white, moist cheese rather like mozarella, and a range of sweet products including *dulce de leche* and the best *cajeta de leche* in the country. Fruit jams are another regional product which can be bought in town or at any of road side stall. Heading north from Zarcero, the road falls rapidly twisting and winding down through the western limits of the Cordillera Central and the eastern edge of the Cordillera de Tilarán.

Zarcero
Colour map 2, grid B2
Population: 3,904

In town, it is the bizarre topiary creations filling the main square that draw the crowds. Travel guides and brochures go into linguistic spasms trying to describe and explain these creations of Zarcero's most famous son, Evangelista Blanco Breves. Given the job of maintaining the central plaza in 1964, Evangelista set about the task with a few simple ideas that have grown, been clipped, grown and clipped again. He has created animals, couples

Central highlands & the surrounding area

dancing, a helicopter, baskets and many Henry Moore-like sculptures still in metamorphosis. According to Evangelista, the inspiration and the idea for these naturally evolving artworks comes from *"El Maestro"* – the great celestial Master who also happens to reside in the white twin-towered church at the end of a topiary double-arch leading through the plaza. Within the church, colour and motifs use just a pinch of artistic guidance from the *carreteras* of Sarchí.

Sleeping and eating Your only choice of accommodation is **B-C** *Don Beto*, on the northern side of the church, T/F463-3137. 8 clean rooms, some with private bath and views over the plaza, in a family home. Several *sodas* and small restaurants are dotted around the plaza.

Transport Zarcero is the gateway to the northern lowlands with buses heading to **Ciudad Quesada** (San Carlos) and from there beyond. Buses from **San José** leave the Coca-Cola Terminal 8 times a day, with others heading for Ciudad Quesada also passing through the town.

San Ramón
Colour map 2, grid B1
Population: 14,122

San Ramón, known locally as the 'City of Poets', is easily reached from the Pan-American Highway, some 76 km from San José. As the most western town of substance in the Central Valley, the town developed through market trading and still has a vibrant street market on Saturday mornings. The history of the stark neo-Gothic metal church which replaced the previous building destroyed by earthquake in 1924, can be viewed at the **Museo de San Ramón**, on the north side of the church. Also has a smattering of local history in black-and-white photos. ■ *Free. Mon-Fri, 0830-1130, 1300-1700, Sat, 0830-1130.*

Sleeping and eating **B-C** *La Posada*, 400 m north of the cathedral, T/F445-7359, hoteles@racsa.co.cr 13 good rooms, with private bath, hot water and cable TV. Full use of kitchen and laundry, and small patio complete with rattan rocking chairs to while away the time. Plenty of parking. Recommended. **C** *San Ramón*, 100 m east of Banco de Costa Rica, T44-2042. 30 spotless rooms (but some with pretty unpleasant décor), each with private bathroom, hot water and cable TV. Parking available. **E** *Gran Hotel*, 150 m west of central park, T445-6363. Big rooms with private bathrooms, hot water, clean. Good open TV area and friendly as well. **F** *Hotel Nuevo Jardín*, 5 blocks north of the Central Park, T445-5620. Simple, clean and friendly. **F** *Washington*, T445-7349. Dark, dirty, unfriendly and possibly one of the worst sleeping options in the country!
 Restaurants dotted around town, with a few *sodas* close to the bus station.

Transport Heading north by car the road forks, the right leading to Zarcero (20 km) and finally to Ciudad Quesada. The left fork heads north to La Tigra and Fortuna passing the Los Angeles Cloudforest Reserve (see below). Many buses going to San Ramón continue to **Puntarenas**. They leave from the Empresarios Unidos stop in **San José** at C 16, Av 10-12, 10 a day. There is also a service via **Alajuela**.

Los Angeles Cloudforest Reserve

Twenty kilometres north of San Ramón is the 800-ha Los Angeles Cloud forest Reserve. This privately owned reserve attracts far fewer visitors than the better known Monteverde. Its prominence is in part due to the fact that it is owned by former President of Costa Rica, Rodrigo Carazo and his wife, Estrella. It gives the visitor a realistic day trip to a cloudforest – something which is very difficult to do with Monteverde.

The reserve has a couple of short trails, with a longer one requiring about eight hours and probably an overnight stop, passing waterfalls and good views. ■ *Entrance to the park US$15, with optional guided walks, horse riding and a canopy tour extra. One-day visits from San José can be arranged direct or through tour operators in the capital.*

Sleeping At the edge of the Los Angeles Cloudforest Reserve is **L-AL** *Hotel Villablanca*, from San Ramón head north to Los Angeles and follow the signs, T228-4603, F228-4004, www.villablanca-costarica.com *Casitas* set a rustic tone, but the small houses are fully equipped with private bathroom and hot water. The buffet-style restaurant is big enough to cater for groups which are most welcome. Guided treks from US$20, horse riding US$12 per hr, and canopy adventure tour US$38. Further along the road to La Tigra/Fortuna road at San Lorenzo is **L** *Valle Escondido Lodge*, at San Lorenzo on same road, T231-0906, F232-9591, www.valleescondido.com Comfortable rooms with private bath, set in 100 ha of primary forest. Additional cost for food around US$35 for 3 meals. Activities include riding, fishing, birdwatching and a canopy tour.

South of the Pan-American Highway, 7 km from San Ramón, is the small town of Palmares. This quiet town has an exceptionally overgrown main square squashed up to a rather bleak, albeit ornate, church with a façade that betrays the beauty and details of the stained glass windows of the interior. General comings and goings give way to **fiesta** for 10 days in the middle of January with carnival rides, music, dancing and non-fatal bull fights.

Palmares
Colour map 2, grid B2
Population: 5,622

Sleeping and eating About 6 km southeast of Palmares in the town of **Rosario de Naranjo** is **LL** *Vista del Valle Plantation*, T450-0800, F451-1165, www.vistadelvalle.com 11 guestrooms of varying size and styles, each with private bathroom and a balcony, are set in beautiful surroundings on the boundary of the Río Grande Nature Preserve. Former Peace Corp worker Mike Bresnan and his wife Johanna have made every effort to create a sustainable operation involving the local community in tourism activities. In addition to the mosaic-tiled pool, you can wander through the grounds at will where you will find a 100-m waterfall. Horse riding and birdwatching are also possible. Ask for directions when booking.

There are no cheaper accomodation options in Palmares

Heredia and surrounding area

On the lower slopes of Volcán Barva just 11 km north of San José, Heredia enjoys a history entrenched in the growth of coffee throughout the central highlands. Founded in 1706, the town fought for dominance of the country alongside Cartago against Alajuela and the eventually victorious San José at the time of independence. Today, though, the quiet town is in danger of losing its position as the fourth city of the republic to more vibrant growth areas such as Liberia or Turrialba. However, Heredians don't seem to be too concerned – traces of colonial heritage and the youthful energy of the Universidad Nacional (National University) give the town a busy grace. This 'City of Flowers' has a quiet charm that seems to say San José is welcome to the spotlight.

In the town you can explore the few sights that exist in a couple of hours. Staying longer is also an option with a few respected language schools in the area. The town offers the best access to Volcán Barva (2,906 m), the main destination for trekkers and hikers in Parque Nacional Braulio Carrillo.

Colour map 2, grid B3
Population: 30,968
Altitude: 1,200 m

Heredia has its own website with a mixture of history, what's on and general information – www.heredianet.co.cr

Ins and outs

Getting there Buses to and from **San José** leave the capital for the 20-40-min journey every 10 mins and every 20 mins from Av 2, C 10-12 and Av 2, C 12-14 close to La Merced Church. Buses arrive on Av 4 and C Central, one block south of the Central Plaza. A taxi to Heredia from San José is about 2,000 *colónes* (US$7). From the **airport**, expect to pay between US$10-15. Buses to other destinations leave from close to the market place, three blocks south of the Central Plaza.

Sights

The sights of Heredia can be seen from one spot through judicious position-ing in the northeastern corner of the main plaza – face north. Over your right shoulder is the **Basílica de la Inmaculada Concepción**, with a short squat design that has helped the structure weather several earthquakes since com-pletion in 1797. External weathering has taken its toll, but the inside is a com-plete contrast, starkly crisp and bright-white, proof positive that beauty lies within. Looking north is **El Fortín**, a single turret complete with gun slats overlooking a small park. Unfortunately the tower is closed to the public, but keep hoping. On the northern side of plaza is the **Casa de la Cultura**, a beauti-fully restored colonial house that was once the residence of President Alfredo González Flores (1914-17). Today in addition to being a fine example of period architecture with beautiful woodcarvings inside, the Casa de la Cultura houses exhibitions and concerts. Keep an eye out for events or just turn up and see what is going on.

Heredia

■ Sleeping	● Eating	8 Le Petit Paris
1 América	1 Bulevar Bar	9 McDonald's
2 Colonial	2 Café Azzura	10 Pizza Hut
3 El Parqueo	3 Cowboy	11 Pollo Frito
4 Heredia	4 El Gran Papa	12 Vishnu
5 Las Flores	5 El Príncipe	
6 Pensión Herediano	6 Fresas	
7 Valladolid	7 La Rambla	

Tour complete, spin round and explore the **Central Plaza** which has a light, airy feel with enough mango trees to provide shade, but not too many to block the light completely. And of course take time to join in the traditional pastime of sitting around for a while, contemplating the issues of the day, catching up with news from friends new and old, and generally doing nothing.

A couple of blocks south, the market is a cacophonous hub of trading. For marine biologists the **Museo Zoológica Marina** at the School of Marine Biology at the Universidad Nacional campus on the eastern side of town has specimens reflecting the marine diversity in Costa Rica's coastal waters. ■ *T277-3240. Mon-Thu, 0800-1200, 1300-1600. Free.*

Essentials

Sleeping
■ *on map*
Price codes:
see inside front cover

AL *Valladolid*, C 7, Av 7, PO Box 1973-3000, T260-2905, F260-2912, valladol@ sol.racsa.co.cr 11 spacious and smart rooms, all with a/c, private bath, telephone and cable TV. Some rooms and suites have microwave and fridge. The 5th floor has a sauna, jacuzzi and the *Bonavista Bar* with its fine views overlooking the Central Valley, is open to non-guests. *La Rambla* restaurant is next door and there is a travel agency to help organize tours. The best option in town.

A-B *Apartotel Vargas*, Apdo 510-3000, Heredia, 800 m north of Colegio Santa Cecilia and San Francisco Church, to the west of the town centre, T237-8526, F260-4698, lmasis@hotmail.com 15 large, well furnished apartments with kitchenette, bathroom, hot water, laundry, TV and enclosed patio. Garage with ample parking and nightwatchman, English-speaking staff and collection from the airport can be arranged with Sr Vargas. Excellent value for money, recommended for language students. **B** *America*, C Central, Av 2-4, T260-9292, F260-9293, www.hotelamerica.net The style and grandeur of Hollywood greets the guest in this former cinema now converted into a hotel. Sadly the rooms don't match the splendour but each has a private bathroom, hot water and telephone with cable TV. Handy for the centre of town and there's an ATM in the lobby.

D *Heredia*, C 6, Av 3-5, T/F238-0880. 10 rooms, some quite dark, but all have private bath and hot water. A simple hotel that receives few plaudits other than staff who, if not able, are at least keen. **D** *Las Flores*, Av 12, C 12-14, T260-8147. Each room with private bath, hot water and parking available. A friendly place, regularly recommended.

E *Colonial*, Av 6, C 4-6, T237-5258. A simple and clean family-run hotel. Shared bathrooms, with hot water, could do with a good scrub. Wooden panelling makes the rooms pretty dark, but it is very safe. Breakfast, coffee and *refrescos* available. If money is really tight, try **E** *El Parqueo*, C 4, Av 6-8, T232-2882. The rooms on the street side are slightly better. Shared baths with cold water *Pension Herediano*, is a good deal with private or shared bath.

Out of town

LL *Finca Rosa Blanca*, 1.6 km from Santa Bárbara de Heredia, to the north of Heredia, T269-9392, F269-9555, www.finca-rblanca.co.cr An absolutely divine hotel, on a bluff overlooking the Central Valley. 10 deluxe suites in an architectural orgasm of style, artistry, romance and exclusivity at the very extremes of imagination. Each suite is unique, capped off with the fantasy romance of the Rosa Blanca suite – a small turret with a four-poster bed central to a room with floor to ceiling windows. Total relaxation continues at the pool, and the body is cared for with fruit and vegetables from the hotel's organic garden. Probably one of the best hotels in the world. **L-AL** *Bougainvillea*, Santo Tomás de Santo Domingo, 9 km east of Heredia and just 10 mins out of San José, T244-1414, F244-1313, www.bougainvillea.com An exquisite and warm hotel with 83 large rooms each with a desk, cable TV, a/c, with crisp lines and fine classic décor leading to a balcony looking out onto the Central Valley. Blue-and-white tiled bathrooms

Central highlands & the surrounding area

complete with hairdryer. The hotel is decorated with ceramic pieces, local art and 12 acres of gardens replete with bougainvillea attracting hummingbirds and butterflies. If relaxing in the gardens and by the pool isn't hard enough work for you, there are tennis courts. Free shuttle service to San José.

Eating
● on map

Mid-range *Cowboy Restaurant*, C 9, Av 5, is a mid-range grill option where the mid-west meets Costa Rica. It's not all meat, but probably best avoided by vegetarians. Lively bar in the evenings and credit cards accepted. *El Gran Papa*, C 9, Av 3, has a gentle buzz and gets the majority of lunchtime business trade, but without being stuffy. There's a good range of *bocas*, pastas and cocktails along with international and national dishes. From US$10.

Cheap *Café Azzura*, on the corner of C 2 and Av 2, modern café serving great fast-food snacks, ice cream to die for and good coffee. A good meal for around US$5. On the edge of the Central Plaza, it's an ideal spot for people-watching. Good noticeboard outside with apartments and general local information for anyone thinking of staying in town for a while. *El Principe*, C 5, Av Central-2, truly international menu ranging from Chinese to pasta and local dishes. From US$8. *Fresas*, C 7, Av 1, T237-3915, diner-style restaurant serving everything you could possibly want including snacks, sandwiches, breakfast, full meals, fresh fruit juices and strawberries. TV in restaurant but you have to wear headphones! Will also deliver. Dishes from US$3. *La Rambla*, C 7, Av 7, T260-2905, has a formal décor but friendly service with a good mix of *comida típica* and international dishes. Prices from US$8. With more style, finesse and effortless charm than most nations can muster, *Le Petit Paris* on C 5 and Av Central-2, is a little piece of France in the heart of Heredia. Amidst Doisneau photographs and 1930s posters of gay Paris, the ambience shifts between the bar, restaurant and patio café. The food is French and, it goes without saying, divine. Live music on Wed. From US$4 upwards. *Vishnu*, C 7, Av Central-1, good wholesome vegetarian served fast food-style out front or a little more leisurely out back.

Seriously cheap *Pollo Frito*, west of Parque Central, is a 'cook it quick and serve it cheap' comedor specializing in fried chicken A hungry look on your face will get you a smile and a large plate of chicken for about US$3.

Cafes, bars,
& clubs

Bulevar Bar, Av Central, C 5-7, is one of the happening places, a fact that becomes blatantly obvious as soon as you're within one block of the neon and noise. Lively bar upstairs with balcony, fast food and *bocas* available. *Le Petit Paris*, C 5, Av Central-2, stylish French bar and café-restaurant well worth a visit. *Océano*, C 4, Av 2-4, is another popular student bar.

Shopping

Siglo 21 on Av 4, C Central – 2, sells *Fuji* and *Kodak* film.

Sports

Swimming is possible at the sports stadium at the end of Av Central. *Club Sports Herediano* football team are based in Heredia.

Transport

Buses In **San José** buses depart from Av 2, C 10-12, every 10 mins between 0500-0015, then hourly through the night until 0400, US$0.40. Through the day buses also leave from Av 2, C 12-14, every 20 mins. Buses from Heredia to the capital leave from Av 4, C Central-1 Local buses leave from Av 8, C 2-4 by the market. Buses to **Barva** leave every 30 mins. To **San José de la Montaña**, every half an hour, US$0.35 and **Porrosatí/Sacremento** at 0630, 1230 and 1600, US$0.40 for the 1-hr journey. **Taxis** are widely available.

Banks Branches of several banks dotted around town. *Banco Nacional* has a branch on the corner of Av 6 and C 6, *Banco de Costa Rica* is at Av 6, C1, and *Banco Popular* is east of the church at Av Central, C 3. Most banks have ATMs, but the most central one is probably in Hotel America, C Central, Av 2-4. **Communications** Internet: expect internet cafés in Heredia to change ownership and location, as the current ones look quite temporary. If those listed have closed, ask locally. *World Net Café*, C 7, Av 1-3, open every day, 0800-2200, US$2 per hr. *Internet Café*, Av 2, C 5-7, Mon-Fri 0830-2130, Sat 1000-2000, Sun 1200-1800, US$2 per hr, 15 mins US$1. Includes "delicious glass of iced tea with lemon"! **Post**: the Post Office is on the north side of the plaza, next to the fort. **Cultural centres** *Casa de la Cultura* facing the northeastern corner of the plaza at Av Central and C Central, has a good schedule of events covering all the performing arts and a few of the observational ones. **Medical services** *San Vicente de Paul Hospital* is at Av 8 and C 14, T261-0091, the *Red Cross* is on the corner of C Central and Av 3. Several pharmacies can be found on the streets between the market area and Central Park. **Language schools** *Centro Panamericana de Idiomas*, in San Joaquín de Flores, PO Box 151-3007, T265-6866, F265-6213, www.cpi-edu.com Also has schools in Monteverde and Playa Flamingo. Intensive classes of 5½ hrs a day focussing on grammar and conversation, with supportive oral and written work. Maximum class sizes of 4 covering all levels. Full range of cultural activities, tours and a volunteer programme. University credits available. Also have a seminar programme on special subjects. 4 hrs a day, US$340 with homestay, US$215 without, 5½ hr day, US$420, US$295. *Instituto Profesional de Educación*, T238-3608, F238-0621, www.learnspanishcostarica.com Founded in 1984, multiple levels with maximum class sizes of 6. Wide range of cultural activities support the classroom studies. Homestay strongly encouraged. US$320 a week with homestay, US$255 without. *Intercultura Costa Rica*, Apdo 1952-3000, Heredia, Costa Rica, T260-8480, F260-9243, www.spanish-intercultura.com Language tuition in small classes covering all levels from beginner to advanced, with a good varied cultural activities programme and options for homestays and a volunteer programme. Also have a school in Sámara on the Nicoya peninsula if you want to move around. University credits also available. Prices from US$245 week without homestay, US$345 with. All schools offer discounts for more than 1 week. **Laundry** Self-service washes possible at *Sol y Mar*, Mon-Sat, 0830-1900, Sun, 0830-1400. Wash 5kg for US$2 and dry it for another US$2. Service-washes cost a little more. **Useful addresses** In an emergency call 911.

South of Heredia

On the road to Santo Domingo is **INBio Parque**, an educational and recreational centre which explains and gives insight into Costa Rica's biological diversity and the country's national parks. In a remarkably small area you can visit the ecosystems of the Central Highland Forest, Dry Forest and Humid Forest, with a couple of trails set out for bromeliads and guarumo. The construction of a wetland area has added to the localized diversity and new interactive exhibits are planned. Guides are available, and there is a rolling programme of courses and talks covering a range of subjects. Excellent for students, and interesting for the generalist. Restaurants, cafés and all amenities on sight. ■ *T244-4730, F244-4790, www.inbio.ac.cr/inbioparque Daily from 0730-1600. US$18, under-12s free. Pick-up easily arranged from hotels in San José. If travelling by car, 400 m north and 250 m west of the Shell petrol station in Santo Domingo.*

North of Heredia and Volcán Barva

Café Britt coffee plantation tour Heading north from Heredia is the *Café Britt* coffee plantation tour. As one of the largest *beneficios* in the country, *Café Britt* is well suited to provide tours round every aspect of the coffee making process from tending the trees and harvesting, through to processing and packaging. But the skill comes in making this theatre. Professional actors guide you through the whole process and the result is informative and, judging by the look on most people's faces, very enjoyable. The success of the tour is so great that *Café Britt* combine the tour with several other Central Valley activities including visits to Poás Volcano, the Rainforest Aerial Tram and the innovative Coffee Culture Tour in San José's National Theatre. For the true caffeine addict there is a Coffee Lover's Tour with visits to the coffee mill during harvest so it only runs in the high season. ■ *Coffee Tour lasts 2 hrs every day at 0900 and 1100, also 1500 in the high season. Tours can be booked through any tour operator in San José. US$25 from hotels in San José, US$20 if you just turn up. T260-2748, F260-1456, www.cafebritt.com Head north from Heredia and follow the 'Café Britt Coffee Tour' signs.*

A short distance further north from Heredia the town of **Barva** (population: 6,348) has kept an historic charm. The white-washed church overlooking the plaza surrounded by single-storey adobe and tile houses dates back to the 1700s. The **Museo de Cultura Popular** has some examples of the local *bahareque* adobe construction method and several exhibits paying tribute to the town's colonial heritage. Traditional food is served in the rustic setting at weekends and on weekdays with advance notice. ■ *Mon-Fri 0900-1600, Sat and Sun 1000-1700. US$1.50. T260-1619, F261-3462, pdm@una.ac.cr 500 m east of the Salón Comunal de Santa Lucía de Barva.*

Volcán Barva
On a clear day in the dry season the scenery is unforgettable and the climate refreshing, but the green season brings rain, cold and many hotels close down. Check before travelling

North of Barva the road climbs the lower slopes of Barva Volcano (2,906 m) rising to the distinctly chilly and moist climate of the cloudforest. Several comfortable lodges, hotels and mountain resorts are hidden away in the pine forests of the upper slopes.

Getting there From Barva the road forks creating a loop that provides access to Barva Volcano and accommodation in the area. Buses from Heredia use the following route. Taking the right fork, the road reaches **San José de la Montaña** after 6 km. For the next 5 km the road twists and turns as the temperature falls and the road climbs to **Porrosatí** at 1,900 m. The route to the entrance and headquarters of Parque Nacional Braulio for climbing Barva Volcano takes a right fork leading to the town of **Sacramento** (5 km) and beyond, while the road leads downhill via Birrí and eventually back to Barva. Taking the left fork north of Barva as far as Birrí and then taking a right completes the circuit in reverse.

Buses leave Heredia from the market place at 0630, 1230 and 1600 taking 1 hr for the journey to Porrosatí where the bus waits for 1 hr before departing at 0730, 1300 and 1700. Some buses continue to Sacremento reducing the walking time.

Sleeping and eating Heading uphill from Birrí, the first hotel you reach is **A-B** *El Cypresal*, T237-4466, F237-7232. Cypress wood dominates the reception and winding up the hill behind, 24 small and cosy cabins have a fireplace for the cold nights, and a patio for sitting in the sun. Each has a private bath, hot water, cable TV and telephone. Small restaurant for meals with sauna and pool. Food not included. A little further uphill is **A** *Las Ardillas*, T260-2172, a well hidden mountain resort within the pine forest. 18 *cabinas* each with private bathroom, hot water and kitchenette.

Dark beams and wooden floors create a warm ambience in the restaurant which serves international and traditional cuisine. In addition to a sauna and jacuzzi, hypnosis, massage and beauty treatments help you reach that higher plain of relaxation. A short distance further on is **A** *El Pórtico*, PO Box 289-3000, Heredia, Costa Rica, T260-6000, F260-6002. This place continues the Alpine theme. A vast bar/lounge area with one side looking down to the Central Valley is heated by an impressive fireplace warmed with occasional live music. Ideal for groups, 18 spacious rooms with private bath and hot water, lined with cypress panelling on all sides, lead off a network of flagstone-paved corridors. The restaurant is stylish, with dinner starting at around US$10.

All the hotels mentioned above have restaurants and welcome non-guests. In Sacramento, north of Porrosatí heading to the National Park headquarters, *Restaurante Auxilladora* has a basic menu, next door *Restaurant Sacremento* has a little more on offer serving *comida tipica* and a well stocked bar to keep the cold at bay.

Hiking to the summit of Barva Volcano (2,906 m) is one of the best ways of seeing some of the less-explored parts of Parque Nacional Braulio Carrillo (see page 162 for more details). The hike to the top passes through fine cloudforest, with moss-covered trees heavily laden with epiphytes and bromeliads. The area is popular with birdwatchers, and fortunately for them quetzals, king vultures and the three-wattled bell bird, as well as countless hummingbirds. Monkeys, reptiles, poison-arrow frogs and the endemic, and currently endangered, *Bufo holdridgei* toad can also been seen. The summit trek offers spectacular views across densely forested valleys shrouded in swirling mist rising from the lowland valleys. Trails lead to three water-filled craters including the **Danta crater** surrounded by profuse vegetation and almost 500 m across. From the summit, magnificent views stretch across the Central Valley.

Climbing Volcán Barva

Access to Barva is difficult compared to some national parks in Costa Rica. Three daily buses travel to Porrosatí from San José de la Montaña and Heredia, from where a poorly marked trail leads to the summit and then out through the park headquarters. A more common route leaves from park headquarters, 3 km beyond Sacremento. The road is rough and if travelling by private vehicle you will need a four-wheel drive and even then may not make it in the wet season. Entrance fees are payable at the headquarters, from where signs lead to the summit. The 4 km takes a little over one hour depending on your condition. For the serious trekker there is a trail heading north from the top of Barva down to *La Selva Biological Station* near Puerto Viajo de Sarapiquí. The trip takes about four days, covers about 65 km and requires proper planning.

Despite its proximity to San José, groups entering the park do get lost. News of their survival only gets out with them so go prepared – the weather can change dramatically and getting caught in cloud is very disorientating. For all trekking in the park you should have maps, compass, food and water, and appropriate protective equipment depending on the length and duration of your stay. Camping is allowed in the park but there are no services so pack up what you take in. ■ *Headquarters open daily 0800-1600. US$6. In Costa Rica call T261-2619, F261-0257. No tour operators in San José provide this trip at present, but* Ocarina Expeditions *(T221-5322) should be able to help with arrangements.*

East of Heredia towards Monte de la Cruz

A few kilometres east of Heredia, **San Rafael de Heredia** is notable for one of the most impressive churches in the Central Highlands. In a town of just over 11,000 a church worthy of any European capital city stands loud and proud, recently cleansed and purified, it beams in brilliant white. Sadly for the residents who would like to see visitors stay a little longer, it provides only passing interest.

North of San Rafael, Highway 113 leads up the slopes of Barva Volcano eventually reaching Monte de la Cruz. The refreshing climate makes this a popular mountain retreat for the better-off families of the Central Highlands, and private homes and mansions border the road some hidden behind imposing front gates. It is also possible to hike in the region but trails are limited and poorly marked.

When not enjoying the comfort of their homes, residents and day visitors relax at *Castillo Country Club* where membership bestows opportunities for R&R in whatever form takes your fancy. Swimming, sauna and jacuzzi, football, tennis, volleyball and go-carts, the list is long – you can even ice skate! There are plenty of picnic areas outside or you can dine at the restaurant with meals from around US$8. ■ *Day membership Mon-Fri, US$15. Members only Sat and Sun. T267-7111, F267-7114, castillo@sol.racsa.co.cr Ranch-style holiday homes available for rent to members, contact for details.*

Sleeping Just above *El Castillo* is the exclusive hotel retreat of **LL** *La Condesa*, T267-6000, F267-6200, www.occidental-hoteles.com Part of the Occidental Hotels group. 96 rooms and suites all with excellent views over the central highlands. Large standard rooms all have tiled private bathrooms with bath tub, cable TV and minibar and the suites go to suitable extremes. 4 restaurants provide a range of dining options. *Patio de Los Condes*, complete with waterfall, provides informal patio dining ideal for breakfast, *Miramonte* serves light dishes and *Florencia* offers the very best in European cuisine. *El Mirador de la Cava del Conde* is a bar and disco with live music at weekends. Full sports facilities and several meeting rooms make this an ideal conference hotel as well as a refreshing mountain retreat.

The final stopping place for most visitors to the region leads down a mystical avenue of moss-cladden pine trees that block and diffuse the light to create an ethereal corridor leading to **AL** *Chalet Tirol*, T267-6222, F267-6229, www.chalet-tirol.com At a lofty 1,800 m and set in 15 ha of private cloudforest, this piece of Alpine Costa Rica is authentic in almost every detail. 20 or so chalets and suites are hidden within the forest offering unrivalled privacy. In addition to the expected homely comforts, each room has a heater to fend off those winter nights. The French restaurant is strongly recommended. Activities include hiking on trails close to the hotel or taking a guide to Parque Nacional Braulio Carrillo through virgin cloudforest. The hotel is also host to the Whitten Entomological Collection of more than one million forest insects and arthropods, and hosts an annual International Music Festival. It's quite a long way up, but you won't need to go down until you leave.

Parque Nacional Braulio Carrillo

Colour map 2, grid B3 Just 20 km from San José, Braulio Carrillo National Park protects some of the
Altitude: from 36 m country's most rugged landscapes. If you're not inclined to get out and
to 2,906 m explore you're in luck, as you get a good impression of the topography from the San José – Guápiles – Limón Highway that travels through the park. Steep sided gorges eroded by rivers hidden at the bottom of heavily forested valleys border both sides of the road. Clouds drift up the valleys, rising to the volcanic peaks of **Barva** (2,906 m) and **Cacho Negro** (2,150 m) where they deposit rainfall that totals around 4.5 m annually. The result is some dramatic waterfalls, most hardly ever seen by human eyes.

The 47,583-ha park was created in 1978 to protect the region against damage caused by the construction of a new highway to the Caribbean in 1977. Named after the republic's third president Braulio Carrillo, who proclaimed himself dictator for life in 1842, the name at least commemorates Carrillo's attempts to improve communications between the Central Valley and the lowlands. Today, Highway 32 is one of the country's busiest roads making the national park the most popular in the country even if the authorities don't count transient visitors behind the wheel. The vast majority passing through see the road and driving conditions as precarious, dangerous and best avoided if at all possible. Some tours incorporate this journey as part of a visit to the national park. It goes without saying that you will not see any wildlife from a bus, but you can pass over the continental divide just to the south of the Zurquí tunnel, which bores a hole under the slopes of Cerro Zurquí.

The biological stock take is staggering. Estimates suggest that over 90% of the park is primary forest and contains some 6,000 species of plants – over 50% of those found in Costa Rica. While the higher altitudes struggle to support life in the chilled and windy atmosphere, profuse humid rainforest dominates, reaching its greatest diversity at the lower altitudes. Animal and bird life is equally profuse. Over 500 species of migratory and resident birds have been logged including quetzals in the higher altitudes, toucans, king vultures, the umbrella bird as well as the national bird: the sooty robin. Mammals include three species of monkey as well as tapirs, pacas, jaguars, pumas and ocelots. To complete the list, reptiles include two of the deadliest snakes in the world, the fer-de-lance and bushmaster.

For management purposes the parks is divided between the **Quebrada González Sector** and the **Barva Volcano Sector**. The entrance at Quebrada González is 23 km beyond the Zurquí tunnel (easy to drive past, if you get to Los Heliconias butterfly farm or the flag-poles of the Rainforest Aerial Tram you've gone too far). Three short trails lead out from the ranger's station. *Las Palmas* is just a 1.6 km trail taking about 1½ hrs, good for birdwatching. *El Ceibo* is even shorter at 1 km taking just an hour and leading to the some fine examples of the ceibo tree. The *Botarrama* trail is an extension of El Ceibo that leads to the Río Sucio and gets deeper into the rainforest covering 3 km taking about 2 hrs. An animal list stating regular sightings of spiders, white-faced and howler monkeys, toucans, peccaries, tarantulas and snakes makes for an interesting read before and after your trek. ■ *0800-1530 daily, if arriving before the ranger's station opens pay on your way out. US$6. T233-4533 or T257-0922. Take any bus heading east of San José from the Gran Terminal de Caribe north of downtown San José and ask the driver to drop you off at the entrance.*

For the Barva Volcano Sector and climbing the summit see page 160

A short distance beyond the Quebrada González (1½ km) station is **Los Heliconios**, a quiet enclosed butterfly garden. There is a guided tour as well as an insect museum and poison dart frogs. It's a refreshing change from the smooth operations that dominate this part of the market. ■ *Daily, 0800-1600, US$6.*

Rainforest aerial tram

Moving silently through the forest at canopy is the best way of seeing the complexity of the rainforest but is inherently problematic for people. Fortunately the unique attraction of the Rainforest Aerial Tram, the brainchild of Dr Donald Perry and John Williams, gives you precisely that opportunity. Open-air cable cars, with protection from the sun and rain, glide slowly through the forest rising from ground level to drift below, in and above the canopy for an

Central highlands & the surrounding area

up-close and personal view of life above the forest floor. Each car has a bilingual guide, equipped with a radio, who will point out interesting fauna encountered on your journey. As with all good guides, their keen and practised eyes will help spot birds and animals, often long before the casual observer, and you will see the sheer density of plant life and insects found in the upper sections of the rainforest. At the half-way point a short walk leads to a vista stretching to the Caribbean lowlands with views as far as Tortuguero on a clear day. The return journey "flies" just above the canopy, before coming back to land – an unforgettable experience.

Visitors to the park should have realistic expectations. Birds abound and birdwatchers should aim to arrive as early in the morning as possible. It is possible to see monkeys, but don't expect them. Several coatis hang around the departure point, but the best chance of seeing other mammals is by hiking one of the short trails that lead through the 450-ha private reserve used for research.

In addition to being a fascinating ride, the creation of a successful green tourism experience on this scale, with relatively low impact is incredible. The history of the creation and construction of the ride makes for an interesting tale explained in a video shown afterwards. Well worth seeing.

■ *Daily 0630-1600, although most tours arrive after 0900, so travel privately if you wish to visit early. Park entrance and tram ride, adults US$49.50, students with ID card and under 11s US$24.75. Package from San José, including pick-up from most hotels, tram fees, meal and hike adults US$78.50, students and under 11s US$53.75. T257-5961, F257-6053, www.rainforesttram.com Reservations office behind the Aurola Holiday Inn, or 150 m west of the INS building. To get there take any bus heading towards Guápiles from the Gran Caribe bus terminal north of town on Calle Central. If driving, take the San José – Guápiles Highway (32), heading northeast from the capital. Toll booth (US$0.20) en route. Vehicles park in a secure car park and you are shuttled down to the ride, so minimizing disturbance of the area. Upon returning to the boarding station, you can stop for a snack or a meal at the Rainforest Café. Postcards and souvenirs are available at the Rainforest Gift Shop including natural remedies covering everything from headaches and high blood pressure, through to impotence.*

Sleeping In early 2001 the Rainforest Aerial Tram opened 10 new "cozy and inviting cabins. Built over a stone base with wood floors and a balcony", in the heart of the reserve (**LL**). Although not seen, the cabins include 2 single beds, private bathroom with hot water. The Aerial Tram and extensive hiking trails are near, and all-inclusive packages are available which include lodging, meals and riding the Tram. Contact reservations.

Northeast of San José

On the Guápiles Highway, just before the toll booth, is **A** *Villa Zurquí*, T268-8856, F268-5084, hvzurqui@sol.racsa.co.cr Not the first choice hotel in the Central Highlands, but a good one if you're looking to get an early morning start through the Parque Nacional Braulio Carrillo. Twenty nine cabins, a few with fire places for the cold nights, and all with beamed ceilings, tiled floors, private bathroom with a bath rub. Set in pine forests, the cabins are quite charming. The intimate restaurant serves international cuisine in front of a real fire.

Running northeast of San José, but south of the main highway, the road runs to **San Isidro de Coronado**. A dramatic grey church stands starkly bereft of paint despite its Gothic splendour. While the town is a popular summer resort, San Isidro owes its place on the map largely due to the *Instituto Clodomiro Picado* snake farm. Those interested in medical research can visit.

■ *Mon-Fri 0800-1600, snake feeding Fri at 1400, T229-0344, F292-0485. Bus marked Dulce Nombre de Coronado from Av 7, C Central-1 or San Antonio Coronado bus to end of line and walk 200 m downhill.*

From San Isidro the road goes on through fine countryside to **Las Nubes** (32 km), a country village on the boundaries of Parque Nacional Braulio Carrillo which has good opportunities for almost solitary walking and hiking and commands a great view of Irazú.

To the north, a road leads to **San Jerónimo** and onto the valley of the Río Hondura. The century-old stone road now seriously degraded was originally built in the 1880s to transport coffee from San José to the Caribbean coast.

Cartago and surrounding area

The massif of Volcán Irazú dominates the skyline from Cartago, the provincial capital and gateway to the southeastern corner of the Central Valley. Once the ruling quarter of Costa Rica, today the province has a distinctly rural feel dotted with the coffee and macadamia nut plantations of the lower slopes, the less exotic products of potatoes and onions on the volcanic slopes, and the dependable presence of coffee where conditions allow.

Colour map 2, grid C3

Exploring the town, it is difficult to see how this quiet spot once mustered up enough energy to lead the nation. Listless and without direction the town continues apparently unaware or at least with only limited interest in its historical legacy. Volcán Irazú is a highly visible reminder of the forces without and within, last erupting in dramatic style to coincide with the arrival of President Kennedy in 1963. The orchids of Lankester Gardens, and the fine views of the Orosí Valley, make pleasant relaxing trips. While the more adventuresome can hike in Tapantí-Macizo de la Muerte National Park, or get wet whitewater rafting in the Pacuare and Reventazón rivers close to Turrialba. The Guayabo National Monument, to the north of Turrialba, is the country's most important precolombian archaeological site.

Ins and outs

If driving, it's a simple car ride of just over 20 km from San José. From Av 2, head east and follow the signs. There's a small toll along Highway 2. *SACSA* buses leave from C 5 and Av 18-20 every 10 mins taking 45 mins for the journey, T233-5350. Transtusa buses stop at Cartago en route to Turrialba with 15 buses a day leaving from C 13 and Av 6-8. T556-0073.

Getting there

The two areas of interest are only 1 km apart – a gentle stroll unless it is raining. If so, there are plenty of cabs around *Las Ruinas* and the streets surrounding the Basilica.

Getting around

Pilgrimages to the Basilica take place throughout the year, but 2 Aug is the most important date in the pilgrims calendar.

Best time to visit

Sights

Sprawling at the foot of Irazú volcano and surrounded by mountains, Cartago was founded in 1563 by Juan Vásquez de Coronado who also conquered much of the Central Valley. The city's dominant position was frequently tested and finally faltered in 1823 when San José acquired the capital seat after a series of minor civil scuffles. Since then, nature has challenged the city with many tremors and two devastating earthquakes first in 1841 and again in 1910 finally finishing off the architectural heritage of the town.

Today, the town bustles with the energy of a local market and transport hub. But despite attempts to look hard, few find reason to stay for long

Central highlands & the surrounding area

When tried to the limits of physical endurance, faith often comes to the fore and Cartago has one of the finest churches in the country, and certainly the most popular with many thousands completing a personal pilgrimage to the Basílica de Nuestra Señora de Los Angeles.

With the old city destroyed by earthquakes the town's architectural sights are limited to two. **La Parroquia**, locally known as *Las Ruinas*, was once the seat of the first parish of Cartago founded back in 1575. Frequent tremors meant the church was reconstructed several times. Almost completely destroyed in 1841, it was rebuilt only to be destroyed again in 1910, in an earthquake estimated to measure around 6.4 on the Richter scale. What stands now is what remained then. A small ornamental garden fills the space within, but is closed for much of the time. In front of the ruins, the Central Park is a large expanse of pavement, but despite the blandness, it makes for good people-watching, and if you're lucky you may see busking and street performances *Tico* style.

A couple of blocks north of Central Park, the **Central Market** blossoms to become a noisy, smelly, chaotic bundle of trading. Cleaner than it looks, it does have a rough edge that is missing from many of Costa Rica's markets, and so common in other Latin countries.

One kilometre to the east, the **Basílica de Nuestra Señora de Los Angeles** is what the crowds have come to see. To be more specific it is the diminutive **La Negrita**, an Indian image of the Virgin Mary less than 15 cm high, which draws pilgrims from throughout the country and from all over Central America because of her great healing powers. Having arrived at the Basílica, pilgrims take to their knees, inching their way down the aisle towards La Negrita.

It's easy to overlook the finery of the Basílica itself. Destroyed by earthquake it was rebuilt in 1926 in Byzantine style. The interior is ornately decorated with gold leaf, fine carvings and always with fresh flowers. To the side of the church, pilgrims fill La Negrita-shaped plastic containers and *refresco* bottles with holy water to take a little of the curative powers back home.

Cartago

■ Sleeping
1 Dinastía
2 Los Angeles B&B
3 Venecia

● Eating
1 Café Linea
2 La Cazada
3 La Princesa del Mar
4 McDonald's
5 Pizza Hut
6 Puerto del Sol

🚌 Buses
1 Cachí via Ujarra & Paraíso
2 Orosi/Río Machi
3 Paraíso
4 Pitaya, Aguacalientes & Lourdes
5 San José
6 San Juan de Chichúa
7 Tierra Blancas/San Gerardo
8 Turrialba

0 metres 200
0 yards 200

Four kilometres southeast of Cartago, and a short bus ride beyond Tejar, is **Aguacalientes**, a warm-water *balneario* (spa) ideal for picnics.

Essentials

Just north of the Basilica is **B** *Los Angeles Lodge B&B*, Av 4, C 14-16, T551-0957. Despite looking closed is still open. Locals say the rooms are clean and pleasant. At the *Las Ruinas* end of town is **D** *Dinastia*, C 3, Av 6-8, T551-7057, F551-0626. Slightly more expensive with private bath. The rooms are pretty small and definitely basic, and generally better with a window although nosier because they are just north of the central market. One good thing: they take credit cards. Close to the old railway station are **F** *Familiar Las Arcadas*, which rents rooms hourly late into the night and nearby is **F** *Venecia*, basic and with cold water.

Sleeping
There is a dearth of accommodation and eating options in the centre of town. If visiting, it is probably worth a brief stop before moving on

Food options are as uninspiring as accommodations. *Puerto del Sol*, Av 4, C 14-16, is just north of the Basilica and the only option at that end of town. South of Las Ruinas is *Restaurante La Cazada*, on Av 1, C2-4, serves typical food at reasonable prices. Open lunchtimes and evenings. *La Princesa del Mar*, C 1, Av 1-3, serves seafood in a fast food café style. The *Club de Cartago* is a glorious building that has struggled through the town's historic challenges. Sadly it only holds private functions, but it's worth a look to see if there is an impromptu opportunity. *City Garden* serves Chinese food at Av 4, C 2-4. Branches of *Pizza Hut* and *McDonalds* are on or close to Av 4, C 1-3. Many *sodas* in and around the Central Market.

Eating

If the restaurants are unappealing raid *Pali Supermarket* on the corner of Av 4 and C 6 for a picnic in the Central Park.

Aug 2nd sees pilgrims from throughout Costa Rica and Central America arrive in Cartago to pay tribute to *La Negrita*.

Festivals

Fuji has a store at Av 2, C 4-6.

Shopping

Club Sport Cartaginés are the local football team, playing at the *José Rafael "Fello Meza"* stadium. Ask locally for fixtures.

Sport

Mercatur, next to *Fuji* at Av 2, C 4-6, provides local tourist information and can book local hotels.

Tour operators

Driving If travelling by car, roads lead north to Irazú for a pleasant and occasionally cloudy drive to the volcano summit. To the southeast Orosí is along Highway 10, from where a good road leads round Cachí Lake. In Paraíso the road peels off to the right leading to Turrialba. An alternative route to Turrialba takes Highway 233, following the contours of Irazú's misty slopes taking in several quiet rural villages on the way.

Transport

A good **bus** service supplies the surrounding area. **San José**, every 10 mins from Av 4, C 2-4. Arrives and departs San José from C 5, Av 18-20 for the 45-min journey. **Orosí/Río Macho**, every 30 mins from C 6, Av 1-3, journey time of 35/55 mins. **Turrialba**, every hr from Av 3, C 8-10, 1 hr direct, 1 hr 20 collectivo. **Cachí**, via Ujarrá and Paraíso from C 6, Av 1-3, every 1½ hrs, 1 hr 20 mins. **Paraíso**, every 5 mins from Av 5, C 4-6. **Aguacalientes**, every 15 mins from C 1, Av 3-5. **Tierra Blancas** for Irazú, every 30 mins from C 4, Av 6-8.

Closest bus for **Irazú** rides to **San Juan de Chicuá**, still 10 km from the summit. The bus leaves Cartago from north of the central market, Av 6, C1-3, at 1730, returning at 0500 the next day, so in reality you have to spend at least 2 nights on the volcano or in a hotel if you can't get a ride. To visit *Volcán Turrialba* take a bus from C 4 y Av 6 to the village of *San Gerardo*.

Central highlands & the surrounding area

 ## Visiting Volcán Irazú

If you're uncertain whether to visit Irazú and risk being clouded over, heed the words of one traveller who writes: "In the afternoon the mountain top is buried in fog and mist or drizzle, but the ride up in the mist can be magical, for the mountainside is half-displaced in time. There are new jeeps and tractors, but the

herds of cattle are small, the fields are quilt-work, handcarts and oxcarts are to be seen under the fretworked porches of well kept frame houses. The land is fertile, the pace is slow, the air is clean. It is a very attractive mixture of old and new. Irazú is a strange mountain, well worth the ride up."

Directory **Banks** No shortage of banks if funds are running low. *Banco de Costa Rica* has a branch with ATM on Av 4, C 5-7. *Banco Interfin*, on the corner of Av 2, C 2 neighbouring Central Park has Visa and MasterCard ATMs. *Banco Nacional* on Av 2, C 1-3, has a Visa ATM. **Communications** Staying in touch in Cartago is challenging. **Internet**: *Café Linea*, Av 4, C 6-8, is the only internet place in town. While popular, it doesn't strike you as the kind of place that will stay open for long so ask around. **Post**: Post office formerly on C 1, Av 2-4, the post office has moved and nobody appears to know to where! Try "800 m west of Central Park," or better still send postcards and letters from somewhere else. **Medical facilities** *Hospital Dr Max Peralta*, entrance on C 3, Av 7, T5550-1999. *Pharmacies* can be found along Av 4 between Calles 1- 6. **Useful addresses** in emergencies call 911.

Volcán Irazú

Colour map 2, grid B3 On a clear day, the silhouette of Irazú looms above Cartago, on a cloudy day the peak and much of the lower slopes are stuck in the clouds – at 3,432 m it is the highest volcano in Costa Rica. With a road reaching to within a few hundred metres of the dramatic lagoon-filled craters, this is one of the country's most popular national parks. Whether buffeted by freezing winds, or basking in glorious sunlight, the volcano is definitely worth visiting.

This "mountain of quakes and thunder", named after the nearby Indian village of Iztarú which once existed on the volcanic slopes, has a lively history. The first documented eruption was recorded by Diego de la Haya Fernández in 1723, the governor of Cartago at the time. Violent eruptions began in 1963 damaging the crater and sending volcanic material down the western slopes to flood the Río Reventado and the community of Taras. This eruption showered Cartago and the capital San José with ash – a dramatic welcome to President John F Kennedy who was visiting at the time.

As recently as 1994 a sudden explosion on the north wall of the crater sent a landslide down the Río Sucio to within sight of the bridge over the main highway connecting San José and Limón. Today, fumaroles, small lava flows and light tremors are proof that the mountain still quakes and thunders.

Once at the top, the landscape is bare, covered in desolate grey sand which looks like the surface of the moon but for pockets of fragile vegetation slowly colonizing the harsh climate. The temperature range of –3°C to 17°C and the poor soil supports a hardy low scrub with thick leaves and stunted growth to cope with the fierce winds and sudden temperature changes near the summit. There are five craters in total, three of which can be easily visited. The **main crater** is a half-mile cube blown out of the earth 1,050 m wide, vertiginous walls 300 m deep and complete with a sulfurous green lake at the bottom. The **Diego de la Haya crater** is slightly smaller. **Playa Hermosa crater**, slowly being colonized, is a good spot for birdwatching where you may see the ubiquitous *volcano junco* bird but otherwise little wildlife and few plants survive in this hostile desert.

The views, however, are stupendous. In general try to visit as early as possible. The summit is often shrouded in cloud but your best chance of a clear view is in the morning. Even if the lower slopes are cloudy, it is quite possible that the summit is above the clouds. The rainy season is from May to December, but take warm clothing and a wind-proof jacket as protection all year round.

■ *Daily 0800-1530. National Park entrance of US$6 plus US$2.50 to park if you are driving. Most tour operators in San José have day trips to Irazú costing around US$35 per person. Buses Metropoli have one bus on Sat and Sun leaving at 0800 from Av 2, C 1-3, in front of Gran Hotel Costa Rica, US$6. There are buses from Cartago going regularly to Tierras Blancas, and one a day up the slopes as far as San Juan de Chicúa, which leaves a refreshing but enjoyable 10 km hike uphill to the summit. A taxi is also a possibility with a group, and the recommended price is 10,000 colónes (US$32) plus entrance. At the summit there is a small café serving snacks and coffee, as well as a few souvenirs of baseball caps, T-shirts and coffee table books covering Costa Rica's exploding volcanoes.*

If you want to stay on the slopes of Irazú there are a number of options. On the road leading up to the summit in **San Juan de Chicuá** is D *Hotel Gestoria Irazú*, T253-0827, F225-9647, gestoria@racsa.co.cr The rooms are simple with private bath, hot water and extra blankets to help you get through the cold winter nights. Given the monopoly this hotel has on the market, it seems to be missing a great opportunity, but the *comida tipica* is meant to be some of the best around. A little further uphill is *Restaurantes Linda Vista* with spectacular views and apparently good food and drinks. But most people stop to post, stick, pin or glue their business card, or any other personal item, to the wall. Join in, you're in good company. The Dalai Lama popped by but sadly didn't leave a card.

On the western flank of Irazú in the small village of **Rancho Redondo** is **AL-A** *Hacienda San Miguel*, T229-5058, F229-1097. A comfortable lodge with very good views over the Central Valley. Plenty of opportunities for R&R with a pool, horse riding, jacuzzi, steam bath, lake, magnificent views. The continental divide passes through the property so both Pacific and Caribbean birds can be seen.

Sleeping & eating

Jardín Botánico Lankester

An overgrown "hobby" founded by the British naturalist Charles H Lankester in the 1950s, Lankester Botanical Garden has grown to be an internationally renowned collection of epiphytic flora, in particular the orchid, of Costa Rica. The gardens have around 800 species of national and exotic orchids laid out in the 10.7 ha of tranquil gardens. These "showy" flowers come in a great variety of colours and reach peak blooming between February and May when temperatures are highest and rainfall lowest.

Beyond the orchids the gardens also have many examples of bromeliads, ferns, cacti as well as heliconia, palm and bamboo. Nature plays its part with over 100 birds visiting the gardens. It's positively calming, and respectful noise levels are requested, nay expected.

For the orchidophiles and botanists there are programmes of short courses covering care and cultivation of orchids, plant recognition and nature photography to name a few topics. Contact the gardens for details.

■ *Daily 0830-1530, except Jan 1, Maundy Thursday, Good Friday, Easter Sunday and 25 Dec. US$4 for adults, US$0.50 for children. T552-3247, F552-3151. The gardens are 5 km east of Cartago on the road to Paraíso. There is no direct bus service. From Cartago take a bus towards Paraíso, asking the driver* *to let you off at the entrance to "Jardín Botánico Lankester" and from there walk south for 500 m, turning right at the sign. Most tour operators in San José provide tours to the gardens, normally as part of a trip to Irazú. From US$55.*

Orosí Valley

From **Paraíso**, 8 km southwest of Cartago, the road falls away to the hidden secrets of the Orosí Valley. The valley floor is flooded by the waters of the artificial Lago Cachí created by the Cachí Dam which blocks the river before flowing out to the popular whitewater rafting Reventazón river. Surrounded by steep-sided mountains rising up to cloud level, occasionally dressed with the fashionable costume of green-lined coffee plantations, the 30-km road makes a pleasant day trip with restaurants providing scenic opportunities for meals along the way. Longer stays are possible at various hotels catering for all budgets.

East of Paraíso Following the northern shore, the road drops past a look-out post leading to the small community of **Ujarrás** and the ruins of the country's first colonial church built between 1570 and 1580. Legend has it that in 1666, English pirates, including the youthful Henry Morgan, were seen off by the citizens of Ujarrás aided by the Virgin. This miraculous protection is celebrated annually on April 16 or the closest Sunday when the saint is carried in procession from Paraíso to the ruined church. The grounds surrounding the ruins are a popular picnic spot with *Joséfino* families. Over the road are a couple of pools that are positively heaving at weekends. The *Charrara Tourist Complex* is a 30-min walk from Ujarrás, also with direct buses at weekends leaving one block north of Cartago ruins. There is restaurant, swimming pool, boat rides on the lake and a good campsite.

Continuing east, the **Presa de Cachí** (Cachí Dam) is not particularly impressive in scale or detail, unless it's releasing water, but makes for a natural stopping point before heading along the southern shore and the compulsory stop at the **Casa del Soñador** (the Dreamer's House), where Hermes and Miguel Quesada carve figurines and faces using twisted old coffee plant roots and driftwood, offering some for sale. Continuing the sculptural tradition of their father, Macedonia Quesada, who set up the school in 1985, the wooden pieces have a simple charm.

Sleeping & eating If looking for a quiet spot to stay for a few days try **A-B** *Cabañas de Montaña Piedras Albas*, T/F383-1819, in San José T/F253-1019, www.cabinas.co.cr 1,500 m east of the church in Cachí, just a couple of fully equipped cabins high in the hills close to the Río Naranjo. Getting up here needs a 4X4, but the views are incredible and you'll have the 4 trails leading through the forest pretty much to yourself. Excellent birding, telescope for star gazing or just complete relaxation. On the lake shore is *La Casona del Cafetal*, T533-3280, a very popular weekend dining destination open every day, but with an "all you can eat" buffet on Sun for US$13. The à la carte menu starts at around US$6. It's a beautiful setting right on the southern shore of Lake Cachí. After lunch you can take a horse-drawn carriage round the coffee plantation before heading east towards the town of Orosí.

Transport **Buses** to **Cachí**, via **Ujarras** and **Paraíso** leave Cartago from C 6, Av 1-3, every 1½ hrs, taking 1 hr 20 mins for the journey. Ask in Cartago or Paraíso if a bus that circuits the lake has started up. The demand for one is obvious and improved road conditions on the southern shore make it quite likely.

Heading south of Paraíso the views are equally impressive as the road twists and descends into the valley passing hillside pastures, flower farms and the inevitable coffee plantations. From high up on the hillside you can rest and refresh at **B** *Sanchiri Mirador & Lodge*, T/F533-3210, www.sanchiri.com The mid-priced restaurant, serving local and international food is a rustic open cabin setting, is precariously balanced on a bluff and has the best views of the valley. Half a dozen rustic cabins, each with private bath and hot water, also have very good views. Rolling down the hill a few hundred metres is an ICT-owned *mirador* (lookout) complete with picnic spots, and kiosk selling drinks and snacks.

A short distance further downhill, a steep road to the right that requires 4X4 leads for 1½ km down to the valley floor and the secluded setting of **B** *Hotel California*, T/F574-6337. Once down here, you'll probably choose to stay. Although the views have gone, the climate is slightly warmer and in addition to the comfortable rooms, there is a swimming pool, soccer pitch and tennis courts. Horses are also available for hire.

South of Paraíso

A rising star of the valley, Orosí is best known for the 18th-century **Parroquia de San José** built by Franciscan missionaries. Recently restored, the church has weathered the trials of countless earthquake tremors clearly apparent in the strained pitch roof that has warped over the centuries. Across the cloister, the **Museo de Arte Religioso** displays religious artifacts and artwork in the former monastery living quarters. ■ *Tue-Sat 1300-1700, Sun 0900-1200 and 1300-1700. Church open every morning. US$1.*

In town there are hot springs next to Orosí Lodge, and a second set in Los Patios a short distance south of town. Ask locally for directions, but both are very crowded at weekends.

Orosí

B *Orosí Lodge*, T/F533-3578, sites.netscape.net/timeveit/orosilodge A beautiful European-style café with a small balcony greets guests at this carefully maintained lodge. Seven rooms all with balcony overlooking the valley towards Volcán Irazú all have orthopaedic beds, private bath, hot water and kitchenette constructed to European standards. The owners Andreas and Cornelia provide just about everything you could want. Divine home-baked cookies, mountain bikes, kayaks and horses for hire and an internet service. Credit cards accepted. **B-C** *Cabinas Media Libra*, T533-3838, F533-3737. Rather stark and characterless rooms, with telephone, TV, fridge. But clean and friendly service, and good local knowledge. Credit cards accepted. **C-G** *Montaña Linda*, if dialling locally call T/F533-3640, if calling internationally T/F 533-2153. note, it is possible to block international calls in Costa Rica, they probably have a separate line for security reasons. www.montanalinda.com A classic backpackers' place, with a good range of options. Bed and breakfast (**C**) if you just can't get out of bed, dormitory rooms (**F**) and options for camping (**G**). The owners Toine and Sara are friendly and know their patch very well. Trips to local waterfalls, Tapantí Macizo de la Muerte National Park, Purisil trout fishing, and any other local sights are easily arranged and mix perfectly with the Spanish classes at the *Montaña Linda Language School* which uses local teachers trained by the school to get you *hablando Español*. And if you want total linguistic submersion – the best way – there is a homestay option.

Sleeping & eating

Buses from **Cartago** to **Orosí/Río Macho** from C 6, Av 1-3 every 30 mins, journey time of 35/55 mins. 160 or 185 *colónes*.

Transport

A short distance south of Orosí the road splits, the left fork crosses the Río Orosí to the **C-D** *Río Palomo*, T/F533-3057 which has simple rooms, with private bath, a pool, and a well thought of local restaurant.

South of Orosí

Central highlands & the surrounding area

The right fork leads towards Tapantí-Macizo de la Muerte National Park some 9 km from the main road and a number of interesting local sights en route. **Monte Sky** is a private reserve covering 416 ha and bordering the national park. Over 160 birds have been counted to date and the number is growing. A *Monte Sky*, T/F228-0010, or San José T256-1790, F256-1124, www.intnet.co.cr/montesky Space sleeping up to 20 people with basic accommodation, ideal for students and groups, with set programmes provided or you can make your own. Nearby **Purisil trout farm** gives you the chance to catch your supper. You pay for what you catch and they will prepare and cook the fish for you on the spot. A couple of km before the entrance is **B** *Kiri Lodge*, T284-2024, beeper T225-2500, San José T257-8064, F257-8065. There are good trails leading through the lodge's ground to the national park. 6 excellent cabins and breakfast included. Peaceful and very friendly.

Parque Nacional Tapantí-Macizo de la Muerte

Tapantí Macizo de la Muerte is the country's newest national park and one of the wettest parts of the country, some parts reportedly receiving as much as 8 m of rain a year. Approached from Orosí and just 30 km from Cartago the national park is surprisingly easy to reach and packs in the interest.

Covering 58,000 ha, Tapantí-Macizo includes the former Tapantí National Park and much of the Río Macho Forest Reserve. The park protects the Río Orosí basin which feeds the Cachí Dam hydro power plant. Strategically the southern boundary of the park joins with the Chirripó National Park extending the continuous protected area that makes up the La Amistad Biosphere Reserve. The park incorporates a wide range of life zones from lower montane wet forest to montane rainforest with altitudes rising from 1,220 m to over 3,000 m at the border with Chirripó. The diverse altitudes and relative seclusion of the park has created an impressive species list which is currently incomplete due to the recent creation of the park. Tapir, pacas, racoons, and white-faced monkeys make up some of over 45 species of mammal found in the area as well as the elusive jaguar and ocelot. The quetzal nests in late Spring and can be found on the western slopes near the entry point, with the black-faced solitaire, countless hummingbirds and oropendolas contributing to some 260 species of birds recorded so far. The wet conditions are ideal for lizards, snakes – including pit vipers – and frogs.

Until 1992 Tapantí was a wildlife refuge and the elevated status has increased interest but visitor numbers are still quite small and the vast majority are *Ticos* and keen birders. Three trails lead off the principal road providing walks ranging from 30 mins to 2 hrs but don't forget the raincoat or umbrella. There are several waterfalls that are good for swimming and some good picnic spots.

■ *Official park hrs through Tapantí are from 0700-1700 daily. US$6. Local contact details T/F551-2970. Camping is not presently permitted within the park but there are plans to build a campsite and facilities. Restrooms and drinking water are available. There is a small information centre with trail maps and a simple slide show. Getting to the park by car simply follow the directions to Orosí and follow the road to the park headquarters. Buses only run as far as Río Paloma from where it is a 9 km walk uphill. Alternatively take a taxi from Orosí. Several tour operators in San José can arrange trips with guides. It will also be possible to reach Tapantí Macizo from the Pan-American Highway. Contact Genesis II for details.*

Turrialba and surrounding area

A lively local shopping hub that has expanded to fill the river flood plains of the Río Turrialba, the otherwise forgettable town appears in the spotlight not through its own merits but rather by association. With the Reventazón and Pacuare rivers nearby, Turrialba is the Costa Rican centre for whitewater rafting, it's the nearest town of size to the Guayabo National Monument archaeological site, and the world famous CATIE tropical research station is just a few kilometres down the road. Volcán Turrialba National Park offers a quiet high altitude hike for those who like to walk to the top of a volcano.

Colour map 2, grid C4
Population: 33,411
Altitude: 646 m

Ins and outs

By car, Turrialba is easily reached from San José via Cartago. Coming from the Caribbean a wonderfully scenic Highway 10 rises and falls through the mountains and coffee fields from Siquirres on the San José – Limón Highway. By bus, there are about 15 buses a day to Turrialba from San José with Transtusa (T556-0073), leaving C 13, Av 6-8, taking about 90 mins.

Getting there

Turrialba is small enough to walk round, but to keep you on your toes the *calles* start from the Parque Central as with most Costa Rican towns, but the *avenidas* take the

Getting around

Central highlands & the surrounding area

Turrialba

To Albergue Mirador Pochotel, Turrialtico
& Monumento Nacional Guayabo

To Santa Cruz

Municipal Buildings

Av 6/John Allen Taylor

Parque
Central

Av 4/Independencia

C/Jenaro Bonilla

C/Marco Tulio Castro Cardilla

C/Mariano Cortés

Río Turrialba

To San José
& Siquerres

Banco Popular $

Banco de
Costa Rica $

Café Net
Turrialba

Av 2/Panamá

Cine
Norma

Banco
Nacional $

To San José

Local Buses

Av 0/José Monge Dumani

Av 1/Francisco Orlich

Río Colorado

4/Paraíso

To Kingston's Restaurant, Casa Turire, Rancho
Naturalista, La Suiza, CATIE & Siquerres

N

0 metres   50
0 yards   50

Sleeping
1 Alcázar
2 Central
3 Chemanga
4 Interamericano
5 Laroche

6 Turrialba
7 Wagelia
8 Whittingham

Eating
1 Café Gourmet

2 La Garza
3 Nuevo Hong Kong
4 Pizzería Mammamia
5 Pizzería Julián
6 Pizzería Soda Popo's
7 Soda Burbuja

railway as the dividing line. For trips to outer lying areas you will have to take a taxi or explore bus options from the central bus station.

Best time to visit   If whitewater rafting, the higher water makes for better rapids, so visit between May and Nov. But you can raft all year round, and you may prefer not to go rafting in the rain.

Sights

At the confluence of the Turrialba and Colorado rivers, 62 km from San José, the town is a bridge between the central highlands and the Caribbean lowlands and was a former stopping point on the old Atlantic railway between Cartago and Puerto Limón. The disused train tracks to Limón run right through town. Despite the loss of transport links, the streets are busy with villagers from surrounding communities stocking up before heading home. Temperatures are comfortably warm at around 22°C year round and sights in the town are almost nil – even the trailer loads of kayaks that periodically rumble through the town barely turn heads.

Essentials

Sleeping   **AL** *Wagelia*, on Av 4 at the entrance to Turrialba, T556-1566, F556-1596. The best hotel in town, and a little overpriced for what you get. 18 rooms surrounding a central courtyard each with private bath, telephone and safety box. Some also have TV, with fan or a/c. Close to the centre of town, the Wagelia also has a restaurant and bar that could be transported from any small European town. **C** *Alcázar*, C 3, Av 2-4, 25 m north of Banco Norte T393-0767, F556-7397. Clean, tidy, efficient and just a few too many plastic flowers. There is a small terrace upstairs and each room has cable TV, a telephone, fan and a private bath with hot water. Small bar/restaurant downstairs with a frightening colour scheme serving meals from US$2. A classic of this price bracket. **D** *Hotel Turrialba*, Av 2, C 2-4, T556-6396. Clean simple rooms with private bath, hot water and TV. There are also a couple of pool tables and soft drinks for sale. **E** *Laroche*, north of Parque Central on C 1, T556-6915. Simple and basic rooms but friendly with comfortable beds. Small bar downstairs. **F** *Whittingham*, C 4, Av 0-2, T550-8927. 7 fairly dark but OK rooms, some with private bath. An option if other places are full.

In a row facing the old railway line are the following places. **C-E** *Interamericano*, Av 1, T556-0142, F556-7790, www.hotelinteramericano.com In the words of the *Blanca Rosa*, one half of the North American mother-daughter team that run the *Interamericano*, the rooms are "nothing fancy but we do guarantee it's clean." The rooms are indeed spotlessly clean, bright with natural light and good beds. Doubtless this modesty, a keenness to help and excellent local knowledge is one reason people keep coming back. Cheaper without private bath. There's also a small bar, internet access and storage of kayaks free for guests, small charge for non-guests. Good social area for talking things over and excellent noticeboard. Any problems, questions, queries, roll up and ask, even if you're not a guest. **F** *Chemanga*, Av 1. Some rooms OK, some definitely not, the last resort. Add cold water, indifferent service and you feel as if you should be paid not paying. **F** *Central*, Av 1, T556-0170. The rooms are pretty basic. Rooms without private bath are cheaper and its cold water all the way through – which isn't too bad at this altitude. There is a TV in the lobby, some games and drinks available.

Out of town   **LL** *Casa Turire*, 14 km southeast of Turrialba, 2 km before La Suiza, 1 km from main road at Hacienda Atirro, T531-1111, F531-1075, www.hotelcasaturire.com Comfort and elegance in this idyllic tropical setting. With a plantation-style ambience and personal service, the *Casa Turire* is one of the celebrated five 'Small Distinctive

Rafting the Reventazón and Pacuare

A short distance from Turrialba the world-renowned Pacuare and Reventazón rivers crash and thunder down the valleys leading from the eastern slopes of the Talamanca Mountains. Organized trips lasting one to four days run Class III, IV and sometimes V rapids flowing through pristine primary rainforest. This is some of the best scenery in Costa Rica with sheer sided gorges draped in finely woven 100% natural green cloth. Seeing toucans, sloths and spider monkeys is virtually guaranteed, unless it is raining!

But when it rains the river is higher so you'll be paddling so hard you won't have time to look at the animals.

Full equipment is provided for all. For novices, safety briefing and training is provided and any reasonably fit person should be able to handle up to Class IV with good supervision and instruction.

Several organizations run rafting trips in the area. Two of the more experienced companies are **Rios Tropicales** and **Costa Rica Expeditions**. Several local companies also run trips including **Loco's Tropical Tours**, **Jungla** and **Rainforest World**.

Hotels'. 12 luxury rooms with bath and 4 suites are fully equipped with every comfort, including cable TV and telephone. The restaurant is Mediterranean-style, and there is a spring-fed pool, library and parlour games room. The arrival of Lake Angostura now makes Casa Turire a lakeside hotel. Beyond La Suiza is **L** *Rancho Naturalista*, PO Box 364-1002 San José, T430-0400, F430-0398, www.ranchonaturalista.com 12 rooms, most with private bath. Reservations essential for this spot which is very popular with birdwatchers. Price per person includes gourmet meals, horse riding, guided tours, transfers from San José and airport. Programmes organized for birdwatchers and naturalists, to surrounding area and CATIE (US$15). **C** *Turrialtico*, on the road to Limón, T538-1111, F538-1575, www.turrialtico.com On top of hill with extensive views, clean, private bath, comfortable, friendly. On this road in the town of **Pavones** is **D** *Albergue Mirador Pochotel*, T556-0111.

Several cheap restaurants and *sodas* dotted around the main square including *La Garza*, with good, local food and *Pizzería Julián* on the north side of the square, both cheap. *Pizzaría Mammamia* and *Pizzería Soda Popo's* are both fast food style cafés on the east side. *Nuevo Hong Kong*, facing the Parque Central, on the corner of C 1 and Av 4, serves good cheap Chinese. One block south of the plaza on C Central is *Soda Burbuja*, popular family run place open to the street with big portions of local dishes, very good value. Out of town on the road south is the locally popular and mid-price *Kingstons*. | **Eating**

Café Gourmet, opposite *Hotel Wagelia* on Av 4, serves excellent coffee indoors or on the tiny patio just big enough for two to watch the world meander by. *Cine Norma* on C 1, Av 2-6, hardly looks open but you may be in luck. | **Cafés, bars & nightclubs**

Rafting operations in San José like *Costa Rica Expeditions* and *Ríos Tropicales*, have trips that you can meet up with in Turrialba. If you're looking for a local operator try one of the following. *Loco's Tropical Tours*, Apdo 285-7150, Turrialba, Costa Rica, T556-6035, www.whiteh2o.com Not the biggest rafting operation in Costa Rica but, they claim, the friendliest. *Tico*-run, and with a fair amount of experience. Prices from US$55 to US$125 a day. *Jungla*, T/F556-6225, toll free in the US on 1-888-4JUNGLA, www.junglaexpeditions.com Just west of town on the road to CATIE is Jungla. In addition to river rafting, you can do kayak school, mountain biking, canyoning, backpacking and sea kayaking. Day trip and multi-day trips organized. A couple of small local operations include *Rainforest World*, T556-2678, | **Tour operators** www.rforestw.com and *Ticos River Adventures*, T/F556-1231, www.ticoriver.com, which both offer 1-day trips around Turrialba and a few multi-day trips further afield. *Serendipity Adventures*, T558-1000, F558-1010, or in USA T800-635-2325, www.serendipityadventures.com Occupy a niche market in Costa Rica providing hot air balloon tours in the Turrialba area, or to the north around Naranjo or Volcán Arenal. Whichever one you choose it is certain to be a stunning adventure. *Serendipity* also arrange a variety of adventure and nature tours.

Transport **Buses** to San José and Siquirres leave from Av 4, C 0-2. Service to San José runs every ½ hr from 0500 until 2100 taking 90 mins. To Siquirres buses depart every 2 hrs, taking 1 hr 40 mins. Buses to local destinations leave from the terminal on the corner of Av 2, C 2.

Directory **Banks** Several banks mostly along C 3 between Av 2-4 generally open from 0830-1530. *Banco de Costa Rica*, Av 0 and C 3, has Visa and MasterCard ATM. A little to the west is *Banco Nacional* Av 0, C 1-3, ATMs. *Banco Popular*, corner of Av 2 and C 3, with Visa ATM. **Communications** Internet: *Café Net Turrialba*, in shopping mall next to *Banco Nacional*. There is another *internet café* on C 2, Av 2-4, close to the San José/Siquirres bus stop. **Post**: The post office is north of the Parque Central on C 0 just passed Av 8. **Hospital and medical services** The local hospital is on T556-1133, several pharmacies found around the centre of town. **Useful addresses** In emergency call 911.

Parque Nacional Volcán Turrialba

Colour map 2, grid B4

Volcán Turrialba is the least visited and smallest of the central highland volcanoes to merit its own national park. Established back in 1955, the lack of interest means there is no entrance fee – or at least no one to collect it, officially you get a permit in San José – and no services provided.

At 3,328 m, it sits on the eastern most flank of the Cordillera Central, next to Volcán Irazú and on a clear day can be seen from the San José – Limón Highway. Three craters show evidence of lava flows, but while the volcano is partially active with fumaroles and slight seismic activity, the last reported eruptions occurred in 1864 and 1865. Vegetation is characterized by tough, twisted branches and small trees. Mammal populations of armadillos, porcupines, pumas and oncillas are believed to be very low, and recorded bird species, including the black-faced solitaire and several species of hummingbird, number 84.

There are a couple of routes to the volcano. From Cartago a bus runs from C 4 y Av 6 to San Gerardo north of Turrialba, you then walk or hitch a ride to **Finca La Central** which sits in the saddle between Irazú and Turrialba. From Turrialba, take a bus to Santa Cruz and walk up to Finca La Central. Day trips can be organized through tour operators in San José. If you want to stay overnight you can camp. Alternatively 2 km from Finca La Central is **A** (per person) *Volcán Turrialba Lodge* T/F273-4335, www.volcanturrialbalodge.com Accessible only by 4-wheel drive and well signposted if you're driving, but the lodge can also arrange transport. Twelve homey rooms each with private bath and fire stove. Some excellent tour options including treks and horse riding to the crater floor. Wholesome Costa Rican food cooked over an open fire.

Monumento Nacional Guayabo

Colour map 2, grid B4

It's easy to think the country's premier archaeological site Guayabo National Monument is overlooked – many maps don't even show its location. Still barely explored, the Indian ceremonial centre lies 4 km from the town of Guayabo, and 19 km from Turrialba.

Over 3000 years old, the site was occupied from 1,000 BC to 1,400 AD flourishing around 800 AD, the period when many of the stone structures that remain were constructed. Stone roads stretch for considerable distances with mounds of different size and height being used for construction of housing. Petroglyphs have been etched on to many of the stones, their meaning still undeciphered, and centuries-old aqueducts still carry water to the reservoirs.

Underfunded and rarely visited, excavation at the site only began in 1968 despite being re-discovered at the end of the 19th century by Anastasio Alfaro. Today the protected area covers 232 ha, only a very small fraction of which has been excavated. Little is known about the people who lived here beyond the broad notion that the community was multi-skilled with individual specializations, and was ruled politically and religiously by a *cacique* (shaman). The economy was based on agriculture, hunting and fishing, but the reason for selecting the site, and for abandoning it in the 1400s, remains a mystery.

If you are looking for ruins of majestic proportions don't visit. Guayabo does not compare to the great ruins of Central America in Guatemala and Mexico, nor to those of South America. Indeed, archaeologists call this part of the Americas the Intermediate Area lying between those two larger civilizations. If, however, you want to visit a spot where you can still let your imagination run wild with theories and possibilities – with no one around to tell you different – while exploring a couple of trails and enjoying plenty of birds, wildlife and impressive waterfalls, then it is worth making the effort. ■ *Mon-Sun, 0800-1600. US$6. T290-1927, F232-5324. Information available with toilets and drinking water. From Turrialba, there are buses at 1100 and 1710 (returning 1250 and 1750), and an additional bus on Sun at 0900, returning 1700. Check times locally. (If you miss the bus it is quite difficult to hitch as there is little traffic.) If you cannot get a bus all the way to Guayabo, several buses each day pass the turn-off to Guayabo, the town is a 2-hr walk uphill. A taxi from Turrialba will cost about US$15 one-way.*

Camping is reported to be allowed in the site. Drinking water and toilets are provided. Alternatively try **C-D** *Albergue y Restaurant La Calzada*, T556-0465, which has a few rooms and a small restaurant. Best to make a reservation. There are several small cafés in the town of Guayabo. **Sleeping & eating**

CATIE

The Centro Agronómico Tropical de Investigación y Enseñanza (T558-2000 ext 2275, F556-1533, www.catie.ac.cr) more commonly known as CATIE is an international, non-profit research organization about 4 km southeast of Turrialba. Its main purpose is research, higher education and outreach in agricultural sciences, natural resources and related subjects in the American tropics. *Colour map 2, grid C4*

Created in 1940 in response to an acknowledged need to share research and experiences in tropical agriculture across the Americas, the Costa Rican government donated 2,500 ha to CATIE's forerunner, the *Inter-American Institute of Agricultural Sciences*. Today, 11 Latin American and Caribbean nations support CATIE's work carried out by a staff of 120, including 40 with doctorates and 50 with masters degrees. We're talking highly qualified here.

CATIE's philosophy is to "produce while conserving and conserve while producing". Contributions to such broad goals are by their own admittance,

 **Laguna Angostura – a new Arenal?**

South of Turrialba, the construction and completion of the Angostura Dam in 2000 created a minor controversy. Blocking the Río Reventazón upstream of CATIE, the dam has created the 256-ha Lake Angostura and inundated farmland and world-class sections of whitewater which attracted international kayakers to Costa Rica.

Being self-sufficient in energy generation is the goal of most nations and Costa Rica is no different. Beyond doubt the nation's greatest potential lies with hydro-electric power, and there are several large projects dotted round the country.

In return, the state-owned electricity company (ICE) has created the country's largest hydro-electric generator which will produce some 177-megawatts, and in the process has been praised for creating local employment.

But, critics say, most of the power generated will be exported to Panama. Archaeological studies instigated as a result of the project revealed 42 new sites of precolumbian cultures that have now been flooded.

Lake Angostura looks certain to develop into some form of attraction, with suggestions of boat tours and even jet skis. Casa Turire now enjoys a lake side vantage, Pochotel Mountain Hotel has a great view from up high. Beyond the melancholic memories of rafters and kayakers mourning the loss, the price, in addition to the US$390 mn cost of the project, depends on your perspective.

difficult to measure, but CATIE has made significant developments in agro-forestry, integrated pest management and management of tropical crops and tropical nature forests. CATIE also maintains a genetic resource bank of several crops and produce. In short, CATIE is of great interest to tropical agronomists and researchers, with one of the largest fruit collections in the world, and an important library on tropical agriculture.

For less academic visitors it is the landscaped gardens and trails leading through the ecologically varied zones that attracts birders in particular. Visits are welcome, and easily arranged directly or through many of the hotels in the Turrialba area. If you want to stay or organize a group trip, a wide range of **accommodation** options are available including student dormitory rooms, apartments and a couple of guesthouses prices **AL-L**. There is also a gym and a couple of restaurants. Contact CATIE to book accommodation. Day trips are possible and should be booked in advance or through an agency in San José.

Moravia del Chirripó From Turrialba you can get to the village of Moravia del Chirripó, east of Turrialba, where guides and horses can be hired for an excursion into the trackless jungle homeland of the Talamanca Indians, with their legends of lost goldfields. The bus from Turrialba takes 4 hrs, only certain in dry season; in wet season go to Grano de Oro, from where it's a 1 hr walk. No accommodation in Moravia, stay put at the *pulpería* (tavern) in Grano de Oro. ■ *Trips can be arranged to the Chirripó Indian Reserve of Alto Pacuare, east of Turrialba; the reserve is a 2½-hr hike from Río Vereh, and is good for serious naturalists and hikers.*

The northern region

5

180

The northern region

182 The Puerto Viejo Loop

189 San José to Fortuna

190 Fortuna

197 Fortuna to Tilaráni

203 North of Fortuna

206 Reserva Biológica Bosque Nuboso
Monteverde and Santa Elena

Sweeping northwest from San José the mountains of the Cordillera de Tilarán create a number of irresistible opportunities. The Puerto Viejo de Sarapiquí loop takes in good scenery, a host of outstanding wildlife opportunities and adventurous pursuits. Volcán Arenal is the perfect volcano, standing symmetrical clear and tall against the horizon, puffing fumes and exploding against a fine blue sky (if you're lucky), with the expansive Lake Arenal in the foreground. Amongst the lowland towns to the north, Los Chiles close to the Nicaraguan border stands out with the profuse wildlife of the Caño Negro Wildlife Reserve. A few hours south of Lake Arenal or as a cut-through from the Pan-American Highway, bumpy roads lead through simple dairy communities to the reserves of Monteverde and Santa Elena and your chance for more natural encounters.

Things to do in the northern region

- There's no getting away from the high expectations of this region but nature doesn't always perform on demand. If Arenal volcano isn't blowing its top, trek out to the thunderous **Fortuna waterfall** which is always impressive.
- Get to grips with the **cloudforest canopy** of Monteverde and Santa Elena. Calmly explore by foot, ride converted ski lifts through the canopy or zip down steel cables strung throughout the valleys.
- Settle down to the **rhythm of the rainforest** at a lodge in Braulio Carrillo National Park or the lowlands to the north.
- Explore the rarely visited **Tenorio National Park** – services are still limited and basic and it should be a good challenge.

The Puerto Viejo Loop

Ins and outs

Getting there & around
This is neither a recognized district or a geographical region, but a road (Highway 4) which leaves the San José–Limón Highway at Rancho Roberto's restaurant at the edge of Braulio Carrillo National Park, and heads north looping through Puerto Viejo de Sarapiquí passing biological stations, ecolodges and adventure centres, completing the final leg of the circuit through the saddle between Volcán Barva and Volcán Poás directly north of San José.

As the name suggests, it's a circular route – particularly scenic in the section from Varablanca to San Miguel. You can make the journey in one day – a popular choice for tours from San José – or travel at a more leisurely pace stopping off as you wish en route.

Travelling by bus is easy with regular, almost hourly, services travelling the route clockwise and counter clockwise from the Gran Terminal de Caribe in San José. However, some of the places of interest are not on the main road so you may find yourself walking a short distance.

Rara Avis

Booking accommodation in advance is strongly recommended especially in the dry season. T764-3131 or T256-4993, F764-4187 or F257-0438, www.rara-avis.com

Reached through **Las Horquetas**, around 16 km north of the San José–Limón road, Rara Avis is a privately owned reserve with accommodation close to the lower slopes of Braulio Carrillo National Park, developed to show the rainforest can be economically productive and consequently save it from destruction. Once visited, few would doubt the success of the place which provides guests with an intimate experience of the rainforest.

Perched on the eastern flanks of the park at an altitude of 700 m, the diversity of the reserve is staggering. Over 360 birds have been recorded including umbrella birds and the green macaw. You will probably see monkeys, coatis and anteaters, and the really lucky may occasionally get to see spotted tapirs and jaguar – or at least their footprints.

At the reserve itself – reached by a bone-shaking 15-km, 3-hr journey in a tractor-pulled cart (see transport below), an extensive network of trails leads through primary forest. Some are quite rough and muddy so go prepared. You can hike them with a guide or enjoy the solitude and absolute silence by breaking out on your own.

Several ongoing projects at Rara Avis are proving the rainforest can be economically productive (since its creation in 1983, Rara Avis has managed to return a slight profit). Firstly, the lodges bring in a reliable source of income. Other natural projects include a butterfly export programme, cultivation of the rare and endemic stained glass palm ornamental plant and research into the sustainable use of orchids.

A number of accommodation options are available. All prices include transport, 3 daily meals and guides. **L** *River Edge Cabin* is the secluded choice, ideal for birdwatchers and couples, with a couple of double beds, hot water, private bath and solar-powered lighting. Hammocks on the shared balcony look across to the forest. **AL** *Waterfall Lodge*, has 8 rooms, each with a private bath and balcony, in a comfortable but rustic lodge. It's just a couple of hundred metres from the waterfall – hence the name. The cheapest option is

Sleeping & eating

Parque Nacional Braulio Carrillo & Puerto Viejo loop

A *Casitas*, with 2-room cabins sleeping up to 4 people, sharing a cold water shower. It's possible to get even cheaper backpacker rates if there are vacancies.

Traditional country-style Costa Rican meals are served family-style 3 times a day in the open-air dining room.

Transport Catching an early bus from San José you should be in time to get to the hut in Las Horquetas in time to catch the tractor-cart which leaves around 0930. The journey takes 3 hrs, leaving Rara Avis at 0200 in the afternoon in time to catch a bus back if needed. There is parking at the lodge if you are driving.

Isla de las Heliconias

Camping (E) is allowed and the price includes entrance

In the thoroughly missable hamlet of **Montero**, close to the Río Isla Grande bridge, is the pleasant surprise of Heliconias Island, a fantastic collection of over 70 types of heliconia from Costa Rica, Latin America and throughout the world. Rarely will you get the chance to see such variety and diversity in such a small area. Tim Ryan, the owner is rapidly becoming a very knowledgeable self-taught botanist. The 2-ha island is a joy to visit, and you can rest with refreshments in the impressively high, thatched bamboo hut restaurant.

■ *Open daily but call ahead to be sure. US$7.50. F766-6247, heliconia@ sarapiquirainforest.com If driving, Montero is 8 km south of Puerto Viejo de Sarapiquí. Look for the right turn 1 km south of Río Isla Grande bridge and the Isla Grand petrol station. A right turn, followed by a right turn leads down a grassy track which should be signposted. If travelling by bus, ask the driver to drop you at Montero.*

Estación Biológica La Selva

Colour map 2, grid B3

Joining Braulio Carrillo National Park at its northern most boundary La Selva Biological Station is an internationally renowned research station. The species diversity is spectacular and for both the specialist and general interest visitor, La Selva is a natural playground. Over half (436) of the bird species found in Costa Rica have been sighted on the 1,513 ha – just under six square miles – of old growth and disturbed tropical wetforests. Toucans, parrots, trogons, hummingbirds, monkeys, peccaries, agoutis and coatis are regularly seen by visitors. There's even a rather touching warning to keep an eye out for the seven venomous snakes out of a total of 56 species found at the station.

Owned by the *Organization for Tropical Studies* (which also owns Palo Verde in Guanacaste and Las Cruces in southern Costa Rica), the station is first and foremost a research station and focuses on that role. But guests are welcome and usually visit as part of a day trip from San José or Puerto Viejo de Sarapiquí. A 3½-hour 'Experience La Selva' tour leaves at 0800 and 1300. There are also half-day and three-day birdwatching courses – what better start could you get to the subject.

■ *The station is open every day, and begins life at dawn – around 0600. Entrance, including the guided walk is US$20. T766-6565 or in San José on T240-6696, F766-6536. The station is just 3 km south of Puerto Viejo de Sarapiquí. There is a sign but you'll probably drive past a couple of times first. Buses from San José to Puerto Viejo will drop you off at the junction from where you can walk the kilometre or so to the entrance.*

Sleeping Accommodation is available (**AL** per person) in dormitory-style accommodation, with 3 meals a day. Rates are reduced for researchers and students. A dirt road just before the OTS station leads to **E** (per person) *Sarapiquí Ecolodge*, T766-6569 (daytime only), F236-8762. 4 rooms with shared bathroom, food extra. Great spot with good birdwatching, river trips, horse riding, but sometimes closed, so call ahead.

Puerto Viejo de Sarapiquí

It is difficult to believe that Puerto Viejo de Sarapiquí is the largest town in the northwestern lowlands and was once a flourishing port moving people and produce northwards down the Sarapiquí River to join the River San Juan and from there to the Caribbean. There are possibilities for river travel but you will need time, plenty of cash and a fair amount of patience if you want to make it to Tortuguero. For the moment at least, the opportunity to jump on the banana boat has long gone.

Colour map 2, grid B3
Population: 9,864;
Altitude: 70 m
www.sarapiqui
rainforest.com

Today's Puerto Viejo de Sarapiquí is a couple of roads linking the small riverside dock with the bus station and not much of interest in between. You enter town at the junction a few hundred metres west of town. The town limps along in an empty, bored way so common in defunct docks. But it isn't as though people don't visit the area – the road west to La Virgen and the road south to the main highway are littered with ecolodges, private reserves and river rafting opportunities. Whitewater and float trips down the Sarapiquí can be organized locally, but most people book trips from San José.

Sleeping & eating

In town   A-B *El Bambú*, in a blaze of lightbulbs on the north side of the football pitch, T766-6005, F766-6132, www.elbambu.com 16 rooms, all with a/c, TV, telephone, hot water and private bath. Smart restaurant looking out to the garden. No great surprise, but there's bamboo furniture throughout. Plans for a pool and a small gym. The best in town, but still overpriced. On the very western outskirts of town, just left of the main junction is **B** *Posada Andrea Cristina*, on the western outskirts of town, just left of the main junction, T/F766-6265. With small, comfortable cabins, set in tropical gardens. Good local knowledge. **C** *Mi Lindo Sarapiquí*, on the west side of the park, T/F766-6074, lindo@sarapiquirainforest.com 6 spotless rooms with hot water private bath and fan. Nothing flashy but a good deal. **F** *Cabinas Monteverde*, next to *El Bambú*, T766-6236. Rooms have private bath, but are pretty dirty. **F** *Hospedaje Gonar*, on the road to the dock above the hardware store, T766-6207. Basic rooms, the ones with windows are better, but they're all pretty grubby.

On the **southern bank of the Río Sarapiquí** is **AL-B** *El Gavilán Lodge*, reached by taxi, T234-9507, F253-6556, www.gavilanlodge.com 13 tidy rooms with tiled floors and simple wooden furniture sleeping 2-4 people all with hot water private bath and a/c. Well tended gardens beside the open-air restaurant serving international and Costa Rican dishes. The 75 ha private reserve has 3 trails round the hotel where you can see spider, capuchin and howler monkeys, and a bird list currently standing at around 120. Boat trips down the Sarapiquí River to the Costa Rican border organized through *Peace Rainbow Travel Agency*.

In **Trinidad**, reached by boat down the River Sarapiquí on the San Juan River is **D** *Cabinas La Trinidad*, T/F259-1679, with simple cabins in a quiet spot, meals included.

Choices of places to eat in town are simple with *Mi Lindo Sarapiquí* serving a wide selection of cheap dishes and super-cold beer. Good cheap food at *El Muelle* by the river with good views from the dockside.

Transport

Bus Almost hourly buses connect with **San José** from the Gran Terminal del Caribe with Empresarios Guapileños, T710-6155. Buses travel north from the capital through **Heredia** and **Vara Blanca**, 3½ hrs, US$2.50. Alternatively, buses head directly east through **Braulio Carrillo National Park** and **Horquetas**, 1½ hrs, US$2.50. Regular buses also go to **Guápiles**, **Horquetas** and **Río Frio**. There are also services from Puerto Viejo to **Ciudad Quesada**, five daily, 2½ hrs, US$1.50.

Car Following the San José–Limón Highway, after passing over and through the Braulio Carrillo National Park, Highway 4 turns north at Rancho Robertos for 33 km. A

The northern region

more scenic, but longer, route heads north through Heredia and Vara Blanca, heading east through La Virgen and on to Puerto Viejo.

Boat The cost of a launch to Tortuguero is about US$300 to US$350 for between 1 and 10 people. The whole trip takes about 5 hrs. There is an outside chance that you may find a boat making the journey – the prices vary depending on your luck from US$40 to US$75. There is a daily launch service to **Trinidad** on the San Juan River, leaving at 1230, returning the next day at 1000.

Tour operators There are no really established tour operators in town. *Peace Rainbow Travel Agency* works out of *El Gavilán Lodge* and provides trips down the **Sarapiquí River**.

A fledgling chamber of tourism is promoting the charms of the region, but the unified approach is yet to arrive. Several stores offer tourist information. One store is run by William Rojas who also runs *Oasis Nature Tours*, T766-6108, T380-9493 (mob), oasis@tourism.co.cr They offer 2-day, 1-night tours to **Tortuguero** including transport, lodging staying at *Ilan Ilan*, meals and jungle walks. US$175 per person, with a minimum of 4 people, or 3 days and 2 nights for US$215.

Other recently introduced tours include trips to a nearby **banana plantation** which takes you through the whole process from planting to packing. Contact T768-8683, F768-8137, www.sarapiquirainforest.com/bananatours Walk-ins are possible in the high season at US$10 per person, starting at 0800, 1000 and 1300. You get to see bananas being bagged, harvested and packed. Call in advance to make a reservation and for transport arrangements.

Directory **Banks** *Banco de Costa Rica* and *Banco Nacional* have branches in town. **Communications** The *ICE telephone* office and **post office** are both beside the football pitch. An **internet** service has opened on the road out of town.

West to La Virgen and San Miguel

Head west young man (or woman) and you'll find several **lodges** ideal for relaxing, birdwatching and adventure lining the road from Puerto Viejo to San Miguel.

The first option is **C** *Ara Ambigua*, turning right after the cemetery 1.5 km from Puerto Viejo, T766-5026, F766-6281, www.sarapiquirainforest.com/ara_ambigua A low-key set-up of 13 clean rooms and rustic lodges – some with flagstone flooring, all with private bath. Three small lakes and a few trails make it a pleasant stopover, with a restaurant and bar littered with old farming tools. A little further along the road is **E** *Cabinas Yacare*, T766-6691, with 11 simple and rather tired rooms.

Selva Verde Lodge Set in 200 ha of lowland rainforest Selva Verde Lodge is a popular stopover for the day or, if time allows, for a few days. Joining Braulio Carrillo National Park and La Selva Biological Station it's a great little spot good for birding, nature tours and river trips. There's a short self-guided tour through the grounds, or you can go on longer trips along the multitude of trails – focussing on botany, birding, orchids or butterflies – with a resident bilingual naturalist. The River Sarapiquí, which runs through the property, is a scenic and gentle boat journey or further upstream an adrenaline pumping challenge.

What separates **L** *Selva Verde Lodge*, from other lodges is the ease of access and the very clear attention to detail and service. 40 rooms and 5 bungalows in a dozen clusters connected by a network of covered walkways, all have tiled hot water private bath and wooden flooring. A hint of Sarchíesque décor adds a pleasant touch to the simple rooms which are raised off the ground to understorey level.

Buffet-style Costa Rican dishes are prepared by local women making the most of local resources. There's a small gift store, and rubber boots are available for your jungle hikes. Many careful touches are clearly designed to make your stay unforgettable – you'll discover them when you stay.

Next door, the **Sarapiquí Conservation Learning Centre** T766-6482, F766-6011, www.sarapiquirainforest.com/learning_center, works to ensure that the local community get to learn about and benefit from the secrets of the rainforest. Extending education about the rainforest to the local community is an essential link if the desire to reduce deforestation is to be effective at the grass roots level. A good library is available in the Learning Centre, and there is a volunteer programme teaching English.

Islas del Río is a multi-activity centre owned and operated by *Aguas Bravas*, focussing mainly on river trips down the Sarapiquí River. The put-in upstream of La Virgen is Class III+, lower down, the river is a beautifully scenic float. Most of the trips run out of San José, but if you're passing and you want to hook-up with a trip make arrangements through the office and you may be able to work something out. T292-2072, F229-4837, www.aguas-bravas.co.cr

A smallish Costa Rican family run country inn **A** *La Quinta Sarapiquí*, 4 km from La Virgen, 12 km from Puerto Viejo, T761-1052, F761-1395, www.laquintasarapiqui.com Located on a curve along the Sardinal River, the 23 rooms are pleasantly spacious, clean and all have private bath with hot water, silent fan (good for trying to sleep) and a shaded porch with chairs. The open-air bar and restaurant serves home-made food with a view out to the rainforest. The place is low key in its approach and marketing but a good little secret with an impressive bird list (115 and counting), a small poison arrow frog trail and a butterfly garden. You can stop by for the day, or just visit if travelling the Fortuna–Puerto Limón route.

L-AL *Centro Neotrópico SarapiquíS*, T761-1004, F761-1415, www.Sarapiquis.org More of an experience than a hotel. The Centro is creating a lot of interest, set out to be a model project for sustainable development but without scrimping on comforts – too bad a powercut prevented a meaningful tour of the place. Twenty four rooms, with hot water private bath, ceiling fans and telephone, in three 18 m high thatched roof *palenques* create the theme of comfort with complete consideration for the environment. The central *palenque* is home to the buffet-style restaurant and bar with stunning views to the mountainous highlands.

The design and layout is based on a precolumbian 15th-century village. With such respect paid to cultural heritage the discovery of precolumbian tombs shortly after construction began seems totally appropriate. A rainforest museum, botanical gardens and the 350-ha **Tirimbina Biological Reserve** provide ample setting for exploring the lowland Caribbean rainforest and aims to be a place to relax, learn and be challenged physically and mentally. Behind the scenes sustainable eco-perspectives employ local people, use solar energy to provide electricity and a biological waste water treatment plant. All in all, proof positive that environmental consideration doesn't have to compromise comforts and service levels.

La Quinta

Centro Neotrópico SarapiquíS

The northern region

La Virgen The small town of La Virgen, 9 km north of San Miguel, suddenly appears and disappears along the roadside.

One good reason to stop is the home of Ken and Leona **E** *Rancho Leona*, T/F761-1019, www.rancholeona.com Rooms and dormitory accommodation are rustic and clean, decorated with stained glass created by Leona and Ken with shared bathroom. The main attraction is **kayaking on the River Sarapiquí** from beginner to advanced level with 2 nights' accommodation included in the all-inclusive price of US$75. A quiet patio for reading in the truly lush gardens, an Indian-style sweat lodge, excellent local knowledge of nearby attractions, musical instruments for jamming sessions and, unique to Costa Rica, a 5-computer LAN with Starcraft, Unreal Tournament and Ages of Empire. All this fuelled on a healthy but filling menu of dishes served in the open-air restaurant. They sell top-quality and home-made gifts including T-shirts and, naturally, their fine stained glass pieces, which are not cheap, but worth it. In the truest sense of the phrase *Rancho Leona* is low-key and homey – a good choice for students, groups, art retreats, language learning or just relaxing. Also try the *Sarapiquí Outdoor Centre*, T/F761-1123, sarapiquiout@hotmail.com, which offers a range of full- and half-day trips down the Sarapiquí, Toro and Pacuare rivers. There are cheap rooms (**F**) and you can **camp** (**G**).

Continuing south the road reaches San Miguel. From here the road climbs the scenic **Sarapiquí Valley** with several stopping places, including the popular **La Paz waterfalls**.

West and north from San Miguel

From San Miguel a road that alternates between bad and OK reaches **Venecia** which has an interesting church, one clean and cheap hotel (**F**) and *Restaurant El Parque*, near the church providing good local food. Nearby are the **precolumbian tumuli of Ciudad Cutris**. A good road goes to within 2 km of Cutris, from where you can walk or take a four-wheel drive. The ruins, which are of limited interest to all but the most devoted, are on private property and you need a permit from the local *finca*.

West of Venecia the road continues to follow the contours of Platanar Volcano arriving at **Aguas Zarcas** where the road splits. Heading west the road leads to Ciudad Quesada (San Carlos) (see below). Heading north then west is a slightly more direct route to Fortuna (see also below). Heading directly north, via **Pital**, the road descends to the rainforest lowlands, reaching the Río San Carlos after 40 km, and the town of **Boca Tapada** which has the extremely remote **A-B** *La Laguna del Lagarto Lodge*, T289-8163, F289-5295, www.adventure-costarica.com/laguna-del-lagarto The lodge has 20 rooms with hot water and ceiling fan, a couple with shared bath. The open-air restaurant, with daily meals working out at around US$25, looks directly out to the unspoiled rainforest and private 500-ha reserve. Some 365 bird species, including the great green macaw have been recorded on the property. You can roam through over 15 km of trails with locally trained guides or head out on your own. Beyond the sheer comfort of the place, you can take canoeing trips on a couple of nearby lagoons, a boat trip to the nearby San Juan River on the border with Nicaragua or go horse riding. A member of *The Ecotourism Association*, Lagarto is constantly recommended by the great and the good.

San José to Fortuna

Leaving the fertile soils of the Central Highlands where coffee is king, the roads passing through San Ramón or Zarcero quickly descend to the northern lowlands where citrus groves and ranching dominates. Small towns along the way can make an interesting stopover whether for a few hours, or maybe overnight.

Ciudad Quesada (San Carlos)

Just 24 km from Zarcero and the continental divide, Ciudad Quesada – also called San Carlos – is the main transport hub for the northern lowlands. While the town is of limited genuine interest for the traveller, you may find yourself passing through or even needing to stop the night as it is a natural junction when travelling between Fortuna, Los Chiles and Puerto Viejo de Sarapiquí and to San José. If driving, watch out for the one-way system.

Colour map 2, grid B2
Population: 34,875
Altitude: 657 m

By Costa Rican standards Ciudad Quesada is a fairly large town, but even so it has a distinctly small-town country feel, with the leathery faces of the workers and the occasional stetson affirming the genuine link. There is really little need to move more than a block or two from the main plaza, which is densely packed with trees and palms. To the east is a cavernous church with an impressive sculpture of Christ hanging above the altar inside.

C-D *Don Goyo*, just south of the main plaza, T460-1780. 13 clean, well lit rooms, with private bathrooms. Restaurant and bar serving a good selection of dishes. Best value in town. **C-D** *La Central*, on the plaza, T460-0301, F460-0391. Popular mid-range hotel, rooms with private bath, hot water and TV, but some a little dark and cramped. Casino and small bar. **D** *El Retiro*, also on the plaza down a small dirt road, T460-0463. Clean and comfortable rooms, with bath, hot water. Nothing flashy but popular with local business people. **D** *Hotel Ambientes*, close to the *Banco de Costa Rica*, T460-6714. New hotel, with clean rooms, TV, fan hot water and parking. **D-E** *Hotel Del Norte*, 1½ blocks north of the main plaza, T460-1959. Clean and secure rooms with fan and colour TV. Rooms with shared bath have more natural light. Next to the new bus terminal north of town is **F** *Cabinas Balneario San Carlos*, T460-6857, F460-2145. Part of a sports complex, *cabinas* with cooking facilities, overlooking an athletics track, and with good swimming pool. Very good value, close to the bus terminal, but a long way from town, and probably very quiet at night. All **F**: several basic *pensiones* line Av 1, C 2-4, around corner from *Banco Popular*. *Diana*, T460-3319, and *Fernando*, T460-3314, which is probably the best of

Sleeping

Ciudad Quesada

To Bus Terminal
To Florencia, Fortuna & Los Chiles

Av 5
Av 3
Av 1
Banco Popular
Banco Nacional
Av 0
Mercado de los Artesanías
Plaza Central
Banco de Costa Rica
Av 2
Tribunales de Justicia
Municipal Buildings
Fuji Shop
Av 4
To Aguas Zarcas
To Zarcero, San Ramón, Alajuela & San José

■ **Sleeping**
1 Ambientes
2 Cristal
3 Del Norte
4 Diana
5 Don Goyo
6 El Retiro
7 Fernando
8 La Central
9 Lily
10 Plaza
11 Terminal

● **Eating**
1 Coco Loco
2 Cristal
3 Los Geridianos
4 Pollos Jeffry

N

0 metres 100
0 yards 100

The northern region

the bunch if you can get one of the new rooms. **G** *Terminal*, is by the old bus station at the northeastern corner of the plaza. T460-2158. Dark rooms, uncomfortable beds, musty and probably due to close quite soon. The benefits – it's the cheapest in town.

Out of town If you're driving, an excellent hotel 4 km on the road to Fortuna is **D** *Hotel La Mirada*, T460-2222. Sitting on the bluff with incredible views of the northern lowlands and Arenal volcano. The rooms, recently refurbished, are clean and comfortable with a private bath and hot water. Excellent value.

Heading east to **Aguas Zarcas**, 8 km along a bumpy road is the luxurious **LL-AL** *Melia Occidental El Tucano Resort and Thermal Spa*, T460-6000, F460-1692, www.occidental-hoteles.com 90 comfortable rooms and suites. Total comfort resort with a large pool, jacuzzi, sauna, horse riding and tennis. Hot mineral and sulphur pools provide for a host of indulgent beauty treatments, all with the background of exuberant tropical forest. Complete indulgence hidden away from the crowds.

Eating & drinking On the western side of the plaza is *Coco Loco Steak House*, complete with wild west swing door. Mid-price, evenings only. *Los Geridianos* is a hip bar and restaurant serving good bocas at US$2, it's the place to be seen in Ciudad Quesada whether young or older. *Pollos Jeffry* serves good basic food, although the décor is all plastic, there's a friendly atmosphere to the place. Cheap. *Restaurant Cristal*, on the northern side of the plaza, sells cheap fast food diner-style, with snacks, ice cream and good fruit dishes.

Shopping If you've time to kill, you can wander round the *Mercado de los Artesanías* on the main plaza which sells a selection of souvenirs. The opening hours are erratic and its oversized for the region, but you may find a bargain.

Transport **Bus** The new terminal is about 1 km north of the plaza. To **San José**, buses depart hourly from 0500-1830, 2½ hrs, US$2. Buses from San José leave from the Atlántico Norte Terminal, Av 9, C 12, T256-8914. Buses to **Fortuna**, leave at 0600, 1030, 1530, 1715 and 2000, 1¼ hrs, US$1. Buses to **Tilarán**, which also pass through Fortuna, depart at 0630 and 1600, 4hrs, US$2.30.

Heading north, buses leave for **Los Chiles** every hour between 0500-1900 and every hour for **Pital**. Heading east, buses go through **Aguas Zarcas**, **La Virgen** and **Chilamate** to **Puerto Viejo de Sarapiquí**, 5 a day between 0500 and 1730, 2½ hrs, US$1.30.

Directory **Communications Internet**: *Café Internet*, on Av 1, C 0-1, US$1.30 for 30 mins, 0900-2100 Mon-Sat, 1500-2000 Sun, also *punta.com* at the post office. **Post**: a small post office is on Av 5, C 4-6. **Medical facilities** The hospital provides services for the whole of the northern lowlands, T460-1176. There are several pharmacies close to the centre of town.

Fortuna

Colour map 2, grid B1
Population: 7,658;
Altitude: 254 m

A steady supply of humans attracted to the glowing lava of Arenal volcano like moths to the flame has changed the once-sleepy backwater of La Fortuna to an occasionally lively hive of activity. Unsure of how to handle the influx of tourists a flurry of energy engulfs the arriving visitor with tour operators keen to sign you up for a trip to the volcano. Shortly after, a strange calm prevails, giving you a chance to explore the town, taking time to relax and mull over your options. Head out to the spectacular waterfalls, explore the lake and national park by foot, horse or bike, visit the nearby caves and of course with so much volcanic activity, there are several thermal baths in the area.

Ins and outs

Travelling by road, all routes to Fortuna are very scenic. From the south leaving the **Getting there**
Pan-American Highway near San Ramón, a good road leads north for 73 km. An alternative and longer route passes through Zarcero and Ciudad Quesada. Arriving from
Tilarán to the west, a pot-holed road follows the north shore of Lake Arenal with great
views across the lake to the volcano. Buses to Fortuna depart from all the places mentioned above and from San José.

Fortuna is small enough to stroll around. Those with the energy and inclination can **Getting around**
hire mountain bikes, horses or even quads to explore further a field. For shorter local
journeys there are plenty of taxis.

If seeing the volcano is the main reason for your visit, the skies are most reliably clear **Best time**
between Dec and Apr. Otherwise take into account greater rain between Aug and Nov **to visit**
– the waterfall will be more impressive, but walking trails will be muddier.

Sights

With the football pitch in the centre and the simple church to the west, sights in *There is a fledgling*
Fortuna are limited. A couple of kilometres west of town is a small **snake farm** *tourist office in*
with a collection of 40 specimens found throughout Costa Rica. A little further *Fortuna on the south*
west the *Albergue Ecoturístico La Catarata* has a small **butterfly farm**, *paca* *side of the main*
breeding project and medicinal plants which is free for guests, US$5 for visitors. *square. Sunset Tours*
 Heading south, **Río Fortuna waterfall** plunges 70 m from lush forest to the *on the main square*
pool below creating a swirling hazy mist. From the entrance it is a steep and *or Aventuras Arenal,*
sometimes slippery path down to the falls, so wear good shoes. A short dis- *on the main road*
tance below the falls there are a couple of good swimming spots. ■ *US$3. You* *heading east, are*
can easily walk or drive to the falls from town following the road for 1.7 km before *also worth visiting*
taking a 4 km bumpy road through yucca and papaya plantations. Alternatively
take a half-day horse riding tour, US$22.

The northern region

Fortuna

To Volcán Arenal, Lago Arenal & Tilarán

Sunset Tours □ ■ Desafio
Eagle Tours
Banco Tours
From Tilarán 🚌 ⑨ Ⓢ Banco Nacional
Álamo Car Rental
Football Pitch
Banco Popular ⑦
Ⓢ ⑩ ✉ (Pol) Aventuras Arenales
Sunset Tours
Soccer Table 2000
Laundrette
⑤ ② ⓘ ④ ⑥ ⑪ ③ ⑤ To/from San Ramón, Ciudad Quesada, San José, to Tilarán
① Canopy Fortuna
② ⑨ Pharmacy Banco de Costa Rica
Ⓢ Coocique
⑧ ④
⑥
⑦ Las Jicaritas @
Río Burío
∨ To the Waterfall & San Ramón

To Ciudad Quesada (San Carlos), Los Chiles & San José

N

0 metres 100
0 yards 100

■ Sleeping	8 Fortuna	2 Choza de Laurel
1 Burío Inn	9 La Posada	3 El Jardín
2 Cabinas Guacamaya	10 Las Colinas	4 La Casa de Hara
3 Cabinas Hervi	11 Luigi's Lodge	5 Las Brasitas
4 Cabinas La Amistad	12 San Bosco	6 Lava Rocks
5 Cabinas Manuel		7 Nene's
6 Cabinas Monte Real	● Eating	8 Pizza Luigi's
7 Cabinas Sissy	1 Angel Azul	9 Rancho Cascada

Essentials

Sleeping

It is worth bearing in mind that although the cheapest accommodation is in Fortuna itself, you will have to pay in the region of US$25 to get to the northern side of the volcano where you can see the eruptions. In the green season some of the hotels in this area may well be within your budget. If you have a car, it's definitely worth looking at some of the accommodation on Lake Arenal's north shore.

Generous discounts in the green season are common. Although many hotels have volcano views, eruptions cannot be seen from town

Centre of town **A** *Luigi's Lodge*, a couple of blocks west of the church, T479-9636, F479-9898, www.luigislodge.com 20 comfortable rooms with private bath, tub, hot water and coffee machine. Email service for guests. Small balconies overlooking a pool, with good views of the volcano. Comfortable but lacking in character. **A-B** *San Bosco*, T479-9050, F479-9109, www.arenal-volcano.com All rooms with private bath, quiet, signs on main road, clean, friendly, gardens with terrace, pool and view of the volcano, excellent service and attention to detail, slightly less without a/c. Best of the bunch in town. **B** *Cabinas Guacamaya*, T479-9393, F479-9087, www.cabinasguacamaya.com 10 good sized rooms sleeping 3 or 4, all with private bath and hot water, fridge and a/c. Clean and tidy, with plenty of parking. Close to town but away from the busy area. **C** *Cabinas Monte Real*, 1 block west and south of the main plaza, T/F479-9243. Big rooms with private bath and hot water, a quiet spot next to the river. Ample parking. **C** *Las Colinas*, at the southeastern corner of the central park, T/F479-9305, hcolinas@sol.racsa.co.cr 20 tidy rooms, with private bathroom, the ones on the top floor with excellent views. Friendly owners with good local knowledge and good discounts in the low season. Recommended. **D** *Cabinas Hervi*, south of church on road to the river, T479-9430, bright rooms, private bath with hot water, a/c or fan. Balcony with view of the church, some tourist information and good discounts in the green season. **D** *Cabinas La Amistad*, T479-9364, clean, friendly with hot water and hard beds. **D** *Rest Fortuna*, 1 block southeast of the central park, T479-9197, simple bare rooms, but very clean. Price includes breakfast. **E** *Cabinas Carmela*, on the south side of the church, T/F479-9010, www.hostelling-costarica.com 12 rooms with private bath, hot showers, floor and ceiling fans, some with fridge. Very central, good tourist information, discount for youth hostel members. Apartment sleeping 5 available **E** per person.

F *Cabinas Manuel*, T479-9079, basic wood-panelled rather dark rooms with a shared bath in a family home. Also some cabins with private bath. **F** *Burio Inn*, down small driveway next to *Canopy Tours*, T479-9454. Shoddy rooms, but clean, with hot water in shared bathrooms. **F-G** per person *Cabinas Sissy*, office is 100 m south and 100 m west of church, T479-9256. Quiet spot beside the river, with a number of options. Basic rooms with private bathroom, some with shared bath, others with access to a kitchen and camping spaces (US$2 per person). Simple but friendly. **G** per person *La Posada*, a couple of blocks east of the central park, T479-9793. 4 simple, but spotless rooms, shared bath with hot water, fan, but mosquitoes reported. Small communal area out front, and the friendly owner, Thadeo, is very helpful. The cheapest spot in town. For camping options see Los Lagos and Arenal National Park page 197.

Listed in the order that you come across them heading out of town

West of town towards the volcano **B** *Albergue Vista Arenal*, 700 m west of town, T479-9808. 12 spacious wooden cabins, in a quiet spots with private bath, a/c, hot water and TV. There's a small terrace outside ideal for sitting around as the evening drifts by, but you'll have to move elsewhere for food and drink. A few hundred metres further on is a rash of hotels, bars and restaurants in the community of **Zeta Trece** starting with **C** *Hotel Arenal Rossi*, T479-9023, F477-9414, cabrossi@sol.racsa.co.cr with breakfast, friendly owner, hot water, fan, volcano views from the garden, horses for hire, good value. 2 km on road towards the volcano is **C** *Cabinas Las Flores*, T479-9307, F479-8042. Clean, basic but a little overpriced. Finally **A-B** *La Pradera*, has

10 rooms with private baths and a/c. **A** *Albergue Ecoturístico La Catarata*, 1.7 km from town down a rough road, T479-9522, F479-9168, in San José on T/F286-4203, www.agroecoturismo.net 8 cabins, reservations essential, organic garden, home-made soaps and shampoos, good fresh food, taxi US$2 to town, hot water, laundry, all meals. There's also a small butterfly farm, *paca* breeding project and a selection of medicinal plants. Part of the *Cooprena* co-operative.

East of town A couple of good places for families with plenty of space for parking and fine views of Arenal are **B** *Cabinas Villa Fortuna*, 500 m east of the bridge, 1 km from the central plaza, T/F479-9139. 10 bright and tidy cabins using wood throughout sleeping 2 or 3, with neat bathrooms, fans or a/c, nice pool, jacuzzi and simple gardens with a poolside café. 500 m beyond is **A** *Las Cabañitas*, T479-9400, F479-9408, www.cabanita.com 30 beautifully finished wood cabins with pristine bathrooms, a couple of pools, as well as a souvenir shop and laundry service. The open-air restaurant Arana is a bit pricey but has some good dishes.

South of town **AL** *Arenal Country Inn*, T479-9670, F479-9433, www.costaricainn.com Once a working hacienda now with 20 large, fully-equipped *cabinas* with unimposing décor, private tiled bathrooms, safebox, a/c and minibar and spread out among pleasant tropical gardens. Complementary breakfast is served in the open-air dining room – once a cattle-holding pen – and you can rest by the pool before heading out to explore. The atmosphere in the family-run inn is calm, the service excellent and it's probably the best in Fortuna. 10 km south of Fortuna, up a very bumpy road to **Chachagua** is **L** *Bosque de Chachagua*, T231-0356, F290-6506, chachagua@novanet.co.cr 22 wooden cabins, complete with balconies and swinging hammock set in beautiful tropical forest. A working ranch, with plenty of landscaped gardens for relaxing, a couple of trails to nearby waterfalls and 64 species of birds counted so far. Spectacular service throughout with fine dishes in the restaurant and barbecues in high season. You'll need a 4-wheel drive to get there, and probably won't use it when you arrive, so a package from San José is a good idea.

Angel Azul, serves good, cheap vegetarian food in a café atmosphere with a couple of chairs outside for the lucky few. Open all day. *Choza de Laurel*, west of the church, T479-9231, serves typical food in a rustic open-air setting with occasional visits from passing hummingbirds. Breakfast, lunch and dinner available, US$2-US$4.50. *El Jardín*, on the main street opposite the gas station. Good varied menu with a mix of local and fast food, *menu del dia* US$4. It's a good place to watch the world go by but success seems to have jaded the personal service and raised the prices. *La Casa de Hara*, round the side of *Hotel Fortuna*, very good local food, fast service and normal prices – where the locals eat. *La Fortuna*, open-air restaurant in the hotel of the same name, serving good, simple food, quiet spot but nothing special. *Las Brasitas*, open-air restaurant at the western end of town serving pizza and pasta in a laid-back European café-style. *Las Jicaritas*, near bridge, simple food, nice setting, (slow) internet service. *Lava Rocks*, south side of the church, smooth open-air café-restaurant serving excellent coffee, good food with chilled music and reasonably priced. Travel agency on site for any questions. Definitely worth a visit. *Nene's*, good food, pleasant service, not expensive. Recommended. *Pizza Luigi's*, formal open-air restaurant with distinctly Italian pretensions toward pizza and pasta. Good wine list for Fortuna. Mid-range and above. *Rancho Cascada*, on corner of Parque cannot be missed with high conical thatched roof, good *bocas*, films shown in evenings. Mid-range.

Eating

West of town Just over 500 m towards the volcano a few generally mid-range restaurants have gathered. *La Vaca Muca*, is a grill-bar with a mixed menu of fish and

The northern region

meat dishes, and a bar area popular with locals. *Nene*, has a good international selec-
tion with a tendency towards Mexican, all reasonably priced. *Steakhouse Arenal*, is a
mid-priced steak house with all the décor of Texas, and a few other dishes to keep the
options open. *Vagabondo* is the most laid-back on the strip serving cheap and
mid-priced pizza and pasta.

Bars, clubs & There are a couple of bars in town and many of the restaurants tend to have bar areas.
entertainment The only nightclub as such is the *Mountain Look* 4½ km north of town next to Baldi
Thermae hot pool. The club is open – when it opens – Fri and Sat. Ask locally before
heading out. In town *Soccer Table 2000* provides table soccer like you've never seen it
before. A break from the endless bars and restaurants. 0700-2100 daily.

Shopping Several souvenir shops dotted around town sell a selection of T-shirts, carvings and
postcards. If you're looking for a hammock, *House of Hammocks* 500 m west of town
has a good selection with sitting hammocks starting at US$13.

Tour All tour operators can provide the basic trips to the **volcano**, **waterfall**, **caves** and
operators **Caño Negro Wildlife Reserve** – see 'Excursions' below. Trips going to **Santa Elena** and
Monteverde are more problematic. Reports suggest that horses are being over-
worked and trips often change at the last minute due to unforeseen problems. Be pre-
pared for this eventuality and seek assurance from your operator and guide. Prices
tend to be fairly consistent across operators. *Aventuras Arenal*, on the main street,
T479-9133, F479-9295, www.arenaladventures.com The main tour operator in town
and one of the few with a national presence. Reliable information on the local area and
they can advise on trips to other parts of the country and will make bookings where
appropriate. *Canopy Fortuna*, on the main street opposite the gas station,
T/F479-9769, www.canopyfortuna.com With a number of short trips in the area
involving horseback, mountain bike and quad tours. As the name suggests, a canopy
tour is also possible starting with an horseback journey from Fortuna, US$45. *Desafio*,
just off main square by thatched restaurant, T/F479-9464, www.desafiocostarica.com
Full range of tours, also with an office in Monteverde. *Eagle Tours*, one block east of the
park, T/F479-9091, aguilas@sol.racsa.co.cr Helpful tour operator, with usual array of
options. *Sunset Tours*, behind Rancho Casado and on eastern corner of the central
park, T479-9415, F479-9099, www.sunset-tours.com Reliable, long standing com-
pany with a good selection of tours, including fishing on Lake Arenal. Recommended.

Transport **Bus** There are daily buses at 0615, 0840, 1130, from Terminal Atlántico Norte, **San
José**, 3½ hrs, via **Ciudad Quesada**, US$2.80, return at 1245, 1445; 6 buses a day from
Ciudad Quesada, 1 hr, US$1, 4 different routes; 2 buses a day to **Tilarán**, 0800 (connect-
ing to 1230 bus Tilarán-Santa Elena/Monteverde and 1300 bus Tilarán-Puntarenas)
and 1700, US$2.90, 4 hrs; 3 buses daily to **San Ramón** at 0530, 1300 and 1600, making
connections to Puntarenas. Subject to demand and normally daily in the high season,
there are direct minibuses to Monteverde and Tamarindo (US$25 per person, min 6)
with *Grayline* and *Interbus*. **Taxis** in the area do their best to overcharge. Agree on price
before travelling. **Car hire** *Alamo* have an office in town,T479-9722.

Whether travelling by bus or car, it is possible to get from Fortuna to **Santa Elena**
and **Monteverde** (via **Tilarán**) in a day, but set out early to make your connection with
the 1230 bus in Tilarán and to avoid driving in the dark.

Directory **Banks** *Banco Nacional*, *Banco Nacional de Costa Rica* all have ATMs and will change
TCs with a US$1 commission. *Banco Popular* has a Visa ATM as does *Coocique*, which is
open Sat mornings 0800-1200. **Communications** Internet: prices in Fortuna are gen-
erally prohibitive and connections poor. If desperate ask round town for the best current

operator, or ask at Post Office (punta.com). **Post**: the post office is down the main street and shares the building with the police so don't risk a hold-up. **Laundry** *Lavanderia La Fortuna*, 0800-2100, Mon-Sat. US$5 wash and dry 4 kg. **Medical facilities** *Farmacía Dr Max*, east down the main street, 0730-2030, Mon-Sat, 0800-1200 Sun.

Excursions

By far the most popular excursion is a trip to see the lava flows and eruptions of Arenal Volcano. While there are variations on a theme, most trips leave in the late afternoon to get you to the best viewing spot for dusk. As darkness cloaks the region, the dust plumes that skirted down the bare slopes through the day reveal themselves to be glowing lava tumbling, crashing and smashing down the volcano slopes in a spray of natural fireworks. The sight is spectacular and the sound decidedly eerie.

Volcán Arenal
All trips can be done independently or with a tour operator

Arenal was a sleeping giant until 1968 when a massive eruption devastated the western flank of the volcano killing 78 people. With that abrupt interruption, Arenal reignited a pattern of growth characterized by periods of explosive activity and lava flows followed by inactivity for hundreds of years. Since 1968 Arenal has been erupting almost continuously with the most recent major eruption in August 2000 resulting in the death of two people (the greater extent of lava flows has seen a more cautious approach to volcano viewing put in place).

Arenal is a classic Stromboli-type stratovolcano, creating a symmetrical cone formed by layers of volcanic material. It is the youngest of the stratovolcanoes in Costa Rica with no rock dating more than 2900 years. Research by OVISICORI at the *Arenal Observatory Lodge* has produced a wealth of data including the mind-boggling notion that the magma chamber that feeds the eruptions is just 5 km below the surface.

You will be permitted to visit safe areas – the current spot used by groups is at El Silencio, 2 km west of Tabacón Resort – but take advice, some of those

Volcán Arenal

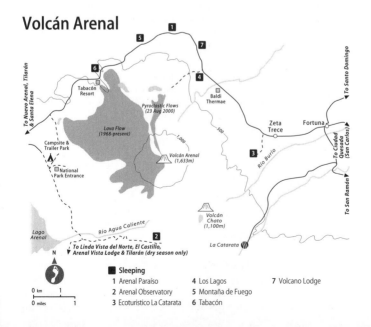

Sleeping
1 Arenal Paraíso
2 Arenal Observatory
3 Ecoturistico La Catarata
4 Los Lagos
5 Montaña de Fuego
6 Tabacón
7 Volcano Lodge

The northern region

who have chosen not to have not returned alive. After viewing the volcano, groups head down to one of the nearby thermal baths for a relaxing soak before returning to Fortuna around 2100. ■ *Trips organized daily through any tour operator in Fortuna, cost US$25 if visiting Baldi Thermae, US$60 if going to Tabacón. Take torch, good shoes, rain and swimming gear including towel.*

Parque Nacional Arenal Dominated by the conical cones of the volcano, Arenal National Park covers an expanse of 12,106 ha. Upgraded from a reserve to a national park in 1994, the park protects the valuable watershed that maintains water levels in Lake Arenal and the micro-climate created by the volcano.

Beyond the volcano the park has five interesting (and safe) trails starting at the national park entrance. The trails range from 25 minutes to a couple of hours and provide good opportunities to see heliconias, birdlife and howler monkeys. Las Coladas involves a bit of scrambling over old lava flows but provides good views of the lake and the extinct Volcán Chato. ■ *Open daily, 0800-1600. US$6. Heading west from Fortuna follow the signs to Arenal Observatory Lodge. While trekking solo is permitted and, subject to current advice, safe, hikes and treks can also be arranged through tour operators in Fortuna.*

Sleeping Opposite the national park entrance is a small camping area, **G** per person, with cold water and hook-ups for trailers. Excellent views of the volcano.

Hot springs A number of hot baths in the area offer the chance for some serious rest and relaxation. Closest to town is **Baldi Thermae**, which has a number of pools starting at a comfortable 37°C rising to an egg-poaching 63°C. ■ *Open daily 1000-2200. US$7. 4½ km north of town you can walk there, and take a taxi back when you're fully relaxed for US$2.50.*

Considerably more fancy is **Tabacón Resort**, with pools, waterfalls, wet bars and utter self-indulgent luxury. ■ *Open daily 0700-2200. US$17, US$13 after 1800. 12 km from Fortuna, taxis charge US$4.50 for the trip. Also see below.*

Across the road is a cheaper option at just US$6, open Mon-Fri 1000-2130, Sat-Sun 0800-2130. For a completely natural experience follow the road for 1½ km to **Quebrada Cedeña**. It can be difficult to find as there are no signs, but it's completely free – look for local parked cars.

Venado Caves About an hour from Fortuna the small community of Venado is home to limestone caves dripping with **stalactites**, dried out river beds, small tunnels you can get stuck in and of course bats. Be prepared to get wet and dirty. ■ *Local entrance is US$3, with hard hats, rubber boots, torches and guides available for rent. All inclusive trips from Fortuna cost around US$35. Buses to Venado and Guatuso leave from Ciudad Quesada. A dirt road leaves the north shore of the lake heading to Venado. An alternative route heads north from Tanque heading west close to Jicarito.*

Lake Arenal, fishing & the Botanical Gardens Formed in 1974 to provide hydroelectric power for the country the lake flooded the Arenal valley. While the wall damming the River Arenal, which flows east to the northern lowlands, is at the eastern end of the lake near Fortuna, the generating plant is at the western end at Tronadora close to Tilarán, where water flows through Guanacaste irrigating lowland areas before reaching the Nicoya Gulf. Trips on the lake are easily arranged through tour operators or by going down to the northern end of the dam and talking to local boatmen. Sport fishing on the lake for rainbow bass (guapote) and machaca is possible throughout the year, with the best months for bass between Mar and Jul. Prices start from US$150 all inclusive for a half day and can be arranged through tour operators in Fortuna.

An interesting trip on the north shore of the lake is to **Arenal Botanical and Butterfly Gardens**, 4 km east of Arenal town, with many flowers, birds, butterflies. It's a delightful place and continuously developing and evolving. ■ *0900-1600 (closed Oct), US$8. T694-4273.*

Just under 50 km north of Fortuna Caño Negro Wildlife Reserve close to the town of Los Chiles at the border with Nicaragua is a popular day trip. The wetlands are host to many waterbirds and you are certain to see monkeys, sloths and caiman. ■ *US$35-45. Organized through tour operators in Fortuna. It's a 1½ hr bus journey to Los Chiles and the boat trip lasts about 4 hrs. You can visit independently if you prefer. For more information see page 204.* **Caño Negro Wildlife Reserve**

According to the Costa Rica rafting guide by Mayfield and Gallo, the Peñas Blancas, south of Fortuna, is, "one of the recently discovered whitewater gems of Costa Rica". For the beginner there are Class III to Class IV rapids which can be tackled on half- and one-day trips from Fortuna costing between US$37-38. Conditions vary greatly depending on rainfall, with the best months being from July to September and occasionally through to December so check for local information. **Whitewater rafting**

The northern region

Fortuna to Tilarán

From Fortuna in the east to Tilarán at the western end of Lake Arenal the road is scattered with a number of hotels offering trails and adventure sports, or seclusion and quiet privacy. A number of comfortable options sit on the lower slopes of the volcano – most on the north side – with good views of the eruptions. A dirt road struggles along the southern shore giving access to a few comfortable hideaways. But the majority of places line the good road that heads around Lake Arenal's north shore west to Tilarán.

The hotels and restaurants are listed as you encounter them from Fortuna – if arriving from Tilarán, start at the end of the section (see page 202) and read backwards!

The eruptions of Aug 2000 have restricted access to the **A-C** *Los Lagos*, 5 km north of Fortuna, T479-8000, F479-8009. Once the universally favoured spot for viewing the lava flows, it is still a very comfortable option with great views – it's just that safety is considered more important than gasps of wonder. The grounds cover a wide area and include a couple of lakes (the flows of August 2000 reached within metres of one), camping areas and several trails with currently restricted access. There is a selection of large rooms and villas with kitchenette sleeping 2-4 people, with a/c, cable TV, private bathroom and hot water. A swimming pool complete with waterslide, thermal pools, and all in the shadow of Arenal, make this a spectacular place to stay and one of the best places to watch the volcano at night. Deeper into the property there are a number of simple cabins for hire (**C**), with picnic areas and **camping** (**G**) is possible in the grounds, costing US$2.75 per person. Day tickets for the resort are available (US$6.50). **AL** *Volcano Lodge*, 6 km from Fortuna, T460-6080, F460-6020, www.costarica volcanolodge.com A new, comfortable option with 20 spacious rooms each with private bathroom, a/c and stunning views from the balcony. For a change, take to the pool or jacuzzi which have equally good views of the lava flows. Popular with groups, there is also a good open-air restaurant with a spectacular fish pool to complement the aquatic theme. The food is surprisingly cheap and if you sit on the right side **Sleeping options around the volcano** you can watch the volcano while you dine. The best of the strip as far as views are concerned. **AL-A** *Arenal Paraíso*, 1 km north, T460-5333, F460-5343, www.arenalparaiso. decostarica.co.cr 20 all-wooden cabins and suites with private bath, a/c and balcony. Good views of the volcano and tours arranged. 8 km out of Fortuna is **L-AL** *Montaña de Fuego*, T460-7340, F460-7338, www.montanadefuego.com 52 full-service bungalows and rooms, all with views of the volcano set in lush gardens. Next door is the elegant and expensive *Restaurant Acuarelas*, serving a fine mix of international and Tico dishes in a stylish setting.

Tabacón Resort   Someone has got seriously carried away with Tabacón Resort. The focus of the resort is a series of mineral pools that vary in temperature offering soothing relaxation and while the thermal-heated waters are 100% natural the rest is pure kitsch. Soft lighting illuminates the hazy mist that settles over the resort at night as guests take a drink at the wet bar, supposedly falling hopelessly in love as the romance of the place washes their troubles away. Enjoy the waters, take a meal at the surprisingly reasonable restaurant and relax. The *Iskandria Spa* has a daunting array of treatments and massages which are certain to have you leaving the resort feeling like a new body. And if all this relaxation is just a little too much, take to the air with the new canopy tour. ■ *Open daily, 0700-2200. US$17, US$13 after 1800. 12 km from Fortuna, taxis charge US$4.50 for the trip. Massages and canopy tour are extra.*

Guests staying at the **LL-L** *Hotel Tabacón*, T256-1500, F221-3075, www.tabacon.com have full access to the spa and a choice of 73 comfortable rooms with large bathrooms and a small balcony (not all with volcano views) and 9 full-service suites.

South shore of   On the northwestern side of the volcano, 4 km after El Tabacón, a signposted gravel
Lake Arenal   road heads towards the lake eventually leading to the **AL-B** *Arenal Observatory*
Hotels on the southern   *Lodge*, T695-5033, F257-4220, www.arenal-observatory.co.cr 4-wheel drive recom-
side of the lake are   mended along this 9-km stretch (taxi-jeep from Fortuna, US$12). With origins dating
slightly cut off but   back to 1973, the observatory was once purely a research station for the Smithsonian
have fantastic views   Institute but now has 42 rooms and growing in separate blocks. Rooms vary from cab-
of the lake   ins with bunk beds and bath to newer rooms with queen size beds. All use the proxim-
ity of the volcano (which is frighteningly close) to provide stunning views across the
Río Agua Caliente valley and Lake Arenal. Fortunately, the lava flows on the other side
of the volcano. There are several trails in the observatory's grounds through the pine
forest and options for trips to Cerro Chato crater lake. While no comfort is spared, recy-
cling is strongly encouraged where possible. Recommended.

On the gravel road, taking the right fork (not to the observatory) that follows the southern lake shore leads to **AL-A** *Linda Vista del Norte Lodge*, T380-0847, F479-9443, www.lindavistadelnorte.com A selection of comfortable rooms and suites sleeping 2-4 people with hot water and stunning views over the lake. Set in a 250-ha *finca* (farm), there are a number of good, unspoilt trails through the forest, with opportunities for horse riding tours and trekking. Recommended. Further along the road is **B** *El Castillo*, T233-9232, F383-7196, cabinitaselcastillo@yahoo.com 10 simple rooms with private bath, fans and TV, with great views. Children under 10 US$5 extra. Simple food in the restaurant and breakfast included. Fording the Río Piedras Negras you reach **AL-B** *Arenal Vista Lodge*, T221-0965, F221-6230, www. arenalvistalodge.com the last hotel before the bumpy dry-season only road contin-ues along the south shore to Tilarán. 25 angular rooms sleeping 2-4 people make the most of the views providing a small balcony, each with bath and hot water. There's a small pool and bar overlooking the lake and boat trips, riding and hiking. Rooms are considerably cheaper for 4 people.

Around Lake Arenal north shore and west to Tilarán

A mostly paved road twists and winds round the northern shore of Lake Arenal, leading to Tilarán via Nuevo Arenal. The views are great and it makes for a fine leisurely drive if you have the time. The lakeside road has improved greatly in recent years, but some sections are still unpaved. The main hazard is the winding road and some seriously pot-holed sections. There is plenty of good accommodation around the north shore, mostly in the higher price brackets. *Colour map 1, grid B5*

With only a couple of buses a day, and limited traffic, getting off the bus for a look will almost certainly delay you for a day. But if you can stop between Fortuna and Nuevo Arenal, an excellent café for a meal and drink in a prime spot over the lake is **Toad Hall**. It is also one of the best souvenir craft shops in the country – some items are modern, some traditional, many desirable.

Working round the lake from Fortuna, 400 m north of the dam wall and 2½ km up a very steep road is **L-AL** *Arenal Lodge*, T/F383-3957, www.arenallodge.com The lodge is at a higher altitude than any other accommodation around the lake and has glorious views south to the volcano and north to the lowlands. A selection of chalets and suites provide complete luxury but not all have the views. As you go up in price rooms have views and kitchenettes. From the main lodge, the excellent but expensive restaurant has fine views of the gardens. **Sleeping**

Continuing west, **A** *Hotel Los Héroes (Pequeña Helvecia)*, T228-7468, F228-1472, heroes@racsa.co.cr A wonderful blend of idiosyncratic *Tico* hospitality and Swiss patriotism – if Costa Rica is the Switzerland of Central America, Los Héroes is its Geneva. 12 good rooms with private bath, with a couple with space for 6, some with a terrace. The restaurant serves *fondues*, *wiener schnitzels* and other Swiss classics, but no credit cards accepted. Devotion to all things Swiss include a 60 cm gauge railway with a couple of diesel engines travelling up the hillside crossing two bridges and going through a couple of tunnels for 2 km (US$3, three times a day), and a small yet beautiful private family chapel. Day trips are possible starting from San José, US$28, travelling, of course, in a Swiss double-decker bus.

Next stop is the divine **Toad Hall** café and gift shop. Serving a heady mix of California-style food with home-grown salads, tropical fruit juices and divine chocolate and macadamia nut brownies, the views of the lake and volcano are heavenly and you won't find a better place to stop for a break. Next to the café, the gift shop is one of the best in Costa Rica selling a mix of ceramics, including Cecilia Figueres ceramics, paintings, banana paper products and a hot-spot of modern *artesanía*. Open daily, 0730-1700. T381-3662, F694-4373, www.toadhall-gallery.com

Complete relaxation is provided at **LL-AL** *La Mansion Marina & Club*, T384-6573, www.lamansionarenal.com This consists of 14 split-level bungalows colourfully decorated with original paintings offering different levels of luxury. The tiled-pool appears to flow directly into the lake and there's a strong emphasis on relaxation – all rooms come with a CD player and you can borrow discs from the hotel. Price includes luxury breakfast with champagne if you wish, served in your room or on the terrace restaurant specializing in European cuisine. Horses and canoes are available for guests to hire for a small charge.

A little further west is **C** *La Alondra*, T384-5575. Simple basic rooms sleeping up to 4 provide the cheapest option at this end of the lake. Great views, friendly *Tico* owners. Nearby is the woefully underrated cheap, simple and tasty **Sabor Italiano** restaurant, serving pasta and pizza and fabulous Argentine-style *parrillada* grills served in a fine earthy setting, T/F385-1474.

A *La Ceiba*, overlooking Lake Arenal 6 km east of Nuevo Arenal, T385-1540, F694-4297, www.bbb.or.cr/ceiba *Tico*-owned and run, good, helpful, great pano-

The northern region

ramic views, spectacular ceiba tree in front of the lodge, good breakfast. **Arenal Botanical and Butterfly Gardens**, is 4 km east of town. It's a delightful place with a selection of flowers, birds and butterflies and is continuously developing and often recommended. ■ *0900-1600 (closed Oct), US$8. T694-4273.*

The last option east of the village is **L-AL** *Villa Decary*, T383-3012 (mob), www.villadecary.com 8 rooms and bungalows, each with a private bath and some with balcony, decorated with Guatemalan fabrics and Chorotega Indian ceramics set in beautiful gardens. Breakfast of fruit and home-made breads included. Set on 7 acres of a former coffee farm, the grounds have a troop of howler monkeys and over 400 species of birds. Good views of the lake and a distinctly relaxed atmosphere.

(Nuevo) Arenal With a head count of just over 2,500, Arenal is a small town with not much to see. The town is 'nuevo' because the old one currently lies deep below the surface of the lake. The population moved prior to the flooding of Arenal in 1974.

Sleeping and eating A little out of town down a truly appalling road locally called Río Seco (Dry River) is **AL** *Joya Sureña*, T694-4057, F694-4059, joysur@racsa.co.cr On a former working cattle farm, with 28 big rooms with private bathroom – some with bath tubs – telephone, fridge and safe box. Breakfast is included and the mid-priced restaurant has a mix of *Tico* and international dishes. Owned and run by Canadian Jim Swan, there's a gym, pool, jacuzzi and sauna, with options for horseriding and fishing. **A** *Aurora Inn B&B*, T694-4245, F694-4262, www.hotelaurorainn.com Rooms with private bath, pool and jacuzzi overlooking Lake Arenal. Breakfast included. In the centre of town by the soccer pitch is **A-B** *Arenal Inn*, with lake views from the rooms, breakfast included. The rooms are a little overpriced, but you do have direct access to the liveliest (karaoke) bar in town (popular with locals). Visa and MasterCard accepted. Almost next door is **E** per person *Cabinas Rodriguez*, the cheapest place in town. Basic but clean, with private bath and hot water.

Pizzería e Ristorante Tramonte, for Italian cuisine, excellent food and very friendly. *Tipico Arenal*, T694-4159, good local dishes with seafood and vegetarian options. They have a large room upstairs (**C**) with private bath and hot water. The best mid-price place in town.

Sport Fishing: several places rent fishing tackle, but if you want a boat, guide and full package try calling *Joya Sureña*, the *Aurora Inn* or *Rainbow Bass Fishing Safaris*, run by Dave Myers, US$200 a day for 2 anglers, fishing licence US$30 for 2 months, PO Box 7758-1000, San José, T229-2550, F235-7662.

Directory *Banco Nacional* beside the football pitch.

Continuing west to Tilarán Some 2 km west of Nuevo Arenal up a flower-festooned driveway is **A-B** *Chalet Nicholas*, T/F694-4041, members.aol.com/ceiliam/chaletnicholas.html (no www) Breaking out from the flowers, the beautiful chalet sits in a clearing with fine views over the lake. 3 guest rooms have orthopaedic mattresses, private baths and plenty of hot water. Run by New Yorkers Cathy and John Nicholas, the day starts with an American-style breakfast prepared using fruits grown on the property. You can hike trails or ride horses on the property and trips to the surrounding area are easily arranged. Non-smokers only. Recommended.

The best restaurant for miles is mid-price *Willy's Caballo Negro*, T694-4515, serving vegetarian, Swiss and seasonal fish dishes with organic salads. Warm family atmosphere in an isolated modern-day rancho. No credit cards.

A few kilometres west of Arenal, up a winding, occasionally misty 3 km road backing onto **Tenorio National Park** is the **AL-C** *Lake Coter Eco Lodge*, T257-5075,

F257-7065, www.eco-lodge.com An Eco-lodge popular with birdwatchers and adventure seekers, with activities including hiking along 18 km of trails, canoeing, mountain biking, horse riding, and all the usual regional tours as well. There's also a good canopy tour open to non-guests (US$45, 2½ to 3 hrs). 21 rooms in the lodge have private bathrooms and there are another 16 much brighter rooms with balcony views of nearby Lake Coter. Generous meals are served in the buffet restaurant with an open fire and a games room nearby. Back on the main road is **A-B** *Rana de Arenal*, T/F694-4031 with several rooms and an apartment.

Moving towards the western end of the lake, the predominant winds channelled through the region make this a world-class spot for **windsurfing**. Consequently many lodges and hotels target that market and offer deals for longer stays.

Bar y Restaurant Los Lagos is a simple local bar serving typical food for a couple of dollars. Up the hill behind the bar is **E** *Los Lagos*, which occasionally responds to loslagos@hotmail.com and should not be confused with the hotel of the same name in Fortuna. Grubby rooms with cold showers. In desperate need of a bit of TLC but the cheapest option round the lake. Perched on a bluff overlooking the lake is **B** *Villas Alpino*, T/F695-5387. 4 basic but fully-equipped cabins sleeping 2-4 people. Complete with kitchenette and a small balcony, it's a great spot for a few days and especially popular with windsurfers. A good deal.

AL-B *Rock River Lodge*, on the road skirting the lake, T/F695-5644, www. rockriverlodge.com 6 tidy rooms sleeping 4 and bungalows ideal for 3 offering comfortable lodgings and good views of lake. It's a real activity spot popular for windsurfing (US$35 rental for the day), mountain biking, fishing tours and a big open-fire in the communal area with a restaurant serving a healthy mix of *gallo pinto*, pancakes, fresh fruit and fast food. A quieter option is **A-C** *Vista Inn*, 700 m east of Río Piedras, T661-1840. Clean and tidy rooms sleeping 2-5 people, with a balcony set in quiet gardens. In the hamlet of Río Piedras there's a couple of small stores and a café.

Continuing towards Tilarán is the unassuming *Equus* bar and restaurant. Barely worth a passing glance in the day, at night it erupts in a frenzy of barbecue grills, music and drinking. If you're staying in the area, this is *the* place for lively nightlife. **A-B** *Mystica Resort*, T692-1001, F692-1001, members.aol.com/mysticacr (no www). Lodgings in comfortable wooden cabins, each with a private bathroom and roomy veranda, sleep up to 4 people. The pizzerria restaurant has a spectacular view across the lake and it's a fine way to start the day, with the tropical breakfast included in the price – also open for lunch and dinner. Windsurfing, mountain biking and horse riding trips can also be easily arranged.

The last option – or the first depending on which way you're travelling – 8 km north of Tilarán is **L-AL** *Tilawa*, T695-5050, F695-5766, www.hotel-tilawa.com With décor and wall-paintings evoking images of ancient Greece, the Tilawa stands out as multi-activity resort. 24 comfortably large rooms all have a pair of queen-sized beds, private bath, ceiling fan and telephone. There are also 4 suites, sleeping up to 4 people, with kitchenette, and a restaurant serving *Tico* and international cuisine. Activities make for a long list including fishing, boat tours visit Tabacón hot springs and the volcano using the hotel's catamaran to make the 20-mile cross lake journey in just 45 mins, and trips to the botanical gardens. Tilawa's forte is anything that combines wind and water – windsurfing, kitesurfing, wakeboarding and whatever the latest trend yet to be invented. If it sounds a little too specialized for the beginner, the windsurfing school will get you up on the board – and if it's not fun, it's free – money back guarantee. You can explore the hotel grounds on foot, horse or mountain bike, watch birds, play tennis or take to the pool. Throw in a Spanish school and even a micro-brewery and there's little reason to move too far from the resort.

Just over 1 km from Tilarán, heading north from the town towards Tronadora, a poor dirt road spurs to the right following the southern shore of Lake Arenal – the

The power of wind

When the rising waters of Lake Arenal slowly flooded the Arenal valley it is difficult to imagine that the engineers could have contemplated the truly staggering effect on the area. Beyond the multitude of secluded hotels and lodges around the lake's shores, and the hydroelectric power produced by the Tronadora dam, the wind that shoots down the length of the lake has created a host of new opportunities.

East to west trade winds move from the Caribbean and northern lowlands and are channelled through the narrow gap between the Cordillera de Tilarán to the south (which includes Arenal Volcano and Monteverde Cloud Forest Reserve) and

Cordillera de Guanacaste to the north. As the winds rise, they dump almost 4½ m of rain on Arenal Volcano National Park at the eastern end of the lake but by the time they reach the western limits of the lake, rainfall is down to a mere 1½ m. One final push over the western hills and the drained winds rush over northern Guanacaste creating conditions ideal for the dry tropical forests of Santa Rosa National Park.

While the winds existed before the manmade lake, the opportunities for world class windsurfing – with winds regularly reaching 60 mph – are a recent development, as are the wind turbines churning away along the western ridge of the valley.

---

road makes a great route for mountain biking. 1½ km down the road is **B** *Bahía Azul*, T/F695-5750. 14 clean rooms with TV, private bathrooms, but in need of sprucing up. A wide range of activities including pedalos, a pool and the only hotel actually on the lake. A short distance further on is **L** *Arenal Country Club*, T693-1001, F653-0248, www.arenalcountryclub.com 5 large terraced townhouses with kitchen, 3 bedrooms and 3 bathrooms which works out as a very good deal. A large swimming pool, gym, a couple of tennis courts and a relaxing restaurant make this a good family spot. It's also up for sale so book in advance to be sure – or buy it and guarantee your reservation.

Tilarán

Colour map 1, grid B5
Population: 9,526
Altitude: 550 m

Tilarán is a small agricultural community in a fairly modern town, which is largely indifferent to the visitors fanning out in all directions. In reality, as far as most visitors are concerned, the town's importance lies in its role as the transport hub linking Cañas on the Pan-American Highway, with Santa Elena and Monteverde Reserve to the south and Lake Arenal and the volcano to the east.

Sleeping
If circumstances should find you needing to stop for the night there are a few options in town. **B** *Naralit*, on the south side of the church, T695-5393, clean, new buildings. **C-D** *Hotel Guadalupe*, a block south and east of the church, T695-5943. 25 pleasant rooms with bath, hot water and cable TV. Recommended. **D** *Cabiñas El Sueño*, one block north of bus terminal/central park, T695-5347, clean rooms around central patio, hot water, fan, TV, friendly and free coffee. Good deal. **D** *Hotel Restaurant Mary*, south side of church, T695-5479. Small pleasant rooms with bath. Recommended. **E** *Central*, round the back of the church, one block south, T695-5363. Rooms with shared bath, noisy.

Eating
Stefanie's out of the bus station to the left on the corner of the main plaza is good and quick if you need a meal between buses. There is also *Restaurant Hotel Mary* which does a steady trade. *La Carreta*, round the back of the church, is the place to go and relax if you have a couple of hours to spare. Excellent pancakes, coffee, Italian dishes and good local information – good value.

La Fortuna or Monteverde?

From Tilarán, deciding whether to head for La Fortuna or Monteverde can be a dilemma, especially in the green season when clouds may obscure views of the volcano. It's little consideration when you realize that at the same time, Monteverde and Santa Elena may equally well be shrouded in cloud. In reality, the decision is best based on your interests and consideration of what is on offer. In the green season, the weather changes rapidly and taking local advice about recent weather is of limited value. But bear in mind you can make the journey between La Fortuna and Monteverde by foot or horse.

Buses Direct bus from **San José**, 5 daily, 5 hrs, from Terminal Atlántico Norte. Two daily buses to **Ciudad Quesada** via **Fortuna** at 0700 and 1230. To Fortuna, 3 hrs, US$2.00. Daily bus to **Santa Elena** (for Monteverde), 1230, 2½ hrs, US$1.65, return 0700 daily. **Tilarán-Puntarenas** 0600, 1300, 3 hrs, US$3. 5 daily buses to/from **Cañas** (to at 0500, 0730, 1000, 1230 and 1530, 40 mins, US$1.25), where buses head north and south along the Pan-American Highway. If you get the 1230 **Tilarán-Liberia** bus, you can get from there to the **Nicaraguan border** before it closes. **Transport**

Banco Cootilaran, a couple of blocks north of the Central Park, has a Visa and MasterCard ATM, and there is also a *Banco de Costa Rica* in town. **Directory**

North of Fortuna

A quiet route to the north leads from Fortuna to **San Rafael de Guatuso**. You can come back to the lake either by turning off before San Rafael through Venado (for the caves), or from San Rafael itself. There are a couple of basic hotels (**D-E** *Albergue Tío Henry*, T464-0211). The roads are in fairly good condition, and go through lovely countryside with beautiful views, especially approaching the lake.

Three kilometres from **Colonia Río Celeste** 20 km west of San Rafael de Guatuso is the **B** *Montaña Magil Forest Lodge*, Apdo 3404-1000, San José, T221-2825, F233-5991, memmora@sol.racsa.co.cr Set in 240-ha on the foothills of the 1,916-m **Tenorio volcano**. The volcano is part of 12,871 ha national park with thermal waters, boiling mud and unspoilt forest. (It is best visited from Bagaces, see page 225.) Price includes meals. 10 rooms with private bath. It is reportedly difficult to find – call in advace.

Buses to San Rafael leave **San José** at 1545, returning at 1000, taking 4 hrs, from Av 3-5, C 12, US$3.50 (Transnorte de Upala - T221-9022). Local services are available from **Ciudad Quesada** and **Fortuna**.

A reasonable road continues north for 35 km towards the **Nicaraguan border** and the agricultural community of **Upala**. It's a small town with a population of just over 13,000. There's little to see or do, but a road leading out west to La Cruz, and a couple of roads heading southwest to the Pan-American Highway via Bijagua or to Bagaces make for an interesting journey. There is also a poor road leading east to Caño Negro, with a bus service, when conditions allow.

The northern region

Sleeping and transport Accommodation in Upala is limited, the best cheap option being **F** *Buena Vista*, T470-0186, which has simple rooms with food available. There's a daily bus from San José at 1500, returning at 0500, taking about 4 hrs, from Av 3-5, C 12, US$4.30 (*Transnorte de Upala* - T221-9022). Several buses make the 1¾ hr trip from Cañas. There's an airstrip as well, but no scheduled services.

North to Los Chiles

From Ciudad Quesada, a paved road quickly drops to within a 100 m of sea level and runs northwest to Florencia (service station). At **Platanar** is **AL** *Hotel La Garza*, 8 km from Florencia, T475-5222, F475-5015, www.hotel-lagarza-arenal.com Twelve charming hardwood and spacious and airy bungalows with bath and fan, constructed from local hardwoods, with a balcony overlooking river, set in beautiful but not overtended gardens. It's a great spot, hidden and secluded – ideal for a quiet getaway – with good views of Arenal. The 230-ha hacienda is still a working dairy and cattle ranch owned and run by the Cantillo family since 1947. While very comfortable, the family is keen to welcome people with an interest in the realities of hacienda life rather than simply being an 'adventure park'. Excursions to nearby sights can be easily arranged.

Continuing north for 13 km to **Muelle San Carlos** is **L-AL** *Tilajari Resort Hotel*, T469-09091, F469-9095, www.tilajari.com Fifty luxurious rooms, and 26 suites, all with a/c and comfortable private bath. It's a popular place with families and groups providing a good range of activities including tennis courts, two pools, sauna, bar and restaurant, horses, boat trips and other excursions organized.

Los Chiles

Colour map 1, grid A6
District population: 10,013
Altitude: 70 m

Heading through the northern lowlands, a good road carves through rich red laterite soils in an almost straight line for 74 km through the Guatuso Plains where the shiny leaves of citrus fruit plantations shimmer in the bright tropical sun. If coffee is king in the highlands, citrus wears the crown in the northern lowlands. Just short of the Nicaraguan border is Los Chiles, the departure point for boat trips through dense, tropical vegetation into the 10,171 ha Caño Negro Wildlife Refuge. Birdwatchers flock to the northern wetlands to see the amazing variety of birdlife which feast at the seasonal lake created by the floodwaters of the Río Frío.

Los Chiles is a small town on the banks of the Río Frío, a few hundred metres west of Highway 35. Close to the border, Los Chiles sees a lot of Nicaraguans passing through looking for season agricultural work and the townspeople reflect upon the merging of nations. The central plaza, with an unassuming modern church on its eastern side, is also a football pitch, mixing fun and faith seamlessly. Most places of interest are within a block or two and the days pass slowly as children chuck themselves off the dockside into the Río Frío a couple of blocks to the west in the heat of the afternoon sun.

Sleeping The best place in town is **C** *Rancho Eco-directa*, one block west of the central park opposite the immigration office, T471-1414, F471-1197, ecodos@racsa.co.cr It has 8 big, clean and well appointed rooms with ceramic floors, bath and hot water, making this the most comfortable option in town – there's even a small desk and a lamp in most rooms. Good thatched ranch-style restaurant serves breakfasts and dinners (parking at the back). *Eco-directa* is a good source of information on the region, and can arrange tours in the area including river safaris and fishing trips. The manager Oscar Rojas has been recommended as a guide, and is useful for information on travelling to Nicaragua. A good budget choice is **E** *Cabinas Jaribú*, (**F** for Youth Hostel members) 100 m from the bus stop, a few blocks east of central park, T/F471-1055, www.hostelling-costarica.com Good rooms with tropical motifs on the walls, private bathrooms, fan, some with TV. Parking, postal service, internet, fax and laundry and a range of interesting tours. You can sort out the cheapest option to Caño Negro (US$20 per person, min 3) with the *Servitur* agency which has its office here. The best of the budget range **G** *Carolina*, is close to the main highway, T471-1151. Small, fairly dark rooms and a few blocks from the centre but very clean and well maintained. Off the strip facing the football pitch your best bet is **G** *Onassis*, on the southwest corner of main plaza, T471-1001. Basic rooms, clean, shared bath and a fan if you ask nicely.

South of town B *Albergue Caño Negro*, 17 km south of Los Chiles on a rough dirt road ideally suited for 4-wheel drive, T460-0124, F240-5460. Rustic rooms on the banks of the Río Frío.

Eating In addition to *Rancho Eco-directa* and *Cabiñas Jabirú*, the eating options are *Restaurant El Parque* on the main plaza, with good home cooking and *Los Petates*, on the road running south of the central park, which has cheap food with large portions. Supermarket *El Chileno* has some basic supplies but is reportedly unfriendly and overcharges.

Tour operators Ask about guides at *Rancho Eco-Directa*, at the *Servitur* office in Cabinas Jabirú or *Restaurant Los Petates* if you want to organize your own trip to Caño Negro. Local prices vary greatly depending on demand but start at around US$20 per person for a minimum of 3 people. Oscar Rojas at *Eco-Directa* and Manfred Vargas at *Servitur* can help organize trips to **El Castillo** and **San Juan** in Nicaragua and could help with arrangements for travelling down the Río San Juan to the Caribbean. In Fortuna *Aventuras Arenal* and *Sunset Tours* run trips to **Caño Negro**.

Transport **Bus** Direct buses to **Los Chiles** leave from San José Terminal Atlántico Norte at 0530, 1530, 5 hrs, US$4, returning to the capital at 0500, 1500. There is a frequent service between **Ciudad Quesada (San Carlos)** and Los Chiles. If travelling from Fortuna, take the bus to San Carlos, alighting at Muelle and wait for a bus heading towards Los Chiles. You may feel stranded, but it'll shave at least an hour off your journey.

Boat There is a daily boat to **San Carlos** on the River San Juan, leaving daily at 0800 or when full. US$5, 45 mins. From San Carlos you can take a boat down the Río San Juan travelling to Trinidad or further downstream to Greytown but there is no border crossing to Costa Rica.

Directory **Banks** *Banco Nacional*, with ATM, on central park. **Communications** Postal and internet services are available at *Cabiñas Jabirú*, see above. **Immigration** Half a block up from the dock, open 0800-1600 every day.

Excursions

Refugio Nacional de Vida Silvastre Caño Negro Covering 10,171 ha **Caño Negro National Wildlife Reserve** draws birds and wildlife to one of Costa Rica's most important wetland regions and visitors flock to the Reserve to see the wildlife. At its heart is Lake Caño Negro, a shallow seasonal lake covering 800 ha no more than 3 m deep, that completely disappears towards the end of the dry season in April and May. Swamps, gallery forest and marshes attract a wide range of migratory birds to the area, many of which are endangered. The reserve is home to the largest nesting colony of

Neotropical cormorants in the country and is the last permanent refuge in the country of the Nicaraguan grackle. The roseate spoonbill with its mildly humourous spatulate bill is a common sight, and you may catch a glimpse of the huge jabirú standing almost 1½ m tall – Central America's largest bird. Travelling in a covered canoe chartered from Los Chiles, the floating safaris follow the Río Frío through primary forest taking 3-4 hrs for the trip. With luck you'll see three of the four Costa Rican monkeys – the howler, spider and white-faced, along with sloths and reptiles including caiman. ■ *Most people take the tour from Fortuna, which costs around US$45, lasting around 8 hrs in total. Tours organized from Los Chiles are cheaper at US$20 and pick-up can be organized with tour operators in Fortuna or you can make up the numbers in town. However, in the green season this may be more difficult.*

Fishing   Freshwater fishing is an option from Los Chiles with 25 kg **tarpon** often taken from the lake Caño Negro. Landing one of these silver kings is unforgettable and you can try your luck and take a trip from Los Chiles for around US$350 for two people, tackle and refreshments included, or organize a trip from San José which will set you back a little more.

Reserva Biológica Bosque Nuboso Monteverde and Santa Elena

Colour map 1, grid B6
Population: 2,363
Altitude:1400 m

www.monteverdeinfo.
com is a useful
regional website

With its head often shrouded in mist, the appalling roads leading to Monteverde Cloud Forest Reserve will keep you (literally and metaphorically) on the edge of your seat in anticipation of the experience of one of the world's premier nature destinations. Milk urns stacked at the roadside awaiting collection give clues to the real identity of this agricultural community that hides cut off on all sides from the rest of Costa Rica. But this isolation has preserved something special in the surrounding hills: the seed of Monteverde Reserve has germinated to create a host of natural experiences that encapsulate the very essence of Costa Rica – diversity, seclusion and at times exhilaration.

The secret that was Monteverde Reserve in the 1970s when it was founded, is now a well trodden path. True to the uniqueness of the reserve, despite the visitors, there is still a rough charm to the area. Santa Elena is a scruffy town of barely three streets and much more appealing for the way it seems to trundle along, like nature, in a state of organized chaos. The settlement of Monteverde lines the bumpy road that leads up to the reserve. For the visitor, reserves, protected forests and more adventurous activities await.

Ins and outs

Getting there   Monteverde straddles the single road leading up from Santa Elena, which is reached
Before you curse   along a number of bone-shaking roads. If driving, there are a number of options.
the poor roads,   From the Pan-American Highway at Km 149, turning right south of the Río Lagarto.
it's worth bearing in   Continue for about 40 km on mostly gravel road (allow 2½ hrs) to Santa Elena. Parts
mind that they have   of the road are quite good, but in wet weather 4-wheel drive is recommended for the
been fundamental   rough parts – make sure your car rental agreement allows you to travel to the
in preserving the   Monteverde. A shorter route is to take the Sardinal turn-off from the Pan-American
cloudforest by   Highway north of the Río Aranjuez. At the park in Sardinal turn left, then via Guacimal
preventing rampant   to the Monteverde road.
development of
the region

You can also drive from Tilarán along an equally poor road – a journey that takes a couple of hours. En route you can visit the quiet watefall Las Cataratas de Viento Frío, 800 m down a very steep road, followed by a 400-m walk.

A couple of buses leave San Jose for Santa Elena daily. A bus comes from Puntarenas via the Km 149 route. There are also buses from Tilarán to the north, linking with Fortuna and Volcán Arenal, and Cañas on the Pan-American Highway.

Getting around Walking is by far the simplest way of getting around the area, and is certainly feasible around Santa Elena. A bus makes the journey up the hill from Santa Elena through Monteverde to the reserve leaving town at 0600 and 1100, getting workers and independent travellers up to the reserve. Taxis are available from Santa Elena charging around US$6.85 for the journey. The smart choice is to get transport up the hill and walk down enjoying the views as you go. Of course, if you have your own vehicle moving around is a lot simpler.

Best time to visit The driest months in the region are from Jan to May, with the best months for birdwatching being Feb, Mar and Apr. This also coincides with lower rainfall, the wettest months being Sep to Nov. As this is cloudforest, remember that mist is common and rain can occur throughout the year.

History and background information

Monteverde owes its formation to the pursuit of ideals. Back in 1951, a group of Quakers from North America left the USA to avoid the draft. Buying land in Monteverde and clearing the forests for dairy farming, the community soon realized that the forest cover was essential to protect the watershed of the area and created a protected area of 541 hectares. In 1972 George Powell and his wife, after a period studying the birds of the cloudforest, set out to protect more of the region, joining forces with the long-time resident Wilford Guindon to promote the creation of a reserve. Combining the Quaker reserve with a further 328 hectares, the Monteverde Cloud Forest Preserve was created in 1972.

Tedious though the facts and figures may be, those ideals have grown with the size of the reserve. Without the backing of large environmental organizations, Monteverde moved from individual passion to global awareness through the medium of rumours and television nature documentaries. Slowly, the notion of ecotourism began to reap rewards, and the Preserve spawned a myriad of reserves, protected areas and conservation projects in the region and across Costa Rica.

A visit to Monteverde or any of the many other private reserves is an opportunity to see nature in grand profusion. Plants grow on every available space, insects breed, birds feed and mammals loiter and stalk. Without a trained eye nearby, you may see only insects and hear a bird take flight, but the experience is no less enjoyable. Even with a guide you'll be lucky to see mammals.

Today, there is much discussion about the future of Monteverde and other reserves in the area. Some residents want to see the appalling roads upgraded to improve access. Others want to restrict the potential damage that may be caused, believing that development has already reached unacceptable limits. You can decide for yourself whether visiting Monteverde is about quality or quantity. Personally, a little hardship makes for a far better reward.

The northern region

The Settlement of Monteverde

There is no official tourist office in Santa Elena or Monteverde, but several private tour operators and hotels in Santa Elena can help with general inquiries and arranging tours

Strung out along the road climbing to the cloudforest, the settlement at Monteverde – between Santa Elena and the Reserve - was founded by American Quakers in the 1950s. Without a centre as such, it started life as a group of dairy farms providing milk for a co-operative cheese factory. The cheese factory, now privately owned, still operates selling excellent cheeses of various types, fresh milk, ice cream, milkshakes to die for and *cajeta* (a butterscotch spread). Today, Monteverde maintains an air of pastoral charm, but tourism provides more revenue for the town than dairy produce ever could.

Monteverde & Santa Elena

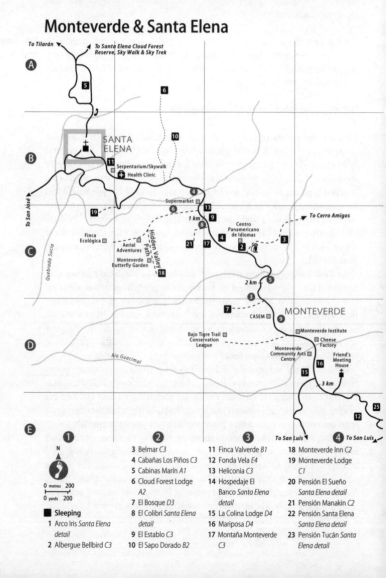

Sleeping
1 Arco Iris *Santa Elena detail*
2 Albergue Bellbird *C3*
3 Belmar *C3*
4 Cabañas Los Piños *C3*
5 Cabinas Marín *A1*
6 Cloud Forest Lodge *A2*
7 El Bosque *D3*
8 El Colibri *Santa Elena detail*
9 El Establo *C3*
10 El Sapo Dorado *B2*
11 Finca Valverde *B1*
12 Fonda Vela *E4*
13 Heliconia *C3*
14 Hospedaje El Banco *Santa Elena detail*
15 La Colina Lodge *D4*
16 Mariposa *D4*
17 Montaña Monteverde *C3*
18 Monteverde Inn *C2*
19 Monteverde Lodge *C1*
20 Pensión El Sueño *Santa Elena detail*
21 Pensión Manakin *C2*
22 Pensión Santa Elena *Santa Elena detail*
23 Pensión Tucán *Santa Elena detail*

Essentials

Sleeping
■ *on map*
Price codes:
see inside front cover

While accommodation in Monteverde and north of Santa Elena is somewhat spread out, there are several good accommodation options within walking distance of town

In Santa Elena   A-D *Arco Iris*, T645-5067, F645-5022, www.arcoirislodge.com   A mixed bag of rooms and fine cabins all with bath. There's a restaurant serving good healthy breakfasts and meals in high season. Horses are available for rent and there's plenty of parking. **B** *Finca Valverde*, 300 m east of *Banco Nacional* up hill on road to the reserve, T645-5157, F645-5216, www.monteverde.co.cr   Comfortable cabins and rooms set in the forest, sleeping 2 or 4 people. Each room has private bath, some with a bath tub. Coffee is still grown on the finca (which is a good spot for birdwatching) and the restaurant serves good *Tico* food. **D** *Pensión Tucán*, T645-5017. A good budget option with clean rooms, some with private bath, or **E** in basic cabins with shower (and sporadically hot water), friendly management, good breakfast and restaurant recommended but closed Sun lunch. Bargain for lower price in the green season. You can also try **D** *Gary Diller*, T645-5045 late afternoons/early evening, an American guide who rents rooms in his house. Highly recommended. **E** *El Colibrí*, is clean and friendly in a timber-built house. Some rooms with balconies – there are reports that it may be closing down. **E** *Pensión El Sueño*, T645-5021. Very friendly, with small but nice rooms, some with private baths and hot showers. Meals are available, but they seem a bit pricey, and there is parking. The proprietor Rafa Trejos does horseback trips into the mountains to see quetzals, US$35. **E** *Pensión Cabinas Marín*, 500 m north of the centre past the Agricultural College, T645-5279. Spacious rooms, with room 8 providing a nice view, good breakfasts, friendly. **E** *Pensión Santa Elena*, T645-5051, F645-6060, www.monteverdeinfo.com/pension.htm   Very popular spot with backpackers and budget travellers. The rooms are clean, with simple doubles and others sleeping up to eight. The place has a lively atmosphere, with a restaurant serving good food (**C** price category includes 3 meals), and a kitchen if you want to cook yourself. Excellent source of information for the area, have a look at the website, Jacques does the hard sell but he knows his stuff.

In the very centre of town is **F** per person *Hospedaje El Banco*, with clean rooms and hot showers. Family-run, friendly and with English spoken it's a good source of information. Recommended.

Approaching Santa Elena from Tilarán AL-A *Mirador Lodge San Gerardo*, 6 km north of Santa Elena, T645-5087, F645-6087, miradorq@

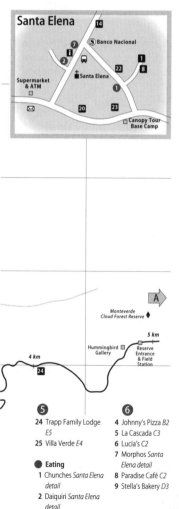

Santa Elena

14
Ⓢ Banco Nacional
7
ℹ️
2
22
1
✝ Santa Elena
8
Supermarket & ATM
1
✉
20
23
Canopy Tour Base Camp

A ▶

Monteverde Cloud Forest Reserve ◆

5 km

Hummingbird Gallery □   Reserve Entrance & Field Station

4 km

24

⑤
24 Trapp Family Lodge *E5*
25 Villa Verde *E4*

● **Eating**
1 Chunches *Santa Elena detail*
2 Daiquiri *Santa Elena detail*
3 El Bosque *C2*

⑥
4 Johnny's Pizza *B2*
5 La Cascada *C3*
6 Lucia's *C2*
7 Morphos *Santa Elena detail*
8 Paradise Café *C2*
9 Stella's Bakery *D3*

The northern region

sol.racsa.co.cr or www.monteverdesangerardolodge.comFrom May to Nov you probably need a horse not 4-wheel drive to get here down the dirt track. Rustic cabins with private bath or dormitory accommodation (**C**) in grounds set in the private reserve, popular with birdwatchers. Being so cut off, the home-cooking in the restaurant is essential rather than an option. **B** *Miramontes*, a couple of kilometres north of Santa Elena, T645-5152, F645-5297, www.multicr.com/miramontes A little piece of Switzerland, with 6 comfortable rooms in wooden cabins, all with private bath and hot water. A couple of the rooms have a veranda looking out across the forest. True to form, the Swiss-run *Spaghettería* restaurant provides cosmopolitan specialties from Italy, Switzerland, Austria, France and of course, Costa Rica. **B** *Sunset Hotel*, 1½ km on road to Tilarán, T645-5048. On top of hill with fine views in a good location, friendly, clean, warm showers, good breakfast, German spoken. **B** *Monte Los Olivos Ecotourist Lodge*, 6 km north of Santa Elena on road to Quebrada Grande and Tilarán, T/F286-4203, www.agroecoturismo.net 4 cabins with private bathroom, 5 with shared bathroom, one of 3 lodges run by community association and supported by WWF Canada and CIDA Canada.

The hotels are listed in order heading up the hill

Uphill to the reserve A single dirt road leads up to the reserve passing through the spread out agricultural settlement that is Monteverde. Hotels and lodges are dotted along the road, many in wonderfully secluded settings with good views. The majority are in the mid- and upper-price brackets, but there are a few exceptions.

Climbing the hill a road to the right leads to one of the trilogy of hotels in the country owned by *Costa Rica Expeditions*. **L** *Monteverde Lodge*, T645-5057, F645-5126, toll free in USA T800-633-4734, www.crexped.co.cr/monteverde.html The spacious rooms all have a private bath, with solar-heated water. It's a graceful hotel, which impresses from the outside with a vast lobby complete with open-fire. The environmental considerations extend to the solar-heated jacuzzi, baked in natural light set in a large glass atrium. The lodge gardens, complete with running stream and a small waterfall, are relaxation itself, and there's a small look-out for viewing the surrounding forest and wildlife. Packages including meals are available, and children under 10 sharing a room go free. Recommended.

Back on the main road, a fork leads to **A** *Cloud Forest Lodge*, T645-5058, F645-5168, www.catours.co.cr 18 immaculate rooms set in 9 double cabins, each with private bath. The lodge is up on the hill set in a private 30-ha reserve with 5 km of trails, and stunning views (on clear days) to the Pacific from the restaurant which bakes bread daily. It's also home to the *Original Canopy Tour* which can be arranged at the hotel, or in the office on the main hill up to the reserve.

Another steep road to the left arrives at **AL** *El Sapo Dorado*, T645-5010, F645-5180, www.cool.co.cr/usr/sapodorado With the *Tico*/US owners reflecting the synthesis of Costa Rican and Quaker traditions, 30 comfortable suites with private bath and private porch entrance, surrounded by tropical gardens. You can choose from Sunset Suites, overlooking the Nicoya Peninsula, Fountain Suites or the 10 Classic Suites, which all have an open fire. The restaurant is widely recommended. International and national dishes merge vegetarian and vegan options with more traditional dishes.

Just beyond the village supermarket is **L-AL** *Heliconia*, T645-5109, F645-5007, heliconia@sol.racsa.co.cr The hardwood chalet is a theme reflected throughout the comfortably furnished rooms, complete with private bathroom and veranda. The restaurant serves excellent food. Next door is **A** *El Establo*, T645-5110, F645-5041, www.establo.com 20 carpeted, brick wall rooms with private bathroom. Home cooking is served in the restaurant, with flagstones and a fireplace in the large sofa-laden reception area. Service is reported to be excellent and it's a popular choice for groups. The 50-ha farm has nature trails through the primary forest, with guides available for birdwatching, and horses available for hire at the stables.

The northern region

What is cloudforest?

Simply put, it's forest that spends much of the year blanketed in cloud creating conditions of high humidity. In Monteverde, trade winds from the Atlantic force moist air up the Tilarán Mountains, cooling the air as it rises which condenses to create clouds.

The result is an abundance of plants and epiphyte growth with tree trunks and branches covered in dense blankets of mosses and lichens, with twisting vines, fallen trees and giant tree ferns.

The cloudforest is an almost magical place, like the forests of fairy tales. Take away the path and imagine how quickly you could get lost.

Opposite the *Heliconia*, a gravel road leads to **E** *Monteverde Inn*, close to the Butterfly Garden, T645-5156. The rooms are basic, and could do with smartening up, but it is a quiet budget spot away from town with good views down the valley, and access to a a 2-hr trail down the Hidden Valley.

Just beyond Establo, a short road leads to **D-E** *Pensión Manakin*, T645-5080, F645-5517, manakin@sol.racsa.co.cr 10 simple rooms, a few with private bath, or **E** with shared bath. Filling breakfast and evening meals are available, in a family atmosphere which is great for sharing stories with other guests. A small balcony at the back makes for a calm place to sit and relax. The Villegas are very knowledgeable about the area, and will help arrange tours and transport up to the reserve if required.

AL *Hotel de Moñtana Monteverde*, on the main road, T645-5046, F645-5320, www.ticonet.co.cr/monteverde 32 comfortable rooms with hardwood floor, some with fireplaces. The cabin-style restaurant serves *Tico* dishes, and you can take to the Jacuzzi or sauna for complete relaxation enjoying the views out to the Nicoya Peninsula. The 15 ha gardens include several short trails and the gardens provide excellent birdwatching opportunities.

Across the road set in fine landscaped gardens is **B-C** *Cabanas Los Piños*, T645-5252, F645-5005, www.costaricanet.net/lospinos A selection of clean rooms with bare brick walls sleeping 2 to 6 people, all with private bath and some with kitchenettes. It's a quiet spot, and a good deal for groups and families.

Just before the gas station is the new **E** *Alberque Bellbird*, T/F645-5026. Half a dozen rooms in mainly dormitory-style accommodation, with shared bathrooms. It's a clean place, and well situated close to the *Belmar* for treks up the Cerro Amigos, if you don't want to be in Santa Elena.

300 m behind the service station up in the hills is **AL** *Belmar*, T645-5201, F645-5135, www.hotelbelmar.com This Swiss chalet-style hotel perched on the hillside has spectacular views of the Nicoya Peninsula and 34 comfortable rooms with private bath and hot water, some with balconies. There is also a restaurant and bar so you don't have to go down the hill for any reason.

Restaurant El Bosque, on the main road marks the turning for **B-D** *El Bosque*, T645-5158, F645-5129, www.bosquelodge.com Set in pretty gardens are 26 low-key rooms with private bath. A good spot, with fine views. There's a short trail through the gardens, ample parking, and helpful staff are happy to help arrange tours.

B-C *Mariposa*, T645-5013. In a single block are 3 simple rooms sleeping up to 3 people, with private bath. A family atmosphere, with breakfast included in the price and dinner by arrangement make this a very relaxed place to stay even if there are no frills.

Next is **B-C** *La Colina Lodge*, T645-5009, F645-5588, www.lacolina.com One of the original settlement homes complete with uneven floors, head-crackingly low doorways and a cozy fireplace decorated with agricultural antiquities. There are 14 good rooms sleeping 2-4 people with private bath, and some with a balcony. There's also 4 bunk rooms (**D**) and you can **camp** at the back (**F**). The restaurant serves the

The northern region

standard regional fare. Marvin Rockwell, the former owner and one of the original Quaker settlers, stills pops in to give talks when requested. The lodge also owns La Colina in Manuel Antonio and will happily arrange transport between the two.

Within a couple of kilometres of the reserve entrance is **L-AL** *Fonda Vela*, T257-1413, F257-1416, www.centralamerica.com/cr/hotel/fondavel Spread around 7 buildings are 25 beautiful rooms and suites, all with huge windows giving great views to the forest, 2 double beds and a private bathroom with hot water. Some rooms are in elevated multiplex wooden cabins. The 14- ha farm has trails leading through the forest with good birding. There are 2 excellent restaurants open to public, a bar, TV room, art gallery and conference room and all just 25-min walk, or a 5-min drive from the reserve.

A *Villa Verde*, across the street from *Fonda Vela*, T645-5025, F645-5115, monteverdehotelvillaverde.freewebspace.com (no www) A selection of rooms and suites with hot showers, shared bath and some with kitchenettes. It's a popular spot with groups, having a large restaurant, a games room and fine views across the valley.

High on a hill without a lowly goat herd, but closest to the reserve is the **AL** *Trapp Family Lodge*, T645-5858, F645-5990, www.trappfam.com Beyond the entrance, floor to ceiling hardwoods make this a fine, elegant choice with 10 immaculate rooms, each with private bath and hot water. The upper rooms have a balcony, the lower rooms a terrace, so all you need is a comfortable chair and your binoculars for excellent birdwatching. The restaurant is open for breakfast and dinner and the friendly and helpful hosts will help arrange tours.

San Luís Beside *La Colina Lodge* a road heads south to **AL** per person *San Luis Biological Station and Ecolodge*, a 40 min drive from Monteverde, call ahead to book, T/F645-5277, or T385-3255 (mob), www.monteverdeguide.com/ecolodgesanluis On 66 ha of farmland and cloud forest in the San Luis Valley, bordering the Monteverde Cloud and Children's International Cloud Forest, the activities of research, farming and eco-tourism are combined in the valley of the San Luis River. Set in the forest with a bird count pushing 250, and a good list of mammals including occasional sightings of puma and tapir, the options are wide and varied. Come just to look and learn, staying in a comfortable cabin, get your hands dirty working on the tropical farm complete with coffee, banana and fruit trees, or get totally emerged working as a research assistant. The cheaper options include staying in a bunkhouse which is ideal for large groups, or the bungalow which can sleep up to 16. Treks through the forest and horse riding are optional extras if you've got the energy.

Eating There are several places right in the centre of Santa Elena. *Chunches*, is a popular place to hangout opposite *Pensión Santa Elena*. Good espresso bar and snacks in addition to a pile of used books, magazines and a laundry service. On the main street *Daiquiri* is another popular spot serving pizzas and traditional food, and Morpho almost next door, has a good, friendly atmosphere serving a range of snacks in a café atmosphere.

Uphill to the reserve In addition to the excellent hotel restaurants at *Monteverde Lodge*, *El Sapo Dorado* and *Fondo Vela*, **Johnny's Pizza**, is on the main road between Santa Elena and Monteverde. Good pizzas cooked in a wood fuel-oven in a relaxed café atmosphere. A few tables on the balcony add precious time for wildlife encounters, and after dining visit the small souvenir shop. *Lucia's* down the road opposite *Heliconia*, is a heaven-sent piece of Italy with tasty lasagne, and countless recommendations. The new **Paradise Cafe** opposite El Establo, serves vitamin busting fruit juices, good coffee and snacks. *Restaurant El Bosque*, next to *CASEM Shop*, has good food and is one of the cheaper options up the hill to the reserve, open from 0630. *Stella's Bakery*, opposite *CASEM*, has excellent wholemeal bread, cakes and good granola to take on hikes, or there's a small garden café if you want to eat in.

Several hotels provide **slide shows** featuring images from renowned photographers such as Michael & Patricia Hogden. Ask in your hotel for schedules. **Entertainment**

At night *Paradise Café* drops the shutters, pops the corn and becomes **Cinema Paradiso**, with a find blend of Hollywood blockbusters, art house and kids movies. It's a new place in town and schedules will need to settle down, but plans are for screenings at 0600, 0800 and matinées at weekends. US$2.50 Dancing and partying happens up the hill at *La Cascada* until the early hours.

Monteverde Music Festival, is much more than a few musicians getting together for a jam. Classical and jazz concerts with performances by local, national and international musicians, performing at sunset between Jan and Apr. Programmes from hotels or the Monteverde Institute, T645-5053, www.mvinstitute.com Entrance US$9. **Festivals**

Many hotels have a small souvenirs shop. *CASEM*, is a co-operative gift shop, just over **Shopping** half way up the road to the reserve, close to El Bosque restaurant. It sells embroidered shirts, T-shirts, wooden and woven articles and baskets. The shop next door sells Costa Rican coffee and you can also get used coffee sacks if they have any in stock. *Bromelias* is a new gallery in the area, close to Stella's bakery, which is worth a visit but still evolving. *Galería Extasis*, a short distance south of CASEM, exhibits and sells sculptures by the Costa Rican artist Marco Tulio Brenes.

Bus From **San José** a direct bus runs from Av 9, C 12, just outside Terminal Atlántico **Transport** Norte, daily at 0630 and 1430, 4½ hrs, US$4. Return buses leave Monteverde from *Hotel Villa Verde* also at 0630 and 1430, picking up through town, stopping at Santa Elena bus stop. Be early. Check times in advance, Sat bus does not always run in low season. *Transportes Tilarán* T645-5032 in Santa Elena, T258-5674 in San José for information. This service is not 'express', and stops to pick up passengers all along the route, and is not a comfortable ride. Keep your day-bag with you at all times; several cases of theft reported, acknowledged by the bus company by the signs in the bus! Bus from **Puntarenas**, with *Terminal Empresarios Unidos* (T222-0064), leave daily at 1415, with an occasional service at 1315 as well, returning at 0600, 2½-4 hrs, US$2.20. This bus arrives in time to catch a bus to Puerto Quepos for Quepos and Manuel Antonio. From **Tilarán** buses leave at 1230, the return bus leaving Santa Elena at 0700 (US$1.80, 3 hrs). Going to Tilarán the 0700 connects with the 1230 bus to **Fortuna** and others to **Cañas** for the Pan-American Highway, **Liberia** and the **Nicoya Peninsula**.

Taxis Available in the centre of Santa Elena for rides up to the reserves and other destinations. Arrange a pick-up time for the return trip.

If you are **driving**, there is a service station roughly half way between Santa Elena and the reserve open Mon-Sat 0700-1800, Sun 0700-1200.

Jeep to La Fortuna If you're heading to La Fortuna, you can avoid the rather tedious 8- hr bus journey via Tilarán by taking a jeep to Lake Arenal, then a boat, and a jeep for the last stretch. It's 3 hrs, US$25, and more scenic. *Pension Santa Elena* can organize the journey or talk to your hotel.

Horse Several places rent out horses for short local trips, longer excursions – out to the San Luis Biological Station to visit waterfalls US$35 – and some travel to La Fortuna. It's a tough journey to Fortuna, and complaints that the horses are overworked are common. Look for signs between Santa Elena and Monteverde or ask at your hotel.

Banks A branch of *Banco Nacional* in Santa Elena is open 0900-1500, for changing **Directory** travellers' cheques and cash advances against Visa. There is also an ATM machine for

The northern region

What a waste

It's a stark truth that people create rubbish. While it's easy to see garbage in the street, what happens to the waste we flush down pipes which is washed away and quickly forgotten? In a place like Monteverde this can create serious problems for water quality.

Stewart Dallas, a research engineer at the Monteverde Institute recently installed an ecological sanitation system (eco-san) in the grounds of the Monteverde Community Arts Centre. Solid waste goes into a composting toilet to be broken down by natural bacteria and micro-organisms before being returned to the soil as an organic fertilizer. Greywater, from showers, kitchen waste and laundry, goes through a reedbed system which

removes the nutrients, before flowing to a small pond where sunlight and aeration further improve the quality, and finally soaking through to water-loving plants such as bananas and sugarcane.

The system treats all the water and recycles all the nutrients. The programme has worked so well that Dallas has installed a project in a four-house site in Santa Elena. The local water authority are keeping an interested eye on the project, which is being monitored by local school children, for its potential to be used elsewhere and the early signs are promising. This is real conservation with real impact. In time, Dallas says, we might start to see an improvement in this precious environment.

Visa in the supermarket. **Communications** Internet: access is opening up in several places. Prices are quite high at around US$6/hr, but should come down as competition increases. **Post**: The post office is at the southern end of town. **Cultural centres** Artists may want to contact *Monteverde Studio of the Arts*, T645-5434, in the US on 800-370-3331, www.mvstudios.com Arranges for students of all ages and abilities to study with local artists in a broad range of materials from basketry and ceramics, to papermaking and photography. Classes are usually 20 hrs over a week, but shorter day courses are possible. US$235, excluding materials. The *Monteverde Institute*, T645-5053, F645-5219, www.mvinstitute.org An educational and cultural organization that works to blend international study and research with opportunities for the local community. The Institute organizes and promotes, along with others, the annual International Music Festival, and supports several projects including the Community Arts Centre which provides courses for local and visiting artists. The Institute is also involved in conservation and preservation including the Boehm/Rockwell house, where the Arts Centre is located, the oldest house in Monteverde. Innovative projects like the reed-bed grey water system and the construction of a composting toilet which have been installed at the Arts Centre (see box), which together treat all sewage and used water to reduce pollution of local rivers, and promote nutrient recycling as well. The Quakers maintain an *English library*, ask at the Friend's Meeting House. **Medical services** Available from the *Red Cross* to the north of town. **Language schools** *Centro Panamericano de Idiomas*, in Monteverde on the road up to the reserve, T645-5441, FT645-5448, www.cpi-edu.com Submersion language courses from 2 to 4 weeks are available. Accommodation with local families and volunteer opportunities arranged if requested. With schools in Flamingo and Heredia, you can balance study with seeing a range of places in the country. Prices from US$215 a week, US$340 with homestay. **Laundry** At many hotels, or try *Chunches*. **Useful addresses** The Guardía Rural are in the centre of town.

Monteverde Cloud Forest Reserve

Getting there The reserve entrance is at the very top of the road by the field station. A bus from Santa Elena leaves at 0600 and 1100 making the return journey at 1400 and 1700. Entrance fee US$14 (students with ID half-price) valid for multiple entry during the day, cannot be purchased in advance. Office open 0700-1630 daily; the park opens at 0700 and closes at 1700.

Ins & outs

The total number of visitors allowed in the reserve at any one time is 150, so be there before 0700 to make sure of getting in during high season. If you want to book a guide, hotels will book a place for the following day. Alternatively you can just turn up and see if there are spaces on any tours.

Contact details For all information, guided tours and refuge reservations contact the reserve offices on T645-5122, F645-5034, montever@sol.racsa.co.cr   www.cct.or.cr

Straddling the continental divide, the 10,500-ha Monteverde Cloud Forest Reserve is privately owned and administered by the *Centro Científico Tropical* (Tropical Science Centre) – a non-profit research and educational association. The reserve is mainly primary cloudforest spending much of the year shrouded in mist, creating stunted trees and abundant epiphytic growth. It contains over 400 species of birds, including the resplendent quetzal, best seen in the dry months between January and May, especially near the start of the Nuboso trail, the three-wattled bellbird and the bare-necked umbrella bird. There are over 100 species of mammals, including monkeys, baird's tapir and all six endangered cats found in Costa Rica – jaguar, jaguarundi, margay, ocelot, tigrillo and puma – reptiles and amphibians. The reserve includes an estimated 2,500 species of plants and more than 6,000 species of insects. The entrance is at 1,530 m, but the maximum altitude in the reserve rises to over 1,800 m. Mean temperature is between 16° and 18°C and average annual rainfall is 3,000 mm. The weather changes quickly and wind and humidity often make the air feel cooler so take a light jacket and rain gear in case.

Best months are Jan-May, especially Feb, Mar and Apr

Be warned that travellers have told us there is little chance of seeing much wildlife. As with all nature experiences, set your expectations realistically

The northern region

Monteverde Cloud Forest Reserve Trails

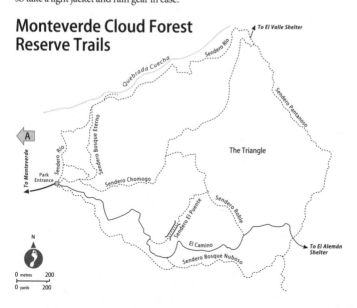

Trails & treks The commonly used trails are in good condition and there are easy, short and interesting walks for those who do not want to hike all day. Trail walks take about two hours but you could easily spend all day just wondering around. Trails may be restricted from time to time if they need protection. There is a trail northwards to Arenal volcano that is increasingly used, but not easy. Free maps of the reserve are available at the entrance along with an excellent self-guided Nature Trail with a guide booklet (US$2). Follow the rules and sign the register, indicating where you are going in case you get lost. Stay on the paths, leave nothing behind, take no fauna or flora out, no radios or tape recorders allowed.

Essentials **Equipment** Recommended equipment includes: binoculars (which are available for rent at the entrance – US$10); a good camera with 400-1,000 ASA film; insect repellent; sweater and light rainwear. Rubber boots or good walking shoes are a must for the longer walks, at all times of year but especially in the rainy season, and can be rented at the park office for US$0.80 or at hotels.

A guide is a good idea if you want to see wildlife – the untrained eye misses a lot **Guides** Natural history walks with licensed biologist guides leave from close to the entrance every morning and afternoon, 3-4 hrs, US$16 (children half price) plus the entrance fee. Tours also include a short 30-min slide show. Advance reservations can be made at the office or through your hotel and are strongly recommended particularly in between Jan and May. An experienced and recommended guide is **Gary Diller** (Apdo 10165, 1000 San José, T645-5045), but there are 25 others with varying specializations and experience. If you use a private guide you must pay his entrance fee. **Tomás Guindon** offers an excellent **night tour** in the reserve where you will almost certainly see tarantulas and anything else Tomás can seek out. Trips leave at 1900, T661-1008, US$13. You will need to arrange transport to and from the reserve through your hotel or organize a taxi.

Shopping There is a small shop at the office sells various checklists, postcards, camera film (print, slide and APS film up to 400ASA – but don't rely on it), slides, gifts and excellent T-shirts, the proceeds of which help towards the conservation project. There is also a **café** serving coffee and snacks which helps dust off the morning cobwebs for those with a problem rising so early in the day.

Sleeping There are 3 refuges in the reserve with basic facilities which provide a chance to get to some of the less well visited parts. Facilities cost US$3.50 or US$5 a night, in addition to the reserve entrance fee, for each night spent in the park, plus a key deposit of US$5. You will need a sleeping bag, flashlight and supplies to make your own meals. Dormitory-style accommodation for up to 40 people is available at the entrance to the reserve, **C** *Albergue Reserva Biológica de Monteverde*. Reservations are required for all reserve accommodation (usually booked up by groups).

Volunteer work If you are interested in volunteer work, from non-skilled trail maintenance to skilled scientific assistance work, surveying, teaching or studying on a tropical biology programme, contact the reserve office at the address above. US$14 per person, board and lodging, 2 weeks minimum.

Donations These are welcome and can be made at the reserve office or Tropical Science Centre (Apdo 8-3870-1000, San José, T225-2649, F253-4963, www.cct.or.cr) at El Higuerón, 100 m Sur y 125 m Este, Barrio La Granja, San Pedro.

The northern region

El Bosque Eterno de los Niños

Adjoining and in the past surrounding the Monteverde Cloud Forest is the *Colour map 1, grid B6*
Children's Eternal Rainforest, established in 1988 after an initiative by Swedish
school children to save forests. Currently at 22,000 ha, the land is bought and
maintained by the Monteverde Conservation League with children's donations
from around the world. The **Bajo del Tigre trail** is about 3 km taking 1½ hours,
guides can be arranged or you can go on a self-guided tour. Trips deeper into
the forest can also be arranged to the **San Gerardo Field Station**, in the western
part of the reserve, where there are 7 km of trails leading through primary, sec-
ondary and regenerating forests and a spectacular view of Arenal Volcano
(when clear) and the surrounding rain forest. The **Poco Sol Field Station** is at
the eastern end of the protected areas near **Poco Sol Lagoon** and reached on the
road from San Ramón to Fortuna, with almost 10 km of trails visiting a beautiful
waterfall and excellent opportunities for birding. Accommodation is available
at both field stations, **C** per person for groups of 6 people or more, **B** for 5 people
or less. The price includes entrance, 3 meals, sheets, blankets, towel, soap, and
toilet paper. ■ *0800-1600, entrance US$5, students US$2. Contact the
Monteverde Conservation League for reservations at San Gerardo or Poco Sol
Field Stations. T645-5003, F645-5104, www.acmonteverde.com*

Donations are welcomed to continue the work of the Monteverde Conservation **Donations**
League. Children from over 44 nations have raised money to buy land. Funds are used
for purchasing additional land and for maintaining and improving the existing Reserve
area. *Asociación Conservacionista de Monteverde* (Monteverde Conservation League),
Apartado Postal 10581-1000, San José, Costa Rica, T645-5003, F645-5104,
www.acmonteverde.com).

The highest point in the region at 1,842 m reached via the Hotel Belmar, **Cerro Amigos**
makes for a pleasant walk lasting a couple of hours. It's uphill all the way pass-
ing through forest with fine views stretching across to the erupting Arenal vol-
cano from the top on a clear day.

Santa Elena Cloud Forest Reserve

One kilometre along the road from Santa Elena to Tilarán, a 5-km track is
signposted to this 310-ha reserve, managed by the Centro Ecológico Bosque
Nuboso de Monteverde. It is 83% primary cloudforest and the rest
17-year-old secondary forest at 1,700 m, bordered by the Monteverde Cloud
Forest Reserve and the Arenal Forest Reserve. There is a 12 km network of
paths with several lookouts where you can see and hear, on a clear day, Arenal
volcano. The 'canopy tour' is recommended, you climb inside a hollow stran-
gler fig tree then cross between two platforms along aerial runways 30 m up,
good views of orchids and bromeliads, then down a 30-m hanging rope at the
end. The Centro Ecológico Bosque Nuboso is administered by the local com-
munity and profits go to five local schools. It was set up by the Costa Rican
government in 1989 with collaboration from Canada. There is a small infor-
mation centre where rubber boots can be hired and a small café open at week-
ends. The rangers are very friendly and enthusiastic and there are generally
fewer visitors here than at Monteverde. Hand-painted T-shirts for sale.
■ *0700-1600, entrance US$8, students US$4, T/F645-5390, www.
monteverdeinfo.com/reserve.htm for information. It is a long, steep hike from
the village, alternatively hire a taxi, carload US$6.50.*

The northern region

Activities and excursions

Most of the attractions are spread out in the region. While the honey-pot Monteverde is the main attraction there are many other places well worth exploring

Five kilometres north of Santa Elena, off the road to Tilarán, **Sky Walk** uses six suspension bridges to take you through the cloudforest at canopy level, the highest being 42 m above the ground. ■ *Daily 0700-1600, US$12, student US$10, child US$4, for information T645-5238, www.skywalk.co.cr* **Sky Trek** is arguably even more popular and a breathtaking experience, as you fly through the air on a system of cables strung out from giant forest trees. On clear days the view from the highest tower is unbelievable and has been known to induce a fair amount of knee-wobbling in even the hardiest characters. ■ *Daily 0700-1500, US$35, student US$28, T645-5238, www.skywalk.co.cr*

Very close to Santa Elena, at the start of the climb to Monteverde, is the **Serpentarium** with specimens of snakes and amphibians found in the nearby cloudforest. ■ *Daily 0700-1700, US$3, T/F645-5238.*

The **Original Canopy Tour** in Santa Elena is in the grounds of Cloud Forest Lodge and gives you the chance to explore the forest canopy while zipping down steel cables between five platforms, ending up with a rappel. ■ *Tours leave from the office in Santa Elena daily at 0730, 1030 and 1430. Adults US$45, students US$35, children US$25. T645-5243, F645-5645, www.canopytours.com*

A hundred metres beyond *Hotel Sapo Dorado* is the **Orchid Garden**, with about 400 species collected by Gabriel Barboza. ■ *Open daily 0800-1700, US$6.*

A dirt road opposite the *Hotel Heliconia* leads to the **Monteverde Butterfly Garden**, a beautifully presented large garden planted for breeding and researching butterflies. ■ *Open daily, 0930-1600, US$7 including guided tour, best time for a visit 1100-1300, wolfej@sol.racsa.co.cr* Near the Butterfly Garden is **Finca Ecológica**, which has three trails totalling around 5 km with bird lists for birdwatchers and a good chance to see other wildlife in this transitional zone between cloud and tropical dry forest. Guides available and night tours can be arranged. ■ *0700-1700 daily, US$5, free trail map, T/F645-5363.* Down the same path is **Aerial Adventures**, a ski lift-style ride travelling slowly through the treetops. Ideal for birdwatching. ■ *Daily 0700-1800, US$12, T645-5960, wmvargas@sol.racsa.co.cr*

From the *Heliconia* to the reserve is a steep 45-min walk uphill (about 4 km) but there are lovely views looking towards the sea and the **Nicoya Peninsula**, particularly in the evening (when you are coming down and can appreciate them).

Reserva Sendero Tranquilo, is a quiet reserve set on 200 ha between the Monteverde Cloud Forest Reserve and the Guacima River, near the Monteverde Cheese Factory. Tours are limited to small guided groups. ■ *Open daily, book through El Sapo Dorado on T645-5010. Entry restricted to 12 people at any one time.*

Quietly churning away, the cheese factory marks time as it has for several decades. Now privately owned, producing and selling excellent cheeses of various types, fresh milk, ice cream, milkshakes to die for and *cajeta* – which is either divine or sickly sweet depending on your taste. ■ *Shop closes 1600.*

Just before the entrance to Monteverde Cloud Forest is the **Hummingbird Gallery**, where masses of different hummingbirds can be seen darting around a glade, visiting feeding dispensers filled with sugared water. ■ *0930-1700, slide shows daily at 1630 (3 times a week sometimes), US$4, T645-5030. Outside the entrance is a small shop and photo gallery selling pictures and gifts.* There is also a slide show at *Hotel Belmar*, 'The Hidden Rainforest', by Bobby Maxson, 1930 daily except Friday.

Guanacaste

Guanacaste

222 Ins and outs

222 Pan-American Highway

223 Cañas

224 Excursions

225 Parque Nacional Volcán Tenorio

225 Bagaces & Volcán Miravalles

226 Parque Nacional Palo Verde

227 Reserva Bioloógico Lomas Barbudal

227 Liberia

230 Parque Nacional Rincón de la Vieja

233 Parque Nacional Santa Rosa

236 Parque Nacional Guanacaste

237 La Cruz

238 Bahía Salinas

239 Peñas Blancas and the border with Nicaragua

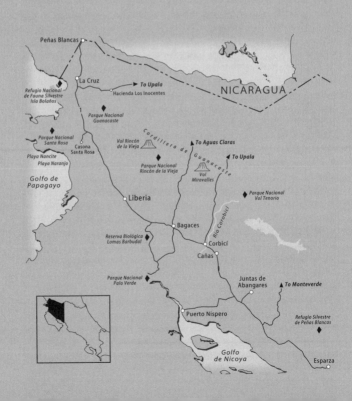

Toasted as the cultural heart of Costa Rica, Guanacaste is home to dry rolling flatlands that have fed cattle since the 1600s. Although largely confined to the realms of history, the tough life of the sabanero – the man of the plains – has become an integral part of the regional and national identity. Moving through the territory on horseback, the sabanero would take his shade under the broad branches and dense leaves of a guanacaste – the national tree. But these people are also open, hospitable and fun-loving. If you're visiting in January and February check out the fiestas throughout the area.

With considerably less rainfall than almost any other part of the country, it is easy to see why the expanses of dry, open land, broken only by the dramatic volcanic silhouettes of the Cordillera de Guanacaste, would be more appealing than the hot, insect-infested jungles of the rest of the country. However, in the 1950s and 1960s, vast areas of the region were cleared for ranching in an attempt to increase meat exports. Only a combination of foresight and falling meat prices protected the last remaining stretches of less-dense dry tropical forest.

Cut-off from the Central Valley and hemmed in by the mountains to the east, the region's proximity to Nicaragua has made it the site of numerous infractions between the two nations – not least a vote at the time of independence which annexed Guanacaste to Costa Rica. Liberia is the area's largest town but it's the national parks of Tenorio, Rincón de la Vieja, Palo Verde and Santa Rosa that pull in visitors. While most people go to the Nicoya Peninsula in search of beaches, there are a few quiet and beautiful ones in the far north for the truly independent of spirit.

Things to do in Guanacaste

- Visit the water wonderland of **Palo Verde National Park** with thousands of waterbirds wading through the wetlands.
- Explore the mudpools, steaming vents and wildlife of **Rincón de la Vieja National Park** where the old woman of legend still throws tantrums, spitting mud and geysers.
- Take to the saddle like a *sabanero*, strike out on your own whistling a tune and imagine your very own frontier experience.
- Trek to the golden **Playa Naranjo** – one of the country's most beautiful and remote beaches - and camp surrounded by rare Pacific dry forest.

Ins and outs

Rainfall is moderate: 1,000-2,000 mm a year, with a long dry season from Nov to May. But the lowlands are deep in mud during the rainy season

The simplest way to get to the region is to fly to **Daniel Oduber Quirós International Airport**, 13 km west of Liberia. Daily flights with *Sansa*, T221-9414, www.flysansa.com, and *Travelair*, T220-3054, www.travelair-costarica.com Flights start at US$66.

Good bus services ply the Pan-American Highway from the capital and Puntarenas as far as the Nicaraguan border, although you may have problems getting to some of the more out of the way national parks. The best way of exploring Guanacaste is in your own car – you can head down the Pan-American Highway peeling off at will to explore quiet spots. From San José the road winds gently to San Ramón before beginning a meandering descent of 800 m to Esparza (31 km). There are fine views but heavy traffic and mist often make conditions treacherous. The Pan-American Highway sets a north-westerly course for the Nicaraguan border after descending from the central highlands to the coast close to Puntarenas.

Pan-American Highway

Esparza
Colour map 1, grid C6

An attractive town with a turbulent history Esparza was once an important trading post on the Camino Real from the highlands to Nicaragua. In the 17th century the town was repeatedly sacked by pirates, belying its peaceful nature today. With grand larceny now out of favour, only the relative quiet of the place is likely to hold you.

Sleeping and eating The most comfortable option is **E** *Hotel Castañuelas*, T635-5105, F635-5769. Quiet place with a/c, a cooler alternative to Puntarenas. **F** per person *Pensión Córdoba*, T635-5014. Clean and modern.

Beyond Esparza is the bar-restaurant *Mirador Enis*, a popular stopping place for tour buses breaking the journey at a service station with fruit stalls nearby, before a left turn at Barranca for Puntarenas, 15 km. In **Barranca** is the good **D** *Hotel Río Mar*, with bath, restaurant.

If going from San José to Monteverde, it is possible to change **buses** in Barranca, rather than going all the way to Puntarenas, if you leave the capital before 1230.

Refugio Nacional Silvestre Peñas Blancas

Peñas Blancas National Wildlife Refuge is one of the quieter protected areas of Costa Rica. Created to protect the regional watershed, the 2,400-ha reserve is distinctive for the rugged terrain of volcanic origin and white rock deposits of diatomite – a white, porous sedimentary rock composed of algae skeletal deposits. Covering altitudes from 600 to 1200 m, the refuge includes areas of tropical dry, semi-deciduous and at higher elevations, pre-montane moist forest. The region was selectively logged before gaining protected status, but visitors will still enjoy the birds and butterflies in the region, and may even see peccaries, pacas or red brocket deer.

■ *Getting to the refuge is difficult without private transport. Leave the Pan-American Highway 6 km north of Esparza heading to Miramar, where there is some simple accommodation. From here, a 14 km track leads east, then north to Peñas Blancas via Sabana Bonita. Alternatively, leave the Pan-American Highway east of Esparza at Macacona, and head north direct to Peñas Blancas. There is a trail to the refuge leaving from Peñas Blancas, but you should take a good topographical map. There are no services in the park but camping is permitted so it's a good opportunity for wilderness camping despite the denuded landscape.*

From the Pan-American Highway at Rancho Grande, just after the Río Aranjuez, a bumpy, dramatic and at times very scenic route heads north, climbing to Santa Elena and Monteverde. Alternatively take a slightly longer, but better, road leaving the highway at Yomale (Km 149), just south of the Río Lagarto. See page 206. **To Monteverde & Santa Elena**

Crossing the provincial border and entering Guanacaste proper, a good road leads to Juntas de Abangares, a small town with a population just short of 10,000, that briefly came to fame in the late 19th century when gold finds attracted prospectors to the town. A century on, a few prospectors still mine for gold, but the main attraction is a mining museum at **La Sierra de Abangares** with mining artefacts from the boom times. ■ *0600-1800 daily, US$1.80.* **Juntas de Abangares** *Colour map 1, grid B5*

This also makes for a good alternative driving route – four-wheel drive recommended – to Santa Elena and Monteverde for those using the Tempisque ferry or coming south from Guanacaste. Buses leave Cañas for Juntas at 0900 and 1400. Basic accommodation and refreshments are available in Juntas.

Four kilometres further north of the turn-off from the Pan-American Highway to Juntas, a left turn goes to the Tempisque car ferry at Puerto Nispero crossing to the Nicoya Peninsula at Puerto Moreno. ■ *T661-8105. Services run from 0430-2400, pedestrians and bus passengers free, motorbikes US$1, cars US$3. The ferry takes a couple of hours off the option of driving all the way, but long queues are common on Sun and holidays with people returning to San José.* **Tempisque ferry**

About 6 km from the Pan-American Highway a road to the right at San Joaquín leads to **A** (per person) *Hacienda Solimar.* A 1,300-ha cattle farm over half of which is dry tropical virgin forest bordering Palo Verde National Park (see below). Near Porozal in the lower Tempisque River basin, the freshwater Madrigal estuary on the property is one of the most important areas for waterbirds in Costa Rica (only guests staying at the hacienda can visit). Also surrounded by gallery forest and with access to the salt pans at Finca Conchal, it is recommended for serious birdwatchers and a good place to spot the endemic mangrove hummingbird. ■ *Reservations essential, T669-0281 or contact Birdwatch, Apdo 6951, 1005 San José, T228-4768, F228-1573, birdwatch@racsa.co.cr 8 rooms with private or shared bathroom, includes meals, minimum 2 nights, transport available on request, local guide, horse riding.* **Hacienda Solimar**

Cañas

Hot and dusty, the town of Cañas is the first settlement of any real size heading north along the Pan-American Highway. There's a modern, but nevertheless rather grubby, church and very little else to hold the visitor for long. The town *Colour map 1, grid B5* *Population: 18,136* *Altitude: 100m*

Guanacaste

has a deserted, windswept feel; only mad dogs and Englishmen go out in the midday sun here. There are several places of interest nearby though, and for the traveller arriving from the north, Cañas is the cut-through to Tilarán with access to Fortuna and Arenal volcano, and Santa Elena/Monteverde. It's also the best way to Tenorio Volcano National Park and on to Upala in the northern lowlands if travelling by bus.

Sleeping On the Pan-American Highway is **B** *El Corral*, T669-1467, F669-1722. The most upmarket choice in town with a/c and private bath. **C** *Cañas*, C 2, Av 3, T669-0039, F669-1294. A popular choice with good rooms. Budget options include **F** *Cabinas Corobicí*, T669-0241. 11 good rooms with bath, parking available. If full, try **F** *Gran*, close to the central park, which has grubby rooms with a fan.

A couple of kilometres north of Cañas on the Pan-American Highway is **C** *Capazuri B&B*, T/F669-0580, www.hostelling-costarica.com Tatty rooms, with private bath and a couple of fans, breakfast included. Has good **camping**, US$3 per person.

Eating *Panchitos* on main square is good and inexpensive. Several good Chinese restaurants, eg *Central*, on main square. The restaurant *Rincón Corobicí*, on the banks of the Corobicí is a clean and pleasant spot to stop and has a small zoo and offers rafting down Río Corobicí, T669-0544. Six kilometres north of Cañas on the Pan-American Highway is, *Hacienda La Pacífica*, T669-0050, F669-0555. A fine restaurant decorated with ranching memorabilia, part of a former working ranch. Mid-range and upwards.

Transport **Bus** Most buses depart from the terminal 500 m north of the centre, except for those to **San José**, which leave from the Pan-American Highway. Buses from **San José**, depart from C 16, Av 1-3, 8 daily from 0400, 3½ hrs, US$2.80, *Transportes La Cañera*, T669-0145. To **Liberia** 10 daily from 0530, 1 hr, US$1.20. To **Puntarenas** 8 daily from 0600, US$2.80. To **Upala** 7 daily from 0500, 1¾ hrs, US$1.50. If going to Arenal volcano and Fortuna or Santa Elena and Monteverde, take the bus to **Tilarán**, 7 daily from 0600, 45 mins, US$0.70, and catch a connection from there. If driving, the turn-off for Tilarán is east at the filling station, no signs.

Directory **Banks** There are a couple of banks in town, including a branch of *Banco Nacional*.

Excursions

Rafting on Río Corobicí & Bebedero Flowing from the upper slopes of Tenorio volcano, the Río Corobicí which lower down becomes the Bebedero, is bordered with gallery forest of ceiba, palm and Guanacaste trees, where you can catch glimpses of iguanas, monkeys and crocodiles. Birds are also very much in evidence; there's a fair chance of spotting parrots, aracaris, mots-mots and kingfishers and occasionally, if you are lucky, ospreys and jabirú.

The slow running rivers are ideal for gentle floats, a more relaxing alternative to high-adrenaline whitewater river runs elsewhere, and far more conducive to watching nature. The *Safaris Corobicí* base is 4 km past Cañas on the Pan-American Highway, 25 m south of the entrance to *Centro Ecológico La Pacífica*, T669-2091, F669-1091, www.nicoya.com They offer float tours down the Río Corobicí, US$35 per person for 2-hr rafting, US$60 for a half day, including lunch. *CATA Tours*, T296-2133, F296-2730, www.catatours. com, has one-day floats down the Bebedero. The river is lined with dense mangroves that open up to reveal seasonal marshes, bordering Palo Verde National Park.

Behind *Safaris Corobicí*, Las Pumas is a small private animal rescue centre **Las Pumas** specializing in looking after big cats, including margay, pumas and jaguar. As with many rescue centres in Costa Rica, the animals end up here as a result of some mishap, misfortune or tragic circumstance which would prevent survival in the wild. While there's no denying the element of sadness that comes with seeing these magnificent creatures caged, their care is tenderly given by the Swiss owners who at times 'play' with the big cats as most people do with a domestic cat. You may even have seen some of them before – they're not strangers to the small screen nature documentary. Entrance is free, but donations are welcome and the bigger the better.

Parque Nacional Volcán Tenorio

Certain to become a popular destination for hiking and trekking Tenorio *Colour map 1, grid B5* Volcano National Park is one of the country's newest, protecting the watershed of Tenorio Volcano (1,916 m) as part of the Cordillera de Guanacaste and 12,871 ha of mixed forest including tracts of primary forest and dry tropical forest. Trails are still developing in the park, and with only basic services and lodging options available it's a rewarding trip for the hardy.

Taking a bus from San José or Cañas, 7 km north of Cañas on the Pan-American High- **Ins & outs** way, Highway 6 heads northeast for 34 km to Bijagua, in the saddle between Tenorio and Miravalles volcanoes.

The most accessible trail leads from **Bijaugua Heliconias Ecotourist Resort** (see below), but you can head for the crater lake, after taking local advice, along trails through cloudforest to the summit with views of Arenal volcano, Lake Nicaragua, and the northern lowlands. You can soak in natural hot springs, and visit the Río Celeste, with heavenly blue waters created by mineral deposits in the rock.

About 3 km out of town on the flanks of Tenorio is **B** *Bijagua Heliconias Ecotourist* **Sleeping** *Lodge*. A simple lodge with 6 cabins, each with private bathroom and hot water, price includes breakfast. The lodge is part of the *Cooprena Community Association*, T/F286-4203, www.agroecoturismo.net Tours can be arranged to Río Celeste, Tenorio and Miravalles volcanos and also waterfalls in the area.

Six kilometres north of Bijagua, a sign points out the 7 km route down a gravel road towards **Santo Domingo** and **AL** per person *La Carolina*, T380-1656, www.lacarolinalodge.com 4 bedrooms, 3 for a couple and 1 for up to 7 people, right on the river. The price is all-inclusive, with 3 meals, guided treks, horse riding, and discounts for children under 12. Home-cooking and juices made from the lodge's own citrus groves and dairy farm. Set on a 70-ha working ranch, this is the most comfortable option for visiting the Río Celeste mineral pools and trekking through the hills of Tenorio Volcano. Other local tours are easily arranged.

Bagaces and Volcán Miravalles

Continuing north along the Pan-American Highway, the small town of *Colour map 1, grid B4* Bagaces set back from the road marks time blissfully ignorant of the traffic that *Population: 8,000* thunders up and down the Highway. There's not much to see in the town that was once a stopping point on the old Camino Real trade route to the north. Today the main reason to visit is to finalize plans for a trip to Palo Verde National Park or the smaller Lomas Barbudal Biological Reserve – see below.

Guanacaste

Route 164 heads north from town climbing slowly to the town of **Guayabo** with thermal pools nearby. The road leads eventually to Aguas Claras and San José but Guayabo is a good spot for hiking to Miravalles Volcano, the highest peak in the Cordillera de Guanacaste at 2,028 m. Services in the area are limited – ask at hotels for details.

Sleeping   There is simple accommodation in Guayabo at **E** *Las Brisas*, which has hot water, bath and fans. At Km 30, you get to **E** *Parador Las Nubes del Miravalles*, T671-1011 ext 280 with tents and mattresses for hire and horse riding. Also in the area is **A** *Miravalles Volcano Lodge*, T673-0823, F673-0350, www.costa-rica-vol-cano-adventures.com The most comfortable option with a/c doubles with private bath and hot water. The nearby **hot springs** complex of *Yoko* is popular for an evening's soak, and hiking trails lead to mineral springs only 15 mins from the hotel.

Parque Nacional Palo Verde

Colour map 1, grid B4   At the northern most limits of the Gulf of Nicoya, the flooded plains of the Tempisque River are protected by Palo Verde National Park, covering 18,651 ha – an area slightly smaller than Washington D.C. in the United States. Subject to extensive seasonal flooding created by poor drainage, seasonal inundation from the Tempisque and Bebedero Rivers and tides from the Gulf, the park has the largest concentration of waterfowl and wading birds in Central America. Add a blend of geological foundations incorporating limestone outcrops, sedimentary and volcanic deposits and the region is one of the most diverse parks in the country. Twelve habitats have been recognized including freshwater and saltwater lagoons, marshes, grasslands, black mangrove, swamp forests and deciduous and evergreen dry tropical forest.

Over 150 species of tree have been recorded in the park including the namesake palo verde or horse bean, with green leaves, branches and trunk. The bird count of resident and migrating species is 275, and includes herons, storks, grebes, ibis and the northern jacana. The park is the only nesting site of the jabirú in Costa Rica. Not to be out-done, land based species also put on a pretty good show; you may well see peccaries, white-tailed deer, white-faced monkeys, turtles and crocodiles.

The area receives the largest concentration of waterfowl and wading birds between September and March, with a distinct dry season between December and March.

There are several trails in the park with good look out points across the Tempisque Basin and the lowlands from limestone outcrops, leading from the **Palo Verde Biological Station**, owned and operated by the Organization for Tropical Studies and accommodation and **camping** is available.

■ *The park office is open 0800-1600. Entrance is US$6, information from the office in Bagaces, T671-1290, F671-1062. Accommodation is available at **B** per person Palo Verde Station, T240-6696, F240-6783, www.ots.ac.cr Getting to the park is only realistically possible in a private vehicle or as part of a tour. The road leaves the Pan-American Highway close to Bagaces, from where a 4-wheel drive makes the last 28 km to the Palo Verde Station. A taxi from Bagaces is a viable option.*

Reserva Biológica Lomas Barbudal

Close to the northern limits of Palo Verde National Park, Lomas Barbudal *Colour map 1, grid B4* Biological Reserve protects precious tree species endangered in much of the rest of the country. Seventy percent of the reserve is deciduous forest and includes mahogany, rosewood and the spectacular cortez tree, which blooms in a riot of colour, a few days after a rain shower in the dry season. Many of the rivers flow throughout the year creating gallery forest in addition to grassy savannahs and extremely dry forest that supports cacti and bromeliads.

Lomas Barbudal is also home to over 130 bird species including the scarlet macaw and great curassows, as well as coatis, howler and white-faced capuchin monkeys. The reserve's great claim to fame, however, is the unusual richness of its insect life, in particular bees and wasps. Some 230 species have been counted to date, including the Africanized bee.

■ *Donation requested for entrance to the park. For information drop in at the reserve office in Bagaces, or call T/F671-1290. The 4-wheel drive track for Lomas Barbudal is just over 10 km west of Bagaces, along the Pan-American Highway, close to the town of Pijije. The reserve administration office, with a small information centre, is 6 km down this road on the banks overlooking the Río Cabuyo. This road continues, eventually joining the road to Palo Verde National Park.*

Liberia

The White City of Liberia stands bright at the junction of the Pan-American *Colour map 1, grid B3* Highway and Highway 21 to the Nicoya Peninsula. While it may be provincial *Population: 36,407* capital, transport and commercial hub and the largest city in northern Costa *Altitude: 150m* Rica, don't expect high rise and hot dogs – it has evolved perfectly to survive the blazing temperatures that bake Guanacaste in the dry season.

The white, mainly single story buildings are designed to reflect the heat. On many of the older buildings a section of wall either side of a corner is replaced by large doors. When left open this distinctive *puerta del sol* allows warmth and ventilation to move freely through the house. Nobody ventures out at high noon, giving the town a deserted feel if you turn up at midday. Rise with the sun, or take an early evening stroll and the streets gently swagger to life.

Liberia has just enough older buildings to give the town a colonial edge, but you won't find them around the central plaza, complete with a rather unattractive triangular modern church, where romantics and promenaders emerging from the shadows gather in the cool breeze at the end of the day. South of town the **Museo del Sabanero**, C 1, Av 6, has a rather disappointing smattering of artifacts and memorabilia in tribute to the horseman of the plains. A privately run tourist office shares the building with the museum, T666-1606. The staff are helpful, knowledgeable and speak English, although the information is not always accurate. ■ *Museum and tourist office open 0800-1200, 1300-1600 Mon-Sat, US$0.45.*

On the Pan-American Highway is **B** *Boyeros*, T666-0995, F666-2529, **Sleeping** www.hotelboyeros.com 70 comfortable rooms, with a/c, private bath and telephone, children under 10 free. There's a good restaurant and a pool – a good choice if driving through. **B** *El Bramadero*, T666-0371, F666-0203. 20 or so rooms, all with private bath, a/c and television, in a lively spot right on the Pan-American Highway – popular with business people. At the southwestern side of town is **B-C** *Hostal Ciudad Blanca*, Av 4, C 1-3, T666-3962, F666-4382. 12 pleasant but grubby rooms with a/c, private bath, hot water and telephone. A small snack-style restaurant and bar serves local food. The

Guanacaste (side margin, vertical)

potential of the building will be utilized at some point, so if you're visiting the nearby *sabanero* museum it may be worth checking out. In a converted old lumber mill is **B-C** *Hotel del Aserradero*, on the Pan-American Highway and Av 3, T666-1939, F666-0475, abalto@sol.racsa.co.cr 16 spacious room with private bath, fans, with some good touches. Plenty of parking, a breezy charm in the reception, reflecting the helpful nature of the owners.

C *Guanacaste*, C 12, Av 3, just round the corner from the bus stations, T666-0085, F666-2287, www.hostelling-costarica.com Clean and friendly, simple rooms most with private bath, but nothing special. Credit cards accepted. There's a cheap snack restaurant, you can change money and there's plenty of parking. As part of the youth hostelling network in Costa Rica, it's a good source of reliable information, organizes tours to Rincón de la Vieja and is generally helpful. On the eastern limits of town is **C** *Daysita*, Av 5, C11-13, T666-0197, F666-0927 A self-contained little complex, with 30 rooms sleeping up to 6 people, making it good for groups. Complete with restaurant and pool, it's a quiet spot, and you won't need to visit the town centre. A couple of blocks south of the main plaza is **C** *La Siesta*, C 4, Av 4-6, T666-0678, F666-2532, ropeflo@hotmail.com With 24 clean rooms with private bathrooms, a restaurant, small pool and good service, this place stands out as a good mid-range option, close to the centre of town.

D-E *Liberia*, T666-0161, F666-4091, maicero@racsa.co.cr Just a half block south of the plaza, 12 basic rooms, some with private bath, in an old house, with a small café for snacks, laundry facilities and a good information board. Recommended. **E** *Cabinas Sagitarios*, Av 11, C 2, T666-0950. A curiously half-hearted attempt at providing accommodation, run by a Dutchman and a Costa Rican, with most of the family helping out. Generally friendly and good choice if you want to see *Tico* life in its fullness. Breakfast and dinner available on request. **E** *La Casona*, Av 6, C Rafael Iglesiash,

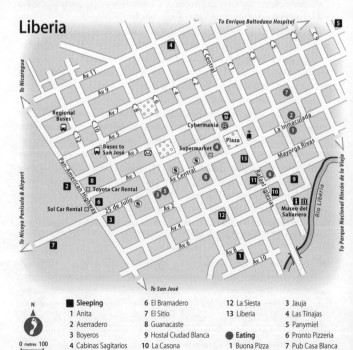

Liberia

N

0 metres 100
0 yards 100

■ Sleeping
1 Anita
2 Aserradero
3 Boyeros
4 Cabinas Sagitarios
5 Daysita
6 El Bramadero
7 El Sitio
8 Guanacaste
9 Hostal Ciudad Blanca
10 La Casona
11 La Posada del Tope
12 La Siesta
13 Liberia

● Eating
1 Buona Pizza
2 Hong Kong
3 Jauja
4 Las Tinajas
5 Panymiel
6 Pronto Pizzeria
7 Pub Casa Blanca
8 Tiffany's (Souvenus)

T/F666-2971, rooms for up to 4 people, shared bath, washing facilities, rooms facing street can get hot. It's a good choice for longer stopovers, with a new annex, **D**, with private bath.

F *Anita*, C 4 y Av 8, T666-1285, F666-3364. Simple rooms, but what can you expect at this price. They're clean, snacks served on the miniscule terrace. Family-run and very friendly. Parking available. Plans for a couple of comfortable rooms out back. The backpacker's natural choice is **F** per person *La Posada del Tope*, C Rafael Iglesias, 1½ blocks south from cathedral, T666-3876, hottope@sol.racsa.co.cr Simple rooms with cold showers, but a host of essential services. Small patio restaurant complete with flaming beacons ideal for resting, chatting and planning. Mountain bike rentals, laundry facilities, baggage storage and the list goes on. The owner Dennis is very helpful, and has good information on visiting Rincón de la Vieja National Park. He also has a telescope for stargazing.

Out of town 2 km south of town on the Pan-American Highway is **AL** *Las Espuelas*, T666-0144, F666-2441, espuelas@sol.racsa.co.cr Good rooms with a/c, satellite TV, swimming pool, round trip bus service from San José, day tour to San Antonio cattle ranch, US$60, Amex accepted. Down Highway 21 towards Nicoya is **AL** *Best Western El Sitio*, T666-1211, F666-2059, www.bestwestern.co.cr 52 comfortable a/c rooms, as you'd expect from Best Western, with a restaurant, pool and gym.

Eating

Buona Pizza, La Immaculada, Av Central, C 3, serves good pizzas baked in a clay oven. *El Bramadero*, part of the Hotel Bramadero on the Pan-American Highway, is a popular spot with grills in the mid-range price, breakfast from 0630 and a lively bar in the evenings. *Panymiel*, next to *Restaurant Jauja* and Av 1, C 2, bakery, snacks and drinks. *Pronto Pizzeria*, C 1, Av 4, good food (not just pizzas) in a charming old colonial house. *Pub Casa Blanca*, on C 5, Av 1-3, is the smartest restaurant in town, with a good mix of international and local dishes, mid-range. *Restaurante Jauja*, Av C, one street west of C 8, pizza and pasta in a lively setting. On the west side of the Plaza is *Soda Las Tinajas*, a great little open-air restaurant looking out on the plaza, specializing in *refrescos*. There are several good Chinese restaurants in town including *Copa de Oro*, next to Hotel Liberia, huge dishes, good value. *Hong Kong*, 2½ blocks east of church, cheap and cheerful.

Shopping

Tiffanys, Av C-2, C 2, is a good one-stop shop if you're looking for a selection of gifts, including T-shirts, ceramics and cigars. *Mini Galería Fulvia*, on the main plaza, sells the *Tico Times*, English papers and books. English spoken and helpful.

Festivals

If you can time it right, visit on **Guanacaste Day**, the *25th Jul*, when the town celebrates annexation to Costa Rica with colourful parades, bullfights, a rodeo, music and general frivolity.

Transport

Air Daniel Oduber Quirós International Airport is 13 km from Liberia along Highway 21. See page 244.

Bus Buses from **San José** leave the capital from C 14, Av 1-3, with an hourly service from 0500 until 2000, 4 hrs, US$4.50. Buses arrive and leave for San José from Av 5, C 10-12. Local buses leave from the local terminal at C 12, Av 7-9. Liberia to **Playa del Coco**. 6 daily, 0530-1815, **Playa Hermosa** and **Playa Panama**, 1130 and 1900, **Puntarenas**, 7 daily, 0500-1530, **Bagaces/Cañas**, 4 daily, 0545-1710 (but you can take any bus heading down the Pan-American Highway), **Cañas Dulces**, 3 daily, 0600-1730, **La Cruz/Peñas Blanca**, 8 daily 0530-1800. To **Filadelfia-Santa Cruz-Nicoya**, 0500-2020, 20 daily.

Car rental *Sol*, T666-2222, F666-2898, sol@guanacaste.co.cr and *Toyota*, T666-7193, www.toyotarent.com, car rental agencies offer a range of similar vehicles for roughly the same prices. A Toyota Rav 4, works out at US$70 a day in the dry season, US$50 in the green season, plus insurance. The weekly rate is US$300 plus US$140 insurance. If you want to cover a lot of ground, you can drop the vehicles off at other offices for an extra US$50.

Taxis Leave from the northern side of the main square, and trips can be easily arranged to nearby National Parks and attractions.

Directory   **Banks** *Banco Popular* and *Bancrecer* both have Visa ATMs. *Banco de Costa Rica* is on the main plaza *Credomatic*, Av Central, MasterCard ATM. If all the banks are closed, try the Hotel Guanacaste for money exchange. **Communications** *Ciberm@nia*, north side of main plaza in the shopping mall, US$2 per hr. The **post office** is at Av 3 and C 8. **Medical services** *Enrique Baltodano Hospital* T666-0011, several pharmacies close to main plaza. **Tour operators** *Tiquicia Travel*, in Hotel Guanacaste, T666-4485. Most of the hotels can arrange tours to local areas including Rincón de la Vieja National Park. *Hotel Liberia* can organize tours, rent out bikes and assist with inquiries. A recommended guide for the nearby national parks is *Alejandro Vargas Rodríguez*, T666-1889.

Parque Nacional Rincón de la Vieja

Colour map 1, grid A4   Geologically formed by the simultaneous eruption of several volcanic cones which eventually merged to become one, Rincón de la Vieja National Park now protects 14,161 ha of ideal territory for hiking and horse riding, and is definitely worth visiting for a few days. The main attraction is the steaming mud pools, hot springs and steam vents in the area, and hiking to the summit with its splendid views (on clear days) across the lowlands. The massif, which rises to a height of 1,916 m at Santa María volcano, is visible from Liberia when the peak is not shrouded in cloud, and the lower summit of Rincón de la Vieja (1,806 m) can be reached on a two-day trek.

Meaning 'Old Lady's Corner', according to Guatuso legend an old witch living on the eastern slopes of Rincón de la Vieja sends smoke skyward whenever she is annoyed. She still gets the hump and last threw really big tantrums in 1995 and 1998, sending ash clouds as far west as Santa Rosa National Park and mudflows down the northern slopes.

Ins & outs   **Getting there** There are 2 routes into the park: the southern route, which has less
Park entrance US$6   traffic, goes from Puente La Victoria on the western side of Liberia and leads, in about 25 km, to the Santa María sector, closest to the hot springs.

The northern route turns right off the Pan-American Highway 5 km northwest of Liberia, through Curubandé (no public transport on this route at present). Beyond Curubandé, you reach Posada El Encuentro, cross the private property of Hacienda Lodge Guachipelín (US$2 for road maintenance), and beyond Rincón de la Vieja Mountain Lodge. Entrance to the park is US$6.

Transport to the park is easily arranged and normally involves sharing a taxi from Liberia at a cost of US$30-40 per cab. Hotels in Liberia will organize the taxi for a similar charge, removing the hassle of arranging a return taxi. *Hotel Guanacaste*, will arrange transport for US$15 per person, minimum 6 passengers, depart 0700, 1 hr to entrance, return 1700, take food and drink. *La Posada del Tope* has similar deals. You can also hitch, most tourist vehicles will pick you up. If you take your own transport a 4-wheel drive is best, although during the dry season a vehicle with high clearance is adequate.

Guanacaste Conservation Area awarded UNESCO recognition

In the world of conservation, the Guanacaste Conservation Area (ACG) is a beacon of hope and in 1999 was created a UNESCO Natural World Heritage Site. The creation of the Santa Rosa National Park in 1971 saw a shift away from ranching to conservation for the coastal region which was complemented by the creation of the Guanacaste and Rincón de la Vieja. The creation of the Rincón Cacao Biological Corridor added the final piece of a migratory corridor that incorporates nine of the 12 Holdridge lifezones found in Costa Rica leading from the Pacific to the 1,916-m volcanic peak at Rincón de la Vieja. Official estimates say the region protects some 235,000 species – more than in the entire continental USA

Proving that conservation is an ongoing process, work goes to protect more of the area and add to the migratory corridor. The rainforest to the north of Rincón de la Vieja is available for purchase and the ACG is seeking support and donations. Contact them on T6665051, F6665020, Apdo 169-5000, Liberia, Guanacaste, Costa Rica, or click on the Rincón Rainforest Campaign at the www.acguanacaste.co.cr website.

Sights For the most part, the park is a calm collection of different ecosystems or lifezones, changing gradually with altitude. The park was created to protect the multitude of rivers and streams that find their source on the volcanic slopes. Four lifezones and over 250 species of birds, including the three-wattled bellbird, great currasows, as well as howler monkeys, armadillos and coatis, ticks and other biting insects are found within the boundaries.

Most places of interest are easily reached from either of the Las Pailas or Santa María Hacienda rangers' stations, which are linked by a path. A number of trails lead from both stations with inspiring names like the 'Enchanted Forest' and the 'Hidden Falls', leading to thermal pools, mudpots and fumaroles. The area is also home to the greatest density of Costa Rica's national flower the *guaria morada* or purple orchid.

Towards the summit, the windy conditions have stunted the growth of the forest. Nearby, the Laguna Jilueros is reported to be a good site for spotting wildlife.

Sleeping Through the **southern route** is **D-E** *Rinconcito Lodge*, which has some basic rooms and cold showers, but you can enjoy the rustic charm of the area by horseback. Transport can be arranged from Liberia – contact the tourist office for details. **G** *Santa María Hacienda* 2 km inside the park. Old, spacious, and basic but refurbished only US$2.50 per person. Bring your own food and bedding, or **camp** (US$2). From the old hacienda you can hike 8 km to the boiling mudpots (Las Pailas) and come back in the same day; the sulphur springs are on a different trail and only 1 hr away.

Accessed through the **northern route**, leaving the Pan-American Highway 5 km north of Liberia at Cereceda is **AL** *Posada El Encuentro*, T/F382-0815, www.guancaste.co.cr/encuentro 6 rooms and small houses. You can set out for the mountains on horseback or simply relax by the pool. Price includes breakfast served in Encuentro's restaurant. Further along this road is **A-C** *Hacienda Lodge Guachipelín*, Lodge T384-2049, office T442-2818, F442-1910, www.guachipelin.com 26 comfortable rooms all with private bath. Meals available at extra cost. Nature guides and horse riding tours are available to waterfalls, hot springs and mud pools in the area, as well as throughout the park, prices around US$15-25. Transport from Liberia arranged, US$25 per person round trip). Includes Kazm Cañon the next step up from a canopy tour, with rappels and Tarzan swings from The Original Canopy Tour company. US$45.

Guanacaste

Continuing up the dirt track you arrive at **AL** *Rincón de la Vieja Mountain Lodge*, T661-8156, F666-1887, mobile 390-8855, www.guanacaste.co.cr/rincon Rustic comforts in 50 rooms with private bath. The restaurant serves traditional dishes, with a small bar and a pool for relaxing. You can use it as a base but most take advantage of the wide range of tours, setting out with guides, on horseback or foot, to explore the waterfalls and scenery of the area.

Leaving the Pan-American Highway 11 km north of Liberia at El Muerto, a steep road leads to Cañas Dulces and eventually to **B** *Buena Vista Lodge*, T/F661-8158, buenavistalodge@altavista.com 69 comfortable log and flagstone floor cabins, with stunning views across to the Nicoya Peninsula. You can trek to Rincón de la Vieja in the dry season. There's a mini-adventure park on your doorstep in the surrounding forest including a mountain water slide, canopy tour, horse riding to several large waterfalls and mud and steam baths.

North from Liberia As you're enjoying new experiences in Costa Rica, 23 km north of Liberia a road heads east to Quebrada Grande and Costa Rica's first commercial **ostrich farm** with blueneck and black breeds. ■ *T228-6646, Javnai Menahen for information on tours.* A further 3 km north is **Quebrada Grande**, 4 km from which is **B** *Santa Clara Lodge*, T391-8766, F666-4047, www.santaclaralodge.com It has 4 rooms using a shared bath, 1 room with private bath. It's a cattle farm with riding opportunities in the

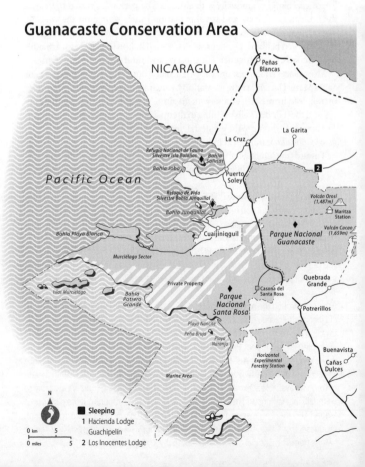

Guanacaste Conservation Area

NICARAGUA

Peñas Blancas

Pacific Ocean

La Garita

La Cruz

Refugio Nacional de Fauna Silvestre Isla Bolaños

Bahía Salinas

Bahía Joba

Puerto Soley

Volcán Orosí (1,487m)

Maritza Station

Refugio de Vida Silvestre Bahía Junquillal

Bahía Junquillal

Cuajiniquil

Volcán Cacao (1,659m)

Parque Nacional Guanacaste

Bahía Playa Blanca

Murciélago Sector

Quebrada Grande

Private Property

Casona del Santa Rosa

Islas Murciélago

Bahía Potrero Grande

Parque Nacional Santa Rosa

Potrerillos

Playa Nancite

Peña Bruja

Playa Naranja

Buenavista

Horizontal Experimental Forestry Station

Cañas Dulces

Marine Area

N

■ **Sleeping**
1 Hacienda Lodge Guachipelín
2 Los Inocentes Lodge

0 km   5
0 miles   5

forest. Also in the area is the Youth Hostel affiliated **C** *Eco Lodge Rincón de la Vieja*, T281-1117, F283-7148, www.hostelling-costarica.com Includes food, pool, camping (US$5). They will pick you up in Liberia if you call in advance. The lodge is on the edge of the park. There are horses to hire, guides, tours. From here it is 3¼ hrs to the volcano. Also in the Quebrada Grande area is **D** *Albergue Nueva Zelandia*, T/F666-4300,www.hostelling- costarica.com Seriously rustic accommodation and genuinely traditional food. You won't be seeking comforts staying here but you will have a genuine experience of Costa Rica *guanacasteco* style.

A **bus** for Quebrada Grande leaves Liberia at 1500 daily.

Transport

Parque Nacional Santa Rosa

Santa Rosa National Park holds a coveted place in the hearts of Tico and international visitors for its historical and natural importance. Tucked in the northwestern corner of Costa Rica, the 38,673-hectare national park has grown to encompass the entire Santa Elena Peninsula and now protects, with the Murciélago Sector to the north, the largest vestige of dry tropical forest in Central America.

Colour map 1, grid A2

The historical significance of the region is also an essential part of the national identity. As early as 1663 the land was treasured for cattle raising with the founding of a ranch in the area. In the 1850s, the prying eyes of US filibuster William Walker saw the Santa Rosa Hacienda -- La Casona - as an essential foothold for his imperialist ideals to take over and reunite Central America. After a brief but fierce battle at La Casona, impassioned Costa Ricans ousted Walker's forces in what was to be the greatest threat to the recently created independent republic. The park and the house have become an essential visit for every Tico. But tragically La Casona was almost completely destroyed by fire in May of 2001.

Guanacaste

Getting there This is easiest by private vehicle, following the Pan-American Highway north of Liberia for 32 km, then heading west at the signpost to the park, and following the entrance road for 7 km. By public transport any bus travelling between Liberia and La Cruz will drop you off at the entrance, from where, with luck, you can catch a lift from someone entering the park. If you're unlucky, it is still a pleasant walk, and if the road is quiet you may even see wildlife.

Ins & outs
For all enquiries contact park administration at the Tropical Dry Forest Investigation Centre on T666-5051, F666-5020, www.acguanacaste. co.cr

Lago de Nicaragua

Santa Cecilia

Brasilla

Birmania

Pitilla Station

Cacao Station

Rincón Cacao Biological Corridor

Von Seebock (895m)

Volcán Rincón de la Vieja (1,806m)

Volcán Santa María (1,916m)

Parque Nacional Rincón de la Vieja

Colonia Blanca

Las Pailas

Santa María

San Jorge

Curubande

Liberia

To San José

Arriving at Playa Nancite – safety in numbers?

Playa Nancite is treasured as the nesting site of three species of sea turtles, the largest at almost 2 m in length being the solitary nesting leatherback and the second largest the green turtle. The smaller olive ridley may lose ground on size but makes up for it in numbers arriving in thousands in an incredible natural phenomenon. At night from August to December, thousands of olive ridleys gather in the offshore waters, enduring a mating cycle that lasts up to nine hours. After mating, the turtles arrive in their thousands over a three to seven night period each depositing between 90 and 120 eggs that incubate in deep nests for 50 days. After hatching the young struggle to the surface, and cross the beach to the treacherous coastal surf. All manner of terrestrial and marine predators feast on the young, hence the vast numbers of mating couples in one small space and the number of eggs produced, which give each individual a greater chance of survival. Estimates suggest that at the peak of the arribadas (arrivals) as many as 75,000 turtles may nest on the beach, before migrating as far north as Mexico and south to Peru. They return every two or three years.

Researchers at the Santa Rosa Investigation Centre have been studying the phenomenon since it was first discovered in 1972. In recent years, figures suggest the numbers of olive ridleys arriving at Nancite are declining – a disappointingly familiar tale – the causes of which remain unknown.

Entrance to the park is US$6. The park is open 24 hrs, but the entrance may be barred to traffic before 0800. The park entrance sells maps, bird lists, a small brochure and museum guide. Entrance to Playa Nancite is restricted to permit holders. Apply to the park authorities for a permit – but expect most permits to be taken by researchers during the mass turtle nestings.

Wildlife The immediate appeal of the park is the abundant and relatively easy to see wildlife. During the dry season from November to May, the mainly deciduous trees shed their leaves and the animals depend on shrinking water holes until they dry up completely. Descending from the park's upper reaches, the open dry tropical forest makes it easier to spot the fleeing white-tailed deer and the dozing howler, spider and white-faced monkeys found within the park. In coastal regions, mangrove swamp is the predominant vegetation. Between August and December on Playa Nancite, the phenomenon of the *arribada* involves thousands of olive ridley turtles arriving on the beach in an orgy of collective reproduction. South along the coastline, Playa Naranjo is one of Costa Rica's most beautiful beaches, and one of the hardest to reach – the sight of a near-deserted beach of golden sand is a just reward for a sterling effort.

To the north the Murciélago Sector, reached through Cuajiniquil, protects over 70 species of bat found in this part of the park.

La Casona Arching roof ridges and straining beams once took the tremendous weight of the century old tiles and history bestowed upon the unassuming hacienda building that has been at the crux of Costa Rican history. First records show the property was created in 1663, but the strategic significance of the region was bought to the fore by the north American filibuster William Walker. An advocate of slavery, Walker believed the independent aspirations of Central America had strayed too far from the interests of its northern neighbour.

Having walked into Nicaragua and gained the presidency, Walker's attention turned to its southern neighbour Costa Rica. His attempts to conquer Costa Rica were founded on and floundered at La Casona.

The Costa Ricans, under the leadership of José María Cañas, defeated Walker's band of filibusters on the afternoon of 20 March 1856. The strategic significance of the area was reinforced again in 1919 when troops marched from Nicaragua to overthrow President Federico Tinoco, and again in 1955 during the presidency of José Figueres Ferrer "Don Pepe". On both occasions the invading troops were defeated.

The arson attack of May 2001, by a couple a vengeful hunters angry that hunting was banned in the park, totally destroyed the collection of military paraphernalia and exhibits recording the lifestyle and events that took place at La Casona. Rebuilding of the structure has begun, but the minimal budget is unlikely to restore the area to anything like its former glory. Behind the hacienda there are good views across the surrounding area.

A number of short trails lead out from the administration area and a detailed **Treks & trails** trail map is available at the entrance. Behind the Casona, the short **Indio Desnudo** (naked Indian) nature trail (1 km), takes a loop through fine stands of dry tropical forest with the red peeling bark of the gumbo limbo tree, with annotated signposts. The **Tierras Emergidas** trail runs parallel to the entrance road. The longest sensible one-day trek is to **Mirador Valle Naranjo**, some 6 km from the administration buildings.

Longer treks to **Playa Naranjo** and **Playa Nancite** require an overnight *Beautiful and* stay and should be booked with the administration offices. (There is a *deserted, access* four-wheel drive track leading to both beaches, but do not rely on being able *to Playa Nancite is* to use it.) The trek descends gently over 12 km, moving slowly through dry *restricted due to* tropical forest and a multitude of butterflies. By the time you've reached the *the importance of* lower altitudes, your eye will be well trained to spotting the iguanas, crabs *seasonal arribadas* and monkeys that are very much in evidence. With luck, you may even see green macaws, white-lipped pecarries, tapir and possibly pumas, which are reported to be increasing in number in the park. A left fork leads to Playa Naranjo which has more trails than Playa Nancite. Towards the southern end, the brackish **Limbo Lagoon** is home to the American crocodile. The beach itself is awesome; stretching for miles around the bay and will probably be deserted. That said, it's a popular surfing spot, and out in the bay, is the surfing mecca of Witches' Rock – one of the oldest geological formations in Costa Rica dated at 680 million years old. Even so you'll still have the place to yourself.

The annexation of the Murciélago Sector has incorporated the whole of the **Murciélago** Santa Elena peninsula within the park boundaries. While access to this section **Sector** of the park is more difficult, it is possible to camp at the entrance to the park and there are several trails. It is possible to get out to Playa Blanca in the dry season in 4WD, but at other times of year you will need permission from park authorities.■ *Access to the sector is 10 km north of the Santa Rosa main entrance, taking the good road heading west towards Cuajiniquil. Buses leave Liberia for Cuajiniquil at 0545 and 1530, returning at 0700 and 0430.*

Close to Cuajiniquil is the airstrip built by Oliver North during the 1980s to supply the Nicaraguan Contras. It was built on a property formerly owned by the Nicaraguan leader Somosa before it was purchased for the national park. The **Bahía Junquillal Wildlife Refuge** is also part of the national park. It's a popular spot with local families and has facilities for **camping**. A dirt road continues north eventually reaching the **Bahía de Salinas** – from personal experience a four-wheel drive vehicle is essential in the wet season.

Sleeping & eating Accommodation in the park is limited and primarily aimed at researchers. **E** Dormitory accommodation is available at the park administration, with a canteen providing food and refreshments. Dormitory accommodation for up to 20 people is also available at Playa Nancite, but you should take your own food and water. **Camping** facilities are available close to the park administration, where tents are shaded under the branches of a huge strangler fig. There is also a small campground at Playa Naranjo. You will need to take food and enough water for your entire trip to Playa Naranjo as sea water has seeped into the freshwater well. Camping is also permitted in the Murciélago Sector.

Parque Nacional Guanacaste

Colour map 1, grid A3 The lynchpin of the Guanacaste Conservation Area, Guanacaste National Park was created in 1991 to protect large expanses of dry and humid tropical forest. Linking two older national parks, Guanacaste protects 34,651 ha, in an area covering Orosí volcano and the summit of Cacao volcano (1,659 m). As with Santa Rosa National Park, the area has a history of cattle ranching but is now very conscious of the fact that ecotourists are likely to provide a more sustainable income than ranching ever could.

Ins & outs Services in the park are limited, with three biological stations – Cacao, Maritza and Pitilla – providing simple dormitory accommodation only with advance booking from park administration at Santa Rosa National Park. If visiting, you will probably have to take your own food unless you can make arrangements with park authorities, T666-5051, F666-5020, www.acguanacaste.co.cr Trails lead from each of the stations.

Trails & biological stations **Maritza Station** is the most comfortable of the stations, and the closest to the Pan-American highway, leaving the highway 10 km north of the turning for Santa Rosa, opposite the turn for Cuajiniquil. It's 18 km to the station (four-wheel drive is recommended throughout the year), from where trails lead through gallery, dry and transitional dry-humid forest. The headwaters of the Tempisque river start close to the station, and to the north the Río Sapoá empties to Lake Nicaragua and eventually the Caribbean. Short trails lead to the petroglyph site close to Cerro El Hacha, you can walk to the summit of Cacao, a long day's walk, or you can hike to the Cacao Field Station.

Higher up the slopes at 1,100 m above sea level is **Cacao Station**. Temperatures are lower, rainfall slightly higher and this part of the park has areas of transitional dry-humid forest and cloudforest. Access is from the Pan-American Highway 23 km north of Liberia at Potrerillos. If you want to trek between the park's stations, bear in mind whether you want to start or end in relative comfort: Cacao station is far more basic, and doesn't have electricity.

Pitilla station may be physically close, but access is 28 km along Highway 4 from the junction with the Pan-American Highway, heading south at Santa Cecilia along 9 km of dirt road. It's a different world – the influence of the Caribbean and nearby Lake Nicaragua creating rainforest with patches of regenerating secondary forest in contrast to the predominant dry forest of the region. It is reported to be one of the best spots for birdwatching in the park, but conditions at the lodge are basic, so go prepared.

Los Inocentes For those that want to visit Guanacaste National Park – or close to it at least – but need a little comfort, head towards **A** per person *Los Inocentes Lodge*, 14 km down Highway 4, a short distance south of La Cruz, T/F679-9190, or T265-5484, F265-4385, www.arweb.com/orosi There are 11 charming rooms with private bath in the main lodge and 12 more modern cabins provide complete comfort. Besides the rooms, the price includes three meals and the restaurant serves simple wholesome food, with excellent service, and heavenly views across the plains to Orosí volcano.

Once a working ranch, just a few head of cattle remain on this fine old hacienda originally built in 1890. Named after the Inocente family who owned the property until 1956, Los Inocentes was completely remodelled in 1982. Today, the breezes that drift through the wide, shady verandas of the two-storey hacienda cool the brows of visitors returning from a morning in the saddle, or one of the nature walks. Los Inocentes' move from ranching to a wildlife conservation and recreation centre, has seen the *sabaneros* of yesteryear become the guides of today. Touring by horseback (or tractor ride), you'll see white-faced, howler and spider monkeys, and a host of other animals.

■ *Tours cost US$20. If you're not staying you can take a 1-day tour including horse riding, and lunch for US$30.*

La Cruz

Almost at the end of the road, 19 km short of the border with Nicaragua, La Cruz has little to draw the casual visitor over and above a branch of *Banco Popular* – the only one for miles. But if you can wangle your arrival for dusk you're guaranteed one of the best sunsets this side of Ursa Minor. The town sits on the edge – literally – of a steep escarpment overlooking the Bahía Salinas, with camping opportunities, a couple of all-inclusive resorts and Isla Bolaños Wildlife Reserve.

Colour map1, grid A3
Population: 9,412
Altitude: 200 m

Guanacaste

By far the best option in town is **C** *Amalia's Inn*, 100m south of the main square, T/F679-9181. A mix of tidy rooms, decorated with original art by the owners, for couples and groups of up to 6 (charged at US$5 per extra person), with private and shared bathrooms. Stunning views from the balcony out to Salinas Bay, with a small pool ideal for a quick refreshing dip. Very friendly and excellent local knowledge. Recommended. **C** *Hostal de Julia*, on the road out to the Pan-American Highway T/F679-9084. 12 motel-style cabins, with private bath, hot water and fans. Ample parking and credit cards accepted. **C-D** *Cabinas Santa Rita*, 150 m south of the central park, T679-9062, F679-9305. A good choice with 36 big rooms with private bath, and a/c or fan. Secure with plenty of parking. A good alternative if Amalia's is full. **G** *Cabinas Maryfel*, opposite the bus terminal but without a sign, T679-9534. 9 cabins, with private bath and parking. The rooms are dark, but clean. The cheapest in town is **G** *Pension Tica*, between the bus terminal and the plaza. Dark rooms, shared bath, quite unpleasant – probably time to consider going home.

On Pan-American Highway 5 km north of La Cruz is **A** *Colinas del Norte*, T/F679-9132. 24 rooms, with private bath, and fan or a/c. A rustic hacienda-style hotel, using hardwood and flagstone flooring throughout. A small pool, disco, and mini golf – but don't expect St Andrews. Will arrange horse riding tours through the nearby forest.

Sleeping

Restaurant Mirador, also known as *Echecatl*, is the place to go for the views. It's also the best restaurant in town, serving healthy fish and grill dishes. *Thelmas* is a popular choice, serving local dishes. Several *sodas* dotted around town. *El Mercadito* at the bus terminal has divine ice creams but don't tell everyone.

Eating

Transport   **Bus**   The terminal is a couple of blocks north of the central square. Buses to **San José** leave every 1½ hrs from 0545, 5 hrs, US$4 – more expensive at the weekend. Transport to Liberia, for the Nicoya Peninsula, leaves 5 times a day, 1½ hrs. Buses heading north to **Peñas Blancas** leave 5 times daily, 30 mins. Buses east to **Santa Cecilia**, passing Hacienda Los Inocentes, leave at 0700, 0930, 1230 and 1500, 1 hr. Buses to **Playa Jobo** west beyond Bahía Solanos leave from close to the main square at 0530, 1030 and 1500.

Directory   **Banks** *Banco Popular*, on the road to the Pan-American Highway, changes TCs, cash and has a Visa ATM. **Communications** The post office is one block west of the central plaza.

Bahía Salinas

Colour map 1, grid A3   West of La Cruz, a good road descends rapidly - and deteriorates equally quickly - passing through old ranch land to Puerto Soley, Bahía Salinas and eventually to the undeveloped beaches of Jobo and Rajada - which locals claim are the best in the country. One of the quieter corners of Costa Rica, the roads are bad and travelling without private transport can be time-consuming.

With tours provided by the two all-inclusive hotels (see below) in the area, it's a good base for families if you're looking for making the occasional trip. The bay also receives reliable westerly winds, so after Lake Arenal, it's the most important **windsurfing** spot in the country.

Sleeping &   After about 8 km is **G** *Playa Morro Trailer Park y Cabinas*, T382-2989. A quiet trailer
eating   park with bathrooms and **camping** close to the beach overlooking the bay. There
Hotels listed in the   are plans for a few cabins. There's electricity and water, and a few BBQ grills, or you
order encountered   can get food from the simple restaurant and bar. You can hire boats for trips to Isla
from La Cruz   Bolaños Wildlife Refuge, or horses for exploring the area.

Following a spur road after about 13 km leads to **LL-AL** *Ecoplaya Beach Resort*, T/F679-9380, www.ecoplaya.com An all-inclusive resort with 88 comfortable villas, some equipped with kitchenettes, with a/c, TVs, telephones, and a patio set in colourful gardens. Seafood, *bocas* and international dishes are served in the thatched roof restaurant where, cooled by winds from the bay, you can sip refreshing cocktails. There's a free form wet bar and a host of activities including horse riding, and trips to the reserve.

An alternative option, targetting families is **A** *Three Corners*, T679-9444, F679-9654,www.threecorners.com 62 rooms in duplex cabins, spread along the small beach. Each room has a couple of beds, a/c and private bathroom with a patio. There's a multitude of things to do, in addition to lazing by the pools or relaxing in the jacuzzi, including kayaking, mountain biking, table tennis, windsurfing – with classes if required, and trips to the reserve. There are also more sedate activities like cards and chess, and of course fishing. The huge thatched roof restaurant serves good meals, with a menu for kids as well.

Refugio de   Sitting in the Salinas Bay, Isla Bolaños Wildlife Refuge is a small island reserve
Fauna Silvestre   protecting just 25 ha of stunted forest that survives on less that 1,500 mm of rain
Isla Bolaños   a year – making this one of the driest spots in Costa Rica. But protected status is afforded to this barren land rising 81 m above the coastal waters, because it is one of the few known nesting sites of the brown pelican in the country, with a colony of 500 or so individuals, and the only known nesting site of the American oystercatcher. You will also see the magnificent and gracefully agile frigatebird. Access to the refuge is restricted – some say denied – but you can walk around the island at low tide. If you wish to visit, contact the *Area de*

Conservación Guanacaste, T666-5051, F666-5020, www.acguanacaste.co.cr
Boat trips can be organized from Puerto Soley or any of the hotels and camp-
sites surrounding the bay.

Peñas Blancas and the border with Nicaragua

From La Cruz it's 19 km to the border with Nicaragua at Peñas Blancas. There
are no hotels or services over and above immigration and customs, and a sim-
ple restaurant. The crossing is open from 0800-1800. For arriving passengers,
there is a small Costa Rica Tourist Board (ICT) office which periodically has
country maps. If crossing by international bus, you are guided through for-
malities by the bus driver. If travelling independently, surrender your pass-
port and immigration form to be stamped, having purchased a *cruz roja* from
the neighbouring window. Nicaragua immigration is a walk of a few hundred
metres, and is straightforward, assuming your papers are in order.

Crossing by private vehicle Rental vehicles are not permitted to cross the border. Leaving by car, just hand
over the printed vehicle permit you were given on arrival and complete the
necessary paperwork. If you are entering Costa Rica by car, first pay your
entrance stamp, then go to the *Aduana Permiso de Vehículo* for your vehicle
permit (state how long you want it to last); at the *Seguro Obligatorio* window,
purchase insurance. Your vehicle is then briefly inspected before you are
allowed to depart. All vehicles are fumigated: cost: US$3 for cars, US$4 for
pick-ups.

Transport There are several express and ordinary **bus** services a day linking with **San José**. Buses
arrive and depart from San José at Av 3, C 16, 100 m north of Coca-Cola terminal, 4 or 6
hrs, US$5. Take an early bus if you want to get from San José to the border before it
closes. Bus from the frontier to **Liberia**, US$1.25, 1½ hrs. There are also buses to and
from **La Cruz**.

Directory **Banks** There is a bank (in the *aduana*, usually changes cash, does not change TCs,
open 0800-1200, 1300-1600) and an exchange to ease your passage. There are plenty
of money changers floating around – shop around to get good rates.

Guanacaste

Guanacaste

The Nicoya Peninsula

7

The Nicoya Peninsula

244 Ins and outs

245 Northern beaches

249 Northwestern beaches and inland

262 Western beaches

269 Southern peninsula

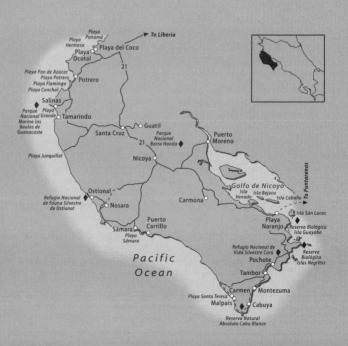

An appendage dangling off the northwest of Costa Rica, the Nicoya Peninsula is a fine contrast to the rest of the country. Although transport links are improving, the Gulf of Nicoya separates the region physically and culturally from mainland Costa Rica. The dry and moist forests that once dominated the landscape have been replaced by open pastures, with only the occasional guanacaste tree providing shade for grazing cattle. With a dependable dry season from December to May, conditions are ideal for lovers of sun, sea and surf.

The peninsula itself is also culturally divided. Small towns, dotted along Highway 21 serve as supply depots for nearby communities, some of the poorest in the country, in surrounding low lying hills. These towns may be close, but they're a world away from the beach resorts of varying comforts that have sprung up along the coastline, pouncing on every inch of beach worth a towel, surfboard or fishing boat.

You can take your pick from bays and beaches covering the length of the western coast – to be honest if you like beaches you'll find something decent everywhere. In almost every bay there are quiet secluded villas and hotels providing mid-range comforts, as well as a couple of cheaper options and a few that are strictly upmarket. Most of these are best reached and explored by private vehicle, but public transport is an option.

Budget travellers using buses should head for Playa del Coco, Malpaís – a surfers' haven – or at the southern end of the peninsula Montezuma, all served by reasonable public transport and enough visitors to keep the party going.

Things to do in the Nicoya Peninsula

- **Beaches, beaches, beaches** – take one four-wheel drive, a map, pin, a free day and a good book and let chance do the rest.
- Learn a new **sport** – scuba diving, surfing, deep-sea fishing. Rappel through the limestone caves of Barra Honda National Park.
- Relax on a sunset **cruise** drifting aimlessly on the Pacific swell.

Ins and outs

Getting there

Air

Dec to May are the most popular months, with endless clear blue skies and temperatures in the high 20s. Booking accommodation is recommended at this time, particularly at Christmas, New Year and Easter

There are enough ways to the peninsula to keep the traveller amused for quite a while. International flights arrive at **Daniel Oduber Quirós International Airport**, 13 km from Liberia along Highway 21. Reopened in 1995 after major renovation, the airport is used for international charter flights. The small, modern terminal decorated with thatched roof for that tropical paradise feel, has full customs and immigration services, a small café and a branch of *Banco de Costa Rica* due to open soon. If you can get a flight, it's a good choice if you want to go straight to the beach. Transport from the airport is limited to taxis, which are readily available. Ask around to get the best price.

Regular domestic flights provided by *SANSA*, T221-9414, www.flysansa.com, and *Travelair*, T220-3054, www.travelair-costarica.com, serve the same airport as well as the smaller airstrips at Carillo, Nosara, Punta Islita, Sámara, Tambor and Tamarindo.

Road & ferry

Road routes starting at the north of the peninsula leave the Pan-American Highway at Liberia, following Highway 21 for 108 km to Carmona towards the south of the peninsula continuing unpaved to Playa Naranjo. If arriving from San José or the south, the **Tempisque vehicle ferry**, T661-8105, plies the gulf waters from Puerto Nispero to Puerto Moreno, cutting a couple of hours off the journey. Services run from 0430-2400. Pedestrians and bus passengers are free, motorbikes US$1, cars US$3. Long queues are common on Sun and holidays with people returning to San José. You can also get a ferry from **Puntarenas** on the mainland to Playa Naranjo towards the south of the peninsula, with access to the north along a potholed road, or to Playa Tambor and Montezuma. See page 284.

Getting around

If driving, the main beaches are clearly signposted from Highway 21

Apart from the main highway, roads through the peninsula are a mix of well intentioned tarmac, sprinkled with varying degrees of potholes – some causing a mild blip, others certain to propel the wheel through the wing of your vehicle. If driving, err on the side of caution, allow plenty of time for your journey and don't take risks crossing rivers. It is often, although not always, possible to move between beaches without returning to the main highway but be prepared to get lost and ask directions regularly.

Public transport follows the main access routes, with **buses** serving the northern route from Liberia, and buses from San José using the Tempisque and Playa Naranjo ferries. Moving around the peninsula can be problematic. You can reach most beach areas with a daily bus service from Santa Cruz or Nicoya. If moving between beaches, you will probably have to improvise your journey over two or three buses, nipping into Santa Cruz or Nicoya. **Taxis** are, of course, an option – as ever, agree the price in advance.

Northern beaches

Playa del Coco

A beach community with a rash of good hotels and restaurants, Playa del Coco is a quiet spot with just enough life to keep things ticking over, without overindulging in all-out partying. The beach is pleasant, although nothing special. With good transport links to the rest of the country, it's a popular destination for Costa Ricans at weekends.

Colour map 1, grid B3

The town has developed to become one of the country's most popular dive spots, with several operators providing courses and dives to more than 30 dive sites within a 20-min boat ride from town. Surfers use this as a departure point for trips out to Witches' Rock to the north, and it's a good base for big game fishing.

AL-A *Coco Verde*, T670-0494, F670-0555, www.cocoverde.com 33 rooms with private bath, a/c, TV, parking lot and security guards. The cleanliness and standard you would expect from a hotel rumoured to be joining the Best Western chain, with a pool, popular bar and casino. A wide range of activities can easily be arranged including fishing and diving. **AL-A** *Flor de Itabo*, on the road leading to the town, T670-0011, F670-0003, www.flordeitabo.com A variety of rooms, apartments and bungalows, all with private bath, a/c and cable TV, some with kitchenette, fridge and coffee machines. The colourfully decorated restaurant specializes in seafood and steaks, with a ceramic tiled pool set in colourful gardens. The hotel specializes in big game fishing, with the pedigree and experience to continue adding to the record breaking catches shown in photographs in the reception. There's also a casino for those who want to ride their luck just a little further. **AL-A** *La Puerta del Sol*, T670-0195, F670-0650, www.lapuertadelsol.com 10 suites, all with a living room, private bath, a/c and fan, telephone and safe box – a couple of larger suites with additional comforts. Hidden down a side road to the north of town, this Italian-run gateway to the sun packs in the services and keeps a family feel to the place. Stylish furniture decorates the bright rooms, the small gym is wonderfully breezy, and the relaxing pool is also used for free scuba try-outs. Excellent home-made pasta in the Italian restaurant. Successful through word of mouth – don't tell everyone!

A *Pato Loco Inn*, T/F670-0145, www.costaricainfo.com/patoloco.html 4 rooms and 2 apartments immaculately presented, decorated with stylish ceramics and paintings. A quiet, unassuming spot leading into town, and one of the

Sleeping

The Nicoya Peninsula

Playa del Coco

Sleeping ■
1 Cabinas Chale
2 Cabinas El Coco
3 Camping Villa El Mar
4 Coco Palms
5 Coco Verde
6 Flor de Itabo
7 La Puerta del Sol
8 Luna Tica
9 Pato Loco Inn
10 Villa del Sol
11 Villa Flores
12 Vista del Mar

Eating ●
1 Bananas
2 Coco Mar
3 Cocos Seafood
4 El Roble
5 Jardin Tropical
6 Jungle Bar
7 L'Angeletto di Roma
8 Mariscos la Guajire
9 Playa del Coco

best restaurants in town. **A** *Villa del Sol*, at the northern end of beach, T/F670-0085, www.villadelsol.com 7 rooms, each with private bathroom, tastefully decorated with bamboo furniture and natural woods. Pool set in gardens just a short distance from the beach, with Italian and French cuisine served in the restaurant.

A-B *Vista del Mar*, at the northern end of town, T/F670-0753, www.larevuenet.com /vistamar 9 comfortable double rooms, a couple with ocean views and private bath, also with a/c or fan – price includes a fruity breakfast. Plenty of parking. A quiet spot with a small patio looking out to the sea. A pool and BBQ spot, make it a good place for relaxing late into the evening. **B** *Coco Palms*, on the main plaza next to the soccer pitch.T670-0367, F670-0117, cocopalm@hotmail.com Comfortable rooms with private bath, set in pleasant gardens complete with pool and popular gringo bar. **B** *Villa Flores*, T670-0269, F670-0787. 7 rooms sleeping 2-4 people, with private bath, TV, a/c or fans – breakfast included. Rooms are a little unkempt but the gardens are pretty, the pool has a wet bar, and you can use the gym, arrange diving and quad-bike safaris. Parking. **B-D** *Cabinas Chale*, north of town, T670-0036. 25 double rooms and villas (sleeping up to 6 with kitchenette), all with private bath and fan or a/c, and a small terraced patio. A good choice for the active with a pool and basketball court. Villas work out as a very good deal, and monthly rentals are possible.

C-D *Cabinas El Coco*, right on the beach front just north of the pier, T670-0110, F670-0167. Plenty of basic rooms, all with private bath, and basic no frills décor, views are good, rooms at the back are slightly cheaper. Office in the restaurant next door. **D** *Luna Tica*, T670-0127, F670-0459. With the *anexo* over the road, 27 rooms with fan and private bath. The rooms are basic, but the best of the budgets, with a small beachfront bar and restaurant. Some villas with kitchenette and fridge available.

Camping **G** *Camping Villa El Mar*, T670-0151. Simple services including bathroom, toilets and kitchen in the heart of town, but the owners are considering closing after 25 years of business. Call in advance to check.

Eating   In a flurry of neon *Cocos Seafood Restaurant* cooks up overpriced surf and turf on the main plaza. *El Roble*, just off the main plaza, is an open-air bar-cum-disco. *Jardin Tropical* is one of the cheapest eateries, with a good mix of *Tico* and snack dishes, and almost open-air. *L'Angoletto di Roma* at *Pato Loco Inn* serves excellent pasta in a cozy atmosphere with Italian style and elegance. Also try the restaurant at *La Puerta del Sol*. *Mariscos la Guajira* is a popular beachfront seafood restaurant. Cheap. *Playa del Coco* on the beach front is a popular cheap spot, opening early at 0600. *Papagayo*, is a regularly recommended, and has good seafood – which was in hiding when visited.

Bars & nightlife   *Coco Mar* is a popular beach front disco. *Bananas* is the current hotspot for drinking, with an open-air balcony overlooking the main road, and dancing until the early hours. *Jungle Bar* is a slightly rougher place with an air-conditioned dance floor.

Shopping   Air-conditioned shops and impromptu stalls dotted around the town are more than happy to relieve you of cash in return for swimwear, beach items, jewellery, and souvenirs.

Sports   **Diving** Playa del Coco, and neighbouring Playa Hermosa have developed a reputation as Costa Rica's main dive resort. Dive operators offer trips to over 30 nearby sites including **Islas Catalina** to the south where you may well see manta rays, and **Islas Murciélagos**, off the Santa Elena Peninsula to the north, where bull sharks are commonly seen. None of the dive operators will deny that visibility in the area is occasionally less than perfect, but seeing whitetip reef and Pacific bull sharks, rays and mantas on a good day could easily compensate.

Tours operators offer roughly the same packages. A 2-tank morning or afternoon dive starts at US$50, with a trip to Catalinas costing US$85, or to Murciélago US$110. Resort courses (ie unqualified) are US$75, PADI training is also available with open water certification costing US$295. For more advanced courses contact dive operators. Prices include tanks, weights, guides and snacks, normally with a minimum of 2 people.

Deep Blue Diving, beside *Hotel Coco Verde*, T670-1004, www. deepblue-diving.com *Rich Coast Diving* T/F670-0176, in the US and Canada 1-800-4-DIVING, www.richcoastdiving.com *Mario Varga Expeditions*, T670-0351, www.divexpeditions.com Also see *Bill Beard's Diving Safaris* in Playa Hermosa, page 248.

Sports fishing While Playa Flamingo to the south gets the main sports fishing business, the *Flor de Itabo* hotel in Coco has a good reputation and all the gear if you want to charter a boat *Agua Rica Charters* operate the 42' *Encantador* Sport Fisher. Trips start at US$850 for a full day, including lunch and drinks. Half days are US$450. T670-0805, F670-0807, www.aguaricacharters.com

Surfing Witches' Rock to the north is the surfing Mecca for disciples of *Endless Summer* and Playa del Coco is as good a departure point as any. *Agua Rica Charters* provide trips with up to 10 boards in a boat for US$400. Also ask at *Cabinas El Coco* on the beachfront.

Buses leave **San José** from C 14, Av 1-3, 0800 and 1400, returning at 0800 and 1400, 5 hrs, US$5.20. From **Liberia** there are 6 daily buses, 0530-1815, returning 0530-1800. **Transport**

Banks A branch of *Banco Nacional* is on the main street. Closed Sat. **Communications** *Café Internet 2000*, on main road town at the entrance to town. Bunch of computer services as well as fine coffee, cakes, bagels and bytes – the only café in town for the time being. The **post office** is on the main plaza. **Useful addresses** The **police station** is in the main plaza. The nearest **pharmacy** is in Sardinal, 8 km east of Playa del Coco. **Directory**

Playa Ocotal

Roughly three kilometres southwest of Coco is the small beach of Playa Ocotal. Without the easy access, it's a more secluded bay than its northern neighbour and better if you've got your own transport. The rocky headlands have developed as a dive site and fishing trips are easily arranged. Snorkelling is OK when visibility is good. *Colour map 1, grid B2*

LL-L *Ocotal Beach Resort and Marina*, At the southern end of the bay, T670-0321, F670-0083, www.ocotalresort.com 59 rooms and suites, all with 2 queen or 1 single king-size bed and a private terrace or balcony with ocean view. Each chic, colourful room has a/c, private bath, cable TV, telephone, safe box and coffee machine. The comforts continue outside with 3 pools, a jacuzzi with spectacular ocean views, and a floodlit tennis court. There are 3 restaurants to choose from, including a minibar on the beach. The resort also specializes in fishing packages, from 4 fully-equipped 32' boats, and diving packages. **Sleeping & eating**

Set back from the beach, in quiet seclusion is the idyllic **AL-A** *Villa Casa Blanca*, T670-0518, F670-0448, www.costa-rica-hotels-travel.com 15 rooms each uniquely decorated in a style as individual as the service is special, set in a charming Spanish-style villa. Whether recovering from a heavenly sleep in a sumptuous canopied 4-poster bed, or any one of the colourful and bright rooms, you can soak in a full-length bath tub, before heading down to a wholesome waffle and pancake breakfast that will see you through most of the day. Comforts include a free-form pool complete with wet-bar, a relaxing patio and landscaped gardens complete with jacuzzi. You will have to venture out for food as there is no restaurant, but Canadian owners James and Janey Seip are happy to order in food. If you want to venture further, trips to places of interest in the region are easily arranged.

The only food in the area is from *Father Rooster Bar & Grill*, with cheap snacks and seafood on the beach.

Playa Hermosa

Colour map 1, grid B2 On the main road from Highway 21 to Playa del Coco, a right spur heads north for a few kilometres leading to Playa Hermosa, a sandy golden beach good for swimming and general water sports spread along a broad bay. With a west facing beach, the sunsets are impressive, and cruises are a popular way to spend the twilight hours (US$50). Without a main centre, the ambience is laid-back with a mix of budget accommodation, and full-service hotels and resorts.

Sleeping & eating The main road parallels the beach with several roads giving access to the beach. The first entrance leads to **A-B** *Hotel Playa Hermosa*, T/F672-0046. 22 spacious rooms, with private bath, hot water, fan and safe box, with pleasant shaded gardens leading to the beach. The patio restaurant has a low-key feel, with an international and *Tico* menu, with a healthy contribution from the Italian owners. A little further along the road is **E** *El Cenizaro*, T672-0186. 7 basic rooms, with hard beds and cold water showers. But next to a *minisuper* (market) and 30 m from the beach.

Back along the main road is the **L-B** *Villa del Sueño*, T/F672-0026, www.villadelsueno.com A mix of villas sleeping up to 4 people, and rooms all with private bath, hot water and ceiling fans. An air of Mediterranean tranquillity hovers over the complex of rooms, with each tastefully decorated with comfortable furnishings that positively radiate calm and relaxation. Dinner is often accompanied by live local music, and occasionally with well known Costa Rican musicians.

The second entrance to Playa Hermosa leads to **B** *Iguana Inn*, T/F672-0065. 9 clean and tidy rooms sleeping up to 4 people making it a good deal for groups, in an easy-come, easy-go atmosphere complete with use of kitchen and laundrette. There's a small pool, if the 100 m walk to the beach is too much, a small bar and snack food in high season. A short distance away is **AL** *El Velero*, T672-0036, F672-0016, www.costaricahotel.net 22 crisply clean rooms, recently refurbished and decorated with Costa Rican textiles and a/c remote control – very flash. A pretty beachside spot, with a pool in the garden leading to the beach. A small bar/restaurant serves fast food dishes with a smattering of national influences. Happy hour – but not too loud – every day, and barbecues on Wed and Sun. Sunset tours arranged US$55 per person.

At the northern end of the bay is **LL** *Condovac la Costa*, T672-0150, F672-0151, condovac@sol.racsa.co.cr Over 100 rooms spaced around the northern hills with every imaginable entertainment. Aimed at the all-inclusive family market and no doubt entertaining if that's what you are looking for.

Tour operators *Bill Beard's Diving Safaris*, T672-0012, F672-0231, www.billbeardcostarica.com One of the longest running dive operations in the country, operates out of Playa Hermosa. With all the normal dive options and some good packages mixing blue activities (wet) with green options inland.

Transport Bus from **Liberia**, Empresa Esquivel, five daily between 0730 and 1900, US$0.80.

Playa Panama

The Papagayo Project is the driving force behind tourism development *Colour map 1, grid B2*
around Playa Panama and the Bahía Culebra. The project aims to convert the
scenic bay into a collection of all-inclusive megaresorts which will see the
growth of high-rise apartments and dramatically change the area – and it's
working. The Mexican company *Grupo Situr*, reported to be investing US$2.5
billion in the project, and European investment companies backing the pro-
ject would see the area become the largest leisure city in Central America with
current estimates putting up to 20,000 rooms in the bay. You don't have to be
an environmentalist or biologist to speculate on the effect that such numbers
would have on the area – north of the peninsula is the Santa Rosa National
Park – and the demand for water in the country's driest regions. Not surpris-
ingly, criticism of the project amongst environmentalists and eco-tourists has
been widespread and has led to the on-off nature of the project. For the time
being, access is still limited although road improvements are proof of plans in
the pipeline.

On the northern side of the bay, the precolumbian site of **Nacascolo** may
be of interest to the truly dedicated explorer of ruins.

LL+ *Giardini di Papagayo*, T672-0067, F672-0223, www.grupopapagaoyo.com No
denying the full luxury and comfort in this exclusive resort, and investment opportuni-
ties for those who wish to fund continued development. **LL-L** *Costa Blanca*,
T672-0096, F672-0239, coragro@sol.racsa.co.cr 28 villas sleeping 4- 8 people. In addi-
tion to the fully-equipped villas, comforts include a pool, jacuzzi and beach access.
L *Blue Bay Village*, T672-0131, F672-0139, www.bluebayresorts.com All-inclusive
resort with hilltop rooms and bungalows scattered around an exclusive bay. The
rooms all have private bath and a/c, with ocean views from the terrace. A couple of
pools, a gym, jogging trails and non-motorized water sports for the hyperactive, and a
couple of restaurants for the dining connoisseur. **L** *El Nakuti Resort*, T672-0121,
F672-0120, www.grupopapagayo.com 40 full-service rooms and 19 big split-level vil-
las sleeping up to 6 complete with kitchenette, all with a/c, telephone and cable TV.
Relaxed and private, there's a pool and jacuzzi or you can get wet water or jet skiing,
snorkelling and diving. The buffet-style restaurant serves international dishes.

**Sleeping
& eating**
*There is no budget
accommodation at
Playa Panama – in
fact chances are
you'll be moved
on unless you look
the part*

The Nicoya Peninsula

Northwestern beaches and inland

Back on Highway 21 the road continues its journey to the heart of the penin-
sula, passing roadside stalls selling distinctive *Chorotega* ceramics and mod-
ern interpretations of the simple, attractive designs.

Thirty-eight kilometres south of Liberia a fork heads west, splitting again
after 24 km at a junction village called Huacas, to several popular beaches,
heading north, west and south. To the north, the road fringes the coastline
passing the beaches of Playa Conchal, Playa Brasilito, Playa Flamingo, Playa
Potrero and the distant Playa Pan de Azúcar. Apart from Brasilito and a cou-
ple of exceptions elsewhere, these beaches mainly target self-catering travel-
lers and public transport is limited.

Straight ahead – directly west – the road leads to Playa Grande and Parque
Nacional Marino las Baulas de Guanacaste. It's a quiet spread out beach area,
popular with surfers, and also the main nesting site for the leatherback (*baula*)
turtle in Costa Rica. You can also reach Playa Conchal, turning right at the vil-
lage of Matapalo.

Most people head south, where the road leads to the laid-back surf town of Playa Tamarindo, with enough happening to keep you busy and active, but still calm enough to be relaxing.

Playa Conchal

Colour map 1, grid B2 The white bay of Shell Beach – created by countless tiny shells – is good for swimming and snorkelling with clear waters easily reached by meandering south along the shore from Playa Brasilito.

Sleeping Activities are overseen by the **LL** *Melía Playa Conchal Beach Resort*, T654-4502, F654-4181, www.meliaplayaconchal.com Over 300 lavish suites with every imaginable comfort. 5 restaurants, reportedly the largest free form pool in Central America, the 18-hole Garra de León golf course and four floodlit tennis courts. In their words, "you can do every activity under the sun". The resort can be reached along the main road to Playa Brasilito.

Playa Brasilito

Colour map 1, grid B2 The beach at Playa Brasilito is not particularly attractive, but good transport and a range of services make it a useful base if you fancy exploring this part of the coast and the budget is tight.

Sleeping **B-C** *Hotel Brasilito*, T654-4237, F654-4247, www.brasilito.com 15 spacious rooms, a
& eating couple with private bath, taking gulps of cooling ocean breeze, all with private bathroom. Comfortable and friendly hotel, close to the beach, with a cheap restaurant and bar. Wide range of activities including horse riding (US$30 for 2 hrs), bikes (US$30 for ½ day) and kayaking (US$10 for ½ day). Also internet service available. On the main road is **C** *Ojos Azules*, T/ F654-4343. 18 cabins, with private bath and possibly the most tasteless décor in the country. Right on the beach is **F** per person *Brasilito Lodge*, T654-4890, F654-4452, www.brasilito-conchal.com Big rooms, good beds and options for **camping** (**G**) in this family home budget option. Tents available for hire if required. Internet, email and tours provided.

La Casita del Pescado has a good selection of reasonably priced fish dishes which have to be consumed quickly as the stools are concrete – ouch! *La Boca de la Iguana*, on the beach, is good value. *Pizzeria Il Forno*, on the main road serves a mean pizza.

Transport **Bus** A daily bus from **San José** leaves the Tralapa terminal at Av 3, C 18 – 20, at 0800 and 1000, passing through Brasilito en route to Playa Flamingo, returning at 0900 and 1400, 5 hrs, US$6.

Playa Flamingo

Colour map 1, grid B2 A few kilometres beyond Brasilito, Playa Flamingo is the sports fishing capital of the peninsula, with the region's largest marina providing services. Once-beautiful white and grey sand beaches have suffered slightly from a spate of developments, but the small town has a good collection of services and comfortable, if rather ostentatious and garish, hotels. The simple charm of the area has gone although there are some more quieter spots to the north at Playa Potrero – see below. Despite the name there are no flamingos – the name is reported to come from mistakenly identifying roseate spoon-bills.

LL-AL *Flamingo Beach Resort*, T/F654-4070, in US and Canada on 1-800-500-9090, www.flamingo-beach.com 91 a/c and large rooms and suites right on the beach. A couple of bars and restaurants, large pool and tennis court. Good for arranging fishing trips and activities in the area. Up the hill with good views is **LL-AL** *Flamingo Marina Resort*, T290-1858 or T654-4141, F654-4035, www.flamingomarina.com 30 deluxe rooms and suites, all with private bath, a/c, TV and minibar. The rooms are a little traditional on the décor. 4 pools, a jacuzzi and the *Sunrise Café* and *Monkey Bar* for sustenance. **L** *Flamingo Bay Resort*, T654-4349, www.flamingobayresort.com 51 mini-suite rooms with ocean views. Popular resort choice, with pool, deep-sea fishing, casino and resident howler monkey wondering around the reception. However, all just a bit too pink and flamingo-ish. **A** *Mariner Inn*, T654-4081, F654-4024, mariner@costarica.net 12 new rooms with bath, a/c and the popular *Spreader* restaurant and bar.

Sleeping & eating

Marie's Restaurant is a popular dining spot open all day serving pancakes for breakfast, burgers and burritos for lunch and a more sophisticated seafood and surf menu for dinner, all washed down with fine cocktails and cool beers.

If you're sailing by contact *Flamingo Marina* T654-4203, F654-4536, www.marflam.com Costa Rica's largest marina providing full services, and information for organizing sportsfishing, sailing and scuba-diving trips.

Sports

Banks In keeping with the popularity of Flamingo there's a branch of *Banco de Costa Rica* with an ATM – the only one for miles. **Language schools** *Centro Panamericano de Idiomas*, T645-5441, FT645-5448, www.cpi-edu.com, have a Spanish school in Playa Flamingo. With schools in Monteverde and Heredia, you can balance study with staying in a variety of places in the country. Prices from US$215 a week, US$340 with homestay.

Directory

Playa Potrero

Beyond the rocky headland the dark sand beach of Playa Potrero stretches north to the distance. At the end of a long bumpy road from the main highways, Potrero is at the limit of comfotable travel if you're using public transport, so accommodation favours those wanting to stay for a number of days or even weeks. If that's what you're looking for the beach is quiet and peaceful.

Colour map 1, grid B2

B-C *Cabinas Cristina*, T654-4006, F654-4128, www.cabinascristina.com A quiet spot, with rooms sleeping 4 people, equipped with private bath, small kitchenette and a small pool in tropical gardens. **C-D** *Cabinas Isolina Beach*, T654-4375, F654-4313, www.isolinabeach.com 11 comfortable simply decorated bungalows with private bath, some with kitchenette, set in fine shady gardens with hammocks for relaxing.

At the northern end of the beach is **C** *Bahía Esmeralda*, T654-4480, F654-4479, www.hotelbahiaesmeralda.com Tidy rooms and villas sleeping 2, 4 or 6, complete with private bath and a/c or ceiling fan. Free form pool in the tropical garden, a short walk from the beach, Italian restaurant and plenty of parking.

At the entrance to the bay is **E** per person *Cabinas Mayra*, T654-4213. Right on the beach, it's a run-down old family home steeped in charm and a good secluded spot. Alvara Chincilla and his family have 5 cabins sleeping up to 8 people, complete with small kitchen, and you can camp on the beach.

Sleeping
Around the bay there are several resorts that flourish and whither with the season

Las Brisas, at the northern end of the beach, is a great spot for a beer, a snack and shooting pool. Surprisingly popular – well, there were 5 people – for the cut-off location. *Costa Azul*, by the football pitch, has snacks and is popular with locals.

Eating

The Nicoya Peninsula

Transport **Bus** From **San José** to Flamingo, Brasilito and Potrero, daily from Av 3, C 18-20, 0800, 1000, 6 hrs, return 0900, 1400. From **Santa Cruz** daily 0630, 1500, return 0900, 1700, 64 km to Potrero.

Playa Pan de Azucar

Colour map 1, grid B2 At the end of the road is the **LL-AL** *Hotel Sugar Beach*, T654-4242, F654-4239, www.sugar-beach.com Bright airy rooms with private bath and ocean views, in a quiet and beautiful sandy forest-fringed bay. The hotel also has a couple of beach houses sleeping up to 10 people. Good open-air restaurant, and fishing packages from the hotel.

Playa Grande

Colour map 1, grid B2 Back at the junction by Huacas the main road leads straight ahead to Matapalo and after 9 km to Playa Grande, a beach popular with surfers and leatherback turtles. Stretching like a speckled golden carpet into the distance, Playa Grande's appeal is as clear as it is beautiful. Along the coast of a small peninsular created by the Tamarindo Estuary, the 485 ha of beach and mangrove swamps are protected in the **Parque Nacional Marino las Baulas de Guanacaste** with an additional 22,000 ha covering the marine reserve. The beach is one of the country's most important nesting sites of the *baula* (leatherback turtle), the world's largest reptile. Growing to a massive 2 m in length and weighing as much as half a ton, fully mature adults arrive at the beach between October and March, when they haul themselves up the beach to deposit between 80 and 100 ping-pong sized eggs, before returning to the ocean exhausted – clearly the turtles of Ninja fame, were the flap-happy juveniles.

Playa Grande is also considered to be one of the best surf spots in the country, with the beach forming the most western point of the Nicoya Peninsula and therefore receiving swells from the north, south and, naturally enough, the west.

Away from the beach, the estuarine waters protect mangrove swamps where all six Costa Rican species of the eight found in the neotropics are found including white, black, the rare tea and the predominant red mangrove. From a gently drifting boat you can see a great deal of wildlife including caiman, crocodiles and the colourful roseate spoon-bill.

Excursions Turtle watching tours are most commonly arranged from and begin in Tamarindo, a short boat trip across the mouth of the estuary. If you are staying in Playa Grande, you will only be charged the US$6 for entering the national park.

If time allows, a visit to **El Mundo de la Tortuga**, on the main road close to the beach, will provide answers to the endless questions surrounding the world of the turtle. ■ *Open in the nesting season. US$6. The MINAE national park office is at the entrance to town. They run trips down the beach in the nesting season. US$13. T/F653-0470.*

Sleeping The main road leads straight to the beach with a right fork heading to the southern tip
& eating of the peninsula – the closest point to Tamarindo. As you arrive, the cheapest option in town is **G** per person *Cabinas/Restaurant Playa Grande*, T384-7661 (mob), or in Heredia on T237-2552. 8 simple cabins sleeping up to 6 people, with a lively bar and restaurant. At the beach is **L-AL** *Hotel Las Tortugas*, T653-0423, F653-0458, www.cool.co.cr/usr/turtles 10 rooms each with private hot water bath, with a/c and cross ventilation. Although close to the beach, the hotel has been constructed to

The Plight of the Baulas

Created to protect the nesting habitat of the leatherback turtle, Parque Nacional Marino las Baulas de Guanacaste has successfully reduced to a minimum the poaching of turtle eggs from the beaches of Playa Grande. But while the local solution may be reduced, the broader global picture does not bode well for this magnificent reptile.

With an evolutionary birth pre-dating the dinosaurs to over 65,000,000 years, the leatherback – like many marine turtles – is critically endangered, threatened by the explosion of coastal developments around the world. Ongoing research is looking to explore the possible causes which range from the disorientation from lighting at beach developments, long-line fishing and drag nets, and the simple garbage of

plastic bags which may be mistaken for the leatherbacks principal diet – jelly fish.

In October of 2000, the United States joined six other Latin American nations as a signatory of the Inter-American Convention for the Protection and Conservation of Sea Turtles. One more signatory will bring the convention into force and will bind members to conserve sea turtle habitat, protect nesting beaches, limit intentional and accidental capture, prohibit international trade in sea turtles and their products, and support sea turtle research.

For now, time is fast running out for the leatherback and other marine turtles which could become nothing more than a memory like the dodo and other species within a generation.

prevent light reaching the beach, and affecting nesting turtles. Louis Wilson, the owner, was involved with setting up the reserve and the rustic nature of the place is designed not to impact the turtles on the nearby beach. Open-air restaurant with a tasty blend of international and Costa Rican dishes from US$8. Pool and jacuzzi at the hotel when not on the beach, snorkelling or exploring the nearby mangroves by canoe or boat. The hotel also has the **AL-C** *Lighthouse Apartments*, with a selection of 1- and 2-bedroom apartments with a/c, sleeping up to 6 people, complete with kitchenette, available by the night or the week.

A left fork takes a pot-holed road running through forests parallel to the beach. It's only a short distance to **C-D** *Lotus Surf Lodge*, T/F653-0490. Targetting the surfers, 10 rooms with hot water private bathroom and fans. A ramshackle old wooden structure scheduled for renovation by the new owners. For the active of mind and body, it has surf and boogie board rental and classes, table tennis, pool and yoga. Next door is *Parque de Agua*, T653-0594, which only opens periodically but may be worth trying. **A-B** *El Bucanero*, T/F653-0480. Close to the beach, with 8 big tidy rooms – 5 with a/c – and an international menu at the bar-restaurant with an ocean view.

Further south, it's a long trip to **AL** *Cantarana*, backing onto the estuary, T653-0486, F653-0491, www.unicaribbean.com 10 air-conditioned rooms with extra fan, patio and pool set in tropical gardens. Also a few 2-bedroom bungalows. Good restaurant with international and national cuisine. The Margrafs are happy to help with arranging trips to other parts of Costa Rica.

At the most southerly tip of the peninsula is **AL** *Villa Baula*, T653-0493, F653-0459, www.hotelvillabaula.com 20 stilted wooden cabins providing a truly rustic experience complete with private bath with hot water, ceiling fan and ocean view. Reasonably priced German and Indonesian food is served at the *Jaguarandi* restaurant, with a couple of pools for complete relaxation.

There is no **bus** service to Playa Grande, the nearest point of access is Huacas, from where a **taxi** costs around US$10. A **ferry** makes the short distance from Tamarindo running until 1600, arriving at the dock beside *Hotel Cantarana*. **Transport**

The Nicoya Peninsula

Playa Tamarindo

Colour map 1, grid B2   Arriving at dusk, the natural response at Playa Tamarindo is to dump your gear or stop the car with a screech of brakes and run for the beach – the sunsets are incredible and all shades of Tamarindo society migrate in daily pilgrimage for the pagan tribute to the sinking sun. Either side of the magic moment, Tamarindo is a flurry of activity.

The beach is attractive, although not stunning, and has strong tides in places so take care if swimming. The main reason to visit is for that happy balance between good services without complete isolation or over development. Three good breaks provide a variety of options for the surf crowd that flock to town. Beyond surf and sun, the most popular excursion is an evening trip to Playa Grande and the leatherback nesting sights. While the town is driven by surfing, there's a good blend of hotels and bars to make it a good beach stop – not too busy, but not so quiet that it's dead.

Ins & outs   **Getting there** There are several daily flights (US$66 one way) from San José with *SANSA* and *Travelair* to Tamarindo airport, 3 km north of town. The *SANSA* office is on the main street. The *Travelair* representative is in Hotel Pueblo Dorado. Direct buses are available from San José, Empresa Alfaro (T222-2666) departs from Av 3, C 18-20 at 0600 in the morning. Additional regular services from Liberia and Santa Cruz. In high season there are also services with *Interbus* and *Grayline Fantasy* bus between Tamarindo and San José and Jacó.

Getting around It's a small enough place to walk around easily, with a main street running parallel to the beach. Mountain bikes, scooters and even quads are available for hire if your legs get too tired. There is an ICT **tourist office** at the north end of town, but it is rarely open.

Best time to visit Surf's up year round if you're looking for board action. Leatherbacks nest at neighbouring Playa Grande between Oct and Mar.

Excursions & activities
See Tour operators, page 257

Look out for copies of 'The Howler', a monthly English-language magazine available in Tamarindo and many other north coast beaches. Good round up of activities in the area, news briefs and surf charts

Quick to seize any new opportunity, Tamarindo is sure to develop the latest craze. Local trips include **turtle watching** tours from November to March to neighbouring Playa Grande. Trips leave late afternoon and cost around US$25 and can be organized through most hotels. **Jungle boat safaris** also head up the mangrove swamps of the Tamarindo Estuary.

Aquatic adventures are many. If you need to hire a **surf** board, there are many outlets in town with short, fun, long and boogie boards – they'll provide you with all the information or just follow the crowds. Staying on top of the water, **sailing boats** leave for sunset tours and **snorkelling** trips. **Kayaks** are available for hire, with tours through the mangrove swamps and out to **Isla Capitán**. **Sports fishing** is a popular option with half and full day trips available from *Papagayo Excursions* or *Tamarindo Sportsfishing*. For those who prefer to get in the water, snorkelling gear is available for hire, and diving can be organized through *Agua Rica Dive Center*, with courses and resort dives.

Everywhere in Costa Rica has to have a **canopy tour** and Tamarindo is no different. *Tamarindo Long Lines Canopy Tours*, T/F653-0597, zips you along seven platforms and four cables – one reaching 500 m in length.

Heading further afield full and half day tours through the hills of the surrounding area are available on **horse**, **mountain bike** and **quad-bikes**.

LL-AL *La Colina Aparthotel*, T653-0106, F653-0303, www.la-colina.com 12 apartments set back from the main street with a fine sea view and complete with every comfort, including kitchens equipped to cook a gourmet meal. Everything is big – the bed, the walk-in fridge, the pool. Good discounts in the green season. **LL-A** *Best Western Tamarindo Vista Villas*, near entrance to town, T653-0114, F653-0115, www.bestwestern.co.cr/bwtamarindo.html Having undergone extensive remodelling in late 2000, the 34 villas and rooms all have a/c. Villas sleeping up to 8 have fully equipped kitchens. Waterfall-filled pool, wet bar, and Jacuzzi, a couple of bars and a restaurant. Internet access for guests. **L-AL** *Tamarindo Diria*, T653-0031, F653-0208, www.tamarindodiria.co.cr Most comfortable option on the main street with 80 a/c rooms, with ceiling fan, cable TV. Fine buffet restaurant and a couple of pools leading directly to the beach. **L-AL** *El Jardin del Eden*, T653-0137, F653-0111, www.jardindeleden.com Set in luxuriant tropical gardens, 18 rooms and 2 villas with private bath and views to the west and the setting sun. The restaurant is one of the best in town, with excellent seafood – expensive but worth it. A couple of pools with a wet bar and a jacuzzi mean you don't even have to walk the short distance to the beach. If paradise is indeed a hotel, it could well be here.

AL-A *El Milagro*, T653-0042, F653-0043, www.elmilagro.com 32 charming wooden bungalows with private bath, a/c or fan and a small balcony. Pleasant pool set in tropical gardens. **AL-B** *Pasatiempo*, T653-0096, F653-0275, www.hotelpasatiempo.com A popular choice with 14 bungalows, with colourfully decorated a/c rooms, private bath and small private patio complete with hammock. Attractive sundeck set in tropical gardens around the pool. Lively bar and restaurant. Recommended. **AL** *Tropicana*, T653-0503, F653-0261, www.tropicanacr.com Comfortable spacious rooms, with private bath, fan, a/c and safety box. While the room décor shows an intense lack of creativity, one of the 3 pools is probably the biggest in town and you can actually do lengths.

A *Villa Amarilla*, T653-0038. A quiet little bed and breakfast on the main road with big, airy rooms and private bathroom with hot shower. The private garden, described as a tropical Eden, backs on to the main beach. **A-B** *Zullymar*, T653-0140, F653-0028, www.tr506.com/zullymar Modern rooms and economy cabins with a/c, fridge, private bath. Close to the beach.

B *Cabinas Marielos*, T/F653-0141. 17 cabins with private bath, fan or a/c and safe box. Shared kitchen and laundry service. Good value deals for groups of 4 or more, and often fully booked. Visa accepted. **B** *Pozo Azul*, at the entrance to town, T653-0280 and T680-0147. Simple basic cabins, some with a/c, cheaper in low season, cooking facilities, clean, good, swimming pool. **B** *Pueblo Dorado*, T653-0008, F653-0013, www.bpecr.com/pueblodorado/ 28 unassuming and simple rooms, tastefully decorated with masks, complete with hot water private bath and a/c. There's a quiet understated charm to the place with a behind the scenes efficiency. Bigger than average pool. Good discounts in green season. **B-C** *La Palapa*, T653-0362. Has three cabins on the beach in a good spot, but the doors sometimes shut early.

C *Frutás Tropicales*, T/F653-0041. A quiet spot with 3 simple, very clean rooms. Cheap restaurant serving local food and snacks out front. **C** *Tamarindo Resort Club*, can be reached along the beach or by car, off the back road. About 40 simple cabins with private bath for 2-4 people. Popular café-style restaurant and bar – a good choice for groups. Plenty of parking.

E *Cabinas Coral Reef*, T653-0291. Basic dark rooms, with scary dog. **F** *Cabinas Roda Mar*, towards the northern end of town, T653-0109. 6 simple rooms, with private bath (cheaper without). *Tico*-owned with a family atmosphere. **F** *Cabinas Tsunami*. Basic but tidy rooms, private bath and use of the kitchen, great value. Turn up and see if there's free space – probably full of surfers more interested in water than comfort. **F** per person *Dolly's*, T653-0017. Basic rooms, some with bath, key deposit required.

Sleeping
■ *on map*
Price codes:
see inside front cover

Book well in advance at Christmas, New Year and Easter. Good discounts in the green season. Area websites include www.tamarindo.com and www.tamarindo.net

The Nicoya Peninsula

Popular budget choice. Lots of rules and regulations and mixed reports – unfriendly if you arrive on a bad day.

South of town Towards Playa Langosto is **LL-AL** *Capitán Suizo*, T653-0075, F653-0292, www.hotelcapitansuizo.com 8 bungalows, 22 rooms and a 5-room

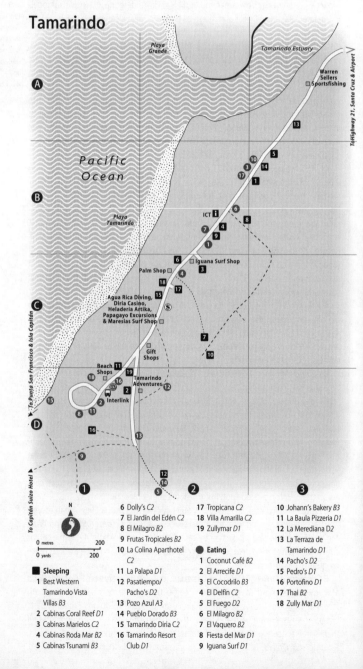

Tamarindo

Sleeping

1 Best Western Tamarindo Vista Villas *B3*
2 Cabinas Coral Reef *D1*
3 Cabinas Marielos *C2*
4 Cabinas Roda Mar *B2*
5 Cabinas Tsunami *B3*
6 Dolly's *C2*
7 El Jardín del Edén *C2*
8 El Milagro *B2*
9 Frutas Tropicales *B2*
10 La Colina Aparthotel *C2*
11 La Palapa *D1*
12 Pasatiempo/ Pacho's *D2*
13 Pozo Azul *A3*
14 Pueblo Dorado *B3*
15 Tamarindo Diria *C2*
16 Tamarindo Resort Club *D1*
17 Tropicana *C2*
18 Villa Amarilla *C2*
19 Zullymar *D1*

Eating

1 Coconut Café *B2*
2 El Arrecife *D1*
3 El Cocodrilo *B3*
4 El Delfín *C2*
5 El Fuego *D2*
6 El Milagro *B2*
7 El Vaquero *B2*
8 Fiesta del Mar *D1*
9 Iguana Surf *D1*
10 Johann's Bakery *B3*
11 La Baula Pizzeria *D1*
12 La Merediana *D2*
13 La Terraza de Tamarindo *D1*
14 Pacho's *D2*
15 Pedro's *D1*
16 Portofino *D1*
17 Thai *B2*
18 Zully Mar *D1*

apartment all with patio or balcony and a/c. The bar and restaurant overlook land-scaped gardens, visited by howler monkeys. Meandering paths lead to the large free form pool. Wide range of tours provided. Excellent service and quality from one of Costa Rica's distinctive hotels.

Playa Langosto LL *Cala Luna*, T653-0214, F653-0213, www.calaluna.com 20 deluxe hotel rooms constructed using tropical hardwoods, and 21 2- and 3-bedroom villas each with a private pool. Complete luxury and stylish ambience throughout the opulent gardens. *Cala Moresca* restaurant serves regional dishes, Italian cuisine and the traditional American breakfast to start your day. **L** *Barcelo Playa Langosto*, T653-0363, F653-0415, www.barcelo.com A 4-star hotel with 135 a/c rooms. A resort-style hotel with pools, restaurant, shopping boutique and games, all right on the beach. All-inclusive packages available.

In addition to the various hotel restaurants mentioned above, there are many restau- **Eating** rants to choose from. At the **northern end of town** is *Coconut Café*, pizzas, pastries and the best fish on the beach. Check the *sodas* for good breakfasts and cheap evening meals. *El Cocodrilo* has nice gardens serving seafood and cool drinks. *El Vaquero* pro-vides a Mexican flavour to national dishes. *Johann's Bakery* is a long-standing favour-ite selling freshly baked bread and bagels. There are also reports of a new *Thai* restaurant next door.

Moving south is *El Milagro* is an atmospheric spot with mid-priced surf and turf among spotlighted gardens. It's a relaxed atmosphere, with attentive service. The pool could be a little too close for comfort if things start getting silly. *El Delfin*, mid-way down the main street, open early for breakfast, serving cheap snacks and dishes throughout the day. *Heladería Artika* serves good ice cream, fine coffee and cigars – probably best not to try them all at once.

Away from the main street is *La Merediana*, T653-0230. Crisp linen table cloths, candles flickering in the gentle breeze rustling through the palms. Heavenly Italian food, served with elegance and charm. Will collect you from your hotel if you call in advance. Expensive, but oh so good.

A small park-cum-turning circle at the south of town is a hive of activity at night. *Bar-Restaurant ZullyMar* (mid-range) is on the beach serving a mix of seafood and national dishes, in a lively setting. *El Arrecife,* popular spot to hang out, for good chicken and pizzas. *Fiesta del Mar* at the end of the road, is a pricey open-air restau-rant. *La Baula Pizzeria* is a lively spot, serving simple fare and pizzas, popular with the beach crowd. *Pedro's Restaurant* at the end of the road right on the beach, is a simple diner serving seafood. *Portofino* is the stopping off point for ice creams.

Following the road inland *La Terraza de Tamarindo* serves good Italian dishes with a fine view from the balcony restaurant. *Pacho's Bar & Restaurant* or *Yucca*, (depend-ing on whether the mood is good or very good) at *Pasatiempo*, positively throbs with the gringo crowd ordering from the truly international menu that squeezes in local, Italian, Tex Mex, Thai and a few other influences. Popular, lively joint with occasional live music.

Across the road *El Fuego* is a charmingly quiet, secluded spot with tables scattered around a plant-filled patio courtyard. Good music in the background accompanies the cheap all-day menu, which flourishes with mid-priced international dishes in the evening. *Iguana Surf* on the road to Playa Langosto is a lively restaurant and bar. Good atmosphere and mid-priced food.

Diving and surfing *Agua Rica Diving Center*, T/F653-0094, www.aguarica.net 2-tank **Tour operators** dive from US$65, resort dive US$115, full certification US$350. *Iguana Surf*, T653-0148, www.tamarindo.com/iguana Specializes in surf gear and all aquatic rentals including jet

The Nicoya Peninsula

skis and hobie cats. They have a couple of offices, a small shack on the main street close to the beach, and the main office, with a restaurant, a couple of blocks inland. Also provide snorkelling tours, kayak tours of the estuary, a surf taxi and surfing lessons.

Fishing *Tamarindo Sportfishing*, T/F653-0090, www.tamarindosportfishing.com *Talking Fish* is a 38' Topaz Express carrying 6 people in the shade. Half day US$575, full day US$975. Captain Randy Wilson is highly recommended. *Warren Sellers Sportfishing*, T653-0186, F653-0248, www.wssportfishing.com, is also highly recommended with over 25 years' experience fishing in Costa Rica. Prices start at US$395 inshore, US$525 offshore.

Cruises Coastal cruises can be taken on *Samonique*, T/F394-4152 www.costarica-sailing.com Sunset cruises start at US$45 including fresh fruit and snacks. Full and half day tours look for dolphins and turtles with stops for snorkelling.

Land and water *Papagayo Excursions*, T653-0254, F653-0227, papagayoexcursions.com A good selection of local tours, with others going beyond the immediate area, including Rincón de la Vieja, Santa Rosa and Palo Verde National Parks and sailing charters and sunset tours. *Tamarindo Adventures*, T653-0108, F653-0640, tamaquad@sol.racsa.co.cr Full range of tours and rentals including boards, kayaks, snorkelling equipment and for transport choose from mountain bikes, scooters, dirt bikes and ATVs (All Terrain Vehicles). **Golfers** can head out to one of 3 courses in the area. The newest in the area is to the south on Playa Langosto where you'll find the *Hacienda Pinilla*, T680-3000, www.haciendapinilla.com North of Tamarindo is the *Royal Pacific* and at the *Meliá Playa Conchal Beach Resort* is the *Garra de León*. You'll be looking at the best part of US$100 for a round with clubs.

Entertainment *Diria Casino* is on the main street hidden behind *Heladería Artika*. *Disco Noai* is the place to spend the night dancing and drinking til the early hours.

Shopping There are several shops and impromptu stalls at the southern end of the main road selling jewellery, T-shirts, sarongs and other beachwear. *Palm Shop* supermarket is a one-stop shop for most things you'll want in Tamarindo. Surf and boogie boards for rent (US$6 and US$4 for ½ day), laundry (US$3.50 per kilo, min 3 kg), turtle tours to Playa Grande and the mangrove estuaries of Palo Seco, and *SANSA* airline representative, T653-0002, F653-0003, altamara@sol.racsa.co.cr *Maresias Surf Shop* is close to the southern end of town.

Directory **Banks** *Banco Nacional*, open Mon-Fri, 0830-1545, Visa ATM. **Communications** Internet: *Interlink* has a couple of much sought after computers. Above *Maresias Surf Shop* there's a new internet service and others can be expected to open up. **Language School** *Wayra Institute de Español*, T/F653-0359, www.spanish-wayra.co.cr 20-hr week-long morning or afternoon courses from US$200. Discounts for longer courses. A couple of student houses in Playa Tamarindo or homestays can be arranged – which is much better for your Spanish.

Santa Cruz

Colour map 1, grid B3 Heading from Liberia down Highway 21, the first town of any real size is Santa Cruz (52 km), with a population of just under 18,000 in the surrounding area. Known as Costa Rica's 'National Folklore City', January is the month for the festival of *Santo Cristo de Esquipulas* with colourful fiestas, dancing and regional food. (July 25 is Guanacaste Day and the town also celebrates this in some style with dancing and music.)

The Nicoya Peninsula

For much of the rest of the year, it's a quiet little town serving as a transport and supply hub for the northern half of the peninsula. If you're heading for self-catering accommodation, Santa Cruz is a good place to stock up on the basics. Activity focuses on a rather bare square called Plaza de los Mangoes. While in town, take a look at the modern **church**, in the main square 600 m south, with its fine stain glass images spraying a rainbow of colours across the congregation. The tower of the old church stands monument to earthquakes that shake the region with reliable frequency.

Sleeping & eating

B *Diriá*, at the entrance to town on the main highway, T680-0080, F680-0442, hoteldiria@hotmail.com Most comfortable option in town with 50 rooms with private bath, hot water and TV. Clean, tidy and spacious, with a couple of pools. The motel-style **C-D** *La Pampa*, 25 m west of Plaza de los Mangoes, T680-0586. 25 simple rooms, some with a/c, all with private bath with *agua natural*. Good and central with plenty of parking. **D** *Plaza*, without a sign above the small shopping mall on the west side of the plaza, T680-0169. Simple rooms, but clean and some spectacular ideas for garish interior design. **E** *Anatolia*, 200 m south and one block west of Plaza de los Mangoes, T680-0333. Small dark rooms, with plywood partitions and dirty bathrooms. One block east of the main plaza is **G** *Pensión Isabel*, T680-0173. Simple box rooms.

Several *sodas* dotted around town. *Coopetortilla*, 200 m south of the main square, is a local institution. A women's cooperative, cooking local dishes of *casadas* and *pinto gallo* on wooden fires. Very cheap and enjoyable.

Transport

Bus Buses leave and arrive from terminals on the north side of Plaza de los Mangoes. Buses leave **San José** from Av 3, C 18-20. 9 buses a day from 0700-1800, 4½ hrs, US$5. An hourly service goes to **Liberia**, 0530-1930, US$1, and **Nicoya**, 0630-2130, US$0,35. Buses to **Tamarindo** leave at 2030, US$1, returning at 0645. Buses to **Playa Flamingo** and nearby beaches every 90 mins with El Folklorico.

Directory

Banks *Banco Nacional*, with ATM, at junction with the main road. **Communications** **Post office** 200 m south of Plaza de los Mangoes.

Excursions

Guatil

An easy and worthwhile excursion meandering through cattle pastures and small settlements, the town of Guatil is out 12 km from Santa Cruz. The neat lines of pots and plates seen laid out along the road in parts of the peninsula are mostly produced in this small town that has retained traditional skills for making the hand-built and oven-baked red and black pieces.

The tiny linear town has a few studios easily found along the road. Drop in and have a look at what is on offer. If you're interested in the manufacturing process, stick your head round the back and nose around – with luck, you'll get the full low-down on the techniques and the plants used to make the dyes. Naturally items are for sale as well, with prices slightly cheaper than stalls along the main road. Buses leave Santa Cruz every couple of hours.

Sleeping, eating & tours

In the community of Bolsón, 22 km east of Santa Cruz, you can stay in simple accommodation with the local families at **B** *CoopeOrtega*, c/o Simbiosis Tours T/F286-4203, www.agroecoturismo.net which is part of the Cooprena network of community-based projects. There are opportunities for exploring the Bolsón, Charco and Tempisque rivers on foot or horseback to see crocodiles, birds and the views of Palo Verde National Park and to experience typical food, dances and music from the region.

The Nicoya Peninsula

Playa Junquillal

Colour map 1, grid C2   The long golden sand beach at Playa Junquillal about 30 km west of Santa Cruz is one of the cleanest beaches in Costa Rica and provides quiet solitude without being so deserted that you feel stranded. The beach has some good surf, and several hotels have gear for hire, but essentially it's more laid-back than many other coastal areas on. Behind the beach, extensive mangroves can be explored. Ask at your hotel, or contact Bernardo Sanchez at *Hotel Playa Junquillal*.

Sleeping
Hotels in order from north to south

AL-A *Iguanazul*, T653-0124, F653-0123, www.iguanazul.com 24 tiled-roof cabins sleeping up to 4 people of varying size and locations some with ocean and poolside views. Ceramic tiled flooring with pleasant wooden touches finish off the comfortable rooms, equipped with private bath, a/c and a fan. A small pool, bar and restaurant with a new daily menu is perfect for relaxing. Popular with surfers for trips to nearby breaks, there's also a surf school package if you want to learn. Activity junkies will be kept happy with kayaking, horse riding, volleyball, pool and table tennis. Fishing trips easily arranged, and a small gift shop selling good souvenirs.

B *El Castillo Divertado*, T653-0428, www.hostelling-costarica.com 7 rooms, all with private bath, hot water and fan. A funky tribute to extravagant architecture in this turreted hotel complete with towers. Slightly cheaper for youth hostel members.

A *Guacamaya Lodge*, perched up on the hill with fine views to the west, T/F653-0431, www.guacamayalodge.com 6 immaculately maintained bungalows and a fully-equipped house. Each bungalow has a private bathroom, with a gentle sea breeze drifting through the airy spacious rooms, and a small terrace. The pool is close to the lofty *Rancho* bar and restaurant serving Swiss and local specialities. A good choice. Next is **A** *El Lugarcito B&B*, T/F653-0436, which looks good but was closed when passing. **A-C** *Tatanka*, T/F653-0426. 10 simple cabins with private bath, in a line facing the pool. Stylish open-air restaurant serving a mix of Italian, French and *Tico* dishes.

Just 50 m from the beach is **B-C** *Hibiscus*, T/F653-0437. 5 big, fresh rooms positively basking in natural light, each with hot water private bath and fan. Well-tended gardens lead to the small restaurant serving seafood and German specialities.

On the beach is **B** *Playa Junquillal*, T653-0432, hotel@playa-junquillal.com 5 cabins sleeping up to 4 people. Fairly basic with a refreshingly chaotic feel to the place, but a good bargain if in a group and the only place actually on the beach. Simple open-air bar and restaurant serving traditional dishes. The manager Bernard Sánchez can organize trips through mangroves set back from the coastal strip.

AL *Land Ho at Villa Serena*, T/F658-8430, www.crica.com/hotels/landho.html 12 spacious rooms and private cabins each with tiled bathroom, a/c and fan. Early morning breakfast room service. Piano bar next to the restaurant serving Costa Rican and international dishes, with *La Tortuga Bar* down by the pool. Wide range of activities including pool, tennis court, full massage services.

Camping At the northern entrance to town – 800 m off the main road down a signposted dirt track after *Iguanazul* – is **G** per person *Camping Los Malinches*, T/F653-0429. Spectacular location up on the bluff overlooking the sea. Clean bathroom and toilets provided. Well worth the effort to get here, but bring all your own food.

Eating   In addition to the hotel restaurants there is *La Puesta del Sol*, T653-0442. The only stand alone restaurant in the bay, but then nothing could compete with the dishes served up that make this a little piece of Italy. US$10-15 a dish in a divine garden setting. Reservations recommended.

Transport   **Bus** Daily bus from **Santa Cruz** departs 1030, returns at 1530.

Nicoya

Colour map 1, grid C3
Population: 25,000

At the heart of the peninsular, Nicoya is a pleasant little market town, distinguished by possessing the country's second oldest church. Like Santa Cruz, Nicoya is an important regional transport and supply centre, with links to the beach communities of Sámara and Nosara to the south, the Tempisque ferry to the east, and Playa Naranjo on the southeastern tip of the peninsula.

The church of **San Blas** has a pulpit dating back to the 16th century, while the actual building was consecrated in 1644. Looking every part its age, the church has undergone periodic renovation, with the latest scheduled for completion sometime in 2001.

For most of the year the town beats to the gently percussive rhythm of commerce. On the 12th Dec the town lets its hair down by celebrating the *Fiesta de la Yegüita*, with dancing parades, fireworks, bullfights and music.

Sleeping

The best option close to town is **B** *Complejo Turístico Curime*, 500 m south of the centre on the road to Sámara, T685-5238, F685-5530. 26 bungalows and rooms, all with hot water private bath. A/c and a fridge in the bungalows, fans in the rooms. The rooms and hotel need a fresh lick of paint but there's a curious blend of luxury options including an airstrip and a 3-m deep swimming pool. Price includes breakfast.

In the centre of town, **D** *Jenny*, or Yenny as the sign says, T685-5050, T686-6471. 24 spotless rooms with bath, a/c, towels, soap and TV. Friendly helpful staff. Cavernous rooms – book in with a friend and play hide and seek. Recommended. **E** *Las Tinajas*, opposite the bus stop to Liberia on Av 1, T685-5081, F685-5777. 28 rooms with bath, modern, clean and good value. **E** *Pensión Venecia*, opposite old church on square, T685-5325, squidgy beds but good value for the price. **F** *Chorotega*, C Central, Av 4-6, T685-5245, with bath (**F** without), very good value, clean, quiet – rooms at back have windows. Clothes washing facilities.

Eating

Many good, simple places to eat around the main plaza. *Daniela* has good breakfast, lunches, coffee and *refrescos*. *Teyo* is good with quick service if you're in a hurry. Opposite *Chorotega* is *Soda El Triángulo* with good juices and snacks, friendly owners. *Café de Blita*, 2 km out of Nicoya on the road to Sámara has been recommended.

Nicoya

Sleeping ■
1 Chorotega
2 Jenny
3 Las Tinajas
4 Pensión Venecia

Eating ●
1 Daniela
2 Soda El Triangulo
3 Teyo

Transport

Bus 7 daily buses with Empresa Alfaro (Av 5, C 15, T222-2666) from **San José**, a couple via the ferry, the rest through Liberia, 4-5 hrs, US$5.20. Hourly service between **Liberia** 0430-1900 and **Santa Cruz** 0630-2130. To **Playa Naranjo** at 0500 and 1300, US$1.45, 2¼ hrs. 5 buses a day to **Sámara**, 1 to **Nosara**.

Directory

Banks An excess of banks with a branch of *Banco de Costa Rica* on the main square with an ATM, and branches of *Banco Popular* and *Banco Nacional* a couple of blocks up Calle 3. **Communications** The post office is on the corner of the main square. **Useful addresses** The *Area de Conservación Tempisque* (ACT) office is on the north side of the square. While there is limited information for visitors, they can help with enquiries about protected areas and visits to nearby Barra Honda National Park.

Parque Nacional Barra Honda

Colour map 1, grid B4   A limestone outcrop to the west of Nicoya creates the largest cave system in Costa Rica and forms the heart of Barra Honda National Park (2,295 ha). Rising to a plateau of just over 500 m, the steep sided hills are the result of fault movements. A network of 42 caves have been discovered to date, with only 19 having been officially explored, making this a focus of attention for the serious spelunker.

Ins & outs   **Getting there** First go to Nicoya, from where there are several buses a day to Quebrada Honda on the road to the Tempisque ferry (first bus 1030, last bus returns for Nicoya 1630, giving you only 2 hrs in the park). Ask the bus driver to drop you off on the road to Barra Honda (Nacaome), from where it is a 1-hr walk to Santa Ana and the park offices.

Entrance If you wish to visit the caves you will need harnesses, ropes and guides as entrance to the cave is from the top. Cost of entrance to the park is US$6, a guide costs US$33, with US$11 per person for equipment. Caving is inherently dangerous in the rainy season (May to Nov), and the dry season is very hot making it essential that you have more than enough water for your stay.

Sights   Because access is fairly difficult, the Barra Honda caves are in excellent condition. Most people enter through the **Terciopelo Cave**, which is richly adorned with stalactites and stalagmites – formed by deposits of calcium carbonate and the trickling of water from the roof of the caves. The flutes of one, *The Organ*, provide accompaniment to the eerie darkness, producing musical notes when gently tapped. **Santa Ana** cave descends for over 240 m, while the **Trampa** cave has the longest single vertical descent at 52 m. The musty aroma is interrupted at the **Pozo Hediondo** (Stinking Pothole) – named after the only cave with a large bat population, whose droppings produce the smell. **Nicoa cave** stands out for mention – human remains and precolumbian artefacts have been found here.

Above ground there are a few **trails** leading up and across the plateau with fine views across the peninsula and the Gulf of Nicoya. One trail leads to **La Cascada** – an impressive waterfall flowing over calcium deposits, but you'll need a guide to get here as the trails are hopelessly muddled by cow paths.

Sleeping   E *Las Delicias Ecotourism Project*, T685-5580. Simple but comfortable accommodation is available in 3 bungalows, owned and operated by the local community at the park entrance. **Camping** is permitted (**F**) with meals at reasonable prices, as well as guided tours.

Western beaches

Nosara

Colour map 1, grid C3
Area website at
www.nosara.com
or www.nosara-
costa-rica.com

Nosara is a small village about 26 km north of Sámara without much to see or do in it – which makes it ideal if you like lying around on beaches. Indeed most people come for the three unspoiled beaches which are a few kilometres from the village. **Playa Nosara** is to the north of the village across the Nosara river, and a site for nesting turtles (see 'Ostional', below). **Playa Pelada**, the prettiest and smallest, south of the river between rocky headlands, is a popular spot for surfers and has a bat cave at one end which is good to explore – ask locally for details. **Playa Guiones** is a long expanse of white sand backed by low dunes and forest, with good, long surf breaks.

Nosara is one of the few places where there is no development on the beach and that contributes in large measure to the appeal of the area. Much of the property backing Pelada and Guiones is owned by North Americans and Europeans, and the hills above Nosara are dotted with the holiday homes of the rich and famous. Some of the expatriate community have joined together to form the *Nosara Civic Association*, which keeps control over development and protects the habitat and wildlife

Unfortunately, Nosara is not a good destination for those on a budget or those without a car. It's popular with surfers and people with money, and it's more of a place to stay rather than somewhere to just pass through.

Nosara village is about 5 km north of Playa Guiones – it's a very long, hot walk and there **Getting around** is no bus but hitching is possible if you're prepared to do it in sections. The roads between the main road and the beach are labyrinthine and finding the beach or your hotel can be tricky; look for signs along the main road indicating where to turn off. For Playa Pelada follow signs to *Olga's Restaurant* or *La Luna*. To get to Playa Guiones, turn off at *Café de Paris* and follow the road straight on to the beach.

The main local attraction is a visit to Ostional to see the mass nestings of the **Sights** olive ridley sea turtles (see below). Other activities include hiking in the privately-owned **Reserve Biológica Nosara**, T682-0035. Most hotels arrange horseback tours along the beaches, through hills or to a nearby waterfall. Boat and canoe trips ride into the mangrove swamps of the Nosara River. Of course fishing is possible and all things beach related – surfing, boogie boards, snorkelling gear – can be rented.

North end High above Punta Pelada with amazing views over both beaches, the ocean **Sleeping:** and the hills behind is **L** *Playa de Nosara*, T682-0121, F682-0123, www. **Playa Pelada** nosarabeachhotel.com A colonial-style hotel with 22 white and wooden rooms, deco- *Hotels in Nosara* rated with wall hangings, dotted around the grounds with a pool, jacuzzi and restaurant. *charge more and offer* Number one for location, trails lead to the beach. Surf packages available. *less than hotels in*

A *Lagarta Lodge*, T682-0035, F682-0135, www.lagarta.com 7 pleasant rooms *Sámara. When* overlooking the ocean, forest and hills, all with bath, hot water and fan. Good restau- *booking, check* rant, pool and tours offered. A beautiful setting, the hotel owns a private reserve and *whether your hotel* has a telescope for wildlife viewing making it a great choice for nature lovers and those *accepts credit cards* in search of a quiet getaway. Recommended. **A-B** *Rancho Suizo*, T682-0057, F682-0055, www.nosara.ch 10 rustic bungalows with bath, and fans, in pleasant trop- ical gardens. jacuzzi, bar and restaurant with good food, breakfast included. A quiet spot, not for raucous party-goers, with eco-friendly tours, boogie boards, snorkels, bicycles for hire. Popular with Europeans but no children under 10.

B *Hotel Almost Paradise*, T/F682-0173, www.nosara.net A rustic, pretty place in the hills above Playa Pelada, with 5 rooms sleeping 2-4 people, with bath, hot water, fan and balcony with superb view. It is a quiet hotel for people who like wildlife and hotels with character, with lots of greenery, art on the walls, a restaurant and bar. Excellent value in the low season. Recommended. Just off the road a couple of kilo- metres south of the village is **B** *Hotel Estancia*, T/F682 0178 or 0176, estangis@sol.racsa.co.cr 10 rooms for up to 4 people with hot water bath, some with fan others with a/c. Quiet and pleasant, there's a pool, laundry and tours service.

The Nicoya Peninsula

Middle **A** *Casa Romántica*, T/F682-0019, casroma@racsa.co.cr A quiet, beautiful hotel near the beach with 8 big rooms good for couples and families, with hot water bath and fan. Breakfast is included in the price, and there's an excellent international restaurant managed by the Swiss owners. Tours easily arranged. Recommended. Run by the same people as Lagarta Lodge is **A-B** *Giardino Tropicale*, T682-0258. Rooms with hot water private bath and fan. Good value in the off season. Restaurant serves good pizza.

B *Rancho Congo*, T/F682-0078. 2 big rooms with bath, hot water, fans and terrace set in natural gardens with lots of native plants. Close to the beach, it's also good for observing wildlife. The German owner provides a very good breakfast for the price, with discounts for longer stays and personalised tours. Excellent value. **B-C** *Gilded Iguana*, T/F682-0259, www.gildediguana.com 4 huge, airy double rooms in the woods with bath, hot water and fan. Owned by a gregarious and cool gringo called Joe, good restaurant and bar decorated with hand-painted ceramic tiles, water sports and tours, especially kayaks and fishing. A bargain – especially the cheaper room.

South end **AL** *Casa Tucan*, T/F682-0113, www.casatucan.net 8 units sleeping up to 4 people have hot water bath and a/c, some with kitchens. Attractive outdoor restaurant and bar, there's also a pool and tours easily arranged. Popular with surfers, it's also a little overpriced. **A** *Villa Taype*, T682-0333, F682-0187, www.villataype.com 32 rooms, some private bungalows, all with bath, a/c, phone, some with TV. Wide range of services with a couple of pools, restaurant and bar, laundry, parking, tennis, table tennis, surf board rental. Large, characterless hotel run by German-Tico family, very close to beach. Overpriced, but popular with surfers. On the road is **A-B** *Hotel de Paris*, T682-0087, F682-0089, www.cafedeparis.net 14 airy rooms and some bungalows – 4 with full kitchen – with hot water bath, a/c or fan. Activity central, there's a pool, pool table, basketball, surf boards and snorkelling equipment. Other services include laundry, car rental, tours, flights and internet. The friendly French-Swiss owners also have a couple of villas with sea views for around US$700 a week. The place is popular with surfers and young groups. Families and groups welcome, and disabled access.

B *Casa Rio Nosara*, T682-0117, F682-0182, www.tropical-holiday.com 6 rustic A-frame cabins about 2 km south of the village, on the river, all with bath, hot water and fan with use of the kitchen and barbecue. Very friendly German owners have lots of animals, including 18 well looked-after horses – they specialize in riding holidays, horseback tours and river tours. Perfect for outdoors and animal-lovers.

D-E *Alan's Surf Camp*, T682-0251, michaelg@sol.racsa.co.cr Rooms almost on the beach with bunkbeds and shared

Nosara

To Playa Ostional

Nosara Village

Airstrip

Playa Nosara

Playa Pelada

Pacific Ocean

Playa Guiones

0 km 1
0 mile 1

N

■ **Sleeping**
1 Alan Surf's Camp
2 Almost Paradise
3 Cabinas Agnell
4 Casa Romántica
5 Casa Tucán
6 Estancia
7 Giardino Tropicale
8 Gilded Iguana
9 Hotel de Paris
10 Lagarta Lodge
11 Olas Grande
12 Playa de Nosara
13 Rancho Suizo
14 Villa Taype

● **Eating**
1 Bambú
2 Disco Tropicana
3 La Dolce Vita
4 La Luna
5 Olga's

bath. It's a very chilled surfer hang-out, very relaxed with a friendly manager and discounts for longer stays. Not for your granny, but good value.

In the village Near the supermarket is **E** *Cabinas Chorotega*, T682-0129. Very clean rooms with shared or private bath, fan, bar and restaurant downstairs, can be noisy. **F** *Cabinas Agnell*, T682-0142. All rooms with bath, cold showers and fan. Recommended.

Camping You can camp at *Olas Grande*, in the middle near the *Gilded Iguana*.

At Playa Pelada, try *Olga's* for seafood on the beach, or *La Luna* slightly up the hill for good food and ambience. The restaurant at *Hotel Almost Paradise* serves good food with a great view. **Eating & drinking**

In the middle section, try *Giardino Tropicale* for pizza, the European restaurant at *Casa Romantica* or the *Gilded Iguana* for gringo food and good company.

South, is the restaurant at *Café de Paris*, recommended, or outdoor *Casa Tucan* towards the beach. *Alan's Surf Camp* does surfers' breakfasts. Finally, south along the road out of town, is *La Dolce Vita* for good but pricey Italian food.

There are plenty of *sodas* in the village, including *Soda Vanessa* which is good and very cheap. Some of the funkier nightlife is in the village as well including *Bambú*, *Disco Tropicana* and various other hang-outs lining the football pitch.

There are several *pulperías* in the village, and a supermarket just beyond the airfield as you drive into the centre. **Shopping**

Most hotels will arrange tours, but if you're not staying at one of them, *Casa Rio Nosara* is recommended for horse or river tours, and *Captain Joe's Jungle Expeditions* at the *Gilded Iguana* for kayaking and fishing. You can also go fishing with *Captain Woody's* charters, T682-0307. For turtle tours, try *Rancho Suizo* or *Lagarta Lodge* who are both sensitive to the turtles and don't exploit or bother them. You can get a healing energy massage from Betty Coe Reiner, T682-0082, by appointment only. **Tour operators**

Air *SANSA* and *Travelair* have early morning daily flights from **San José**, 40 mins, US$66 one way. **Bus** A direct bus from **San José** leaves Av 5 and C 14 at 0600, 6 hrs, US$6. The bus returns at 1245. Tickets available from Soda Vanessa. There is also a daily bus to and from **Nicoya** at 0600, 90 mins. **Transport**

Banks There is no bank in Nosara – change money at hotels. **Communications** Try the *Nosara office centre* - although there are reports that it has closed down – in the village which offers email, fax, international calls and photocopies. Open 0900-1200, 1330-1700, Mon-Fri, 0900-1300, Sat. **Language Schools** The *Rey de Nosara Escuela de Idiomas*, in the village on T682-0215, www.reydenosara.itgo.com They also act as an impromptu information office, with advice about other things to see and do in the area and can arrange tours. **Directory**

Refugio Nacional de Vida Silvestre Ostional

North of Nosara is **Playa Ostional** a wide beach protected for the natural spectacle of the *arribada* when tens of thousands of olive ridley turtles arrive en masse in frenzied acts of nest building. Along with Playa Nancite to the north, Ostional is one of the most important nesting sites for the *lora* (olive ridley turtle) in the world. *Colour map 1, grid C2*

The *arribadas* – literally 'arrivals' – occur between July and November with the largest numbers arriving between August and October, at the end of the

The Nicoya Peninsula

lunar cycle. If for some reason you overlook arranging your vacation around the phases of the moon, don't worry, you can normally see some turtle activity at any time of the month. As with humans, you'll always find one turtle that just has to be different! The beach is also occasionally used by the leatherback and Pacific green turtle.

Ostional is also interesting in that locals are permitted to harvest turtle eggs under a strict, and now well-developed, programme that incorporates conservation goals with the genuine needs and requirements of the local community.

The beach is part of the wider **Ostional National Wildlife Refuge** recently expanded, protecting 352 ha of land reserve, including Nosara beach, with a marine zone of 8,000 ha. The sparse vegetation in the reserve supports mixed deciduous forest species with good populations of howler and capuchin monkeys. On the northern banks of the Río Nosara, large mangrove swamps are home to over 100 species of birds – a good spot to slowly explore by kayak.

■ *Day and evening trips to the nesting grounds are easily arranged through local hotels. If driving, Ostional is a 30-min drive north of Nosara. Visit the MINAE Ranger Station for more details. Four-wheel drive needed in rainy season if coming from Sámara. There is one daily bus at 0500 to Santa Cruz and Liberia, returns at 1230 from Santa Cruz, 3 hrs, US$1.75.*

Sleeping & eating

There is very basic accommodation in cabins next to the village shop, **F** per person *Cabinas Ostional*, with bath, clean, friendly; also *Cabinas Guacamaya*, with bath. Clean, good food on request. You can camp on the beach, but ask locally for permission about where. 1 km south of *Cabinas Guacamaya* is *Mirador de los Tortugueros*, a good restaurant with coffee and pancakes, good atmosphere.

Sámara

Colour map 1, grid C3

Area website at www.samarabeach. com – very good

Sámara is a smallish *Tico* village that has managed to maintain some of its regular way of life alongside steady tourist development. It also has one of the best bathing beaches in Costa Rica. The place is gradually becoming more developed, but it has a relaxed pace and with a gentle trickle of international residents from around the world, the place is genuinely cosmopolitan and is a good excuse to get away for a few days and relax by the sea.

Sleeping

L-AL *Hotel Isla Chora*, T656-0174, F656-0173, www.samarabeach.com/islachora/index.html Tourist complex at the western end of town with 10 a/c double rooms with bath and balcony. 4 apartments sleep up to 4, with bath, a/c and kitchen. Safes available. Pool, disco and restaurant in high season. Price includes breakfast. Overpriced and nothing special. Rising up the hill above the village with great views is **AL** *(Aparthotel) Mirador de Sámara*, T656-0044, F656-0046, www.miradordesamara.com 6 large, cool and comfortable suites with bath and kitchen, all with private balconies, breakfast served in the tower if desired, pool, internet access, tours arranged around Sámara and further afield. German-owned and very friendly. Recommended. East of town on the beach is **AL** *Las Brisas*, T656-0250, F656-0076, www.brisas.net Large, 34-bungalow complex with bath, fan or a/c. Italian-owned. It's a little bland but personal touches and pleasantly landscaped. Pricey restaurant.

On the beach, about 2 km east of the village in a residential area is **A** *Hotel Fénix*, T656-0158, F656-0162, www.fenixhotel.com 6 slightly cramped double units, sleeping up to 4), with fans, hot water private bath, kitchens, very small pool, run by a couple from Seattle. Boat tours and watersports offered. No restaurant, but close to local eateries. **A** *Sámara Beach*, central T656-0218, F656-0326, www.hotelsamarabeach.com 20 rooms for 2-4 people, with fan or a/c, all with bath (some with tub and bidet) and most have balconies. Pool, restaurant, parking, internet access, tours arranged. Generally rather bland and a bit overpriced.

A-D *Cantamar*, (also known as *Cabinas Don Jaime*), T656-0284, F656-0368. A cabin with fan and kitchen on the beach (**A-B**), and other rooms, **B** with bath, **D** without. Don Jaime is an artist who exhibits and sells his work around the country – he's a very interesting man and you can talk to him endlessly about art and other matters. Great for a peaceful or longer stay.

Sloping up the hill is **B** *Belvedere*, T/F656-0213, www.samarabeach.com/belvedere/index.html 10 double rooms sleeping 2-4 people, all with private bath and solar-heated hot water, some with a/c, cheaper with fans. Swimming pool, jacuzzi and a comfortable family atmosphere with very friendly German owners. Also have a couple of flats sleeping up to 4 for longer stays. Ultralite aerial tours reported to be available. Recommended. **B** *Casa Naranja*, T656-0220. 2 rooms available in this funky private French house, both with bath, hot water, fan and breakfast included. A bar and restaurant serving mid-range, mainly French food, are open to non-guests with live music during the season. Very cool and very orange. On the main road is the Italian-owned **B** *Giada*, T656-0132, F656-0131, www.hotelgiada.net 13 pleasantly decorated rooms with attractive bathrooms, hot water, fan and balcony. Hand-painted touches, pool, laundry, dolphin and horse tours offered. Internet access for guests. **B** *Los Chalets*, T656-0219 or T280-5536, F222-5946. Swiss-style chalets with bath and fan. Closed when visited, but has a good reputation. **B** Opposite is *Marbella*, T656-0121, F656-0122, www.marbella.com This recently renovated and German-run hotel has nice grounds, pool and good service.

Sámara

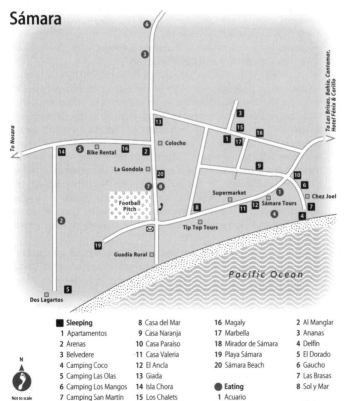

Sleeping		
1 Apartamentos	8 Casa del Mar	16 Magaly
2 Arenas	9 Casa Naranja	17 Marbella
3 Belvedere	10 Casa Paraíso	18 Mirador de Sámara
4 Camping Coco	11 Casa Valeria	19 Playa Sámara
5 Camping Las Olas	12 El Ancla	20 Sámara Beach
6 Camping Los Mangos	13 Giada	
7 Camping San Martín	14 Isla Chora	● Eating
	15 Los Chalets	1 Acuario

2 Al Manglar	
3 Ananas	
4 Delfín	
5 El Dorado	
6 Gaucho	
7 Las Brasas	
8 Sol y Mar	

N

Not to scale

The Nicoya Peninsula

B-C *Casa del Mar*, T656-0264, F656-0129, www.casadelmarsamara.com French-owned hotel near the beach with 11 simple rooms with bath, 6 with shared bath, a/c is US$10 extra. Breakfast is included and there's a safe, laundry, jacuzzi in gardens, and plans to reopen the restaurant. Also a suite for 6 available. The cheaper rooms are an excellent deal off-season. **B-D** *Casa Valeria*, on the beach T656-0511. Various different rooms, some with sea view, all nicely decorated, most with hot water and private bath. Friendly and good value, especially for 3 sharing. Breakfast included, kitchen and laundry available and a small bar. Tours, tickets and car hire arranged.

C *Apartamentos*, next to *Hotel Marbella*, T656-0609. Catering to a predominantly *Tico* crowd, units have bath, fridge, fan and kitchen. Good value and often full. **C** *Bahia*, on the beach near Las Brisas. Tired-looking rooms with bath and fan sleeping up to 3. The *Tico* owner works in the post office – ask if there is room before trekking out there. Restaurant serves *típica* and western food. **C** *Casa Paraíso*. Several high-ceilinged, airy rooms with bath, cold showers and king-size beds. No frills but friendly and well-run by the French owners, better value if sharing with several people.

E *Arenas*, in the centre of town, T656-0320. 12 basic but clean rooms with bath, cold showers, fan, use of sink to wash clothes, friendly *Tico* owner and parrot. *Típica* restaurant in the high season, discounts for longer stays. **E** per person *El Ancla*, T656-0254. Clean and simple rooms with bath and fan on the beach. Friendly and good value. **E-F** *Hotel Playa Sámara*, T656-0190. A large hotel with lots of grimy rooms, all with bath and fan, feels like a scene from Escape from Alcatraz. A last resort. **E-F** *Magaly*. has 7 basic rooms with fan, 4 with bath, 3 sharing. Extremely friendly and very clean *Tico*-owned place Discounts for longer stays.

Camping On the eastern side of the village, on the beach, try **G** per person *Camping Coco*, T656-0496, toilets, electricity until 2200 or **G** per person *Camping San Martin*, T656-0336, same family, same deal, around US$3 per person in highest season. Slightly further from the beach is *Camping Los Mangos*. At the other end of the village, near *Dos Lagartos* disco is *Camping Las Olas*.

Eating There are several cheap *sodas* around the football pitch in the centre of town. Up a notch, but still cheap, is *soda Sol y Mar*, serving a mixture of Costa Rican and western food. Opposite is *Las Brasas*, a mid-scale Spanish restaurant and bar. Other mid-scale restaurants include *Gaucho*, a short walk along the Nicoya road – cheaper *Ananas* is next door. On the beach next to *Cabinas El Ancla* is the very good-value French-owned *Restaurant Delfín*, they also have *cabinas*, **B**, and close by is the untried but newly reopened *Restaurant Acuario* serving *Tico* and snack food. A little way along the road to Cangrejal are *El Dorado*, *Tico* and pizza, and, towards the beach, *Al Manglar*, best pizza – turn left at *Hotel La Chora*. Most hotels have mid-scale restaurants – try *Casa Naranja*. You can buy food at the supermarket and *Boulangerie Chez Joel*, near the campgrounds on the east end of the village, sells excellent bread and *pain au chocolat*.

Bars & nightlife There are a few bars in town. *Bar La Gondola* is a popular hangout and opposite is *Bar Colocho*. *Dos Lagartos* disco is on the beach near Al Manglar and the disco at *Isla Chora* is apparently the place to be during the season – if you like resort discos.

Shopping There are various small shops and stalls selling clothing and souvenirs on the main road. The supermarket, near *Casa del Mar*, is well stocked and you can get fresh bread and croissants from *Chez Joel*, T656-0057. There is no pharmacy but some simple medicines are available in the supermarket.

Tour operators Most hotels will arrange tours for you. You can rent bikes from near the *ferretería* (ironmonger's) on the road to Cangrejal. Recommended, though, is the newer *Tip Top Tours*, T656-0650, run by a very nice French couple, offering the usual dolphin tours

The Nicoya Peninsula

from US$45, mangrove tours US$43 and waterfall tours US$20, naturalist guided tours to Barra Honda and Isla Chora US$70, as well as slightly more unusual trips like 'Journee Cowboy' where you spend a day on the ranch roping cattle and eat with a *Tico* family. Prices based on minimum of 2 people, discounts for groups of more than 4 people.

Air Daily flights to and from **San José** are operated by *SANSA*, US$66. **Bus** There is a **Transport** direct bus to **San José** at 0430 on Mon-Sat, 1300 Sun, up to 6 hrs. A good paved road, with a gas station a little way out of town towards Nicoya, leads from Sámara to **Nicoya** with 5 buses between 0530 and 1630, 1½ hrs. A school bus makes the journey to **Nosara** at about 1600 – ask locally for information on how to get on it. Official and pirate **taxis** stop outside the bus terminal. US$20 to Nosara, US$10 to Nicoya. You can **rent bikes** from a hardware store on the road to Cangrejal.

Banks There is no bank in Sámara, although some hotels will change money. **Com-** **Directory** **munications** Internet: There are no internet cafés in Sámara at present, although some hotels allow their guests to use their connections. **Post**: The post office is by the bus station, almost on the beach. **Telephone**: card operated public telephones are opposite the football field. **Laundry** Most hotels provide a laundry service.

Southern peninsula

From Nicoya Highway 21 continues southeast skirting close to the towns of Holancha and Carmona, before running along the eastern flank of the peninsula with fine views to the gulf, small villages with sodas and cafés for refreshment. Although the road is asphalted, it takes a fair pounding from large traffic and there are some axle crunching potholes on the road that almost stops at Playa Naranjo.

Ins and outs

Regular vehicle and passenger ferries leave Puntarenas for Playa Naranjo and further **Getting there** around the bay to Paquera. See Puntarenas, page 283 for details.

Buses meet the ferries arriving at Playa Naranjo providing transport north to Nicoya **Getting around** and the north of the peninsular. There is also bus transport from Paquera heading west to Tambor and Montezuma, which conveniently avoids the truly appalling dirt road that links Playa Naranjo and Paquera.

Playa Naranjo

Deceptive to the last, there are no oranges and only fair beaches in Playa *Colour map 1, grid C5* Naranjo which is little more than a ferry dock with a few over-priced *sodas*, a restaurant and a gas station.

If circumstances find you looking for accommodation try **A** *Oasis del Pacífico*, **Sleeping** T/F661-1555, www.costaricareisen.com/oasis An old building on the beach with 36 rooms with a/c, hot water bath, a pool and good restaurant. Good discounts in the rainy season. **B** *El Paso*, T/F661-2610, is a clean, slightly cheaper options, with rooms with private bath, cheaper without, and a pool. **D** *Cabinas Maquinay*, 1.3 km northwest towards Jicaral, T661-1763, has simple rooms, with a pool and the attached *Disco Maquinay*.

A small village 22 km along the coast from Playa Naranjo, Paquera is reached **Paquera** overland along one of Costa Rica's more deceptive roads. Seemingly a natural connection to the southernmost tip of the peninsula, the road climbs and falls over and around the rocky headland for the mind-numbingly slow trip towards the main tourist areas. If you're out exploring, a four-wheel drive is recommended for the bone-shaking journey. If you're coming from Puntarenas, get the boat to Paquera where there are a few shops and some simple lodgings, for example *Cabinas Rosita* on the inland side of the village. It is separated from the quay by a kilometre or so, where apart from a good *soda*, one restaurant, a public telephone, a petrol station and a branch of *Banco de Costa Rica*, there are few facilities. You will, however, find transport heading out to Tambor and beyond.

Playa Tambor

Colour map 1, inset From Paquera the road improves – the latest reports say the road has now been paved all the way to Montezuma. Once a quiet fishing village, Tambor makes for a pleasant and quiet stopping point, with a dark sand beach stretching for 6 km around Bahía Ballena. The town itself has a handful of shops and restaurants, but apart from that you'll be entertaining yourself all day lying on the beach and taking walks on the long sandy beaches.

Sleeping **L** *Tambor Tropical*, T683-0011, F683-0013, www.tambortropical.com 10 luxury
& eating cabinas created from tropical hardwoods that glow in the golden light of sunset. The fully-equipped cabinas have a small kitchenette or you can dine in the hotel restaurant. The hotel has a pool with gardens leading through to the beach, a jacuzzi and a positive attitude to encourage guests to do nothing… although tours and activities can be arranged.

AL *Costa Coral*, T683-0105, F683-0016, www.costacoral.com A blaze of colour found throughout the 6 villas with fully equipped kitchenette, private bath, a/c and fans, with a terrace. Bright, attentive service – just like the décor – with a pool and jacuzzi. Lively bar and excellent mid-range open-air restaurant. A refreshing change from the norm. **C-D** *Cabinas Cristina*, T683-0028. Has 6 simple clean rooms, with fans, on the beach. **C-D** *Dos Lagartos*, T/F683-0236, aulwes@costarica.net Good, clean rooms, some with private bath, others sharing, with fans. A small snack restaurant with a flower-filled garden leading to the beach. Good value and recommended. **D** *Cabinas del Bosque*, T683-0039. One of the cheapest options in town.

Out of town On the run into town from the north is **L** *Hotel Playa Tambor*, T683-0303, F683-0317, www.barcelo.com A 5-star all-inclusive resort with almost every amenity available including a private airstrip. With a focus on beach life and water activities, there is also a 9-hole golf course in the neighbouring *Los Delfines Golf and Country Club*. The *Barceló* group of Spain, walked into a storm of controversy with the construction of the *Hotel* and *Golf Club*. Built around a former cattle farm, the resort is alleged to have encroached on the public beach and drained mangrove swamps and wildlife habitats. A second stage is planned at Punta Piedra Amarilla, with a 500-ship yacht marina, villas and a total of 1,100 rooms.

South of town is **LL** *Tango Mar*, T683-0001, F683-0003, www.tangomar.com Full on comforts including their own private golf course and a spectacular waterfall nearby that crashes directly into a coastal rock pool.

Many of the hotels have there own restaurants including *Cabinas Cristina*, *Dos Lagartos* and the mid-range but stylish and excellent *Costa Coral*. The beach front restaurant in Tambor is also very good, serving up big portions of seafood dishes and hamburgers at cheap prices. If you fancy a bit of a walk try the *Bahía Ballena Yacht Club* which has a restaurant and bar that has received recommendations.

Services in the village are limited, with a few shops, a public telephone, a supermarket **Shopping**
and an agency for bicycle hire. *Tucán Boutique* sells a mix of goods including
beachwear, and will help with inquiries.

Air *Sansa* and *Travelair* both have scheduled daily flights from San José to *Tambor*, **Transport**
US$66. **Bus** The **Paquera-Montezuma** bus passes through town, meeting the ferries
to and from Puntarenas. Ask locals for latest times.

Peninsula and Gulf islands

Drifting off the southeastern tip of the Nicoya peninsula, a handful of *Colour map 1,*
sand-fringed islands are easily visited from the peninsula, Puntarenas or San *grid C5*
José. By far the most popular is a luxury cruise to **Isla Tortuga**, a pair of small
uninhabited islands just off the peninsula to the south of Curú with beautiful
white-sand beaches, crystal clear water ideal for swimming, snorkelling and
other aquatic malarkey and just a gentle hint of desert island feel. As one of the
most popular trips in Costa Rica – and marketed accordingly – don't expect
to have the place to yourself. Day tours from San José are available with several
companies, the most respected being *Calypso Tours*, T256-2727, F256-6767,
www.calypsotours.com Tortuga can also be visited with trips starting from
Puntarenas or, if you're on the peninsula, from Tambor or Montezuma.

Travelling from Puntarenas, boats also sail close to the biological reserves
of **Isla Guayabo** and **Isla Negritos**. Guayabo, a huge slab of steeply angled
sedimentary rock and cliffs, is uninhabited and uninhabitable. Fortunately
the 200-300 brown pelicans that use the island as a nationally important nest-
ing site disagree, as do several other marine birds and, in winter, the peregrine
falcon. Access is also denied to Isla Negritos, which protects and supports
marine birds and important fauna.

Isla Gitana, or Isla Muertos as it is also known, is 13 km southwest of
Puntarenas, just off the tip of the Nicoya Peninsula. It's cut off, and the stuff
that tropical paradise islands are made of with white sand beaches, lots of
wildlife and a couple of rustic cabins, **A** per person, including meals. Water
activities are also possible, and the owners will arrange speedboat transfers
from Puntarenas of meet the Puntarenas-Paquera launch. Contact Linda
Ruegg, T661-2994.

Refugio Nacional de Vida Silvestre Curú

Between Bahía Ballena and Paquera the Curú National Wildlife Refuge vies *Colour map 1, grid C5*
for the title of smallest protected area in the country with a mere 70 ha which
nevertheless packs an impressively diverse punch. Rising from the three
beaches, perfect for swimming and snorkelling, there are five different
lifezones, including red mangrove swamps. Mammals are equally diverse
with white-tailed deer, racoons, pacas and capuchin monkeys visible to the
patiently quiet.

■ *The refuge is privately owned and operated, and access is only with advance
permission by telephoning Doña Julieta on T661-2392. Trips to the refuge can be
organized from Montezuma. If you want to try and visit on your own be sure to
telephone in advance. The Paquera-Montezuma bus can drop you at the locked
gate. Basic accommodation is available, but is often booked in advance.*

Little more than a junction for travellers passing through, Cóbano can be **Cóbano**
reached by bus from the Paquera ferry terminal. It's primary interest to visitors

The Nicoya Peninsula

to the area is a branch of *Banco Nacional*, a petrol station and access, by four-wheel drive and in only the best conditions, to the north of the peninsula if the rivers are low enough. Ask locally for conditions – and listen to the answer.

Montezuma

Colour map 1, inset

Once a quiet sleepy hamlet, Montezuma is a small village which has become one of the most popular budget traveller destinations along the coast. Montezuma made its way onto the tourist circuit by virtue of its reputation for having a laid-back alternative life-style – locals call it *Montefuma*. These days it is no longer a secret hideaway and you shouldn't expect to see much of the *Tico* way of life. At busy periods, hotels fill up every day, so check in early.

Montezuma can be reached in 4 hours from Puntarenas if you get the early launch

Although it gets crowded, there are some wonderful beaches, rounded off by rocky points, great for exploring tidal pools. Go for beautiful walks along the tree-lined beach, visit impressive waterfalls and, further afield, Cabo Blanco Nature Reserve, is an easy and enjoyable day trip.

Excursions Tour operators in Montezuma offer a range of tours including kayaking and snorkelling at **Isla Cabuya** (US$25 per person), day trips to **Isla Tortuga** (US$35), horse tours to nearby waterfalls (US$25) and mountain bike rental (US$5 per day). Other trips further afield include whitewater rafting, canopy, sunset and wildlife tours.

If you want to strike out on your own, 20 minutes up the Montezuma River, is a huge, beautiful **waterfall** with a big, natural swimming hole, beyond a smaller waterfall. Intrepid walkers can carry on up to further waterfalls but it can be dangerous and accidents have been reported. North of Montezuma (6 km) is another waterfall with a pool right by the beach – follow the road out to the beach at the north end of town and keep going past three coves for about half an hour until you reach the trail off to the left (you can't miss it).

Montezuma is also the natural base for exploring the nearby **Reserva Natural Absoluta Cabo Blanco**. ■ *Closed Mon and Tue. A shuttle service leaves Montezuma at 0800 and 0900 and picks you up outside the park at 1500 or 1600, US$3.*

Local boatmen can arrange transport further up the peninsula or to the mainland. It's best to try and get a group to spread the cost. Ask locally for details or contact *Aventuras en Montezuma*.

Sleeping
■ *on map*
Price codes:
see inside front cover

L-A *Luz de Mono*, T642-0090, F642-0010, luzdmono@sol.racsa.co.cr Apparently the *Luz de Mono* project has been created with the "revolutionary vision of breaking the schemes of lodging." In fact it's an over-designed complex with 12 rooms, all with thermo-solar heated bathrooms and environmentally sensitive wooden furniture. 8 private cabins offer more privacy and home comforts. There's an open-air restaurant and bar (the wines come from their own vineyard), a jacuzzi, (pool being built) and internet access.

Stretching up the hill behind the village is **AL** *El Jardín*, T642-0548, F642-0074, www.hoteleljardin.com 16 cool, airy rooms, many with sea view and balcony, all with bath, hot water in most rooms, two with a/c are less bright (the rest have a fan). Nice gardens with good privacy, very friendly and well run. A small shop sells clothes, and tours can be organised. Recommended. A short walk south of the centre leads to **AL-B** *Amor de Mar*, T/F642-0262, shoebox@sol.racsa.co.cr Rooms carry different prices (not all have private bath or hot water) but all are bright and comfortable. On the beach amid pleasant gardens, friendly, families welcome, all day breakfast served in restaurant, relaxing atmosphere. Nearby is **AL-B** *Los Mangos*, T642-0076. A large site comprising 9 bungalows (**AL**), each sleeping 3 people with bath and fan. Slightly cheaper are the 10 rooms, some with shared bath, some for 4 people (A or B). Good

Greek restaurant serving 3 meals a day. White and wooden décor with interesting wall hangings. Different and fun. In leafy gardens and on the beach just north of the village is **L-A** *Sano Banano*, T642-0638, F642-0067, www.elbanano.com Accommodation ranging from private bungalows to double rooms, all with bath, hot water, fans, excellent restaurant, café, massage, gift shop, tours. Plush but informal. The recently refurbished **AL-A** *Tajalin*, T642-0061, F642-0527, www.tajalin.com A newish hotel with 11 big rooms with hot water bath, a/c or fans.

B *Mar y Cielo*, T642-0261. 6 rustic rooms sleeping 2-5 people, on the beach, all with bath, fan and sea view. German-run, it's very clean and recommended. The reception is inside the souvenir shop on the corner next to the public phones. On the beach is **B** *El Pargo Feliz*, T388-1731. 8 very clean large and pleasant rooms, all with cold water bath and fan. Upstairs rooms are nicer but all are good value. No reservations – arrive

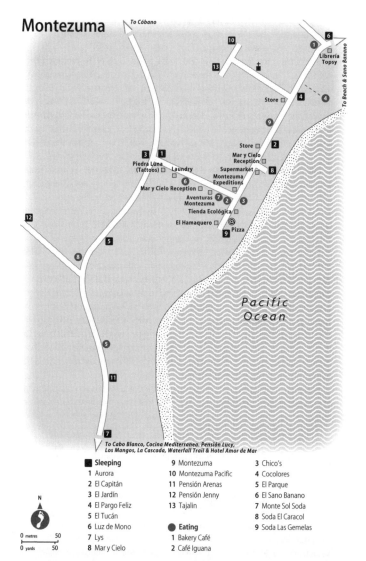

Montezuma

To Cóbano

10

13

†

6

1

Librería
Topsy

To Beach & Sano Banano

Store

4

4

9

Store

2

Mar y Cielo
Reception

3   1

Supermarket

8

Piedra Luna
(Tattoos)

Laundry

6

Montezuma
Expeditions

Mar y Cielo Reception

Aventuras
Montezuma

7   2   3

Tienda Ecológica

El Hamaquero

@   9   Pizza

12

5

8

5

11

7

*Pacific
Ocean*

The Nicoya Peninsula

*To Cabo Blanco, Cocina Mediterranea. Pensión Lucy,
Los Mangos, La Cascada, Waterfall Trail & Hotel Amor de Mar*

N

0 metres   50
0 yards   50

■ Sleeping
1 Aurora
2 El Capitán
3 El Jardín
4 El Pargo Feliz
5 El Tucán
6 Luz de Mono
7 Lys
8 Mar y Cielo

9 Montezuma
10 Montezuma Pacific
11 Pensión Arenas
12 Pensión Jenny
13 Tajalin

● Eating
1 Bakery Café
2 Café Iguana

3 Chico's
4 Cocolores
5 El Parque
6 El Sano Banano
7 Monte Sol Soda
8 Soda El Caracol
9 Soda Las Gemelas

between 1000 and 1200 to secure your room. The friendly owners request quiet – no visitors, and party-goers are not welcome. No credit cards.

A short walk south of the village, on the river close to the quieter beaches is **B-D** *La Cascada*, T/F642-0057. 14 pleasant, simple rooms for 1-5 people, with bath (cold water) and fan. Rooms downstairs seem cooler. Laundry service and a restaurant serving *comida típica*. *Tico*-owned it's particularly good value and recommended. Good deals in off-season.

C-D *Aurora*, T/F642 5551, www.aurora-costa-rica.com Simple rooms, some with private bath and hot water, cheaper without and laundry service. Set back from the road in gardens, complimentary tea and coffee, fridges, books and games for communal use. Perhaps a little overpriced. **C** *Montezuma Pacific*, T642-0402. Quiet rooms with private bath, hot water and a/c.

D *Hotel Moctezuma*, T/F642-0058. 20 rooms with bath and fan and plans for hot water. Clean and helpful, it's very central with sea views from the back, but can be noisy. Reception can arrange tours and change money. Popular bar and restaurant downstairs serving selection of *típica* food – popular with *Ticos*.

One of the oldest hotels in town and on the beach south of the centre is **E** *Lucy*, T642-0273. 10 rooms with fans, some with sea view, shared bath, pleasant balcony with sea view. The ultra-friendly and helpful *Tica* owner is planning to reopen their restaurant. Rooms downstairs slightly better. Recommended. **E** *Lys*, T642-0568. Formerly the *Hotel Liz*, the simple rooms are slated for a possible overhaul. Plans are to stay within the same price bracket, possibly with camping, so worth a look. **E** *Pensión Arenas*, on the beach, T642-0308. Run by Doña Meca, it has rustic small rooms, with fan, shared bath, no frills but pleasant balcony and sea view. Free camping (no services provided).

In the centre on the beach is **E-F** *Hotel El Capitán*, T642-0069. 20 basic rooms sleeping up to 4, with fan and shared bath. A large, rickety-looking hotel, some rooms are a bit pokey and they're cheaper downstairs. Visa accepted. Up the path alongside *Soda Caracol* is **E/F** *Pensión Jenny*, T642-0306. Twelve rooms with fan, shared bath, laundry, kitchen for guests' use, rooms a little dark. Quiet. **E/F** *El Tucán*, T642-0284. Very clean, wood-panelled rooms, with fan and shared bath. Good value.

Out of town **AL** *Horizontes*, 1.8 km north on the road to Cóbano, T/F642-0534, www.horizontes-montezuma.com 7 good rooms with private bath and fine views from this elevated spot. A good restaurant serving local and international dishes, a pool and language school. Highly recommended. **A** *Los Caballos*, 3 km north on the road to Cóbano, T/F642-0124. 8 rooms with bath, pool, outdoor restaurant, ocean views, gardens, 5 mins from beach, horses a speciality. **C** *Linda Vista*, T642-0104, on the hill, units sleep 6, with bath (cold water) and fan, ocean views. **D** *Cabinas Las Rocas*, 20 mins south of Montezuma, good but quite expensive meals, small, seashore setting, isolated. Also the *Mochila Inn*, T642-0030, 300 m outside Montezuma has houses and apartments to rent, for around $350 per month.

Camping You can camp for free at *Pension Arenas* and there is also camping in the high season at *Rincón de los Monos*, on the beach 500 m north of the village – no prices available. Clean, well organized with lockers for rent and many monkeys.

Eating For breakfast, don't miss the *Bakery Café* at the north end of town, which serves bread and cakes and vegetarian food. *Chico's*, popular beach hangout. The best restaurant in town is the *Cocina Mediterranea* (also called *Playa de las Artistas*), mid-range, about 5 mins south of town on the road to Cabuya. For seafood, go to *Cocolores* on the beach behind El Pargo Feliz (closed Mon) or, for a cheaper option *El Parque*, on the beach next to *Pension Arenas*. In town try *El Sano Banano*, a health food restaurant, good vegetarian food, large helpings, daily change of menu, milkshakes, fresh fruit and yoghurt, owned by Dutch/Americans, free movies with dinner. *Los Mangos*, in the hotel of the same name is a good place to eat with Greek food. *Lucy*, is planning to reopen their restaurant. *Pizzería*, next to *Hotel Montezuma*, self-service, good.

Several *sodas* around town, including *Soda El Caracol*, serving good Tico food. *Soda Monte Sol*, recommended for good Mexican burritos, good value, big helpings. *Soda Las Gemelas*, simple local food.

Chicho's Bar appears to be the happening place in town. Many hotels have more sedate bars in their restaurants. **Bars & nightlife**

There are several small souvenir shops in town, including *El Hamaquero* which sells locally-made crafts and puts some of the profits back into the community. *Tienda Ecologica* also provides a post office service, international calls and money exchange. *Libreria Topsy* sells books and maps – Mon-Fri, 0800-1400, until 1200 Sat. **Shopping**

Aventuras en Montezuma, T/F642-0050, www.aventurasenmontezuma.com has very helpful staff who stand in as *de facto* tourist office, and *Montezuma Expeditions*, T/F642-0467, both provide a selection of tours. They can also arrange boat transfers to Jacó or Tamarindo for around US$150 for up to 6 people. **Tour operators**

Buses Montezuma to **Paquera** daily at 0530, 1000 and 1400, connecting with the car ferry. Also at 0815, 1215 and 1600, to connect with the *lancha* to Puntarenas central docks. Tickets available in advance from tourist information centre; be at bus stop outside Hotel Moctezuma, in good time as the bus fills up quickly, US$2.60, 2 hrs. Daily shuttle bus to **Cabo Blanco**, departing 0800 and 0900, returning at 1500 and 1600, US$3. **Taxi** Montezuma to *Cóbano* US$3.50; taxi Paquera-Montezuma US$12. **Transport**

Bank Change money at *Hotel Moctezuma*, *Tienda Ecologica* and sometimes in *Aventuras Montezuma* if they have enough *colónes*. Otherwise go to the *Banco Nacional* in Cóbano. **Communication** There is an internet café in the pizzeria next to *Hotel Moctezuma*. **Language schools** *Horizontes de Montezuma*, T/F653-0359, www.horizontes-montezuma.com **Launderette** There is a launderette in *Pensión Jenny*. **Medical services** If you need a **pharmacy**, you will have to go to Cóbano. **Directory**

The Nicoya Peninsula

A small town 9 km south of Montezuma along the coast road, Cabuya lies close to the southwestern most point of the peninsula, and 2 km from the entrance to Cabo Blanco Nature Reserve. It's a quiet spot with not much to do – and so fantastically relaxing as a result. At low tide, you can wade out to **Isla Cabuya**. A rough four-wheel drive only road leads west to Malpaís. **Cabuya**

A *Celaje*, T/F642-0374, celaje@sol.racsa.co.cr Thatched roof cabins on the beach, with private bath and hot water. Very good Italian restaurant. **D** *Cabinas y Restaurante El Ancla de Oro*, T642-0369. Cabins with private bath, cheaper sharing. Seafood restaurant with lobster dinners and filling breakfasts. Horses and mountain bikes available for hire, and transport from Paquera launch can be arranged. *El Delfín* restaurant at the crossroads is friendly, serving good value local food. On the road west out of Cabuya, *Cafetería El Coyote* specializes in local and Caribbean dishes. **Sleeping & eating**

Reserva Natural Absoluta Cabo Blanco

Neatly covering the southwestern tip of the Nicoya Peninsula, Cabo Blanco Nature Reserve is a precious reserve, both ideologically and biologically. Created in 1963, it is the oldest protected area in the country apart from the frontier corridor to the north with Nicaragua. The reserve is the legacy of Nicolás Wessberg and his wife Karen Mogensen who set out to preserve the stands of *Colour map 1, inset* moist forest as development gradually denuded the surrounding area. The land was finally donated to the National Parks programme in 1994, when Doña Karen bequeathed the land to the state.

Today, the 1,370-ha reserve is easily visited on short trips from nearby Montezuma. The reserve is home to tracts of evergreen and deciduous species in this beautiful moist forest that fringes the beaches and rocky headlands. With roughly 2,300 mm of rain a year, this is one of the wettest spots on the peninsula.

A couple of trails lead through the park, which for its size has a good variety of wildlife including porcupines, armadillos and three species of monkey. The reserve is also an important site for seabirds including brown pelicans, frigate-birds and the largest nesting colony of brown boobies. Just beyond Cabo Blanco is beautiful **Playa Balsitas**, with lots of pelicans and howler monkeys, however, some reports say this area is closed. Ask at the ranger station before visiting. ■ *The park is closed Mon-Tue. Other days 0800-1600, US$6. Contact the ranger station on T/F642-0093 for more details. A shuttle bus runs from Montezuma. Alternatively a taxi will cost in the region of US$7 per person.*

Malpaís, Carmen and Santa Teresa

Colour map 1, inset From Cóbano a road leads west for 11 km to Carmen, splitting to head south for Malpaís, a rocky beach at the northern limits of the Cabo Blanco Nature Reserve. Taking the right fork at Carmen leads to the beach at Santa Teresa, with long white beaches, creeks and natural pools stretching along the coast. This stretch of beach is developing rapidly and is a particular favourite of surfers.

Sleeping **Carmen** At the road junction is **A-E** *Frank's Place*, T640-0096, F640-0071, www.frankplace.com Wide variety of rooms set in tropical gardens with private or shared bath, and self-catering options available. Good range of services and local advice.

Malpaís Heading south is **AL-F** *Mal País Surf Camp and Resort*, T/F640-0061, www.malpaissurfcamp.com Accommodation for every budget and style from comfort-able cabins with private bath sleeping up to 5, to camping with all amenities included. International and seafood served in the lively café-style restaurant. A good choice. **C** *Cabinas Mar Azul*, T642-0298, run by Jeannette Stewart, camping possible, delicious fried fish, shrimp, lobster. Set in attractive grounds is **D** *Cabañas Bosque Mar*, T640-0074, clean, large rooms with hot water shower and a good restaurant on beach nearby.

Set back 2 km from the beach is **AL** *Star Mountain Eco-Resort*, T640-0102, F640-0101, www.starmountaineco.com 20 rooms in a rustic *pueblo* setting with some dormitory rooms making it good for families (children under 6 free) and groups. The res-taurant serves gourmet dining, including fresh fruits and baked breads. All tours in the area are easily arranged including horse riding, surf school and trips to Cabo Blanco.

Santa Teresa Continuing north along the coast from Carmen, the next beach is Playa Santa Teresa with **AL** *Milarepa*, on beach, T/F640-0023, www.ticonet.co.cr/milarepa Great bamboo bungalows, open-air bathroom. **A** *Tropico Latino Lodge*, T/F640-0062, www.centralamerica.com/cr/hotel/tropico 6 spacious Italian designed bungalows that retain and use local materials, all with private bath and hot water, big ceiling fans and tiled floor leading out to a private porch and hammock. The restaurant serves north Italian and local cuisine, naturally using seafood for many dishes, in a thatched *rancho* overlooking the beach side, swimming pool and jacuzzi. Tours easily arranged. **D** *Cabinas Playa Santa Teresa*, T640-0137, 150 m from beach, surfboard rental, horses, German-run.

Transport **Air** *SANSA* and *Travelair* fly twice a day to **Tambor** (US$66) from where the mid- and upper-range hotels will be happy to arrange transport. **Bus** There is a daily bus service between **Cóbano** and **Malpaís**.

The Nicoya Peninsula

Central Pacific

8

Central Pacific

280 Ins and outs

280 Puntarenas

289 Jacó

295 Quepos

300 Manuel Antonio

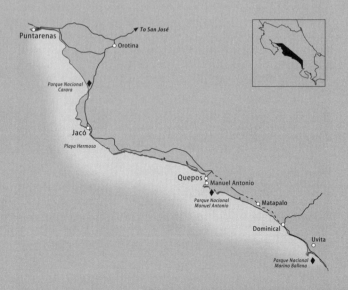

Hiding neatly between the peninsulas of Nicoya and Osa, the central Pacific is a well defined lowland region hugging the western coastal lowlands from Puntarenas in the north as far south as Palmar Norte. The last ripples of the Talamanca mountain range push up to the shore, creating a challenging blend of rocky outcrops and broad sandy beaches.

Much of the region's interest lies, literally, on the beach. The lively surf spots of **Jacó** and **Playa Hermosa** with their reliable waves, golden beaches and gently bustling nightlife, provide low-key entertainment day and night for surfers and beach lovers. The hum of activity surrounding **Quepos** and **Manuel Antonio** is a little more stylish, swanky and upmarket. Further south are the quieter surf and beach towns of **Dominical** and **Uvita**, which have good budget accommodation options, while the more exclusive and secluded hillside accommodation is found further south around the gently developing **Playa Tortuga**.

Protected areas also entice many to the region. **Carara National Park** is a transitional zone between the dry forests to the north, and the humid tropics to the south. Its trails lead through an evergreen rainforest that teems with life. The palm-fringed sandy beaches separated by rocky peninsulas of **Manuel Antonio National Park** make it the most popular park outside the central highlands.

And beyond the beaches, agricultural life toils under the hot sun where endless lines of neatly planted African palms produce oil in plantations that are a world away – economically and socially – from the wealthy, vibrant tourist hot-spots of the region.

Central Pacific

Things to do in the Central Pacific

- Explore the beautiful beaches of **Manuel Antonio National Park**.
- Learn to **surf** in Jacó or Dominical.
- **Trek** from Santa María de Dota to Quepos.
- Gawp at the **architectural follies** of old Puntarenas.
- Visit the wonderful waterfalls of **Nauyaca**.

Ins and outs

Getting there

Air   The only flights in the region are to **Quepos**. There are several direct daily flights from San José, with *SANSA*, locally on T777-0683, www.flysansa.com and *Travelair*, T220-3054, www.travelair-costarica.com   The flight takes just over 30 mins, US$44 one way.

Road   Access to the central Pacific by road is along Highway 34 from Puntarenas, San José or Orotina to the north, San Isidro de El General to the east, and from Palmar Norte to the south. A fine scenic road leads from San Isidro de El General west to join Highway 34 – also known as the *costanera* – at Dominical.

Getting around   The length of the central Pacific is covered by Highway 27 from Puntarenas south close to Orotina, from where Highway 34 runs south, for the most part in good condition, to Palmar Norte. Highway 34 is being upgraded and currently only the 44-km section from Quepos south to Dominical is still a dirt road.

     A regular and reliable bus service connects all major centres and by nature of the region, smaller areas can easily be reached by hailing down a passing bus.

Best time to visit   The dry season runs from Dec to Apr, if it's clear blue skies you're looking for. For the rest of the year – the green season – the greatest rainfall is in Oct and Sep.

Puntarenas

Colour map 1, grid C5
Population: 22,009
Alt: Sea level

Encapsulating Puntarenas is tough – the northern side of this long thin coastal sand spit is a bustling array of scruffy fishing and ferry docks. The southern side – just six blocks away – is a coastal promenade and beach dotted with bars, cafés, restaurants and hotels. Neither aspect is particularly successful – both fishing and beaches are distinctly average.

     Traditionally, the town has survived on trade. These days its main commodity is people. They come to bathe or to move. Ferries go to the Nicoya Peninsula and bus connections head north and south without having to go east. Through a miraculous trick of light, Puntarenas seems to be permanently on the move yet somehow stagnating at the same time.

Ins and outs

Getting there
See 'Transport' page 283 for more details

Puntarenas is the main transport link on the Pacific coast. With the singular purpose of avoiding returning to San José, buses to Puntarenas link with Liberia, Cañas, and Santa Elena/Monteverde in the north, and Quepos, and places en route to the south.

Passenger and vehicle ferries leave Puntarenas for Playa Naranjo and Paquera on the Nicoya Peninsula.

Getting around Barely 6 blocks across, the walk from town to beach is manageable, at over 40 blocks from end to end, you may want to get a taxi if catching the ferry from the northern terminal. Apart from Av Central, the main thoroughfare is the beachfront Paseo de los Turístas.

Best time to visit Weather is reliably good from Dec to May. The main festivity of the year is the celebration of the Festival of the Virgin of the Sea in the second week of Jul. General revelry culminates on 16 Jul with a parade of brightly decorated boats sailing out into the gulf.

Sights and history

For several centuries, Puntarenas has flourished and floundered with the rise and fall of her importance to trade routes. Once the town was the country's main port, until rail links between Puerto Limón on the Atlantic coast and the central highlands moved the spotlight. Her role was reduced still further with the construction of an international container port in the 1980s at Caldera, a short distance to the south of the centre.

Regional website www.puntarenas.com

Puntarenas is like an old maid trying hard to retain her beauty – if the sun is shining, you can see glimpses of it, but with overcast skies the wrinkles appear and only those closest to her feel any real affection. The northern side of the town has the typical characteristics of many ports, with an edgy vibrancy and carelessness that works and plays hard. Take a stroll around the market or the fishing dock on the north of the peninsula and this is *pura vida*. Not the sunset and beach type of holiday brochures, but the real life of hard graft and toil. Stroll a little further, preferably in the day, and you'll discover a world of forgotten, albeit grubby, architectural charms and more than a few follies. The neglect of the port town is so great that someone forgot to pull down the older buildings, which now could be renovated to glorious effect. This is the heart of Puntarenas (around **Calle Central**), with its banks, the market, a few hotels and fishing docks.

The southern side is made up of the **Paseo de los Turístas**, drawing crowds to the hot, sometimes dirty beach, especially at weekends. It's a pleasant enough stroll down the promenade, which is home to several hotels, as well as restaurants, bars and has a generally laid-back seafront beach atmosphere. There is a public swimming pool at the western end of the point (US$1 entrance), close to the ferries, and reportedly good surfing off the headland. The **Museum of Marine History** in the Cultural Centre is by the main church and **tourist office**. ■ *Mon-Fri 0830-1200, 1300-1630 daily, US$1.80.*

The appeal of Puntarenas is limited though there is talk of a long overdue face-lift, which would be a huge task. It's not the stuff of idyllic vacations, but there's a gritty realism to the place. With time, a stay here would probably be more rewarding than in most glitzy *Tico* towns.

Excursions Charter vessels and cruisers leave Puntarenas for day trips to **Isla Tortuga**, with most people starting out from San José. See page 271.

Variations on the sailing theme offered by *Calypso Tours* take you out to **Punta Coral**, a small deserted beach on the eastern-most point of the Nicoya Peninsula, with trails through dry forest and opportunities for snorkelling in the crystal clear waters or relaxing in a shaded hammock in the peaceful private reserve. An alternative trip sails the 60-ft catamaran *Lohe Lani* to **Isla San Lucas**, Costa Rica's own Alcatraz, described as the dreaded Devil's Island due to the

Central Pacific

prison island's terrible reputation. It was eventually closed in 1991. Trips take in a visit to the cells, visits to the bird sanctuary islands of **Pan de Azúcar** and the **Reserva Biológica Isla Guayabo** and also stop at a couple of beaches. ■ *Prices are US$99, or US$150 from San José, transport and food included.*

Essentials

Sleeping
■ *on map*
Price codes:
see inside front cover

Hardly adding to the appeal of Puntarenas, hotel prices tend to be higher and service levels lower

AL-A *Tioga*, on the beach front between C 15 and 17, T661-0271, F661-0127, www.hoteltioga.com 46 rooms, all with private bath, a/c, TV and telephone. The best hotel in town with a restaurant, swimming pool, casino and good service. Rooms with balconies are much better and have good views. **AL-A** *Yadran*, almost at the western limit of the peninsula at C 37, T661-2662, F661-1944, www.puntarenas.com/yadran A mid-sized complex with comfortable rooms all with private bath and a/c. There are 2 pools – 1 for the kiddies, 3 restaurants and a disco. Trying hard, but somehow not quite making it. **A** *Las Brisas*, on the waterfront between C 31-33, T661-4040, F661-2120, www.puntarenas.com/brisashotel 20 smart motel-style rooms, with a/c and TV. Small restaurant serving Greek, Mexican and *Tico* cuisine and a pool. Small multi-lingual book swap. Price includes breakfast and tax. A little overpriced, but comfortable.

B *Michael's Hotel*, on the waterfront on the corner with C 29, T661-4646, F661-4647, michaelh@sol.racsa.co.cr 6 tidy rooms, with private bathroom, a/c, fan and TV. Small pool, with bar and snacks. Good deals for groups and families. Nothing special but friendly and nice quiet spot. Parking available. **B-C** *Las Hamacas* on beach front between C 5-7, T661-0398. Rooms are OK, but noisy when the bar is in full flow. Small pool and gym. With a lick of paint it would be quite pleasant but for now it is overpriced.

C *Cayuga*, C 4, Av Central-1, T661-0344, F661-1280. 31 rooms with private bathroom, a/c, some with TV and fridge. The rooms are pretty dark; as respite you can sit in the small patio garden but it's hardly paradise. **C** *Gran Imperial*, on the beach front, in front of the Muelle de Cruceros (dock), C Central-2, T661-0579. Pleasant rooms in an old building, although a little dark, but clean, with private bath and fan. Small garden patio and a very chilled atmosphere. Good spot and handy for buses. **C** *La Punta*, good position 1 block from the ferry dock to the Nicoya Peninsula at Av 1-3, C 35, T661-0696. Good rooms with private bath and a/c. Mixed reports, but seems to be improving. Small bar and a restaurant. Pool out back. **C-D** *Ayi Con*, C 2, Av 1-3,

Puntarenas

Sleeping
1 Ayi Con
2 Cabezas
3 Cayuga
4 Gran Chorotega
5 Gran Imperial
6 La Punta
7 Las Brisas
8 Las Hamacas
9 Michael's
10 Pensión Monte Mar
11 Río
12 Tioga
13 Yadran

T661-0164. 44 rooms, some with a/c and private bath (**C**), private bath and fan, or shared bath and fan (**D**). Pretty grotty rooms but clean. **C-D** *Gran Hotel Chorotega*, on the corner of C 1, Av 3 near the banks and market, T661-0998. 38 clean rooms with private bath, cheaper if shared. Efficient and friendly service. Popular with Costa Rican business types. A good deal.

D *Cabezas*, Av 1, C 2-4, T661-1045. 23 simple, no-frills rooms, but bright and clean, some with private bath, cheaper without. With friendly service this is a good deal. **D** *Río*, down a side street off Av 3 between C Central and 2, near market, T661-0331, F661-0716. Countless rooms with shared or private bath and fans. Friendly Chinese owners who are very keen to help. Lively area, sometimes noisy but popular place.

G *Pensión Monte Mar*, Av 3, C 1-3, T661-2731. Very basic, some rooms with fan. Bearable on a budget, a fine study in cardboard partitioning.

Out of town On the neck of the peninsula at Cocal is the *Yacht Club*, T661-0784, F661-2518, cryacht@sol.racsa.co.cr Caters for members of international yacht clubs. Nearby is **A** *Porto Bello*, Av Central, C 68-70, T661-1322, F661-0036. With bath and a/c. Pool in pleasant gardens, clean and quiet with excellent food in the restaurant and a helpful Italian owner.

Paseo de los Turístas sparkles and twinkles in the evening breeze, inviting you to walk and explore the restaurants, bars and karaoke clubs. Explore until you find something that meets your mood. *Aloha*, on the seafront at C 17, is worth checking out. *Casa de Mariscos*, C 7-9, is a popular mid-range seafood restaurant on the seafront. *Jardin Cervecero Bierstube*, at C 23-25, is good for snack sandwiches, hamburgers and a finely chilled beer. *La Yunta* at C 19, is a good mid-priced steakhouse. *Soda Macarena*, opposite the Muelle de Cruceros close to the bus stops, makes good cheap *empañadas*, ideal when waiting for the bus. **Eating & drinking**

Moving away from Paseo de los Turístas towards the north side of the peninsula, *El Kayte Negro* is on Av 1, C 17, has cheap, good local food. Next door *Mariscos Kahite Blanco* is an excellent and locally renowned cheap seafood restaurant. Around the central market area there are many *sodas* and snack bars, with good cheap food from the market stalls. *Soda Brisas del Mar*, on C Central, Av 2-4, is good for a snack.

A number of Chinese restaurants on Av Central and C 1 (eg *Mandarín*, good value).

Central Pacific

Eating
1 Aloha
2 Brisas del Mar
3 Casa de Mariscos
4 El Kayte Negro
5 Jardín Cervecero Bierstube
6 La Yunta
7 Mandarín
8 Mariscos Kahite Blanco

Puntarenas **Carnival** takes place over 10 days in the middle of *Feb* with decorated parades, wandering musicians, concerts and processions ending in bull fights and fireworks. Later in the year **Fiesta de la Virgen del Mar** has a week of festivities leading to a carnival and regatta of decorated fishing boats and yachts on the Sat closest to 16 Jul. **Festivals**

Puntarenas is home to *Puntarenas FC*, a first division team that flirted with winning the championship over 20 years ago. Ask locally for details on matches. **Sport**

Bus *Empresarios Unidos* (T222-0064) buses between **San José** and **Puntarenas** leave San José from Terminal Puntarenas C 16, Av 10-12, 0600-1900. In Puntarenas the **Transport**

Parque Nacional Isla del Coco

On the internet www.cocos-island. org is packed with fascinating information about Coco Island

For distant island destinations the diving paradise of Isla del Coco – one of the largest uninhabited islands in the world – has to be the best option around. Over 550 km southwest of Costa Rica, the volcanic island rises from the sea floor at the western tip of the Coco Plate. With an area of just nine square miles, most of the coast is lined with steep cliffs, rising to the highest point of 634 m at Cerro Yglesias. The rugged terrain creates numerous watersheds and rivers, which in turn create waterfalls some of which plunge directly into the ocean. Only the bays of Wafer and Chatham make the island accessible.

Temperatures of 30°C and rainfall close to 7 m guarantees almost permanent cloud cover over the islands and produces lush premontane rainforest. But while preserved as a National Park and a UNESCO World Heritage Site, the island itself is considered to be impoverished in terms of diversity when compared to the mainland, largely due to its isolation. But every cloud has a lining, and a number of endemic species exist. Of the 87 bird species, three – the Cocos Island flycatcher,

cuckoo and finch – are endemic, as are two species of reptile. Insects proliferate and hawksbill, green and olive ridley turtles occasionally visit the undisturbed bays.

Offshore, the protected waters of 97,000 ha are rich with coastal reefs and emergent islands. Over 300 species of fish are found in these waters, but the real interest lies in the hammerhead sharks that school in their hundreds, and the abundance of white-tipped sharks, whale sharks and manta rays.

If the image is one more of prison than paradise, you're getting the idea. In fact the island was a prison for a couple of years between 1872 and 1874. An exploratory trip in 1898 to reopen the penitentiary ended up being a scientific expedition which realized the importance of protecting the area.

History has added spice to the islands which showed no signs of habitation prior to the arrival of the Spanish in the new world. Poorly marked on navigational maps, only experienced sailors could find the islands. Myth and legend claims the

terminal is at C 2, Av 2-4. Buses leave every 40 mins from 0415-1900. Buses to other locations leave from close to the San José terminal on the Paseo de los Turístas and Calle 2. Heading north there is a daily bus to **Santa Elena** for Monteverde at 1315, with an occasional bus at 1415. Buses go to **Liberia** 5 times daily, first at 0530, last 1500, 2½ hrs. There are a couple of buses to **Tilarán** via **Cañas** leaving at 1130 and 1630. Heading south, buses leave for **Quepos**, via Jacó, at 0500 and 1000, and 1430 in high season.

Boat There are ferry services across the Gulf of Nicoya to the Nicoya Peninsula from 2 docks. The most commonly used dock is at the northwestern end of Puntarenas, on Av 3, between C 33 and 35.

Conatramar, T661-1069, F661-2197, provide a passenger and vehicle service between **Puntarenas** and **Playa Naranjo**. Ferries depart at 0315, 0700, 1050, 1450 and 1900 for the 90-min journey. Ferries return at 0510, 0850, 1250, 1700 and 2100. Prices: pedestrians US$1.60; motorbikes US$3; cars US$12. Buses meet the arriving ferry in Playa Naranjo providing connections to **Nicoya**, via **Carmona**, and beyond.

A couple of passenger and vehicle ferries also head for **Paquera** on the southern side of the peninsula. Ferries leave at 0845, 1400 and 2015, returning at 0600, 1115 and 1800. Buses to **Tambor**, **Cóbano** and **Montezuma** meet the ferry. *Hotel Playa Tambor* operates the *Barceló Naviera Tambor*, T661-2084, F661-2160, naviera@sol.racsa.co.cr primarily for guests. Non-guests can use the service, subject to availability, which leaves Puntarenas at 0500, 1230 and 1700, returning at 0800, pirates Benito Bonito, William Davies and Captain Thompson buried significant quantities of treasure here between the late 1600s and 1821, including the Lima Booty which is supposed to include a life-size (and rather heavy) statue of the Virgin Mary and Child in solid gold. Since then, over 300 expeditions have visited the island in search of the elusive 'X'.

Diving deals Marine life is the main draw and most people visiting are serious about diving and arrive on live-aboard dive boats. Trips normally last at least a week as the boat journey to the islands takes 36 hrs. May-Nov is the rainy season and considered the best time of year for diving but conditions are generally good all year round. Once in the area, diving is guided and organized by the divemaster and subject to the weather. If conditions allow, there are trips to explore the island and visit some of the many waterfalls. Due to cooler waters and strong currents, dive operators advise that Coco Island is not suitable for beginners.

The **Okeanos Aggressor** is a 110-ft steel vessel with berths for 21 guests, all

fully carpeted, with a/c and private bathrooms. The comfortable salon has an entertainment centre with TV and video for relaxing. Meals are served buffet style and on the top deck there is a wet bar. Departing from Puntarenas, the Aggressor offers 9-day, Sat-Mon, charters with 6 days of diving and 10-day, Tue-Fri, charters with 7 days of diving, with most guests making up to 3 dives a day. Prices start at US$2,795 for 9 days, US$2,995 for 10 days. T228-6613, F289-7334, in the US toll free on T800-348-2628, www.aggressor.com

Central Pacific

1430 and 2030. Transport is available for guests, and you may be able to get a ride as far as the hotel to the north of Tambor.

A smaller pedestrian and motorbike launch makes the journey from the dock behind the central market, directly north of the bus stop. Departures at 0600, 1100 and 1515, returning at 0730, 1230 and 1700. Pedestrians US$1.50, bikes US$0.80, motorbikes US$1.60. Tickets sold on a first come first served basis when vessel is docking. T661-2830.

Banks *Banco Nacional* and *Banco de Costa Rica* on Av 3, C 1-3 near the central market, both change TCs and have ATMs. **Communications** Internet: *Millenium Cyber Café* on the beachfront with C 15. sOnly one in town and popular, 1000-2000, US$3 per hour. Free coffee if you're lucky. **Post**: Post office on Av 3, C Central-1, close to the central market. **Telephone** ICE and Radiográfica on Av C, C 2-4. **Tour operators** See under San José Tour Operators page 119 for cruises in the Gulf of Nicoya. **Directory**

South to Orotina

Heading for the Central Pacific, Highway 27 links Puntarenas with the town of Orotina. At Roble, 10 km east of Puntarenas, there are a few quiet accommodation options. **Roble**

Sleeping B *Villa del Roble*, T663-0447. By the sea, with 12 quiet rooms – a charming stop with a small pool. Near the regional hospital is **B** *Casa San Francisco*, T663-0148. Another friendly place run by a couple of Canadian women, with clean rooms, a pool. Breakfast included and laundry facilities. For food and drink try *María Vargas* with good food and reasonable prices in a friendly setting.

Mata de Limón On the old San José-Puntarenas railway, near the new port of Caldera is Mata de Limón. It's a simple resort with a beach and mangrove swamps nearby. The fishing nearby is reported to be good. Once a quiet spot, the peace has been shattered by the traffic from the nearby port.

Sleeping The following are options if circumstances find you looking for lodgings. **E** *Casablanca*, Av 14, C 2-4, T222-2921, which can provide full board. **E** *Manglares*, near the former train station, is a reasonable option with a good restaurant. South of the village there are several very basic places to stay, all **F**, including *Viña del Mar*, *Villas Fanny* and *Villas América*.

Inland to The road from Caldera heads inland along the broad valley of the Cuarros and
Cascajal Tárcoles rivers. A dirt track leads to the coast at Tivives with mangrove swamps popular with bird-watchers and a good surfing spot.

Sleeping Close to Cascajal on the road inland to Orotina is **AL** *Dundee Ranch Hotel*, in San José on T267-6222, F267-6229, www.dundee-ranch.com A 23-room working ranch with private bathroom, a/c, pool and restaurant. Not surprising that the place is big on horseriding, but there's also a range of other activities including bird-watching, hiking and of course lazing by the pool.

Orotina Once an important rail road and transport junction, the 9,000-strong lively town of Orotina still maintains a role as an important transport hub with good links to the port at Caldera, the agricultural industry along the Pacific coast and the central highlands. However, there's not much here to keep you for long.

Sleeping If stopping over try **C** *Cabinas Kalim*, near the plaza, T428-8082. Just north of Orotina in **San Mateo** is **AL** *El Rancho Oropendola*, T/F428-8600. Cabins with private bath or rooms with shared bath, rustic and peaceful, pool, nature trails. West of San Mateo, at **Higuito de San Mateo**, is *Las Candelillas*, T428-9157, F428-8434, a 26-ha farm and reforestation project with fruit trees and sugar-cane. There is a **camping** area with showers, pool and riding.

Iguana A short 14 km south of Orotina, Iguana Park offers a refreshing approach to
Park the issues of conservation and the endangered status of the green iguana. By studying the green iguana the founder Dr Dagmar Werner and her team have found that the reptile needs buffer forest to thrive and survive. The outcome of the research has been the release of over 80,000 iguanas in the first five years of the project, which has helped the iguana recover in the area, and the realization that the iguana can be farmed and used to provide meat, giving preservation of the forest a much needed economic value.

A trip to Iguana Park incorporates an audio-visual presentation, 4 km of trails, a chance to see the green iguana, a souvenir shop and a restaurant – not surprisingly iguana is on the menu. The park has also successfully bred and released scarlet macaws into the neighbouring Carara National Park. ■ *0800-1600, US$15 entry, US$10 for guided tour, T240-6712, F235-2007.*

Iguana Park is also home to the *Original Canopy Tour* company with a tour going through three different lifezones. The third platform rests on a strangler fig over 30 m in height which links to a fourth on a 44-m high kapok tree. An entertaining way of learning about the rainforest. ■ *Tours last 3½ hrs, Open 0800-1600, with last tour leaving at 1330. US$45 plus entrance to Iguana Park. All inclusive trip from San José, US$60. T257-5149, F256-7626, www. canopytour.com*

Orotina to Jacó

South from Orotina, the central Pacific region becomes clearly defined. The predominant dry forest of the north gives way to moist forest, and Highway 34 becomes a coastal road proper, or *costanera*, travelling from Orotina to Jacó. The road is in good condition – maybe too good, watch your speed. The wide swinging roads just invite you to floor it but the policeman on the road round the corner is not waving you on your way with a smile, he's pulling you over for a ticket.

If you're driving, one of the most popular free experiences in Costa Rica is to dangle over the side of the **Río Tárcoles bridge** to see the opaque, sediment-filled waters broken only by the bony backs of the somnolent crocodiles below. It's easy to find the spot to stop, as parked cars cram the roadside, especially at dawn and dusk when scarlet macaws can be seen returning to their roosts from Carara National Park on the southern banks of the river.

■ *You can get a closer look by taking a **boat tour** with* Jungle Crocodile Safari, *T292-2316, F225-4852, or* Crocodile ECO Tour, *formerly the Crocodile Man Tour, T/F637-0426. US$25 per person from the dock in Tárcoles, US$39 round trip from Jacó.*

Next to Carara National Park is **La Catarata**, a private reserve with an impressive waterfall with a drop of close to 200 m with natural pools for bathing. It's a steady hike and you'll need to take food and refreshments but it's definitely worth the effort. ■ *Open 0800-1500, Dec to Apr, US$7.50, T236-4140. There are signs on the main road. Take the gravel road up the hill beside* Hotel Villa Lapas. *5-km hike to the entrance, 2½-km hike to the falls and pools.*

Parque Nacional Carara

Incredibly close to San José (just 90 km away, or a couple of hours by road), *Colour map 1, grid C6* Carara National Park provides some of the most accessible primary forest in the country and is one of the most popular protected areas. Lying in a transitional zone between the dry forests to the north and moist forests to the south, the average temperature of 27°C and annual rainfall of 2.8 m creates a staggering diversity of plants with over 750 species recorded to date in the park. The region was once part of Hacienda el Coyolar, one of the largest land titles in the country, before it was protected in 1978. The park also protects numerous **precolumbian archaeological sites**, some dating back to 300 BC.

A few trails lead through the park, which you can explore on your own, but a good guide will be able to point out some of the wildlife which includes scarlet macaws, spider monkeys and the typically Costa Rican black and green **poison arrow frog**. A couple of trails just over 1 km leave from the ranger's station at the southern boundary of the park. The longest trail, at the northern boundary of the 5,242 ha park, takes up to four hours and skirts the gallery forest along the Río Tárcoles passing an ox-bow lake carpeted with water hyacinths home to waterfowl, wading birds including the roseate spoonbill and dozing crocodiles.

Central Pacific

■ *T383-9953, F636-6399. The park is open daily from 0700-1700. From May-Oct the hours are 0800-1600. Entrance is US$6. The entrance to the park is a couple of km south of the Río Tárcoles bridge. Travelling by regular bus from San José or Puntarenas, ask the driver to drop you off at the entrance or the bridge.*

WARNING Regular letters appear in the weekly *Tico Times* recording the latest innovative scams of car thieves who empty vehicles while drivers watch the crocodiles from the bridge of the Río Tárcoles. Vehicles parked in the ranger's station have also been targetted. An increased police presence on the bridge has reduced the problem, but the police clock off at 1600! Make sure your vehicle is locked at all times, and avoid leaving valuables in the vehicle if possible.

Sleeping & eating

AL *Villa Lapas*, on the southern side of Carara National Park beside the Río Tarcolitos turn, T637-0232, F637-0227, www.villalapas.com 47 comfortable but uninspiring rooms, all with private bath and a/c. Each room has a terrace with views of the river, garden or pool and a Jacuzzi. International and local dishes are served buffet style in the *Toucan Restaurant*. Over 2.5 km of trails connected by hanging bridges meander through the hotel's own private reserve.

Playa Tárcoles C *Cabinas Carara*, T/F637-0178, basic, 16 cabins with bath, small, simple restaurant, pool, superb bird-watching at mouth of Río Tárcoles about 5 km along this road. 3 km from Tárcoles is *El Tico*, a good seafood restaurant. **AL** all-inclusive per person *Tarcol Lodge*, T430-0400, F430-0398, www.ranchonaturalista.com A handful of rooms in a small, rustic lodge with hot water shared bath, and meals using fresh seafood. The main appeal of the area is the bird life which flocks to the mud flats as the tidal waters recede.

Punta Leona L+ *Villa Caletas*, T257-3653, F222-2059, www.distinctivehotels.com Perched high on a cliff above the ocean and surrounded by lush rainforest, this place is, as they claim, close to heaven. There are 8 rooms and 13 villas, all luxuriously decorated throughout. Many of the rooms have views out to the Pacific, with villas and junior suites offering greater space, and the suites and master suite even have private swimming pools. Don't worry, the shared pool is no less elegant. A couple of restaurants serve international gourmet cuisine. As befitting a place of such elegance, *Villa Caletas* hosts an **International Music Festival** every Aug.

AL *Punta Leona*, T661-1414 or in San José on T231-3131, F232-0791, www.hotelpuntaleona.com A full service resort with over 200 rooms and apartments set in 300 ha of rainforest. All rooms have a private bath, a/c, TV, telephone, fridge and safety box. But it's the activities laid on that will appeal most: tennis, mini-golf, aerobics, dance classes and a wide range of nature tours and watersports provided by *JD's Watersports*. Ideal for families and the activity-obsessed.

Bahía Herradura is the next beach south before Jacó and you may know it better than you realize as it was used for location filming for the gloriously over-produced movie *1492: Conquest of Paradise* starring Gerard Depardieu. Over 500 years later golfing enthusiasts enjoy **L** *Los Sueños Hotel and Golf Club*, T290-3311, F231-6040, www.los-suenos.com As part of the *Marriott* chain, you should expect the very best in standards and services. Over 200 rooms with apartments and a marina with moorings for 300 yachts. Still evolving, there are plans for sportsfishing charters, international bill-fishing competitions, day and sunset cruises.

Watersports at *Los Sueños* are provided by *JD's Watersports*, T257-3857, F256-6391, toll free in the US on T1-800-477-8971, www.jdwatersports.com JD's – who also have a base at *Hotel Punta Leona* – are watersports specialists. Wherever there is water in the vicinity they'll do something on, in or with it, from Jungle River Cruises up the Tárcoles River, sunset cruises, scuba diving courses and sportsfishing. Also a wide range of beach watersports with equipment rentals available.

Jacó

The original surf capital of Costa Rica, Jacó continues to be a major attraction as the closest real beach to San José. That proximity makes it a popular choice for Ticos and international visitors alike and the population feels far larger than official figures suggest. While the place is hardly paradise, the sandy beach is pleasant enough and long enough to find a relatively quiet spot.

Visitor numbers are sufficient to ensure a good range of activities and a fair amount of partying if you're looking to start your vacation with a bang or grab a few last rays of sunshine at the closest point to San José before heading home.

Population: 3,552
Colour map 2, grid C1
Altitude: Sea level

Ins and outs

Jacó is a few hundred metres west of the *costanera* which runs parallel to the beach, some 117 km from San José – look out for the signs if driving. A good road links to the capital make driving these simple. Buses (3 daily) take just over 2 hrs from the Coca Cola Terminal. There are also services to Quepos, Puntarenas and Orotina.

Getting there

From north to south the bay of Playa Jacó is just over 3 km in length. The walk down the beach or the main road is a fair old trek. Naturally enough, taxis are available if the walk is too much or if you want to go further afield. Bikes and cars are also available for hire.

Getting around

There is no official tourist information in Jacó, as the thriving private sector does a fine job. Keep an eye out for *Jacó News*, a monthly English language publication with snippets of news and tide tables.

Tourist information

Temperatures and climate for the beach lover reach ideal in Jacó from Dec-Apr with offshore breezes keeping temperatures in the mid 20s. The surf is best in the rainy season from May-Nov but is good all year round according to locals.

Best time to visit

Central Pacific

Sights

Jacó is the kind of place where you do rather than see. Activities mostly relate to water and naturally enough **surfing**. Surf stores and schools exist in profusion to serve both the experienced and the rookie surfer. The *Terraza del Pacífico*, based in Playa Hemosa a short distance to the south, tries to organize a monthly surfing competition at different venues which is open to both local and international entrants.

Kayaks are available for hire for a different type of messing about on the water. Deep sea **fishing** and sunset **cruises** are easily arranged. Beyond this **horseriding** is popular and can be organized through most hotels. The latest addition to the scene is **paragliding** and boat-plane tours with private beach drops.

There is of course an exception, which in Jacó's case is the **Butterfly Fantasy** which gives you the chance to observe the lifecycle of the butterfly. ■ *Closed Mon, US$5.*

Surfers (and mere mortals) can catch local information on Jacó and Playa Hermosa on the web at www.rovercam.com

Excursions Tours to regional attractions – **Carara National Park**, **La Catarata waterfalls** and **Tárcoles crocodile tours**, and to nearby **Playa Hermosa** to the south – are easily arranged from Jacó. *Chiclets Tree Tour* canopy tour operates out of *Terraza del Pacifico Hotel* in Playa Hermosa, a few kilometres south of Jacó. Contact them on T643-3222, F643-3424, www.jacobeach.co.cr

Essentials

Sleeping
■ *on map*
Price codes:
see inside front cover

Accommodation in Jacó is over-priced Look for discounts May-Nov

L *Jacó Fiesta*, at the southern end of town, T643-3147, F643-3148, jacofies@racsa.co.cr Popular medium-size resort with comfortable rooms, 4 pools, tennis courts, pool tables, and countless other activities. Popular with groups, English, German and French spoken. Could do with a fresh lick of paint. Generous discounts (**A**) in the green season.

AL *Club del Mar*, at the southern end of the beach, T/F643-3194, balcon@racsa.co.cr 10 rooms with kitchenette, fridge and ceiling fans, but were undergoing extensive renovations. You can lounge by the pool, or set out on your own adventure with rented bikes, boards and cars. **AL** *Copacabana*, on the beach just north of the centre, T643-1005, F643-3131, www.copacabanahotel.com Canadian-owned with 30-odd rooms all with hot showers and fans. Lively relaxation with a pool, complete with wet bar, an open-air restaurant, access to the beach and gentle whoops of the howler homo sapiens from the sports bar. Underwent major renovations in late 2000. Popular choice. **AL-A** *Best Western Jacó Beach Resort*, at the northern end of town, T643-1000, F643-3246, toll free in the US on T1-800-528-1234, www.bestwestern.co.cr/bwjaco.html Big comfortable *Best Western* rooms with private bath and tub, cable TV but no awards for creativity. Big pool and beach-front bar and restaurant. Activities include tennis court and free use of bikes for guests. Good deals available, but most expensive internet in the country. **AL-A** *Cabinas Tangeri*, T643-3001, F643-3636. 24 a/c chalets (9 hold up to 8

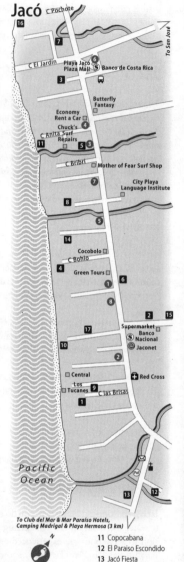

Jacó

To San José

To Club del Mar & Mar Paraíso Hotels,
Camping Madrigal & Playa Hermosa (3 km)

0 metres 200
0 yards 200

■ **Sleeping**
1 Alice
2 Apartotel Gaviotas
3 Best Western Jacó
  Beach Resort
4 Bohío
5 Cabinas Emily
6 Cabinas La Cometa
7 Cabinas Las Palmas
8 Cabinas Tangeri
9 Camping El Hicaco
10 Cocal
11 Copacabana
12 El Paraíso Escondido
13 Jacó Fiesta
14 Los Ranchos
15 Paraíso del Sol
16 Pochote Grande
17 Zabamar

Eating
● Bananas
2 Chatty Cathy's
3 Emily's
4 La Hacienda
5 La Ostra
6 Pizza Hut
7 Sunrise Grill Breakfast
  Place
8 Wisbone

Central Pacific

people) with private bath, TV and fridge. 3 pools – 1 for children – set in pleasant gardens leading to the beach. Good BBQ grill and restaurant with cocktails. Nothing special, but excellent value for groups. **AL-A** *ZabaMar*, central and close to the beach, T/F643-3174. 20 large rooms some with a/c, cheaper with a fan. A small pool which seems to be more popular than the beach. Helpful American owners, small restaurant and bar, reservations recommended.

A *Cocal*, on the beach near the centre of town, T643-3067, F643-3082, cocalcr@racsa.co.cr Neat and tidy throughout, the 44 rooms have a/c and private bath. 2 pools, an open-air restaurant and claims to have the largest casino in Jacó. **A** *Mar Paraíso*, at the southern end of town, T/F643-1947, www.hotelmarparaiso.com Tidy rooms in a mid-range resort, in a quiet spot at the southern end of town. **A** *Paraíso del Sol*, east of main street close to centre, T643-3250, F643-3137, www.rovercam.com Apartments sleeping 2-6 people with kitchenette, pool and parking. Recommended and good for groups. **A-B** *Apartotel Gaviotas*, T643-3092, F643-3054. 12 self-catering apartments with kitchenette, TV and parking, some with a/c, cheaper with fans. Big pool and easy-come, easy-go atmosphere. **A-B** *Pochote Grande*, north of town, T643-3236, F220-4979, www.centralamerica.com/cr/hotel/pochote.htm A simple 2-storey villa with 24 spacious rooms all with hot water, private bath and fridge, with a terrace or balcony. The fine tropical gardens include a pool partially shaded by an incredible 500-year old *pochote* tree, with direct access to the beach. Quiet little bar and restaurant, with good secure parking. A good choice in this price bracket.

B-C *Cabinas Las Palmas*, north end of town, T643-3005, F643-3512. Simple tidy rooms, some with kitchenette, all with bath and fan, clean, set in pretty gardens – shame about the lime green colour scheme. **B-C** *El Jardín*, at the north end of town, T/F643-3050. Close to the beach, 10 rooms in quiet spot, friendly with small pool. Readers have recommended the new **B-C** per person *El Paraíso Escondido*, 150 m east of the Catholic church on C Los Cholos, T643-2883, F643-2884, paraisoescondido@racsa.co.cr All the tiled floor rooms have a private bath, patio and a/c – there are some cheaper rooms with fan. There is a swimming pool set in fine quiet gardens. Good service, attention to detail and the friendly owner often meets arriving buses. Central and close to the beach is **B-C** *Los Ranchos*, T643-3070, F643-1810, cobjm16@racsa.co.cr 4 bungalows, complete with kitchenette, and 8 rooms sleeping 4-8 people. Lively spot with a small pool, a short walk from the beach.

C *Alice*, south of centre, T/F643-3061. Tidy rooms with private bath, small terrace and pool. **C** *Bohío*, central and near beach, T643-3017. Simple accommodation with private bath, cold water and fan. **C** *Cabinas La Cometa*, on the main street in the centre, T/F643-3615. Good rooms with fan, hot water shared bath, very clean.

D *Cabinas Emily*, T643-3513, behind the restaurant of the same name not far from buses. Simple rooms, with private bath and fan. Good value and *Tico* owned. **D** *Cabinas Gipsy Italiano*, near beach to the north of town, T/F643-3448, with bath, hot water.

Camping *Camping El Hicaco,* slightly south of the centre, is **G** per person with *Restaurant Los Hicacos* nearby, both down same access route to the beach. *Camping Madrigal*, at the southern end of the beach, is a quiet spot.

Jacó is the classic stroll-and-discover beachside town. Meandering down the main street you'll find a restaurant or bar that takes your fancy and then move on. In addition to the many *sodas* throughout Jacó, *Bananas* and *Chatty Cathy's*, on the main drag, are popular dining spots. *Emily's*, just within the centre to the north, has simple décor without the razzmatazz of many places in town, with unassuming, cheap and mainly fish *Tico* food. *La Fragata*, at the northern end of town, has been recommended for pasta and fish. *La Hacienda*, northern end, good bar and restaurant serving mid-priced snacks. There's a breezy balcony and gentle rock standards drifting through the

Eating

background. *La Ostra*, good fish in this pleasant open-air restaurant open all day. The clue's in the name at *Sunrise Grill Breakfast Place*, which has breakfast from 0700 until 1200. Closed Wed. *Wishbone*, on the main street, serving big plates of Mexican in a fine Tex-Mex *cantina* setting, with a small terrace. Prices from US$6.

Bars & nightclubs Discos in town come and go and moods change. *Central*, close to the beach, is one of the most popular places. Close by is *Los Tucanes*.

Shopping A wide range of beach shops in the centre with scary names like *Mother of Fear Surf Shop* and the more enticing *Cocobolo* provide all your heart's desires including surf gear, beachwear, oils and lotions. Several supermarkets in the centre for stocking up on basics and supplies if you're in self-catering accommodation. If your addiction is shopping malls, try *Playa Jacó Plaza Mall* to the north of town.

Tour operators There are several tour operators down the main street. A recommended one is *Green Tours*, T643-2773, F643-2439, juniorbenito@racsa.co.cr who arrange local and national tours.

Transport **Bus** The bus terminal is at the north end of town by the *Playa Jacó Plaza Mall*, close to Pizza Hut. From **San José** there are 3 direct daily buses a day at 0730, 1030 and 1530, from the Coca-Cola terminal, 2¼ hrs, US$2.40. Buses return at 0500, 1100 and 1500 with a 1300 service on Sun. 4 buses a day for **Quepos** to the south and also for **Puntarenas** to the north. For information about services call T643-3135.

Car Rental *Economy*, next to the *Jacó Best Western*, T643-1719, F643-1098, www.economy.co.cr *Elegante*, T643-3224, www.eleganterentacar.com *Budget*, T/F643-2665, www.budget.co.cr have opened an office at the *Jacó Best Western*.

Directory **Banks** *Banco Nacional* in centre of town. **Communications** Internet: *Jaconet* on main road, but not really established – look out for new places. **Post**: The post office is at the southern end of town near the *municipalidad* offices. **Language schools** *City Playa Language Institute*, T643-2123, F643-2122, www.cityplaya.com offers Spanish classes with 2 weeks for US$310, add US$120 per week for homestays. **Medical services** *Red Cross* in the centre of town, T643-3090. **Useful addresses** *Chuck's Surf Repairs* will sort out any serious damage to your board.

Playa Hermosa

Colour map 2, grid C1 A rocky headland and 3 km separate Jacó from Playa Hermosa, a far more sedate and arguably better surf hang-out – for both the surfing and the atmosphere if you like a quieter spot. The *costanera* skims the coastline where you'll see a huddle of hotels – check in and get your board out.

In 1998, 10 km of dark sand beach from Playa Hermosa south was declared a Wildlife Refuge to protect the nesting site of marine turtles which arrive on the beach between July and December. Although conservation efforts are in the early stages, ask at local hotels to see if night tours are available for visitors.

Sleeping **L** *Casa Pura Vida*, T/F643-2039, www.casapuravida.com 4 apartments with a couple of rooms sleeping up to 4 people. A/c, hot shower and kitchenettes, but breakfast is included. A graceful and quiet Mediterranean-style villa, with a pool with direct access to the beach – a good relaxing choice. **L** *Terraza del Pacífico*, T643-3222, F643-3424, www.jacobeach.co.cr 43 big rooms with tiled floors, high wooden ceilings and private bathroom. The mid-price open-air bar and restaurant overlooks the sea. There's also a

Central Pacific

souvenir shop and internet service. Although it's a comfortable resort-style hotel, complete with a big pool and wet bar, the atmosphere is more genuine than most with this much to offer. *Chiclets Tree Tour* canopy tour operates out of the hotel, with 10 platforms set between 60 and 132 ft above the ground. Contact the hotel for bookings. US$55.

AL *Fuego del Sol*, T643-3737, F643-3736, www.fuegodelsol.com 18 rooms with hot water private bath, a/c and telephone in a 2-storey villa overlooking the pool, gardens and to the beach. 3 suites also have a kitchenette and fridge. The pool has a wet bar and the restaurant looks directly out to the beach and the coast. **AL** *Villa Hermosa*, T643-3373, F643-3506, www.surf-hermosa.com Right on the beach with 10 fully-equipped, a/c *cabinas*, in lush gardens sleeping 24 people. There's a swimming pool, bar and sundeck close to hand and the hotel will help arrange trips further afield.

B *La Iguana Perezoza*, T643-1042, www.lazyliz.com Popular surf place with 6 rooms, all with hot water private bath, a/c and ceiling fans. Lounge around the pool, the open air bar and restaurant or stroll a short distance to the beach. Good for surfing and fishing trips, a good comfortable choice.

C *Las Olas*, T/F643-3687, www.cabinaslasolas.com Cabins with hot water and fridge and ranches with a kitchenette sleeping 2-6 people. Small pool and a beach-front café in a quiet if slightly cramped spot. **C-D** *Ola Bonita Aparthotel*, T643-3990, www.olabonita.com Basic rather uninspiring rooms sleeping 4 with a pool.

E per person *Las Arenas*, T/F643-3508. 6 basic surf cabins with microwave and fridge – what else do you need? The *Tico* owner Chino speaks English and is a keen surfer and is happy to talk about local breaks. Good snack restaurant and bar

Heading fast toward the stuff of legend is **F** per person *Rancho Grande*, T645-3529, a funky wood and bamboo house that makes a home away from home run by the friendly Rhonda and Brian from Florida – get the top room if you're in a group. 7 rooms of varying size which fill up with surfers. Private baths have cold water, shared baths are hot. Stereo goes to the person with the best music.

Costa Nera is a well thought of mid-range Italian restaurant serving Italian food cooked by… Italians. Neat eh! *Las Arenas* is a good spot for an ice-cold beer and snack food. Also try *Jungle Surf Café*, which has a chalked up menu based on what's available but normally includes fish, burger snacks and a few cheap local dishes. **Eating**

Playa Esterillos and beaches south to Manuel Antonio

South of Playa Hermosa, the *costanera* heads inland and the coastline is filled with row upon row of African palm. The dense plantations are dark and vaguely threatening, devoid of both character and local features. Hidden from view and all but the most curious of drivers and surfers, it almost requires a leap of faith to believe there is a long stretch of fine beaches some 20 km south of Jacó. *Colour map 2, grid C1*

The secluded accommodation is available across a range of budgets – perfect for a quiet hideaway and definitely for those with the resources to keep themselves amused. While independent travellers can walk down any of the access roads and will love the seclusion, you will probably feel quite cut off once you get there as services are limited.

C *La Felicidad Country Club*, T770-8332, F779-9960, lafelicidad.com (no www). A low-key place with comfortable rooms with private bath, some with kitchens and balconies overlooking the endless beach. A private pool, comfy chairs and hammocks for relaxing. There's a small bar and restaurant, and a couple of *sodas* and seafood restaurants on the beach front. **Playa Esterillos Centro**

Central Pacific

Playa Esterillos Este	**A-B** *Auberge du Pélican*, F779-9236, www.aubergedupelican.homestead.com A very comfortable small French-Canadian owned hotel with 11 rooms all with hot water, private bath, cheaper if shared, and safe box. There's a small pool and a range of water sports activities for messing about on the beach, good restaurant service and a small airstrip right on the doorstep – literally.
Playa Bejuco	An even quieter beach, Playa Bejuco is home to **A** *Hotel El Delfín*, T/F770-8308. With 15 a/c rooms with private bath, many with balconies. Small cheap restaurant serving seafood dishes.
Playas Palma & Bandera	A popular choice with *Tico* families, Playa Palma is a popular surf beach with a gently humming village life, which at some point heading south along the shore becomes Playa Bandera. **B-C** *Cabinas Maldonado*, T286-1116, F227-5257. 6 cabins sleeping 4-10 people, all with private bath. Facilities include fan, kitchen and fridge. Small pool, Jacuzzi and BBQ grill just a few metres from the beach. **D** *Finca Don Herbert*, T779-9204, beeper T296-2626. Good spot for families. 5 equipped cabins with a small pool with waterslides and a café snack bar. **E** *Rooms/Restaurant Alex*, with simple rooms is 2.6 km south towards Playa Bandera. **F** *Las Brisas*, T779-9238, T372-4220 (mob). Simple rooms with private bath and a small restaurant.
Parrita	The first and only town of any real size between Jacó and Quepos is Parrita, a bustling low-level supply town serving nearby agricultural communities. Not much to see, but there's a *Banco Nacional*, a *Banco de Costa Rica* with an ATM, a gas station and a few basic hotels and stores – handy if you're staying at a nearby beach.
Isla Palo Seco	A road heads south at Parrita for 5 km to Isla Palo Seco with more fine sandy beaches, mangrove swamps and canals to explore. **Sleeping AL** *La Isla*, T779-9393, F779-9494, www.hotel-laisla.com 16 furnished and fully equipped self-catering apartments complete with TV, fan. There's a pool and Jacuzzi, and horses for riding along the beach, and canoes for exploring the mangroves. **A** *Beso del Viento*, T779-9674, F779-9675, www.besodelviento.com A better choice, this French-owned hotel has large open villas, with stylish decorative touches and 4 self-catering apartments sleeping up to 6. The pool is quiet and there are kayaks and horses for rent. The beach is close to paradise – stretching for miles into the distance.
Parrita to Quepos	South of Parrita the road continues for 22 km to Quepos down a mainly good but pot-holed road that travels through endless stretches of African palm plantations, broken only by the occasional village of two-storey, balconied houses laid out around a central football pitch, a church of normally Evangelical denomination and the obligatory branch of Alcoholics Anonymous. Most of the villages look tired, destitute and forgotten. Driving through, it would appear that some of the community are getting their spirit from various different sources.

Driving the *costanera*

From Orotina to the Pan-American Highway at Palmar Norte, Highway 34, colloquially known as the costanera, follows the coastline for 230 km. Serving popular beaches, agricultural industries and communities alike, it is a busy road and a crucial lifeline to the rest of the country. It's a fascinating road, drawing a line through varied sections of Costa Rican life.

Considering the importance of the region, the paving of the costanera *has been slow in coming, which has probably reduced development of the area. But now,*

only the 42 km section between Quepos and Dominical remains unpaved and that will probably be completed soon.

One word of warning if driving. While the roads – even the dirt ones – are good, many of the bridges in the middle section are single carriageway. More than one rented vehicle driver fresh out of Quepos has misjudged speed and space, ending up crashing down to the riverbed below.

The road is not dangerous – but some of the drivers are. Drive with caution at all times, especially at night.

Quepos

With a legacy in name at least to the Quepo Indians who inhabited the region at the time of the Spanish conquest, Quepos today pulsates with the crowds that converge on the small town, arriving in search of palm-fringed beaches and wildlife encounters. The main attraction, reached by a winding 7 km road that climbs and falls over the rocky Punta Quepos peninsula, is the justifiably popular Manuel Antonio National Park.

Quepos has successfully moved beyond a dependency on banana exports – the raison d'être behind the now largely empty port development – which crippled the town after plantations in the region were overwhelmed by disease in the early 1950s. The oil-producing African palm has replaced banana agriculture in the region, and tourism has provided employment. The lively bars and restaurants buzz and hum in the warmth of a cool ocean breeze sustained by a considerable expatriate community and visiting tourists. But hanging silently in the background, the atmosphere of an old port town remains.

Population: 14,674
Colour map 3, grid B1
Altitude: Sea level

Central Pacific

Ins and outs

Several daily flights with *SANSA* and *Travelair* from San José, with taxis meeting incoming flights for the 4-km journey to Quepos. There are 8 buses a day from San José to Quepos. Direct buses take 3½ hours, normal service 4½.

If driving, Highway 34 – the *costanera* – passes Quepos a couple of kilometres to the east – watch out for the signs or follow the traffic. From the north it's a good road for most of the 192-km journey. To the south, the road is in poor condition as far as Dominical.

Getting there

Quepos is certainly small enough to walk around without any trouble. If heading for Manuel Antonio, a half-hourly bus service makes the 7-km journey from town. The road is lined with hotels, bars, restaurants and stores – tell the bus driver where you want to get off and he'll stop at the nearest safe point. Taxis to Manuel Antonio cost about US$3 on a good day and are meant to be cheaper on the return journey but that is probably being too optimistic.

Getting around

Best time to visit Ask a *Quepolandian* and their rose-tinted view on the world will say any time is good, but the dry season runs from Jan-Mar, when clear skies and temperatures in the high 20s are guaranteed. For the rest of the year, life is still pretty good, with the heaviest rainfall between Aug and Oct.

Tourist information There is no tourist information office but drop into *Lynch Travel Services* or *Iguana Tours* for a full run-down on the latest offerings and information. Keep an eye out for *Quepolandia*, www.quepolandia.com a locally produced free English language magazine dripping with advice, tips and permanently positive quips.

History

The earliest interactions with the Quepo Indians of the peninsula took place in 1519, but it was not until Juan Vásquez de Coronado began his exploits in Costa Rica in 1563 that the Spanish conquerors got a foothold in the country. By 1570 the first mission in the country had been created in nearby San Bernadino. Fortunes waned for the Indians and the population declined rapidly and the mission closed in 1747.

Activity in the region recommenced with the small-scale planting of bananas in the area in the early 1900s, which was later adopted by the *United Fruit Company* who began large-scale plantation production in the 1930s. Development of the port and docks began at the expense of mangrove clearance. Sigatoka disease hit in the 1940s followed by Panama disease in the 1950s, which virtually wiped out the industry. Partial economic recovery

Sleeping	
1	Best Western Kamuk *B2*
2	Cabinas El Cisne & Sensación Tropical *A6*
3	Cabinas Hellen *C4*
4	Cabinas Mary *C5*
5	Ceciliano *C4*
6	Doña Alicia *B5*
7	El Malinche *B2*
8	El Parque *C2*
9	Hospedaje La Mancha *B6*
10	Majestic *C2*
11	Mar y Luna *B2*
12	Quepos *C5*
13	Sánchez *C4*
14	Sirena *B2*
15	Villas Sol y Mar *B5*

Eating
1 Café Milagro *A2*
2 Dos Locos *C2*

0 metres (approx) 100
0 yards (approx) 100

came with the introduction of African palms which produce oil used in margarine and soap.

The seeds of tourism were planted in the 1970s and early 1980s when a few isolated cabins enjoyed the unspoilt beauty of the area. The rest is history.

Essentials

In general, accommodation in Quepos is cheaper than on the road south to Manuel Antonio. With regular buses to the park, you may want to base yourself in Quepos if you're on a tight budget.

Sleeping
■ *on map*
Price codes:
see inside front cover

It can be difficult to find accommodation on Sat, Dec-Apr and when local schools are on holiday

Out of town On the *costanera* close to the airstrip is **L** *Rancho Casa Grande*, T777-0330, F777-1575, hotelrcg@racsa.co.cr Lovely yellow *casitas* in tropical gardens, with a/c, private bath and TV. Pleasant mosaic-tiled swimming pool with thatched *palapas* strewn around the sundeck. Good open-air restaurant and bar. **B** *Viña del Mar*, a few blocks north of the centre in *Boca Vieja* on the road into town, T/F777-0070. Rooms with bath, fan, pool and a restaurant. A good spot but badly in need of refurbishment.

In the centre **A** *Best Western Kamuk*, T777-0811, F777-0258, www.kamuk.co.cr 35 uninspiring but comfortable rooms with a/c, cable TV and private bath. Some of the rooms have ocean views and there's a sports bar and restaurant at street level. For this money, you will get more in Manuel Antonio. The same is true of **A** *Hotel Sirena*, T/F777-0528. A newish hotel with 14 fair-sized rooms, with a/c, hot water and private bath. The pool is rather cramped and only just outdoors. The restaurant serves breakfast and there's a small bar.

B-D *El Malinche*, T/F777-0093. 27 clean and good sized rooms, simply decorated. Some new rooms with a/c but much cheaper without. **E** *Cabinas Kali*, 200 m northeast of bus station, T777-1491. Nice rooms, family-run, clean, friendly, safe but noisy. **E** *Majestic*, T777-0294. Noisy with shared bath. **E** *Mar y Luna*, T777-0394. With or without bath, quiet, clean and popular place – but no prizes for being friendly.

F per person *El Parque*, on the waterfront, T777-0063. Clean and friendly place with private bathroom and fan. A bit rundown but good value. **F** *Sánchez*, T777-0491. Without bath but OK.

There are also various hotels towards the **eastern side of town**, on the road leading to Manuel Antonio but still in town and within walking distance. **B-D** *Ceciliano*, T777-0192. Quiet, family-run hotel with small rooms and private bath. **C** *Cabinas El Cisne & Sensación Tropical*, T777-0719. Motel style accommodation in a family-run hotel. Safe with secure parking. Bigger rooms on the left. **C** *Hotel Quepos*, T777-0274. 20 simple

3 El Banco Sports Bar *B2*
4 El Gran Escape *B2*
5 Escalofrío *C2*
6 Isabel *B2*
7 L'Angolo *C2*
8 La Cueva del Marisco *B2*
9 La Fuente *B2*
10 La Marquesa *B2*
11 Pizza Gabriel's *B2*
12 Pueblo *B2*
13 Rickshaws La Tropical *C2*
14 Soda Nahomi *C5*

Central Pacific

rooms devoid of all trimmings with bath, **D** without. **C** *Villas Sol y Mar*, T777-0307, F777-0562. 8 rooms with private bath and hot shower. Relaxed spot and plans for a refurbishment. Parking. **D** *Cabinas Hellen*, T777-0504. 24 quite small but clean rooms with private bath and fan. Plenty of parking. **D** *Cabinas Mary*, by the football pitch close to *Iguana Tours*, T777-0128. Clean, friendly, with parking. OK. **F** *Doña Alicia*, T777-0419. Big cabin with bath, friendly, quiet and parking. Clothes washing allowed. **F** *Hospedaje La Mancha*, next to post office on walkway by the football pitch, T777-0216. Cheapest place in town, very basic but clean.

Eating & drinking	*Café Milagro*, on the waterfront, best espresso and coffees, cakes and shakes. Also Cuban cigars, souvenirs and freshly roasted coffee for sale. *Dos Locos*, popular place open to the street with big portions of Mexican food. Occasional live music which drifts towards impromptu karaoke. From US$5. *El Banco Sports Bar*, long bar with bright neon, and a good line in Tex Mex. TV screens for the all-important sports games. *Escalofrio*, pizza, pasta and ice cream to die for from US$4. *El Gran Escape* is a lively restaurant serving Tex Mex with a tropical twist. Good food, recommended. Dishes from US$10. *Isabel*, on the seafront is a good breakfast choice, with good food, helpful staff and a bulletin board.

La Cueva del Marisco, opposite *Hotel Sirena*. Pokey looking, small fish restaurant, cheap and very clean with much sought after chef who refuses to go and work for the bigger hotels. Recommended. *La Fuente*, upstairs with several balcony tables, this new Chinese restaurant is very popular. Dishes around US$8. *La Marquesa*, very good and popular with cheap *casados* and many other dishes to choose from. Good for breakfast. *L'Angolo*, opposite *Dos Locos*, excellent Italian delicatessen with pasta, cheeses, bread and meats – will make up subs… a little pricey, but enjoy. *Pizza Gabriel's*. A popular little spot with a lively undercurrent – quiet not dead. Fine looking pizza and pasta from US$6. *Rickshaws La Tropical*, a bustling Chinese, popular with locals away from the bright neon and loud music. Cheap. Recommended. *Soda Nahomi*, on the road out to Manuel Antonio, next to *Lavanderías de Costa Rica*. Good sandwiches and great choice of ice creams.

There are also many good restaurants along the road towards Manuel Antonio.

Bars & nightclubs	Many of the restaurants above are equally happy if you just want a drink. Specific bars include *Tio Fernando*, a tiny little joint in the centre, normally packed, playing jazzy little tunes and serving chilled beers. The best kind of place to get stuck in for the night. *Restaurant Pueblo* is a lively bar with karaoke for the exhibitionist in you.

Shopping	Try the municipal market for fruit and bread at the bus station, as the *Super Mas* supermarket is generally poorly stocked. *L'Angolo* serves an absolutely divine mix of breads, olives, hams and everything you'd need for self-catering in style.

If you like the coffee at *Café Milagro* you can buy some to take home or order some for delivery online at www.cafemilagro.com For gifts and souvenirs try *Galeria Regalame II*, the gift store branch in Quepos of the excellent *Si como no* hotel in Manuel Antonio.

La Buena Nota, on road near the beach in Manuel Antonio, sells English language newspapers and beachwear.

Tour operators	Two first class operations are *Iguana Tours*, close to the church on the football pitch, T777-1262, www.iguanatours.com Excellent local knowledge with all the locally available tours. Friendly and helpful. Also *Lynch Travel Services*, right in the centre of town, T777-0161, www.lynchtravel.com Good information on local tours and the best one-stop shop for making travel arrangements including *SANSA* and *Travelair* flights.

*A*migos del Río, tours, good guides, T777-0082, F777-2248, amigorio@racsa. co.cr or www.amigosdelrio.com Provides Class III-IV whitewater rafting on the nearby Savegre and Naranjo rivers.

Blue Fin Sports Fishing Charters, next to *Hotel Quepos*, T777-1676/0674, www. bluefinsportfishing.org offers sports fishing charters in Quepos, Playa Flamingo and Drake Bay, and can organize a range of local tours. *Canyoning Tours*, T/F777-1924, www.canyoningtours.com will send you down or up waterfalls trussed up in all the safety gear – refreshing exhilaration. *Costa Rica Dreams* has an office on the waterfront, T777-0593, www.crdreams.com 30 years of experience in the area, custom trips and week long packages from US$1000.

Outdoor Expeditions, in the centre of town, T777-0100, F777-3079, www.canopy-tour.com Operate the canopy tour and ATV rainforest adventures. Life on the ocean waves, for a half a day, a sunset or moonlight tour with food and drinks all included with *Sunset Sails*, T/F777-1304, www.sunsetsails.net/home.htm Adults US$59, children US$49.

Air There are 8 daily flights from **San José**, 4 with *SANSA* (US$44 one way) and 4 with **Transport** *Travelair* (US$40 one way). Book in advance. In Quepos the *SANSA* office is under *Hotel Quepos*, T777-0683. Minibuses and taxis meet arriving flights at the airport, which is about 4 km from Quepos.

Bus Buses leave the capital from the Coca Cola Terminal. There are 2 express buses a day leaving San José at 0600, 1500, returning at 1230, 1900, 3½ hrs, US$4.50, book a day in advance, 6 regular buses, 4½ hrs, US$4. From **Quepos** there are buses northwest along the coast to **Puntarenas**, 3½ hrs, 0430, 1030 and 1500, return 0500, 1100, 1430, US$2.10. Two daily buses via Dominical to **San Isidro de El General**, 0830 and 1700, 3½ hrs, US$2.50, connections can be made there to get to the Panamanian border, return 0700, 1330.

Car rental *Elegante* have an office in Quepos, T777-0115, www.eleganterentacar.com *Alamo*, 100 m north of the post office, T777-3344, F777-3355, www.alamocostarica.com

Taxis Congregate opposite the bus terminal, just up from *Dos Locos* restaurant.

Banks Several branches in town including *Banco Nacional* which has a Visa ATM, as **Directory** does *Banco Popular* and *Banco San José*. The best place to exchange TCs or US$ cash is at *Distribuidora Puerto Quepos*, opposite Banco de Costa Rica, open 0900-1700, no paperwork, no commission, all done in 2 mins, same rate as banks. **Communications Internet**: access available from above *Iguana Tours* on the road out of town. Fast machines. Also at *Jungle Net Café*, above restaurant Dos Locos. **Post**: the post office is on the walkway by the football pitch, open 0800-1700. **Language schools**

Central Pacific

There are a couple of schools on the road out to the national park. *Escuela D'Amore* is in a great setting overlooking the ocean, half-way between Quepos and the national park, T777-1143, www.escueladamore.com US$850 for 2 weeks, US$980 with homestay. *Centro de Idiomas del Pacifico*, 2 km from town, T777-0805, www. escueladelpacifico.com US$440 per week with homestay, maximum class size of 4. **Laundry** *Lavanderías de Costa Rica*, near the football pitch on the road out to Manuel Antonio. **Medical services** The **hospital** is out of town near the airstrip, call T777-0922, or the **Red Cross** on T777-0118. **Useful addresses** **Immigration**: on the same street as the *Banco de Costa Rica*. **Police**: T777-0196.

Excursions

Activities in the region are developing fast. Iguana Tours and Lynch Travel Services will be able to arrange any of the trips mentioned here

Beyond lazing on the beach, **surfboards** are available for hire from rental outlets in front of the beach near the park. Local tour operators can organize **surf taxis** to nearby locations on request.

Guided walks of Manuel Antonio National Park lasting 2½ hours can be arranged through your hotel or at the entrance to the national park. Wildlife tours head out to the mangroves of nearby **Damas Island**, with caiman, sloths, monkeys and many birds. The more active can head out on tour by **kayak**.

Tours of the nearby forest are a popular activity. **Horseriding** gives you the best chance of seeing wildlife. One option heads inland to **Rancho Los Tucanes**, touring the quiet hills, valleys and waterfalls near Londres.

Raising the heart rate slightly, **whitewater rafting** trips head out to the Class III and IV Naranjo and Savegre rivers, passing through serene jungle scenery when not pumping adrenaline to fight the rapids.

Canyoning tours are one way of getting even more intimate with the rivers of the area, with rappels up and down the face of nearby waterfalls.

Noisy, and potentially dangerous, **All-terrain Vehicle (ATV) tours** are more exciting, but you'll only see wildlife if you run it over.

With all the activity, the best way to wind down at the end of the day is with a **sunset tour** of the coastal waters in one of the fine yachts that cruise the bay, sipping an ice-cold beverage as the sun sinks below the western horizon.

Rain Maker Nature Reserve

High up in the treetops is where you'll find the real activity of the rainforest, and Rain Maker, a short trip northeast of Quepos, will get you there. A network of suspended cable bridges hung between trees and linking platforms affords a unique bird's eye view of the canopy and this fascinating world. Accompanied by a local guide the trip starts with a steep – but manageable – climb to the first bridge. The 540-ha reserve protects ecosystems ranging in altitude from 200-1100 m above sea level, and your guide will point out some of the 40 butterfly and 300 bird species found in the reserve.

■ *Open daily, call in advance. T777-0777, F777-1093, www.rainmaker. co.cr Most people visit the reserve on trips from Quepos and Manuel Antonio. If you want to make your own way there, head for San Rafael Norte, leaving the costanera at Pocora, 10 km east of Parrita.*

Manuel Antonio

Colour map 3, grid A1

From the southeastern corner of Quepos, a road winds up, over and round the peninsula of Punta Quepos, passing the hotels, restaurants, bars and stores that have flourished along the length of this rocky outcrop. Travelling the road for the first time, you can't fail to be impressed by the beauty of the views. And at night,

Education in Manuel Antonio

At times the insatiable desire to make a fast buck is unpalatable, especially when made at the expense of rainforest which is at the very heart of Costa Rica's appeal. Local and international residents – and visitors too for that matter – all play a role in creating the demand that involves the destruction of rainforest.

Breaking down the relationship between conservation, preservation and economic growth is a complex affair fit for academia, and its endless international conferences and papers, but you can be certain that youngsters will keep things simple.

Kids Saving the Rainforest is a non-profit association founded by a couple of elementary schoolchildren in Manuel Antonio. With a variety of local charity events money has been raised with the simple goal of trying to save the local rainforest and the remaining squirrel monkeys found in the area. Funds raised have purchased monkey bridges which should help the monkeys move from one side of the busy main road to the other without having to cross by ground or resort to using the electric cables which straddle the road.

Donations welcome. Kids Saving the Rainforest, Apdo 297, Quepos, Costa Rica, T777-2252, www.amazingarts.org Or drop in at the Mono Azul.

---

you can't help being blinded by the neon and bright lights that speckle the hillside – evidence of the vibrant tourist trade. At times it is difficult to believe a national park flourishes on the other side of the watershed.

Ins and outs

A regular bus runs from Quepos to the end of the road at Manuel Antonio, leaving every 30 mins, US$ 0.35.

Getting around

Central Pacific

History and background

With the arrival of the Spanish, the threat to the region's natural wealth began in earnest. Long after the indigenous peoples had been sold as labourers or wiped out by illness, land was cleared for agriculture. While much of the region was used for banana plantations, the spectacular vistas of the peninsula were acquired by foreigners. With locals denied access, state authorities became aware of rumoured plans to clear the region for agriculture. In haste, the area was declared a national park in 1972.

Since then tourism development has been broadly limited to either side of the access road to the west of the national park. While there is no denying the fact that a flourishing tourism industry and a national park make uncomfortable neighbours, the extent of the damage depends on your perspective. For the time being at least development is confined – the future could be very different depending on who you talk to.

Excursions

Down towards Manuel Antonio is *Marlboro Stables*, T777-1108 offering a range of **horseriding** trips in the area. Also try *Equus Stables*, T777-0001, www.mansionesverdes.com who have **beach** horseriding trips (US$35) and trips into the **rainforest** (US$60). **Surfboard rental** is available from several beachside outlets down in Manuel Antonio.

Also see 'Excursions' in Quepos, page 300

Essentials

Sleeping
■ *on map*
Price codes:
see inside front cover

Some hotels shut in
the low season; those
that stay open offer
generous discounts

Hotels are listed in order from Quepos to Manuel Antonio. Many of the hotels along the road are in the higher price bracket. In high season, it is best to book ahead. The area is full to bursting at weekends with many locals camping on the beach.

Deciding where to stay could take all vacation. Beyond budget, it's probably simplest to work on the basis of proximity to the beach. If you want to go to the beach every day, head for the very end of the road. If you're happy mixing relaxing by the pool (if your hotel has one) with the occasional trip to the beach, then any of the hotels along the main road will suffice. Beyond these simple options, each hotel has a range of goodies and attractions designed to entice.

From Quepos one of the first and cheapest hotels you encounter is **C** *Cabinas Pedro Miguel*, T/F777-0035, pmiguel@sol.racsa.co.cr 16 simple rooms in a *Tico*-owned hotel, complete with a small pool. Credit cards accepted. The owners are down-to-earth and very helpful – a world away from the slick service found up the hill.

AL-A *Plinio*, T777-0055, F777-0558, www.hotelplinio.com 12 rooms of varying sizes, facilities and comforts and a jungle house, climbing up the hillside in a flourish of tropical hardwoods, with a nature trail leading to an observation tower. Comfortable restaurant serving *Tico*, Italian, German and north American food. Good bar and a pool set in shady tropical gardens. **AL** *El Mirador del Pacifico*, T/F777-0119, www.elmiradorcostarica.com A total of 25 rooms and villas, all with private bath, fan, a/c and balcony, some with an ocean view. The popular *Billy's Bar* and restaurant has a range of lively dishes and offers, including happy hours and live music. The pool and Jacuzzi mean you don't have to wonder out to the beach unless you really want to and they're happy to help book tours. **AL-A** *Mimo's*, T777-0054, F777-2217, www.hotelmimos.com 10 big rooms sleeping up to 4 people in a large villa, with hammocks on the veranda. Pool with bar and Italian restaurant set in pleasant gardens.

A-B *Mono Azul*, T/F777-1954, www.monoazul.com 20 rooms with private bath, with a little extra for TV and a/c. Wide range of services including a couple of pools, games room, small library and internet café. In a world controlled by the seasons, the full service bar and restaurant is open daily from 0600 until 2200 – 365 days a year. Actively involved in trying to limit further development in the region with 10% of profits going to *Kids Save the Rainforest* charity. For that very special holiday romance, co-owner Jennifer Rice is a minister. For weddings please bring your passport and birth certificate.

Hidden up a side road is the newly opened **L-A** *Villas Mymosa*, T/F777-2454, www.villasmymosa.com 10 airy villas with refreshing cross-ventilation, with fully equipped kitchenette. Big pool with moody dark blue mosaic tiling. Good discounts in low season. Recently refurbished, a bargain at these prices – get in while the going's cheap. A little further up the hill is **AL-A** *Hotel California*, T777-1234, F777-1062, www.hotel-california.com A fine view from the 22 rooms, all with private bathroom, a/c, minibar and telephone, which were undergoing extensive refurbishment when visited. There will also be a new fitness centre.

AL-A *Villa Teca*, T777-1117, F777-1578, www.hotelvillateca.com A/c rooms with a private terrace, pool, Italian restaurant and a useful free shuttle service to Manuel Antonio and the beaches. **AL** *Tres Banderas*, T777-1871, F777-1478, www.hotel-tres-banderas.com/costa-rica 14 rooms with private bath and tiling throughout, finished off with local hardwood touches. All rooms have a balcony, some with a view over the big pool, others to the rainforest. **AL-B** *La Colina*, T777-0231, F777-1533, www.lacolina.com Rooms, apartments and suites, with garden terraces and fine ocean views. Relaxing 2-tier pool complete with waterfall and wet bar. Also have a popular place in Monteverde. **A-B** *Flor Blanca*, in the middle of town – if there is such a thing –

Central Pacific

Manuel Antonio

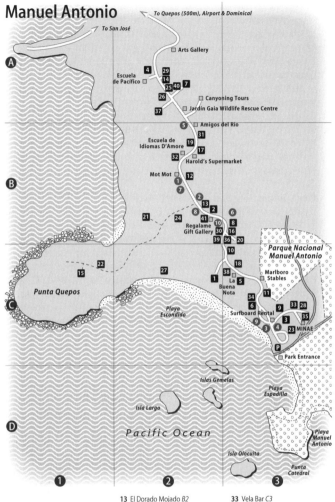

To Quepos (500m), Airport & Dominical

To San José

☐ Arts Gallery

Escuela
de Pacifico ☐

4
29
14
25 **40** **7**
26
37
☐ Canyoning Tours
☐ Jardín Gaia Wildlife Rescue Centre
5 ☐ Amigos del Río
31
Escuela de
Idiomas D'Amore
19
32 **17**
☐ Harold's Supermarket
Mot Mot ☐ **12**
1
7
2
13 **2**
8 **6**
24 **41** **10** **8**
Regalame **30** **16**
Gift Gallery **39** **36** **20**
21 **10**
18
22 **38** Marlboro
27 **5** ☐ Stables
15 **1** La **5**
Buena
Punta Quepos Nota **11**
34
Playa **6** Surfboard Rental **9** **33** **28**
Escondido **9** **3** **35**
3 **4**
23 MINAE
P
☐ Park Entrance

*Parque Nacional
Manuel Antonio*

*Playa
Espadilla*

Islas Gemelas

Isla Largo

Pacific Ocean

*Playa
Manuel
Antonio*

Isla Olocuita

*Punta
Catedral*

Central Pacific

N

0 metres 500
0 yards 500

■ **Sleeping**
1 Arboleda *C2*
2 Byblos *B2*
3 Cabinas Espadillas *C3*
4 Cabinas Pedro Miguel *A2*
5 Cabinas Piscis *C3*
6 Cabinas Ramírez *C3*
7 California *A2*
8 Casitas Eclipse *B3*
9 Costa Linda *C3*
10 Costa Verde *C3*
11 Del Mar *C3*
12 Divisamar *B2*

13 El Dorado Mojado *B2*
14 El Mirador del Pacífico *A2*
15 El Parador *C1*
16 Fila Verde *B3*
17 Flor Blanca *B2*
18 Karahe *C3*
19 La Colina *B2*
20 La Quinta *B3*
21 Makanda by the Sea *B2*
22 Mansion Inn *C1*
23 Manuel Antonio
   & Restaurant *C3*
24 Mariposa *B2*
25 Mimo's *A2*
26 Mono Azul & Restaurant *A2*
27 Nature's Beach Front *C2*
28 Playa Espadilla *C3*
29 Plinio *A2*
30 Si como no *B2*
31 Tres Banderas *B2*
32 Tulemar Bungalows *B2*

33 Vela Bar *C3*
34 Verde Mar *C3*
35 Villabosque *C3*
36 Villa Nina *B3*
37 Villa Teca *A2*
38 Villas de la Selva *C3*
39 Villas Mogote *B2*
40 Villas Mymosa *A2*
41 Villas Nicholás *B2*

● **Eating**
1 Barba Roja *B2*
2 Café Milagro *B2*
3 Del Mar *C3*
4 El Mono Loco *C3*
5 Fiesta del Mar & B21 *B2*
6 Gato Negro *B3*
7 Karola's *B2*
8 La Terraza Bar & Grill *B2*
9 Mar y Sombre *C3*
10 Pickle's Deli *B2*

close to *Harold's Supermarket*, T777-1633, F777-0032. 10 fairly pleasant rooms some with a/c, cheaper with fans, in a *Tico*-owned hotel.

Arguably the most luxurious option around is **LL** *Tulemar Bungalows*, T777-0580, F777-1579, www.tulemar. com Every luxury you can expect at this level, with floor-to-ceiling windows with panoramic views of the setting sun. Beautiful pool, nature trails and an exclusive beach.

AL-A *Divisamar*, T777-0371, F777-0525, www.divisamar.com The rooms are meant to be fairly large with private bath and a/c – but then I wasn't allowed to look at them. Popular casino which could be the main attraction. Seems overpriced from the outside. Just past the *Divisamar* there is a sign pointing to **L-B** *Nature's Beachfront*, T777-1473, F777-1475, www.maqbeach.com/natures.html The beach-front property has large studios sleeping 7, a smaller studio for 4 and standard double rooms all right on the beach. Guests who have stayed here rated them very highly.

Punta Quepos A dirt road opposite *Café Milagro* leads to Punta Quepos, which has some of the area's most exclusive (and expensive) hotels. First up is **LL-L** *Mariposa*, T777-0456, F777-0050, www.lamariposa.com A fine hotel with 35 rooms, suites and villas in a spectacular setting on a cliff overlooking Manuel Antonio beach and Punta Catedral. The restaurant is set out with all the trappings of a Spanish villa and the rooms are comfortably breezy. However, while all this is true, it has indeed seen better days. Further down the road is the exclusive **LL** *Makanda by the Sea*, T777-0442, F777-1032, www.makanda.com Certainly a contender for best hotel in Costa Rica and a winner of most romantic. Meandering paths lead to private studios and villas fully equipped for a stay of pure indulgence. With subtle Japanese influences, conventions such as walls, which restrict the view, are kept to a bare minimum. What remains in the split-level studios is a simply stunning view as the day unfolds from dawn to dusk, seen from the perfectly positioned sofa, hammock or bed. In a doubtless dreamy haze, you can wander to the infinity pool, Jacuzzi, or the nearby almost-private beach. Hopeless romantics positively encouraged.

At the end of the road is **LL** *El Parador*, 2 km from the main road, T777-1414, F777-1437, www.hotelparador.com 80 rooms with all the expected comforts. The success of the *Parador* lies in managing to provide abject luxury while keeping a happy fresh face on the place. Chatty but always courteous staff tend your every need, 4 dining rooms cater for every mood and moment include the *Queen Elizabeth*. Beyond are the comfortable rooms with fine views of the ocean and the gardens. A pool and bar, tennis courts and a gym will keep you in fine trim. If you want to visit the beach, there's a free shuttle bus. Every imaginable luxury – including helipad, but cross-winds can make for a lively take-off.

CASA LYDIA

- 5 Bedroom luxury villa rental
- Private pool
- Fantastic views of the Pacific Ocean and jungle
- Under 1 mile from pristine beaches and Manuel Antonio National Park
- Daily maid service
- Walking distance from the best local restaurants

CASA LYDIA
Manuel Antonio, Costa Rica
www: casalydia.com
email: casalydia@yahoo.com

Back on main road to Manuel Antonio AL-A *El Dorado Mojado*, T777-0368, F777-1248, www.maqbeach.com/dorado.html Set back in the forest with 8 rooms – 4 fully equipped villas and 2 studios and a couple of standard rooms. **L** *Byblos*, T777-0411, F777-0009, www.byblos.co.cr Quirky little rooms with some outrageous décor. Freeform pool surrounded by rainforest and a rancho style bar and restaurant. Overpriced. **LL-A** *Villas Nicolás*, T777-0481, F777-0451, www.villasnicolas.com 12 comfortable and spacious rental suites. If the stylish furnishings and relaxed touches feel homely that's because all the suites are someone's home, rented out when not used. Mind you, if my home was this good, I'd be reluctant to let anyone else use it. **LL** *Si como no*, T777-0777, F777-1093, www.sicomono.com A wave of refreshing originality greets the visitor staying in one of 40 rooms with ocean or forest views. With more cool touches than a polar bear on Christmas Day, the hotel sparkles with the reflected light of stained-glass windows. Comforts include a solar-heated Jacuzzi, pool and wet-bar. Of course you can dine as well at the *Claro Que Seafood* restaurant or the *Rico Tico* bar and grill. And naturally a small 40-seater cinema. Yes, why not. One of the 'Distinctive Hotels of Costa Rica', with all the best intentions to be environmentally sensitive – expensive, but worth every cent. **L-AL** *Hotel & Villas Mogote*, T777-0582, F777-1043. Comfortable rooms and villas with a bar, swimming pool, Jacuzzi and seclusion. **LL-A** *Casitas Eclipse*, T/F777-0408, www.casitaseclipse.com White-washed villas and suites drifting down the hillside, with space for 2-5 people. All rooms equipped with private bath, a/c and telephone and no less than 3 freeform pools to choose from. **B** *Fila Verde*, T777-1585, F777-1324. The closest to budget accommodation in this area. Basic rooms with private bath and small pool.

A-C *La Quinta*, up a completely missable driveway, T/F777-0434. 5 simple rooms, some with kitchenettes, with unrestricted views overlooking the bay. Up above most of the activity, this is a charming spot away from the mêlée. Recommended by humans, squirrel monkeys and Hungarians alike. In unmistakable bubblegum pink, **AL** *Villa Nina* is a bit of a landmark, T777-1221, F777-1497, www.hotelnina.com 10 hideously decorated rooms, but pleasant pool and friendly.

The World War II aeroplane – decked out as the new *Ollie's Folly Bar* – perched at the brow of the hill marks the downhill run to the beach and the imminent arrival of **LL-AL** *Costa Verde*, T777-0584, F777-0560, www.hotelcostaverde.com Booking in at the train carriage reception you're led to one of 5 multi-storey apartment blocks with comfortable to luxurious suites all with ocean or jungle views. A couple of pools have spacious sundecks with Pacific views, and trails lead through the nearby forest which apparently still has "more monkeys than people". You'll certainly be woken by howler monkeys as they crash through the trees, before heading to the *Anaconda* restaurant for breakfast with fine ocean views and national and international dishes. Across the road *La Cantina* is a bar, restaurant, disco and sports bar all rolled into one.

B-D *Arboleda*, TT777-1385, F777-0092, www.hotelarboleda.com Cabins sleeping 2-3 with bath and fan. On the hillside leading right down to beach, there's a Uruguayan restaurant, swimming pool, squash court and 8-ha wood to explore – beware snakes, crabs and monkeys in the yard at night. Recommended. **L-AL** *Karahe*, T777-0170, F777-1075, www.karahe.com *Tico*-owned and run, 32 pleasant rooms set in tropical gardens within walking distance of the beach. Set on a steep hillside, some of the cabins have lovely views. Fishing trips arranged using the 32-ft *Trinidad*.

Next to *La Buena Nota* is **B-C** *Cabinas Piscis*, T777-0046, with a dozen simple rooms, handily close to the beach. Getting closer to the beach with every step is **B** *Hotel del Mar*, T777-0543. Simple rooms with private bath. **AL** *Verde Mar*, T777-1805, F777-1311, www.maqbeach.com/verdemar.html 20 rooms with kitchenettes, fridge, personable service and a funky little pool. **C** *Cabinas Ramírez*, T777-0003. A simple option with private bath. Hammocks and camping possible. Guests can help with cooking in exchange.

At the very end of the road where buses and vehicles can easily turn is **C-D** *Hotel & Restaurant Manuel Antonio*, T777-1237. Looking straight out to the beach, has a few simple rooms where location is more important than décor. You can **camp** in the parking lot next to the restaurant. A handy spot, but naturally you'll need to watch your gear.

A small side road – made prominent by a cluster of *sodas*, surfboard rental shops, tour operators and information kiosks – leads to a handful of popular hotels.

E per person *Costa Linda*, T777-0304, double rooms or **F** per person in 6-bed dormitories with fan and cooking facilities, fan. Reports of raccoons raiding the outdoor kitchen in the night, good breakfasts. **AL** *Cabinas Espadillas*, T/F777-0416, www.espadilla.com/cabins.html A good family choice with fully equipped cabins sleeping up to 4 people, complete with kitchenette – a good deal if you can get the numbers together, shares the facilities of the *Hotel Playa Espadilla*. **B-C** *Hotel Vela Bar*, T777-0413, F777-1071, www.velabar.com 11 rooms including a fully equipped house, with private bath, fans, porch and safe box. The restaurant is very good. Open all day serving a mix of international, Costa Rican and vegetarian dishes. At night, the bar is also a popular spot. **L-AL** *Hotel Playa Espadilla*, T/F777-0903, www.espadilla. com 16 rooms, a dozen with hot water bath, cable TV and a/c set in pleasant gardens. 4 fully equipped rooms have a kitchenette and fridge. A wide range of activities including pool table, tennis, as well as a restaurant, bar, swimming pool and wet bar. **AL** *Villabosque*, T777-0463, F777-0401. 18 comfortable but unexceptional rooms all with a/c, private bath and hot water. Good range of services including a pool, bar, restaurant and parking, but just a little too cramped.

Eating
In order from Quepos to Manuel Antonio

Fiesta del Mar is a fairly new place in town yet to become established, serving seafood. *Barba Roja* restaurant and bar in a popular spot, with happy hour either side of sunset. Good mix of seafood, grills, burgers and snacks. Credit cards accepted. Open 0700 until 2300. Mid-range and up. *Karola's*, T777-1557, is one of the best restaurants in the area with a mind-boggling international menu. Naturally seafood dominates, but there's something for everyone. Mid-range and up.

Café Milagro serves good coffee and homemade baked goods, with a selection of international newspapers and magazines. *Sunset Poolside Bar & Grill*, T777-0442, at *Makanda by the Sea* hotel is a classy dining choice for a special evening. Expensive.

Next stop on the perched on the main road is *La Terraza Bar & Grill*. Indeed a terrace bar and grill with a fine view out west. Stop for a beer, a snack or in the evening choose something from the grill menu. *Pickle's Deli* is a dreamy surprise if you've been on the road for a while, with mouth-watering fillings packed into subs and sandwiches. Fresh baked goods, fruit smoothies and of course coffee. A little further on is the newly opened *Restaurant Gato Negro* which is worth a visit. *La Cantina BBQ*, T777-0384, at *Costa Verde* positively hums with activities. If you're keen on live music, it's worth stopping by for the lively atmosphere before heading elsewhere.

Approaching the beach area, in a small lay-by, is *Bar & Restaurant Mar y Sombre*, T777-0003, good *casado especial* and jumbo shrimps with shady tables on the beach and sun-loungers for hire. On the main road towards Quepos is *Restaurant del Mar* T777-0543, which rents surfboards, sells drinks and light meals and has a collection of English novels to read in the bar. Almost at the end of the road is *El Mono Loco*, serving up a full menu of international dishes and lively in the evenings.

Shopping
Harold's Supermarket is pretty much in the middle between the national park and Quepos. Well stocked, in their own words "if we don't have it, you don't need it". *Mot Mot* next to *Barba Roja* sells a good selection of souvenirs, with some good original T-shirts. *Regalame* is one of the best gift shops in Costa Rica, with a great collection of souvenirs and goods, all made in Costa Rica and all made by genuine artists. *La Buena Nota*,

Booking accommodation

*Communications in the south and central region of Costa Rica are less well developed than in many other parts of the country. If you want to book accommodation in advance, and the contact details provided fail to get a response try using the **Selva Mar** booking service. Their office is in San Idisro de El General or you can contact*

them on T771-4582, F771-8841, www.exploringcostarica.com

*Also look up **Brunca Tours**, T771-3100, F771-5159 www.ecotourism.co.cr/ bruncatours They can arrange a number of local tours, based from their office in San Isidro de El General.*

T777-1002, F777-1946, buennote@sol.racsa.co.cr One-stop shop for newspapers, magazines, books, beachwear, postcards, information and the odd bar of chocolate.

Language Schools Next door to *Cabinas Pedro Miguel*, is the *Escuela del Pacífico*, **Directory** T777-0805, www.escueladelpacifico.com Class sizes limited to 4 people, usually just 2. A fine spot to touch up on your Spanish, with options for homestays at US$440 per week, a private room at the school or more conventional hotel accommodation. Another option further along the road is the *Escuela de Idiomas D'Amore*, T777-1143, F777-0233, www.esueladamore.com which subscribes to the immersion technique, US$850 for 2 weeks, US$980 with homestay.

Parque Nacional Manuel Antonio

Universally acclaimed as one of the most scenic landscapes of Costa Rica, *Colour map 3, grid B1* Manuel Antonio National Park is a gem of tropical wilderness. Whether a lover of pristine sandy beaches and crystal clear waters, or wandering through tropical forests teeming with wildlife, there is something in this park for you.

The park protects just 638 ha – making it one of the smallest in the country – with a further 55,000 ha of marine preserve. But it packs quite a punch. High annual rainfall (close to 4 m) makes this an area of humid forest with sections of untouched primary forest and secondary forest slowly undergoing regeneration. The diversity is complemented by stands of red, white and buttonwood mangrove. Offshore, a dozen coastal islands provide refuge and nesting sites for seabirds.

Rocky outcrops feature strongly in the headland. **Punta Catedral**, once an island, is now connected to the mainland by a sandy link or tombolo, slowly deposited over time by opposing currents sweeping along the coastline. A **trail** climbs steeply through the point, with viewing points conveniently placed so you can catch your breath. The former island is home to primary and secondary forest and a quiet early morning walk will find you face to face with surprisingly timid wildlife including pacas, agoutis and iguanas. With a guide you'll see a lot more. A couple of longer trails head east along the coastline passing the tree-fringed beaches of Manuel Antonio, heading out to **Playa Escondido** and beyond to **Punta Serrucho** and **Playa Playitas**. The trails are the best place to see the monkeys, which are fairly easily seen in the park, including white-faced capuchins and the rarer and endangered squirrel monkey.

The second main attraction in the park involves strolling just beyond the entrance to the park and plonking yourself on a beach. There are five beautiful sandy beaches, fringed with the attractive but poisonous **manzanillo** tree, with gentle gradients good for swimming. ■ *T777-0644, F777-0654. The park is open 0700-1600, Tue-Sun. Closed Mon. US$6. The entrance to the park is*

Central Pacific

across the tidal estuary of the Quebrada Camaronera. If the tide is too high to wade across, small boats will ferry you for a small fee. On the land side of the river, there is ample parking. US$5 for the day. The half-hourly bus from Quepos ends at the parking area. Guides can be arranged at the entrance to the park, or you can make arrangements at your hotel.

Quepos to Dominical

From Quepos the *costanera* continues its journey down the coast along a dirt road which is the last remaining stretch left to be upgraded. It's an interesting drive as much for what you don't see as anything – with almost no tourist services for the 42-km journey to Dominical, just endless neat lines of African palms glistening and rustling in the coastal breeze. If you're driving, there are many single-width bridges that are not signposted which have been the site of many accidents – drive carefully.

Matapalo
Colour map 3, grid B2

Of course life would be dull without exceptions like Matapalo, about 24 km south of Quepos – look out for the sign on the main highway. A small Swiss community has seized on the beauty of this almost uninhabited stretch of fine sandy beaches, all good for swimming. It's a great place to stop for truly quiet relaxation, yet it's close enough to visit attractions near Manuel Antonio to the north and Dominical to the south.

Smaller places tend to close down in the green season – call ahead

Sleeping and eating **A-C** *El Coquito del Pacifico*, T/F384-7220, www.elcoquito.com 6 big bungalows and the same number of rooms, all kitted out to comfortable European standards. The bungalows, decorated with Latin American wall hangings, get fresh cross-ventilation from the sea breezes. The French-influenced Swiss restaurant serves excellent fresh food from a menu tailored to the guest's request. Big pool and pleasant gardens right on the beach – a good choice.

B *Alberque Suiza*, T/F382-7122. 3 big rooms with tiled floors and bamboo furniture with terraces and private bath in a large villa. Quiet little balcony restaurant upstairs services a fusion of reasonably priced European and *Tico* cuisine. Horses and mountain bikes available for rent. **B-C** *Piedras Blancas* T771-3015. 5 reasonably comfortable wooden bungalows. Owned by one of the longest resident expats in town, the place is evolving slowly and with a chaotic charm. Good international menu at the restaurant and plans for a small beachwear boutique.

A couple of cheaper places that are periodically open include **D** *El Oasis*, with 10 cabins and **E** *Terraza del Sol*, with a handful of beach-front cabins. Out on the main road, *Express del Pacifico* is a good stopping point for a snack and refreshments if you're driving through town. International and local cuisine and a first for Matapalo – ping pong … just what you need after driving down the response- testing *costanera*.

Dominical

Colour map 3, grid B2
www.dominical.net

A small town of no more than a few hundred people at the mouth of the Río Barú, Dominical owes its success to the fine surf that pounds the coastline. If you want to surf, or learn, it's a great spot. Other breaks nearby add a touch of variety if the board is your guide, and there are several locals who will happily offer advice and suggestions on places to go.

Beyond surfing, the beaches in the area are quite pleasant. There are also tours and trips to *Hacienda Barú* private reserve to be investigated, complete with canopy tours and nature trails and nearby waterfalls and trails through the forest on foot or horseback.

Dominical is small enough to walk through in 5 mins. The access road is on Highway 34, with most hotels and restaurants along the road or lining the beach. **Getting around**

Hacienda Barú is an eco-friendly adventure park set in a privately owned **Excursions** National Wildlife Refuge. The owner Jack Ewing and his wife arrived in the area in 1972 at a time when Costa Rican conservation was in its infancy. By the end of the 1980s, the cattle-man turned conservationist – a reasonably common conversion – had the opportunity and foresight to buy and formally protect the remarkably diverse property. In an area of just 1.92 sq km, over 310 species of bird have been recorded – the whole of the United States has 996.

A sense of personal discovery is created by the use of interpretive pamphlets that allow you to wander through the trails alone. Going as slow as you like – and the slower the better – you can soak up the complexities of the rainforest at your own speed. Guides are also available if you prefer. Trails lead through primary and secondary forest, to the mangroves along the beach and to an observation tower where you may see three-toed sloths, white-faced capuchin monkeys and peccaries.

Beyond the trails activities include tree climbing, trussed up in harness and safety gear, a full day guided nature walk through primary forest or a night spent in the jungle – an eerie experience under a dark moonless sky. The beach is also used by solitary nesting olive ridley, and increasingly rare hawksbill, turtles that arrive from July through to October. ■ *Open daily, guided walks start at US$20 per person, rising to US$50 for a night in the jungle. Contact Hacienda Barú on T787-0003, F787-0004, www.haciendabaru.com Barú is about 2 km north of Dominical. Accommodation is available (B) in simple, fully-equipped cabins. A pleasant open-air restaurant services refreshments and Tico dishes for guests and visitors.*

There is a volunteer work programme run by the local conservation group *Asociación de Amigos de la Naturaleza del Pacífico Central y Sur* (ASANA) which is working to develop a wildlife corridor project – the Tapir Biological Corridor – between Manuel Antonio and the Osa Peninsula. Placements cost US$75 a week for food, working on trail maintenance, tree nurseries, planting and other tasks. Contact Franklin Sequeira at ASANA on T787-0254 or Jack Ewing on T787-0001, jeewing@racsa.co.cr, or to work on the turtle project asanaturtles@yahoo.com

Ten kilometres along the road to San Isidro, a road leads to a couple of water- **Waterfalls** falls, the largest being the 50-m high Nauyaca Waterfalls reached by horseriding tours through the rainforest. Trips can be organized from Dominical or direct with Don Lulo on T787-3187, F771-2003, www.ecotourism.co.cr/nauyacawaterfalls

A-B *Tortilla Flats*, a stone's throw from the beach, T/F787-0033, www.ecotourism. **Sleeping** co.cr Formerly *Cabinas Nayarit*, 19 rooms, sleeping 3 people, private bath and hot water. Overpriced in the high season, but good discounts for rest of the year.

B-C *Río Lindo*, at the entrance to town, T787-0028, F787-0078, www.dominical. net/hotelriolindo Clean, tidy rooms with a balcony or terrace, run by the affable Paco. Each room has a private bath with *agua natural*, fan or a/c. Big pool and sundeck with a lively bar in high season.

C *Diuwak*, T787-0087, F787-0089, www.diuwak.com Popular mini-tourist complex, comfortable rooms or fully equipped bungalows sleeping 2-6 people, which are smartly if rather uncreatively decorated. Good range of services including (pricey) internet access, a small supermarket, and international telephone service. Credit cards

Central Pacific

accepted. **C-D** *Albergue Willdale*, T787-0023. Rooms with fan and bath. Bikes, boat trips, fishing and horse rental available. Reported to be winding down or taking only month-long bookings. **C-D** *Cabinas San Clemente*, on the beach, T787-0026, F787-0015. 12 *cabinas*, both with and without a/c, sleeping 3-5 people. Also 6 surf rooms, where your interests should lie beyond where you're sleeping. Friendly US-owned place, with same owners as the restaurant on the main street. There are cheaper rooms (**E**) above the bar with shared bath and fan.

D *Posada del Sol*, on the main street next to *Diuwak*, T/F787-0085. Owned by local historian Mariela Badilla, 20 or so well kept and tidy rooms, with bath, fan and a small patio with hammocks. A quiet spot, and good value. At the end of the road is **D-E** *Cabinas El Coco*, T787-0235, F787-0239. 20 rooms, the 10 that are close to the beach front are OK with private bath. **Camping** is possible (**G**) per person.

Close to the town About 500 m from the beach upstream along the Río Barú at the northern end of town and reached through the main entrance road is **AL** *Villas Río Mar Jungle and Beach Resort*, T787-0052, F787-0054, www.villasriomar.com 40 thatched roof bungalows meandering up the hillside, all with kitchenette, bathrooms and a small terrace with hammock. The complex focuses on a big pool, with a wetside bar and a huge thatched roof restaurant serving local and international specialties. A tennis court for the active, it's good spot for families and groups.

On the beach front 1 km south of Dominical, more easily reached along the main road, is **A** *Hotel Roca Verde*, T787-0036, F787-0013, www.hotelrocaverde.com Tropical rooms with a/c and a small balcony or terrace. Good quiet spot in a secluded cove, with a pool, big bar and restaurant.

Eating Down the main (er, only) street there is *Soda Nanyoa* and a little further on *Restaurant Coco* which serves good cheap food.

La Capanna, near the entrance to town, T787-0072, is universally acknowledged as the best restaurant in town with authentic Italian and Mediterranean dishes. Open daily 1100-1500, 1700 until late. Closed Mon. *Mono Loco* restaurant and bar at *Tortilla Flats* is on the beach front with divine gourmet sandwiches (teriyaki chicken!) open for breakfast and full dinner. Cheap. *San Clemente Bar & Grill* is a lively Tex-Mex sports bar with mid-range dishes and huge portions, a pool table and satellite TV. Recommended. *Thrusters* positively heaves – it's the hip spot for the surf crowd.

Jazzy's River House T787-0023, is a beautiful laid-back dining option which soothes the soul. Throws and cushions create a relaxed homely atmosphere away from the loud music and noise of other bars. Fine food is accompanied by live music performed by ... you. Bring your instruments and join in the open-mike which sometimes takes place after dinner. There's also folk dancing and basket weaving classes (yes, really) – drop in and find out about the latest developments.

Transport Dominical is a bit of a transport hub. Highway 34 meets the only good road from San Isidro de El General and the highlands for its entire length just north of the town.

Bus There are 3 daily buses to **Quepos** at 0545, 0815, 1350 and a 1450 at weekends, 2 hrs. Heading south, 5 daily buses go to **Uvita** from 0950 to 2100, 45 mins. A couple of buses head further south to **Ciudad Cortés** and **Ciudad Neily**, for connections to the Osa Peninsula, at 0420 and 1000.

Heading inland, there are 4 daily buses to **San Isidro de El General**, from where there are frequent buses to San José. A direct bus to the capital leaves at 0545, with an additional weekend bus at 1340.

If driving, it is a good 34-km scenic road that climbs slowly through the mountains arriving eventually at San Isidro de El General.

Communications There are a couple of public telephone boxes in town, but for long distance calls visit *Diuwak* who also have an **internet** service.

South of Dominical

Newly paved road stretches south to Uvita and beyond to Palmar opening up a number of comfortable roadside options and secluded hideaways to the privileged few who get this far south by road. The main appeal of the area is to slow down to a state of total and abject relaxation venturing out to the few beaches found down the coastline when the mood takes you or to the undeveloped Parque Nacional Marino Ballena. As is true for much of Costa Rica's west coast, the sunsets are simply beyond words.

Public transport is available to Uvita. Outside of this immediate area most – though not all – hotels are away from the main road making private transport a necessity. The recently paved *costanera* improves access to the area substantially and is certain to lead to more visitors. New hotels are opening and most are tasteful in style so look out for any new and pleasant surprises.

On the east side of the road, 3½ km south of Dominical, hills give way to a small, grassy area and a dirt road, more suited to walking than driving, climbs steeply to Escaleras. The road winds through good forests, ideal for a bit of independent exploring if you've got the confidence to strike out alone. While the gradient is challenging, four-wheel drive will get through, and the road leads to Finca Brian y Emilia (see below).

Escaleras
Colour map 3, grid B2

Sleeping A *Finca Brian y Milena*, T396-6206, Apdo 2-8000, San Isidro de El General, Costa Rica, for a 2-day minimum, all meals included. A working farm with simple accommodation that has been "making paradise a reality" for 25 years. A couple of cabins and some rooms set in a forested area, with *Tico* dishes. Good hiking in the grounds. Also a good volunteer programme which you can work for a week or even longer. A little further up the hill with unbelievable views is **B** *Bella Vista Lodge*, T388-0155, or through *Selva Mar*. A handful of rooms and fully equipped *casitas* in a large wooden house with broad balconies perched on the edge of the forested escarpment looking out to the Pacific. Filling national dishes keep the energy levels up for the moments of exertion which naturally include hiking and bird-watching, and further afield horse-riding to the Barú River falls. Even further up the hill is **L** *Villas Escalera*, T/F385-1526, www.villas-escaleras.com Top of the range comforts are available in this luxury, fully equipped house with 4 rooms large enough to take up to 10 people. Vaulted ceilings, beautiful hardwood flooring, Spanish tile floors and white-wash walls decorated with fine textiles. Quiet and secluded, with a freeform pool, it's a great spot to hide away either on your own, or in a group.

Around the town of Uvita, a few small communities including Bahía and Colonia provide simple accommodation popular with budget travellers seeking quiet and solitude on the Pacific coast. If you want rainforest with occasional beaches go to the town of Uvita; if you want beaches, head for Bahía or Colonia.

Uvita
Colour map 3, grid B2

Sleeping Uvita The entrance to Pueblo Uvita is marked by the *El Viajero* restaurant. A short distance up the hill on the left is **D** *Cabinas Los Laureles*, with 3 *cabinas* with private bathroom, simple and quite good. A little further on is **C** *Coco Tico Ecolodge*, with 6 clean *cabinas* sleeping 3, with private bathrooms and trails out the back. A steep signposted uphill hike of a couple of km – it's not that bad really – leads to

Central Pacific

E-G *Cascada Verde*. Sorry, no telephone in the jungle, but just turn up and you're certain to find space of sorts in this educational retreat and permaculture farm. Beds, hammocks and camping are allowed and you can actually work on the farm to offset your accommodation expenses. Vegetarian meals work out at US$8 a day, and every 7th night a meal is free. Seeking utopia, all sorts of relaxation techniques for mind and body drift through the nature-first philosophy. Up in the hills, the place is close to walking trails, waterfalls and swimming pools. If you like this kind of place, you'll love it – the people staying certainly do.

Sleeping Bahía **E** *Cabinas Punta Uvita*, closest to the beach opposite *Restaurant Los Almendros*, T770-8066. Simple, basic *cabinas* with private bathroom. Also provide tourist information, arrange horseriding and snorkelling and scuba diving. Moving away from the beach is **F** *Cabinas Betty*, with 3 simple cabins, and **F** *María Jesus*, on the road from the main highway. **F** *Villa Hegalva*, T382-5780. In a permanent state of evolution, the 14 basic rooms are clean and a good deal. **Camping** is permitted for a small fee, and hammocks rock gently in the breezy shade of the pleasant gardens. Small bar and restaurant to keep you going and plans for a kitchen but don't rely on it.

Colonia has a beautiful, grey sand beach and is normally completely deserted

Sleeping Colonia A comfortable choice in the area is **B-C** *Cabinas El Chamán*, 2 km south on the beach, T771-2555. Good location with 8 simple *cabinas* all with private bathroom. **Camping** permitted at US$4 per person. Nearby is **D** *Villa Marie Luisa Lodge*, T/F236-6185, with simple cabins.

Transport **Bus** Services in the area are increasing as transport becomes easier. Buses leave from **San José** Coca Cola Terminal at 0500 and 1500, returning at 0500 and 1300, 7 hrs. From **San Isidro de El General** there are daily services at 0900 and 1600, returning at 0600 and 1400, 2 hrs. From **Dominical** buses leave at 1000 and 1700. From the south, buses leave **Palmar Sur** at 0700, 1300 and 1700, returning at 0430, 1100 and 1500, 2 hrs. Buses do a trawl of the area stopping close to Uvita and Bahía. Let the driver know where you are planning to stay and he will drop you off at the closest point.

Rancho La Merced Rancho La Merced is a national wildlife refuge south of Uvita, with over 500 ha of primary and secondary tropical rainforest as well as mangrove estuary, adjacent to the Marino Ballena National Park. The area can be explored easily, ideally on horseback, with trips going down the beach, to the mangroves or around the ranch as you get to be cowboy for a day, driving and roping cattle and checking calves and cows. There are also walking tours to nearby waterfalls. ∎ *Prices from US$30 for a half-day walking tour.*

Sleeping Accommodation is available at **A** *Cabina El Kurukuzungo*, which has space for 6 people with a couple of bedrooms, kitchen and living room and *The Old Farm House*, with a capacity for 10 with 5 bedrooms, a bathroom and kitchen. There are 3 Costa Rican country-style meals included in the price, with electricity provided by a generator from 1800-2100. Book through *Selva Mar*.

Parque Nacional Marino Ballena

Colour map 3, grid B2 The vast majority of Ballena (Whale) Marine National Park is coastal waters – 5,161 ha against 116 ha of protected land – which may go some way to explaining why there isn't a lot to see on land at this, one of Costa Rica's least-developed national parks.

The underwater world is home to coral reefs and abundant marine life that includes common and bottle-nosed dolphins as well as occasional visits from humpback whales, at times seen with their calves.

Offshore, **Las Tres Hermanas** and **Isla Ballena** mark the southernmost boundary of the park providing nesting sights for frigate birds, white ibis and brown pelicans. To the north, at **Punta Uvita**, sandy deposits have created a tombolo linking the former island with the mainland.

Although there is a rarely staffed ranger's station in Bahía (T/F786-7161), and signposts line the *costanera*, the infrastructure in the park is non-existent. There is a nominal entrance fee of US$6 which is rarely collected. Along the beach at Bahía is a **turtle nesting** project administered by the local community. As with the park itself, the organization is very ad hoc – visitors and volunteers are welcome. **Beachcombing** is good, as is **snorkelling** when the tides are favourable. **Boat trips** to the island can be arranged from Bahía, and **diving** is starting up with the most recommended local being Maximo Vásquez, or Chumi as he is known.

The beaches continue south, sprinkled with the ornate shapes of bleached white driftwood. Currents are strong and ever changing due to tides and the influence of the Río Terraba with its main outlet to the south. The area around the town of **Ojochal** and **Playa Tortuga** has sprouted a modest harvest of comfortable hotel and dining options – many of them with French-Canadian owners.

Around Ojochal

Sleeping First stop, about 12 km south of Uvita, is **A** *Paraíso del Pacífico*, T788-8280, F786-6335, sindys@racsa.co.cr 11 comfortable, if slightly sparse cabins with private bath and hot water and small balcony set on the hillside. Excellent views with an open air restaurant to watch the setting sun and pool and sundeck. A slightly livelier option than most places nearby.

A little further on is **AL** *Villas Gaia*, T/F788-8676 or T/F256-9996, www.villasgaia. com A Dutch-run hotel with 12 colourful wooden cabins perched up on the hillside. Each cabin has private bath, orthopedic beds for 3 and a superb view from a balcony that looks straight out to the forest. The restaurant is a colourful scene of murals and plants with good food at reasonable prices. A big pool has beautiful views across the Pacific to the west and a drink from the bar will finish off what is certain to have been a perfect day.

B *Villas El Bosque*, mobile 398-2112, F786-6358, pages.infinit.net/miring/costa/ rica/ Also with a fine view from the bluff overlooking the beach below, with just a couple of cabins surrounded by forest sleeping 4 and a double room. Private bath, hot water and kitchenettes are available. The balconies look directly over the cliff – giving a bird's eye view of the birds' eyes. A small pool and a small trail make this a great, intimate little spot.

Just south of the turning to Ojochal is the new home of 'Gringo Mike', **B** *Posada Playa Tortuga B & B*, T384-5489, in San José on T220-2410, ptortuga@racsa.co.cr 10 elegantly decorated and spacious rooms, all with private bath, an air of relaxed sophistication and fine ocean views. Mike's genuine and apparently effortless charm blends excellent service with an inherent knowledge of the weakness in us all – the desire for fine food and good times. A full breakfast starts the day, with evening dishes several nights a week if there's enough interest. With excellent local knowledge, Mike is one of the original expat arrivals to the area and one of the best hosts.

Central Pacific

Ojochal North of Posada Playa Tortuga a road heads inland to the small community of Ojochal, which by planning or default is overwhelmingly French-Canadian.

Sleeping **AL-C** *Rancho ô Soluna*, T788-8351, solunacr@yahoo.com A couple of rooms decorated with celestial influences, and a pair of small houses with kitchenette. Pleasant gardens are now home to a new swimming pool or take the more natural approach in the Río Balsa – an idyllic setting for swimming in the shallow pools or **camping**.

Several other good options in the region lead further inland – but many close or wind down for the rainy season so be sure to book in advance. They include **A-B** *El Perezoso*, T786-6358, **A** *Papagayo*, T/F788-8210. One of the best restaurants in the area is *Gringo Mike's* (see *Posada Playa Tortuga B & B* above), which apparently does some of the best pizza in the New World.

If the place is all just a bit too quiet you can interact with the outside world at *Café Dulce Lucy* which is a cyber café, with super cuisine. It is a bit pricey but you are a long way from anywhere and it's all done by a satellite sitting on the roof – latest news is that telephone lines are coming to town, but maybe they'll keep the dish as a local landmark. The French-Canadian owners are also very helpful and can help with any inquiries.

The southern region

9

The southern region

318 Southern Pan-American Highway

318 Route of the Saints

319 Pan-American Highway

320 Pan-American Highway

321 Cerro de la Muerte

322 San Isidro de El General

326 San Gerardo de Rivas

327 Parque Nacional Chirripó

329 Pan-American Highway

331 Palmar Norte and Palmar Sur

333 Ciudad Neily

334 Paso Canoas

335 Valle de Coto Brus

335 San Vito

336 Parque Nacional La Amistad

337 Wilson Botanical Gardens

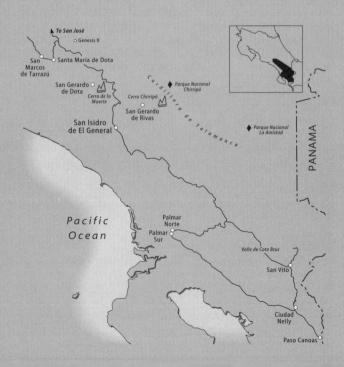

Tell a Tico *you're going south along the Pan-American Highway through the Cordillera de Talamanca and the look of bewilderment that spreads across the face is unfailing and immediate. From south of Cartago to the Osa Peninsula, the central southern district of Costa Rica is almost an undiscovered, or more likely forgotten, region – for some with good reason. Your journey takes you through* **Siberia** *and beyond to* **Cerro de la Muerte** *– the Hill of the Dead – hardly names to inspire a journey through paradise. Beyond División the road makes a slow and steady descent through the valley of the El General river.*

But the southern zone has some very real charms, which for some will be the highlight of their visit. This is where the smart money goes for guaranteed **quetzal** *sightings. The highest point in the country,* **Cerro Chirripó** *at 3,820 m, is a steady and rewarding hike from San Gerardo de Rivas, close to San Isidro de El General. For the entire length of the* **Talamanca Mountains** *stretching beyond the border with Panama, only a handful of opportunities exist to explore this vast protected area.*

Further south, culturally depleted **Indian communities** *struggle to adapt to an ever-changing world. From San Vito in the far south, it's a short trip to the world famous* **Wilson Botanical Gardens,** *from where a spectacular road drops rapidly to the western lowlands around* **Ciudad Neily.**

> ## Things to do in the southern region
>
> - Aim for the top of the world – well the top of Costa Rica, at least – by trekking to the summit of **Cerro Chirripó**. And set your sights on the Pacific, hiking from **Santa María de Dota** to **Quepos**.
> - Survive a hike to the **Cerro de la Muerte** – the Hill of the Dead – and experience the cloudforest wonders of Genesis II.
> - Visit the indigenous **Terraba** and **Boruca** communities of the southern valley, taking time to hear their version of progress in Costa Rica.
> - Drift slowly through the rarely visited **Coto Brus Valley**.

Southern Pan-American Highway

From San José, Highway 2 – the only section of the Pan-American Highway not called Highway 1 – heads southeast towards Cartago, shying south of the city and beginning the steep climb through switchbacks, with only clouds and heavily laden trucks for company.

Accommodation is dotted along the road, and signposting – as in much of the country – is more a statement of intent as opposed to a reliable indication of direction and destination. Hotels advertise their location in relation to kilometres from San José. While kilometre markers are erratic, the system does work, even if it does occasionally mean getting involved in advanced algebra as you try to work out precisely where you are.

Sleeping
These first couple of options along the Pan-American Highway are really only of interest to bird-watchers

B-C *Cerro Alto*, at Km 46, T/F551-5428. Simple A-frame alpine cabins sleeping up to 4 people with kitchenette and a café-style restaurant. Popular with *Josefiños* at weekends, you'll have the place and views of the volcanoes and valleys to yourself in the week. The same is true of **C** *Cabanas de Montaña*, at Km 51, set back 1.6 km off a 4-wheel drive road, T382-4148. Very quiet and basic cabins with real fires at a chilly 2,200 m above sea level. Beautiful cloudforest with several trails leading through the moss-laden trees.

Route of the Saints

Forgotten in time – and barely one hour's drive south of San José – the so-called 'Route of the Saints' makes for a popular day-trip from the capital or an interesting detour if heading south. You can visit the area heading directly south from San José through Aserrí along Highway 209.

It's a curious collection of small towns and cut-off communities that take their name from various saints. Some are set in broad valleys, while others sit clinging to hillsides surrounded by neatly planted lines of coffee. Youthful streams have carved steep-sided valleys, often shadowed by challenging roads that provide spectacular scenery and occasionally unexpected views – especially when lit by the soft light of dawn or dusk. As the name suggests, saintly guidance takes on an ecclesiastical sheen and the churches of the towns are as varied in style as the wildlife of Costa Rica. They are not the kind of places you 'must see', rather a pleasant collection of experiences.

Santa María de Dota
Colour map 3, grid A2

Taking the turning west at Km 51, south of Empalme, a winding road descends to the town of Santa María de Dota (population 4,713). A simple white-washed church basks in the spacious main plaza.

The southern region

To the Pacific Coast – direct

From Santa María de Dota and San   *the route is a popular mountain bike route*
Marcos de Tarrazú, rarely used trails lead   *and an interesting hike which is reportedly*
west through fine scenery to the Pacific   *manageable in 10 hours, but probably*
coast just north of Quepos. Only suitable   *more enjoyable spread out over two or*
for 4-wheel drive vehicles in the dry season,   *three days.*

Sleeping and eating If staying the night the best choice is the incredibly friendly **D** *Cecilia's Cabinas*, 15 mins' walk southeast from the plaza T541-1233. 7 simple, clean cabins with hot showers. Highly recommended. In the centre of town is **F** *Hotel and Restaurant Dota*, 25 m north of the plaza, T541-1026, without bath. **F** *Hospedaje Fonda Marieuse*, by the bus stop, T541-1176. Shared bath, clean but very basic. Has seen better days, but still OK.

No shortage of *sodas* in town and if you are short of cash there's a *Banco Nacional*.

Sliding down the steep slopes of the Río Pirrís valley, a 6-km road leads to San Marcos de Tarrazú with its fine cream-coloured church perched on the hillside and a community that might be auditioning for a John Ford western. | **San Marcos de Tarrazú**
Colour map 3, grid A1

Sleeping D *Tarrazú*, close to the main square, T546-6022. Simple rooms with private bath, hot water and parking. Next best is **E** *Continental*, T546-6225, with shared bath and cold water. Finally, try **F** *Zacateca*, T546-6073, with bath and hot water. | *Accommodation here is generally unappealing*

Several *sodas* around town and the fine *Pizzeria Las Tejas* round the back of the church. Branches of *Banco Nacional* and *Banco de Costa Rica* in town.

Further southwest **San Lorenzo** has a thoroughly modern church which, in a complete break with tradition, isn't on the main plaza. North of San Marcos, **San Pablo de León Cortes** has a modern, polygonal church with fine carpentry.

Bus 13 daily buses from San José to *Santa María* via *San Marcos*, US$2.10, 1½ hrs, from Av 16, C 19-21, Terminal Los Santos. | **Transport**

East of Santa María, the road climbs the Pirrís valley to Copey, 7 km from the Pan-American Highway at Km 58, with a fine, rickety old tin church that defies nature and the elements, and somehow remains standing. | **Copey**
Colour map 3, grid A2

Sleeping Just outside town is the very comfortable **A** *El Toucanet Lodge*, T/F541-1435, www.ecotourism.co.cr/eltoucanetlodge 4 rooms sleeping 3, in a beautiful wooden stilted house built by the owner Gary Roberts. Each room has a private bath, hot water and a small terrace. After a day exploring the nearby *páramo* (see page 329) and cloudforest biological reserve looking for quetzals and other birds you can feast on international and *Tico* dishes before resting by the fireside to ward off the chill that accompanies the night at 1,950m.

Pan-American Highway

Four-and-a-half kilometres east of Km 58 (marked by the prominent mustard yellow church in Cañón) is *Genesis II*, a privately owned National Wildlife Refuge protecting 40 ha of cloudforest at 2,360 m above sea level, bordering Tapantí-Macizo de la Muerte National Park, Costa Rica's newest | **Genesis II**

The southern region

 ## Surviving the Talamanca Mountains

Compared to the comfortable warmth of the lowlands, the cold of the highlands can be quite a shock. Night-time temperatures at lodgings along the higher sections of the Pan-American Highway are often below 10°C – even lower at high altitudes – so make sure you have plenty of warm clothing.

national park. The project, which has been running for almost 20 years, aims to preserve tropical cloudforest by living in it. A simple, inspirational and, by general consensus, highly successful idea. Not satisfied with simple preservation, Steve and Paula Friedman (with a considerable band of volunteers and supporters) have also embarked on a reforestation project to recreate the forest.

Hiking trails lead through the fairytale-like cloudforest which drips with epiphytes and mosses, and whether guided or simply exploring the maintained trails unaccompanied, you'll see many of the 153 bird species recorded close to the lodge including the Resplendent Quetzal, as well as several endemic plant species found only in this part of the Talamanca Mountains. The newest attraction is the **Talamanca Treescape**, which allows the gravitationally challenged to "fly" through the canopy between platforms – no one ever said conservation has to be boring. ■ *Genesis II is open daily. Entrance and hiking costs US$10 for a 2-hr guided tour, or for the day unaccompanied. The Talamanca Treescape is US$45 per person, US$36 for students with ID – this price includes entrance to the reserve.*

Further information For more information and complete details contact Genesis II, T/F381-0739, or look at the award-winning website www.genesis-two.com For postal enquiries in Costa Rica, Apdo 655, 7.050, Cartago; or in the USA, #SJO 2031, Unit C-101, PO Box 025216, 601 NW 97th Ave, Miami, FL. 33102-5216. A well structured and organized **volunteer programme** is available at US$150 a week, all inclusive, 4 weeks minimum, with free time allocated for trips.

Getting there Driving to Genesis II is easy along the Pan-American Highway. While you can make the journey from Cañón on your own, the signposted route goes down the second-worst road in Costa Rica – and it is possible that if you do arrive, you'll be leaving the vehicle as a donation. While I'm sure the Friedmans will happily accept donations of all kinds, it is best to call in advance to receive directions to a good road providing access for "normal" vehicles. Any bus travelling the highway will drop you at Cañón, where you can arrange to be collected.

Sleeping Accommodation is available at the all-inclusive **AL** per person *Genesis II Lodge*. 4 rooms with a couple of simple beds, with room heaters, heated towel rails and hot water bottles. Meals are served "home-style" in the dining room. **Camping** is possible on covered wooden decks. US$3 per person with your own tent, US$5 to rent a tent, with a small additional charge for facilities.

Pan-American Highway

Continuing south, there are a few points of interest worth stopping at. At Km 62 is the **AL** *Tapantí Albergue de Montaña*, T290-7641, F232-0436. Spanish-owned, 10 quite good, large rooms sleeping up to 5, all with private bathrooms, hot water and some with balconies. It's a good choice for groups with a fireplace in the cosy restaurant and fine views across the nearby hills.

As the name suggests, **Finca Eddie Serrano Mirador de Quetzales** is *the* place to see the brilliant red and emerald green colours of the quetzal – in fact it's almost guaranteed – as are the fine views down the Valle de los Santos. A short 3-km self-guided trail leads through forests of giant oak to a couple of waterfalls and a look-out point. ■ *Tours take a couple of hrs, US$6.* ***Accommodation (B per person) is available in 8 rustic cabins, including breakfast, dinner and the tour.***

The rather neglected **Casa Refugio de Ojo de Agua** at Km 78 was once an historic pioneer home. The now creaking wooden building is certain to collapse under the environmental battering dealt out by the harsh climate of the region, but on a fine day, it's a good place to stop for a picnic or just to break the journey.

A steep, dramatic and scenic road at Km 80 heads down the valley that gives birth to the mighty Río Savegre, leading to the small valley community of San Gerardo de Dota. If it were just a little warmer, the crashing waters of the Savegre and the lush forest of the narrow valley could be the Garden of Eden. Naturally the bird-watching is excellent, there is some fishing in the area and there are trails for walking and horseriding.

San Gerardo de Dota
Colour map 3, grid A2

Ins and outs It's a steep road if you're driving, 4-wheel drive recommended. There is no public transport down here, but pick-ups can be arranged from the highway if arriving by bus.

Sleeping **A** *Trogón Lodge*, T223-2421, F222-5463, www.grupomawamba.com 16 fine wooden cabins each with private bath, small balcony set in beautiful landscaped gardens connected by paths frequented by dive-bombing hummingbirds. International and national dishes are available in the wood-panelled restaurant. There are 3 trails – the longest lasting 2½ hrs – fanning out from the lodge. Bilingual guides available on request.

Further down the valley is **AL** per person *Hotel de Montaña Savegre*, T771-1732, www.ecotourism.co.cr/savegrelodge Boldly claims to be "the best place in Costa Rica to see the quetzal". The 26 rooms are fairly simple and the buffet restaurant reminiscent of a college café, but then you'll be outside most of the time walking trails, riding horses or fly-fishing for trout.

Also in the area is the **C** *Cabinas El Quetzal*, T771-2077. 4 cabins with private bath. At the bottom of the valley is **D-F** *Los Ranchos*, T771-2376. Rooms sleeping up to 4 people or **camping** in perfect surroundings.

Cerro de la Muerte

Highway 2 continues the climb to the highpoint of the Pan-American Highway reaching its apex at **Km 89.5** and the nearby Cerro de la Muerte (3,419 m) – enticingly translating as the 'Mountain of Death'. Driving rain and mist often create the conditions that would clearly have been life-threatening when most transport was by foot. Barren *páramo* scenery dominates, shrivelled by the wet, windy and cold climate. If you want to climb La Muerte, stop at **E** *Hospedaje Georgina*, Km 95. This is Costa Rica's highest hotel, and has simple double rooms. Many of the buses making the journey between San José and San Isidro stop at the Georgina, which also serves good and hearty cheap meals.

Colour map 3, grid A2

It's downhill all the way to the Pacific from here, but on the way leaving the Pan-American Highway at División at Km 107, heading west down a 4-km bumpy gravel road is *Avalón Private Reserve*, T770-1341 or T380-2107, murrybear@earthlink.net It's worth a stop if you have time. The 151-ha

Reserva Privada Avalón

The southern region

reserve is mostly primary forest with areas of stunted elfin forest, and has great opportunities for highland bird-watching, a few trails leading to waterfalls and, on clear days, views to the Pacific.

Still undergoing development – which is part of the charm – the potential for ecotourism and research is promising. A number of orchids found in the reserve have attracted the interest of several US-based botanical gardens.

Sleeping Accommodation (**A-B**) is in a couple of private cabins each with private bath and hot water, or 4 shared rooms with shared bath. One cabin is dormitory style accommodation with shared bath. Meals served in the restaurant with views of the El General valley cost between US$4-8, and there is also a **volunteer programme** if you're interested in staying a while. Contact Avalón in advance for details.

The road then twists and turns to the broad Río General valley with sweeping views to the Talamanca Mountains and Cerro Chirripó to the east. Soak up the view at Km 119 the *Restaurant Mirador Vista del Valle*, T384-4685, whose fine food accompanies the scenery perfectly. The owners also have plans for accommodation.

San Isidro de El General

Colour map 3, grid B2
Population: 45,145
Altitude: 702 m

Easily the largest town south of San José, San Isidro de El General rests at the base of a broad fertile valley created by several rivers – the largest being the Río General. Completion of the Pan-American Highway in the 1950s has seen the quiet town grow as a service centre of the agricultural hinterland and a transport hub for journeys north, south and east. Tourism has seen the town develop as the departure point for ascents of Costa Rica's highest peak, Cerro Chirripó, and descents of the Río General whitewater rapids. Happy to wear several hats, the town also has several names – San Isidro is a less challenging and useful contraction, and Pérez Zeledón is the name favoured by bus companies.

Ins and outs

Getting there
See also 'Transport' page 322

The Pan-American Highway slices through San Isidro draining and supplying the town with a constant flow of produce and people from the north and south. A road heads west to Dominical and the Pacific coast. Regular buses ply all routes with terminals on or close to the highway.

Getting around

The main areas of interest in the town – hotels, restaurants and bus terminals – are within a 7-block square, all easy walking distances.

Best time to visit

With regard to temperature and climate, the best time to visit is from Dec-Apr, when skies are clearest. If you're in town in Feb you may catch the livestock and agricultural festival. On 15 May the death of San Isidro Labrador, the patron saint of the town and agricultural workers is celebrated. The anniversary of the city's founding is celebrated on 9 Oct.

History and sights

The rapid but low-key growth of recent years has left the town surprisingly devoid of history, bar one major fact and highly significant event. According to the Museo Nacional in the capital, **José María Figueres** used the town as a foothold from which to launch the short civil war of 1948. The events of that year led to the creation of the modern political era in Costa Rica and to the abolition of the nation's armed forces.

In the mid-1950s, completion of the startling **cathedral** in honour of San Isidro Labrador was consecrated. From the "provoke a response" school of architecture, for some the concrete structure is a bold statement, for others nothing short of sacrilegious. Inside the temple is light, bright and breezy with a few refreshing approaches to religious iconography. The mood continues in the town, with more shops touting religious statuettes than you're likely to find anywhere else in Costa Rica.

After the religious fervour, head for the **Museo Regional del Sur**, in the old marketplace, now the *Complejo Cultural*, Calle 2, Av 1-0, with local displays. ■ *Mon-Fri, 0800-1200, 1330-1630, free.*

San Isidrio de El General

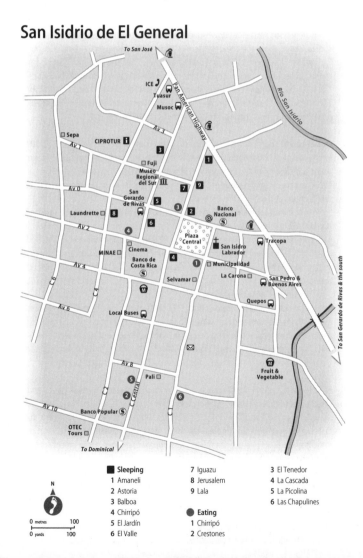

The southern region

	Sleeping	7	Iguazu	3	El Tenedor
	1 Amaneli	8	Jerusalem	4	La Cascada
	2 Astoria	9	Lala	5	La Picolina
	3 Balboa			6	Las Chapulines
	4 Chirripó	●	**Eating**		
	5 El Jardín	1	Chirripó		
	6 El Valle	2	Crestones		

Essentials

Sleeping One of the best options in town is **D** *Hotel/Restaurant Amaneli*, T771-0352. 41 quite good rooms with private bathroom, fan, some noisy and a diner style café. Another fair choice is **D** *Hotel Iguazu*, above *Alacén Super Lido*, Calle Central, Av 1, T771-2571. 20 or so smart rooms with just a hint of interior design. Hot water private bath, clean rooms with cable TV, safe place with secure parking.

E *El Valle*, C 2, Av Central-2, T771-0246, F771-0220. Claiming to be "a new concept in friendly hotels", the 32 rooms, each with private bath and TV, are certainly better than most in town for this price. **E-F** *Astoria*, on north side of square, T771-0914. Expansive impersonal hotel with 50 tiny but clean rooms. Some rooms with private bath, cheaper without. A justifiably popular choice is **E-F** *Hotel Chirripó*, south side of Parque Central, T771-0529. Plenty of rooms in this multi-storey hotel, which is bright and airy. It's nothing special but the odd plant and picture make the world of difference. Many combinations of rooms sleeping up to 4 people, with or without bathroom. Very good restaurant downstairs, free covered parking – recommended.

F *El Jardín*, above the cheap restaurant of the same name, Av Central, C Central-2, T771-0349. Rickety old building showing age more than the charm of history. Small rooms, clean with shared bath. Upstairs rooms are brighter. **F** *Hotel Balboa*, C 2, Av 1-3, T771-0606. Simple rooms with shared bath, close to centre. **F** *Lala*, C Central, Av 1, T771-0291. Very basic and simple – just like the Teletubby. **F** *Pensión Jerusalem*, a dozen grubby rooms sharing a couple of baths – the last resort.

Out of town South on the Pan-American after 6 km is **A-B** *Hotel Del Sur*, T771-3033, F771-0527, www.hoteldelsur.com A mini-resort style complex with almost 60 rooms, suites and cabins. Some rooms are very spacious, with bath, hot water, telephone and TV. Others are distinctly unkempt but are in a process of being redecorated. Large pool, tennis courts and other activities. Reasonable restaurant.

The road to San Gerardo de Rivas, 6 km east of San Isidro, is home to **A** *Rancho La Botija*, T/F770-2146, www.ecotourism.co.cr/labotija 3 comfortable cabins with private bath and hot water sleeping 4 people. The rustic style of the restaurant, decorated with agricultural implements and shards of *botijas* around a central *trapiche* or sugar mill, serves a mix of Mexican and national dishes at good prices. Small pool overlooking the jungle in a fine setting, very friendly owners. Several interesting tours – see 'Excursions' below. Recommended.

Nearby is **A** *Talari Mountain Lodge*, T771-0341, talaripz@sol.racsa.co.cr 8 rooms, each with private bath and hot water, set on an 8-ha farm with trails leading through virgin, regenerated forest and fruit orchards. The mid-range restaurant serves healthy and varied dishes with fresh fruit from the daily harvest. There's also a couple of pools – one for kids. Note that they close for a couple of weeks, usually in October.

Eating & *El Tenedor*, C Central, Av Central-1, is a popular choice for mid-range pizzas and a
drinking selection of traditional dishes. *La Cascada*, on Av 2 and C 2, is the balcony bar where the bright young things hang out. *La Picolina*, T771-8692. Good pizza, to eat in or delivered to your door. *Las Chapulines*, south of the main square opposite Pali. Good tortillas and snacks in a pavement café. *Restaurant Crestones*, a few blocks south of the main plaza. Nothing special, but serves a good mix of snacks and drinks. It's popular with locals and makes for lively company at night. *Chirripó*, south side of the main plaza, gets the vote from the current gringo crowd, with a patio terrace for people watching. *Soda J&P*, in the indoor market south of the main plaza, is the best of many.

Entertainment **Cinema** San Isidro has the distinctive honour of having the only true cinema in Costa Rica south of San José. See local notices for listings.

La Carona supermarket has a good selection of food if you want to stock up for the **Shopping** Chirripó summit, as does *Pali* a few blocks south of the main square. For fruit and vegetables try the *market* on the south side of town on Thu and Fri. *Fuji* slide film is available from Av 1, C 2-4.

CIPROTUR, the Centro de Información y Promoción Turística del Pacífico Sur, C 4, Av **Tours** 1-3, T771-6096, F771-2003, www.ecotourism.co.cr A regional tourist board working **operators** hard to promote the attractions of the south. *Selva Mar*, C 1, Av 2-4, T771-4582, F771-8841, www.exploringcostarica.com General tours and the main contact for out of the way destinations and hotels in the southern region.

Bus Buses from **San José** with *Tuasur*, T222-9763 or T771-0419, and *Musoc*, **Transport** T222-2422 or T771-0414, leave the capital from C Central, Av 22-24, every hour on the ½ hour from 0530 to 1630. Return buses have similar times for the 3-hr journey, US$3.30. Most destinations south of San José pass through San Isidro so try *Tracopa*, Av 5 and C 14, T222-2666, as well.

Local buses tend to leave from the newish bus terminal to the south of the main plaza. Buses to **San Gerardo de Rivas** and **Cerro Chirripó** leave at 0500 and 1400, returning at 0700 and 1600.

Leaving town, most long-distance bus companies have their terminals on the Pan-American Highway. You can either turn up and wait for the next hourly bus passing through or get the precise times from your hotel. Timetables vary depending on road conditions and it is normally not possible to buy tickets in advance as buses may be full. *Tracopa* have services heading south to **Buenos Aires, Palmar Norte, Paso Canoas,** 4 daily, **David, Panama, Golfito, Puerto Jiménez** and **San Vito**.

Transportes Blanco Lobo at the southern end of town has services to Uvita and Quepos via Dominical (1½ hrs) on the coast. To **Uvita** at 0900 and 1600 for a journey of 2½ hrs, returning at 0500 and 1400. To **Quepos** at 0700 and 1330 taking 3½ hrs, returning at 0500 and 1330.

Banks *Banco Nacional*, on north side of plaza, Mon-Fri, 0830-1545. *Banco Popular*, **Directory** Mon-Fri, 0815-1700, with a Visa ATM. **Communications** Internet: *Bruncanet*, on the north side of plaza, provides good reliable internet access as do the southern regional travel specialists *CIPROTUR*. **Post**: The post office is 3 blocks south of the church. **Telephone**: *ICE* office on C 4, Av 3 – Pan-American for international calls. **Language Schools** *SEPA*, about five blocks west of the main plaza, T770-1457, F771-5586, www.sabalolodge.com/sepa.html has Spanish language classes – it's a far quieter option than San José and recommended by several volunteer organizations. From US$190 a week for 20 hrs of classes a week. **Laundry** There's a launderette a couple of blocks west of the main plaza. **Useful addresses** The *MINAE* office, a couple of blocks west of the main plaza, T771-4836 or T7713155, F771-3297, is useful for booking accommodation and making reservations to climb Cerro Chirripó .

Excursions

An interesting trip that involves a short hike goes to **Centro Biológico Las Quebradas**. This 750-ha community-protected reserve is host to mosses, bromeliads, butterflies and birds of the Quebradas River basin, which ranges from 1,000 to 2,500 m above sea level. It is this river basin that supplies San Isidro with drinking water, so while the development of the park and almost 3 km of trails is useful for educational purposes, there is a genuine interest in protecting the reserve. ■ *Open Tue-Fri, 0800-1400, Sat and Sun, 0800-1500. US$6. T/F771-4131, or contact* Ciprotur, *T771-6096,*

F771-2003, www.ecotourism.co.cr Take the bus or drive to Quebradas (5 km) from where it's a 2.5 km walk to the centre.

Rancho La Botija is more than just a hotel. Trails lead from the hotel through grassland and forest to **precolumbian petroglyphs** and the mysterious **Rock of the Indian**, which the owner believes were etched from the stone by the Chiripoyas. ■ *T/F770-2146. Weekdays 1400-1700, weekends 0900-0500, US$5 adults, US$3 children. Head south before taking the road to San Gerardo de Rivas and keep an eye out after about 6 km. See page 324 for more details of the hotel's facilities.*

Los Cusingos, 30 minutes journey southeast of San Isidro in Quizarrá de Pérez Zeledón, is a small but highly significant bird reserve which is home to one of the best known ornithologists in Costa Rica, Dr Alexander Skutch, who co-authored the seminal field guide *A Guide to the Birds of Costa Rica*. The reserve of 76 ha was threatened with encroaching deforestation when the Tropical Science Center purchased the land from Dr Skutch with the assurance that the forest would be protected permanently. Visits by appointment only are limited to researchers, students, naturalists and bird-watchers. ■ *T253-3267, F225-2649, www.cct.or.cr*

Whitewater rafting is a popular pastime round these parts. The El General river is widely recognized as the largest whitewater river in Costa Rica, with over 100 miles of paddleable streams according to the experts Mayfield and Gallo. While the valley is scenic, the novice rafter tends to head for the spectacular forested sections of the **Pacuare** and **Reventazón**, leaving the Class III to V rapids of the General, ideal for playboating, to the specialists. Trips can be organized locally through *Selva Mar* or from San José with *Ríos Tropicales* or *Costa Rica Expeditions.*

San Gerardo de Rivas

Colour map 3, grid A3

Of the myriad small communities that dot the General valley, San Gerardo de Rivas stands out as the entrance to Chirripó National Park and the base for hikes to the summit of Cerro Chirripó Grande (3,820 m).

Situated in a cool, pleasant spot at the confluence of the Río Blanco and the Río Pacífico Chirripó, the town is spread up a steep slope that only gets steeper once you start the climb proper. The surrounding scenery is impressive with whitewater streams crashing and tumbling over huge boulders in the steeped sided valleys pocked with agricultural smallholdings (where gradient allows). But in all honesty, you wouldn't visit the palce unless intent on hiking, bird-watching, or more specifically conquering the summit of Cerro Chirripó.

Supplies in San Gerardo are limited. If you are hiking, buy in San Isidro before arriving in the area

You can book accommodation through the telephone in the village store T771-1866

Hot springs close to the town are rather handy for weary legs after the stiff climb if you're planning to stay in town an extra night. ■ *Before crossing the new concrete bridge at the bottom of town, turn left towards Herradura. After a 10-min walk, look for the sign after Parqueo Las Rosas; go down the suspension bridge, cross the river and continue for 10 mins to the house where you pay.*

Sleeping & eating

Starting at the bottom of the hill on the right just after the cemetery is the new **A** *Chirripó Pacífico*, www.riochirripo.com 8 comfortable rooms in bamboo buildings and a vast conical-roofed, thatched *palapa* communal space with restaurant and fireplace. Mainly a yoga and Watsu retreat, guests welcome when workshops have not taken all the rooms. Perched on a steeped sided hill is the **D** *Pelicano*, T382-3000. 10 rooms in a large wooden lodge, with shared bathrooms. Loosely decorated with idiosyncratic wooden creations. It's a fine setting with trails leading to the nearby mountains, good for bird-watching.

The southern region

Fancy a run?

A marathon is a challenging distance for anyone to run. With training and a hearty dose of enthusiasm, 26 miles and a few hundred yards is manageable. But if you need a real challenge, turn up at San Gerardo de Rivas in February and join the annual race to the refugio *and back – 38 km (just under 24 miles) over steep and uneven terrain. Fifty-year-old Francisco Elizondo Badilla of Cabinas El Descanso – one of 176 entrants to the race in 2000 – has been the first runner from the village for the last 12 years, completing the course in in 3½ hrs . Go on… have a go.*

Clustered beside the *MINAE* national park office is **D** *Marín*, which has 8 basic, rather dark, but OK rooms, with shared bath and hot water. Nearby is **E** *Cabinas Bosque*. Scruffy looking from the outside, the 8 rooms – 1 large enough for a group of 7 – are spotless. Some rooms have a balcony with hammock overlooking the River Chirripó Pacífico and down the valley – a divine spot especially at sunset.

Over the bridge you arrive at the home of local hill-running legend Sr Francisco Elizondo Badilla. **F** per person *Cabinas El Descanso*. 10 clean and tidy rooms, 6 doubles and 4 singles. A few hammocks for hanging around and a cosy restaurant complete with fireside for late night tale telling. Next door is **E** *Elimar*, with 4 good *cabinas* with private bath and hot water. Simple restaurant and a small pool.

The original 'hard rock' café **E-F** *Roca Dura*, opposite the football pitch, is the highest point you can reach by bus. Built on a huge boulder, the 8 rooms are a little on the dark side, but popular. Rooms are for 1, 2 or 3 people, some with private bath, others shared, all with hot water. Good café serving a full menu and good coffee. And the name? The foundations are one huge boulder which forms a rather dramatic feature in at least one of the rooms.

If driving, continue to the very top of the road and stay at **D** *El Urán*, T388-2333, the closest hotel to the park entrance just a few metres from the start of the trail. Rooms are basic with shared bath, but friendly staff will send you up the hill with a hearty breakfast at some unearthly hour, and will store luggage until you return.

Buses to San Gerardo leave **San Isidro** at 0500 and 1400, returning at 0700 and 1600. If driving, the 20 km route to San Gerardo leaves the Pan-American Highway a short distance south of San Isidro. **Transport**

Parque Nacional Chirripó

For seekers of the highest spot or even just in search of a good, hard walk, a two-day trip to Chirripó National Park (50,150 ha) is the place to go. As far as boot-busting, foot blistering walks go, it's a pretty tough number. It's up all the way up and down all the way down. Without a good pair of hiking shoes you'll be hurting your heels all the way up and stubbing your toes as you descend. *Colour map 3, grid A3*

But is it worth it? Yes. Chirripó is the icing on the cake that is Costa Rica. Climbing steadily from a starting altitude of 1,400 m, the path skirts through evergreen forest, floats among cloudforest, eventually leading to the barren open *páramo* savannahs. Along the length of the route the fauna and birdlife is constantly changing and the views from the top to the Atlantic, the Pacific and down the spine of the Talamanca range are spectacular, especially at sunrise.

Entrance to the park is US$6, with each night at the refuge costing a further US$6. Accommodation at the refuge is booked through *MINAE* which has offices in San Isidro (T771-4836, F771-3297) and San Gerardo (T770-8040). The refuge does fill up **Ins & outs**

The southern region

particularly in the dry season from January to April, and at weekends, so book in advance if possible. Sleeping bags and small gas stoves are available for rent at a small fee.

If all you want to do is climb the peak and let someone else do the organization, most tour operators in San José will arrange it, costing around US$500 for the 4-day round trip. Alternatively contact the regional specialists *Selva Mar* who will organize your trip, T771-4582, F771-8841, www.chirripo.com

A simple map of the park is available from MINAE for US$0.80. It is possible to complete a circuit of the park but you will need a guide or good topographical maps, available from the *Instituto Geográfico Nacional* and Lehmann book store in San José.

You can rent horses to carry your equipment to the refuge in the dry season. Bags for 2 people costs US$20 – but you will still need to carry a day pack. Make arrangements in your hotel.

The national park
Chirripó National Park is Costa Rica's second largest national park. With neighbouring La Amistad International National Park – the largest – Chirripó protects the Talamanca Mountains from south of Cartago down to the border with Panama.

In a world of subtle tropical variations, the presence of classic glacial formations like u-shaped valleys, moraine deposit and glacial lakes appear out of place. But the hint of an ice-age remains with bitter winds and temperatures that drop, at their lowest, to -9°C. From around 3,000 m, the barren *páramo* landscape is of stunted forest and savannah covering broad open plateau. The dominant oak landscape just below the summit area is severely scorched and slowly recovering from a fire in 1992. Around the summit, trails lead to Cerro Crestones – a rocky outcrop slowly developing spiritual significance as a site of pilgrimage – the **Valles de los Conejos** (Valley of the Rabbits) and the **Sabana de los Leones** (Lion's Savannah).

Parque Nacional Chirripó

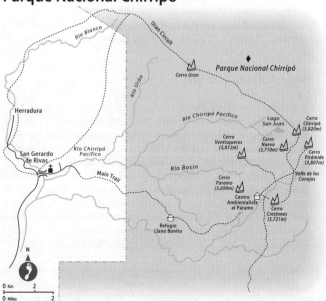

At lower altitudes, and warmer temperatures, cloudforest dominates with incredible diversity of flora and fauna – in particular the birdlife, of which there are over 400 species.

Technically and navigationally the climb up Cerro Chirripó Grande is straightforward. A well marked trail leads to the **Centro Ambientalista el Paramoa** or *refugio* at 3,400 m above sea level, where there is basic accommodation. It's between eight and 10 hours for the average trekker to the *refugio*, from where it's a couple of hours, mostly on the flat, to ascend the last 400 m of the hike. Other trails in the area are easily navigated, although you may feel more comfortable with maps or a guide.

Climbing Cerro Chirripó Grande

Organizing the two-or three-day trip is straightforward. The *refugio* has around 80 dormitory rooms with four beds, and a kitchen for preparing food. You'll need food for the trip depending on how many days you plan to take. Temperatures at the refuge and the summit are close to freezing around nightfall and warm clothing is essential, as is rain gear from May to December.

Day 1 Start the trek early around 0600 or earlier if possible, and aim to get to the refuge in one day. It is a long, uphill trek with barely any level, let alone downhill sections to break the monotony. While the scenery compensates, you don't want to be struggling towards the top with nightfall approaching

Water is available at the very basic, open-air Llano Bonito lodge at 2,500 m reached after about three hours. It is possible to stay at Llano Bonito but the conditions vary and are not reliably clean.

Day 2 Another early start leaving the refuge around 0330 from the refuge goes through the mainly flat trek to the final summit push – a rock scramble of a couple of hundred metres – to the peak for sunrise. If short of time and keen to move on, you can head downhill and you should be able to make the 1600 bus to San Isidro. If not, take things a little slower and enjoy the simple trek to Cerro Crestones and other peaks and valleys in the area. Most people follow the main trail.

Pan-American Highway

A slow descent from San Isidro meanders gently through the broad valley – this is possibly the best bit of road in Costa Rica, permanently shadowed by fine views of the Cordillera de Talamanca. Coffee plantations merge with eucalyptus groves giving way, close to Buenos Aires, to the distinct sweetness and aroma of pineapples that cover vast fields as far as the eye can see. If driving, there are plenty of side roads to explore.

Buenos Aires
Colour map 3, grid B4

Buenos Aires, with a population of 15,577 in the town and surrounding district, owes its prominence to the huge Del Monte cannery that sits at the junction of the town and the Pan-American Highway. The town itself is a few kilometres off the main highway. It's the main place to stay if heading for the Durika Biological Reserve further east in the Talamanca mountains, seeking a bus to the Boruca Indian Reserve to the southwest, or changing for a bus south to San Vito.

A few simple options in town include **F** *Cabinas Violeta*, next to the fire station 200 m west of the plaza, T730-0104. Clean, simple, central and OK if you're stuck for the night. An alternative is **F** *Cabinas Mary*, 800 m south of the centre close to the Aradikes office, T730-0187. A quiet spot which at least tries to be clean.

Sleeping & eating

Several *sodas* in town around the main square including the popular *Soda Kriss* on the east side of the plaza.

The southern region

Transport Regular *Tracopa* buses from San José heading south to **Ciudad Neily** and **Paso Canoas** pass through town or the *bomba* on the highway. Buses head inland to **Ujarras** at 0600 and 1200, taking 2 hrs. Buses to **Boruca** leave at 1100 and 1530, 1½ hrs.

Directory **Banks** A large concentration of banks with branches of *Banco Nacional*, *Banco de Costa Rica* and *Banco Popular* (open Sat mornings), all with ATMs.

Reserva One of the few chances to spend time in the depths of the Talamanca moun-
Biológica tains is in the Durika Biological Reserve, a private reserve of almost 800 ha,
Durika 17 km east of Buenos Aires reached by four-wheel drive along a dirt track. The community aims to encourage conservation and reforestation of the region and ecotourism plays a part in that process. Good trails through the area and to the nearby Cerro Durika (3,280 m) give an insight into this rarely visited part of Costa Rica.

Don't expect pristine wilderness – deforestation has led to serious erosion in the rainy months. But according to the Durika Foundation the environmental education programmes are beginning to reap rewards. T730-0657, www.gema.com/durika

Sleeping Accommodation is available in 5 comfortable but rustic cabins (**B-C**) and includes 3 vegetarian means a day. All sorts of healthy pursuits for mind and body with short hikes to *campesino* and Indian communities, longer hikes to the mountain peaks and yoga and meditation classes.

Boruca The small community of Boruca is the focal point of the Boruca Indians. For
Colour map 3, grid B4 much of the year, the small village of several hundred people is almost lifeless - a loose collection of simple homes scattered around dusty lanes, that twist and wind around the elevated and rather scruffy church. The steady erosion of the traditional culture in the region began in earnest with the arrival of the Jesuits in 1649. Today a simple cultural museum, sitting in the shadow of the church, is a sad (and true) reflection of the value placed on indigenous people in the country. Black and white photographs with peeling edges, desiccated by winds blowing through the dilapidated structure, show images of a steady decline in traditional life.

But each year on the last day of December and the first two days of January the hardships of agricultural life are discarded in the colourful celebrations of **La Danza de los Diablitos** – the Dance of the Devils. Dressed in fine masks and colourful costumes an elaborate game of tag sees the bull destroy the devils. On the third day, the devils rise again to stalk and eventually kill the bull. The bull symbolizes the colonization and persecution of the lands and indigenous people at the hands of the Spanish, offering the hope that, one day, the Indian communities will be victorious.

The festival sees the continuation of a tradition that has lasted for centuries, and is the culmination of months of quiet, behind-the-scenes preparation. Similar but quieter celebrations are held in the nearby town of **Rey Curré**, starting on the last day of January, also lasting for three days.

If you can time your visit to coincide with the festival, visitors are welcome. If not, a visit is still worthwhile. There are waterfalls nearby and several villagers still carve masks, bows and arrows which you can buy.

Sleeping and transport Accommodation in town is limited to the **F *Boruca***, with basic rooms, a small restaurant and bar with a pool table. Buses from **Buenos Aires** depart at 1100 and 1530. If driving, take the road east from the Pan-American

ARADIKES

The latest estimates put the Amerindian population of Costa Rica at just 1% of the total. Consistent with tendencies worldwide, the plight of indigenous groups has not been uppermost in the minds of government officials. While the national government ratified the international agreement for the rights of indigenous people in 1992, indigenous communities believe that as a minority, their rights are constantly being infringed – with the invasion of their private property, illegal logging and unauthorized cattle roaming. Other projects like the proposed hydro-project on the Río General add pressure on communities to sell land and slowly relinquish the few ties that still exist with their history.

The six communities close to Buenos Aires – Térraba, Boruca, Rey Curré, Salitre, Ujarrás and Cabagra – have created the Asociación Regional Aborigen del Dike (ARADIKES) a non-governmental organization that aims to strengthen indigenous communities in the region. They have a small office in Buenos Aires if you are interested in their work.

ARADIKES has a programme for volunteers genuinely interested in the rights of indigenous peoples, conservation developments and community programmes. Applications should be made in advance to Aradikes, Apdo Postal 24-8100, T/F730-0289, F730-1189, www.aradikes.org

---

Highway at Brujo, or from Puerto Nuevo on the section connecting Paso Real and Palmar Norte.

Most of the rain that falls on the western side of the Talamanca mountains from División to the north and the Panama border to the south is channelled through Grande de Térraba river valley that cuts through the coastal mountain range to Palmar Norte and the Pacific. The Pan-American Highway follows the river heading west to the Pacific. A poorly maintained bridge over the Térraba provides access to the Coto Brus valley, San Vito and the Wilson Botanical Gardens. **Paso Real** *Colour map 3, grid B4*

Palmar Norte and Palmar Sur

At a major junction on the Pan-American Highway, Palmar Norte is of particular interest to people fascinated by big trucks. The whole town, tucked in the elbow behind a right-angled sweep to the south in the highway, is one big truck stop. Roads lead southeast to Golfito and the Panama border, south to Sierpe, northwest to follow the Pacific coast and east to head inland, eventually reaching San José. Such convenient access makes this an important transport hub and it should be used accordingly. *Colour map 3, grid B2*

If passing, one regional appeal is the impressive, mysterious and perfectly spherical stone carvings left by the Diquis culture. The region is littered with these curious objects which are most easily seen outside the **Instituto Agropecuario** in the Palmar North or in the central square of Palmar Sur – on the opposite bank of the Térraba river, a couple of kilometres to the south – which is littered with the spheres.

As with much of Costa Rican archaeology, the construction and purpose of the *esferas piedras*, believed to be around 2000 years old, is still very much open to debate. Significant detail relating to the Diquis culture is lacking and the subject is desperately in need of detailed and dedicated study. The largest stone carving in the region, at about 1.7 m across, is estimated to weigh 9 tons.

The southern region

If you want to visit, the gravel track leaves the Pan-American Highway opposite the entrance to Palmar Sur. After about 4 km, just before the second concrete bridge, an overgrown path leads for a hundred metres to the sphere. If you get lost, ask in the local smallholdings – no one knows where it is, but you'll make some good friends along the way and get there eventually.

Sleeping & eating

D *Cabinas Tico Aleman*, on the Pan-American Highway, just east of the gas station, T786-6232. 25 rooms with private bath – pay a little more and you get hot water, a/c and TV. A couple of blocks back from the highway is the popular **D-E** *Hotel y Cabinas Amarilla*, T786-6251. 16 *cabinas* and 19 single rooms in a big yellow clapboard house on the west side of the park. The service is largely indifferent but the rooms are clean and well kept. **G** *Hotel Xinia*, T786-6129. The cheapest and worst in town – could well be sold or closed by the time you read this.

Several *sodas* and Chinese restaurants in town and close to the various bus stops. Try *Marisquería* opposite the gas station, for hearty portions of fairly simple cuisine.

Transport

Air *SANSA*, T221-9414, www.flysansa.com and *Travelair*, T220-3054, www.travelair-costarica.com, have a daily return flight serving Palmar Sur from **San José**, US$66.

There are several daily express buses to and from **San José** with *Tracopa* from Av 5, C 14, T222-2666, between 0525 and 1645, 6 hrs. Regular buses also pass through **San Isidro de El General** throughout the day; 5 daily buses go to **Sierpe** leaving at 0700, 0930, 1130, 1430 and 1700, 45 mins – you'll need to get the first one if you're trying to get a regular boat from Sierpe to Drake. Heading south there are buses to **Ciudad Neily** (over 20, 1½ hrs), **Golfito** (1230, 1½ hrs) and **Paso Canoas** (1100 and 1830, 1¾ hrs). Heading north a bus leaves Ciudad Neily for **Dominical** at 0600 and 1430, passing through Palmar around 0730 and 1600.

South from Palmar Norte

At **Chacarita**, 33 km, the only access road to the Osa Peninsula heads southwest. Ten kilometres further on, at **Briceño** a barely noticeable junction leads to *Esquinas Rainforest Lodge* in **Parque Nacional Piedras Blancas**. One of the few remaining areas of moist tropical forest on the Pacific, the park was created in 1991 by presidential decree. As with many parks, legal protection did little to stop the reality of private landowners selectively logging the area – the land needed to be purchased. As the local communities realized the newly created park challenged their way of life, the growth in interest in the region's preservation saw the Austrian government, with particular support from the well known classical violinist Michael Schnitzler, a part-time resident of Costa Rica, begin to purchase land, creating the 'Rainforest of the Austrians'. By 2001, over 13,000 Austrian individuals had donated more than US$1.5 m, enabling the purchase of over 28 sq km of rainforest. The property, most of which had exploitation permits for logging, has been donated to the Costa Rican government and become part of new Piedras Blancas National Park.

Sleeping In the meantime, the 14,025 ha park can be explored along a 10-km network of paths that lead from the **AL** *Esquinas Rainforest Lodge*, T/F775-0901, www.esquinaslodge.com 10 cosy rooms, with tiled floor, ceiling fans and hot water private bath with verandas overlooking the tropical gardens and forest. The large thatched bar and restaurant serves local and Austrian dishes and there's a pool for cooling off after a day's hiking. As part of the programme to alleviate the economic pressures for logging, the lodge employs local people, and uses all profits to support community projects in the small community of nearby La Gamba, such as the repair of the water system, roads and bridges, planting of cash crops, reforestation or environmental education.

The southern region

Transport It's 4 km to Esquinas from the Pan-American Highway, or you can approach from Golfito from the south along a hairy and occasionally impassable road – especially in the wet season.

Ciudad Neily

Of passing interest to the driving visitor, you could easily fly past Ciudad Neily on the Pan-American Highway, without noticing or indeed missing anything. 15 km from Río Claro and the turning for Golfito, and 16 km from Paso Canoas on the Panama border, the town sits in a broad valley created by the River Corredor. The small-town agricultural feel supporting the banana and African oil palm plantations to the south, belies the nominal district population of almost 22,000. Close to sea level, the town is uncomfortably hot and humid in the wet season.

Colour map 3, grid C5

Bus travellers will take more interest in Neily, as it's an important transport hub for bus services linking to all points on the compass.

Sleeping & eating

Probably the best place in town is **C** *Hotel Andrea*, in front of the *ICE* office, T/F783-3784. 18 clean *cabinas* with private bathroom, a/c or fan and TV. Pleasant open-air bar and restaurant serving mid-price dishes. Parking available. Popular place with *Ticos* and handy for the bus terminal. Another good choice is **D** *Cabinas Helga*, T783-3146. 13 spotless *cabinas* sleeping up to 4 people. Some with a/c, others with fan. Well maintained and friendly owners. In need of a coat of paint is **D** *Centro Turístico Neily*, T783-3301. 41 reasonable rooms sleeping 5, with hot water private bath, a/c and TV. There's a couple of pools and a small disco – probably the best choice for a family if you have to stay in town. The same owners neglect **D-E** *El Rancho*, T783-3060, F783-5435. It has 50 uninspiring rooms with private bath, a/c and TV. **E-F** *Cabinas Heileen*, T783-3080. 10 simple *cabinas* with private bath and fan. **F** *Cabinas Fontana*, T783-3078. Simple but OK rooms recommended by one reader. **F** *Hotel Musuco*, T783-3048. 18 basic rooms with good beds, some with a view. As a last resort, try **F** *Elvira*, T783-3057, which offers the curious luxury of parking despite being very grim.

Plenty of *sodas* in the town. Next to *Cabinas Fontana* is **Pizza Internet Los Colegios** for chips and bytes all in one handy package.

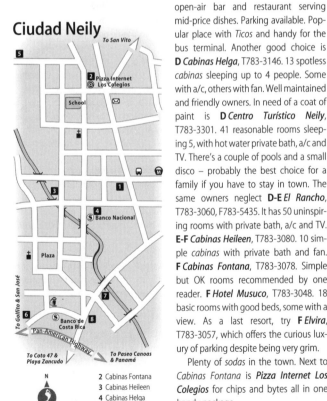

Ciudad Neily

To San Vito

Pizza Internet
@ Los Colegios

School

Banco Nacional

Plaza

Banco de
Costa Rica

Pan-American Highway

To Golfito & San José

To Coto 47 &
Playa Zancudo

To Paseo Canoas
& Panamá

N

0 metres 100
0 yards 100

■ **Sleeping**
1 Andrea
2 Cabinas Fontana
3 Cabinas Heileen
4 Cabinas Helga
5 Centro Turístico Neily
6 El Rancho
7 Elvira
8 Musuco
9 Villa

Transport

Air *SANSA*, T221-9414, www.flysansa.com has a daily return flight to **Coto 47**, a few kilometres south of town, from San José.

The southern region

Bus 5 daily buses from **San José** head for Ciudad Neily and on to **Paso Canoas** from 0500 to 1800, 7 hrs, US$6 with *Tracopa* T783-3227. Hourly buses leave for **Paso Canoas** from 0500-1800.

Heading towards the Osa Peninsula buses to **Golfito** leave every 30 mins from 0600-1930. *Transportes Térraba*, T783-4293, have a service to **Puerto Jiménez** at 0700 and 1400, 3 hrs, US$3.

Heading north, buses head for **Palmar** and **Dominical** at 0600 and 1430, 3 hrs.

Inland of Neily is **San Vito**, served by 7 daily buses, 2 hrs.

Directory **Banks** *Banco de Costa Rica* has an ATM and there is a branch of *Banco Nacional* in town.

Paso Canoas

Colour map 3, grid C5 If you could stereotype a border town, Paso Canoas would probably be the outcome. A few thousand people, scratching out a living from the cross-border price differential on goods such as CDs, sunglasses and other items, live huddled together in a town that feels like it could be dismantled at a moment's notice.

But it is a long way to come for CDs, so you'll probably only end up here if you're heading for Panama or entering Costa Rica. If circumstances find you seeking a bed, there are some surprisingly acceptable options.

Sleeping **D-E** *Real Victoria*, T732-2586. 33 rooms with a/c or fan, and cable TV throughout.
& eating Credit cards accepted and a popular swimming pool open to the public. **E** *Cabinas Jiménez*, T732-2258. 18 quiet good *cabinas* with private bath, fan, a/c and TV. Very clean. **E** *Hilda*, T732-2873, has some clean rooms. A friendly cheap option is **E-F** *Cabinas el Interamericano*, T732-2041. The rooms are big and clean – upstairs rooms even have windows. **F** *Cabinas Jiménez Annexe*, T732-2258. A scruffy option if the rest are full. **G** *Cabinas El Paso*, T732-2740. 14 freshly decorated rooms with a/c. Excellent bargain while it remains clean.

Brunca serves fairly unappealing but filling and cheap meals if you're waiting for a bus out of town or with a hole in your stomach. Several other options close to the hotels.

Transport *Tracopa* buses to **San José** leave at 0400, 0730, 0900 and 1500, 7 hrs, US$6.50. An hourly service goes to **Ciudad Neily** with connections to the Pacific coast, the Osa Peninsula, and to **Golfito** from 0500-1830, 2 hrs, US$1.

Directory **Banks** Services are limited to the branch of *Banco Nacional*, although naturally cash can easily be changed around the border with money changers. **Communications** The *post office* is close to the border crossing. A new *internet* service was opening up when visiting.

Border with **Immigration** The border is open from 0600-2200, with the customs and
Panama immigrations office on the left side of the road as you enter town. Border formalities, including the purchase of the exit *cruz roja* are straightforward and completed in one stop. Don't forget Costa Rica is 1 hr behind Panama.

Immigration in Panama is open 24 hrs. The crossing is quick and painless for international buses. For private vehicles, there are maps of Panama available at the IPAT tourist office.

Valle de Coto Brus

The sharp bend in the Pan-American Highway at Paso Real marks the conflu- *Colour map 3, grid B4* ence of the El General river to the north and the Coto Brus river to the south. Highway 237 crosses the Térraba and climbs slowly towards San Vito. If driving towards the southernmost point of the country, this route – as opposed to the Pan-American Highway – is considerably more enjoyable. The journey takes longer even though the distance is shorter, but the views of the Talamanca mountains are impressive and the dramatic descent from San Vito to Ciudad Neily is nothing short of spectacular with fine views across the southern lowlands to the Osa Peninsula.

A short distance south of the bridge a dirt road heads north for 18 km to **C** per per- **Sleeping** son *Monte Amou*, T256-6149. A serious contender for 'Most Out-There Accommodation' in Costa Rica the road passes through the town of Portrero Grande and beyond Lucha (15 km). There are 4 simple wooden cabins sleeping up to 7 people and a handful of rooms. The rooms, bar and restaurant are genuinely rustic. Simple mid-range meals are available and there are several trails leading close to La Amistad National Park and nearby waterfalls. Generator supplied electricity cuts off around 2200. It's an excellent spot for bird-watching and wildlife spotting. Call in advance to make sure there is space. By the time you get up the road, you expect to be greeted by applauding jaguars and quetzals perching on your car singing a welcome chorus – would be an awful shame to find the place full!

The good road south towards *San Vito* is dotted with the occasional hamlet – often little more than a few houses and sometimes a simple café.

San Vito

Climbing close to a vertical kilometre from Paso Real or Ciudad Neily, San *Colour map 3,* Vito has a distinctly comfortable climate compared to the lowlands to the *grid C5* south – one of the reasons Italian settlers founded the town in the 1950s. *Population: 14,732*
Altitude: 970m

Today, San Vito is a regional commercial and agricultural centre with limited interest to the casual visitor. The main centre of the town is a two block long street running downhill from the triangular plaza. South of town towards Cuidad Neily, are the world-renowned **Wilson Botanical Gardens** – definitely worth a visit, see page 337.

The southern region

C *El Ceibo*, just off the main plaza, T/F773-3025. Easily the best place in town, 40 or so **Sleeping &** neat rooms with hot water private bath and TV. Good, slightly pricey restaurant, serving **eating** Italian and local dishes. Parking available. **D-E** *Cabinas Rino*, right in the centre of town, T773-3071. 10 clean, well kept rooms with a few simple touches, hot water private bathroom, cable TV and secure parking. Facing the plaza is **F** *Colono*, T773-4543, with new management trying to sweep out the old tired ways – would appear to be working as it's essentially clean, although some of the beds are a bit lumpy. Cheap restaurant.

Arriving from San Isidro, close to the gas station you will find **F** *Cabinas Firenze*, T773-3741. 6 basic *cabinas*, sleeping 5, with private bathroom – pretty grim. Not much better a little further down the side road is **E** *Cabinas Las Huacas*, T773-3115. 13 rooms which are reportedly OK, with hot water private bath and TV. Closed when visited.

On the road to Sabalito is **F** *Hotel Pitier*,½ km out of town, clean with bath. **F** *Las Mirlas*, T773-3714, on the opposite side of the road, is slightly more attractive with half a dozen small cabins overlooking woodlands.

Best place in town for a meal is the mid-range and very Italian *Hotel El Ceibo*. *Lilianas*, close to the plaza, is true to the Italian heritage of San Vito, serving good, cheap pasta dishes. *Jimar* has a pleasant spot with a small patio on the road out to Paso Real serving cheap food. *Restaurant Nelly*, near the gas station on the west side of town, serves good wholesome truck driver's fare *Tico* style complete with a smile.

Shopping On the road south out of town towards Ciudad Neily is ***Finca Cántaros***, T773-3760, specializing in local arts and crafts, including Chorotega pottery and more modern pieces from the capital. Woven textiles and hand-crafted wooden products from the Guaymi and Boruca and coffee fresh from the harvest in the Coto Brus valley. With carvings and *molas* (brightly coloured appliqué embroidery) from neighbouring Panama adding an international flavour, Cántaros is one of the best craft shops in Costa Rica – worth a look even if you don't buy anything. The owner, Gail Hewson Gómez and her husband have planted over 5,000 trees in the property which has a short trail to a lake, a fine lookout and a small nature trail that attracts many species of birds – entrance US$2.

Transport **Air** *SANSA*, T221-9414, www.flysansa.com, have plans to provide flights to **San Vito** – enquire for details.

Bus Long distance buses leave from the *Tracopa* terminal the centre of town,T773-3410. Direct buses from **San José** leave at 0545, 0815 and 1130 (8 hrs) with a direct bus at 1445, 6 hrs, US$7. Return buses run at 0500 (direct), 0730, 1000 and 1300. Services leave **San Isidro** at 0530 and 1400, returning at 0645 and 1500, 3 hrs.

Local buses leave from a separate, but fairly close terminal. There are 7 buses a day to **Ciudad Neily** taking all sorts of circuitous routes via **Sabalito** and **Cañas** leaving from 0530 to 1700. Take a direct bus for **Wilson Botanical Gardens**. If going to Ciudad Neily sit on the right going down, the left going up to admire the wonderful views.

Buses head north for villages including **Santa Elena**, **Roble**, **Guinea** and **Mellizas**.

Directory **Banks** Surprising selection of banks to choose from with branches of *Banco de Costa Rica*, *Banco Nacional* (with ATM) and *Banco Popular* (also with an ATM). **Communications** Post and internet: the post office is at the northern end of town and should provide internet through the *punta.com* service in the near future. **Telephone**: the *ICE* telephone office is a few metres west of the main plaza, 0730-1700.

Parque Nacional La Amistad

Colour map 3, grid B4 As the largest protected area in Costa Rica La Amistad National Park protects the Talamanca Mountain range of south-central Costa Rica – easily the largest park in the country covering an area of 199,147 ha. In some respects La Amistad is the perfect national park. Secluded, difficult to reach and lacking in significant services La Amistad is a hothouse of diversity which goes beyond national boundaries and receives very few visitors.

Ins & outs Visiting the park is difficult to say the least. There are 3 ranger's stations at Tres Colinas, Estación Pittier and Altamira. Access to them is tricky and there is no guarantee that the stations will be manned when you arrive. Your best bet is to contact the park services in San Isidro de El General, T771-4836, F771-3297, for the latest information. On the Pacific side of the mountains your best bet is at *Monte Amou* (see page 335). For serious trekkers, ATEC based in Puerto Viejo on the Caribbean coast have a strenuous trans-Talamanca trek taking 10 days. You will be carrying your own food and equipment, so hope the weather is bearable as you make the journey and book at least a week in advance.

La Amistad National Park is the cornerstone of the International Amistad Biosphere Reserve, created by the United Nations in 1982. The reserve includes Tapantí-Macizo de la Muerte National Park (just south of Cartago), Chirripó National Park, four Indian reserves and several other protected areas covering an area slightly smaller than the state of Delaware in the US. When Panama created the neighbouring La Amistad National Park across the border in 1990, the entire Talamanca Mountain range became a World Heritage Site.

The park is the very epitome of how Costa Rica demonstrates the convergence of North and South American flora. Its varied climate and soils create an inventory of species that reads like a What's What of the neotropics.

The **Talamancas** are the highest non-volcanic mountain range in Central America, created by uplift of the earth surface which was subsequently eroded by glacial activity and heavy rainfall. That rainfall – up to 6 m a year in places – has created steep sided slopes that have left some areas of the park devoid of any human intervention. Temperatures range from 25°C down to –9°C. Eight of the 12 lifezones found in Costa Rica are present in the park, including lowland tropical rainforest, cloudforest and paramo forests. Altitudes range from 3,820 m (Cerro Chirripó) down to 50 m above sea level. Over 9,000 flowering plants are found in the park, as well as all six species of feline occuring in Central America, the quetzal, the three-wattled bellbird, the umbrellabird and the harpy eagle. In the words of the United Nations, "it has been suggested that no other park in the world possesses as many species and such a wealth of fauna".

From San Vito a good gravel road, paved in places, runs via **Sabalito** (*Banco Nacional*) to the Panama border at Río Sereno. There are buses from Sabalito to San José.

Frontier with Panama

Wilson Botanical Gardens

In 1961 Robert and Catherine Wilson moved from their botanical gardens in Miami, Florida, down to Costa Rica with the aim of setting up a botanical garden and a commercial nursery. Some 40 years later, the legacy of that vision has created the Wilson Botanical Gardens – one of the world's premier collections of tropical plants open for day visits, overnight stays and research.

Colour map 3, grid C5

The gardens are open from 0800 to 1600 daily. Cost US$6. T773-4004, F773-3665, www.ots.ac.cr The gardens are 6 km south of San Vito, easily reached by car, bus or taxi.

Ins & outs

A few kilometres south of San Vito, the 10-ha gardens feature a network of trails and paths designed by the Brazilian landscape architect Roberto Burle Marx. The success of the gardens lies in their location. At an altitude of 1,100 m, the gardens receive around 4,000 mm of rain a year from May to December when the area can be shrouded in heavy fog and is regularly watered by afternoon clouds.

Lasting from 20 minutes to 2½ hours, self-guide leaflets provide snippets of information allowing you to wonder aimlessly through the gardens at your own pace. Alternatively you can use a guide who will point out some of the 700 species of palms found in the garden – there are a total of 1,000 in the neotropics. Resident birds species total 331 and mammals are also found the gardens.

The Wilson Gardens are part of the *Las Cruces Biological Station*, owned and operated by the *Organisation for Tropical Studies*. As with La Selva and Palo Verde, the station is a focus for biologists, students, birders and naturalists keen to take advantage of the phenomenal diversity of the region.

Sleeping **AL** accommodation is available at the reserve. 12 beautiful airy cabins with hot water private bath and a small balcony. The price includes 3 meals at the fine café-style restaurant with a small balcony and library.

10

Golfito and the Osa Peninsula

Golfito and the Osa Peninsula

342 Ins and outs

347 Puerto Jiménez

352 Parque Nacional Corcovado

354 Golfito

358 Beaches north of Golfito

359 South of Golfito

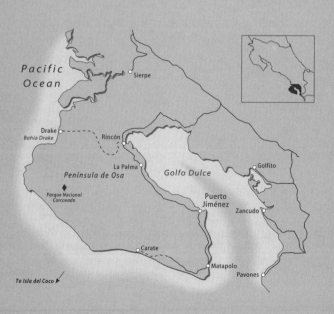

Pacific Ocean

Sierpe

Drake
Bahía Drake

Rincón

La Palma

Península de Osa

Golfo Dulce

Golfito

Parque Nacional Corcovado

Puerto Jiménez

Zancudo

Carate

Matapalo

Pavones

To Isla del Coco

The Osa Peninsula is the smaller of Costa Rica's two Pacific protuberances. But while broadly similar in shape, the landscape could hardly be more different. All lush, verdant tropical exuberance – Corcovado National Park is the place to visit in Costa Rica if you're looking for a rainforest wilderness experience. On the western side of the peninsula, Corcovado makes you work for your pleasure and requires a demanding trek which you can do on your own or as part of a group. Beyond rainforest hikes, it's a fairly active place and kayaking, diving and surfing are all popular options at several points around the peninsula.

On the mainland, the regional centre of Golfito is an important town, flourishing as a tax-free trade centre, and also the most convenient stepping-off point for other beaches around the Golfo Dulce to the north and south. Zancudo is a fine beach and a base for some of the best deep-sea fishing in the country, with Pavones providing the ultimate surf experience.

All around the Gulf and the peninsula, hotels and lodges hide in exclusive bays basking in comfortable temperatures for much of the year.

Things to do in the Osa Peninsula

- Test yourself to the limit **trekking** through the rainforest heat and humidity in Corcovado National Park.
- **Kayak** through coastal mangroves around Puerto Jiménez or Sierpe.
- **Watch dolphins** and **whales** in the warm waters of Gulfo Dulce or Drake Bay.
- **Touch**, **see**, **smell** and **taste** the wonders of the rainforest at Casa Orquideas near Golfito.
- Experience the **relaxation** of Zancudo and world-class **surfing** at Pavones. Splash out on some of the very best deep-sea **fishing** in the country out of Zancudo.

Ins and outs

Getting there

Air & bus Once the luxury of the cash and time rich, the region is now accessible to all budgets. There are 3 main access points served by air and road transport. From the north daily flights with *SANSA*, T221-9414, www.flysansa.com, from **San José** to **Palmar Sur** (US$66) with connections to **Sierpe** from where boats head along the northern coast to **Drake**. Regular buses leave San José for Palmar Sur.

Travelair (T220-3054, www.travelair-costarica.com) also fly to Palmar Sur and have seasonal flights direct to **Drake** (US$70) and **Carate** (US$75) in the high season.

Daily flights and buses leave **San José** for **Puerto Jiménez** (US$66) on the eastern side of the Osa Peninsula. Across the Golfo Dulce, **Golfito** receives a daily flight (US$66) and regular buses from the capital, with ferries linking to the peninsula and other beaches up and down the coastline.

Overland you can drive or take a bus to **Sierpe**, **Golfito** or **Puerto Jiménez** from **San José**. In the dry season there is road and bus access to **Drake**.

Getting around

Moving around the region is easiest using local boats, taxis and bus services. Many of the more expensive lodges will provide comfortable transport from the nearest airport by boat and/or taxi to whisk you to comfort with the least possible inconvenience. Those on a tight budget will need to use local bus services which are limited but get you to most places eventually.

Best time If best equals more sun and less rain, visit between Jan and Apr, with temperatures in the
to visit mid-20s. But if you've always dreamt of experiencing a tropical storm that lights up the sky in a way that leaves Hollywood's shambolic attempts in the dark, pick Oct and Nov – this is nature in its stunning, powerful and thoroughly soaking glory. There is over 5.5 m of rainfall annually in parts of the peninsula, although it is normally short and fierce.

Sierpe

Colour map 3, grid B3 A maze-like gravel road leads south for 12 km from Palmar Sur to Sierpe
Population: 3,707 through endless lines of banana plantations and African palms that produce a
Altitude: sea level natural oil for cooking, sunblock and skin cream. The small town on the banks of the Río Sierpe, with a population just short of 4,000, is surprisingly pleasant in a laid-back, indifferent way. However, most people normally just pass through en route to Drake.

Keen to capitalize on regional attractions, trips to nearby Isla Violin, Isla del Caño, Corcovado and tours of the largest area of mangrove swamps in the country can be arranged from here.

Should circumstances find you seeking a night's accommodation the best option in the heart of town is **B** *Oleaje Sereno*, one block west of the park, T786-7580, F786-7111. Neat and tidy after a recent renovation, 10 good rooms with private bath, hot water and a/c. The small restaurant overlooking the river is a fine spot to relax. **F** *Margarita*, two blocks north of the park, T786-7574. 5 clean and simple *cabinas* with fan and private bath or a bakers' dozen rooms in the **G** category. The rooms with windows are bright and breezy, and the owners are very friendly.

Out of town (2.1 km) across a rather hairy suspension bridge is **A** *Eco Manglares Sierpe Lodge*, T786-7414, F786-7441, www.ecotourism.co.cr/ecomanglares 7 rustic cabins for 3-4 people, with private bath and hot water. Pleasant gardens and an open-air restaurant serving mid-priced Italian and *Tico* dishes.

A *Río Sierpe Lodge*, T284-5595, F786-6291. 14 rustic but comfortable rooms with private bath near the mouth of the Sierpe river. Good spot for nature tours of the mangrove swamps and an ideal location for billfish and wahoo fishing in Pacific and snook and roosterfish in the tidal basin.

Bus Buses to **Sierpe** leave Palmar Norte at 0700, 0930, 1130, 1430 and 1700. Buses to **Palmar Norte** leave Sierpe at 0530, 0800, 1000, 1300 and 1530. Most hotels in Drake provide transport from Sierpe. Space allowing, you can get a ride for US$15 per person, boats leave around 1100. If you have missed the boats you can charter a local vessel for around US$70 for up to six people.

Isla Violin is home to some beautiful beaches and couple of treks. Further offshore you can visit **Isla del Caño** a popular destination for divers and snorkelling, with several *esfericos de piedra* to beguile the onlooker. Tours of the Térraba-Sierpe mangrove swamps (22,008 ha) – the largest area in the country – can also be arranged from Sierpe. For more information contact the Osa Conservation Area office in Palmar Norte on T/F786-7161.

Bahía Drake

A crescent shaped bay on the northern end of the Osa Peninsula, Drake (pronounced *DRA-kay*) Bay is named after Sir Francis Drake, the English bucaneering seaman who in March 1579 careened (deliberately beached) his ship on Playa Colorada in Bahía Drake. A plaque commemorating the 400th anniversary of the nautical aberration was erected in Aguijitas, but such drastic action is no longer required with the alighting point of preference now being the landing stage at Aguila de Osa Inn.

The main attraction of Drake is **diving off Isla del Caño** – where the water is exceptionally warm (around 25°C) – and for access to Corcovado National Park. Life in the bay is quite pricey and once you include transport you're looking at US$100 for one night without including any tours. Consequently, it's not a great option if on a tight budget, and many people come as part of an all-inclusive deal arranged from San José. If you want to dive, there are PADI dive centres with courses for beginners and experienced divers.

Sleeping & eating

Transport

Excursions

Colour map 3, grid C3

Walking around the length of the bay takes about 20 mins, otherwise, all transport is by boats arranged by the hotels

Golfito and the Osa Peninsula

Sleeping & Hotels in Bahía Drake are hugely overpriced in comparison to the rest of the country.
eating Prices quoted are per person not per room and include 3 meals unless otherwise
stated. It's a good idea to book, especially in the high season from Jan-Apr. Some
places offer discounts in the green season. Most hotels offer tours directly or will
arrange them on request.

L *Aguila de Osa Inn*, T296-2190, F232-7722, www.aguiladeosa.com A plush hotel in
nice gardens with 11 spacious rooms and 2 suites, all with hot water private bath and
fan. Open-air restaurant and bar serving international dishes. Good views and a mainly
US clientele. **L** *Drake Bay Wilderness Camp*, opposite *Aguila de Osa*, T/F770-8012 or
T256-7394, www.drakebay.com Large cabins, sleeping up to 5, with hot water and
private bath with splendid ocean views. Generous discounts for children and package
deals out of San José. **L** *La Paloma Lodge*, Next to *Drake Bay Wilderness Camp*,
T239-2801, F239-0954, www.lapalomalodge.com 4 rustic but elegant rooms sleep-
ing 3, and 5 bungalows sleeping 5, all with private bath and hot water. Perched up on
the hill and set in pleasant grounds the magnificent views look out to the Bay and Caño
Island in the distance.

AL *Jinetes de Osa*, T/F385-9541, crventur@costaricadiving.com, www.
costaricadiving.com A cool and funky hotel at the southern end of the bay, run by 2
brothers from Colorado. Rooms are spacious and airy, all with bath, hot water and fan –
some practically have waves lapping at the door. Open-air restaurant serves meals fam-
ily style with fresh bread. A new canopy tour has opened – the first and only one cur-
rently in Drake Bay. Recommended. **AL** *Pirate Cove*, at the northern end of the beach,
T380-3670 or T281-3260, piratecove@hotmail.com Very pleasant tent-like cabins,
some with bath, emulate an outdoor experience minus the mud. Large open-air restau-
rant serving *comida típica* with a hint of Swiss. *Caño Divers* is based here.

A *Jade Mar*, 5 mins up the hill along the road behind the *pulpería*, T384-6681,
F786-6358. Breezy simple rooms with bath and fan, **D** for a bed only. Good open-air
restaurant with views and tours available. **A** *Rancho Corcovado Lodge*, roughly in the
middle of the beach, T240-4085 (in San José) or T786-7059 (in Sierpe). Simple, rustic
rooms, many with views, all with bath. Pleasant restaurant on beach serves *comida
típica*. Good value tours offered. Friendly *Tico* owners are planning to remodel.

B *Cabinas Mirador Lodge*, up the hill just north of *Rancho Corcovado* and follow
the signs, T387-9138, F735-5440, www.lanzadera.com/javargase Pleasant, airy and
rustic rooms, all with bath. Restaurant serves *comida típica* using only fresh food –
good choices for vegetarians. The owner, José Antonio Vargas, is an ecologist and
there are trails on the property for bird-watching. Recommended.

The only real budget option in town is **C/D** *Bella Vista Lodge*, sometimes also
called *Cabinas Cecilia*, on beach at the southern end of the bay, T770-8051. Basic and
rather disappointing rooms, some with bath, 1 with a fan.

Outside Bahía Drake LL *Delfín Amor Eco Lodge*, a short boat journey just over 1 km
west of Drake, T394-2632, or T/F786-7636, www.divinedolphin.com 5 simple
screened cabins with a couple of double beds, set in lush jungle surrounded by wild-
life. The set-up is guided by a passion for dolphins and whales that visit the Drake Bay.
A 9-day package from San José is US$1250 or you can visit for just a few days. Superb
website, if you like dolphins and a well organized volunteer programme.

L *Corcovado Adventures Tent Camp*, set in forest right on Playa Caletas (4 km
southwest of Drake), T384-1679 or T289-3595, www.corcovado.com Large tents
with comfortable beds complete with babbling brook. Good choice for those who like
the outdoor with lots of tours and snorkelling and boogie boarding from the beach.
L *Marenco Beach and Rainforest Lodge*, set in 600 ha of private reserve a little further
west, T258-1919, F255-1346, www.marencolodge.com 17 rustic bungalows and 8

rooms, all with bath and sea view. Meals in restaurant from a menu with a good selection. The hotel has several km of private trails and supports students and research with discounted rates, exploring the options for tourism and conservation working successfully side by side. Packages offered out of San José including guided tours, all meals, transfers and accommodation. Very friendly.

AL *Poor Man's Paradise*, in Playa San Josecito southwest of Drake, T/F786-6150, www.mypoormansparadise.com 8 clean, rustic and pleasant cabins with bath. Also provide tents so you can **camp** at **B** or you can pitch your own **F**. Prices include 3 meals. Transfers from Sierpe US$20 per person.

Almost at the **San Pedrillo** park entrance to Corcovado National Park in a 69 ha private reserve is **LL** *Casa Corcovado Jungle Lodge*, T256-3181, F256-7409, www.casacorcovado.com 10 very comfortable and separate thatched bungalows with tiled floors, ceiling fans and beds draped with mosquito nets. A good luxury choice, it mainly offers packages at US$795 per person, including transfers from and to San José, 3 night's accommodation, all meals and tours to Corcovado and Caño Island.

Camping Options include **F** per person at *Rancho Corcovado* including use of electricity and bathrooms, or *Pirate Cove* (see above) which has no fixed price but a small charge for use of baths.

Most hotel restaurants only cater for guests. Hotels that might make an exception if **Eating** you give a little advance notice include *Jade Mar*, *Rancho Corcovado*, *Mirador Lodge* and *Pirate Cove*. All food tends to be expensive because supplies have to come by boat from Sierpe. There is a *soda* on the beach in the village, but it's nearly always closed. Otherwise, the *pulpería* stocks a few basics.

As with dining, the nightlife is mostly arranged by the hotels, but you could try *Bar Mar* **Bars** *y Sombra*, up some steps from the beach between *Jinetes de Osa* and *Bella Vista Lodge*.

Most people arrive at Bahía Drake by boat from **Sierpe** (see page 343), having arrived in **Transport** Palmar Sur on 1 of the daily *SANSA* flights. *Travelair*, T735-5062, F735-5043, www.travelair-costarica.com (US$70) announced plans to fly direct to Drake from San José for the first time in 2002, so make enquiries. It is possible to drive to Drake leaving the Pan-American Highway at **Chacarita**, following the road to Rincón from where a right fork leads to Aguijitas. This road is 4-wheel drive and only passable in the dry season.

Excursions

Drake is good for swimming, but the beach is pebbly and lots of hotel boats use the water. Day trips to **Isla Caño**, **Corcovado National Park** and the mangroves of the **Sierpe-Térraba estuary** cost around US$70 per person but prices fall considerably if travelling in a group.

Diving in the area is mainly to view fish rather than coral and you may well see white-tipped sharks, manta and sting rays. Two places offer diving. *Jinetes de Osa* at the southern end of the bay offer 5-day PADI courses (US$325), full-day dives with 2 tanks dives and resort dives (US$130). Also recommended are the very friendly *Caño Divers*, at *Pirate Cove Hotel* a short walk north, who charge US$110 for a two-tank day's diving at Isla Caño. If you're not staying at either of these places, you can arrange your dive with them through your hotel. When not diving, there is good snorkelling at several places in the area.

Golfito and the Osa Peninsula

Dolphins and whales can be seen year round, but the best time is mid-Nov-Apr, which fortunately coincides with the dry season

The continuous research of the *Delfin Amor Eco Lodge*, who hope to set up a marine reserve here, has recorded 24 species of **dolphins** and **whales** in Drake Bay, including humpback whales, bottlenose dolphins, pilot whales and sea turtles. The lodge offers tours and packages to see dolphins and whales, T394-2632, F786-7642, www.divinedolphin.com/costaricadolphins Green and hawksbill **turtles** nest to the north and south of Bahía Drake in the green season, but egg-poaching is a problem – ask locally for tour information.

Several hotels arrange **sportsfishing**. Prices starting at US$200 per person.

Reserva Biológica Isla del Caño
Colour map 3, grid C2

Some 20 km west of the Osa Peninsula, *Caño Island Biological Reserve* is a popular day trip from Sierpe with a single path on the island and good opportunities for snorkelling close to the coast. The 300 ha island rises to a height of barely 110 m above sea level with much of the coastline created by high cliffs. Wildlife is relatively scarce on the island although you may see bird species such as osprey and brown booby, and pacas, four-eyed opossums and boa constrictors are also present on the island.

The island's main interest – on land at least – is archaeological. There is evidence that the island was used as a precolumbian cemetery. The perfectly round stone spheres found throughout the Diquis Valley on the mainland are also present on the island, adding to the mystery of how and why these stone spheres were created.

The 2,700 ha marine portion of the reserve protects marine platforms of low coral reef, large pelagics (large fish) and the regionally endangered lobster and giant conch.

Pan-American Highway to Puerto Jiménez

Rincón
Colour map 3, grid C3

A good road leaves the Pan-American Highway at Chacarita and shadows the southern shore of the peninsula climbing with each rocky headland. The small town of Rincón is marked by the stylish *La Ventana* restaurant (mid-range) and the author of the *Southern Costa Rica Guide*, Alexander del Sol lives next door. He's local, knowledgeable, passionate about southern Costa Rica and welcomes visitors.

Sleeping At the southern end of town, *Soda El Puente* and the bridge of the Río Rincón mark the (dry season only) road route to Drake Bay. Along this road is the **B** person *Centro Juvenil Tropical*, T735-5522. It's probably of only passing interest to ecotourists unless you're a teacher, in which case go and explore the environmental education centre that targets Costa Rican kids. Good, simple dormitory accommodation ideal for groups with great access to the rainforest. The centre is run by *Fundación Neotrópica*, who can be contacted in San José at C 20, Av 3-5, T253-2130, www.neotropica-tyc.org

La Palma
Colour map 3, grid C3

Fourteen kilometres beyond Rincón is the town of La Palma and the road heading west for access to the *Los Patos* ranger's station of Corcovado National Park. Along this road is the **B** *Albergue Ecoturístico Cerro de Oro* T/F286-4203, www.agroecoturismo.net As part of the *Cooprena* cooperative, you'll be contributing to the grass-roots economy by staying in one of the six rooms with shared bath, or the cabins which sleep up to six people. A good spot for exploring the Río Rincón and surrounding area. Breakfast included.

Puerto Jiménez

Once the gold-mining centre of the Osa Peninsula, with a single, dusty main street fringed by a few stores and bars, Puerto Jiménez still has the faint feel of a lawless frontier town, even though the prospectors that rolled into town from throughout the peninsula were cleared from Corcovado National Park in 1985.

Colour map 3, grid C4
Population: 2,500
Altitude: Sea level

Today, Puerto Jiménez is a popular destination with its laid-back but occasionally lively atmosphere, reasonable beaches nearby and, of course, the beautiful national park not far away. A particular charm of Puerto Jiménez, barely five blocks square, is its relative freedom from road traffic. There's plenty of budget accommodation, good local walks to the jungle, beaches, and mangroves only a couple of blocks from the main street, where you will see monkeys and many birds. But if you want to see wildlife you don't even have to go that far – Scarlet macaws roost in the trees around the football pitch, cheering on the local team.

Ins and outs

A daily flight from San José touches down on the southeastern side of town. A regular – and long – bus journey from the capital leaves early in the morning, and ferries cross the Gulf of Dulce to Golfito a couple of times a day. If you're driving, the 79 km road from the Pan-American Highway follows a good road to Rincón, from where the 35 km reasonable dirt road heads south to Puerto Jiménez. There are many bridge crossings so check locally for conditions.

Getting there & around

If you're staying in town, you can walk everywhere without inconvenience. If your accommodation is out of town, make arrangements with the hotel to be picked up from the airstrip, ferry dock or bus station.

Regular *colectivos* (pick-ups) make the journey to Carate from Puerto Jiménez, from where you can make trips to the national park.

There is no **tourist information** but you won't go wrong if you pop in to *Caroline's* and talk to the people at *Escondido Trex*.

Essentials

AL-C *Doña Leta's Bungalows*, just beyond *Let George Do It*, T735-5180, www.donaleta.com 7 fine wooden framed bungalows sleeping up to 5 people equipped with a small kitchen, private bath and hot water. A/c comes with sea breezes from the beach barely 30 m from the open-air restaurant. All this set in pleasant gardens and with kayaks free for guests to explore nearby coves and the mangroves. A good choice for groups and families.

Sleeping
■ *on map*
Price codes: see inside front cover

A-B *Agua Luna*, right in front of you if arriving by ferry, T/F735-3593, agualu@racsa.co.cr 14 uninspiring but comfortable rooms equipped with TV, telephone, fridge and optional a/c. Strangely, only cold water in the private baths. Good service and fishing tours arranged.

B-C *Los Manglares*, T/F735-5002, F735-5605. 10 clean and well maintained cabins with private bath. A small bar and simple dishes are available. On the river banks close to the mangroves, capuchin monkeys visit for breakfast, scarlet macaws roost in nearby trees and the odd crocodile basks in the grounds by the river. Good place to relax, very friendly and recommended.

E *Oro Verde*, T735-5241, F735-5468, oroverde@racsa.co.cr 10, big and comfortable rooms with bath and fan, some overlooking the street. Friendly efficient service, can and will arrange tours.

Golfito and the Osa Peninsula

F (per person) *Cabinas Marcelina*, T735-5007, F735-5045, www.hostelling-costarica.com 6 rooms with bath. Big, clean and basic. Nice front yard for relaxing and small discount for youth hostelling members. **F** *Iguana Iguana*, on the road into town, T735-5158, 2iguanas@racsa.co.cr Simple rooms with private bath and a small bar. Swimming pool in high season.

On the gulf shore with good views is **G** per person *Cabinas Puerto Jiménez*, T735-5090, F375-5215. 10 big, spotless rooms sleeping up to 4 people. Private bath, fan and small table. Very friendly – possibly *the* best cheap place in Costa Rica. **G** *Cabinas Thompson*, T735-5910. Quiet spot off the main street, dark rooms but essentially clean, with a small patio for relaxing. **G** (per person) *Pensíon Quinter*, T735-5078. Very simple old wooden building with a dozen rooms and share bathroom. Bit grubby but generally clean.

Camping The gloriously titled **G** *Puerto Jiménez Yacht Club* is more commonly known as *Let George Do It*, T735-5313. While George's main focus is tours, you can camp in the grounds which push up to the beach, with showers and bathroom provided. Great spot.

Playa Platanares Outside Puerto Jiménez, 5 km south, behind the airstrip is the grey sand beach of Playa Platanares. Quiet and secluded with good swimming, it's a good spot for groups and particularly popular with the European crowd. As part of the Preciosa Platanares National Wildlife Refuge, plans are underway to develop a turtle project and ensure the protection of the beaches used by olive ridley, hawksbill and green turtles. **AL** *Iguana Lodge*, T735-5205, F735-5043, www.iguanalodge.com Right on the beach, with 4 stilted cabins built from bamboo and local hardwoods complete with private bath in fine landscaped gardens. Price includes meals. Business is booming so they've also taken on the place next door and renamed it *The Pearl* – make enquiries for details. **A** *Playa PreciOsa Lodge*, T735-5062, F753-5043, www.playa-preciosa-lodge.de 4 funky round cabins with a double bed and a couple of singles. The restaurant has a fine panorama overlooking the gulf, and when not eating, you can hang in the hammocks and relax all day. Right on the beach, it's ideal for swimming and surfing.

Dos Brazos Out of town on the way out towards the mainland a road leads after 4 km to Dos Brazos. Local gold mine workings can be visited here by climbing the road that goes uphill beyond the town. In the wet season, the road has puddles the size of small lakes – call ahead for bookings and to enquire about road conditions, which apparently were repaired shortly after the rented mini-submarine was returned.

AL *Bosque del Río Tigre*, F735-5045, www.osaadventures.com A small lodge set in the forest on the Río Tigre on the outskirts of Dos Brazos, with trails nearby. Targetting the traveller looking for a little luxury in the middle of the forest, the rustic and peaceful lodge sleeps a maximum of 10 people. Not great at "tooting their own horn", the naturalist owners have built up a reputation for a family-like atmosphere, good food and great guiding with about 300 bird species spotted within a 30-min walking radius of the lodge. **D** *Namu Woke*, T265-7475 (owner's sister in Heredia) or just turn up (if the road is good). 6 basic cabins sleeping up to 3 people with private bath, and while it could do with some new bedding, it is clean. Restaurant serving basic meals.

Eating Dining options in Jiménez are hardly endless. *Carolina's* on the main street is a good and cheap, recommended for fish and as a place to gen up on tour options with the guys at *Escondido Trex* at the back of the restaurant. At the northern end of town is *El Rancho* with good pizzas a bar and music until the early hours. Across the street is *Pizza Rocks* which hardly needs explanation. The best restaurant, and most expensive in town is *Agua Luna* with linen cloths and tiled flooring overlooking the bay (mid-range).

Escondido Trex in *Restaurant Carolina's* on the main street, T/F735-5210, **Tour operators** www.escondidotrex.com Open daily and you'll normally find someone around in the evening. They have developed a full range of tours on the Osa Peninsula and around the Dulce Gulf. You can head out in kayaks at sunset to paddle alongside black-spotted, spinner and bottle-nose dolphins before watching the sunset from your kayak. Also hiking in the southern region and Corcovado National Park and many other options. Trips start at US$40 a day. Good on general information and with a small book swap. *Osa Peninsula Tours*, T/F735-5135, osapentours@racsa.co.cr Provide a range of kayak and hiking tours, as well as bird-watching trips, canopy climbs and a small book swap. You can *Let George Do It* at the *Puerto Jiménez Yacht Club*, T735-5313, F735-5051, with dolphin and whale watching tours. George also has kayaking tours and bikes for rent. *Osa Natural* T735-5440, F735-5045, www. osanatural.com Opposite the football pitch but seem to be more interested in the internet connections than helping clients – for the timebeing at least.

Puerto Jiménez

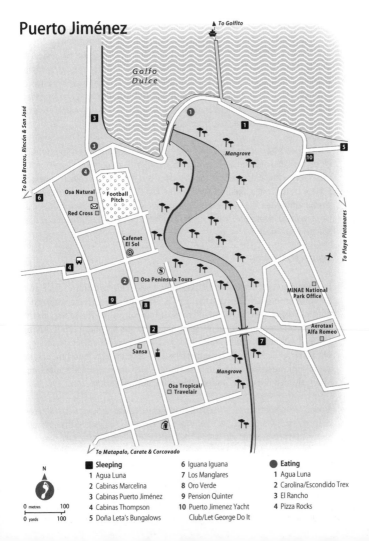

Sleeping	
1 Agua Luna	6 Iguana Iguana
2 Cabinas Marcelina	7 Los Manglares
3 Cabinas Puerto Jiménez	8 Oro Verde
4 Cabinas Thompson	9 Pension Quinter
5 Doña Leta's Bungalows	10 Puerto Jimenez Yacht Club/Let George Do It

Eating	
1 Agua Luna	
2 Carolina/Escondido Trex	
3 El Rancho	
4 Pizza Rocks	

Golfito and the Osa Peninsula

At the southern end of the main street *Osa Tropical*, T735-5062, F735-5043, www.osatropical.com is the *Travelair* agent in Puerto Jiménez. *Osa Tropical* also acts as booking agents for several secluded and privately owned houses to the south of the peninsula.

If planning to book accommodation in Corcovado National Park you will need to make reservations at the MINAE office facing the airstrip. T735-5036, F735-5276.

Transport **Air** Daily flights with *SANSA*, T735-5017, F735-5495, www.flysansa.com (US$66) and *Travelair*, T735-5062, F735-5043, www.travelair-costarica.com (US$75). The airstrip is at the southeastern corner of town. Alongside the airstrip are the offices of *Alfa Romeo Aero Taxi*, T/F735-5112, which provide alternatives to getting to out of the way places including Drake Bay and Carate.

A café by the bus stop opens at 0430 when you can get a cheap but reasonable breakfast

Road From **San José** buses leave the Terminal Atlántico Norte (C 12, Av 9-11) with *Autotransportes Blanco Lobo* and make the 8 hr journey to **Puerto Jiménez** at 1200, US$6.30 passing through **San Isidro**, **Buenos Aires**, **Palmar Norte** and **Palmar Sur**. The return bus leaves at 0500. Buses leave for **Ciudad Neily** at 0530 and 1400, 3 hrs, US$3.

A couple of *colectivos* depart daily for **Carate** from outside *Restaurant Carolina* at 0530 and 0600, cost US$7. Services may be restricted in the wet season.

To reach Puerto Jiménez by car leave the Pan-American Highway at Chacarita, 33 km south of Palmar Norte. The road is paved to Rincón – although there are some precipitous drops (and great views) – with a fairly good gravel road for the remaining distance.

Boat A boat leaves the *muellecito* (small dock) from **Golfito** for Puerto Jiménez at 1120, US$2.50, 1½ hrs. The ferry leaves Puerto Jiménez at 0600. Alternatively you can charter a boat – US$60 for up to 8 passengers.

Directory **Banks** There's a branch of *Banco Nacional* in town. **Communications** Internet: *Café el Sol* provides a pricey internet service (US$8 per hr). *Osa Natural* is cheaper but the machines are much slower. **Post**: the post office is at the northern end of town opposite the football pitch. **Medical services** The *Red Cross* is beside the football pitch. **Useful addresses** The **police station** is at the northern end of town on the main street. *www.soldeosa.com* is a source of Osa-related online news that has taken a few tentative early steps.

South to Carate

From Puerto Jiménez, a dirt road continues for 33 km to Carate, which gives the southernmost road access to the park. The route skims the coastline dipping and rising with the rocky outcrops and crossing a handful of streams that are normally passable in the dry season but rise quickly after rain. If driving, proceed with caution, take local advice and be prepared for delays. *Osa Tropical*, T735-5062, F735-5043, osatropi@sol.racsa.co.cr, in Puerto Jiménez acts as the booking agents for a number of lodges and cabins in the Matapalo area. Many, though not all, are aimed at the self-catering market.

Matapalo Around 17 km from Puerto Jiménez the road rises steeply to pass over Cabo Matapalo.
Colour map 3, grid C4 **LL** *Lapa Ríos*, T735-5130, F735-5179, www.laparios.com 14 spacious thatched bungalows using hardwoods and bamboo furniture from top to bottom. Each bungalow has a private deck with views to the ocean or rainforest, and a private bathroom with solar-heated shower. Set in 400-ha private rainforest reserve, the open-air restaurant serves divine international cuisine, complete with a full bar providing cooled drinks you can sip from the observation deck with fantastic views. Full range of tours available and a pool to contemplate the paradise. All this comes at a quite a price, but the guiding principals for this eco-conscious hotel ensure that only locals are employed. If you

ever needed inspiration to work harder and earn more money this is it. Too bad such relaxing natural comforts are not available for everyone – if they were nature conservation would be a far easier nut to crack.

Nearby you will find **L** *Bosque el Cabo Rainforest Lodge*, T/F735-5206, www.bosquedelcabo.com White-washed with terracotta tiles, each breezy bungalow has a fantastic view out to the Pacific from the idyllic location perched on the cliffs of Cabo Matapalo. Set in beautifully tended gardens – with enough space to think you have the place to yourself – it would be easy to spend the days just lounging in the hammock listening to the sounds of the rainforest as the day slowly passes. But venture from such comforts and you'll find a pool and a fine open-air restaurant serving national and international dishes.

Several places in the Matapalo area are booked and managed by *Osa Tropical* in Puerto Jiménez, T735-5062, F735-5043, www.osatropical.com You can choose from **A** *Casa Matapalo*, www.casamatapalo.com, which has a large, fully equipped cabin sleeping 4 adults set in tropical rainforest. All bedding and netting provided. **A** per person *Encanta la Vida*, www.encantalavida.com 3 thatched roofed cabins, comfortably furnished with tiled floors and hardwood furnishing, or a 4-bedroom, 2-bathroom house. Privacy and seclusion for honeymooners and large groups. The price includes 3 meals a day. **C** per person is *Casa Tortuga*, www.costarica.com/tortuga, sleeping up to 6 people, with a 2-day minimum stay. Good choice for surfing off Matapalo Point. *Casa Matapalito* is in fact couple of comfortable houses for rent, sleeping up to 5 people. All modern amenities and the all-essential balcony with hammock for lazing away the day – contact *Osa Tropical* for prices.

The closest point approaching Corcovado National Park from the south, Carate has fairly good links with Puerto Jiménez to the east. There's a clutch of good accommodation in the area which is great for simply relaxing and equally good for use as a base for short trips to the national park and the surrounding rainforest.

Carate
Colour map 3, grid C3

Close to Carate is **L** (per person) *Luna Lodge*, T/F380-5036, www.lunalodge.com 7 thatched roof bungalows climbing up the valley of the Carate River, each with a couple of double beds, private bath and a viewing deck. Set in gently landscaped gardens, over half the property is primary rainforest with trails leading to several nearby waterfalls. A fine *rancho* restaurant is the setting for international cuisine, and a great spot for mulling over the wonders of days past and yet to come.

AL (per person) including 3 meals *Lookout Inn*, T/F735-5431, www.lookout-inn.com 3 comfortable tiled-floor rooms complete with bamboo furniture and nature scene murals on the wall have a fine breezy feel, with hot water private bathrooms.

Golfito and the Osa Peninsula

Luna Lodge

- *Private baths with hot water*
- *Located on the mesa above the Carate River, 1 mile north of the airstrip at Carate*
- *7 Cabinas, built of native material*
- *very large rancho which houses the restaurant, cantina, store and reception area*
- *60 acres of rainforest*
- *The Lodge borders Corcovado National Park and shares the same ecological environment.*
- *Howler monkeys, Toucans, Scarlet Macaws & Sloths are prevelent.*
- *The Lodge provides a true "Rainforest adventure."*
- *The Lodge can arrange for charter flights to the airstrip at Carate-Also, flights can be arranged by commercial-Sansa Airlines-which flies to Carate and then a taxi service delivers guests to Carate- Arrangements can be made in the United States by contacting Don Wedmore at toll free-888-409-8448*

Phone & Fax at the lodge 011-506-3805036
www.information@lunalodge.com

International and local dishes naturally incorporate fresh fruit and lots of home cooking served on the roof top observation platform with spectacular views of the rainforest and the ocean. Now with a swimming pool. **AL** *Terrapin Lodge*, T735-5211, F735-5049, www.terrapinlodge.com A new set-up. 5 wooden screened cabins, some with ocean views, surrounded by rainforest and powered by solar panels. Dining in a central wooden *cabana* complete with bar. **AL** *Corcovado Lodge Tent Camp*, 30 mins' walk west along the beach, T257-0766, F257-1655, www.costaricaexpeditions. com Part of the impressive *Costa Rica Expeditions* set-up, the camp is a creative and comfortable camping option. If camping isn't your style then you've clearly not seen the 20 walk-in tents, each with a couple of comfortable camp beds and a small front porch, set in a beautiful coconut grove yards from the beach with the rainforest climbing up the hills nearby. Shared bathrooms are a short walk from the tents. Meals are served in a large thatched roofed dining room, and there's a hammock house for relaxing. As ever, the *Costa Rica Expeditions* team provide bilingual experts to guide you through their 161 ha private reserve and wildlife viewing platform some 100 ft off the ground. You can follow trails to wonderful views of the bay or you can go on longer treks to and through Corcovado National Park. Multi-day packages available from San José or starting locally. The whole place is highly recommended.

Just before town **A** *Carate Jungle Camp*, has simple cabins and shared showers, meals included. The only **budget** option available is to camp at the *pulpería* in town run by Gilberto Morales and his wife, who will let you camp for a small fee.

Parque Nacional Corcovado

Colour map 3, grid C3   *For many the most magnificent jewel in the priceless green crown that is Costa Rica, Corcovado National Park protects roughly one third of the Osa Peninsula (42,469 ha). After Monteverde and Arenal, Corcovado National Park is probably the most recorded part of Costa Rica. National Geographic Discovery Channel, the BBC and countless other esteemed naturalists have recorded the delights of the area, and with good reason. Although selectively logged until its creation in 1975, and finally cleared of gold prospectors in 1985 the national park protects the largest area of humid tropical rainforest in the country.*

For wildlife watchers the place is a paradise, for people who want to hike on their own it offers one of the few opportunities in Costa Rica for long-distance treks through lowland rainforest that really stretch your legs. To follow the coastal path from San Pedrino to La Leona will take at least three days – without allowing for extra time spent exploring shorter trails close to Sirena.

Ins and outs

Getting there   There are 3 ranger's stations providing access to the park. **San Pedrillo**, to the north is reached through Drake from where you need to charter a boat or walk round the headland. **Los Patos** in the centre of the peninsula is reached from La Palma, accessed by buses travelling from the Pan-American Highway to Puerto Jiménez. The final option is through **La Leona** to the south, reached from Carate which in turn has road access from Puerto Jiménez.

If the budget stretches that far you can get an air taxi from Puerto Jiménez to **Carate**, **San Pedrillo** and even **La Sirena** for as little as US$99 per person with 5 people. Just think of the views – go on, it's worth it.

If short of time and/or money, the simplest way to the park is to take the pick-up truck from outside *Carolina's* in Puerto Jiménez to Carate, from where you can go on short treks in the south of the park.

Getting around You can travel through the park using any combination of entrance and exit points. Entering through Carate and exiting through La Palma – or vice versa – is probably the simplest and cheapest option.

Entrance & sleeping Entrance to the park is US$6 paid at the ranger's station. Basic accommodation is available at the ranger's stations San Pedrillo, Los Patos, La Leona and, the most commonly used, La Sirena at **F** a night. Bring a sleeping bag and mosquito net. Camping is possible at US$2 a night. Meals are available US$3 for breakfast (served promptly at 0500), US$6.50 for lunch and dinner. Accommodation and meals should be booked in advance with the *MINAE* office in Puerto Jiménez, T735-5036, F735-5276. If trekking alone, get topographical maps from the IGM in San José.

Sights

Wildlife As ever it's the combination of temperatures in the high 20s and rainfall as high as 5.5 m that has created eight different lifezones. Cloudforest on some of the higher summits gives way to montane forest, which covers over half the park. With swamp forest around Corcovado lagoon and mangrove forests along the river estuaries there are over 500 species of tree in the park including the 70-m high silk cotton or ceiba tree – probably the largest in the country.

Wildlife is equally diverse. Corcovado is home to the largest population of scarlet macaws in the country. All six cats in Costa Rica are found in the park, and the beach to the north at Llorona is used as a nesting site by four species of sea turtles. The wildlife inventory is staggering – 140 species of mammals, 367 of birds, 177 amphibians and reptiles and 40 freshwater fish – but you'll need a guide, patience and a good deal of luck to tick significant numbers off your list.

Trails About 40 minutes beyond Carate is **La Leona** station. It's about 18 km (6 hours) from Carate to Sirena which you can make in one day as long as the tides don't work against you – check with the wardens so you don't get stuck. From

You will find both hiking boots and sandals useful if you are walking any distance in the park

Parque Nacional Corcovado

Golfito and the Osa Peninsula

La Leona to the end of Playa Madrigal is another 2½ hr walk, part sandy, part rock with some rock pools and rusty shipwrecks looking like modern art sculptures. At points the trail rises steeply into the forest and you are surrounded by mangroves, almonds and coconut palms. A couple of rivers break the beachline. The first, **Río Madrigal**, is only about 15 minutes beyond La Leona. Clear, cool and deep enough for swimming about 200 m upstream, it's a refreshing stop if you're walking out and a good place to spot wildlife.

The best place for viewing wildlife – although increasingly popular in the dry season – is **La Sirena**, where there are several short trails lasting from 30 minutes to a few hours exploring the network of paths inland and Corcovado lagoon. It's definitely worth staying a couple of nights at La Sirena ranger's station, if time allows. More than one visitor to Costa Rica records staying here as the highlight of their trip.

From Sirena you can head inland on a trail to **Los Patos** (20 km, six to nine hours depending on conditions) passing several rivers full of reptiles on the way. The ranger station at Los Patos has a balcony which is a great observation point for birds especially the redheaded woodpecker. From Los Patos you can carry on to the park border, before criss-crossing the Río Rincón to **La Palma**, a settlement on the opposite side of the Peninsula (13 km, six more hours). From La Palma there is transport to Puerto Jiménez (see above).

Alternatively, from La Sirena you can walk north along the coast to **Llorona**, with waterfalls nearby, continuing north on a forest trail and then along the beach to the station at **San Pedrillo** on the edge of the park. You can stay here and eat with the rangers if you've made a reservation.

Golfito

Colour map 3, grid C4
Population: 15,157
Altitude: Sea level

Tiny in comparison to the Golfo Dulce, the diminutive Golfito built its success on the long and sheltered bay that lines the town. These perfect conditions saw the town flourish as a major banana exporting port when the United Fruit Company *set up operations in the town in the 1930s. Bust followed boom when the*

Golfito

N

0 metres   500
0 yards   500

■ Sleeping
1 Cabinas Marlin
2 Cabinas Playa Cacao
3 Del Cerro
4 El Gran Ceibo
5 Golfo Azul
6 Las Gaviotas
7 Mar y Luna
8 Sierra

● Eating
1 Siete Mares

company pulled out in 1985 leaving behind the skeleton of a prosperous town. Golfito, stretched long and thin between the coastline to the west and steep, forested hills to the east, still seems a little on the skinny side. With bare bones showing, it's difficult to warm to the place and you'll probably be just passing through to get elsewhere – the Osa Peninsula, northern beach resorts or Playa Zancudo and Pavones to the south.

The affluence and services that do remain owe their success to the tax free zone or depósito libre *set up in 1990.* Ticos *and resident expats travel half way across the country to get items at about 60% of prices in the capital – what a bargain!*

Ins and outs

Getting there

Daily flights from San José with *SANSA* and *Travelair* arrive on the airstrip at the northern end of town. If driving, the paved Highway 14 leaves the Pan-American Highway at Río Claro, 15 km north of Ciudad Neily. A daily bus service plies the Pan-American Highway from San José, with a more regular service between nearby Ciudad Neily. If you're out on the peninsula at Puerto Jiménez you can catch a ferry across the Gulf.

Getting around

Moving around Golfito without your own transport is, quite frankly, tedious. It's almost 6 km from the first hotel on the sea front to the *depósito libre*. There is a local bus that commutes the main drag in a hail and ride system for US$0.30 a trip. Beyond that, taxis are readily available.

Sights

The *United Fruit Company* history of the town has left a distinctive mark on Golfito, which is strung out along the shore in clusters. Arriving from the south, the road encounters a few of the better hotels in the area. Further north the administrative centre of the town, complete with rusting locomotive and a statue in weary tribute to a banana labourer, has a few old clapboard hotels and bars making it the main focus for a stay. At the northernmost point, a few old management buildings of the *United Fruit Company* create a sense of

Golfito and the Osa Peninsula

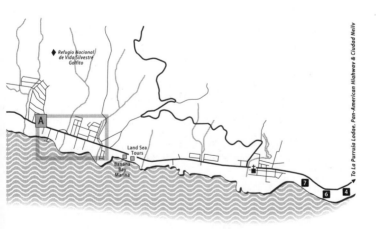

Related map
A Golfito detail,
page 356

elevated grace completely overshadowed by the gaudy nature of the rush to buy domestic appliances and hi-fi systems at the *depósito libre*.

Essentials

Sleeping
■ *on maps*
Price codes: see inside front cover

Hotels are listed in order from the south

Hotels in the area don't exactly bend over backwards to win business – people visiting the town are here for the discounted goods. Although there are a couple of exceptions, don't expect too much in the way of service.

On the road to Golfito, 4 km before the coastal strip is **D** *La Purruja Lodge*, T/F775-1054, www.purruja.com 5 simple uninspiring duplex cabins with bath. Good for **camping** at US$2 a tent. There's also a small outhouse with a couple of hammocks. Small restaurant, pool table and darts board. Lots of safe parking.

Arriving at the coastline, the first place in town is **B-D** *El Gran Ceibo*, T/F775-0403, www.ecotourism.co.cr/elgranceibo Reasonable rooms, some with a/c, some with TV, and cold water private bath. The plus is a small pool – perfect on hot, breezeless days. **B** *Las Gaviotas*, T775-0062, F775-0544, lasgaviotas@hotmail.com Probably the best place in town, it has 21 tidy cabins and rooms strung out along the waterfront, all with TV, telephone, fridge and safe box. Fine pool with sundeck and an open air restaurant serving dishes (mid-range) and a bar to keep you entertained day and night. A short distance further on is **D** *Mar y Luna*, T775-0192, F775-1049. 8 good rooms sleeping 2-4, with bath and fan. Unassuming and simple, the restaurant sits on stilts above the sea. Quiet spot, friendly staff – a good deal.

A couple of kilometres further down is the administrative centre of the town. **E-F** *Delfina*, T/F775-0043. Basic rooms with fans. Rooms with a private bath are much better, and rooms on the street can be noisy. Parking available. **F** *Cabinas Melissa*, behind *Delfina*, T775-0043. 4 simple, clean and tidy rooms, with private bath and small terrace with views of the bay. Safe parking available – a great bargain. **F** *Golfito*, T775-0047. Quiet and central with a couple of rooms overlooking the bay. A little run-down but not a bad deal. **F** *Costa Rica Surf*, T775-0034. 25 dark rooms, most with private bath, which are probably filled with noise when the big bar downstairs gets going. **G** *El Uno*, above the restaurant of the same name, T775-0061. Very basic, in a clapboard house from the 1940s – mildly amusing if you fancy pretending to be a banana in a packing case. That said, it is very friendly.

Golfito detail

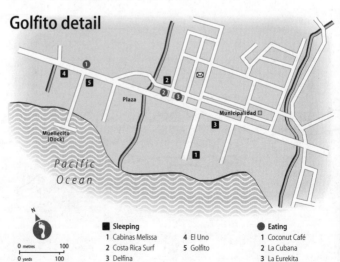

N

0 metres 100
0 yards 100

■ **Sleeping**
1 Cabinas Melissa
2 Costa Rica Surf
3 Delfina
4 El Uno
5 Golfito

● **Eating**
1 Coconut Café
2 La Cubana
3 La Eurekita

Close to the docks is **D-E** *Del Cerro*, T775-0006. 20 simple rooms sleeping 1-6, with private bath. Small restaurant, bar topped off with wonderfully indifferent service. **F** *Cabinas Marlin*, a couple of streets back from the bank, T775-0191. Small neat rooms with fan and hot water private bath. *Tico*-owned and very friendly in the old part of town.

At the northern end of town near the airport and free zone is **B** *Sierra*, T775-0666, F775-0506. 72 double rooms with a/c, a couple of pools and a restaurant. Rooms are better than the place looks from the outside, but still overpriced. **C** *Golfo Azul*, T775-0871, F775-1849, golfazul@racsa.co.cr 20 comfortable and large rooms with private bath, a/c and cable TV in a homely setting. Breakfast included.

Coconut Café is the main gringo gathering point with good cheap breakfasts and snacks, a book swap, good local knowledge and a notice-board for messages. Internet planned. *Cubana*, near the post office, services excellent local dishes at seriously cheap prices. Nearby *El Uno* services good, reasonably priced seafood. *Delfina Restaurant*, is in the centre serving cheap breakfasts from 0700, snacks and home-made baked goods. *Le Eurekita* is a popular cheap place with locals in the centre serving a mean breakfast of *huevos rancheros* (fried or scrambled eggs served with chopped tomato).

Eating & drinking
There are many seafood restaurants along the seafront

There are several lively bars and clubs around the central area. Start at the bar in the *Hotel Costa Surf* and then follow your instincts.

Land Sea Tours, to the south of the centre of town, 0730 to 0500, Mon to Fri, 0800-1300 Sat, T/F775-1614, landsea@racsa.co.cr A one-stop shop. Whether you're looking for local information, to organize a personalized local tour, book accommodation in some distant hideaway, rent a car or arrange national or international flights, Tim and Katie and their team can help.

Tour operators

If you needed any other reason to drop by they also have a good book swap, internet service and fresh coffee permanently on the go.

Marina services are available at Golfito with *Land Sea Tours* (see above) and *Banana Bay Marina*, T775-0838, F775-0735, bbmarina@sol.racsa.co.cr

Air Several daily flights, mostly in the morning, with *SANSA* (US$66) and *Travelair* (US$75) (local agent *Land Sea Tours*, T/F775-1614), via **Coto 47** or **Puerto Jiménez**. It's an all weather runway, but the landing is reported to be a little on the tight side between the trees.

Transport

Road Services to **San José** with *Tracopa*, T775-0365, leave the capital from Terminal Alfaro at Av 5, C 14, at 0700 and 1500 (direct, 7 hrs), returning at 0500 and 1300, US$6. Buses travel down the Pan-American Highway through **San Isidro**. Alternatively, take any bus heading south, alighting at the junction at **Río Clara**. Hourly buses travel to and from **Ciudad Neily** and **Paso Canoas**, US$1.25.

Boat A ferry (locally called *la lancha*) makes the 1½ hr journey across the Dulce Gulf to **Puerto Jiménez** leaving the *muellecito* (small dock) beside *Restaurante El Uno* at 1120, returning at 0600, US$2.50. There is also a launch service to **Playa Zancudo** – ask at *Land Sea Tours* or the *muellicito* for the latest timetable.

For boat journeys further afield *ABOCAP* (Asociación de Boteros, T775-0712), opposite the ICE building, provide **water taxis** in and around Golfito. A boat to Puerto Jiménez is about US$60 for up to 6 people, US$45 to Playa Zancudo. Make enquiries for other destinations.

Communications Banks The *Banco Nacional* in town seems to enjoy the novelty of being able to change travellers cheques, although the service can be slow. **Internet**: services are available at *Land Sea Travel* but expect to see others opening up soon – try the *Coconut Café*. **Post**: the post office is in centre of town beside the football pitch. **Telephone**: *ICE* telephone office is a little further up the street opposite the small dock.

Directory

Excursions

The steep slopes to the east of Golfito and the northern peninsula constitute the 1,309 ha **Refugio Nacional de Fauna Silvestre Golfito** (Golfito National Wildlife Refuge). Created to protect Golfito's watershed, the tall evergreen forest receives heavy rainfall and is rich in rare and medicinal plants. Bird and mammal residents in the refuge include jaguar, coatis and peccaries but in real terms research in the refuge has been limited to date.

On the positive side, this makes it a great opportunity for surprises on treks which can be organized through *Land Sea Tours*.

Thirty minutes by water taxi from Golfito at Playa San Josecito, you can visit **Casa Orquídeas**, a family-owned botanical garden with a large collection of herbs, orchids and local flowers and trees with an entertaining 2½-hr tour explaining details about the various edible, medicinal and ornamental plants with the chance to smell, touch and taste your way through the gardens. ■ *Book through Land Sea Tours, T775-1614, entrance US$5 including a 3-hr tour, open Sun-Thu.*

Further north, **kayak** tours to the mouth of the **Río Esquinas** explore the mangroves with ideal conditions to see monkeys, dolphins, freshwater and sea turtles, and caiman. Trips also run south of the bay to the mouth of the **Río Coto Colorado**.

For serious **deep sea fishing**, you're best off heading south to Playa Zancudo (see below) and making plans with the lodges there.

Beaches north of Golfito

Golfito has little to offer in the way of beaches and genuine relaxation, but across the bay at Playa del Cacao, and just outside the bay on beaches to the north of Golfito, there are a number of small bays that break the line of rocky outcrops that make up this part of the coastline. While visits to the beaches can easily be arranged from Golfito, most are only visited by people staying in lodges nearby.

Playa de Cacao Across the bay from Golfito, or around the north shore of the bay is Playa de Cacao – the closest beach to beachless Golfito, its just a small strip of sand but worth a visit if you are in town and need a few hours sun or sea. You can pop over on a taxi boat from Golfito for US$2.50 or, road conditions permitting, follow the bay round in a four-wheel drive.

Sleeping B *Cabinas Playa Cacao*, T382-1593, T/F256-4850, www.cabinas-playa-cacao.co.cr 6 bright, conical thatched huts bright and breezy complete with hot water baths, fridge, kitchenette, hammocks and fan. Fine views across the bay in a wonderfully quiet and secluded spot. A good location for exploring other places in the area and you can take a few Spanish classes from Isabel the owner. In the same bay is the popular *Siete Mares*, a good, cheap restaurant.

Playa San Josecito Beyond Playa de Cacao, the next beach north – and outside the protected bay is Playa San Josecito. A couple of activity jungle retreats occupy the rocky bay.

L *Golfo Dulce Lodge*, T383-4839, F775-0573, www.golfodulcelodge.com Set in 300 ha of private reserve bordering the Piedras Blancas National Park are 5 spacious wooden bungalows, with fan and sun-heated water in the private bathrooms, each sleeping 3 people. There are also 3 rooms. Everyone gets a private veranda with hammock and rocking chair to suffer the free-wheeling thoughts while stuck in paradise or waiting for European influenced meals served in the thatched restaurant. An observation platform and self-guided tour are close and local tours easily arranged. **AL-B** *Dolphin Quest*, T382-8630 (mob), F775-0373, www.dolphinquestcostarica.com A secluded jungle adventure centre and rainforest retreat, with a selection of *cabinas*, thatched roof *ranchitos*, room and dormitory lodgings. Set in 280 ha of mountainous rainforest, with trails and waterfalls nearby. A seemingly endless range of land- and sea-based activities – even a birthing raft in case of unexpected arrivals. Volunteer opportunities available.

LL *Rainbow Adventures*, 30 mins northwest of Golfito, at Playa Cativo, T690-7750, F690-7735, www.rainbowcostarica.com A mix of rooms and apartments, with hot water private bath in an impressive 3-storey wooden jungle lodge surrounded by exuberant tropical vegetation. The rustic feel doesn't scrimp on the comforts which include a fresh-water chlorine free swimming pool. Gourmet meals using fresh fish, fruit and home-made bread will keep you energized for a daunting list of activities including jungle treks in the nearby Piedras Blancas National Park. **Playa Cativo**

South of Golfito

Leaving the bay of Golfito and heading south you cross the mangrove estuary of the Río Coto Colorado and eventually arrive in Zancudo, with not only some fine beaches but great sports fishing facilties (the best in the country). Further south is Pavones, a surfing Mecca with Costa Rica's longest left hander.

Playa Zancudo

Arriving at dusk along the overland route that meanders through endless groves of African palm, the setting sun shoots golden beams through the jauntily angled coconut palms that blind and hypnotize simultaneously. For beach lovers Zancudo has a captivating charm that has attracted a mixed bag of ex-pats who have created a fine balance of laid-bag comforts whilst avoiding any complicated trappings. For fishing junkies, you probably don't care beyond the two top-notch fishing lodges that will take you to deep waters which offer up world-record sized fish. *Colour map 3, grid C4*

For anglers Most people staying at these lodges are on part of a fishing package. **LL** *Golfito Sport Fishing*, T776-0007, F776-0018, www.costaricafishing.com 8 screened cabins with a/c and tiled bathrooms. The menu's emphasis is on wholesome, filling food. Set in comfortable gardens backing on to the Río Coto Colorado so when you're not fishing out in the bay, you can drop a line out back. **AL-A** *Roy's Zancudo Lodge*, a short distance further south, T776-0008, F776-0011, www.royszancudolodge.com 4 comfortable suites and a growing number of rooms, all with a/c and private bath, set around a floodlit swimming pool in pleasant gardens dotted with palms. Fine bar and restaurant serving all-you-can-eat meals family style. Plenty of stuffed fish just in case the fishing yarns are lacking – which is highly unlikely given that the lodge's guests have held over 40 world records. **Sleeping**

For the rest **AL-A** *Zancudo Beach Club*, T776-0087, www.zancudobeachclub.com 3 cabins, a couple of rooms and an apartment sleeping 3 to 6 people. The spacious and airy accommodation has private bath and the beautifully maintained cabins have a

Golfito and the Osa Peninsula

fridge, microwave and coffee machine. Spectacular views from the rooms and restaurant looking out to the beautiful beach. The friendly owners, Gary and Debbie Walsh, serve pizza from an extensive menu and are happy to share their piece of paradise with guests. There are plans to set up horse riding trails through the nearby forest.

A-B *Los Cocos*, T/F776-0012, www.loscocos.com A handful of cabins – some of which were originally for banana plantation workers – with kitchenettes, small terrace and big "windows" to let the ocean breeze cool. On the beach front, it's a very laid-back choice ideal for perfect privacy. Bikes, boogie boards and beach chairs available for guests. Andrew and Susan also run *Zancudo Boat Tours* with a taxi service to Golfito and local boat tours. Recommended.

B-C *Coloso Del Mar*, T/F776-0050, www.coloso-del-mar.com 4 all-wood cabins in a great little spot just a few metres from the beach. A big rancho in the beach front garden is ideal for watching the sun go down, and the new restaurant serves local and Caribbean dishes. **B-C** *Sol y Mar*, T776-0014, F776-0015, www.zancudo.com The 4 screened cabins and 3-story rental house are comfortable and relaxing, complete with private bath. The restaurant serves meals from 0700 until 2200. The appeal of the place is as the activity centre of Zancudo. The beach front is littered with sports equipment, the bar is the focus point of nightly gatherings and there's a gentle energy that bubbles through the place. Highly recommended.

E *Pensión Fin del Mundo*, over *Restaurant Tranquilo*, has 6 simple rooms with fan, mosquito net and shared bath. Clean. Another cheap *Tico*-owned place in town is **F** *Hotel Pitier*, which has some simple rooms.

Eating Most hotels providing food for guests. *Macondo* is a new, Italian restaurant that is locally recommended. Mid-range. The open-air **Bar y Restaurant Tranquilo** is a lively spot between *Zancudo Beach Club* and *Coloso Del Mar*. Cheap.

Tour operators In addition to *Roy's Zancudo Lodge* and *Golfito Sport Fishing*, *Arena Alta Sportfishing* also operate out of Playa Zancudo. Prices vary depending on the package, but a 5-day round trip from San José with 3 days fishing, accommodation, food, drinks and equipment included will set you back around US$2300 per person. Get a group together and prices fall considerably.

Zancudo Boat Tours run by Andrew Robertson at *Los Cocos*, has tours down the Río Coto Colorado behind town, and to Casa Orquídeas north of Golfito. US$40 for a 4 hr tour. They'll also take you over to Puerto Jiménez for US$15 per person, minimum 2 people. No service down to Pavones – the big waves make the landing too hairy.

Transport Without doubt the best way to town is by **water taxi**. Contact *Zancudo Boat Tours*, T776-0012, US$12.50 per person, minimum US$25. Alternatively visit **Land Sea Tours** office in Golfito, T775-0838, who will arrange transport from town.

It is possible to **drive** to Zancudo from Paso Canoas, or cutting through on the Golfito / Río Claro road 10 km from the Pan-American Highway turning right at *Bar El Rodeo* and catching the ferry across the Río Coto Colorado. Either way be prepared to get lost as signposts are poorly marked. A **bus** leaves **Golfito** for **Zancudo** at 1400, 3 hrs, US$2.50. Transport to **Pavones** can be arranged locally, US$50 for two.

Pavones

Colour map 3, grid C4 Moving further south, the sleepy little surf village of Pavones is growing quickly as surfers arrive in droves to ride the country's longest left hander. The main activity in the area is surfing – but fishing, horseback riding and hiking to waterfalls in the area can easily be arranged through local hotels. If you want a quiet beach, Zancudo is a better choice.

B *Pavones Surf Lodge*, in San José on T222-2224, F222-2271. 2 cabins with bath, 6 rooms with shared bath including meals. **B** *Cabinas La Ponderosa*, T384-7430 or in the USA on T407-783-7184 www.ccgnv.net/ponderosa Large cabins with private bath and fan, owned by a couple of surfers. Fishing, diving and, naturally enough, surfing. **C** *Mira Olas*, T393-7742, tomello@racsa.co.cr A couple of cabins with private bath and use of the kitchen. A pleasant jungle setting with access to beach.

A number of places in the centre of town offer accommodation – most of it fairly basic. **C** *Cabinas Willy*, across from the football field, has clean rooms with private bath. **E** *Cabinas Mendoza*, **E** *Esquina del Mar* and **F** *Cabinas Carol* are all in the centre of town with basic rooms and shared bathrooms.

You can get cheap, traditional *Tico* fare from *Doña Dora* in town and in *McRonalds* in the cantina on the beach side of the football field. *Pesto del Sol*, nearby does a good line in Italian food.

Arte Nativo is a craft shop selling locally produced art with the eventual aim of creating art workshops. In the meantime, the owner Candyce Speck is the main communication link with the outside world, and a good source of local information. T/F383-6939, tomello@racsa.co.cr

Sleeping & eating

Shopping

Burica Adventures, T388-3630, www.buricaadventures.com, is a regional based tour operator with tours to nearby waterfalls, sea kayaking trips, snorkelling and sunset tours in the Pavones area, the wider gulf and across to the Osa Peninsula and Corcovado National Park. They can also arrange transport to Pavones from Golfito (US$60).

Tour operator

As with Zancudo, driving is possible, but a **water taxi** from Golfito is eminently more convenient. A **bus** leaves **Golfito** for Pavones at 1400, returning at 0500, 3hrs, US$2.50.

Transport

South of Pavones, at the mouth of the Golfo Dulce is Punta Banco with the incredibly remote tropical retreat of **L** *Tiskita Jungle Lodge*, T296-8125, F296-8133, www.tiskita-lodge.co.cr A collection of 16 cabins and rooms set in 223 ha of private biological reserve. Probably the ultimate "escape from it all" lodge in Costa Rica, you can go no further south – in this country at least. Cabins are comfortable, as you would expect, with broad balconies and quite spectacular natural bathrooms. Hearty national dishes using the freshest fruit and produce are served 3 times a day in the open air restaurant.

Local activities include a new swimming pool, natural tide pools, trails leading through the nearby primary and secondary rainforest – and a home-made table tennis table. Trips head further afield to Corcovado National Park and Sirena across the Gulf.

Arriving at Tiskita is normally by chartered plane arriving on the Lodge's private airstrip. All part of the can-do survival frontier spirit that is an integral part of the place.

Punta Banco

Golfito and the Osa Peninsula

Caribbean lowlands

11

Caribbean lowlands

366 Ins and outs

366 Highway 32 to Puerto Limón

370 Puerto Limón

375 The North Caribbean

376 Parque Nacional Tortuguero

385 South Caribbean

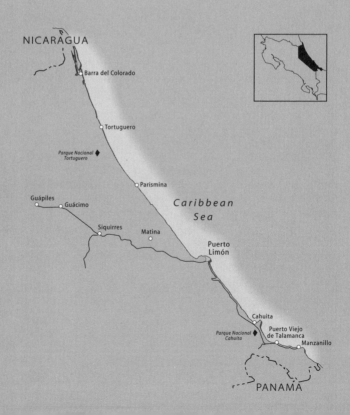

At times the Caribbean lowlands of Costa Rica are like a different country. The links with the Ticos of the central highlands and the Pacific are as minimal and symbolic as the single road that links the region with the highlands.

Bananas replace coffee as the temperature rises and the climate gets wetter. The Latino lifestyle gives way to Caribbean culture, the marimba is replaced by reggae, and the casada is pushed out by the coconut as the rivers run steadily to the coast. Friendly informality is preferred over quiet courtesies – so you will find the Caribbean distinctly laid-back compared with her western compatriots.

Transport links are the single greatest way of understanding the Caribbean of Costa Rica. The region was closed to the rest of the country until the opening of the railroads in the 1890s and only the creeping line of roads, electrification and telecommunications have now slowly opened up the region to visitors. And while the passing tourist sees beaches and nature, the main source of employment is still bananas.

From the chaotic charms of Puerto Limón, the northern lowlands of Tortuguero are a nature lover's paradise, remote and cut-off, even from the Limón. South of the city, beautiful beaches line the coast with the settlements of Cahuita and Puerto Viejo drawing visitors down to the relaxed atmosphere.

Things to do in the Caribbean lowlands

· **Travel silently** along the coastal canals of Tortuguero exploring the birdlife of the rainforest, and stumble along the cratered beach after dark, listening out for nesting turtles in the dead of the night.

· Marvel at over a million **migrating** raptors that stream down the coastline between September and November, returning in March and April.

· Don't try and learn to **surf** on the coral-based wave of Salsa Brava, Puerto Viejo de Talamanca - it will hurt. Start out at softer spots further north.

· Mix a **pampering** paradise with all-round adventure staying at *Selva Bananito*, or camp deluxe at *Almonds and Coral Tent Camp*.

· Dive off a kayak into Gandoca Lagoon, or take the ultimate challenge – the Trans-Talamanca **trek**. Ten tough days trekking out of Puerto Viejo – no frills.

Ins and outs

Getting there

Air   Air transport is limited at present with a daily service from San José to **Tortuguero** and **Barra del Colorado** in the north of the lowlands.

Road   From the central highlands, the main route to the Caribbean lowlands follows Highway 32 from San José through Braulio Carrillo National Park and then directly east to arrive at Limón. Alternative routes join Highway 32 swinging round the northern flanks of Barva Volcano through Puerto Viejo de Sarapiquí, and from the south through Turrialba joining the highway at Siquirres.

Getting around

Road   To the south of the Limón Highway 36 runs along the coastline to the border with Panama at Sixaola. For the most part the road is in good condition. Driving in the region is easy by private vehicle and regular buses provide links up and down the coastal highway. Opportunities for moving inland are limited and restricted still further by roads that deteriorate rapidly.

Boat   North of Limón, the Tortuguero Plains are a maze of banana plantations and waterways. The main areas of interest to visitors – the coastal strip around Tortuguero – are reached and explored by boat. All-inclusive packages normally include transportation, but independent travel on boats is easily arranged from Limón and Puerto Viejo de Sarapiquí.

Best time   Temperatures in the Caribbean lowlands are in the upper 20s for most of the year.
to visit   Rainfall varies slightly to the Pacific coast with rain throughout the year, but at its lightest in Feb, Mar and again from Aug to Oct. Annual rainfall varies from 3-6 m, falling most heavily in the north.

Highway 32 to Puerto Limón

From the misty ridges and peaks of the Braulio Carrillo National Park and beyond the Rainforest Aerial Tram (see page 163), Highway 32 continues east along the flat lowlands toward Puerto Limón. The road is straight and the scenery has just a smattering of activity, the profiles of Irazú and Turrialba breaking the skyline to the south. Just north of the main highway, the banana towns of Guápiles, Guácimo and finally Siquirres are hardly inspiring. As you head east, all this inactivity simply provides you with more time to contemplate the differences between the regions.

Places of interest are spaced along the road, and beyond the main towns, accommodation options require a vehicle – or energetic legs.

On Highway 32, 6 km after the junction at Santa Clara which heads north to Puerto Viejo de Sarapiquí, **Río Danta Restaurant and Reserve** is part of *Grupo Mawamba*, who also own a lodge at San Gerardo de Dota. The 10-ha reserve is a fairly recent acquisition for the group and is currently a stopover for all-inclusive trips travelling to Tortuguero. But if you want to stop, there are good birding trails pushing up to Braulio Carrillo National Park. ■ *T223-2421, F222-5463, www.grupomawamba.com, US$4 for the trail.*

Further down this road is **Tropical Magic Forest** canopy tour, T280-5200. Nine platforms with wires travelling over the secondary forest of a former *finca*. You can take a dip in the nearby swimming pools on the river, or explore a few trails. It's makes a pleasant low-key change from some of the high profile canopy tours. ■ *Open daily, US$40, T280-5200.*

Restaurant Ponderosa, west of the bridge over the Río Blanco 6 km west of Guápiles, is the marker for more off-road adventure to the south. Just over 1 km down the pebble-dashed road is **A** *Casa Río Blanco*, T382-0957, F710-2264. Space for 12 guests in perfectly rustic, but comfortable cabins. Each cabin has a small terrace and looks over the Río Blanco, creating a cool micro-climate that has produced a bird list of over 300. Old jars collecting dust exhibit several other local inhabitants – many of which you'd probably rather not see. Vegetarian meals, with breakfast included in the price, and supper optional. A good place to stop for a few days' genuine relaxation.

Two kilometres further uphill on a worsening road is **A** *Happy Rana Lodge*, T385-1167, F710-6309. Rustic stilted and screened cabins overlooking the river. Price includes breakfast and transport can be arranged from Guápiles or San José if booked in advance.

If staying in the area the two main **restaurants** in the area are *Rancho Robertos*, at the Santa Clara junction, T710-4609. A fine old rancho serving grills, traditional dishes in an open-air restaurant. Mid-range. Just before the Río Blanco is *Restaurant Ponderosa*, a recommended local choice, popular for meat dishes.

West of Guapiles

Guápiles

A regional transport hub for travel in to the network of banana plantations to the north, Guápiles is a lively centre with… little of inherent interest. The most budget-minded of travellers may stop here en route to Cariari, then GEEST Casa Verde from where a regular morning boat makes the journey to Tortuguero National Park.

Colour map 2, grid B4
District population: 19,686
Altitude: 260m

AL *Hotel Suerre*, at eastern end of town, T710-7551, F710-6376, www.suerre.com A large country club hotel with spacious tiled rooms with touches of wooden décor, and TV, safe box, telephone and a/c. The services are impressive with an Olympic size pool, a couple of indoor tennis courts as well as a casino, large conference rooms and open air restaurant.

C *Centro Turístico Río Blanco*, on the main road at the entrance to town,

Sleeping & eating

Caribbean lowlands

 ## Costa Rican bananas, global markets and fair trade

Next time you're in the supermarket, look at the sticker on the label of the bananas and there's a one in five chance that they came from Costa Rica, the second largest producer of bananas in the world. Bananas are the main agricultural export of Costa Rica earning the country over US$600 million in 2000 for exports of two million tonnes. This despite a drop in the prices of bananas in real terms of 35% in the last 15 years – a fall in price that has not been reflected in supermarkets of the West.

Ever since Minor C Keith founded the United Fruit Company *at the turn of the 19th century and began growing bananas to pay for railroad expansion, Costa Rica's fortunes have been linked with those of the banana.*

Since those early days the industry has been in the hands of US-based international companies. The United Fruit Company *has expanded and grown to become* Chiquita, *while the* Standard Fruit Company *is now commonly known as* Dole. *More recently* Del Monte *has* become a significant exporter. All companies have been accused of poor working conditions, creating job insecurity, confrontational labour relations and falling wages. But while workers fought to improve conditions, bureaucrats were meddling with the industry and trade lawyers on both sides of the Atlantic were having a field day.

In 1993 the creation of a single market in the European Union created a limit on imports of "dollar" bananas from Latin America, in favour of producers with whom the EU has historical ties. The majority of bananas grown in Latin American are sold by Dole, Chiquita and Del Monte, and the cheapest come from the world's largest producer, Ecuador. The formation of the World Trade Organisation in 1995 set out to liberalize and promote international free trade. Blocked from European markets Chiquita pressurized the US to take the EU to the World Trade Organisation for contravening the rules of international trade.

T710-7857. Simple rooms with bath and fan. OK if needing somewhere to stop. **C** *Cabinas Car*, 50 m west of the church in the centre of town, T710-0035. 10 clean and tidy rooms with hot water private bath, fan and TV. **E** *Cabinas de Oro*, northeast of the bus terminal, T710-6663. Clean rooms with hot water private bath, even cheaper without and a restaurant downstairs. **F** *Hotel Cariari*, on the road into town just north of the church, T710-6048. A bit unkempt, but essentially clean with shared bath and restaurant and laundry downstairs. The best budget deal in town – until the renovation wears off – is **G** *Hotel Alfaro (El Tunél)*, 50 m west of the bus terminal, T710-6293. Clean simple rooms with no frills, reached by way of a rather funky aluminium stairway – open 24 hrs!! Good value. Several *sodas* and snack bars around town – nothing particularly worth mentioning.

Transport **Bus** Hourly buses pass through town going to **San José** (2 hrs, US$1.70) and **Limón** (1¾ hrs, US$2). Buses to **Puerto Viejo de Sarapiquí** leave every 2½ hrs, US$1.30. There are also regular buses to **Cariari** (1½ hrs, US$2) for connections to **GEEST Casa Verde**.

Guácimo

Colour map 2, grid B4 Heading east for 12 km leads to Guácimo where rail and road once merged and created the important regional town with just short of 10,000 people in the surrounding district.

Nearby is *EARTH* (Escuela de Agricultura de la Región Tropical Húmeda). Disregarding the lengths some will go to for a natty acronym, this private international school receives graduates specializing in tropical

After judging against the EU and being subject to US$200 million in economic sanctions, the trade dispute in effect ended in July of 2001 after the EU came to an agreement with the US and Ecuador.

According to the National Chamber of Independent Banana Producers in Costa Rica, the cost of liberalizing and promoting international free trade to the industry in Costa Rica will be paid by finding a balance between the labourers in Costa Rica and Ecuador. The hard fought for minimum wage in Costa Rica is US$240 a month, while workers in Ecuador receive just US$90 a month – even though the official minimum wage is US$170.

The implications of the new regime are uncertain but the outcome looks bleak for independent producers in Costa Rica. In 1999 and 2000 dozens of independent producers had their contracts cancelled by the multinationals. Then in 2001 the multinationals further reduced the price paid to Costa Rican growers. Consequently the future of the Costa Rican banana industry – which used to directly employ around 50,000 people – is in perilous danger.

At this early stage it is difficult to assess the implications of the global restructuring of the industry on Costa Rica. But one thing is certain – the cost of liberalizing and promoting international free trade will not come from trade lawyers or appear in the price of bananas on supermarket shelves. The savings will be found in the plantations of banana producers in Costa Rica and throughout the world.

So when driving through the plantations while travelling to Tortuguero, an uncomfortable wrench rises in the stomach as you realize the cost of two-nights in one of the all-inclusive lodges costs the same as a banana worker receives in a month.

Can you make a difference? Yes, as one UK newspaper recently put it, "Change the world with your shopping trolley". Buy fair trade bananas, buy fair trade coffee and everything else fair trade for that matter.

agriculture from throughout Latin America. Guests are welcome to visit and stay (**A**), with tours around the forest reserve, banana plantation and packing plant, and botanical gardens costing US$22 for the day. ■ *T713-0000 ext 5006, F713-0005, www.earth.ac.cr*

The only real choice in the area is **B** *Río Palmas*, 1 km east of *EARTH*, T760-0330, F760-0296. 30 rooms all with private bath and hot water. A good restaurant and relaxing pool add to the pleasures of a 200-ha property that includes an ornamental plant farm with a few trails through rainforest.

Sleeping & eating

Siquirres

You'll be getting the idea by now when, after another 25 km, the town of Siquirres marks another banana town. The largest town along the lowland section of Highway 32, and almost half way, it also marks the junction with the old Pacific highway joining from the south and the route of the Pacific railroad.

Colour map 2, grid B4
District population:
29,781
Altitude: 80m

Not normally a stopping point, you can tour **La Esperanza banana plantation**, which exports Dole bananas, seeing the process from harvesting to packing. There is also talk of the introduction of the banana train from Siquirres to Matina – ask locally for details. ■ *Ideally aimed at groups, walk-ins are possible in high season on Thu and Sat, US$10 per person. Contact Banana Tours on T768-8683, F768-8137, www.sarapiquirainforest. com/bananatours*

Also nearby is **Parque Nacional Barbilla** with 11,944 ha of humid and premontane tropical forest. Created in 1982, the park has crept silently through the national park system and still has no facilities.

For the car crazy, Siquirres is the access town for the closest point by car to Tortuguero. The route, according to residents of Tortuguero, is as follows: head north through Carmen and Maryland for 37 km to Caño Blanco marina where you can safely park your vehicle while in Tortuguero.

Sleeping **D** *Centro Turístico Pacuare*, T768-6482, on the main road, renovated with large pool. **D** *Don Quito*, 3.3 km from Siquirres, T768-8533. Pleasant choice with a good restaurant. **F** *Alcema*, 50 m east of the market, T768-8157. Clean rooms, some a little dark, with fan and shared bath.

Matina

Colour map 2, grid B5

Last stop on the banana train line before the coast is Matina, 26 km east of Siquirres, a short distance north of Highway 32 at the locally known junction of "techo rojo". Just short of 7,000 people in the surrounding area, Matina still has the air of a small town village with the train station as the focal point of activity.

Most all-inclusive trips to Tortuguero pass through Matina travelling to the docks, before heading north through the canals.

A few kilometres east of Matina the 800-ha **Pacuare Nature Reserve**, a privately owned reserve that protects the nesting sites of marine turtles. Leatherbacks nest from Mar to Jun, with the green turtle arriving between Jun and Aug. A volunteer programme is available with accommodation in a fine lodge complete with balcony. Outside the nesting season, it is possible to stay at the lodge, for a minimum of one week. Away from the beach, the reserve is a quiet and secluded spot for bird-watching and exploring nearby waterways. The programme is run in conjunction with *Rainforest Concern*. ■ *www.rainforest.org.uk For volunteer work contact Carlos Fernández, Corporación de Abogados, Avenida 8-10, Calle 19, No 837, San José, T233-0508, F221-2820, fdezlaw@sol.racsa.co.cr The charge for the volunteer programme is US$100 a week, including food and lodging, with a minimum stay of one week. **Accommodation** at the reserve is **AL** per person, including transport to the lodge and 3 meals. Book through* Conselva *in San José, T/F253-8118.*

Puerto Limón

Colour map 2, grid B6
Population: 61,494
Altitude: sea level

Arriving in Puerto Limón, you can almost feel the difference in atmosphere and it isn't the high humidity or almost daily rains. A rocky outcrop in an almost featureless coastline, Limón has born the brunt of its Caribbean prominence. Columbus dropped anchor on Isla Uvita off the coast, waves of labourers arrived from the Caribbean and China to work on the railroads, creating a cultural diversity unique to Limón, and a ready labour supply for the banana plantations and burgeoning eastern port.

With fortunes rising and falling, Limón had and still has all the problems and nefarious energy associated with the transient populations of port towns worldwide. For most, Limón is tolerated or hated and visited only in passing – if driving you don't even have to do that if heading for the south Caribbean as the coastal road heads south before town.

But for all this negative talk, on the right day, with the right attitude Limón is a refreshing change and a challenge. The town cares little for the tourist and the tourist cares little for Limón. For the visitor, it's a rare chance to slip in to

The rebirth of Puerto Limón

In mid-2001 the Ministry of Tourism announced dramatic redevelopment plans for Limón which should see the creation of a new dockside promenade, and the regeneration of the central park and the surrounding area.

Investments totalling close to US$450,000 will also see the potential of

Uvita Island developed with the creation of regular boat services, visitor facilities and the creation of some simple trails. The year 2002 is the 500th anniversary of Columbus' arrival at Isla Uvita and the project should be completed in time for celebrations. Watch the developments and ask locally for details.

community life without being pampered or feted for your precious tourist dollars – unless you arrive for carnival.

Ins and outs

Getting there & away
Flying to town is not an option unless you charter a plane – the international airport south of town was closed several years ago in an attempt to limit drug trafficking between South America and the US. If driving, head east on Highway 32 and don't stop until you reach the docks at Limón. Highway 36 from the south hugs the coastline as far south as Manzanillo. Regular buses from San José arrive in a compressed little mêlée of activity ripe for a rip-off or under-cover scam. If heading north or south, you have to head across town to catch your connecting bus.

Getting around
Limón is small enough to walk round. But the beaches north of town and the docks at Moín for Tortuguero definitely require transport. Regular buses leave from behind the cathedral for Moín and taxis cruise the streets looking for business – as ever, only go with an official taxi and use a meter or get a price before travelling.

Best time to visit
Allowing for seasonal variations, Carnival, culminating on Oct 12, is the best time of year to be in town.

Security
Limón has a history of causing hassles and problems for visitors. While care and sensible precautions should keep you out of most difficult situations, there is a 24-hr police booth on the main square if you have problems.

Sights

Parque Vargas is a tired old park of straggling palms and plants that muster up a rustle when a coastal breeze rolls in. Sadly rundown, a colourful mural depicts the town's turbulent history and woeful neglect while a paint-peeling pagoda stands waiting for the band that never arrives. Craning the neck upwards through the trees, you may see the sloths that are said to meander their way through the upper reaches – but then it could be a town-wide joke. A promenade looks out to Isla Uvita where Columbus dropped anchor and you can't help thinking why he bothered.

South of the park, the **cargo docks** are busy with cargo vessels and international crews making regular journeys, as well as the pristine floating palaces that cruise the Caribbean.

The **central market** is the main focus of activity, with most Limeños drifting through the plaza several times a day. To the south of the plaza, the small – and rarely open – **Museo Etnohistórico de Limón** supposedly features

Caribbean lowlands

displays on local history. ■ *C 2, Av 2. Official opening hours are Mon-Fri, 0900-1200, 1300-1600.*

It's all rather weary, unless you happen to roll up when a drumming band is practising in the street. Three dozen young men appear in their finest bandannas, crisp ironed shirts unbuttoned revealing finely toned and tanned bodies. The trees perk up to hear the vibrant life, bored of municipal gestures, and the dreary cloud dissolves, replaced instead by the optimistic glow of dusk-lit neon.

Essentials

Sleeping
■ *on map*
Price codes: See inside front cover
Remember Limón is a port town and there are often drunks staggering about the streets especially at weekends. Hotels fill up at carnival time – book in advance

A-B *Park*, Av 3, C 1-2, T798-0555, F758-4364, rlyxie@racsa.co.cr Overlooking the bay with 34 rooms, this is a neat little hotel. Sea-facing rooms are quiet and cool. Good restaurant (mid-range) with seafood and sea views. Recently renovated – head and shoulders above everything else in town.

B-C *Acón*, on northeastern corner of the main square, C 3, Av 3, T758-1010, F758-2924. 39 big, clean rooms with private bath, a/c, telephone and safe box. Good restaurant downstairs. Popular daily *Aquarius* disco, except Mon. In need of sprucing up and overpriced for Limón.

C *Tete*, overlooking the main square, Av 3, C 4-5, T758-1122. Clean, bright rooms with good beds and private bath. Some sleeping up to 6 and some with balconies overlooking the street and the square. Good value and friendly, helpful staff.
C-D *Miami*, next to *King* on Av 2, C 4-5, T/F758-0490. Reliable mid-range hotel with 35 clean rooms with private bath. Some with a/c, others with fans. Secure and efficient. Credit cards accepted. **C-D** *Caribe*, facing Parque Vargas at Av 2, C 1-2, T758-0138. Big,

Puerto Limón

To Springfield Restaurant (400m),
Hospital, Portete & Moín (for Tortuguero)

Caribbean Sea

Paseo Juan Santamaría

Radio Casino
Fuji Film
Plaza Caribe
Cathedral
Plaza Central
La Casona · Parque del Parque · Vargas
Laundry
Mercado Artesanal Caribeño
Film Supplies
Baseball Park
Museo Etnohistórico
Customs
Muelle Nacional

To San José

To Swimming Pool (300m), Airport & Cahuita

0 metres 100
0 yards 100

■ **Sleeping**
1 Acón *B2*
2 Caribe *B3*
3 Continental *A2*
4 Costa del Sol *A1*
5 El Paraíso *B2*
6 El Sauce *B2*
7 Internacional *A2*
8 King *B2*
9 Miami *B2*
10 Ng *A2*
11 Palace *B2*
12 Park *B3*
13 Pensión Costa Rica *B3*
14 Pensión Los Angeles *B2*
15 Tete *B2*
16 Wilson *B2*

● **Eating**
1 Antillita *B1*
2 Brisas del Caribe *B3*
3 Diplo's *A1*
4 Doña Toda *B2*
5 Marisquería El Cevichito *B3*
6 Monte de Oro *A2*
7 Palacio Encantado *C2*
8 Soda Mares *B2*
9 Soda Yans *B1*

🚍 **Buses**
1 To Cahuita, Puerto Viejo & Sixaola (south) *B2*
2 To Moín (for Tortuguero) *B2*
3 To San José *B3*

immaculate rooms all with private bath, hot water and swamp fans you could use to fly a kite. Good deal.

D *Palace*, one block north of San José bus stops, C 2-3, Av 2, T758-0419. Family-run hotel, with 33 mostly big rooms. Pretty clean, balcony overlooking street, popular with travellers and good place to make up groups for Tortuguero.

E *Continental*, a few blocks north of the centre, Av 5, C 2-3, T798-0532. 25 big, clean rooms some good for groups, with private bath and ceiling fans. Safe parking outside. **E** *International*, opposite the *Continental*, Av 5, C 2-3, T758-0434. 24 tidy rooms with private bath, some with a/c, others with fan. Some rooms are a little dark. **E** *King*, next to post office near the main square on Av 2, T758-1033. 23 simple rooms, a handful with private bath. Pretty dark, but safe, friendly and essentially clean. **E** *Pensión Costa Rica*, Av 2, C 1-2, T758-0241. Small, dark rooms wonderfully finished with a fan! **E-F** *Costa del Sol*, Av 5, C 5, T798-0808, F798-4545. Growing rapidly with endless combinations in the 30 rooms, some with a/c, telephone and private bath.

F *Hotel Wilson*, Av 3, C 4-5, T758-5028. Clean, tidy and central. **F** *El Paraíso*, Av 2, C 4-5. Spectacularly sad hotel with plyboard partitions dividing a once-beautiful house in to tiny, dark, box rooms. Hardcore roughing it – it's time to go home or get a job.

G *El Sauce*, C 5, Av 2-3, T758-1068. Very simple and basic rooms, pretty grubby bathroom and toilet. **G** per person *Ng*, C 4, Av 5-6, T758-2134. 15 basic rooms some with bath, cheaper without. Basic and a bit untidy, but friendly. Good for the price. Also has **E** *Cabinas Cerro Mocho*, 1 km west of town, which may be an option at carnival time. **G** *Pensión Los Angeles*, Av 3, C 4-5, T758-3576. 15 dark rooms with shared bath and fan. A rickety old family home with a friendly charm.

Eating
● *on map.*
With a couple of exceptions, most places to eat in Limón are cheap

Antillita, C 6, Av 4-5. Caribbean rice, beans and meat. Popular local choice, open evenings only. *Brisas del Caribe*, facing Parque Vargas, Av 2, C 1. Wide range of dishes including noodles, meat, seafood. Good service and a popular drinking spot in the evenings looking out to the park. *Diplo's*, Av 6, C 5-6. The cheapest and the best genuinely Caribbean food in town. Not aimed at tourists so take it as you find it. *Doña Toda*, near the market on the main square. A cheap street *soda*, perfect for people-watching and hanging out. *Marisquerías El Cevichito*, Av 2, C 3-4. Fish, fish, fish with excellent *ceviche*. Good spot for watching the world drift by relaxing in the bamboo café chairs.

Cheap food is also available in the central market, *casados* in the market in the day, outside at night. Try **Milk Bar La Negra Mendoza** with good milk shakes and cheap snacks. Try *pan bon*, spicy bread from Creole recipe.

Monte de Oro, Av 4, C 3-4. Good local dishes in a rough and ready atmosphere. Handy while waiting for buses going south. Seriously cheap. *Palacio Encantador*, 50 m east of Baseball park, good Chinese. *Park Hotel*, Av 3, C 1-2. One of the best dining options in town with a full menu, reasonable prices and a sea view. Mid-range. *Sabor Pizza*, just off the main square on the corner of Av 3 and C 4 in *Plaza Caribe*. Good pizza by the slice. *Soda Mares*, on the south side of the market square. Good Chinese and local dishes, in a décor of Asian meets Caribbean. All rather confusing – like Limón. *Soda Yans* along Av 2, C 5-6, is a popular spot. *Springfield*, a 15-min walk north of town opposite the hospital, is a stylish restaurant serving a mix of *Tico* and international dishes. Best restaurant in the area. Mid-range.

Bars & clubs

The main activity is at *Aquarius*, the nightly disco at the *Acón* hotel. Things don't get going until around midnight so pop down to *Brisas del Caribe* on Parque Vargas for a couple of drinks to start with.

Festivals

Carnival or *carnaval* as it is known in Limón is on *Oct 12* with the preceding days building steadily to the big *El Día de la Raza*. The town suddenly appears to have a degree of desirability as the sedate highlanders flock to the Caribbean to join the music, dancing

Caribbean lowlands

and celebrations. The biggest celebration in the country, the costumes are out in full as the country has a moment of genuine unity of *Tico* and Caribbean influences.

Shopping Perfectly positioned to meet and greet alighting cruise passengers, *La Casona del Parque* and *Mercado Artesanal Caribeño* are on the west side of Parque Vargas. They sell a mix of standard crafts and a few tasteful items but nothing particularly inspiring.

Fuji film is available at the a/c store on C 5, Av 4-5. Other films can be purchased at *Rafael Barrantes* camera shop on Av 2, C 6, close to the baseball park.

Transport **Bus** Regular buses travel Highway 32 from **San José** to Limón. Buses leave from the Gran Terminal del Caribe at least hourly, 0500-2000, 2½ hrs, US$3. Buses are direct or stop off at **Guápiles**, **Guacimó** and **Siquirres**. Buses with *CoopeLimón*, T233-3646, T758-1476, and *Caribeños*, T222-0610, T758-2575, arrive and depart from C 2, Av 1-2, one block east of the main square.

For destinations south of Limón, buses leave from Av 4, C 3-4, close to Radio Casino, with *Mepe*, T758-0618. There are 9 daily buses to **Sixaola** on the border with Panama, stopping at **Bananito**, **Cahuita**, **Puerto Viejo** and **Bribrí** en route.

Buses north to **Moín** to catch boats down the coastal waterways to **Tortuguero** leave every 20 mins from behind the cathedral.

Boat Boats for independent travel to **Tortuguero** leave the small canal dock (Terminal de Desarollo) at **Moín**, at around 1000, US$50 return. You will have to pay for all accommodation, food and tours once you arrive in Tortuguero. Just turn up or contact Sebastian Torres on T798-3059 or T297-1010 (beeper). It's a 2½ hr journey with no stops. You can also get a boat to **Barra del Colorado** for about US$75, minimum 4 people.

Directory **Banks** Usual banking hrs (roughly 0830 to 1500) and services and all with ATMs at *Banco de Costa Rica*, Av 2, C 1, *Banco Nacional*, Av 2, C 3, *Banco Popular*. C 3. Av 1-2. *Banco San José*, Av 3, C 3-4. **Communications** Internet: services are slow in arriving to Limón. Ask around for any new places, but a well established choice is *Eductec Internet*, on the 2nd floor above *Plaza Caribe*, US$2.40/hr. **Post**: the post office is opposite the central market. **Telephone**: calls can be made from *ICE* on Av 2, C 5-6 and at C 3, Av 4-5, open Mon-Thu, 0800-1700, Fri 0800-1600. **Medical services** The regional **hospital** (Dr Tony Facio) is north of town on the road to Moín, opposite *Springfield Restaurant*, T758-2222. **Laundry** At Av 2, C 5-6. Price per item so not that cheap but a 2 hr turnaround – handy if you want to skip town fast! **Useful address** The police booth on the main plaza is open 24 hrs a day if you have problems to report.

Excursions

Despite the potential, Limón has so far comprehensively failed to pick up on any tourism opportunities – there are no tour operators in town. If you want to arrange a boat out to **Isla Uvita** ask in your hotel.

Trips to **Tortuguero** can be arranged – again make enquiries with your local hotel. One local company is *Tortuguero Odyssey Tours*, T/F758-0824, which charges US$60 per person. The tour is unlikely to get to Tortuguero proper – more likely a trip through some of the southern canals.

North of Limón

Playa Bonita some 5 km north following the coastline, has the best beaches close to Limón if circumstances find you staying in town. A handful of houses form the town of **Portete** where fishing boats are moored in the protected little bay, and further on over the hill, **Moín** is the location of the new international docks where modern day banana boats are loaded with hundreds of containers used to export most of Costa Rica's 2.1 million tonnes of annual banana exports. Of passing interest if you like big boats, dull as ditchwater if you don't.

At the eastern end of **Playa Bonita**, is **C-D** *Maeva del Caribe*, T758-2024. 12 cabins **Sleeping** and a couple of pools. Looks good value, but the owner is selling up so things may **& eating** change. On the rocky **Punta Piuta** headland is **AL** *Maribú Caribe*, T758-4543, F758-3541. 50 comfortable rooms in thatched roof, circular bungalows, with fine wooden furniture. A couple of pools in the rather cramped grounds, but the Caribbean views from the buffet restaurant are dreamy. Close by is *Restaurant Placeres*, a popular local choice. Mid-range.

Continuing west is **A** *Matama*, T758-1133, F758-4499, matama@racsa.co.cr Straddling up the hillside this rather eclectic tourist complex has 16 comfortable rooms, kitted out with modern fittings including a/c, cable TV and telephone. Price includes breakfast in the palm-roofed *ranchos* housing the bar and buffet style restaurant, with a couple of trails and a large botanical garden for a bit of activity. They can arrange trips to Tortuguero. Really targetting large Costa Rican family gatherings, it's the best place in the area, and up for sale.

Across the road is **B** *Cocorí*, T798-1670, F758-2930. 24 darkish rooms, most with a/c, with hot water private bath and cable TV. Price includes breakfast served on the pleasant balcony restaurant looking out to the beach and rocky headland with some tasty looking options on the menu for dinner. Looking far better on the outside than it is inside, but it's nothing a fresh coat of paint wouldn't put right. A short distance further west is **B-C** *Albergue Turístico Playa Bonita*, T798-3090, F798-3612. A good, friendly little choice with just 7 rooms with hot water private bath, a/c and TV. Small garden patio in a great little hotel, just 200 m from the ocean.

In **Moín** is the **C** *Moín Caribe*, T758-1112. Uphill from the dock to Tortuguero, it's reported to be friendly, nice and clean although it doesn't look it. It is, however, a handy place to stay before heading out to Tortuguero.

Boats to **Tortuguero** leave the small canal dock (Terminal de Desarollo) at the bottom **Transport** of the hill around 1000, US$50 return. Just turn up or contact Sebastian Torres on T798-3059 or T297-1010 (beeper). Charter boats to **Barra del Colorado** are US$75, minimum 4 people.

The North Caribbean

Tantamount to an offshore island, the north Caribbean between Limón and the Río San Juan on the Nicaraguan border, is an adventure to reach and a rainforest paradise to visit. Reached by air skimming over the Caribbean lowlands or river travel through the inland waterways and canals surrounding Tortuguero or Barra del Colorado it is the largest area of tropical wet forest in Costa Rica. The coastal canals of the northern Caribbean were built in the mid-1960s to connect the indigenous communities living along the rivers and lagoons of the region. While the canal network improved access to the communities dramatically, this is still one of the least accessible parts of the country.

The beaches of Tortuguero are a major natural attraction as one of the most important green and leatherback turtle nesting sites in the country. Inland, the natural rivers and manmade channels draped with the dense growth of riverine forests are flooded with rains of up to 5 m a year. The traditional 'jungle' of buttressed root forest giants and stilted trees are home to abundant wildlife, mostly seen from the comfort of a small launch drifting silently

Caribbean lowlands

Independent travelling to Tortuguero

Most people visit Tortuguero National Park as part of a 2 or 3-day package tour leaving from San José and staying at one of the lodges close to but not in the village of Tortuguero. These trips can be expensive if you are on a tight budget.

But contrary to what agencies tell you, it is possible to get to Tortuguero, find accommodation and organize a guide independently. There are a couple of budget options and what's more it is far better for the local economy.

The cheapest is to catch the 1330 banana boat from GEEST Casa Verde, a short bus ride from Cariari, which is

reached on the 0900 direct bus from San José's Gran Terminal del Caribe – in total around US$13.50 from San José! One word of warning – this boat may not run if there is too much or too little water in the rivers.

Alternatively you can catch a regular boat from Moín, north of Limón. Boats leave the small dock at 1000 and cost US$25 one way.

There is plenty of accommodation in the village, some of it is perfectly OK, and local guides can be arranged for a small fee. For more information contact the Tortuguero Information Centre, T392-3201, safari@racsa.co.cr

through the narrow creeks.

Ins and outs

Getting there **Air** Daily flights to **Tortuguero** and **Barra del Colorado** (costing US$55) with *SANSA*, T221-9414, www.flysansa.com, and *Travelair*, T220-3054, www.travelair-costarica. com Most visitors arrange accommodation before arriving and transport from the airstrip is provided. In Tortuguero *SANSA* offers a boat service to the town for US$3 per person. If flying with *Travelair*, call the Tortuguero Information Centre or Ronald Artavia Corea T223-3030 (beeper) to arrange a ride.

Boat Transport by boat is easily arranged. The simplest option is from **Moín**, a few km north of Limón from where you catch a boat heading up the coastal canal. It is also possible to catch a boat from **GEEST Casa Verde**, a short bus ride from Cariari. Finally you can charter a vessel from **Puerto Viejo de Sarapiquí** – the most expensive option. Most all-inclusive packages leave from a small private dock close to Matina.

Parque Nacional Tortuguero

Colour map 2 Tortuguero National Park is one of the great treasures of Costa Rica. The 29,068-ha area is made up of a network of flooded waterways that twist and meander through the vast alluvial plain created by rivers flowing off the central highlands' eastern slopes. By the time the rivers reach the coast they have slowed almost to a standstill and with high rainfall, the dense tropical forest is often flooded. Essentially flat, the landscape is bursting with vegetation and trees which crowd up to the edge of waterways, only occasional gaps providing a glimpse of the world within.

The main focus for visitors to the park is the small town of Tortuguero which lives, as it has for centuries, in co-existence with the turtles that nest on its beaches. According to guides, the community made a living selling turtles, a stay-fresh source of meat, to mariners that sailed the Caribbean. And indeed, Tortuguero – meaning 'turtle seller' – still makes a living from its turtles. While conservationist, Archie Carr, one of the park's main proponents, set out to encourage the local *community to take a long-term view of the nesting turtles, it seems their welfare will always be directly related to the welfare of the community.*

Ins and outs

Entrance to the park is US$6 per person for 1 day. A 4-day pass is US$10, which is paid **Entrance** to the headquarters at the southern end of the town before beginning any trip through the waterways. A few usually muddy trails lead out from the park office. Night-time trips along the beach are coordinated through the lodges or the information kiosk in town.

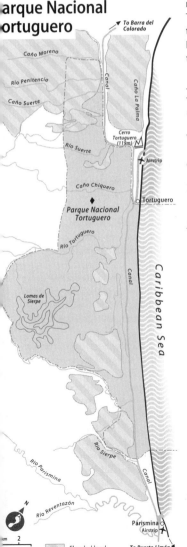

With an average temperature of 26°C and **Best time** rainfall between 4.5 and 6 m a year, **to visit** Tortuguero is one of the wettest spots in the country. While rainfall is slightly less in Feb and Mar there is a high chance of getting wet throughout the year.

According to the information centre Jul to Oct is the best time to see green turtles nesting. The Leatherback or *baula* nests between Mar and Jun.

Wildlife

Tortuguero is one of the country's most diverse national parks and home to over half the bird and reptile species found in the country. It also just so happens to be the most important nesting site of the green turtle in the western Caribbean. The looping flight of the keel-billed toucan crossing the open waterways is a common site as are Northern Jacanas, oropendolas and herons. Less rarely spotted is the endangered green macaw which also resides in the park. Needless to say, wildlife viewing in the area is spectacular and best seen from a boat moving silently through the myriad channels. Mammals are also numerous with howler monkeys and sloths commonly spotted, while hidden within the undergrowth the tracks of jaguar, ocelot and tapir go unseen by most as does the endangered manatee that explores and grazes the watery channels. If you're particularly lucky you may see the fishing bulldog bat, a large bat with a 60 cm wingspan that hunts on the waters of the canals. Reptiles and amphibians are on the scene in large

Caribbean lowlands

numbers – you may well see crocodiles, and if you are very lucky glass and poison dart frogs and the bug-eyed gaudy leaf frog.

The main reason for travelling to Tortuguero is to see nesting turtles. The green turtle uses the beaches in significant numbers, with visits from leatherback, hawksbill and occasionally loggerhead turtles. As with much of Costa Rica, getting the timing right to see this natural phenomenon is essential. The green turtles lay their eggs at night between June and October, with the hatchlings emerging from the depths of their sandy nests until November at the latest. Leatherbacks can be seen between March and June. While access to the beaches is unrestricted, trips to look for nesting turtles are carefully monitored and you must be accompanied by a licensed guide at all times. See 'Excursions' below.

Tortuguero town

Colour map 2, grid A4 The small town of Tortuguero on the southern tip of a sandy spit with a few hundred *Ticos* and no cars, is the main focus of the area. At the confluence of the Río Tortuguero and the coastal canal, the town is vibrant and pulsates to a distinctly Caribbean beat. Dotted around the network of sandy paths and lush vegetation, the town itself has a creaking old church, a general store, football pitch, a couple of gift shops and half a dozen accommodation options.

Ins & outs Most people visit Tortuguero as part of a 2 or 3-day package tour from San José, flying to the airport in Tortuguero, or by bus and then catching a lodge boat from Matina. However it is possible to travel to Tortuguero independently – see box.

In the centre of town there is a small booth with **information about the turtles** and the area. You need to register here for beach tours if you are not part of a lodge package.

Sights Flowing north from the town is the **Laguna de Tortuguero** which leads for 5 km to the Caribbean. Either side of the thin waterway – and on the canal running parallel further inland to the west – comfortable all-inclusive lodges have spread along the river banks.

First populated in the time of pirates when turtles provided a ready supply of meat for the ship-bound mariners, the turtle harvest and trading patterns continued until research by Archie Carr, the founder of the *Caribbean Conservation Corporation*, in the 1950s suggested that the green turtle was probably heading for extinction.

Today the nesting grounds attract attention for a different reason, bringing tourists from around the world. While some members of the community invariably benefit from tourism-related employment, others are clearly having difficulties adapting to the new world which puts the conservation of the turtle above all other issues. The introduction of a recycling programme probably seems like a good idea to the majority of visitors who stay in the all-inclusive lodges, but looks rather out of place in Tortuguero. Sharing out some of the benefits of the region's attractions throughout the community is probably a better idea. It's difficult not to see a big divide between the comfort of the lodges and the basic lifestyle of the village community.

Sleeping Accommodation options are simple. Lodges and hotels of varying comforts are scattered around the lagoon. Most lodges, with the exception of Mawamba and Laguna Lodge, require transport to get to and from Tortuguero. In Tortuguero village there are limited accommodation options, which will be more appealing to the budget traveller.

In town A *Casa Marbella*, in front of the catholic church, T392-3201, safari. jumptravel.com (no www). A new bed and breakfast with 4 small rooms, with private bath, solar assisted hot water and ceiling fans. Right on the river with a dock for bird-watching and views of the setting sun over the forest. Run by adopted local guide Daryl Loth who also provides tours and advice on local travel – fills a great niche of providing comfort without having to go for an all-inclusive lodge option.

D *Mary Scar* has 23 simple rooms with foam mattresses. Most have a shared bath, although there are couple with private bath. There's a restaurant in the high season, friendly enough if other places are full. **D** *Miss Junie's*, T710-0523. 12 good cabins at the northern end of town at one of the town's old favourites. **D** *Cabinas Sabina's*, winding down for eventual closure, 16 simple cabin style rooms with good views looking out to the Caribbean. **D** *Cabinas Tortuguero*, has 5 little cabins, each sleeping three with a private bath set in pleasant little gardens complete with hammocks – a good spot. **D** *Yoruki Lodge*, T233-3333 (beeper), new rooms which looked like they would be clean and simple, overlooking the river. There are also several very cheap *cabanas* in the **E-F** range dotted around town.

Out of town The closest lodge to town is **AL** *Mawamba Lodge*, T710-7282, in San José on T223-2421, F222-5463, www.grupomawamba.com 50 or so rooms connected by covered and well lit walkways with fine gardens to lookouts over the lagoon. Rooms are wooden cabin-style with a fan, private bath, hot shower, and a small balcony and veranda. Tasty and healthy meals are served buffet style in the restaurant and you can relax in the freeform pool. There's a small but well stocked gift shop and a conference room which is put to good use before and after nature trips, an honour-bar and quiet games room. Dip through a little hole in the bushes and you're walking along the nesting beaches, or you can head south for the short walk to town – a good choice. 2 nights and 3 days all-inclusive for US$280.

A little further north you will find **A** *Laguna Lodge*, T710-0355, F283-8031, www.lagunalodgetortuguero.com 52 rooms sleeping 2 or 3 people, each with private bath and a small balcony. The restaurant serving buffet meals has a fine view and location over the lagoon. There's a small pool and a bar, close to the newly planted garden which is designed to attract butterflies. A 2-night tour is US$235 per person.

Across the lagoon from Tortuguero is **AL** *Pachira Lodge*, T256-7080, F223-1119, www.pachiralodge.com 34 comfortable rooms decorated with bamboo furniture all with private bath and ceiling fans. Meals served buffet style, and a large sundeck surrounds a rather amusing turtle-shaped pool. 2 nights and 3 days package US$239.

Continuing north along the western bank of the lagoon is **A** *Jungle Lodge Hotel*, T233-0133, F233-0778, www.tortuguero.com 50 big, wood panelled rooms with a small balcony and private bath. Meals are served buffet style, there's a pool complete with wet bar, and a separate bar with a disco – a worrying development that hopefully won't be copied by all the lodges. Part of the large *Grupo Papagayo*.

D *El Manati*, T/F373-0330 and booked through *Ecole Travel* in San José, (T223-2240, F223-4128, www.travelcostarica.net) Just 8 simple cabins, with a budget and homely atmosphere where you can truly relax without feeling the need to dress for dinner – because there isn't any unless requested in advance. Boats are easily arranged if you want to pop over to town, and there's a small bar and thatched roof rancho overlooking the river for relaxing in the grounds. Plans for a small project to study and preserve manatees is the inspiration for the name. 3 days, 2 nights from Puerto Moín, US$125. Good value. **D** *Ilan Ilan*, through *Agencia Mitur* in San José, T255-2262, F255-1946, www.mitour.com 24 rooms in a line, with private bath and slightly offensive décor. But the service is good and friendly, with big helpings served in the screened buffet restaurant, and a new pool, Jacuzzi and riverside bar. Can also

Caribbean lowlands

be arranged through *Oasis Tours* in Puerto Viajo de Sarapiquí, T766-6108. 2 days all-inclusive US$215.

The most luxurious choice on the lagoon at the northern most point is **L *Tortuga Lodge and Gardens***, T257-0766, F257-1665, www.costaricaexpeditions.com 22 big, bright and breezy rooms, set in a couple of 2-storey lodges, each with hot water private bath, and a balcony or veranda complete with hammock overlooking the gardens and the lagoon. The restaurant is *à la carte* in an area of buffet preference and there's a wine list worth exploring. On the quiet days you can relax around the free form pool or wonder at will round a couple of trails. As with all the lodges, tours are included in the price but with Tortuga you decide where you go and when. Several eco-touches to limit the impact on the region including solar-heated water and a closed-water pool system. Expensive, but very comfortable. 3-days, 2 nights, US$379 per person.

One channel west from the lagoon is **B *Caribbean Paradise Eco-Lodge***, T221-4420, F221-4315, caribbeanparadis@racsa.co.cr *Tico*-owned and run by Carlos Bruno and his wife Ana, this is ecotourism and comfort combined, and the only lodge that is actually in the National Park. The 16 rooms are spacious and pleasantly decorated with fan and hot water private bath. The porch balconies look across a tended garden which has a natural feel, with a stream complete with turtles and caiman. Personable service creates meals to your liking, drawing on national and Caribbean influences, served family-style. Carlos is proud to say there are no set itineraries – the guests choose what they want to do and when. Add 1500 m of trails out the back, and active support of the almond tree reforestation for green macaws, and this place gets the thumbs up. 3-days, 2 nights, US$237 per person.

A little further north is **B *Tortuguero Caribe Lodge***, with breakfast and dinner, **E** without, T385-4676. 10 simple cabins, friendly *Tico* run and owned. Book direct or arrange a package through *Ecole Travel* in San José.

Volunteering   North of Tortuguero the *Canadian Organization for Tropical Education and Rainforest Conservation*, T381-4116 or in Canada T905-831-8809, home.interhop.net/~coterc/ has the **Caño Palma Biological Station** which aims to provide leadership in education, research and conservation, providing accommodation and services for visiting researchers and students. A volunteer programme exists with simple tasks like path maintenance and horticultural based opportunities. There are basic rooms for volunteer staff, **F** per person, including meals. It's a good place for serious naturalists or just for unwinding, accommodation for up to 16 in wooden cabin, freshwater well for drinking and washing. Minimum stay 2 weeks at roughly US$100 per week.

Eating   All lodges, apart from *El Manati*, provide 3 meals a day. In town you'll find the following
Good food is limited   places. *El Dolar* is a simple, cheap restaurant with good *casados* despite the small menu. *La Casona* is a new place serving fish and pasta dishes. Within the realms of legend *Miss Junie's* at the north end of town has good local Caribbean dishes and a reservation is normally necessary. *Miss Miriam's* is a new place on the north side of the football pitch, serving cheap and tasty *Tico* and Caribbean dishes. Miss Miriam has plans to open 6 cabins. *The Vine* serves a mix of baked goodies and fruit smoothies with tables out the back where you can sit, sip and enjoy the setting sun. A simple menu of pizzas and sandwiches from US$3.

Shopping   *Paraíso Tropical* by the dock steps sells a large selection of souvenirs and general goods. There is a small general store a few metres north. *The Jungle Shop* specializes in handicrafts selling the odd T-shirt, postcard and nature book.

Lodge bookings are generally arranged through tour operators in San José – see **Tour operators**
respective lodges for details. Tours from San José will include transport, meals, guides
and boat trips for between US$125 (from Moín) and US$395 per person.

Local tour operators and guides can be arranged on arrival. If you want to arrange a
guide for an independent trip in advance try: Daryl Loth *Tortuguero Safaris*,
T392-3201, safari@racsa.co.cr; or Barbara Hartung of *Tinamon Tours*, T223-3030
(pager – extension 3761, www.tinamontours.de, an English, German and Spanish
speaking biologist who has been strongly recommended for boat, hiking and turtle
tours in Tortuguero. Both charge roughly US$5 per person per hr.

Providing tours from Limón is *Viajes Laura*, T758-2410, who have been recom-
mended and provide a daily service with an open return by boat for US$60 from Moín.

Air Daily flights from **San José** with *SANSA*, T221-9414, www.flysansa.com, and **Transport**
Travelair, T220-3054, www.travelair-costarica.com, US$55. The airstrip is about 4 km
north of the town. You will need to arrange transport from the airstrip to your hotel if it
is not included.

Boat All-inclusive packages provide the transport links, normally by boat from a pri-
vate dock near Matina. For independent travellers there are 2 main options. From
Limón on the Caribbean coast take a bus to **Moín**. Tell the driver you are going to
Tortuguero and he will drop you at the dock. An almost daily service is provided by
Alexis Soto and Sebastien Torres (beeper T297-1010) to and from Tortuguero leaving
at about 1000, charging US$25 one way, US$50 return. The boat returns from
Tortuguero at 1000 providing plenty of time for an early morning trip before returning
to Moín, arriving around 1300.

Alternatively, head for **Cariari** on the 0900 direct bus from Terminal Gran Caribe in
San José. From Cariari take a bus to **GEEST Casa Verde**, telling the driver you want to
go to Tortuguero. For US$10 you get a gentle slow journey to Tortuguero arriving
around 1500. Boats return at 0700 in the morning so you will probably need to stay 2
nights if you want to do an early morning tour. This service is subject to the vagaries of
river level and cannot run if the water is too high or too low. If in doubt contact the
Tortuguero Information Centre on T392-3201.

Transport can also be arranged from **Puerto Viejo de Sarapiquí** – see page 185.

If you need to charter a vessel there are several options. Willie Rankin, T798-1556,
travels from Moín to Tortuguero. Ruben Bananero also provides a charter service –
T382-6941.

There are no banks or other significant services in the town apart from a quiet old post **Directory**
office which opens sporadically. However, direct telephone lines are meant to be arriv-
ing in town at the end of 2001. Locals are planning to get internet access which should
provide a greater degree of contact with the outside world.

Excursions

The Caribbean beaches of Tortuguero National Park protect the nesting sites **Turtle**
of the green turtle and also, in smaller numbers, the huge leatherback, **watching**
hawksbill and loggerhead turtles. To see one of these magnificent creatures
emerge from the ocean surf, haul itself up the beach and dig a nest in which to
store its precious cargo is an unforgettable experience. Likewise, seeing the
tiny hatchlings emerge dazed from their sandy birthplace before heading
frantically like some wind-up mechanic toy for the ocean is truly memorable.

Tours to see nesting turtles take place at night. Strict rules govern the tours
which are only carried out by authorized local guides. You must be

accompanied at night. Torches, cameras, video cameras and smoking are prohibited – one of them may kill you, all of them are deemed bad for the turtles. Tours last for a couple of hours – the elderly may find trudging blindly along the beach difficult after a while – and you are advised to wear dark clothes and closed shoes. This list is designed to limit disturbance to any turtles, so naturally being quiet is also advised.

Keep an eye on the tagged turtles on the net at www.cccturtle.org

While exploring the palm-fringed beach struggling under growths of icacao and sea grape, the nest craters and driftwood make the area look more like a bomb-site than a sensitive nesting site. The understanding of the beach and its importance to the green turtle began with the work of Archie Carr – one of the prominent figures in the Costa Rican conservation movement. The work and study that began with *The Brotherhood of the Green Turtle* continued with the creation of the *Caribbean Conservation Corporation*, T224-9215, www.cccturtle.org Carr's work and energy were crucial in the creation of Tortuguero National Park. Today the Corporation has a small exhibition centre to the north of town and continues tagging work with eight tagged turtles monitored by satellite which can be seen on the CCC website. ■ *Open daily, 1000-1200 and 1400-1730, entrance by donations but 300 colónes as a suggestion. Turtle tours are arranged through your lodge or the information kiosk in Tortuguero. Visit the kiosk and sign up. The fee is US$6 for entrance to the park and US$5 for the guide per person.*

Touring the waterways
From the Tortuguero Lagoon a network of smaller channels are accessible by launch. Exploring these channels gives a window on the rainforest and if you travel in silence and with a good guide, you are certain to see much wildlife. Most tours leave early in the morning when bird life is most in evidence and the chance of seeing mammals is also higher.

Tours with lodges are normally included in the price. If you organize your own tour you have a slightly greater variety – the secret to a good tour is being quiet. On a self-organized tour you can take a guide that uses paddle power.

Note Most boats use petrol engines to get to the quieter channels. Once entering the park they are legally required to switch to electric engines to reduce noise and wave wash damage to the banks. Keen to maximize the clients time spent wildlife viewing – and to keep tourists happy – many guides stay in the channels as long as they can, switching to petrol motors when they leave. Looking behind the boat you can see the waves crash against the banks. Only by visitors discouraging such activity will such misdirected good intentions be stopped – feel free to speak out.

Cerro Tortuguero
At the mouth of Tortuga Lagoon, Cerro Tortuguero rises to 119 m. While the height is not staggering, in an area that is overwhelmingly flat, the views from the top are spectacular. Walks up the hill can be arranged through lodges and local guides.

Less rarely visited, the **Lomas de Sierpe** lie to the west of Tortuguero – a good day trip for those wanting a more challenging trek.

Parismina

Colour map 2, grid B5

Perched at the mouth of the Río Parismina, the small riverside hamlet of Parismina is just a passing glance for boats heading north to Tortuguero. The Parismina picks up the Reventazón and many other tributaries flowing off the slopes of Turrialba Volcano on its steady eastward journey to the Caribbean.

While Parismina is close to the southern limits of Tortuguero National Park, the riverside hamlet prefers to concentrate energies on its reputation as one of the best places in the world to fish for tarpon and snook.

To reach Parismina, take a ferry from Moín – see Tortuguero above. If you have booked accommodation, the lodge will arrange transport.

Sleeping & eating
All accommodation is open year round

LL *Rio Parismina Lodge*, T798-0918, F229-7597, toll free on T1-800-338-5688, www.riop.com A full comfort fishing lodge with 12 wooden cabins, restaurant and bar located at the mouth of the Parismina. For added comfort there's a pool and Jacuzzi in the hotel grounds. The fishing is aboard custom-designed v-hull ocean craft making ocean fishing in the choppy coastal waters an alternative to exploring the inland canals. Weekend fishing packages start at US$1800 per person, a full week will set you back US$3250. **LL** *Jungle Tarpon Lodge*, locally on T380-7636, in the US on T907-262-4515, F907-262-8797, toll free on 1-800-544-2261, www.jungletarpon.com Big rooms with beamed ceiling and tiled floors and private bathrooms. Catch and release tarpon are beyond doubt the target out in the ocean or in flat-bottomed boats in the jungle lagoons. 5 days and 4 nights start from US$1495, a full week is US$1995.

L *Caribbean Expedition Lodge*, T232-8118, or in the US on T361-884-4277, www.costaricasportfishing.com A slightly less luxurious feel, but still very comfortable in the tiled floor cabins, with private bath. The screened dining room serves north American and local dishes, but as ever the action is out in the water with ocean and inland water vessels. A 5-day snook and tarpon package will set you back US$1345. Can also arrange jungle tours and trips up the Tortuguero.

There are a few more affordable choices, but they are certainly not budget, and the options for getting around are limited.

Barra del Colorado

Colour map 2, grid A4

The village telephone number is T710-6592

Tucked up in the northeastern corner of the country, Barra del Colorado is reached by a couple of daily flights or a bumpy boat journey of several hours to the northern most limit of the man-made coastal canal. Barra del Colorado is one of the most cut-off parts of the country. Activity – if that's what life can be called in this relaxed, sleeping backwater – is based in the divided waterside hamlet of Barra del Colorado which straddles the Río Colorado. Barra del Sur has the airstrip, lodges and the jaguar's share of available services. Barra del Norte enjoys the honour of being on Isla Calero – the largest island in Costa Rica. In addition to providing services for tourists, locals of Caribbean and Miskito (from neighbouring Nicaragua) origin make a living fishing for spiny lobster. Two major draws attract visitors to the region – excellent sportsfishing for snook and tarpon fishing and the Barra del Colorado Wildlife Reserve.

Refugio Nacionales de Vida Silvestre Barra del Colorado is a fair mouthful and at 81,213 ha is also one of the country's largest protected areas, much of it covering the border with Nicaragua along the Río San Juan. A drenching 6 m of rain a year in parts and temperatures averaging 26°C create conditions very similar to those in Tortuguero. Established in the mid-1980s much of the area had already been disturbed by logging but the potential for nature tourism in the area remains largely untapped. If you have the time and the money – Barra is more expensive than Tortuguero – the opportunities for exploring the quiet waterways and backwaters are incredible.

Local advice says that fishing is good all year round, but the best is from September to April. Accommodation is available at a number of lodges dotted throughout the area, some of them close to Barra del Colorado – some requiring a short boat ride.

Sleeping & eating

In the town One of the oldest lodges in the country and certainly in Barra is **LL** *Rio Colorado Lodge*, T710-6897 or T232-4063, F231-5987. Comfortable rooms built back in the early 1970s with private bath are connected by a maze of covered pathways, and happy hour at bar, equipped with a TV and video keeps the mood rolling along. The main focus is on fishing but non-fishing guests are also welcome. **LL** *Silver King Lodge*, T381-1403, F381-0849, in the US on 1-888-682-7766, www.silverkinglodge.com Widely regarded as the best and most luxurious lodge on the north Caribbean coastline, with big comfortable screened cabins and private bath with hot water. The food has been compared to that produced in a gourmet restaurant. Lots of little touches make it a great places to stay – an open bar, free laundry, a pool and Jacuzzi. Hardly surprising that the fishing is equally impressive using ten v-hull centre console boats in open water and unsinkable Carolina skiffs in inland waters. They also accommodate nature tourism and non-fishing guests, with canoes available for use with knowledgeable English speaking guides available.

B *Tarponland Lodge*, T710-6917 or on the village phone at T710-6592, is the cheapest option in town with 12 basic rooms, a periodically neglected pool and a few fishing options available. It's also the closest to the airstrip.

Outside Barra A couple of km north of Barra del Colorado facing Laguna Agua Dulce is **LL** *Casa Mar Lodge*, T714-578-1881, F714-525-5783, toll free in the US on 800-543-0282, www.casamarlodge.com 6 duplex cabins, each with private bath and showers, are set in 7 acres of tropical garden. Home-cooked north American buffet meals are served with a few local dishes for variety, and naturally plenty of fruit. Eddy Brown is a very experienced and well known local fisherman, and 22-ft centre console vessels for inland water angling. Five days fishing will set you back US$1785.

6 km south of Barra del Colorado on the Samay Lagoon and very isolated is **L** *Samay Lagoon Lodge*, T384-7047, F383-6370, www.samay.com 22 beautiful single and double rooms with private bath. After dining in the restaurant the open run bar should help the tall tales grow. Fishing is the primary business using 24 ft Carolina skiffs costing around US$1000 for 4 days and 3 nights. The opportunities for nature tourism in the area have been seized with a 3-day, 2-night nature safari that starts in San José and heads out to the *Samay Lodge* via Puerto Viejo de Sarapiquí and the Río San Juan returning after several treks and tours, US$278.

Arguably the best way to find the best fish is to keep moving, easily done on the **LL** *Rain Goddess*, T231-4299, F231-3816, www.bluwing.com, which unashamedly follows the fish. The 65-ft customized houseboat is finished with wood-panelling in the 6 rooms. Meals are served with wine and the bar never closes in this flotel which merges quality and comfort. What about the fishing? 16-ft Jon boats work the rivers and backwaters, with larger 20-ft vessels for fishing the river mouths. 5 day's and 3 night's fishing will set you back US$1750 per person, non-anglers, US$850.

Transport

Air Daily flights from **San José** are available with *SANSA*, T221-9414, www.flysansa.com, and *Travelair*, T220-3054, www.travelair-costarica.com, US$55.

Boat Boats can be arranged from Tortuguero, taking 1½ hrs. Costs vary widely ranging from US$30 if arranged by a lodge you're staying at to US$100. Ask around. It is also possible to arrange a boat from **Puerto Viejo de Sarapiquí** – see page 185.

Border with Nicaragua – Barra del Colorado

The Río San Juan – the southern banks of the river to be precise – mark the border between Costa Rica and Nicaragua. Technically when travelling this route you are entering Nicaragua and should travel with your passport at all times. In reality if you are simply travelling to Puerto Viejo de Sarapiquí you can travel without having to complete border formalities.

Crossing the Río Colorado to Barra del Norte (which in fact is the south arm of the Río San Juan delta), the truly adventurous can, in theory, walk to San Juan del Norte in Nicaragua along the coast. It is a long 30-km beach walk, requiring food and lots of water. Seek advice from locals in Barra before setting out – you may be able to get a ride off a boat heading that way.

South Caribbean

From Limón to the border with Panama, the southern Caribbean coast is dotted with quiet beaches and small communities that until quite recently have been cut-off from much of the rest of Costa Rica.

Once the preserve of Bribrí and Cabecar Indians who lived in the southern Talamanca mountains, the indigenous populations were joined by Afro-Caribbean groups who built the railroad and worked on banana plantations. This single means of transport was the only line of communication until the late 1970s when the road from Limón crept south slowly linking the isolated villages. Only in 2001 did the tarmac road finally arrive in Manzanillo.

The slow advance of progress has had some benefits limiting the voracity of coastal developments, retaining an element of cultural diversity and keeping a generally relaxed and laid-back atmosphere to the area.

Of course, this being Costa Rica, natural events always have a part to play. On the 22nd April 1991 an earthquake hit the area, raising some parts of the southern coastline by over a metre. Rivers were re-routed and temporary crossings replaced the bent and broken bridges ruined in the tremors. Ten years later almost all the bridges have been replaced but at points along the coast, you can still clearly see the shelf in the land.

Accommodation is focussed in the towns of Cahuita and Puerto Viejo de Talamanca but a particular appeal of the region is the (generally pleasant) sprawling of individual lodges in quiet hideaways filled with character, charm and imagination as varied as their owners – many of them expatriates from around the globe who have fallen for the south coast's idyllic ambience.

Best time to visit Rainfall along the coast ranges from 3 to 2.5 m annually. Just to keep everyone on their toes, and to underline the fact that the south Caribbean is a little different to the rest of the country, the traditional dry season doesn't quite work here. The dry "pockets" are from Feb to Apr and Sep and Oct – ideal if you want to escape the rains in the rest of the country. But in reality, you'll find it could rain on any day. Temperatures average out at about 26°C.

South to Cahuita

Highway 36 begins it's coastal journey south to Cahuita just west of Limón. A thin line of palms breaks the view of the beautiful beaches which hide dangerous currents found down the stretch of coastline north of Cahuita.

Selva Bananito Lodge Heading inland at Bananito a challenging road leads to extreme seclusion of **LL** *Selva Bananito Lodge*, T/F253-8118, www.selvabananito.com A family-run rainforest lodge that is probably winner of the 'Most Difficult Lodge to Reach' award, Selva Bananito is beautifully remote, close to Cerro Muchilla on the border of La Amistad Biosphere Reserve. More than a holiday stop, it's a place for body, mind and soul. 11 exquisite cabins are made from earthquake-salvaged hardwoods. Tiled bathrooms with solar heated water, lead from terracotta-tiled rooms with a balcony complete with hammock, opening to spectacular views to the mountains. Without electricity, the evenings are lit by candles and the days start with the sun and the dawn chorus of the nearby rainforest. Meals cater for vegetarians and non-vegetarians taking influences from the highlands and the Caribbean. Beyond the tree-hugging calmness, you can also enjoy some serious activities if you're up to it: tree climbing and rappelling; mountain biking; hiking; waterfall swimming; horseriding; or the more sedate pleasures of bird-watching and simply enjoying the gardens. Getting here can be amusing and involves crossing 4 rivers – 4-wheel drive is essential, but Selva Bananito will pick you up or provide a map if you want to drive yourself.

Aviarios del Caribe A few kilometres north of Penshurst is **AL** *Aviarios del Caribe*, T/F382-1335, aviarios@costarica.net 6 spacious rooms and suites, with private bath and hot water, with breakfast included. Beyond the comfortable lodging Aviarios has become the main sloth rescue centre in the country. Buttercup is the first among equals of a cherished family of 2- and 3-toed sloths that turn up through various tales of misadventure to be nursed back to health and then, with a bit of luck, returned to the wild. Judith and Louis are passionate about sloths, which are just crying out for serious research. Beyond indulgence in one of the deadly sins, the 60-ha island delta of the Estrella River has created a tropical paradise alive with otters, monkeys, caiman, poison-dart frogs, and butterflies. The bird list has topped 318. A 3½-hr tour is US$30 and worth every cent. There's a volunteer programme as well – contact Aviarios for details.

Reserva Biológica Hitoy Cerere From Penshurst, a road heads inland climbing the Estrella Valley eventually arriving at Hitoy Cerere Biological Reserve. The 9,950-ha reserve stands out for what biologists are speculating may provide some of the greatest diversity in Costa Rica which has created interest in the park for natural remedies. For the time being, the reserve offers some tough day-hikes.

Rainfall in the park is a steady 3.5 m a year, with temperatures in the high 20s creating perfect conditions for wet and premontane tropical forest. Three trails lead from the ranger's station through the spectacular forest rich with epiphytes and many streams, rivers and waterfalls. Wildlife is profuse with sloths, howler and white-faced monkeys to be seen, while on the ground you may see otters, peccary, even jaguar and tapir. Over a hundred birds have been spotted in the park.

■ *Getting to the park is strictly 4-wheel drive for the tough drive. Buses leave Limón for the Estrella Valley, but still leave you 15 km short of the ranger station. The easiest and simplest way to visit is on a tour from Cahuita or Puerto Viejo. You can contact the reserve office on T758-3996, F758-3996.*

Cahuita

Colour map 3, grid A5 Blink and you'll miss Cahuita which is hidden a few hundred metres down an unassuming road off Highway 36, 10 km south of the petrol station at Penshurst. The small town which supports a district population of 4,200 epitomizes the south Caribbean – laid-back but with just enough energy to keep things ticking along. Don't rush, don't hibernate, do something in-between.

The predominantly Afro-Caribbean town sitting on a small rocky peninsula – the first protuberance of significance south of Limón – is barely larger than a football pitch. Heading north out of town, a bumpy dirt road shadows the dark sand beach of Playa Negra drifting passed quiet hotels and lodges. South of town, a small creek leads to the golden sands that mark the northernmost point of Cahuita National Park (see below), home to some of the best coral reefs in the country.

Warning Cahuita and Puerto Viejo de Talamanca have suffered from what locals believe is a lack of support and investment from central government. An under-current of problems, partially based on the misconception that everyone on the Caribbean coast takes drugs, does mean that you may be hassled for drugs. If you are not interested, just say no. You should be aware there have been several violent attacks in the area and in March 2000 a couple of female students were murdered. The shock of this event after so many difficult years has produced some positive responses from the government and local community.

If you want a little more life in the evenings, choose somewhere central. The quieter, and generally more expensive places, are on the road north out of town along Playa Negra.

Sleeping

■ *on maps*
Price codes:
see inside front cover
Hotels and lodges,
especially those out
of town, will give
discounts for stays
of over 1 week

In town Right on the border of the national park at the southern end of town is **B** *Kelly Creek*, T755-0007, kellycr@racsa.co.cr 4 big rooms in an old plantation style wooden house complete with broad eves and shaded veranda. Decorated with colourful textiles, the bathrooms are spacious with lots of light, and the ceiling fan and louvered windows are perfect for getting a sea breeze moving through.

C *Brisas del Mar*, T755-0011. Just 4 simple rooms, each sleeping up to 4 people, with a ceiling fan and a small desk. Tiled veranda and hammocks outside. Elisha the owner is very friendly – the dog is very loud. **C** *Cabinas Palmar*, T755-0243. *Tico*-run, clean, friendly and very helpful. A few hammocks around the place for chilling and can arrange trips. Internet café out front. **C** *Jenny's Cabinas*, T755-0256, jenny@racsa.co.cr Canadian owned *cabinas* for singles, doubles and triples, in a quiet spot with sea views. Breakfast is served from the seaview terrace and they specialize in kayaking trips down the Río Sixaola. **C-D** *National Park*, T755-0244, F755-006. 14 rooms with just a bit too much plastic to be enjoyable. Some rooms upstairs have good views, the grudging friendliness ruins a good spot, but the restaurant on the beach is probably enough to compensate.

D *Cabinas Seeside*, on the beach close to *Jenny's*, T755-0027. A lively spot, with brightly decorated rooms – you'll either love it or hate it. **D** *New Cabinas Arrecife*, right on the coast, close to *Miss Edith's*, T/F755-0081. Rooms with private bath, hot water and ceiling fan could be a little bigger, but OK for the price. A good quiet spot with good views from the restaurant.

E *Cabinas Smith*. Simple clean rooms, with hot water private bath and ceiling fans. Not much better than basic, but good for the price. Facing the school is **E** *Cabinas Surf Side*, T755-0246. Clean rooms, good value and with safe parking. **E** *Sol y Mar*, T755-0237. 9 big rooms with ceiling fans, the ones upstairs have lots of light. Clean, friendly and family run. **E** *Vaz Cabañas*, T755-0218. 24 rooms, with private bath, hot water and ceiling fan, laid out in a big garden. Nice bright rooms and easy come, easy go atmosphere.

F *Albergue Room*, T755-0192. 12 basic rooms owned by Carlos who permanently laments the absence of business. The room are basic but clean – enough said. **F** per person *Cabinas Safari*, opposite *Cabinas Palmar*, T755-0078. Basic rooms with fan and shared bath. Friendly owner, clean and good value.

North out of town along Playa Negra (Places listed in the order that you come across them) **C** *Cabinas Tito*, T755-0286. With a distinct Hansel and Gretal feel about the place, these "little houses" are clean, safe and quiet, with hot water, private bath, fans and some pleasant personal touches. Quiet spot, good for families. **D** *Cabinas*

Caribbean lowlands

Belo Horizonte, T755-0206, has a couple of good, quite simple rooms on the beach. Don't ask for discount – business is tough. Also home to the *Caribe Spanish Language and Cultural Centre*.

A *El Encanto*, T/F755-0113, encanto@racsa.co.cr 3 beautifully decorated cabins with choice textile hangings set in well tended gardens. The open-air restaurant is in a Spanish-style villa and the owners are French – that figures.

Down a side road is **F** *Cabinas Arco Iris*. Clean and basic with private bath – OK for the price. A little further on is **D-E** *Cabinas Margarita*, T775-0205. Simple rooms, quiet spot, nice atmosphere and clean. Credit cards accepted.

The next side road leads to **C** *Paradise Colibri's*, T755-0180. A pair of funky hexagonal wooden cabins each with 3 beds and hot water private bath. Shared use of the kitchen. A good spot but the path is rather dark.

Cahuita

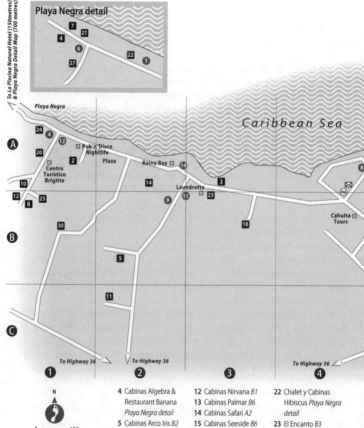

N

0 metres 100
0 yards 100

■ **Sleeping**
1 Albergue Room *C6*
2 Atlantida Lodge *A1*
3 Belo Horizonte *A3*
4 Cabinas Algebra & Restaurant Banana *Playa Negra detail*
5 Cabinas Arco Iris *B2*
6 Cabinas Brisas del Mar *A6*
7 Cabinas Cocal *Playa Negra detail*
8 Cabinas Iguana *B1*
9 Cabinas Jenny *B6*
10 Cabinas Mambu *A1*
11 Cabinas Margarita *C2*
12 Cabinas Nirvana *B1*
13 Cabinas Palmar *B6*
14 Cabinas Safari *A2*
15 Cabinas Seeside *B6*
16 Cabinas Smith *B5*
17 Cabinas Surfside *B5*
18 Cabinas Tito *B3*
19 Cabinas Vaz *C6*
20 Camping Koutiki *A1*
21 Casa Anahi *Playa Negra detail*
22 Chalet y Cabinas Hibiscus *Playa Negra detail*
23 El Encanto *B3*
24 Jaguar *A1*
25 Jardín Tropical *B1*
26 Kelly Creek *C6*
27 Magellan Inn *Playa Negra detail*
28 National Park *C6*
29 New Cabinas Arrecife *A5*

Caribbean lowlands

A *Atlantida Lodge*, T755-0115, F755-0213, www.atlantida.co.cr 30 rooms with private bath, terrace and ceiling fans in what is the closest to a resort in Cahuita. Big restaurant and bar, pool and Jacuzzi, massage rooms, gym all in over-tended gardens. Safe parking. Popular with groups. Very pleasant, but not very Cahuita.

A small track leads to **C-D** *Centro Turístico Brigitte's*, www.brigittecahuita.com A small cabin sleeping 2, but more about providing excellent local information. A good small restaurant for breakfast snacks, and lots of tours arranged on bikes and horses. There is also an internet service. Recommended.

A little further down the road a huddle of hotel options. **C** *Cabinas Mambo*, T/F755-0033, has rooms with an optional kitchen for an extra US$5. **D** *Cabinas Nirvana*, T755-0110, nirvana99@racsa.co.cr 7 simple wooden cabins sleeping 2-4 people, some with shared bath, others with private bath, balcony and hammock.

A-C *Jardin Tropical*, T/F755-0033, jardintropical@racsa.co.cr Looks can be deceptive, but deep within the undergrowth are some fine self-catering *cabinas*, and a couple of simple, but well equipped rooms. Seeing a couple of poison dart frogs on leaving, the penny dropped – this is a tropical garden.

B-C *Cabinas Iguana*, T755-0005, F755-0054, iguanas@racsa.co.cr Swiss-owned with a selection of houses and rooms to rent, some with fully equipped kitchen and balcony. All very neat and tidy with a mosaic-tiled waterfall fed pool and probably the best book swap in the country with every conceivable language on offer. Very good value, recommended.

On the main road **A** *Hotel Jaguar*, T755-0238, F226-4693, jaguar@racsa. co.cr is woefully overpriced with peeling paint and drab concrete paths.

D *La Piscina Natural*. A place so laid back it's horizontal. 5 simple rooms, with a small patio. A sea-fed lagoon creates a natural swimming pool, and tables and hammocks are dotted round the rocky coastline and garden. Sounds good enough to make a reservation. However, Walter the owner is not going near that telecommunications stuff.

AL *Magellan Inn*, T/F755-0035, www. web-span.com/tropinet/magellan1.htm 6 comfortable carpeted rooms offer the most luxurious and relaxed comfort in Cahuita. The garden is filled with the perfume of the bella dona by day, ilan ilan at night and plenty of birds. The unimposing pool is a mere 10,000 years old, courtesy of some fossils that have been uncovered. Recommended.

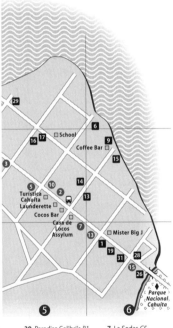

30 Paradise Colibri's *B1*
31 Sol y Mar *C6*

● **Eating**
1 Café Cristina *Playa Negra detail*
2 Caribbean Roots *B5*
3 Cha Cha Cha *B5*
4 Ciao's Paradise *A1*
5 El Palenque *B5*
6 La Casa Creole *Playa Negra detail*
7 La Sodas *C5*
8 Miss Edith's *A4*
9 Piccolo's *B2*
10 Pizza Cahuita *B5*
11 Pizzeria El Cactus *B2*
12 Reggae *A1*
13 Robertos Restaurant & Tours *C6*
14 Sobre Las Olas *A2*
15 Vista del Mar *C6*

C *Chalet y Cabinas Hibiscus*, T755-0021, F755-0015. A mini-resort with a handful of fully equipped cabins, a small pool, pool table and volleyball court. Popular with families. **A** *Casa Anahi*, T755-0470, is a very well equipped thatched roof house with everything ready to go. Sleeping up to 7 people, it's a good choice for a couple of families and often booked in advance. There's a balcony for lounging, a dining room if the mosquitoes get too bad. Everything is in good order, the bath, shower and comfortable bedrooms. A good choice. Next door **E** *Cabinas Cocal*, T755-0470, has some simple rooms sleeping 4 and a big house sleeping 10.

C *Cabinas Algebra*, T/F755-0057. 1 big and 1 small fully equipped house, each sleeping up to 4 people. Nothing fancy, but full of character and a quiet spot.

Camping At *Kontiki* T755-0261, **G** per person, opposite *Centro Turístico Brigitte*, with laundry, showers and toilets, and *Paradise Colibris*, out of village close to Playa Negra. Camping is also possible in Cahuita National Park (see below).

Eating **In town** *Cha Cha Cha*, international menu, great food and service, refreshing chic
● *on map* décor, very good pasta. Cheap. *El Palenque* has the distinctly tropical feel with spilt bamboo walls, sand floors and a good menu. Cheap. Almost legendary *Miss Edith's*, delicious Caribbean and vegetarian food, nice people, good value, no alcohol licence, take your own, many recommendations for breakfast and dinner, but don't expect quick service. *Pizza Cahuita*, right in centre, more than pizzas with good pasta, hamburgers and a fairly standard menu. *Sol y Mar*, good value, open 0730-1200, 1630-2000, need to arrive early and wait at least 45 mins for food, red snapper and volcano potato especially wicked, US$5, also good breakfasts, try cheese, egg and tomato sandwich. Seriously cheap. *Vista del Mar*, facing entrance to Park, good fish and Chinese dishes. Cheap.

Out along **Playa Negra** *Piccolo's* serves a good mix of local dishes and snack food. Cheap. *Pizzería El Cactus*, good pizzas in an open-air restaurant. Cheap. *Sobre las Olas*, right on the beach serving *Tico* and Mexican food from midday and a popular bar in the evening. Mid-range. *Reggae Restaurant* laid-back bar serving a mixed bag of dishes. *Ciao's Paradise*, good little reggae bar looking out to the beach, with oropendola nests hanging out too. *La Casa Creole*, next to the *Magellan Inn*, 2 km north of Cahuita, is a culinary feast of French and Creole creations and the best restaurant in the area. Open 0600-0900, closed Sun. Call T755-0104 for reservations. Mid-range. Recommended. *Restaurant Banana*, at the top of Playa Negra, has a good restaurant and bar popular with the semi-resident gringo crowd. Recommended and worth the walk.

Nightlife *Casa de Locos Assylum* and *Cocos Bar* are right in the centre of town. *Coffee Bar*, on the shore near *Cabinas Jenny*, is a good reggae spot.

Out of town places to get a drink include *Sobre Las Olas*, *Pub'n'Disco Nightlife*, the *Reggae Restaurant* and *Ciao's Paradise*.

Tour operators Beyond heading to the beaches of Cahuita National Park there are several popular tours. Locally it is easy to rent mountain bikes to explore on your own, or go horseriding. Contact *Centro Turístico Brigitte's*, along Playa Negra, T/F755-0053, www.brigittecahuita.com. Also on the Playa Negra road is *Rainy Bay* with surfboards to rent and a surf school, aimed particularly – but not exclusively – at women.

Reef tours in glass-bottom boats leave the town for a 5-hr tour with guide to see the corals off Cahuita National Park. US$25 per person. A 1-day trip to **Hitoy Cerere Biological Reserve**, promoted as the 'Pharmacy of the World', can be arranged. It's a 1½ hr trip to the reserve for 3 hrs walking to waterfalls including food and entrance. The latest adventure sport is **body rafting** on the Class I Río Sixaola, which is easily

Caribbean lowlands

combined with a trip to the **KeKöLdi Indigenous Reserve** and the **green iguana farm**. US$60 per person.

Trips further afield go up to **Tortuguero** for a 2-day, 1-night trip staying at *Laguna Lodge*, costing around US$160 per person, or you can arrange transport. Likewise, you can head south to the clear waters and sandy beaches of **Bocas del Toro** in **Panama** for a couple of days.

There are a number of tour operator right in the centre of town. Try *Cahuita Tours*, T758-0000, F758-0082. *Turística Cahuita*, T/F755-0071, dltacb@racsa.co.cr Arranges sea fishing trips, US$45 for 4hrs, and snorkelling. Also try *Mister Big J Tourist Service*, T755-0328, or *Roberto Tours*, T755-01178. None of these places stands out particularly but they are all close to each other, so walk around and see which one takes your fancy.

Bus A direct service from **San José** from Terminal del Caribe with *Transportes Mepe*, at 1000, 1330 and 1530, return 0730, 0930, 1130, 1630, 4 hrs, US$4.10, T257-8129, and from **Puerto Limón**, in front of Radio Casino, 0500-1800, return 0630-2000, 1 hr, US$0.80, T758-1572. Both continue to **Bribrí** and **Sixaola** on the Panamanian border (US$1, 2 hrs). | **Transport**

Banks There is no bank in Cahuita. Money exchange is difficult except occasionally for cash dollars (*Cahuita Tours* changes dollars and TCs). Take plenty of *colónes* from Limón. Nearest bank is in Bribrí (20 km) but several places accept credit cards. **Communications** Post: post office, next to police station at northern end of town. Internet: *Cyberbet*, part of *Cabinas Palmar*, US$1.60 per hr. **Laundry** There is a launderette in town and also on the Playa Negra road. **Language schools** *Caribe Spanish Language and Cultural Centre*, T/F775-0417, operates a language school in the area. Call or make inquiries at *Belo Horizonte*. **Useful addresses** The police are at the northern end of town. | **Directory**

Parque Nacional Cahuita

If the Caribbean means beaches to you, the palm-fringed golden sands stretching from the southern limits of Cahuita will be tough to beat. The beaches are postcard perfect, shaded by jauntily angled coconut palms reaching out to the ocean and a very short walk from the southern end of Cahuita town. | *Colour map 3, grid A5*

There are 2 rangers' stations giving access to the park. At the southern end of Cahuita town, **Kelly's Creek** station works on a voluntary donation system designed to limit the cost of visiting the beach area of the national park. **Puerto Vargas** ranger's station at the southern end of the park charges the usual national park entrance fee of US$6. **Camping** is permitted in the park at a designated campsite on the south side of Punta Cahuita. | **Ins & outs**

Entering the park from Cahuita gives good access to the beaches, but be warned that valuables go missing if left unguarded. As tedious as this is, either leave all your belongings apart from essentials in your hotel, or have them watched by someone you can trust.

Cahuita National Park was created in 1970 to protect the coral reef that lies of Punta Cahuita. As the best example of coral in the country, snorkellers who swim or join a tour to the reefs will see brain coral and leafy sea fans in the crystalline waters, and colourful coral fish darting nimbly amongst the corals. The reef has suffered considerably at the hands of the earthquake of 1991 and the chemical run-off from banana plantations and increased sediment run-off due to deforestation. The marine portion of the protected area covers over 22,400 ha, the land portion is much smaller measuring at just 1,106 ha. | **Sights**

Caribbean lowlands

A path follows the coastline around Punta Cahuita moving through the coconut palms and entering the mixed forest where you have a good chance of seeing howler monkeys, coatis, racoons, snakes and butterflies. Areas of swamp are good places to see green ibis, yellow-crowned night herons and northern boat-billed herons. Walking the 7 km trail between Cahuita and Puerto Vargos to the south takes about 3 hours, allowing for stops to nose around and take a dip.

Options for visiting the park are varied. You can stroll through a small portion of the park by entering from Cahuita, turning around after you've been far enough. Walking through, which makes for a comfortable day's walk, you eventually arrive at Puerto Vargas and the junction with Highway 36 from where you can catch a bus back to Cahuita. There is also a small tourist complex in Puerto Vargas with a couple of *sodas* and a simple restaurant. Alternatively, take an early morning bus heading south, ask the bus driver to drop you at Puerto Vargas and walk back heading north to end up in Cahuita.

Samasati Lodge

South of Cahuita, Highway 36 loses interest in the coastline and heads inland at *Hotel Creek* travelling through Bribrí for Sixaola and to the Panamanian border. Travellers with youthful energy will head straight on for Puerto Viejo de Talamanca. Those seeking an overall more calming state of mind should consider following the signs to **L** *Samasati Lodge & Retreat Center*, T224-1870, F224-5032, www.samasati.com Filled with enough healthy options to send the caffeine addict packing, Samasati is a genuinely relaxing lodge perched on the hill overlooking the Caribbean. 9 beautifully constructed hardwood bungalows with private bathrooms, all with balconies looking across to the ocean or to the rainforest. Chorotega pottery in the vegetarian restaurant emits a state of calmness, with trails for walking the forest where over 200 birds have been recorded, but the real focus of the retreat is yoga, meditation and other therapies given in the wonderful setting of the meditation hall – deep within the privacy of the rainforest.

Puerto Viejo de Talamanca

Colour map 3, grid A5
Area websites:
www.greencoast.com;
www.puertoviejo.net

Puerto Viejo de Talamanca, 17 km south of Cahuita, is a popular spot where the laid-back relax and surfers seek out the glorious Salsa Brava wave which peaks from December to February. Out of the water, a dark sand beach stretches to the west. To the east the more enjoyable golden beaches of Playa Cocles, Playa Chiquita, Punta Uva, and Manzanillo offer a quieter retreat along a road blessed with countless hotels and restaurants. Away from the beach botanical gardens invite you to explore, you can visit the nearby KeKöLdi indigenous reserve or enjoy countless other activities.

An early morning stroll through the streets puts you face to face with sleepy individuals dazed by the bright sunshine scuffling along while scratching ruffled hair. Whether hyper-active surfers who have risen too early or late night wanderers who forgot to go to bed is unclear. As you will soon find out, Puerto Viejo, with its good beaches, excellent surfing and vibrancy has become the main party town of the Caribbean coast. With the steady arrival of expatriates setting up homes in quiet backwaters, the Afro-Caribbean make-up of the town is slowly diluting – the town is changing, and changing fast.

Sleeping
■ *on map*

In town B *Coco Loco Lodge*, at the southern end of town, T/F750-0281, www.clubs.privateweb.at/karibikbungalows (German language only). 5 thatched roof cabins spread out in expansive garden. The cabins are well fitted out, comfortable and in a great spot. **C** *Cabinas Casa Verde*, T750-0015, F750-0047, www.greencoast.

Tough times in the Talamancas

Asociación Talamanqueña de Ecoturismo y Conservación – the Talamancan Association of Ecotourism and Conservation (ATEC) – have developed a couple of interesting and challenging activities. One- or multi-day trips head by motorized dugout canoe up the Río Sixaola to the indigenous community of Yorkin, some 20 km west of Puerto Viejo on the Costa Rica – Panama border. Trips staying more than a day get to hike through the forest learning about indigenous lore, handicrafts and staying in very simple lodgings.

The ultimate challenge is a no-frills transcontinental crossing of the Talamanca Mountains. It's a tough 10-day trek and you carry all your own gear. It's only a hunch, but this has the potential to become one of the great hikes in Costa Rica. For the time being you can do it for just US$400 for up to 3 people. Contact ATEC for details.

com/casaverd.htm Comfortable rooms with hammocks, private bath, cracked tile showers in beautiful gardens. All very pleasant and far too relaxing. **C** *Cabinas Grant*, T750-0292 or T758-2845. 11 large clean rooms, with private bath, fan and a small terrace with a fine view of… the parking lot. **C** *Cabinas Guaraná*, T750-0244, www.hotelguarana.com 12 rooms all with private bath and hot water overlooking a small patio garden. **C** *Cabinas Tropical*, T/F750-0283, rblanke@sol.racsa.co.cr Spotless rooms, with good mattresses, private bath and hot water. Pleasant gardens with a shaded rancho in the for relaxing, small bar/café. The German owner, Rolf Blancke, is a tropical biologist and runs tours. Recommended. **C** *Maritza*, T/F750-0003, www.hostelling-costarica.com Simple rooms in cabins with private bath, hot water and fans. Affiliated to the Youth Hostel Association. English spoken and recommended. **C-D** *Pura Vida*, T750-0002, F750-0296. Spotlessly clean Swiss-run hotel, with hot water and private bath. A quiet spot with plenty of shade, although lacking in any real character.

D *Cabinas Popular*, T/F750-0087. A few rooms with private bath, and a balcony or terrace. A fair choice. **D** *Jacaranda*, T750-0069. A very relaxed place set in beautiful gardens. Some rooms have a private bath and some of the mattresses are a bit on the thin side. The locally well thought of *Garden Restaurant* is due to reopen soon. **D** *Los Sueños*, T750-0369. A great little spot with just four rooms sleeping 2-3 people. Brightly painted with a couple of windows in each room. A good choice.

E *Cabañas Yoli*. Clean, basic with a fan. OK – one of the last *Tico*-owned places in town. **E** *Cashew Hill*. Classic backpacking hideaway. Quiet, very chilled, easy-come, easy-go atmosphere with basic cabins. **E** *Puerto Viejo*, in the centre of town. Rooms sleeping 1-5. Popular with surfers. **E** *Sol y Sombre*, T750-0267. 5 clean rooms with fan, mosquito nets, a small restaurant and just enough style to make it clear the owner French.

F *Cabinas Diti*, T750-0311. 3 rooms with private bath, cold water and ceiling fan. Credit cards accepted. **F** *Cabinas Salsa Brava*, on the seafront. Popular with surfers. **F** *Kiskadee*, T750-0075. Small jungle lodge with 2 dormitories, kitchen available, American-run, about 200 m south of football field, from where it is signposted, take torch and rubber boots. Recommended.

Out of town (west) Heading west along the black sand beach the first accommodation is **AL-A** *El Pizote*, T750-0227, F750-0088, www.hotels.co.cr/pizote.html 18 cabins and bungalows, many with kitchen. Nice gardens with a couple of pools. Good mid-range restaurant if you want to stop by. A comfortable choice and close to town.

B sleeping up to 4 people *Cabinas Playa Negra*, down the same road as the Botanical Gardens (see page 396), T750-0063. Basic equipped houses, close enough to the

Caribbean lowlands

beach for access, but far enough away to feel as if you're living in the middle of nowhere. They prefer long-term bookings – a good budget choice for a group.

A-C *Chimurí Beach Cottages*, turning north on the road on the opposite side of the river to Puerto Viejo, T/F750-0119, www.greencoast.com/chimuribeach.htm 3 fully equipped bungalows in a wonderfully quiet setting 1.5 km from Puerto Viejo. A good place to check in and be left to your own devices. Next door is **A** sleeping up to 6 people *Black Sands*, T750-0124, F750-0119, www.greencoast.com/bsands.htm Great old wooden house perfect for a group who want to spend quiet days on the beach and long evenings telling tales over home-prepared food and drinks.

B *La Perla Negra*, at the end of the road, T750-0111, F750-0114, www.laperlanegra.com Mini-resort style place with 3 clapboard houses, 8 rooms in each, all with tiled bathroom. Price includes breakfast. There's a pool and bar – a lively spot in the evenings.

Puerto Viejo de Talamanca

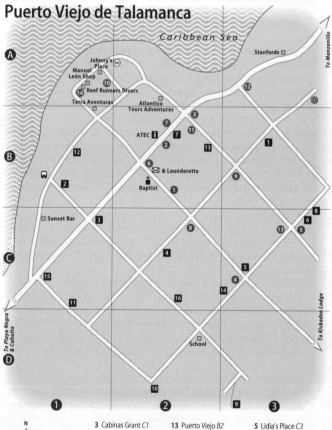

0 metres 50
0 yards 50

N

■ **Sleeping**
1 Cabinas Casa Verde *B3*
2 Cabinas Diti *B1*
3 Cabinas Grant *C1*
4 Cabinas Guarana *C2*
5 Cabinas Jacaranda *C3*
6 Cabinas Popular *C3*
7 Cabinas Tamara *B2*
8 Cabinas Tropical *C3*
9 Cashew Hill *D3*
10 Coco Loco Lodge *D2*
11 Los Sueños *C1*
12 Maritza *B1*
13 Puerto Viejo *B2*
14 Pura Vida *C3*
15 Sol y Sombre *C1*
16 Yoli *C2*

● **Eating**
1 Café Pizzería Coral *B2*
2 El Dorado *B2*
3 El Parquecito *B2*
4 Esmeralda *C3*
5 Lidia's Place *C3*
6 Marcos Pizzería *B2*
7 Marisquería Marley *B2*
8 Mister Patt *C2*
9 Oro *B3*
10 Pan Pay *A1*
11 Pizzería Caramba *B2*
12 Soda Britain *A3*
13 Soda Miss Sam *C3*
14 Soda Luisa *A1*

Out of town (east) Heading east the road travels to Manzanillo. Within easy walking distance of town is **D** *Cabinas Yucca*, T750-0285. Nice beach garden, parking, German-run. **C** *Cabinas David*, has clean tidy rooms within walking distance of town. Slightly off the main road is **C** *Calalú*, T750-0042, private bath and hot water, with thatched roof cabins. Nearby is the clean **D** *Monte Sol*, T750-0098, most with private bath.

D *Escape Caribeño*, 500 m along road to Punta Uva, T750-0103. Well furnished bungalows set in pleasant gardens sleeping 2-4. 10 mins' walk from town is **C** *Hotel Casa Blanca*, T750-0001. Simple rooms cooled by ceiling fans, hot water private bath, hammocks on the terrace and snorkelling gear and boogie boards for hire.

Café Pizzería Coral, south of centre, does good breakfasts from 0700, and good pizzas and meals for the rest of the day. Not cheap but recommended. *Bambú*, on the beach at the eastern end of town has good food. *Pizzeria Caramba* has excellent pizzas and other Italian dishes. *El Parquecito*, facing sea in the centre, nice breezy atmosphere, specializes in cheap fish and seafood dishes (evenings only). *Garden Restaurant*, in *Cabinas Jacaranda*, good Italian and Caribbean food, opens 1700. Highly recommended. *Johnny's Place*, on the beach front, serving cheap sushi by day and a disco open Tue-Sun, by night. *Lidia's Place* has good cheap food and to-die-for chocolate cake that does not hang round for long. *Marcos Pizzería* does what it says on the tin. *Pan Pay*, good bakery on beach front. *Piranha* restaurant at the Puerto Viejo Hotel claims to serve the "fattest plates in Costa Rica," and reasonably priced. Hold them to that! *Salsa Brava*, Spanish food and seafood. Recommended, closed Sun. *Soda Miss Sam*, south of the centre, good local food piled high, seriously cheap. *Tamara*, on main street, open 0600-2100, local good fish dishes, popular throughout the day, packed at weekends – the life and soul of the place. **Eating**

East of town, within easy walking distance is the stylish Italian restaurant *Amimodo*, T750-0257, with fresh bread and pasta (mid-range). *Der Schwabe*, is a German restaurant across the road

Partying is a profession in Puerto Viejo – not for wimps and not for those who like an early night. *Stanfords* is the place to end up at the end of the night when the reggae keeps thumping out. *Johnny's Place* comes alive at weekends and further east along the seafront is the *Sunset Bar*. On the main street *Tamara* and *El Dorado* next door are good places to start the evening with a drink or two. **Nightlife**

The **South Caribbean Music Festival** is a new introduction to the calendar bringing together local and national musicians and performers in the months leading up to Easter. Ask locally for details or contact *Playa Chiquita Lodge*, T750-0062, see below. **Festivals**

Growth in recent years has seen rapid changes in the area. *ATEC* (*Asociación Talamanqueña de Ecoturismo y Conservación*, the Talamancan Association of Ecotourism and Conservation), T/F750-0191, www.greencoast.com/atec.htm Set up in 1990 to tackle some of those issues and now provides advice and organizes many trips in the area and has by far the broadest offering (see box). Building on the popularity of the area *Atlantico Tours Adventures*, T/F750-0004, offers a range of trips as do *Terra Aventuras*, T/F750-0426, terraventuras@hotmail.com **Tour operators**

Diving in the area can be organized through *Aguamor Adventures*, based in Manzanillo, T391-3417, F750-0191, www.greencoast.com/aquamor.htm, who have been providing courses and dives since 1993. *Reef Runners Divers*, T/F750-0480 in Puerto Viejo is a new dive operation in town.

Caribbean lowlands

Riptides rumble Russian rouser

He may have turned the tide of Communism in the former Soviet Union, but Mikhail Gorbachev came a cropper like Canute while swimming off Costa Rica's southern Caribbean coast close to Manzanillo in June, 2000. After getting into difficulties in a strong current that was taking him out to sea, he was finally rescued by a local Red Cross lifeguard.

Local businesses are setting up a lifesaving programme. There are good and bad spots for swimming – always seek local advice.

Transport **Bus** There are 4 daily buses from **San José** from Gran Terminal del Caribe at 0600, 1000, 1330 and 1700, returning at 0700, 0900, 1100 and 1600, 4½ hrs, US$4.80. 9 daily buses from **Limón** between 0500-1800, 1½ hrs, US$1.30. 30 mins from **Cahuita**, US$0.45. Three daily buses to **Manzanillo** at 0700, 1530 and 1900, 30 mins, US$0.80. Five daily buses to **Sixaola** 0545-1915, 1½ hrs.

Directory **Banks** There is no bank in town, although there is speculation that a branch of *Banco Nacional* is coming to town. The only alternative is to change cash and TCs at Manuel Leon's general store on the beach, although commission on TCs is a painful 11%. **Communications** Telephone and internet: *ATEC* is the communications hub of the town until the new telephone line is installed. You can visit them for telephone calls, faxes and internet. There are also a couple of public telephones outside their office. *Cibercafé* just south of Stanford's has a couple of internet connections. **Post**: the post office is half a block south of *ATEC*. **Useful addresses** **Police** can be contacted on the seafront.

Excursions

Watersports Naturally, a lot of activities in the area involve water. **Surfing** is best from November to March. You can also rent **snorkelling** gear, sea **kayaks**, **boogie boards** and **mountain bikes** from several places in town.

Staying with the water, a couple of **dive** operations head out to the corals dotted down the coastline between Puerto Viejo and Manzanillo to the east. A two-tank boat dive costs about US$55 needing at least two people. *Aquamor* down in Manzanillo will take singles out for beach, night and kayak dives starting at US$30. They also organize dolphin observation tours in **Gandoca-Manzanillo Wildlife Refuge** with local captains.

On land A popular trip goes to the **KeköLdi Indigenous Reserve** just east of Puerto Viejo. You can visit the reserve on your own paying a small fee to see the green iguana farm or join an *ATEC* organized tour that includes a 4-hour guided hike through the reserve and a traditional meal. Twitchers can join **bird-watching** tours in the surrounding hills and further south in Gandoca-Manzanillo Wildlife Refuge.

The **Botanical Garden** just a few hundred metres west of the town is a fascinating experience with self-guided jungle trails that loop through the forest with flowering plants, medicines and over 60 kinds of fruit trees. In addition to learning about the forest pantry, there's a good chance of seeing toucans, sloths, butterflies from the treehouse and four different species of poison dart frog that live naturally in the area. Peter and Lindy are a mine of information, genuinely passionate about their work and incredibly knowledge. ■ *Open Fri to Mon, 1000-1600. US$3 for the trail, US$3 for the treehouse which is good for bird-watching. T750-0046, www.greencoast.com/garden.htm*

If you're based in the area for a while, most tour operators can organize trips to **Tortuguero** and **whitewater rafting** around Turrialba, or trips south for a few days to **Boca del Toro** in **Panama**.

Puerto Viejo to Manzanillo

Heading east from Puerto Viejo the road to Manzanillo provides a wide range of accommodation. Seclusion, family homes and must-avoid resorts. The strip is developing quite quickly, despite the restriction of the Gandoca-Manzanillo Wildlife Refuge.

Most accommodation is aimed at mid-range and above

About 4 km away through Playa Cocles, which has some of the best surfing on this coast, is Punta Cocles. A further 2 km is Playa Chiquita with many places to stay. Next is Punta Uva, unattractively translating as 'Grape Point', and eventually Manzanillo followed by the white sand beaches and rocky headlands of Punta Mona and the Gandoca-Manzanillo Wildlife Refuge.

D *Cabinas El Tesoro*, T750-0128, www.puertoviejo.net/cabinaseltesoro.htm Has a handful of cabins and a couple of small houses. The cabins sleep up to 4 people with use of shared bathroom and kitchen. Good friendly spot, close to town and beach. **B** *La Isla Inn*, T/F750-0109, www.puertoviejo.net/laisla.htm A stone's throw from the beach in front of Cocles Island, with 5 comfortable rooms with great views from the balcony. Breakfast available at a small extra charge.

Sleeping: Playa Cocles
Places listed in geographical order

Italian style comes to Playa Cocles at **A** *Cariblue*, T750-0035, F750-0057, www.cariblue.com Beautiful gardens surrounded by rainforest are home to 11 bungalows, some of dark hardwoods, and all with thatched roofs. Spacious inside and out with a balcony. The private bathrooms are all decorated with colourful cracked-tile mosaics. The new restaurant has a Swiss chef. Bikes available for rent. **C** *Cabinas Garibaldi*, T750-0101, is a cheap option with seven rooms to choose from.

"Rustic elegance" is what the brochure says and that is what you get at **A** *La Costa de Papito*, T/F750-0080, www.greencoast.com/papito.htm 10 bungalows of personal design with personal touches you'll barely notice. The grain and cut of the wood is intrinsic to the design of the spacious cabins, all with cracked-tile bathrooms and a small balcony complete with hammock. Breakfast is available, and bought to your door if requested. Relax, your host Eddie Ryan knows exactly what he is doing.

One hundred metres beyond the Río Caño Negro is **A** *Yaré*, T/F750-0106. A complex of 22 rooms, with fan and hot water. Half with kitchenette – the other half can dine in the restaurant serving international and local dishes.

On the beach side is **A** *Casa Camarona*, T750-0151, F222-6184, www.casacamarona.com 18 rooms in a two-storey house with balconies and porches looking out to the sea. Quiet little gardens and a selection of games for the young and old – special prices for groups. *El Rinconcito Peruano* is a small Peruvian seafood restaurant serving a mean *ceviche* at good prices. **C** *Olé Caribe*, T750-0455, has eight simple cabins sleeping up to four people in a quiet family home.

If you can't stand hard wood flooring try the **AL** *Villas del Caribe*, T750-2200, F750-0202, www.villasdelcaribe.net Two storey apartments looking out to the sea, with fully-equipped studio kitchens and a lounge for relaxing.

Hidden down a small driveway is the brightly painted *Tico*-owned **A** *La Caracola*, T750-0135, F750-0248, accionya@racsa.co.cr 14 rooms all with hot water private bath, with good access to the sea. It's a quiet spot and a good choice.

At the start of Playa Chiquita is **AL** *Hotel Punta Cocles*, T750-0338, F750-0336, www.novanet.co.cr/cocles 60 cabins hidden among the trees in a starkly unpleasant setting. Great for families who need constant stimulation, not good for quiet

Playa Chiquita

relaxation. 6 km from Puerto Viejo is **AL** *Hotel Kasha*, T/F750-0205, kashahotel@ hotmail.com Ten quiet bungalows surrounded by gardens and tropical forest. Satellite TV, pool, open-air gym and Jacuzzi if the relaxation gets too much.

Looking through the keyhole, this is clearly the home of an artist and someone seeking to find a genuine affinity with nature. Come to think of it, there were no keyholes at **A-B** *Miraflores Lodge and Restaurant*, T/F750-0038, mirapam@ racsa.co.cr Ten rooms throughout the spacious lodge, with shared bath. Upstairs a visionary shared area looks out directly to the rainforest and you just have to relax. Pamela Navarro is making all efforts to support the ideals of sustainable tourism and it shows. While it may be a little too rustic for some, it's a great spot and recommended.

El Duende Feliz, T750-0356, is a popular Italian restaurant. Nearby is *Café Negra* and the next dining stop is *Elena's Restaurant*, T750-0265, serving Caribbean style food washed down with cool beers to the sounds of reggae.

C *Villas Paraíso*, T750-0322, has eight double rooms with fan, hot water private bath, and a shared cooking area. Plenty of parking.

B *Playa Chiquita Lodge*, T/F750-0062, www.playachiquitalodge.com A dozen tranquil cabins nestled in the tropical garden, each with screened windows, ceiling fan and private bathroom. The open-air restaurant serves local dishes, and you're just a short walk from the beach. Naturalist guides available for tours. The Lodge is also home to the South Caribbean Music Festival which takes place every year in the months before Easter.

Positively oozing comfort is **AL** *Shawandha Lodge*, T750-0018, F750-0037, www.shawandha-lodge.com A luxury complex designed and laid out like an old village, with 12 bungalows fitted with refinement and comforts in a neo-primitive style. Wonderful ambience from the restaurant at night with dishes created by a French chef. Pricey, but worth it.

Punta Uva *Selvin* has a restaurant and some simple (**E**) cabins, and budget travellers can head for *Walaba Travellers Hostel* with simple dormitory accommodation.

AL *Las Palmas*, T750-0049, F750-0079, hpalmas@ racsa.co.cr with 60 ocean view rooms, and **AL** *Suerre*, T750-0181, F710-6376, www.suerre.com with over 40 rooms complete with TV. Both glitzy resorts have pools and every imaginable recreational activity. They are fine, but not very Puerto Viejo. The refinement that is **AL** *Almonds and Corals Tent Camp*, T272-2024, F272-2220, www.almondsandcorals.com brings a warm glow to the soul. Luxury camping in screened cabins with private bath and hot water – it's like camping without the mud. To be woken by the hum of the jungle in the morning but knowing it can't get in is a special feeling that should be compulsory for all visitors to Costa Rica. Excellent open-air restaurant serving filling tasty local and seafood meals. Many activities available and the elevated walkways lead to a beautiful beach.

Manzanillo

Locally simply known as the 'End of the Road', Manzanillo is little more than a turning circle for buses, but opportunities for laid-back activity are numerous.

Tour operators & excursions *Aquamor* have been operating a **diving** and **kayak** centre out of Manzanillo since 1993 and have now established over 100 dive sites in the surrounding waters including diving trips to the **Gandoca lagoon** by kayak. While the general criticism of poor visibility in Costa Rica stands true in the area there are times when the diving can be world-class, the reef diving in particular. In general the diving is best in September and October, April and May, although opportunities always arrive outside these months. Two-tank dives start at US$55, a beach dive is US$30. A full PADI course is US$300.

When not playing with tanks, the *Aquamor* team are **surfing on sea kayaks**, something they claim they'll have you doing in no time. More genteel kayak adventures can be found in small rivers and lagoons.

Dolphin-watching trips using local captains and guides can also be arranged through *Aquamor*. US$25 *Aquamor* T391-3417, F750-0191, www.greencoast.com/aquamor.htm

C *Pangea B&B*, beeper T224-2400 (code: 'Pangea'), behind *Aquamor*, has a couple of good rooms. Round the back of the village store *Mas x Menos* is **D** *Cabinas Las Veraneas*, T75-2298, with 13 clean and tidy rooms, most with private bath.

Restaurant Maxi's is well known in the area for very good seafood and Caribbean dishes, but locals say the prices have been bumped up too high and few people eat there these days. The bar has the potential to be lively when everyone's not glued to the TV. 5 simple rooms downstairs are ideal for beach lovers, **E**.

Sleeping & eating

Express bus to **Manzanillo** from **San José**, Terminal Sixaola, daily, 1600, returning at 0630. Buses travel between **Puerto Viejo de Talamanca** and **Manzanillo**. They leave Puerto Viejo at 0700, 1530 and 1700, returning at 0500, 0830 and 1700, 30 mins, US$0.60.

Transport

Refugio Nacional de Vida Silvestre Gandoca-Manzanillo

At the southeastern corner of Costa Rica Gandoca-Manzanillo National Wildlife Refuge protects some of the country's most important wetlands. While many areas in the country suffered from intervention before their value was realized, it looks as if Gandoca-Manzanillo's wealth has been recognized before it has been damaged. A combination of geographical, historical and cultural factors have limited human impact on the moist tropical forest and the inland and coastal waters have been left largely unscathed.

The 5,103-ha land portion of the refuge protects creeks, lagoons and the only natural population of mangrove oysters on the Central American Caribbean. The inland waterways are home to manatee, crocodiles and caiman, while the forests provide a refuge for jaguar and tapir, howler, capuchin and spider monkeys. Over 300 bird species have been recorded in the area including the vivid green emerald toucanet.

The coastal waters are equally diverse. White sandy beaches to the south of Punta Mona are used by nesting leatherback, loggerhead, green and hawksbill turtles. Below the surface, the 4,436 ha of marine reserve protects large areas of coral, including 11 species of sponges endemic to the area.

Marine and freshwater fish species throughout the reserve are estimated to number over 500 and mammals are topped off with three species of resident dolphins – the bottlenose, Atlantic spotted and the little-known species, the tucuxi. All in all, Gandoca-Manzanillo is a natural wonderland and a magnet for wildlife lovers.

Visiting the park is easy enough and can be arranged through the park offices in Manzanillo, T/F754-2133. While exploring the coastline is pretty straightforward, a guide is strongly recommended if you intend to go inland. Trips to the land sections of Gandoca-Manzanillo can be organized through ATEC, see page 395.

Several organizations work in the area to ensure that tourism and nature interact with minimum impact. *The Talamanca Dolphin Foundation*, T406-586-9942, F586-0995, www.dolphinlink.org, was established to create a greater awareness of the dolphins in the area and has subsequently developed guidelines for interaction between dolphins and people. The *TDF* and *Aquamor* have trained local captains and guides in

Ins & outs

Caribbean lowlands

dolphin etiquette with the aim of keeping the impact of dolphin watching to a minimum. Likewise, the nesting sites of the leatherback turtles is overseen by the local organization *ANAI*, T750-0020 or T224-3570, F253-7524, anaicr@racsa.co.cr **Volunteer programmes** exist with both organizations. *ANAI* require a commitment of at least 1 week, and charge from US$6 per night camping in the community of Gandoca. Lodging with local families is also available.

Bribrí At Hotel Creek, north of Puerto Viejo, the paved road heads through the hills to the small village of Bribrí, the municipal hub of the region and really only of interest to the visitor because it has a bank.

The town is at the foot of the Talamanca Mountains and the Talamanca Indian Reserve. Access to the park is limited, the most viable option being to plan a trip in conjuction with *ATEC* in Puerto Viejo.

Sleeping **D-F** *Cabinas El Piculino*, T751-0130, has 14 clean and tidy rooms, some with a/c and
& eating TV, cheaper without. **F** *Bar Restaurant El Mango*, T751-0054, also has a simple room when the mood takes them. There are several restaurants and *sodas* around town.

Transport Local buses depart for **Shiroles** 4 times a day, providing transport to the villages of **Chase** and **Bratsi**.

Sixaola

Colour map 3, grid A6 From Bribrí Highway 36 struggles valiantly through the potted road that passes through line after line after line of banana plantations. Company plantation villages of clap-board houses, with schools, football pitches and playgrounds for the children spring up from time to time, between the banana packing plants and the churches of the Seventh Day Adventists. It's a funny old road that leads you to Panama.

The border town of Sixaola has absolutely nothing going for it. Only over-optimistic curiosity and Panama as your eventual destination could be the reasons for coming. If you do need to stay, there is some simple accommodation, but you'd be better off timing your journey to pass straight through.

There are no banks in Sixaola, but it is possible to change money in the supermarket, but rates to the US dollar are very poor. Shops near the border in Panama will accept *colónes* but shops in Changuinola and beyond do not.

Sleeping At the entrance to town opposite the police station is **E** *Imperio*, T754-2289, with 8 basic cabins with fan and shared bath. **F** *Cabinas Sánchez*, 200 m before the bridge, 100 m block south, T754-2105, is clean and tidy, with private bath, fan and TV. Parking available and the best option in town. **F** *El Siquirreño*, 200 m before the bridge, T754-2224, with shared bath. Has just changed owners so could get better... or worse. **F** *Hotel Doris*, T754-2207. 8 basic rooms with fan and parking.

Costa Rican The border is open 0700-1700. The immigration office is just before the railway bridge
immigration over the Sixaola river which marks the border with Panama. The *cruz roja* required to leave the country can be bought from the supermarket for 300 *colónes* – immigration do not sell them. All formalities are quick and straightforward. Remember to advance your watch by 1 hour on entering Panama.

Transport Direct buses leave Terminal del Gran Caribe in **San José** at 0600, 1000, 1330 and 1530, 6hrs, US5.80, returning at 0700, 0830, 1300 and 1530. You can also join the buses at **Limón**, **Cahuita**, **Puerto Viejo** and **Bribrí**.

Background

12

Background

403 History

413 Government and the modern country

417 Culture

420 Land and environment

423 Wildlife of Costa Rica

History

Population of the Americas began somewhere between 40,000 and 15,000 years ago, when mankind first crossed the Bering Straight from Asia. A slow southerly migration steadily peopled the continent, and evidence suggests that humans first appeared in what is now Costa Rica roughly 10,000 years ago.

Early human settlement developed in this intermediate zone without a single dominant cultural group. The region was very much part of a north-south divde, taking its influences from both the Maya civilizations of modern-day Mexico and from several smaller groups in South America.

Farming, which began in earnest around 1000 BC, is the greatest indicator of this division. The Chorotega Indians, who lived in the northwest of Costa Rica on the Nicoya Peninsula, present day Guanacaste, were the largest and most advanced tribe in the country at the time of conquest. Arriving from Chiapas in southern Mexico around the 13th century, they cultivated beans and maize and developed a tradition of ceramics influenced by the Mesoamerican cultures of the Maya and later the Aztec. However, people on the Caribbean coast and in southern regions were more influenced by South American cultures, leading to the dominance of tuber cultivation, in particular yucca or manioc. Likewise, the dominance of jade, an influence from the north, waned with the decline of the Maya between 500-800 AD, encouraging the influence of gold from cultures of the south.

With increased food supplies, social organization and hierarchy developed to manage the increased populations. Regions of Costa Rica were divided into *cacicazgos* which were the basis for exchange of goods within the country and further afield. Rivalry and competition were intrinsic to the hierarchy, and dominance of an area was directly related to military ability and population. Likewise, dominance relied on the creation and development of strategic alliances to overcome and dominate the enemy.

Archaeological evidence of early settlements in the country are scarce. The largest single precolumbian site in the country is the Guayabo National Monument, close to Turrialba, which is believed to have been ruled by a *cacique* or shaman. Inhabited from 1000BC to 1400AD, the economy of Guayabo was based on agriculture, hunting and fishing. The reasons for abandoning the site remain a mystery, as do explanations of the country's other main archaeological remains, the stone spheres found dotted around the Diquis Valley in the south of the country.

Population estimates prior to the arrival of the Spaniards vary dramatically. Early studies put the population as low as 27,000, but these are almost certainly estimates made after the first wave of diseases impacted the region. More recent studies put the figure somewhere between 250,000 and 400,000.

The Genoese explorer Christopher Columbus introduced European influences to the country when he dropped anchor off the coast of Puerto Limón at Isla Uvita on September 18, 1502. After 17 days exploring the coastal area, teased by the prospect of Indians decorated in gold, Columbus and his men moved south calling this section of the coast of 'Veragua' *costa rica* – the rich coast. The precious metal never materialized in significant quantities but rumours travelled far and fast at the turn of the 16th century.

For almost 60 years the Spanish made half-hearted attempts to settle the region, with the primary intention of taking rich pickings of gold and easy labour, only to be hampered by difficulties. The conquest of Central America was launched from Panama to the south, and following Cortés' successful defeat of the Aztecs, from Mexico to the north. Using Panama as a base **Diego de Nicuesa**, appointed governor of

Veragua in 1508, launched the first attempt to establish a settlement in Costa Rica on the Caribbean coast. Nicuesa's expedition floundered off the coast of Panama and ground troops that attempted to march north endured sickness, hunger and encountered hostile tribes who denied the Spaniards food and slaughtered the invaders when the opportunity allowed, eventually forcing them to retreat. In 1513 the governor of Darién in Panama, **Vásco Núñez de Balboa**, led his forces across the isthmus and became one of the first Europeans to see the Pacific Ocean. Following the difficulties of colonizing the Caribbean, the focus now shifted to the Pacific coastline. Coastal forays explored the Pacific coastline reaching the Nicoya Peninsula and by 1522 **Gil González Dávila** had established good relations with the Chorotega Indians. After a trip that continued further north to Nicaragua and Honduras, Dávila returned to Panama with a cargo of gold and equally importantly, the souls of several thousand converted Chorotegas. However, a couple of years later, when Francisco Fernándo de Córdova established the first Spanish settlement of **Villa Bruselas** to the north of present day Puntarenas, the site had to be abandoned within three years as a result of starvation and further attacks from Chorotega Indians.

Despite the successes, the pattern of exploration, settlement and desertion continued as Spanish attempts to colonize through coercion met with resistance. Not until 1561, under orders from King Philip II of Spain, was an attempt at conquest successful when **Juan de Cavallón** managed to move through the territory from east to west for the first time, establishing a permanent settlement in the northwest of the central highlands at Garcimuñez. But it is **Juan Vásquez de Coronado** who receives the credit for establishing the first truly permanent settlement in the central highlands. Forging temporary alliances and utilizing rivalries between different indigenous groups – a technique that proved successful for Cortés in Mexico and Pizarro in Peru – Vásquez de Coronado founded Cartago in 1563. He established a settlement of sufficient numbers in the relative comfort of Cartago with plenty of fresh water and fertile volcanic soils for agriculture, and away from the sweltering heat and fetid coastal waterways of the Caribbean.

Despite Vásquez de Coronado's less bellicose approach to settlement, he too faced problems of indigenous uprisings. The energy and resources of the governor was all but depleted and the city nearly abandoned in 1568, when the next governor **Perafán de Ribera** arrived with extra supplies, manpower and enthusiasm for the conquest. Still searching for precious metals, Ribera attempted to pacify the Indians of the Talamanca region, but the Indians resisted and attempts at settling the region were quickly abandoned.

Once Cartago was secured, the division of land between settlers began. While land was divided between Spanish gentry and commoners, the relatively low indigenous populations and the absence of mineral wealth in any substantial quantity denied the Spanish landholders many of the comforts afforded landlords in other parts of the Spanish empire. While the gentry provided leadership in municipal government, the reality was that most were simple farmers, forced to work the land themselves. Some historians suggest this is the bedrock of the liberal sentiments that created the social advances and democratic traditions of Costa Rica.

The absence of labour was partly the Spaniards' own doing. Indigenous population numbers were first decimated by the microscopic killers of smallpox, measles and a host of other new diseases introduced to the new world by the Europeans against which the indigenous people had no immunity. The indigenous population was then reduced still further by the discovery of gold and silver wealth in South America. A strong demand for labour in the ports of Panama meant many men of working age were sold to work as slaves. Once the conquerors had settled, the *encomienda* system which allowed the new landlords to extract labour and produce from the indigenous population in return for protection and religious guidance, lacked the labour that fuelled the system. By the 1560s, the indigenous population had been reduced by as much as 95% and the Indian population that remained, had already demonstrated their resistance to Spanish advances.

Europeans settling the land

The new settlers land had hardly made an encouraging start and the absence of labour and mineral wealth placed Costa Rica in a colonial no-man's land. The Spanish system of administration was arranged regionally and tiered. Costa Rica answered first to the Audiencia of Guatemala which included land from Chiapas in Mexico to the southern border of Costa Rica and ultimately to Spain. While Costa Rica's size did not warrant her involvement in the detailed financial administration of empire, the province was deemed too remote to manage at distance. Apart from taxes and salaries, which were collected and paid from Nicaragua, Costa Rica was left to govern herself without much interference.

The small size of the population settled in Costa Rica limited the development of an internal market and the aspirations of settlers were quickly lowered. Brief moments of optimism broke the gloom. Mules bred and raised to the north were fattened in the Central Valley before heading to Panama to shift cargo across the isthmus supply route. In Guanacaste, cattle were raised and slaughtered for tallow and leather, planting the seeds of ranches throughout the region. Small concentrations of cacao plantations rose up around the Caribbean port of Matina, responding to a demand around the Caribbean and in Venezuela, and was actually encouraged and promoted by the actions of the governor Diejo de la Haya Fernández (1718-27). But in general opportunities were rare and the outlook bleak. For a brief time in 1709, money was so scarce that the cacao bean was temporarily used as currency.

Attempts to extract labour from the remaining indigenous populations saw a two-pronged approach with missionary and military expeditions to the Talamanca region attempting to extract the remaining indigenous population and culminating in the last significant Indian uprising in 1709 and the eventual execution of the Indian leader **Pablo Presbere**. The absence of labour, the growth in cacao production and trade with the Caribbean created the first wave of Afro-Caribbean migration as slaves were imported from Jamaica. However, by the 1750s, the demand for cacao and consequently slave labour had fallen due to increased competition from regions throughout the Caribbean.

The slow growth and brief periods of prosperity through the 1700s saw the founding of the fledging settlements of Heredia (1706), San José (1736) and Alajuela (1782). The award of a monopoly to Costa Rica for tobacco production for the whole of Central America in the late 1700s was the catalyst for growth in smallholdings in the central highlands and the first signs of an internal economy. The establishment of the trading centre for tobacco in San José stimulated the growth of the town and was to prove significant when a second crop introduced at the turn of the 18th and 19th centuries also played a significant role in the nation's development. Coffee was introduced from Cuba in the late 1700s – although the official date for introduction is often reported as 1808 – and planted in the volcanic soils of the Central Valley. The sleepy colonial territory was eventually waking, and a new phase of Costa Rican history was just beginning.

Background

Independence from Spain by post

On the eve of independence the population of Costa Rica had grown to 63,000 – still easily the smallest of the provinces of the Audiencia de Guatemala and just one 20th of the total. (The province amounted to little more than the principal settlements of Cartago, Heredia, San José and Alajuela.) Following the near decimation of the indigenous populations, the mixed blood *mestizo* population of Costa Rica was whiter than in neighbouring countries and with less than 10% of Costa Ricans being able to

 ## The Walker affair

In 1855, at a time when Costa Rica was beginning to enjoy the fruits of her independent labours in the presidency of Juan Rafael Mora Porras, one William Walker entered the Central American stage from the United States. Guided by the Monroe Doctrine which made all Latin American developments the business of the US, a thinly veiled attempt to protect US business interests and the reintroduction of slavery, Walker made a post-dated attempt to reunite Central America.

With an impressive academic record drifting through medicine and law, he moved to journalism before embarking on his ill-fated adventures to the south.

Arriving in Nicaragua in 1855 at the invitation of Liberals, Walker declared himself President of Nicaragua. He set about implementing his expansionist plans as Central American nations took arms to defeat the progress of the ambitious filibusterer.

News reached Mora Porras that a small band of Walker's forces had taken La Casona ranch in the northwestern province of Guanacaste and he hurriedly gathered together the armed forces, enlarged by volunteer peasants and labourers, to led a victorious battle in March of 1856. Costa Rican forces marched on to Rivas in southern Nicaragua where Walker's troops were defeated in a bloody battle which saw the young Alajuelan drummer boy Juan Santamaría rise to the status of national hero by torching the mercenary's military headquarters.

Walker eventually surrendered to British forces in 1857, and after several attempts at talking his way out of his predicament, colonial powers tired of his meddling, handed him over to Honduran authorities who tried and sentenced him to death by firing squad in 1860.

For Costa Rica, the Walker affair proved a defining moment. The country lost one tenth of it's population from the battle and cholera epidemic that returned with the forces, and the Battle of Rivas distilled a sense of nationalism in what was still a young state.

trace a pure Spanish heritage, the friction between the Costa Rican born and the Spanish born and bred authorities lacked the heat found in some Latin American countries. This mutual disinterest could hardly be illustrated better than when independence for the nations of the Central American isthmus was granted on 15 September 1821. Such was the importance to Costa Rica, and the loss to the motherland, that pronouncement of independence is reported to have taken a month to arrive from Guatemala City.

Independence created problems for Costa Rica which were to impact the country for almost 20 years. Mexico declared independence a few weeks before the Central American provinces. **General Agustín de Iturbide** invited the provinces to join a Mexican Empire, which set the four towns of Costa Rica in to a tailspin. Cartago and Heredia favoured joining the Empire, while San José and Alajuela preferred federal relations with the Central American provinces or better still, complete independence. A brief civil war broke out in late 1822 in which the republican forces of San José and Alajuela emerged victorious, rejecting domination from Mexico. While the fighting was in vain as Iturbide's imperial aspirations collapsed in early 1823, it did expose the rivalry between the towns of the Central Valley.

With the collapse of the Mexican Empire, Costa Rica joined the newly formed Central American Federation. The rivalry between the towns meant that the conservatives of Cartago and Heredia resented the decision made by liberals of San José and Alajuela. As the prospects for peaceful integration through the Central American Federation waxed and waned with varying degrees of violence, the people of Guanacaste chose to secede from Nicaragua in 1824. Meanwhile in Costa Rica the four main towns fought over the dominance of the nation in a series of regional quarrels. In desperation, in 1834 the head of state **José Rafael de Gallegos** approved the somewhat bizarre Law of Movement which rotated the capital seat every four years. But the conflicts continued and Gallegos resigned to be replaced by the forceful leader **Braulio Carrillo Colina**, who firmly established San José as the capital.

Disgruntled by the imposition of a liberal, Cartago, Heredia and Alajuela rose up against San José in a league of capitals. The **War of Leagues** in 1835 was victorious for Carillo and eventually put an end to the rivalry for the capital seat.

Elected as the first head of state by Congress in 1824 **Juan Mora Fernández** governed over a period of economic stability which saw the construction of state schools and houses, the founding of the national mint and government promotion of coffee cultivation. Following the introduction of coffee at the end of the 18th century the importance of coffee to the economy grew steadily and by 1829 coffee had overtaken cacao, tobacco and sugar to become the nation's major source of foreign revenue. When Braulio Carrillo Colina became head of state in 1835, he encouraged cultivation of the coffee industry still further, donating publicly owned land to anyone who would plant it with coffee trees, and the construction of roads to bring coffee to market.

The golden bean & social progress

The breakthrough for Costa Rican coffee occurred in 1843, when an English captain seeking ballast for his return journey to Liverpool, took on board sacks of coffee beans. The cargo was well received in England and Costa Rican coffee no longer stopped in Chile to be blended with inferior beans, but was shipped direct to Europe. This boom in coffee production and exports to Europe funded social developments for much of the 19th century.

When Carrillo declared himself dictator for life in 1841, his conservative opponents sought out the Honduran General **Francisco Morazán Quesada**, the former leader of the Central American Federation to remove Carrillo from office. Morazán's tenure as head of state was briefly popular until he imposed direct taxes with the aim of funding a Costa Rican army and relaunching his ideal of the regional federation. He was overthrown and later executed in San José's Central Park.

Morazón's execution cleared the way for a number of developments which were a result of liberal enlightenment that balanced the vested interests of the coffee élite, with a belief in improved education, public works and more efficient government.

A new constitution in 1844 attempted to introduce direct election, removing the process from the meddling of Congress dominated by influential families. In 1847 Congress named the youthful 29-year-old **José María Castro Madriz** the first president of the republic. Castro officially declared Costa Rica a republic in 1848, drawing a line under the perennial discussions amongst the ruling classes on the subject of joining the Central American Federation. Castro's wife, Doña Pacifica, is credited with designing the national flag. As a co-founder of the University of Santo Tomás in 1843, Castro pushed the importance of education, and as a believer in democracy he encouraged the freedom of the press. But while his achievements appear noble with the benefit of hindsight, his reforms eventually trod on the toes of the coffee élite and a replacement was provided.

When **Juan Rafael Mora Porras** rose from the coffee aristocracy to become president in 1849, the role of the coffee élite in society and the economy was established and influenced the development of the nation through the defining years of the 19th century.

The growth of the nation was facilitated by the excellent reputation of Costa Rican coffee in Europe. While the majority of small holdings were family owned – a fact that is still true today – a brief crisis between 1847 and 1849 assisted the

Background

tendency of coffee barons to add to their wholesale role by acquiring property. Simple economies of scales exacerbated the differences with every trade cycle and the birth of an ever stronger coffee élite increasingly influenced society. The arrival of Porras as president in 1849 marked the beginning of the rule of the coffee barons which lasted until 1870. Liberal government policies continued to improve the general well-being of the nation while nurturing the coffee industry.

With every shipment of the golden bean to Europe, vessels made the outward leg of the journey from Europe with an increasing supply of European goods. Styles of fashion, entertainment, architecture and culture – exemplified in the extravagance of the Teatro Nacional paid for by a direct coffee tax and inaugurated in 1897 – all took their lead from Europe. For Iván Molina and Steven Palmer, contemporary Costa Rican-US historians, it is the "European disposition" of the new coffee élite that saw the introduction of liberal ideals to Costa Rica.

However, the continued domination of the political and economic future of the country by the coffee families led to the coup of 1870 which saw General **Tomás Guardia Gutiérrez** take the presidency. Guardia ruled as authoritarian dictator determined to break the power of the coffee barons redistributing land from some of the larger landowners and introducing taxes on personal wealth. He introduced a new constitution in 1871 which extended the voting to an electoral college and abolished the death penalty. But his programmes continued the liberal tradition of extending education, stimulating trade and encouraging greater production of coffee and sugar. Guardia also set in place the construction of the Atlantic railroad.

Guardia succeeded in breaking the power of the coffee families, only to replace them with his own nepotistic successions. On Guardia's death in 1882 his brother-in-law Próspero Fernández Oreamuno ruled as president until his death in 1885, when his brother-in-law Bernardo Soto Alfaro took the presidential position. But despite continuing the dictatorial style, Soto introduced free and compulsory education, the national library, the Red Cross and promised to abide by congressional elections at the end of his term in 1889. With freedom of the press, the first truly honest and open election in Costa Rica's history took place. Soto set himself up as the victor, but lost.

The 1890s marked a shift in the political and economic landscape of the country beyond the introduction of a considerable improvement in the democratic process. The church also re-entered the political arena tired of the consistent undermining of their role as the educatorsl and moral guide of society. As early as 1825 the income of the church through the state collected taxes was cut, abolished and eventually the clergy were demanded to pay taxes on their income. In the presidency of Fernández civil marriage and divorce were introduced, religious instruction in schools was prohibited and the Jesuits were expelled from the country. The creation of the Partido Unión Católica (Catholic Union Party) in 1891 intended to defend the interests of the church.

The banana boom

When Guardia instigated the construction of the railroad link from the Central Valley to the Atlantic coast, the simple logic was to speed up and reduce the cost of transporting coffee to European markets. Guardia contacted Henry Meiggs who had experience of railroad building in Chile and Peru. Almost £4 million was borrowed from British banks to finance the construction.

The first tracks were laid in 1872, but due to mismanagement and corruption, construction was regularly delayed. The task actually fell to Meigg's nephew **Minor Cooper Keith** who completed the line in 1890 having managed to secure some generous concessions along the way in return for taking on the debts of the railroad. Keith moved in political and social circles that saw him negotiate a 99-year lease on the railroad, purchase land for banana cultivation alongside the track and marry the daughter of former president Castro Madriz. In the process of construction over 4,000 workers died and labourers from China, Italy and then from Jamaica were recruited to work on the railroad. By the time the railroad opened in 1890 foreign capital had gained a strong foothold in the Costa Rican economy, the economic profile of the country had shifted and the social make-up of the country had been dramatically altered.

With the completion of the railroad a permanent link to the Caribbean was established and the banana industry grew rapidly. Keith created the *United Fruit Company* (today known as *Chiquita*) in 1899 and many of the labourers that worked on construction of the railroad moved to work in the port of Limón or the banana plantations. The coffee élite of the highlands avoided investing in bananas, leaving the industry to develop in almost complete isolation. Between 1910 and 1920, exports had grown to equal coffee in value and control of the Caribbean lowlands was almost entirely in the hands of the company which colloquially became known as *Yunai*.

On the back of the prosperity of the late 19th century, increased affluence for agricultural élites, an increasingly educated populace enlarged by considerable migration from Spain, Germany and Italy, and ever-greater hardships for plantation workers and the urban working class sowed the seeds of resentment in the early years of the 20th century. The constitution was nudged gently towards direct elections and eventually produced President **Alfredo González Flores** (1914-17). When he proposed the Liberal reforms of a state bank and direct taxes as gestures towards reducing growing inequalities and tackling problems with the public finances produced by coffee prices which had been falling since the early 1900s, González lost popular support and was ousted in the military coup of **Federico Tinoco Granados** in 1917. Events conspired to remove Tinoco as the US withdrew support for the regime and further loss of German markets due to World War I crippled public finances. Populist sentiment removed him from power in 1919.

Protest movements and revolutions springing up in Russia, Mexico and closer to home in neighbouring Nicaragua added noise to the ever-louder cry for better working conditions. Economic hardship between the two world wars, culminating in the depression of the 1930s led to greater social conflict. Widening influence on the political process, fuelled by the well educated and opinionated population, saw the introduction of ideology to the Costa Rican political process. The **Reformist Party**, which promoted unions, an end to state monopolies and control over foreign capital, was created in 1923, founded by Jorge Volio a politician and a priest credited with the introduction of the Christian Socialist policies to national politics. The **Communist Party** was founded in 1931, and under the leadership of Carlos Fallas led strikes that paralysed the banana plantations of the *United Fruit Company* in 1934. One outcome of the strike was the introduction of a minimum wage. However, economic recovery towards the end of the 1930s was abruptly halted by the outbreak of war in Europe and once again the immediate loss of markets for bananas and coffee. But despite the economic problems, government investment in health and education continued to improve health provision and reduce illiteracy.

The 1940s saw tensions between agricultural and urban forces rise to boiling point and the eventual outbreak of civil war. The elections of 1940 awarded **Rafael Angel Calderón Guardia** of the Partido Republican Nacional (PRN – National Republican Party) the presidency. Calderón favoured government intervention in social and economic affairs and marked a slight shift in the liberal tradition. Early reforms proposed by Calderón were unsuccessful but raised the suspicions of many landowners, and stimulated thought in a small band of modernizing liberals who suggested it was the structures and institutions of governments that needed to be changed for the good of the

Seeds of democratic reform

Civil war

Background

country overall, not just the policies. Costa Rica's early declaration of war against the Japanese and shortly after with Germany and Italy earned Calderón greater criticism that he had overstretched the country's position without having the means to defend itself. One vocal critic of Calderón was **José Figueres Ferrer**, a landholder with sympathies towards the modernizing factions, who denounced the president. Figueres was promptly exiled to Mexico. Calderón's social intervention increased with a swathe of reforms called the 'Social Guarantees' which improved job security, proposed health insurance and introduced a mild series of land reforms. The suspicions of Calderón's opponents were increasing and with elections approaching in 1944, Calderón looked to sure up his political support. The church gave tacit support to Calderón approving his social reforms and the reintroduction of religious instruction in schools. An unholy alliance was created when rumours of a coup pushed Calderón into the arms of the renamed and toned down Communist Party, thus gaining valuable support of labour movements which led to the prompt introduction of a minimum wage, an eight-hour working day and trade union rights for workers. While the reforms further ostracized the ruling élites, young professionals and liberal moderniszers, opposition to communism was widespread and growing.

Constitutionally barred from standing for two consecutive terms Calderón's puppet-candidate Teodoro Picado Michalski stood for election for the PRN and held the presidency from 1944-48.

After two years in exile in Mexico the vehemently anti-Communist **Figueres** returned in 1944 to find the communist party still played an increasingly significant role in national politics. With no direct political heritage of his own, Figueres formed allegiances with Calderón's adversaries. Civil liberties were increasingly restricted through the Picado presidency and civil unrest rose to new heights when government forces killed two protesters. Picado promised to abide by the outcome of presidential elections in 1948, but few were convinced. **Figueres**, calling on Central American allegiances he had made while in exile, planned for military intervention if democratic elections failed.

The elections of 1948 set Calderón against **Otilio Ulate Blanco** who occupied the anti-Calderón ticket. The election produced a victory for Ulate, but as feared alleged voting irregularities led congress to award the presidency to Calderón.

Figueres justified a military uprising in defence of democracy and began a brief but bloody civil war. His **Army of National Liberation**, supplemented with soldiers and weapons flown in from Guatemala, quickly made progress from San Isidro de El General, via Limón and eventually to the decisive battle at Ochomogo, outside Cartago. The five-week battle resulted in 2000 deaths before government troops surrendered in April 1948.

'Don Pepe', as Figueres later became known, assumed the position of head of state for a period of 18 months leading the Junta of the Second Republic. Against expectations, he retained many of the reforms of Calderón and extended them further. The Junta prised power away from the ruling élites by nationalizing the banks controlled by the coffee oligarchy, creating the *Costa Rican Electrical Company*, public bodies to administer health insurance, public utilities and social security and increasing taxes. The army was abolished and a new constitution extended suffrage to women, blacks and Indians and created the Supreme Electoral Tribunal to remove the possibility of electoral fraud. With the new constitution designed to redistribute power away from established élites and remove institutional corruption, Figueres stood down in 1949 peacefully handing power to the elected president Ulate.

Historians continue to explore different interpretations of the reforms of the 1940s, but the legacy of a nation without armed forces has been enduring. The shift of political power away from social élites combined with improved education fuelled the growth of urban middle classes. The post-1949 era was to be defined by the acceptance of public involvement in the economy, an informal acceptance of centrist politics and the introduction of free and open democratic elections.

Following the divisions of civil war and global economic expansion after World War II, Costa Rica enjoyed a period of extended growth. The presidency of Ulate set the country on a sound economic footing before embarking on infrastructure developments. With the unifying anti-Calderón forces removed, Figueres founded the *Partido Liberación Nacional* (PLN – National Liberation Party). **The birth of modern Costa Rica**

The strength of Figueres' character, and the absence of any meaningful opposition handed Don Pepe – as Figueres is affectionately known in Costa Rica – the presidency with an overwhelming mandate. Investment in public bodies and services was funded by increased taxes on the *United Fruit Company* and individuals with higher incomes. The tax increases were at the expense of popularity and the party lost the presidency to **Mario Echandi Jiménez** (1958-1962) of the *Partido Unión Nacional* (PUN – National Union Party), but the PLN still strongly influenced congress and Echandi was unable to reduce the spending deficits incurred by Figueres or the programmes.

Through the 1960s and 1970s, despite healthy growth in the economy, governments battled to balance the books which needed to fund a burgeoning welfare sector and social security system. Investment in education, health and infrastructure saw the number of public sector employees expand to 33% of the working population, making the state the single largest employer and fuelling the development of an increasingly urban society. Banana exports and coffee prices grew rapidly providing increased tax revenues through the state banking system. Tax incentives incubated a domestic manufacturing industry to move away from the vulnerable exposure to commodity prices.

Beyond the city, small farmers struggled to adopt the efficient technologies of larger landholdings and many left the land for the bright lights of the city, focusing even greater pressure on the provision of public services in the city. At the same time, agricultural expansion led to widescale deforestation with the loss of almost 50,000 ha annually between 1963 and 1973 – the highest rates in the world at the time outside the Amazon Basin.

The return of Don Pepe to the presidency from 1970-1974 saw the continuation of PLN policies to invest in public services. The oil crisis of 1973 deflated the economic growth bubble of Costa Rica and after a brief rise in coffee prices in the mid-1970s, the drop in revenues from poor global commodity prices and the global economic recession exacerbated the difference between public spending and income. The presidential term of **Daniel Oduber Quirós** (1974-78) marked the first continuation of power within the same party and saw a continued deficit in public finances. The presidency of **Rodrigo Carazo Odio** (1978-82) saw the economic crisis worsen as annual inflation reached 90%, the economy shrank and relations with international lending agencies were stretched to the limit. During Carazo's administration public foreign debt rose to US$3 bn. In September 1981, with debt repayments already suspended, Carazo reluctantly agreed to austerity measures imposed by the IMF in return for a reduction in public spending and price controls.

With the Nicaraguan revolution to the north, **Luis Alberto Monge Alvarez** (1982-86) negotiated a financial aid package from the ally-seeking US that trod the difficult line between structural adjustment of the economy and avoiding complete social meltdown. First attempts at reducing the large number of public employees made minimal inroads. Despite pressure from the US which came with large sums of money to prop up the economy, Monge declared Costa Rica's neutrality in the Nicaraguan conflict and managed to avoid being drawn directly into events north of the border. With increasing pressure from the US, **Oscar Arias Sánchez**

Background

(1986-90) proposed and successfully negotiated a Central American peace plan between Nicaragua, Costa Rica, Honduras, El Salvador and Guatemala. It seems entirely appropriate for a country that disbanded its army almost 40 years before to be the seedbed for a regional peace process that eventually led to elections in Nicaragua, and discussions between governments and rebels in El Salvador and Guatemala. Arias Sánchez received the Nobel Peace Prize in 1987 for his efforts.

By 1987 the country's burgeoning national debt had risen to US$4.7 billion – more than the country's gross domestic product. The challenge facing governments of the 1990s was to reduce public spending, reschedule debt repayments while somehow managing to hold on to education, health and social security benefits that made Costa Rica stand out from most countries in Latin America.

In 1990 **Rafael Calderón Fournier** of the *Partido Unidad Social Cristiana* (PUSC – Social Christian Unity Party), the son of the 1940s reformist president Calderón Guardia, won the presidency and introduced austere measures that restricted public spending and saw limited trade liberalization. One casualty was the closure of the Atlantic railroad 100 years after it had first opened, although any debate on the subject terminated the huge earthquake which hit the Caribbean lowlands in 1991 taking the railroad out of action permanently. The broader social impact was dramatic, with some 38% of Costa Ricans judged to be living below the poverty line in 1993, labour protests increased accordingly.

The early 1990s also marked a greater focus on the potential for tourism and the introduction of quotas for banana exports to the European Union in 1993 beginning a trans-Atlantic trade dispute that set Brussels and Washington on an economic collision course at the cost of uncertainty and job losses in the Costa Rican banana industry (see box page 368).

José María Figueres Olsen of the PLN, continued the pain of readjustment from 1994-98, repeating history by following a Calderón administration as his father Don Pepe had done almost 50 years previously. Plans to minimize the pain of restructuring were quickly shelved by the collapse of the *Banco Anglo Costarricense*, the country's oldest bank. The loss of confidence rocked the economy which drifted into recession in 1996. Figueres proposed a new range of reforms which tinkered with the restructuring of debts, the sale of two state banks and the privatization of RACSA, the state-owned telecommunications company. Most reforms never materialized due to Congressional obstruction and Figueres left office with some of the worst approval ratings in Costa Rican history. However, he is credited with the stabilizing impact of removing the link between the economic and electoral cycle and attracting the US microprocessor *Intel* which opened a manufacturing plant in the central highlands in 1998 with an investment totalling US$500 million (see page 415).

Disillusionment with politics saw a largely disinterested electorate in 1998 hand the presidency to the US-trained economist and lawyer **Miguel Angel Rodríguez** of the PUSC. Economic progress continued in the first two years, with the number of tourists exceeding one million for the first time in 1999 and the benefits in the growth of high-tech manufacturing beginning to filter through. A program of reforms pursuing the opening up of the telecom, electricity and insurance sectors to private investment was initially supported by Congress but eventually led to widespread public protest and the plans were shelved. Traditional products of coffee and bananas also took a battering as commodity prices and industry developments dramatically reduced the value of exports. Global factors also highlighted the frailty of the economic market with the brief surge in the price of oil in 2000 threatening to squash economic progress, the global downturn in the high-tech market threatening to undermine the recent successes of the fledgling industry in the country, and the, as yet unknown, impact of events in New York and Washington on September 11th 2001.

The elections scheduled for February 2002 look certain to see another close-run outcome fought between the liberalizing policies of the PLN and the PUSC. An electorate broadly against the economic restrictions enforced by the international community will have little to choose from, with many voter viewing the policies of the PLN and the PUSC to be largely the same.

Government and the modern country

Government

The president is the head of state and government, elected for a four-year term and cannot be re-elected. Legislation is passed through the single-chamber Legislative Assembly with 57 deputies who, like the president, hold their positions for four years and cannot be re-elected.

The current president, **Miguel Angel Rodríguez**, of the *Partido Unidad Social Cristiana* (PUSC – Social Christian Unity Party) assumed the presidency in May 1998 and will relinquish the position in May 2002. The ruling PUSC has a majority of 27 in the assembly with the *Partido Liberación Nacional* (PLN – National Liberation Party) having 23 deputies. The remaining seven seats are held by five smaller parties. With neither of the main political parties possessing an absolute majority, legislation is easily blocked and government has shown tendencies towards stalemate when confronted with difficult legislation.

Growing support to lift the ban on re-electing the president, campaigned for by the former president Oscar Arias Sánchez, was rejected by the Supreme Court in 2000. It looks certain to be an ongoing issue with some 74% of Costa Ricans reported to be in favour of re-election.

Provinces

Background

🐾 Costa Rica's provinces

Province	Size – km²	%	Population	%	Density/km²
San José	4,959	10	1,356,442	35.5	274
Alajuela	9,753	19	716,935	18.7	74
Cartago	2,657	5	432,923	11.3	163
Heredia	3,125	6	354,926	9.3	114
Guanacaste	10,141	20	264,474	6.9	26
Puntarenas	11,277	22	358,137	9.4	32
Limón	9,188	18	340,756	8.9	37
Total	**51,100**	**100**	**3,824,593**	**100**	

Administratively the country is divided into seven provinces, 81 cantons and 449 districts. Over half the population lives in the central highlands which includes sections of the provinces of San José, Alajuela, Cartago and Heredia.

Government reforms

One of the government priorities for this term was the reform of ICE, the state-owned electricity and telecommunications monopoly. The Rodríguez administration had hoped to reform the 11,000 strong state body to improve efficiency and facilitate the faster development of better telecommunications, especially important in light of the growth of the internet economy. Congress was strongly supportive of the reforms, the three deputies of the Fuerza Democrática successfully mobilized public support leading to protests and road blocks throughout the Central Valley. Opponents to the reforms believe that the Costa Rican electricity and telecommunications market would be taken over by global companies, siphoning off jobs and profits that have been one of the driving forces behind the nation's prosperity. Supporters of the reforms believe the telecommunications sector in particular is not capable of providing the level of service required for the Costa Rica to capitalize on the importance of the internet.

Nicaraguan border dispute

Relations between Costa Rica and her northern neighbour have periodically been difficult. After one spat in the 1950s, Figueres is reported to have told the Nicaraguan dictator Somoza García to "grow up." One political success of the Rodríguez government has been the diplomatic resolution of the ongoing dispute with Nicaragua, who prevented Costa Rican police forces from travelling on the river with standard weapons.

Prior to the Nicaraguan revolution in 1979, the Sandinistas were alleged to be using bases to the south of the shared border to launch attacks on the country and Nicaragua closed the border. After the revolution, the same region was used as a base by Contras fighting against the Sandinistas which were now in government. As early as 1858 the Nicaragua-Costa Rica border was defined as the southern bank of the San Juan River, although Costa Rica was permitted access for patrols.

More recently tension mounted when the Costa Rican police forces began patrolling the river to prevent illegal immigration. The border crossing close to Los Chiles was closed until a few years ago and this situation was just short of outright conflict in 1998 when Costa Rican police forces using the river with standard weapons, were judged to be threatening Nicaraguan sovereignty. The diplomatic resolution has secured navigation rights for Costa Rican police when agreed in advance with Nicaraguan authorities.

Economy

Economically the country is undergoing a slow revolution, with every year bringing a steady shift away from traditional agricultural production, and a move towards manufacturing, the electronic economy services and tourism.

The national economy experienced strong growth in the last years of the 1990s, with gross domestic product growing by 8.4% in 1999, taking the average for the decade up to a steady 5% a year. Predictions by the World Bank made in the first half of 2001 put growth at 5.2% per year between 1999 and 2003. In the light of the downturn in the global economy and the reduction in banana quotas in mid-2001 these would appear to be optimistic targets.

The picture is dampened even more by inflation, which hovers around 11%. Constraints in some sectors of the economy have seen unemployment rise to 6% and underemployment to around 8%. And foreign debt, in 1999 totalling US$4.2 billion, continues to be a big drain on the nation's finance.

Coffee

Stimulating the growth of the nation through most of the 19th century and the early 20th century, coffee continues to be an important part of the economy, but the drop in commodity price in recent years has seen the value of exports fall by one third on the previous year to US$289 million in 1999.

Costa Rica is one of the largest producers of arabica coffee in Central America, with cultivation concentrated in the central highlands. The industry is made up of over 50,000 coffee farms cultivating an area of roughly 100,000 ha. Over 90% of smallholdings cover less than 5 ha and are owned and farmed by approximately 125,000 families, giving the industry considerable significance beyond its presence in the national identity.

Current coffee prices are at the lowest they have been since 1973, with prices at US$95-85 for a 60 kilo bag. The *Costa Rican Coffee Institute* (ICAFE) estimates prices need to be around US$100 a bag to break even. However, Costa Rica is a member of the *Association of Coffee Producing Countries* which agree to retain coffee in government warehouses if the prices falls below a certain rate.

Bananas

As with coffee, bananas are an intrinsic part of the national economy and identity. Exports of 2.1 million tonnes in 1999 earned US$630 million – a three fold economic increase in the last decade. Figures for 2000 show a dramatic decline of roughly 15% in just one year due to the impact of the global trade war between the US and European Union over access to European markets for banana producers.

In the trans-Atlantic trade war, the certain losers in the global market for greater competition are the independent growers of Costa Rica who sell to the multi-national companies *Chiquita, Dole* and *Del Monte*. Hard fought for, and reluctantly given, concessions have slowly improved working conditions and job security for banana industry workers. At present, banana labourers account for 14% of agricultural labourers, but just 3% of the total work force. After the industry has readjusted to the new trade regulations, employment figures are expected to be substantially lower. For more detailed information on the banana wars see page 368.

Other agriculture

Many traditional industries have also suffered with recent economic developments. The contribution of cattle rearing to the national economy has dwindled to just US$20 million, creating additional problems of increased unemployment in Guanacaste.

Manufacturing

An unquestionable economic success has been the attraction of *Intel*, the US microprocessor manufacturing to the central highlands. The plant, which opened in 1998 with the creation of 2000 jobs, is believed to have made a significant contribution to

Background

the surge in economic growth in 1999. The success in attracting this major high-tech company is placed at the door of the country's education system. The hope is that the arrival of *Intel* will reap multiple rewards, encouraging high-tech employment opportunities, and early signs already indicate that other companies are considering opening plants in Costa Rica.

Tourism Equally spectacular has been the growth in tourism. In 1999 more than one million tourists visited Costa Rica contributing more than US$971 million to the economy. The figures in 2000 increased by just under 10%, and in the first six months of 2001 over 609,000 tourists had visited. According to the *Camara Nacional de Turismo de Costa Rica* (CANATUR – National Chamber of Tourism), the tourism industry employs around 140,000 people and accounts for 15% of exports.

Overall, the industry is structured towards the better off-traveller with all-inclusive resorts. The creation of the large scale Papagayo project on the northern coast of the Nicoya Peninsula is such a project which has been widely criticized for damaging environmentally sensitive areas and promoting the kind of tourism that relies on large scale foreign investment, creating very little internal wealth for the country once the projects are operational.

Energy production Almost 70% of the country's electricity is produced by hydroelectric power generation, with the latest addition to the installed capacity of 734 megawatts being the 177-megawatt **Angostura Dam** south of Turrialba, the construction of which was completed in early 2001. Many of the country's hydroelectric projects are initially obstructed by locals and users before construction, the criticisms being that there is a loss of valuable natural resources. One such project is the development of a dam on the lower reaches of the El General river, south of San Isidro de El General, which is strongly opposed by indigenous groups in the area.

Costa Rica has no viable oil reserves and imports its supplies from Mexico and Venezuela. In the early 1990s, concessions were granted for exploration in the southern Caribbean area. This start-stop exploration is being fiercely contested by local residents who believe that it will damage the environmentally sensitive area. The government is keen to see appropriate development of reserves to offset the current spending of US$500 million on petroleum imports.

Society Government-led social investment between the 1950s and 1970s, has pushed Costa Rica to the top of regional league tables in terms of service provision. Education is free and compulsory up to the age of 15, with overall literacy rates of 95% against a Latin American average of 88%. There are three state universities which produce roughly 18,000 graduates each year, and several private universities. Health provision is also a high priority with the social security system providing effective health care to roughly 95% of the population. Infant mortality rates – at 13 deaths per thousand a year – are some of the lowest in the region, and life expectancy is 77 years, as opposed to a Latin American average of 70. Government spending on health fell to 22% of GDP in 1996 from highs of 32% in 1991. Access to improved water supplies has now reached 92% of the population, which is also a significant improvement compared with the regional average, although the extent of drinking water supplies is estimated to reach around three quarters of the population.

With the best education and social security system in the region, at current population growth rates of 2.9% a year, the provision of health and social security is seen as unsustainable. The welfare system is very important to the Costa Rican people. Government proposals to privatize some state-owned bodies were designed in part to fund necessary reforms. Limits on current financial spending combined with resistance against privatization mean reform is likely to be a long and difficult process.

Culture

Pinning down the culture of any nation is always difficult and runs the inherent risk of distilling traits and behaviours down to a single common denominator, taking the all-elusive 'normal' person as your guide. With an amiable tolerance to life, *Ticos* suffer more than many in this respect and risk being misjudged. And yet, to say that there is no culture in Costa Rica is bordering on the absurd. On the whole, what you find is all-encompassing and such an intrinsic part of life as to go almost unnoticed. (The universal reference to Costa Ricans as *Ticos*, for example, is almost second nature. The term is believed to derive from the Costa Rican tendency to use the diminutive in Spanish which places *ito* at the end of the noun.) Likewise, there are many low-key and highly localized indicators of culture.

The cultural foundations of Guanacaste to the northwest lie close to the land and the hardy existence of life on the ranch. The skills and style of the saddle-bound *sabanero* are still tried and tested at rodeos with ironically pacifist non-fatal bull fights. While the regional music – if such a thing exists – is the staccatoed percussion of the marimba, a xylophone-type instrument which despite being technically impressive, is rarely relaxing and almost intrusive as it struggles for harmony. Yet a short flight east to the Caribbean lands you in a world that could not be more different. The energy to work and control the land is replaced by the more compliant and accommodating laid-back rhythms of the Caribbean where calypso and reggae are washed down with a diet of coconut and rum.

And in the heart of the country, *Ticos* perched up in the capital and the central highlands move to the beat of urban life. Patriotism comes out on national holidays and special occasions, but take away the number plates, currency and people and you could almost be in any major city in the world.

People

The 2000 census put the national population at 3.82 million – having doubled since 1974, an annual increase of 2.8% – with the overwhelming majority (94%) considered to be white of mixed **Spanish** descent. The next largest single group is Afro-Caribbeans making up 3%, Amerindian 1%, Chinese 1% and 'others' the remaining 1%. Roughly one third of the population lives in the Greater San José metropolitan area and close to half of all *Ticos* live in the central highlands.

The **Afro-Caribbean** population is almost entirely concentrated on the Caribbean coast, in particular in Puerto Limón and the towns to the south. Originating in the Caribbean, most arrived from Jamaica to build the railroad and later found work on plantations. Likewise, the **Chinese** community can trace its Costa Rican roots to the period of railroad construction in the late 19th century.

Estimates for the number of **Nicaraguans** living in the country either as refugees or temporary economic migrants is as high as 400,000, or 10% of the population. Following Hurricane Mitch, the Costa Rican government announced a general amnesty to all illegal Central American immigrants living in the country. By June of 2000, 156,000 people had qualified for legal residency papers and 95% of them were Nicaraguan. The policy is intriguing and on the face of it a very generous one since most *Ticos* blame illegal Nicaraguans in Costa Rica for every affliction to beset the country, from theft and crime to extended periods of unseasonal rain. (The suspicion is mutual, and Nicaraguans believe that Costa Ricans have an elevated sense of self-importance and superiority.)

A significant but unquantifiable influence on the country is the large number of **'Western' expatriates** who have retired or emigrated to Costa Rica to work. Residency rules stipulate that retired persons need an income above US$600 a month and that business investment requires a minimum start-up capital of US$75,000. The

Background

transportation of ideas, lifestyles and standards of living has an obvious effect in tourist areas. Throughout the Pacific coast, enclaves of German, Italian, Swiss, Canadian and, the most popular, US communities have sprung up, bringing with them all the traits of home – good and bad – and a few new ones that have evolved locally.

The **indigenous population** has been in steady decline ever since the arrival of Europeans. Those that did not succumb to new diseases, being sold to work in other parts of Central America or being subject to forced labour, retreated to the highland areas of the south. Today there are eight recognized indigenous cultures or tribes: Huetar, Bribrí, Cabécar, Guaymí, Chorotega, Boruca, Guatuso and Térraba, with land protected in 22 reserves, covering 1,240 square miles – just over 6% of the national territory.

The indigenous population have five recognized languages. The northern Chorotega culture had great influence from Mesoamerican cultures and spoke the Nahuatl language of the Maya and Aztecs. The Boruca, Bribrí, Cabécar, Guaymí, Huetar and Guatuso spoke a language with its roots further to the south, which became more complex as the Arawak and Caribe cultures moved in to permanent settlements on the Caribbean coast adding their sounds.

The Bribrí and Cabécar are the only cultures that have been able to keep religious myths pure, outside of major influences from social and cultural changes, with the Sibú being the supreme god and creator of their world.

The *Comisión Nacional de Asuntos Indígenas* (CONAI – National Commission for Indigenous Affairs) is a government institution created in 1973 to uphold indigenous law. Indian affairs should have taken a turn for the better in 1977 when the

Indigenous reserves

1 Reserva Indígena Guatuso (Maleku)
2 Reserva Indígena Matambú
3 Reserva Indígena Quitirrisí
4 Reserva Indígena Zapatón
5 Reserva Indígena Nairi-Awari (Barbilla)
6 Reserva Indígena Chirripó
7 Reserva Indígena Bajo Chirripó
8 Guaymí/Península de Osa
9 Guaymí/Conte Burica
10 Guaymí/Coto Brus
11 Guaymí/Abrojos Montezuma

12 Reserva Indígena Curré
13 Reserva Indígena Boruca
14 Reserva Indígena Térraba
15 Reserva Indígena Ujarrás
16 Reserva Indígena Salitre
17 Reserva Indígena Cabagra
18 Reserva Indígena Taymí
19 Reserva Indígena Telire
20 Cabecar - Talamanca
21 Bribri Talamanca
22 Reserva Indígena Kekuldi (Cocles)

government created the system of Indian reserves, but the government retained the land titles. Consequently whenever an issue relating to land use has arisen, the government has the upper hand. Several hydroelectric projects on indigenous land are in a permanent state of reappraisal. In 1992 the Costa Rican government went one step further, signing the International Labour Organization which ratifies the constitutional rights of Costa Rican indigenous people. However, disenchantment is widespread. While the government provides education and health to many indigenous communities, the services are generally provided in Spanish by teachers from other cultures which automatically undermines the fabric of community life.

Indigenous communities are realizing that their best hope of retaining a sense of cultural identity is through fighting for their rights politically. The creation of organizations like *Aradikes* (see page 331), in the Buenos Aires area of the western Talamancas, fight for the rights of indigenous communities on several fronts, although it must be said that progress is limited and painfully slow.

It is possible to contribute to keeping the cultures alive with several indigenous groups still producing goods as they have for hundreds of years. In the north it is still possible to buy ceramics in the Chorotega style and Guatuso stonework. In the south you can buy the textiles of the Guaymi, and the *jicaro* engraved gourds of the Bribri.

Religion

It is said that around 90% of *Ticos* would judge themselves as **Roman Catholics**, and a small survey of taxi and bus drivers, hotel staff and chance encounters do little to change this perception. Certainly the churches are packed to bursting on Sundays.

A particular feature of the *Tico* Catholicism is the annual pilgrimage on August 2 to the Basílica de Nuestra Señora de Los Angeles in Cartago to see the revered image of the Virgin Mary. Around 600,000 pilgrims were estimated to have made the journey in August of 2001.

Moving away from the central highlands, the rise and rise of **evangelism** of varying denominations is apparent, with small churches often evident in quiet roadside communities.

Sport

Nothing reflects better the ability of Costa Ricans to adapt their interests to the moment than sport. **Claudia Poll** made Olympic aficionados of Costa Ricans overnight after winning the country's first gold medal in the pool at the Atlanta Olympics in 1996. Although she was unable to repeat the feat at Sydney 2000, she returned home with a couple of bronze medals won in the 200 m and 400 m freestyle and still had the streets lined with welcoming crowds.

Football, however, is the greatest passion, and many a *Tico* still get starry eyed thinking about Costa Rica's qualification to the final stages of the World Cup in 1990, and even more incredibly progressing to the second round taking Scottish and Swedish scalps on the way and making it to the last 16. For a country the size of Costa Rica, this was an impressive achievement which had the nation's football fans dancing in the streets.

More recently, the peregrinations of Paolo Wanchope in the English Premiership (currently dissatisfied at Manchester City and expected to move shortly) are followed with intense scrutiny on the sports pages of the Costa Rican press.

Arts

Those looking to find a country draped in colonial creative arts will leave Costa Rica disappointed. Lovers of contemporary expressionism, however, are quite spoilt for choice with the capital in particular being an outpouring of individualism, or an eclectic mess, depending on your point of view.

Painting and sculpture The first Costa Rican sculptures emerged in the 19th century and, using wood as their medium, mainly worked on religious themes. Francisco

Background

Zuñiga is the most well known artist in this field and achieved international fame after a period living in Mexico.

Painting blossomed from the 1930s and by the 1960s was taking influence from Western abstract painters. Reflecting the concerns of the left, most painters at the time were politically and socially conscious and some, including Manuel de la Cruz González, Loda Fernández and Juan Luis Rodríquez, achieved international recognition for their work.

More recently, the 1980s saw the creation of the Bocaraca school of *Tico* painting influenced by Francis Bacon and informal Catalan art. For a more detailed look at Costa Rican art, get a copy of *Historía Crítica del Arte Costarricense* by Carlos Francisco Echeverría (Editorial Universidad Estatal).

Literature   Literature in Costa Rica is still relatively young and lacks the struggles and challenges that inspired many Latin writers. Carlos Fallas has perhaps the most well known works in *Mamita Yunai* looking at life on the *United Fruit Company* banana plantations.

Contemporary writers include **José Leon Sánchez** and **Carlos Cortéz Fernando Contreras**, and poetry lovers should seek out **Jorge de Bravo**.

In Costa Rica, the *Librería Internacional in the Multiplaza* in Escazú has a section dedicated to Costa Rican writers. Internationally, *Costa Rica – A Traveler's Literary Companion* by Barbara Ras, is a good starting point.

Theatre & dance
For events and listings look in the Viva section of 'La Nación' on Thu or the 'Tico Times'

What Costa Rica lacks in literature it makes up for in a thriving theatrical and contemporary dance scene. The golden age of the theatre was the 1970s, when Chilean and Argentine playwrights lived and worked in Costa Rica to escape the right-wing regimes of the time. Their influence on professional and amateur groups in San José has helped them reach some of the highest levels in Central America, a tradition maintained by the requirement for local theatres to perform at least two plays a year written by local playwrights. Some of the best theatre productions are performed by the *Companía Nacional de Teatro*, but also keep a look out for smaller amateur productions which tackle every subject from classics to contemporary comedy.

For dance, see the *Companía Nacional de Danza*, who perform in the Museum of Contemporary Arts) and *Danza Universitaria* and *Danza Una* in the Universidad Nacional de Heredia.

Land and environment

Geography

The Republic of Costa Rica covers 51,100 sq km (19,730 sq miles), roughly half the size of the state of Kentucky in the United States, or one 10th the size of Spain. The country is part of the Central American isthmus ranging from 8° to 11° longitude north of the equator. The international boundary with Nicaragua to the north covers 309 km and is marked for much of the Caribbean slope by the southern bank of the Río San Juan which flows from Lake Nicaragua. To the south the boundary with Panama stretches for 330 km.

Geology   Geologically the region from southern Nicaragua to Colombia is the bridge between North and South America. The archipelago that stretched through the region was forced upwards by the subterranean forces of plate tectonics around 5 million years ago creating a land bridge between the north and south. These tremendous forces continue to effect the country, as the Cocos Plate to the west is forced against the

Caribbean Plate which holds the land mass of Costa Rica. Moving at different speeds and in different directions, tension builds to breaking point between the two plates, eventually shifting and creating earthquakes. Massive pressures can force land upwards as is the case with the Talamanca Mountains to the south of the country. Likewise, one block of land may be forced below another creating a subduction zone. Release of pressure causes earthquakes and the super-heated friction forces molten rock to the surface, most visible as volcanoes and in some areas producing mudpots and hot springs.

Tectonic events continue to effect the country, and low magnitude earthquakes are reasonably common, the vast majority having no damaging effects. Naturally, there are occasionally devastating exceptions. A large earthquake hit Cartago in 1910, leaving the church in ruins. It was the third and last time the city was destroyed by earthquakes and the church ruins stand more or less as they were left after the last tremors. To the north of Cartago, Irazú volcano erupted with such force in 1963 that it showered San José with volcanic ash. Later that decade Arenal volcano woke from its slumber to begin an active phase which continues today with devastating effect – in August 2000, two people were killed by an unexpected lava flow.

In April 1991, an earthquake measuring 7.5 on the Richter scale hit the Talamanca Mountains, resulted in 58 deaths and raised large sections of the Caribbean coastline by around 1.5 m.

In brief, the Costa Rican climate is tropical in the lowlands and temperate in the central highlands. Lowland temperatures drift around the mid-20s with slight seasonal variations taking the temperature higher in March and April. In the central highlands, day time temperatures are in the low 20s cooling off slightly in the evenings. The dry season runs from December to April, with slight variations on the Caribbean coast with a brief dry period in September and October. | **Climate**

In reality, the Costa Rican climate is a complex mosaic relating altitude, rainfall and local factors. Rainfall varies considerably throughout the country. Precipitation is heaviest close to Cerro de la Muerte and the newly formed Tapantí-Macizo de la Muerte National Park where rainfall can exceed 6 m annually. On the Pacific coast rainfall is heaviest around the Osa Peninsula to the south, while on the Caribbean the northern region around Barra del Colorado is the wettest point. Moving south from Barra del Colorado rainfall tails off down to around 2.5 m at Puerto de Viejo de Talamanca. On the Pacific moving north from the Osa Peninsula, the fall is even greater with northern parts of the Guanacaste province receiving just 1.5 m a year.

Variations in temperature are less complex with changes in temperature directly affected by altitude with a change of between 5°C and 6°C with every thousand metres' shift in altitude.

This complex relationship between rainfall and altitude (and consequently temperature) directly effects the plant and wildlife found in an area. In the late 1940s L.R. Holdridge developed a system of classification which divides regions into lifezones. Widely used by botanists, biologists, field workers and probably your guide, Costa Rica has 12 so-called lifezones, the most significant, in terms of area, being **tropical dry forest** (10.3%), **tropical moist forest** (24.2%), **tropical wet forest** (22.6%) and **tropical premontane wet forest** (13.6%) (see page 424).

The creation of a land bridge between North and South America also created a land barrier between the Caribbean and the Pacific. The **Talamanca mountain range** in the south of the country stretches from southwest of San José to beyond the border with Panama and incorporates the highest peaks in the country including **Cerro Chirripó** at 3,820 m where temperatures frequently fall to freezing point. Produced by the uplift of marine areas injected with localized volcanic events, the Talamanca | **The central mountains**

Background

range is geologically the oldest part of Costa Rica. The region varies fantastically, the higher altitudes home to the northernmost occurrence of Andean paramó above the treeline and with only scarce shrub cover.

A smaller coastal range – the **Fila Costeña** – runs parallel to the Talamancas separated by the El General and Coto Brus river systems, which merge to join the River Térraba.

To the east of San José, a line of volcanic peaks stretch northwest to the border with Nicaragua, incorporating three mountain chains: the **Cordillera Central**, **Cordillera de Tilarán** and finally the **Cordillera de Guanacaste**. Seven active volcanoes are found in the region including Arenal, one of the most active volcanoes in Central America.

The central highlands Nature didn't quite manage to join the mountain ranges, and the small gap between the Talamancas and the northern volcanic ranges creates a highland plateau. Detritus from volcanic eruptions and river run-off built up over millennia creating a broad fertile plain at an altitude ranging between 1,000 m and 1,500 m which happens to be perfect conditions for growing coffee. Once Europe warmed to tha taste of coffee in the early 19th century, the central highlands became the economic powerhouse and foundation for the development of Costa Rica. The republic's four main cities – San José, Alajuela, Heredia and Cartago – are all in the Central Valley and all owe their origins, in part, to coffee.

The Caribbean lowlands East of the continental divide – as the line dividing east from west is called – the Pacuare, Reventazón and Sarapiquí are three of many rivers that feed through the lowlands to the Caribbean. To the south, the Talamancas push almost to the coastline creating a thin coastal strip broken only by a few river valleys. To the north, the extensive lowland plains stretch further inland created by vast alluvial deposits from the many rivers flowing off the eastern slopes of the northern volcanic ranges. Naturally the area would be subject to extensive flooding but banana cultivation has led to controlled irrigation of the area.

Much of the Caribbean coast remains undeveloped, compared with the Pacific, with unspoilt areas being the stereotypical image of rainforest or in terms of Holdridge's lifezones, Tropical Moist Forest and to the north, Tropical Wet Forest.

The Pacific coastline The Pacific coastline is far more varied than the Caribbean, although removing the complications, it is possible to see a thin coastal plain running the length of the country. To the south the **Fila Costeña** runs parallel to the coastline broken only by the Río Térraba, which, having collected most of the rainfall on the western slopes of the Talamancas, flows out to the Pacific, close to Palmar through the Diquis Valley and the extensive mangroves around Sierpe. The rocky Osa Peninsula and Dulce Gulf are areas of high rainfall with tropical moist and premontane rainforest. To the south the **Coto Colorado Valley** is extensively farmed mainly with African Palm.

Moving north, rainfall drops rapidly with the Río Tárcoles marking the dividing line between wet forest to the south and dry forest to the north, produced by the rain shadow created by the northern volcanic ranges and strong seasonal trade winds from the Caribbean southeast. The **Tempisque basin** which feeds through the Gulf of Nicoya is the main drainage system of the area providing extensive wetlands for seasonal and resident birds.

The **Nicoya Peninsula** receives slightly more rain to the south, but essentially extends the climate of the dry forest across its rocky peninsula, although extensive farming and human interaction has considerably altered the region.

National parks

Costa Rica is promoted as a model of conservation with national parks protecting 11% of the country and just over one quarter of the national territory falling within a protected status category of some kind.

See map next page

The country has undergone a dramatic turn around within recent decades. From the 1940s to the 1970s the country had some of the highest rates of deforestation in the world, clearing at a rate that would have stripped the entire country by early in the 21st century. Fortunately the efforts of a dozen or so national and international individuals – among them such guiding lights as Mario Boza, Archie Carr, Leslie R Holdridge, Daniel Janzen and the Organization for Tropical Studies (OTS) – have been successful in highlighting the extraordinary nature of Costa Rica's flora and fauna. Coupled with some rather timely falls in commodity prices, the government moved away from state-sponsored land clearance for ranching and agriculture, favouring instead the creation of the national parks system.

The evolution of protected parks began in 1970 with the creation of the National Parks Service (SPN). The latest reorganization completed in 1995 divided the entire country into 11 regions creating a National System of Protected Areas (SINAC – Sistema Nacional de Areas de Conservación), which is administered as part of the Ministry for the Environment and Energy (MINAE – Ministerio del Ambiente y Energía).

In addition to national parks, the National System protects land within a range of categories including biological and forest reserves, wildlife refuges and a few smaller categories. The goals of the reorganization are to consolidate and guarantee the conservation of the protected areas and the national biodiversity and to control and manage their sustainable use. Many of the national parks have a combined purpose of protecting watersheds which feed the country's essential hydroelectric power system and protecting areas of particular biological interest.

Wildlife of Costa Rica

Costa Rica, considering its size, contains more species of plants and animals than any other country in the world. Indonesia holds the world record for the number of mammal species (515) in any one country, as Colombia, with 1,721 species, does for birds. However, these two countries are, respectively, around 37 and 22 times the size of Costa Rica, so you will have to travel a lot further in those countries to see the same number of animals than you will in tiny Costa Rica. With around 10,000 plant species, 870 bird species (600 or so residents), 205 species of mammals, 215 reptiles, 160 amphibians, 130 species of freshwater fish and some 360,000 insects, the country is home to between four to five per cent of the world's terrestrial species.

In comparison, the USA, about 183 times the size of Costa Rica, has a total of only 996 species of birds and mammals combined, while the UK (about 5 times the size of Costa Rica) has a mere 284 species of mammals, birds, reptiles and amphibians combined.

Costa Rica's amazing biodiversity is partly due to its geographical situation in the centre of the two huge continental masses, partly because it is a barrier between two oceans, and also due to its wide variety of landscapes, including mountains, valleys, coastal plains and prairies. In addition, though wholly within the tropics, Costa Rica has a climatic diversity.

Much of the country's wildlife remains only in the small, but numerous, national parks and reserves which protect over 25% of the country. Elsewhere, most of the forest, home to the majority of the animals, has been cut down, replaced by agricultural land.

Background

A brief description of the major forest habitats in the country and some of the more striking plants the visitors may see will help with a broader understanding of the ecology of the country.

Habitats

Of the many different systems used for the ecological classification of Costa Rica's vegetation, the most widely used is the system of 'Life Zones' devised mainly by L.R. Holdridge, based on a complex inter-relationship between rainfall, temperature and altitude. Under this system, Costa Rica's forests are divided into **tropical lowland**,

National parks

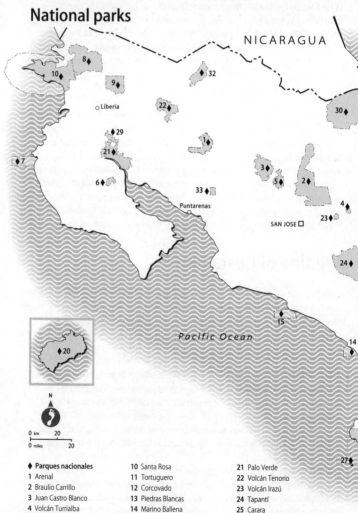

♦ **Parques nacionales**	10 Santa Rosa	21 Palo Verde
1 Arenal	11 Tortuguero	22 Volcán Tenorio
2 Braulio Carrillo	12 Corcovado	23 Volcán Irazú
3 Juan Castro Blanco	13 Piedras Blancas	24 Volcán Turrialba
4 Volcán Turrialba	14 Marino Ballena	25 Carara
5 Volcán Poas	15 Manuel Antonio	26 Gandoca – Manzanillo
6 Barra Honda	16 Cahuita	
7 Marino Las Baulas de	17 Chirripó	♦ **Reservas biológicas**
Guanacaste	18 Internacional la Amistad	27 Isla del Caño
8 Guanacaste	19 Barbilla	28 Hitoy Cerere
9 Rincón de la Vieja	20 Isla del Coco	29 Lomas de Barbudal

tropical **premontane**, **lower montane** and **tropical montane**, with each category subdivided into moist, wet and rain forest types; also included are the dry forests and mangroves. The forest habitats described below have been much simplified and do not follow Holdridge's system.

The lowland wet forests in Costa Rica, found in the northern and southern Caribbean lowlands and in the southern Pacific lowlands, are the classical tropical forests. Tall, semi-deciduous and evergreen trees reach to a height of 40-55 m and even taller, emergent evergreen trees soar above this canopy. A sub-canopy of lower trees is often present, while the ground may be bare or have a sparse shrub layer. While walking through the forest, one of the most commonly seen plants in the understorey and shrub layer are members of the genus **piper**. There are over 90 species in this genus within Costa Rica. All are small trees or shrubs characterized by their erect, candle-like flowering structures, which are generally pollinated by bats. Buttress and stilt roots are common features in these forests. Buttress roots appear as broad ridges attached to the side of a tree trunk and acting as support for the tree, to account for the minimal sub-surface root system. Stilt roots come off the side of a tree trunk, growing down and entering the earth some distance from the trunk to anchor the tree more firmly in the soil.

Palms are common in this type of forest and one species you may well see is *Welfia georgii*, which bears its fruit on its trunk. **Vines** are also numerous; quite common is the passion flower (*Passiflora foetida*), with bright red flowers, and the Swiss Cheese plant (*Monstera deliciosa*), a large-leafed climber in these wet forests and commonly seen as a house plant in European and North American homes. **Epiphytes**, plants that grow on other plants, are frequent in the lowland wet forests and large trees such as the **kapok** (*Ceiba pentandra*) are often heavily laden with them. This tree is massive, often emerging above the surrounding canopy, with a broad, flat crown and a seed that produces a fibrous material often used to stuff cushions and furniture. Epiphytes include mosses, ferns, orchids and bromeliads. The **orchids**, with over 1000 species in Costa Rica, can be spectacular when in flower – indeed Costa Rica's national flower is an orchid, the

♦ **Refugios nacionales de vida silvestre**
30 Barra del Colorado
31 Golfito
32 Caño Negro
33 Peñas Blancas

Lowland wet forests

Lowland wet forest is found in the northern and southern Caribbean lowlands and in the southern Pacific lowlands

Protected areas containing this forest include La Selva Biological Reserve, Cahuita National Park, Manuel Antonio National Park and Corcovado National Park

Background

guaria morada (*Cattleya skinneri*). **Bromeliads** typically have fleshy, often spiky leaves formed into a rosette with a central 'well' that holds water, which is often used as a small pond by a host of animals including snails, worms, insects and even frog tadpoles and adults.

The driving force for change in the lowland wet forest is forest gaps. Clearings created by a tree fall produce a sudden availability of light and various plant species rush to colonize the area, before being gradually replaced by more mature, slower growing species. Within the lowland forest, pioneer species such as the **balsa tree** (*Ochroma lagopus*), grow rapidly in these gaps to reach a height of 30 m. Its light, soft wood is used for making many of the wooden souvenirs available to tourists in Costa Rica. *Cercropia obtusifolia* is another pioneer species, frequently found in lowland forests. Thriving on the light of forest gaps, it has large, umbrella-like leaves, which are a favourite food of sloths. Also found in disturbed areas of the forest, in clearings and along streams are species of ***Heliconia*** which have large leaves resembling those on banana trees and striking red, orange and yellow flowers, shaped rather like lobster claws, pollinated by humming birds.

Lowland dry forest

Protected areas in this region include Palo Verde National Park, Lomas Barbudal Wildlife Reserve and Santa Rosa National Park

This type of forest once covered extensive areas of Costa Rica's northern Pacific coastal plain, but most has now been cleared for agriculture. The rainy season in this region is only six months in length (May to October). By comparison, rain falls year round in the Caribbean lowlands hence the difference in forest type. The dry forest is semi-deciduous, with a canopy at 20-30 m, an understorey of trees 10-20 m tall and a 2-5 m high, dense shrub layer. **Vines** are present, but epiphytes are generally rare. Common or conspicuous plants include the **gumbo limbo tree** (*Bursera simaruba*), which is recognizable by its smooth, red/orange bark. The ***crescentia alata***, a fairly common large, shrub-like tree, has conspicuous hard fruits or gourds growing from its trunk which are eaten by rodents and also used for decoration. **Corteza** trees, in the genus *tabebuia*, are commonly seen but stand out most when in flower as all members of a species flower simultaneously towards the end of the dry season, though for only four days, so you'll have to be lucky to catch them. The flowers are either yellow or pink. **Palms** are not as frequent in the dry forests as they are in the wetland forest, but one palm, *Acrocomia vinifera*, is fairly common; it has long, sharp spines on its lower trunk and occurs particularly in swampy areas and along roads.

Wildlife is often easier to see in these more open, less dense forests than in the thicker, wetter forests, though biodiversity is lower.

Premontane & montane forest

Protected areas with this vegetation include Irazú and Arenal Volcano National Parks, Braulio Carrillo National Park, La Amistad National Park, Monteverde Cloud Forest Reserve, Rincón de la Vieja National Park and the Wilson Botanical Gardens

In the forests at higher elevations, the hot stickiness of the lowland forest areas is replaced by a cooler dampness. The cooler climate is due to the temperature dropping, on average, by 0.4-0.7°C for every 100 m gained in altitude. Mists of cloud or fog enshroud the forest canopy for much of the time, hence the evocative name 'cloud forest' which is often applied to these forests. Light levels tend to be reduced at higher elevations and the foliage drips with water that condenses out of the atmosphere. These forests are less diverse than those in the lowlands, but they are often home to endemic species – ones that are found nowhere else in the world.

These forests occur on the slopes and upper areas of Costa Rica's mountains. In the lower areas the cloud forest is mixed deciduous and evergreen, while at higher elevations it is uniformly evergreen. There are frequent strong winds in the higher forests so the tops of the trees become more even and flat compared to those in the lowland forests. In addition, the trees tend to become gnarled, twisted and multi-stemmed and the leaves are much smaller, narrower and leathery. Canopy height at lower levels is around 30-40 m, declining as elevation increases. There is usually a subcanopy and dense undergrowth. **Vines** and **epiphytes** grow profusely, especially in the evergreen cloud forests; indeed **lichens** can be hanging in curtains from many of the trees. Though also found at lower elevations, **tree ferns** are especially common in the higher forests. Quite a number of the trees and shrubs found at these higher elevations are ones from genera that may be found in temperate regions such as **oaks** (*Quercus*), **buddleia** (*Buddleja*) and **magnolia** (*Magnolia*). Also found in these high forests is the **Winter's bark** (*Drimys winteri*). Growing to about 15 m in height, it has aromatic bark, large, leathery oval yellow-green leaves with a waxy white underneath and clusters of fragrant, small, white flowers and dark purple berries. So attractive is it, that it has been introduced as a garden plant to temperate gardens.

This treeless, subalpine habitat predominates at the highest elevations in Costa Rica. Only grasses and shrubs are found in these areas. Chirripó National Park contains some areas of páramo. **Páramo**

Terrestrial mammals

Costa Rica has only four of the 70 or so species of monkey that are present in the New World. The three larger ones are quite common in many protected areas, while the squirrel monkey is found in only a few lowland wet forests of the southern Pacific slope of the country. **Red-backed squirrel monkeys** (mono tití, *Saimiri oerstedii*) are small (0.6 – 0.9 kg) monkeys, with a golden orange back, hands and feet, a black crown and muzzle and a white mask. Moving in groups of 10 – 20 individuals, they run and jump through the trees feeding on fruits, seeds, leaves and insects. The groups contain several adult females and males, with juveniles and infants. The birth season is in July and the young remain on their mother's back for the first month of their life; after that they spend an increasing numbers of hours away, exploring and playing, until they are finally weaned at 11 months. This species is only found in Panama and Costa Rica and is considered to be in danger of extinction. **White-faced capuchin monkeys** (mono carablanca, *Cebus capucinus*), are medium-sized monkeys weighing between 2.5 – 4 kg. They have a white throat, head and shoulders, while their back and prehensile tail are black. They forage over all levels of wet forests, including mangroves, and may even be seen on the ground. Their diet is mostly fruit, but also includes leaves, nuts, flowers, insects, small birds, reptiles and young mammals. Group size is around 10 – 20, consisting of several males and females, usually more of the latter. These monkeys are probably the most commonly seen in Costa Rica as they occur in dry and wet forests and are active and noisy throughout most of the day. Their threat display includes jumping up and down and shaking branches, which makes them quite difficult to miss! **Geoffroy's spider monkeys** (mono colorado, mono araña, *Ateles geoffroyi*) are definitely the most elegant of Costa Rica's primates. They weigh between 6 – 9 kg and their coat colour varies from light buff to black, usually with black hands and feet. They use their prehensile tail as a fifth limb, swinging, climbing and hanging mostly in the upper canopy of the forest, preferring the wet, evergreen forests to the dry forests. They eat mainly fruit, though include seeds, flowers, leaves and insects in their diet. There are usually around twice as many females as males in a group, though the number of monkeys moving together is very variable (4 – 35) as the troops tends to divide into small foraging parties, especially if food is scarce. Spider monkeys are active during the day, though, like many monkeys, they tend to be less active at midday when temperatures are highest. **Mantled howler monkeys** (mono congo, *Alouatta palliata*) are black except for a fringe of long, gold to buff hairs on their sides. Adult body weight is variable, from 3 to almost 10 kg, males are heavier than females. Even if not seen, these monkeys will certainly be heard by anyone visiting, in particular, the lowland evergreen forests or the dry forests, though they are also present in montane forests. **Primates**

Background

The males, in particular, give loud roaring vocalizations, most frequently at dawn and in the late afternoon, that can easily be heard 3 km or more away. Howlers move relatively slowly and deliberately high in the forest and may well be passed by unnoticed, especially as over 70% of the day can be spent resting. Leaves are the main component of their diet, though flowers and fruits are also taken. Group size is usually 10 – 20, made up of several adult males and females and offspring.

Opossums There are nine species of these marsupials in Costa Rica, occupying all habitats except high mountain areas. Most likely to be seen is the **common possum** (zorro pelón or zarigüeya, *Didelphis marsupialis*), which resembles a large rat, around 42 cm long, with yellowish face, blackish or grey-black body, black ears and a long, hairless, prehensile tail. They are mostly nocturnal, but can be seen active during the day, usually foraging on the ground for fruits, eggs, invertebrates and small vertebrates, though they are also good climbers. They frequent human habitations, foraging in rubbish dumps and eating fruit crops. The smaller **gray four-eyed opossum** (zorro de cuatro ojos, *Philander opossum*) is found in rainforest regions; it has a black face mask with large white spots over its eyes. The **water opossum** (zorro de aqua, *Chironectes minimus*) is also seen quite commonly, often by or in water. This species has a grey body with broad black/brown stripes.

Anteaters Costa Rica has three species of anteater. The most commonly seen is the **northern tamandua** (oso hormiguero or tamandua, *Tamandua mexicana*) which has a brown or yellowish head and legs with a black vest on its belly and back. Its body is 45-75 cm long with a prehensile tail of the same length. It can be found in trees and on the ground in wet and dry forests and in savanna habitats, feeding mainly on termites and mostly at night. The **giant anteater** (oso homiguero gigante, *Myrmecophaga tridactyla*), up to 2.1 m in length (including the tail) and weighing as much as 39 kg, is extremely rare, while the tiny **silky anteater** (serafin de platanar, *Cyclopes didactylus*) standing just 17 cm tall is arboreal, nocturnal and unlikely to be seen.

Armadillos Costa Rica has two of the world's 20 species of armadillos. The more common species is the **nine-banded armadillo** (Armadillo de nueve bandas, *Dasypus novemcinctus*). It has a grey to yellowish, armour-plated body, a long snout, large ears and scales on its head and legs. Around 60 cm in length with a long ringed tail, it is found on the ground in all but the most arid habitats. Its diet is also extremely variable, including insects and small vertebrates, fruit, fungi, tubers and even carrion. It digs to obtain food, to make burrows and to escape predators so it is common to see signs of its presence, even if the armadillo itself is not seen (it and Costa Rica's other species, the **naked-tailed armadillo** (*Cabassous sp*), are nocturnal). Uniquely among mammals, the nine-banded, and some other, armadillos regularly give birth to four genetically identical offspring.

Sloths Costa Rica has two of these strange, slow-moving, upside down creatures:
A visit to Los Avarios del Caribe, a sloth rescue centre close to Cahuita, is a good place to see sloths if you do not see one in the wild
Hoffman's two-toed sloth (perezoso de dos dedos, *Choloepus hoffmanni*) and the **brown-throated three-toed-sloth** (perezoso de tres dedos, perico ligero, cúcula, *Bradypus variegates*). The former is generally a tan colour and has no tail, while the latter is greyish brown with a distinctive grey and white mask and a small, stumpy tail. In moist conditions, the coats of both species may be suffused with green, the colour coming from the blue-green algae that live on their fur and help camouflage them in the trees. Both have three curved claws, or 'toes', on their hind feet, while it is the claws on the forefeet that give them their common names. The three-toed sloth is active both day and night and may move through four or five trees in two days, whereas the two-toed is nocturnal and is often in the same tree for two

consecutive nights. Both species eat only leaves and it may take a month for a full meal to be completely digested. As a result, they need to defecate only once a week and descend to the base of a tree to do so. Young are born throughout the year and are carried by their mother for six to nine months, so its worth looking for an extra, smaller head when you see an adult animal!

All six species of the cat family in Costa Rica are both nocturnal and rare, which makes it unlikely that they will be seen. The smallest, spotted species is the **oncilla** (tigrillo, *Felis tigrinus*), which is the size of a small domestic cat; next in size is the **margay** (caucel, *F. wiedi*) weighing 4 – 9 kg, followed by the medium dog-sized **ocelot** (manigordo, *F. pardalis*) at 11 – 16 kg, and then the large **jaguar** (tigre or jaguar, *Panthera onca*) weighing 57 – 113 kg. The two unspotted cats are the smaller **jaguarundi** (león breñero, *F. yagouaroundi*) at 5.5 – 10 kg, and the **puma** (león montés, *F. concolor*), which is almost the same size as a jaguar. All species are found in forest, though some also occur in scrubland and even savanna. The diet of the smallest, the oncilla, includes large insects, frogs, birds, lizards and small mammals, while even the largest, the jaguar, is not averse to small prey such as fish and frogs, it also takes deer, tapirs, monkeys and peccaries. Most climb trees as well as hunting on the ground and both the jaguar and ocelot are also excellent swimmers. Nocturnal activity is most common though some, for instance the jaguar and jaguarundi, may also be active during the day. Walking at night along trails cleared in the forest will give you the best chance of seeing one of these cats. Wear a headlamp, rather than carrying a torch, as then their eyeshine is reflected back to your eyes and even a brief glimpse of a cat's glowing eyes is exciting.

Cats (*Felids*)
Difficult to spot in the wild, Las Pumas wildlife rescue centre in Guanacaste province north of Cañas, and Profelis, close to Dominical, provide an opportunity to see pumas

The **coyote** (coyote, *Canis latrans*) and the **gray fox** (zorro gris, *Urocyon cinereoargenteus*) are Costa Rica's two species from the dog family. The coat colour of the former, the larger species, varies from grizzled grey to brownish yellow, while that of the latter is silver grey with tawny legs, feet and ears. Both are active during the day and night and both are found in forest or, more commonly, open areas of the northern Pacific lowlands. Both species tend to eat whatever is available, from fruit and insects to small mammals or even deer, in the case of the coyote. The howl of the coyote, consisting of high-pitched staccato yelps followed by a long siren wail, is quite likely to be heard.

Dogs (*Canids*)

Of the six species of raccoon found in Costa Rica; the **white-nosed coati** (pizote, *Nasua narica*) is most likely to be seen; also quite common are the **northern raccoon** (mapache norteño, *Procyon loctor*) and the **kinkajou** (martilla, *Potus flavus*). The **crab-eating raccoon** (mapache cangrejo, *Procyon cancrivorous*), the **olingo**, (olingo, *Bassaricyon gabbi*) and the **cacomistle** (cacomistle, *Bassariscus sumichrasti*) are also present in the country. All but the coati are nocturnal and all are omnivorous, foraging in trees and, in the case of the raccoons and coatis, also on the ground. Generally, these species have pointed muzzles, short legs and long tails. The northern and crab-eating raccoons have a striped tail and a distinctive, black face-mask, the overall coat colour of the former is grizzled grey, while that of the latter is brown. The northern raccoon is more widespread in Costa Rica, the crab-eater being confined to the Pacific lowlands. Both are most commonly seen near water, indeed the latter is considered semi-aquatic. Unlike the other species, coatis are very sociable with the females and their offspring living in groups; the adult males, though, are solitary. Coat colour is grey or brown and they have a long, ringed tail that is often held erect above the body and a highly mobile, upturned and elongated snout. Infants in these species are small and poorly developed when born and they spend their first five or six weeks in a nest built by their mother in a tree. The kinkajou

Raccoons (*Procyonids*)

Background

is the only species uniform in colour (greyish or reddish brown) and without a ringed tail, it also has a shorter muzzle than the others and is decidedly more cute looking! Its tail is prehensile and it has a long tongue used for probing nectar from flowers and obtaining honey from bees' nests. The olingo is similar in habit and appearance, but is smaller with indistinct rings on its bushier (non-prehensile) tail and faint grey markings on its more pointed face, it is also more rare. The cacomistle is found in drier forests, is has a fox-like face, larger ears than the other species in this group and a bushy, ringed tail.

Weasels (Mustelids) There are three species of skunk in Costa Rica, all more likely to be smelled than seen. The **striped hog-nosed skunk** (zorro hediondo raya, *Conepatus semistriatus*) is found countrywide, in forests but more often in cleared areas including gardens and agricultural land, so it is the most liable to be seen. It is black, with a wide white stripe on its head and along its back and it has a large white, bushy tail. It has a bare, elongated snout - hence its name. The **spotted skunk** (zorro hediondo encamanchado, *Spilogale putorius*), and the **hooded skunk** (zorro hediondo encapuchado, *Mephitis macroura*) are much less common. All three skunks are nocturnal and forage on the ground for insects and small mammals, though they also eat fruit, birds' eggs and the like. The smallest species, the spotted skunk (0.5 kg), readily climbs trees. The **tayra** (tolumuco, *Eira barbara*) is a long, slender animal that resembles a mink, it has black or brown body with a tan head and neck and a yellowish patch on its chest. At 4 – 6 kg, it is a lot heavier than any of the skunks. Tayras are often seen in pairs, foraging in trees and on the ground during the day and night for birds, small mammals and fruit. Other species found in Costa Rica are the **grison** (grisón, *Galictis vittata*), which has a smoky grey back and tail, with black legs, underparts and face and a white stripe across its forehead; the **long-tailed weasel** (comadreja, *Mustela frenata*), which resembles the European weasel; and the **Neotropical otter** (nutria neotropical, *Lutra longicaudis*). All three are active both day and night.

Peccaries The **collared peccary** (saíno, *Tayassu tajacu*) and the **white-lipped peccary** (chancho de monte, cariblanco, *T. pecari*) both travel in groups, of up to 50 individuals in the case of the collared peccary and 100 or more for the white-lipped. The groups tend to divide into smaller family groups of adult males, females and their offspring. They are rather pig-like, in both activity and appearance. With a diet of mostly roots, seeds and fruit, signs of their rooting activities can often be found, as can their dung piles, which are used as territory markers, and their mud wallows. The collared peccary weighs about 17 – 30 kg and is black or grey with a band of lighter coloured hair around its neck. It is the more widespread species, occurring in all forest types at low and mid elevations, in shrublands and agricultural areas and it is active mainly during the day. The white-lipped peccary, weighing 25 – 40 kg, occurs only in forests and is active day and night.

Deer The **white-tailed** (venado cola blanca, *Odocoileus virginianus*) is the largest of the two species of deer found in Costa Rica, standing 1 m high at the shoulder, and is seen more commonly. It is a light-, dark-, or greyish-brown deer, with a white belly, white under the tail and often has a white throat. Males over a year old have branched antlers, which are shed and regrown each year. The smaller **red brocket deer** (cabro de monte, *Mazama americana*) is reddish brown, with white under the tail and the males have small, straight antlers. The white-tailed occurs in more open drier forests and on forest edges, while the brocket deer tends to be in thicker, wet forests, both are active day and night. The deer graze on grass and browse on leaves and twigs from trees and shrubs, with the brocket deer also taking fruit and flowers. Brocket deer live singly or in very small groups, while the white-tailed deer are in larger, usually single-sex, groups. When alarmed, both species flee with their tail raised, displaying its white underside. This is the most frequent sighting of the deer - a disappearing rump!

Tapirs

Baird's tapir (danta, *Tapirus bairdii*) is the only tapir occurring in Costa Rica. It is a large, stocky mammal, weighing 200 kg or more. Its coat is sparsely furred with reddish brown hair and it has a short, bristly mane extending along the back of its neck. The tapir has a short, fleshy trunk, derived from the nose and upper lip, which is used to pull leaves and shoots into its mouth. Its sense of smell is excellent, its hearing is good but its vision is not. It is found in wet forests and swampy areas, where it is active mostly at night, feeding on leaves, twigs, fruit and grass. The most likely clue to its presence is its characteristic three-toed track, but tapirs are uncommon and rarely seen in the country.

Rodents

There are 50 or so rodent species in Costa Rica, including mice, rats, pocket gophers, squirrels and others such as the **Mexican hairy porcupine** (puercoespin, cuerpoespin, *Coendou mexicanus*), **paca** (tepezcuintle, *Agouti paca*) and **agouti**, (guatusa, *Dasyprocta punctata*). The agouti, a reddish brown creature which looks rather like a large, long-legged guinea pig, is quite likely to be seen moving on the forest floor during the day searching, in particular, for fallen fruit and also seeds and flowers. They may become nocturnal in areas where they are hunted. The paca is quite similar in shape, but, at around 10 kg in weight, is twice the size of an agouti with white spots on its body. It too feeds on fruit, seeds, nuts and other vegetation but is nocturnal. Mexican hairy porcupines spend most if their time in trees, using their prehensile tails to help them climb and hang on to branches, though they do come to the ground occasionally to feed and to move from tree to tree. They are nocturnal, spending the day on a branch or in a hollow tree. Their diet consists mainly of leaves but also includes fruits, seeds, roots insects and small vertebrates.

Of Costa Rica's five squirrel species, the **red-tailed squirrel** (ardilla roja, *Sciurus granatensis*) and the **variegated squirrel** (chiza, *S. variegatoides*) are the ones most likely to be seen. The former tends to be in wet forests, while the latter is found on forest edges, in drier forests and more open areas including close to human habitations. Both are diurnal, actively foraging for fruits, nuts, insects, leaves and flowers in the trees.

Rabbits

Two or three species are present in the country, including the **eastern cottontail** (conejo cola de algodón, *Sylvilagus floridensis*) and the **forest rabbit** (conejo de bosque, *S. brasiliensis*). The former is found on the forest edge and in more open areas, while, as expected from its name, the latter lives inside forests.

Bats

With over 100 species in the country and all just glimpsed as they swoop past at night, it is very difficult, if not impossible for the casual visitor to identify the species seen. The smallest bat in Costa Rica, the **black myotis** (murciélago pardo, *Myotis nigricans*), weighs just 5 g, with a wingspan of 5 cm, while the largest, the **false vampire bat** (vampiro falso, *Vampyrum spectrum*), weighs 200 g with a 80 cm wingspan. Food items include pollen, nectar, fruit, insects, small vertebrates (including fish, frogs, birds, rodents or other bats) and blood, different species specializing on different items. Daytime roosting sites include hollow trees, caves, tree branches, rock crevices, under bridges and in buildings. The **sucker-footed bat** (murciélago de ventosas, *Thyroptera tricolor*) most commonly roosts in small family groups in rolled up banana or *Heliconia* leaves; unlike most species, they rest head upwards.

Birds

Though the mammals in Costa Rica might be elusive, you can guarantee that you will see birds, and lots of them. They'll vary from all those little brown jobs (LBJs for short) to comparatively massive, colourful macaws and toucans. For anyone with more than a superficial interest, a good bird book is a must as this guide can only touch on a few of the more outstanding or conspicuous species.

Sea & shorebirds Very obvious by the sea is the **magnificent frigatebird** (rabihorcado magno, *Fregata magnificens*), a large (2 m wingspan), soaring, black bird with pointed wings and forked tail. Males have red throat pouches that they inflate during courtship displays. Seeing these frigatebirds stealing fish and nesting material from other seabirds and eating cute young sea-turtles, which have just hatched and are making a dash for the relative safety of the sea, makes you realize that their habits do not live up to their elegant appearance. The **brown pelican** (pelicano moreno, P*elecanus occidentalis*) are much sturdier birds, easily recogniszable by their big throat pouches, which they use as a net to scoop up fish underwater. Though somewhat ungainly looking when on the ground, a group of them flying in formation slowly and silently low over the water or beach is an impressive sight. Less impressive are the many species of shorebirds – plovers, sandpipers, etc, that can be seen scuttling along the beaches. Though not necessarily small, they still tend to be classified as LBJs, of real interest only to ardent birdwatchers!

Waterbirds, herons & egrets Also seen by the sea, as well as in freshwater areas, are anhingas and cormorants – quite similar looking birds, very often seen standing with their wings spread out to dry in the sun. The **olivaceous cormorant** (pato chancho, *Phalacrocorax brasilianus*) is a black/brown bird with a wingspan of 1 m, a longish tail and a long bill ending in a down-curve. The **anhinga** (pato aguja, *Anhinga anhinga*) has a longer neck and a long, pointed bill without a hook; the female has a brown neck. Many other birds, including storks, ibis, herons, egrets and spoonbills can be seen in aquatic habitats. Perhaps most desirable to spot is the **roseate spoonbill** (espátula rosada, *Ajaia ajaja*), a large, pink wading bird with a white neck and distinctive spoon-shaped beak that it opens and swings about underwater, snapping it shut when until it feels a frog, fish or other such prey. Also very distinctive is the **jabiru stork** (galán sin ventura, *Jabiru mycteria*), a very large, white wading bird standing 1.4 m high, with a black bill, a huge black beak and a red area at the base of its neck.

Cattle egrets (garcilla bueyera, *Bubulcu ibis*) precede any river safari through open savanna, taking to the air in flocks in a blaze of feathers, only to roost. The **bare-throated tiger-heron** (garza-tigre, *Tigrisoma mexicanum*) is a far more impressive bird standing 80 cm tall. The juvenile has tiger-like stripes that blend perfectly against the alternating shade and sunlight, which eventually grow out at adulthood.

Marsh & stream birds Included among Costa Rica's marsh and stream birds are such species as the jacana, several rails, crakes, coots and gallinules and the sunbittern. The **northern jacana** (gallina de agua, *Jacana spinosa*) is seen in marshes, wet pastures and on ponds, often walking on top of lily pads or other floating vegetation, its incredibly long toes spreading its weight and preventing it from sinking into the water. It feeds on insects, snails, frogs, fish and some vegetable matter. The adult has a black head, neck and chest with bright brown wings, belly and back and a yellow beak, forehead and unmistakable yellow under its wings. More colourful is the **purple gallinule** (gallareta morada, *Porphryula martinica*) with its bluish, violet head neck and chest, green wings, red and yellow beak, light blue forehead and yellow legs. It too is found in marshes and around lakeshores.

Costa Rica's 15 or so species of ducks includes the **Muscovy** (pato real, *Cairina moschata*), mentioned here as you may well have seen its domesticated form in a farm in your own country. The wild bird is mostly greenish-back, with white patches on its wings and the male has a feathered crest and red warts on his face and beak. It is no longer very common due to hunting pressure and habitat destruction.

Ducks

Not beautiful, but conspicuous and commonly seen are Costa Rica's vultures. There are four species in the country. The more sociable **black vulture** (zopilote negro, *Coragyps atratus*) and **turkey vulture** (zopilote cabecirrojo, *Cathartes aura*) are a frequent sight round towns and villages, both are large black birds, the former with a bare, red head and neck and the latter with a featherless, black head and neck. Larger than either of these, with a wingspan of 2 m, is the **king vulture** (zopilote rey, *Sarcoramphus papa*), which is white with black wings and tail and has a featherless, black orange and yellow head. It usually hunts over forest and wooded areas. Least common and smallest is the **lesser yellow-headed vulture** (zopilote cabecigualdo, *Cathartes burrovianus*). All are carrion eaters, though the king and black vulture do sometimes take live prey.

Vultures

Also known as birds of prey, raptors mostly hunt living animals, usually other vertebrates. They include birds such as hawks, kites, eagles, falcons and caracaras; there are about 50 species of them in Costa Rica. Though often quite difficult to identify as they soar far overhead above all types of habitats, some more conspicuous ones can be picked out. The **osprey** (aquila pescadora, *Pandion haliaetus*) is unusual in that is feeds on fish, grabbing them with its sharp claws from fresh or saltwater. White below and brown above, it is found more or less worldwide. The American **swallow-tailed hawk** (elanio tijereta, *Elanoides forficatus*) can be distinguished from other raptors by its deeply forked, long black tail. It feeds on the wing, grabbing flying insects and snatching small prey such as lizards from trees. The **harpy eagle** (aguila arpía, *Harpia harpyja*) used to be widespread in Costa Rica, but is now very rare – possibly extinct. It is a large, spectacular bird standing around 1 m tall that can grab small monkeys and other mammals from the tree tops as it flies above them. The **crested caracara** (caracara cargahuesos, *Polyborus plancus*) is a large (wingspan to 1.3 m) black bird, with a barred black and white neck, a black, white and red head and yellow legs that is found over open areas and quite commonly seen in groups eating carrion, along with turkey or black vultures.

Raptors

You might be lucky and see one of Costa Rica's 15 species of owl during the day, especially if a local guide knows a roosting site that a particular owl regularly uses, but, as they are mostly nocturnal hunters, you are more likely to just hear them. However, both the **spectacled owl** (buho de anteojos, *Pulsatrix perspicillata*) and the **ferruginous pygmy owl** (mochuelo común, *Glaucidium brasilianum*) can sometimes be seen hunting in the day or at dusk. The former is a large owl, 46 cm high, with a dark brown head and back with a lighter chest and, as indicated by its name, white 'spectacles' and white on its throat. It is found in forest and in more open areas. The pygmy owl is just 16 cm high, commonly hunting during the day, it is a reddish or greyish brown owl with white streaks on its front.

Owls

Nine species of these nocturnal birds are found in Costa Rica, the most common is the **pauraque** (tapacaminos común, *Nyctidromus albicollis*). They inhabit open areas such as farm- and parkland, thickets and forest edges but are most commonly seen as they fly up directly in front of one's car, their eyes flashing a bright red in the headlights. Indeed, their Spanish name means 'common road blocker'. Their mottled brown, black and white colour is an excellent camouflage, ensuring that they are

Goatsuckers or nightjars

Background

almost impossible to spot roosting (on the ground or along tree branches) during the day. The **common potoo** (nictibio común, *Nyctibius griseus*), unlike most other nightjars, adopts a vertical roosting posture, often perching during the day in the open on a dead tree stump, looking very much like an extension of the stump.

Swifts & swallows There are 12 species of swallow and 11 swifts in Costa Rica. Though not closely related groups, they do superficially resemble each other being slender streamlined birds seen swooping through the air catching insects while on the wing. This group will be familiar to most visitors, indeed the **barn swallow** (golondrina tijereta, *Hirundo rustica*) is a common species more or less worldwide.

Hummingbirds Hummingbirds are wonderful little creatures that are a delight to watch and Costa Rica has over 50 species of them. Though easy to recognize as a group, they are actually quite difficult to identify as they dart past at high speed or hover briefly at a flower extracting its nectar. So tiny are some of the species, mostly weighing between 3-6 g, that they can become entangled in spiders' webs or be eaten by praying mantises and frogs. The major part of their diet is nectar, but they also feed on insects to obtain protein. The largest hummingbird in Costa Rica is the **violet sabrewing** (ala de sable violáceo *Campylopterus hemileucurus*), which is 15 cm in length with a down curved bill and white patches at the end of its tail. The male has a violet head and front with a dark green back and wings, while the female has a violet throat but a grey front. Although the **long-tailed hermit** (ermitaño colilargo, *Phaethornis superciliosus*) also measures 15 cm in length, much of this is, indeed, its tail. It is a greenish brown hummingbird, with a long white tipped tail, a down-curved bill, black and light coloured eye stripes and a light brown front that is found in forests and on forest edges. Most 'hummers', including the **crowned woodnymph** (ninfa violeta y verde, *Thalurania colombica*), are less than 10 cm long. The male of this species has a glossy green throat, chest and rump, with a purple head and belly and a dark forked tail and dark wings, the female is greenish with a light grey throat and chest. Both have a straight bill, only slightly curved at the tip. Many hummingbirds act as pollinators for flowers, the flowers generally being red, pink or orange, thereby indistinguishable to insects, and odourless so as not to attract nectar-feeding insects. The flowers also tend to be shaped into long thin tubes adapted to fit the birds' beaks.

Trogons Of the 10 trogon species found in Costa Rica, the resplendent quetzal is the one most people want to see. However, all species are spectacular, particularly the males. They have metallic green, blue or violet heads and chests, with contrasting bright red, yellow or orange underparts. They usually sit erect in the forest with their distinctive tails (long, with horizontal black and white stripes on the underside and a squared off end) pointing downwards. The spectacular male **resplendent quetzal** (quetzal or fénix del bosque, *Pharomachrus mocinno*), is a bird of the cloud forests with an emerald green head, a crest of green feathers and long trailing green plumes extending 45 cm or more beyond his white tail. In spite of their bright colours, trogans can be quite difficult to spot in forests as they blend into the dark green foliage and tend to sit silently waiting to catch passing insects. They feed on small lizards and frogs as well as fruits, especially figs. Other trogons found in Costa Rica are the **slaty-tailed trogon** (trogón coliplomizo, *Trogon massena*) and the **violaceous trogon** (trogón violaceo, *Trogon violaceus*), the latter being found in dry as well as wet forests at low elevations.

Kingfishers There are six species of kingfisher in Costa Rica, mostly seen perched on branches while they scan the water beneath them for fish, though they also seem to favour telegraph lines as perching sites. All have large heads, with long, straight, quite sturdy bills and fairly stubby bodies but they vary in size from 12 to 40 cm. The bigger species eat larger prey and, hence, avoid competition with the smaller ones. They lay their eggs in burrows dug in the banks of rivers or streams. The **ringed kingfisher** (martín pescador collarejo, *Ceryle torquata*), a blue-grey bird, with a brownish front, white neckband and throat, is the largest kingfisher in the country. The smallest is the American **pygmy kingfisher** (martín pescador enano, *Chloroceryle aene*), which has a green back and head, a reddish brown neck-band, throat and chest with a white lower front. The female of this species has a green bar across her chest.

The motmots, relatives of the kingfisher, are very handsome birds, brightly coloured with distinctive, long, racquet tails. Perhaps the most attractive of the country's six species is the **turquoise-browed motmot** (momoto cejiceleste, *Eumomota superciliosa*), a green to brownish green bird, with a black throat, a small black mask round its eyes and turquoise bar above the eyes, its tail and wings are also turquoise. All motmots are more common in low and mid-altitude forests, but they can also be seen in parks, orchards and drier scrub areas. Like the kingfishers, they tend to sit and wait for their prey, mostly insects, but also frogs, snakes and lizards, then swoop down, grab it and return to their perch to beat it to death. Motmots will also eat some fruit.

Motmots

The toucans are a quite unmistakable group – all bearing large, brightly coloured bills that look more plastic than real! There are six species in Costa Rica, two toucans, two aracaris and two toucanets. The **chestnut-mandibled toucan** (dios-te-dé, *Ramphastos swainsonii*) is the largest, both it and the slightly smaller **keel-billed toucan** (tucán pico iris, *Ramphastos sulfuratus*) are mainly black with a yellow face and chest and red under the tail. The former has a bicoloured bill, chestnut below and yellow above, while the latter has an amazing multicoloured bill, red, orange, green and blue. The **collared aracari** (tucancillo collarejo, *Pteroglossus torquatus*) and **fiery-billed aracari** (tucancillo piquianaranjado, *Pteroglossus frantzii*) look somewhat alike, but the former is found on the Caribbean side of the country and in Guanacaste region and the latter on the south Pacific. Both have a black head and chest, a dark green back and a yellow belly with a central black spot, the bill in both is black below, but is bright orange red above in the fiery-billed and pale yellow in the collared. The **yellow-eared toucanet** (tucancillo orejiamarillo *Selenidera spectablis*) and **emerald toucanet** (tucancillo verde, *Aulacorhynchus prasinusare*) are smaller birds, the latter only 30 cm in comparison with the 56 cm of the chestnut mandibled toucan. The emerald toucanet is mostly green, but has a blue throat and is chestnut below its tail. Its bill is black below and yellow above. All species are forest-dwelling, fruit eaters, they tend to be seen in small groups, mostly staying high up in the canopy. Toucans nest in hollow trees, often using holes that have been made by woodpeckers.

Toucans

This group hardly needs describing, as its members will be more or less familiar in overall appearance, at least, to all visitors to Costa Rica. There are 22 species in the country. The most common ground dove is the **ruddy-ground dove** (tortolita rojiza, *Columbina talpacoti*), the male of which is reddish brown with a grey head, while the female is duller. This species is usually seen feeding in open areas, pastures, fields and woodland clearings, searching the ground for food items such as seeds, fruit and some insects. A slightly more unusual looking member of the group is the **Inca dove** (tortolita colilarga, *Columbina inca*), which is a small pale grey bird with black linings on its feathers that give it a scaly appearance, it has a longish tail with white edges and, in flight, its reddish brown wing patches can be seen. Its habitats

Pigeons & doves

are very similar to those of the ground dove. Pigeons' nests tend to be rather scrappy structures, built on the ground, rock ledges or in trees or bushes. Usually only one or two eggs are laid and the fledglings are initially fed on 'pigeon milk', a nutritious liquid produced in the crop of both parents.

Parrots Many of Costa Rica's 16 species are small and green and quite difficult to tell apart unless seen very clearly, but quite unmistakable and very spectacular is the **scarlet macaw** (lapa roja, *Ara macao*). It is a large bird, 84 cm long, with a bright red body, yellow and blue wings, a long red tail and a white face. Sadly, this species has become quite rare, devastated by habitat destruction and hunting for the pet trade. It is found mostly on the southern Pacific side of the country, whereas the similarly sized **green macaw** (lapa verde, *Ara ambigua*) is found on the Caribbean side; this species, too, is endangered in Costa Rica. Most of the parrots are noisy and sociable, feeding on fruits and seeds that they tear apart with their powerful, short, hooked beaks. Breeding usually takes place in hollow trees, with the young of the large macaw species remaining in the nest for three to four months and those of smaller species for three to four weeks. They are very vulnerable at this time as many nestlings are taken and sold as pets. Fairly typical of the smaller species is the **white-fronted parrot** (loro frentiblanco, *Amazona albifrons*), a green bird with red around its eyes, with a white forehead, blue on top of its head and red and blue patches on its wing, though these colours are seen mostly when it is flying.

Woodpeckers Two of Costa Rica's 16 woodpecker species, the **lineated woodpecker** (carpintero lineado, *Dryocopus lineatus*) and the **pale-billed woodpecker** (carpintero picoplata, *Campephilus guatemalensis*) look just like the cartoon character Woody Woodpecker! They both have large, crested heads with varying amounts of red on it (depending on sex and species), large black bodies with white markings and banded, black and white fronts, but only the lineated has white on its head. Both are found in wet forests in the country. Though insects make up most of the diet of the majority of the woodpeckers, fruits, nuts and nectar may also be taken, while the sapsuckers do just that – drill holes in trees and suck the sap. Even if you do not see a woodpecker, you may well hear them as drilling for insects, excavating nests or communicating with each other by drumming. As with the kingfishers, the different sized species avoid competition by taking prey of different sorts or sizes. The smallest of the woodpeckers in Costa Rica is the 9 cm long **olivaceous piculet** (carpenterito oliváceo, *Picumnus olivaceus*), which may be seen in gardens and plantations as well as drier woodlands and wet forests. It has a dull green back and lighter front, with the male having orange streaks on its head. The medium sized species, around 19 cm in length, include the quite similar **Hoffman's woodpecker** (carpintero de Hoffman, *Melanerpes hoffmannii*) and **red-crowned woodpecker** (carpintero nuquirroja, *Melanerpes rubricapillus*). Both have black and white bars on their backs and wings and light brown chests; the former has a yellowish belly and the latter a reddish one. The male Hoffman's has red on the top of his head, while both sexes of the red-crowned have red backs to their necks and the male, in addition, has a red crown while the top of the female's head is white. Both species favour open, wooded sites and are found on the Pacific slope, but Hoffman's occurs in the north and the red-crowned in the south.

Curassows This group, with 13 species in the country, contains the quans and chachalacas as well as curassows, with the larger members of the group weighing up to 4 kg. They are related to such birds as pheasants, partridges and quail – all called 'chicken-like birds', even by serious birdwatchers! Unfortunately, they taste good too so several species, including the **crested guan** (pava crestada, *Penelope purpurascens*), **black**

guan (pava negra, *Chamaepetes unicolor*) and the **great currasow** (pavon, *Crax rubra*) are becoming uncommon outside protected areas. They are quite heavily built birds, with long sturdy legs and often a long tail. They tend to be brown, black, grey or olive though might have some brightly coloured patch such as a red dewlap in the crested guan or yellow knobs on the bill of the male great currasow. Guans and currasows live in forests, the former mostly staying in the trees and the latter on the ground. The chachalacas are aboreal, but are more common on forest edges and clearings. The arboreal birds eat fruit, leaves, buds and some insects; while the terrestrial currasows feed on fruit, seeds and insects, generally moving round in flocks of 10 – 20 individuals except during the breeding season.

Tinamous

The tinamous, 5 species in Costa Rica, look rather like partridges; they have chunky bodies, with short tails and legs and a small head. All are terrestrial, feeding, sleeping and nesting on the ground, except for the **great tinamou** (tinamú grande, *Tinamus major*), which roosts in trees. Their flight is clumsy and they are more likely to run than fly from danger. Tinamous are brown, grey or olive, with darker spots or bars so they are well camouflaged as they scuttle through the forest searching for fruit and seeds, but also taking insects and even small vertebrates. Females lay their eggs in indentations in the ground, generally hidden under a bush. Several females may use the same nest and then it is the male that incubates the eggs and looks after the chicks. They feed themselves as soon as they hatch, but he leads them round the forest and protects them from predators. In spite of being hunted by humans, tinamous appear to be quite common, perhaps because they are so secretive and also because they are adaptable, able to survive in forest that has been partially logged.

Cuckoos & anis

Most commonly seen among the 11 species in this group are the **squirrel cuckoo** (cucu ardilla, *Piaya cayana*), the **smooth-billed ani** (garrapatero piquiliso, *Crotophaga ani*) and the **groove-billed ani** (garrapatero piquiestriado, *Crotophaga sulcirostris*). Unlike the European cuckoo, none of these three lays their eggs in the nest of another species. The squirrel cuckoo, which is a large (48 cm) reddish brown bird, with a bright yellow beak, a grey belly and a long tail with black and white stripes on its underside, is found in wooded areas across Costa Rica. It tends to be quite a secretive bird, feeding off insects and pairing up just for the breeding season. Both sexes build the nest, incubate the eggs and feed the young. In contrast, the anis are noisy, conspicuous, gregarious birds, living in flocks of 8 – 25 individuals in bushy scrub and open areas, often around human habitation. They are often seen foraging on the ground around cattle, eating the insects flushed up by the cows. Both species are black with a large, almost parrot-like grey bill, the smooth-billed being found on the southern Pacific slope and the groove-billed in the northern Pacific and the Caribbean.

Passerines

The groups mentioned above include fewer than half of Costa Rica's birds. All the others are passerines, with feet specialized to grasp and perch on tree branches. They tend to be small land birds, many are LBJs but some are very bright and conspicuous. Included among the passerines in Costa Rica are 16 species of **woodcreepers**, all looking and acting rather alike. They are slender brown birds, with longish beaks and stiff tails, most often seen moving up tree trunks probing under bark and into plants looking for insects. The **antbirds** (30 species), though a more variable group, are not seen often as they are inclined to skulk in the shade low down in the forest. Most males come in shades of black or brown with some white, while the females tend to be olive or brown. Their name comes from the habit that some of them have of following marching columns of ants eating the insects and other small prey that the ants flush out of hiding. Costa Rica's 22 species of **wrens** are all smallish (10 – 20 cm), mostly brown or reddish brown. Their most distinguishing feature is their tail – usually held stiffly upright. They are found in forests, thickets, grassland and marshes, usually hopping or flitting low down searching for insects. Many of Costa Rica's 50 species of **warblers** are migrants from North America. They are small birds, commonly found flitting round gardens and plantations often in the company of other birds such as tanagers and honeycreepers. They can be quite brightly coloured, usually yellowish or greenish with varying amounts of black, grey and white and maybe patches of red orange or blue. They mostly forage for insects but also take some nectar and juice from fruits. The **gnatcatchers**, 11 species in Costa Rica, are small, predominantly grey birds that are very similar in habit to the warblers. Although common and frequently seen, the **sparrows** and **grosbeaks** of Costa Rica are mostly rather dull brown or grey little birds, not a group that most visitors would be particularly interested in searching out. Indeed, most people will be very familiar with one of them the **house sparrow** (gorrión común, *Passer domesticus*), which arrived in Costa Rica in 1974 having spread from North America, where it was introduced by European settlers in the 1800s.

The **thrushes**, 11 species breeding in Costa Rica, also tend to be rather drab birds but you will almost certainly see and can easily recognize the **sooty robin** (mirlo negruzco, *Turdus nigrescens*), as it looks and acts much like the **blackbird** (*Turdus merula*) common across Europe. The male is black and the female dark brown and both have an orange beak, legs and eye-ring. One member of this quite diverse group, the **black-faced solitaire** (solitario carinegro, *Myadestes melanops*) is famed for its singing and consequently its numbers have declined as it is caught for the pet trade.

Another diverse group are the **blackbirds** and **orioles**, included with them are the caciques, cowbirds, grackles, meadowlarks and oropendolas. Around 20 species occur in Costa Rica, distributed through all elevations and most habitats including human settlements and agricultural areas. They vary in size (15 – 56 cm), colour, ecology and behaviour. Widely distributed and conspicuous in the country is the **great-tailed grackle** (clarinero, *Quiscalus mexicanus*), the male is a large black bird with a purple gloss to its foliage and a long black tail. Both sexes have yellow eyes and black bills. The male, reaching 43 cm, is quite a bit bigger than the brownish female (33cm). They occur at low and middle elevations on both the Caribbean and Pacific slopes of the country, mostly in open habitats. The large groups they form outside the breeding season can cause damage to agricultural areas and their roosting sites. Much more spectacular to look at is **Montezuma's orpendola** (oropéndola de Montezuma, *Psarocolius montezuma*), which has a large (50 cm) brown body, with a black head and chest, a yellow-edged tail, an orange tip to its large black bill and a blue patch under its eye. The orpendolas breed in colonies, weaving large bag-like nests, many of which hang from the branches of each tree. Montezuma's orpendola is quite strange in that 3 – 10 males establish a colony in a single tree and then defend the 10 – 30 females that join them to mate and nest there. The dominant male tends to mate with most females, but there is much competition with aggressive displaying and fighting between the males. The **bronzed cowbird** (vaquero ojirrojo, *Molothrus aeneus*) does not bother to make any form of nest; instead, the female lays her eggs in the nest of another species and leaves the other bird to rear her young.

Jays, which are members of the crow family, are some of the largest passerines, reaching up to 71 cm in length. Most are brightly coloured, such as the **white-throated magpie-jay** (urraca copetona, *Calocitta formosa*), which is found in open wooded sites and around human settlements on the northern Pacific slope. This is a large bird, up to 46 cm, brilliant blue above and white below with a conspicuous crest and a long blue tail. In contrast, the slightly smaller (40 cm), more widely distributed **brown jay** (urraca parda, *Cyanocorax morio*) is, as you might guess, brown! It has a pale brown to white chest and belly and its tail is white tipped. Jays are omnivorous, eating just about anything and everything. Their diet includes eggs, nestlings, carrion, insects, fruit and nuts, which are foraged for on the ground and among trees. Both species live in small groups of related individuals and jointly defend a territory. The oldest pair mates, while the others help to nest build and feed the young. There are five species of jay in Costa Rica.

The American **flycatchers** are a very large and diverse group of birds with about 75 species in Costa Rica. Many of the small drab species are difficult to identify but the **scissor-tailed flycatcher** (tijereta rosada, *Tyrannus forficatus*) is both handsome and easily seen as it adopts the typical flycatcher technique, perching motionless on a fence to dart out and grab a passing insect and then return to the same perch to eat it. This flycatcher is a non-breeding migrant found in open areas such as fields, marshes and human settlements on the northern Pacific slope. It is a medium sized, silver-grey bird, about 20 cm in length, with a long (15 cm) black, forked tail, black wings with reddish patches under them and a white chest. Another bright and frequently seen flycatcher is the **great kiskadee** (bienteveo grande, *Pitangus sulphuratus*), which is a medium-sized (23 cm) bird, with an olive brown back, chestnut wings, a bright yellow chest and belly, a white throat and a black and white head. It tends to be found in quite open sites such as in gardens, along the forest edge and in grassland trees. Along with catching insects, the great kiskadee also eats frogs and lizards and even small fish.

Some of the most colourful of Costa Rica's passerines are the 50 or so species of **tanagers** found there; included in this group are honeycreepers and euphonias. They are found in forested and shrubby areas over a wide range of elevations, tending to be in more open places and often seen near human habitation in mixed-species flocks foraging for fruit. Most tanagers are arboreal and most eat small fruits and berries, though some are ground foragers and some eat insects. The honeycreepers eat nectar, making holes at the base of a flower with their beak and sucking out the nectar, they also take insects and fruit. The **blue-gray tanager** (tangara azuleja, *Thraupis episcopus*) is abundant and found over most of the country at all elevations, often near towns and villages, in parks and along forest edges. As its name implies, it is a blue-grey bird, with a darker blue back and bright blue wing and tail, the female is duller in colour. The male **scarlet-rumped tanager** (tangara lomiescarlata, *Ramphocelus passerinii*), is about the same size (16 cm) as the blue-gray tanager, but is black with a conspicuous red rump and pale blue-grey beak. The female is yellowish olive with a grey head and throat and a yellow-orange rump, chest and belly. Euphonia males are typically blue-black above, with yellow foreheads, breasts and bellies, while the females tend to be olive, greenish with duller yellow fronts. Many of the male honeycreepers are brilliantly coloured. Typical of these is the **red-legged honeycreeper** (mielero patirrojo, *Cyanerpes cyaneus*), which is a bright blue bird with a black back, wings, tail and eyestripe, a turquoise patch on top of his head and red legs. The female is overall yellow, greenish, but also has red legs. This species may well be seen in gardens and plantations and also on the edges of drier forests in the north of the country.

Though they are small (9 – 19 cm), stocky birds, male **manakins** are noted for both their colourful plumage and their elaborate courtship diplays. They are very active, forest dwelling birds, foraging in the understorey for small fruits and some insects. One very attractive species is the **long-tailed manakin** (saltarín colilargo, *Chiroxiphia linearis*), which is found in forests on the northern Pacific slope. The male is black with a bright blue back, a red crest on his head and two very long, black tail feathers. The female is olive green, with a more yellow-green front and orange legs and she lacks the long tail feathers. The female **white-collared manakin** (saltarín cuelliblanco, *Manacus candei*) is also a small olive green bird, but the male has a bright yellow belly, black on his wings and on the top of his head, an olive rump and a white throat and chest. This species is found in low elevation, wet forest on the Caribbean side of Costa Rica. During the breeding season, from February to July, manakin males display at particular sites in bushes, on tree branches or on the forest floor; generally several males display in the same area – the lekking site. They try to attract females with both visual and vocal displays, involving elaborate courtship dances, the movements in which are species specific. In some species, including the long-tailed manakin, two or three males do a coordinated dance on the same perch. Once a female has selected the male she considers to be the most spectacular and has mated with him, she goes off to nest build, incubate and rear young on her own.

Closely related to the manakins are the **cotingas**. This is a very diverse group containing bellbirds, umbrella birds, phias and fruitcrows as well as typical cotingas, though there are only 10 species in Costa Rica. The cotingas eat mainly fruit, finding it high up in the canopy of the forest, though some eat insects as well. The bellbirds, though, stick to a strictly frugivorous diet, even, unusually, feeding fruit to their chicks. The nestlings, consequently, take longer to develop as their diet is low in protein. The male **three-wattled bellbird** (pájaro campana, *Procnias tricarunculata*) is a medium sized (20 cm), brown bird with a white head and three odd looking, worm-like appendages or wattles, hanging from his beak. The female is olive-green with a yellow-streaked front. Also strangely ornamented is the male **bare-necked umbrella bird** (pájaro-sombrilla, *Cephalopterus glabricollis*), a mostly black bird with a large red throat sac that is inflated during displays and also an umbrella-shaped black crest. This umbrella bird is only sparsely distributed and is threatened by habitat destruction as it breeds in highland forests, but overwinters in lowland forests, so requires both habitats in the same area and a forest corridor connecting them. Somewhat more common is the **snowy cotinga** (cotinga nivosa, *Carpodectes nitidus*), which is found in wet forests at low elevation on the Caribbean slope and in more open wooded areas. The male is pale grey above and white below, while the female is overall more grey.

Reptiles

Snakes Costa Rica's reptiles comprise 127 snake species. The best place to see the snakes is in a zoo or snake farm – they are not often seen in the wild. Indeed, there are some of them that you will be very glad not to meet at close quarters! The **bushmaster** (matabuey, *Lachesis muta*), for instance, is the New World's largest venomous snake, it can reach 3.5 m in length. It is an aggressive, slender, large-headed snake with a yellowish to tan body with black or brown blotches along it. Another large, reaching lengths up to 2.5 m, poisonous snake to be avoided is the **fer-de-lance** (terciopelo, *Bothrops asper*) as it too can be quite aggressive. It has a triangular head and a patterned olive, beige, black and brown body. Both this species and the bushmaster tend to be found on the ground, though young fer-de-lance may be found in trees. The **eyelash viper** (toboba de pestaña, *Bothriechis schlegelii*) is much smaller, reaching only 75 cm in length and is arboreal. It is very variable in colour: grey, olive, through reddish yellow, to bright golden yellow with or without markings on the body. Its name comes from the two or three horny spine-like scales that jut out above each eye. The last of the poisonous snakes to be covered here is the Central American **coral snake** (coral, *Micrurus nigrocinctus*), which may be found on the floor in forests, but also in more open areas. It is very colourful, with a small, black and yellow head and red and black rings along its body, which may or may not have narrower yellow rings as well. Given just a quick glance, it is quite easy to confuse the non-poisonous **harlequin snake** (coral falsa, *Scolecophis atrocinctus*) and the **tropical kingsnake** (coral falsa, *Lampropeltis triangulum*) with the coral snake. Both have bodies with bands of yellow, red and black, thereby mimicking the coral snake's colouration, perhaps in an attempt to deter predators. It should be noted that the vast majority of Costa Rica's snakes are not venomous and those that are tend to be nocturnal and secretive, so it is really not necessary to worry about being bitten. However, it is still not advisable to poke under rocks and logs or into bushes and pay attention to where you are putting your feet.

Perhaps most conspicuous and certainly largest of Costa Rica's 68 lizard species are the **green iguana** (garrobo, *Iguana iguana*) and **black iguana**, (iguana negra, garrobo, *Ctenosuara similes*). The green iguana is more widespread, found in wet forests at low elevations and along streams and rivers in drier areas on both the Caribbean and Pacific slopes. It can often be seen sunbathing high in trees, especially early in the morning. The black iguana is found only on the Pacific slope, often in drier areas and on the beach, but also in forests. Considerably smaller, but very commonly seen at night in houses are **geckos**, usually grey or brown with large eyes and toes that appear to have little pads on them. Unlike most lizards, they make quite audible squeaks.

Lizards

Of the two crocodilians, the smaller **spectacled caiman**, (caiman, *Caiman crocodiles*), is more common, but the American **crocodile** (cocodrilo, *Crodylus acutus)* is also found in the country. The crocodile has a longer, more slender and more pointed snout than the caiman and also, unlike the caiman, has a tooth on each side of its lower jaw, projecting upwards, that is visible when the mouth is closed.

Freshwater turtles, (there are eight freshwater and six marine species) such as the **white-lipped mud turtle** (tortuga caja, *Kinosternon leucostomum)* are quite a common sight, sunning themselves on logs along rivers. Six marine turtles nest on Costa Rican beaches and with luck and planning you may get to see one or two come ashore to nest on either the Pacific or Caribbean beaches. The small **olive ridley** (lora, *Lepidochelys olivacea*) arrives on the beach of Santa Rosa in spectacular *arribadas* with many thousand turtles arriving to nest over a few consecutive nights at times in the year. The hook beak of the **hawksbill turtle** (carey, *Eretmochelys imbricata*) is a distinctive characteristic of the species, as is the treasured tortoise-shell carapace once used for engravings prized for the subtle patterns. Green turtle soup is fortunately on fewer menus, improving the survival rates of the **green turtle** (tortuga verde, *Chelonia mydas*). The largest reptile in the world is the **leatherback turtle** (baula, *Dermochelys coriacea*) which can grow to over 2 m in length weighing over 500 kg. All marine turtles are endangered and protected, along with their nest sites and eggs, by international law.

Turtles

Amphibians

Around 35 salamanders, 3 caecilians, 14 toads and about 105 frogs are found in Costa Rica. **Salamanders**, which look rather like wet lizards, tend to be nocturnal and secretive, hiding in damp places. **Caecilians**, which are legless and resemble earthworms, are even less commonly seen as they mostly live underground. The largest toad in the country is the huge marine or **cane toad** (sapo grande, *Bufo marinus*), which reaches up to 20 cm in length and 1.2 kg in weight. These toads can be found in forests, in more open areas and in and around buildings. In contrast, Costa Rica's **golden toad** (sapo dorado de Monteverde, *Bufo periglenes*), is only 6 cm in size, the males are golden while the females are black with red spots ringed with yellow. It was found only in the Monteverde Cloud Forest Reserve and has now moved largely in to the realm of legend, believed to be extinct. The reason for its decline, and that of 20 or so other species in the reserve, is unclear. The amphibian

Background

that is probably the best known and most sought after by visitors is the beautifully coloured **red-eyed** or **gaudy leaf frog** (rana calzonuda, rana verde de arbol, *Agalychnis callidryas*). This is 5-7 cm in size with a pale or dark green back, blue-purple patches both on the underside of its limbs and vertical bars on its side, orange fore and hind feet and ruby red eyes. When resting or dormant, only the green colouring shows making the frog virtually invisible. Also much sought after are the brightly coloured poison-dart and poison arrow frogs. These include the **strawberry poison-dart frog** (ranita roja, *Dendrobates pumilio*), which is bright red with varying quantities of black flecks on its body and with red, blue, green or black limbs, the orange and **black poison-dart frog** (rana venenosa, *Phyllobates vittatus*), which is small (2-3 cm) and black with a wide pair of orange stripes on its back and turquoise mottling on its limbs and the **green poison-dart frog** (rana venenosa, *Dendrobates auratus*). This species can be up to 4 cm in size and is very variable in colour – bright blue, turquoise, green or dark green with brownish or black patches. It is found on the forest floor or in low vegetation, mostly in forests at lower elevations. While the vivid warning colours of poison dart frogs and their sensational name suggest otherwise, there is no evidence that their toxic secretions have ever been used to tip darts for hunting in Costa Rica, unlike Choco Indians of western Colombia.

Insects

There is no space in this guide to cover Costa Rica's invertebrates, but try, at least, to visit a butterfly farm and keep your eyes open to search out these smaller creatures in the forests. You might well, for instance, see long marching columns of **leaf-cutter ants** (*Atta spp*), each carrying a piece of leaf back to its nest. These can be very large structures – a mound of leaf mulch surrounded by a considerable area of forest floor cleared of all green vegetation. Probably most impressive of the many butterfly species is the **morpho** (*Morpho peleides*), which has a 15 cm wingspan. The upper side of its wings are bright, shiny blue with a brown edge marked with white, but once it settles and closes its wings, the dull brown underside ensures that it is almost invisible.

Footnotes

13

Footnotes

445 Basic Spanish

448 Index

452 Shorts

453 Maps

453 Advertisers

457 Colour maps

Basic Spanish

Whether you have been taught the 'Castillian' pronounciation (all *z's*, and *c's* followed by *i* or *e*, are pronunounced as the *th* in *think*) or the 'American' pronounciation (they are pronounced as *s*) you will encounter little difficulty in understanding either: Spanish pronunciation varies geographically much less than English.

Using basic Spanish

Pronouns   In the Americas, the plural, familiar pronoun *vosotros* (with the verb endings – *áis*, – *éis*), though much used in Spain, is never heard: two or more people, whoever they are, are always addressed as *Ustedes (Uds)*. The singular, familiar prounoun *tú* is replaced in many areas by the pronoun *vos*; when it is, the accent on the verb tends to move toward the end: instead of *tú quieres*, one hears *vos querés* (though both will be understood).

Expressions of time   Many misunderstandings about engagements stem from terminology rather than tardiness. *Ahora* is often a synonym for *hoy*, 'today', not the 'now' in the dictionary; 'now' or 'soon' are *ahorita*; 'right now' is *ahora mismo* or *enseguida*. In Panamá, *ahora* means 'in a little while', 'in a bit', not 'now'.

While *en la tarde* could conceivably mean at 1230 or 1300 in the afternoon, is more likely to mean 1500 or 1600, even 1730 or 1800. A polite way of pinning down a vague commitment is to ask '*¿A qué hora más o menos?*'

Terms of address   Almost anyone qualified by credentials or custom to a title more elevated than *Sr, Sra*, or *Srta*, uses it. A physician, dentist, or veterinarian is always addressed as *Doctor(a)*, as is any holder of a doctoral degree. Primary school teachers, often not university graduates, are always *Maestro(a)*, as are some skilled crafts people, builders, etc. Secondary school and all university teachers, are always addressed as *Profesor(a)*, or, informally by their students, as *Profe*. Lawyers and university graduates in any of the arts or social sciences are addressed as *Licenciado(a)*, abbreviated *Lic*; graduate engineers, and holders of any degree in a technical field, use *Ingeniero(a)*, abbreviated *Ing*. Architects use *Arquitecto(a)*, abbreviated *Arq*. Protestant clergy are always *Reverendo(a)*, never just *Sr(a)*.

Address male strangers over the age of 20 or so as *Señor*, or, if substantially older than you, as *Don*. Younger men may be addressed as *Joven*. Address female strangers over the age of 20 or so, or younger women if they are obviously accompanied by (their own) children or a husband, as *Señora*. Younger women can safely be addressed as *Señorita*. Address middle-aged or older women as *Doña*. Note that the terms *Señorita* and *Señora* have implications of virginity as well as marital status. An elderly woman who has no children and has never married may well correct you if addressed as Señora. *Don* and *Doña* also enable you to use a person's first name without sounding disrespectful, as in Don Juan or Doña Josefina.

Once you have learned a person's name young people among themselves, as everywhere, use given names or nicknames immediately. Whenever the person addressed is a few years older, however, use the form *Señora González*, or to imply respectful friendship, *Señor Juan*. Where the age difference is substantial, use *Doña Mercedes* or *Don Francisco*. Reply to officials' questions with *Sí, Señor* or *No, Señora*.

Bs and Vs   Travellers whose names include the letters '*b*' or '*v*' (pronounced the same in Spanish) should learn to distinguish between them when spelling aloud as *be larga* or *be grande* and *ve corta, ve chica* or *uve*. (Children often say *ve de vaca* and *be de burro* to distinguish between the two letters.)

Greetings & courtesies	Spanish		
Hello/	Hola/	Yes/no	Sí/no
Good morning	Buenos días	Excuse me/	Con permiso
Good afternoon/	Buenas tardes/	I'm sorry	Lo siento/disculpe
evening/night	noches	I don't understand	No entiendo
Goodbye	Adiós/chao	◀I don't want it	No lo quiero
See you later	Hasta luego	Please speak slowly	Hable despacio
How are you?	¿Cómo está/		por favor
	estás	What's your name?	¿Cómo se llama?
I'm fine	Muy bien gracias	I'm called_	Me llamo_
Pleased to	Mucho gusto/	Go away!	¡Váyase!
meet you	encantado/a	Leave me alone	¡No me moleste!
Please	Por favor	I'm off/leaving	Me voy
Thank you	Gracias (muchas)		

Questions			
Where is_?	¿Dónde está_?	How do I get to_?	¿Cómo llego a_?
I should like	Me gustaría/quisiera	Do you have_?	¿Tiene_?
How much does	¿Cuánto vale?/¿cuánto	Are there any rooms	¿Hay cuartos para esta
it cost?	cuesta?	tonight	noche?
When?	¿Cuándo?/¿a qué hora?	Bring me the bill, please	La cuenta por favor
When does the bus	¿A qué hora sale/llega	Can I have my change,	Deme el cambio, por
leave/arrive?	el autobus?	please	favor
Why?	¿Por qué?	Can I make a phone call?	¿Puedo llamar por
			teléfono?

Basics			
police (policeman)	la policía (el policía)/	bank	el banco
	el carabinero	exchange house	la casa de cambio
hotel	el hotel (la pensión,	exchange rate	la tasa de cambio
	el residencial,	travellers' cheques	los travelers/
	el hospedaje)		los cheques de
room	el cuarto/		viajero
	la habitación	cash	el efectivo
single/double	single/doble	breakfast	el desayuno
with two beds	con dos camas	lunch	el almuerzo/la
bathroom/toilet	el baño		comida
hot/cold water	agua caliente/fría	dinner/supper	la cena
toilet paper	el papel higiénico	meal	la comida
restaurant	el restaurant	drink	la bebida
post office/	el correo/el	mineral water	el agua mineral
telephone office	centro de llamadas	beer	la cerveza
supermarket	el supermercado	with/without sugar	con/sin azúcar
market	el mercado		

Getting around			
on the left/right	a la izquierda/	train/train station	el tren/la estación
	derecha		(de tren)
straight on	derecho	airport	el aeropuerto
bus station	la terminal	aeroplane	el avión
	(terrestre)	ticket	el boleto
bus stop	la parada/el	ticket office	la taquilla
	paradero	luggage	el equipaje
interurban bus	el bus/el	rucksack	la mochila
	camión	bag	la bolsa
urban bus	el micro		

Time

What time is it?	*¿Qué hora es?*
At half past two	*A las dos y media*
Ten minutes	*Diez minutos*
Five hours	*Cinco horas*
It's one o'clock	*Es la una*
It's seven o'clock	*Son las siete*
It's ten to seven	*Son las siete menos diez*
It's 6.20	*Son las seis y veinte*

Medical terms

It hurts here	*Me duele aquí*
I have a headache /stomach ache	*Tengo dolor de cabeza/de estómago*
I don't feel well	*No me siento bien*
I need a doctor	*Necesito asistencia médica*

Numbers Spanish

1	*uno/una*	11	*once*	21	*veintiuno*
2	*dos*	12	*doce*	30	*treinte*
3	*tres*	13	*trece*	40	*cuarenta*
4	*cuatro*	14	*catorce*	50	*cincuenta*
5	*cinco*	15	*quince*	60	*sesenta*
6	*seis*	16	*dieciséis*	70	*setenta*
7	*siete*	17	*diecisiete*	80	*ochenta*
8	*ocho*	18	*dieciocho*	90	*noventa*
9	*nueve*	19	*diecinueve*	100	*cien, ciento*
10	*diez*	20	*veinte*	1000	*mil*

Days/months

Monday	*lunes*	March	*marzo*
Tuesday	*martes*	April	*abril*
Wednesday	*miércoles*	May	*mayo*
Thursday	*jueves*	June	*junio*
Friday	*viernes*	July	*julio*
Saturday	*sábado*	August	*agosto*
Sunday	*domingo*	September	*septiembre*
		October	*octubre*
January	*enero*	November	*noviembre*
February	*febrero*	December	*diciembre*

Key verbs

To go	*Ir*	**To be** (in a permanent state)	*Ser*
I go	*(Yo) voy*	I am	*soy*
you go	*(tu) vas*	you are	*eres*
s/he/it goes	*(Ella, El, Usted) va*	s/he/it is	*es*
you (formal) go	*(Usted) va*	you (formal) are	*es*
we go	*(Nostros) vamos*	we are	*somos*
they/you (plural) go	*(Ustedes) van*	they/you (plural) are	*son*

To have	*Tener*	**To be** (positional or temporary state)	*Estar*
I have	*tengo*	I am	*estoy*
you have	*tienes*	you are	*estás*
s/he/it has	*tiene*	s/he/it is	*está*
you (formal) have	*tiene*	you (formal) are	*está*
we have	*tenemos*	we are	*estamos*
they/you (plural) have	*tienen*	they/you (plural) are	*están*

Index

Letters and numbers in italics after a place name refer to the grid reference on the colour maps at the end of the book.

A

accommodation 43
Aguacaliente 167
Aguas Zarcas 188, 190
AIDS 78
air travel 33, 46
airline offices
  San José 130
airports 39
Alajuela *M2, B2* 143
altitude 76
amphibians 441
Angostura Dam 416
Arenal (Nuevo) 200
Arias Sánchez, Oscar 411
art 419
Atenas *M2, B2* 148
Aviarios del Caribe 386

B

Bagaces *M1, B4* 225
Bahía 312
Bahía Drake *M3, C3* 343
Bahía Herradura 288
Bahía Salinas *M1, A3* 238
bananas 408, 415
Bananito *M2, C6* 385
banks 32
Barra del Colorado *M2, A4* 383
Barranca *M1, C6* 222
bars 55
Barva *M2, B2* 160
Bijaugua Heliconias
  Ecotourist Resort 225
birds 432
birdwatching 58
boat travel 39, 51
  Tortuguero 382
Boca Tapada 188
borders 38
  Paso Canoas 334
  Sixaola, Panama 400
  Barra del Colorado 384
  Peñas Blancas 239
Boruca *M3, B4* 330, 418
Bosque de Paz
  Rainforest Reserve 152
botanical gardens 63
Bribrí 400, 418
Briceño *M3, C4* 332
Buenos Aires *M3, B4* 329
bungee jumping 59
bus travel 38, 50
  Butterfly Farm, La
  Guacima 147

C

Cabécar 418
Cabo Matapalo *M3, C4* 350
Cabuya 275
Café Britt coffee
  plantation tour 160
Cahuita *M3, A5* 386
camping 45
Cañas *M11, B5* 223
Cañón *M3, A2* 319
canopy tours 59
car hire 48
  San José 125
Carate *M3, C3* 351
Caribbean lowlands 363
Carmen *M1, inset* 276
carnival
  Puerto Limon 371
Carrillo Colina, Braulio 407
Cartago *M2, C3* 165, 404
Casa del Soñador 170
Cascajal 286
CATIE *M2, C4* 177
Central highlands and the surrounding area 139
Central Pacific 277
Centro Biológico Las Quebradas 325
Centro Neotrópico SarapiquíS 187
Cerro Amigos 217
Cerro de la Muerte *M3, A2* 321
Cerro Tortuguero *M2, A4* 382
Chacarita *M3, C4* 332
Chachagua *M2, B1* 193
children 27, 71
Chirripó Indian Reserve 178
Chorotega 403,418
Ciudad Neily *M3, C5* 333
Ciudad Quesada (San Carlos) *M2, B2* 189
climate 21, 421
clothing 31, 41
Cóbano 271
coffee 415
  history in Costa Rica 405
cold 76
Colonia 312
Columbus, Christopher 403
conduct 41
Cooprena 45
Copey *M3, A2* 319
Corobicí 224
cost of living 33
credit cards 32
crime 43
currency 32
customs 32
cyber cafés 52
cybercafés
  San José 131
cycling 51

D

Damas Island 300
dance 420
Daniel Oduber Quirós International Airport 40
dengue fever 31
departure tax 40
diarrhoea 74
disabled travellers 27
diving 60
Dominical *M3, B2* 308
Drake *M3, C3* 343
drink 41,54
driving 37, 42, 49, 60
drugs 41
duty free 32

E

eating 54
economy 415
eco-tourism 45, 69
El Bosque Eterno de los Niños *M1, B6* 217
El Mundo de la Tortuga 252
embassies 131
Empalme 318
Escaleras *M3, B2* 311
Escazú 134
Esparza *M1, C6* 222
Estación Biológica La Selva *M2, B3* 184
Esterillos *M2, C1* 293
expatriates 417

F

fauna 427
fax services 53
ferries 51
festivals 57
Figueres Ferrer, José 410
Finca La Central 176
fishing 63
flora 424
food 44, 54
  glossary 55
football 69
Fortuna *M2, B1* 190
Frajines *M2, B2* 150
frogs 442

G

Gandoca *M3, A6* 400
Garcimuñez 404
gay travellers 27
Genesis II 319
geography 420
geology 420
golf 60
Golfito *M3, C4* 354
Golfito and the Osa Peninsula 339
government 413
Grecia *M2, B2* 150
Guácimo *M2, B4* 368
Guápiles *M2, B4* 367
Guanacaste 219
Guatil 259
Guatuso 418
Guayabo *M1, B4* 226
Guaymí 418

H

Hacienda Barú 309
Hacienda Solimar 223
health 31, 71
heat 76
hepatitis 73,79
Heredia *M2, B3* 155
hiking 67
history 403
hitch-hiking 51
holidays 57
hospitals
  San José 132
hot air ballooning 60
hotels 43
Huetar 418

Hummingbird
  Gallery 218
hummingbirds 434

I

Iguana Park 286
immigration 29
immunization 72
INBio Parque 159
independence 405
Indigenous
  population 418
insects 77, 442
insurance 30
internet 52
Isla Ballena 313
Isla Cabuya 272, 275
Isla de las Heliconias 184
Isla del Caño 343
Isla Gitana 271
Isla Guayabo 271
Isla Negritos 271
Isla Palo Seco 294
Isla San Lucas 281
Isla Tortuga 271
Isla Uvita M2, B6 374
Isla Violin 343

J

Jacó M2, C1 289
Juan Santamaría airport
  39, 86
  accommodation 108
Juntas de Abangares M1,
  B5 223

K

Keith, Minor Cooper 408
KeköLdi Indigenous
  Reserve 396

L

La Casona 234
La Catarata 287
La Cruz M1, A3 237
La Esperanza banana
  plantation 369
La Garita M2, B2 148
La Guácima Butterfly
  Farm 147
La Guácima de Alajuela
  M2, B2 147
La Leona 352
La Palma 354
La Palma M3, C3 346
La Quinta 187
La Sierra de
  Abangares 223
La Sirena M3, C3 352,
  354
La Virgen 188

Laguna de Fraijanes 150
language 26
language schools 60
  San José 132
Lankester Botanical
  Garden 169
Las Nubes M2, B3 165
Las Pumas 225
Las Tres Hermanas 313
lesbian travellers 27
Liberia M1, B3 227
Limbo Lagoon 235
Limón M2, B6 370
literature 80, 420
Llorona 354
Lomas de Sierpe 382
Londres M3, A1 300
Los Angeles Cloudforest
  Reserve 154
Los Chiles M1, A6 204
Los Cusingos bird
  reserve 326
Los Inocentes 236
Los Patos 352

M

malaria 31, 79
Malpaís M1, inset 276
Manuel Antonio
  M3, A1 300
Manzanillo M3, A6 398
maps 25
Mata de Limón 286
Matapalo M3, B2 308
Matapalo M3, C4 350
Matina M2, B5 370
media 53
medical facilities
  San José 132
medical insurance 71
medicines 72
meningitis 73
Moín M2, B6 374
money 32, 42
monkeys 427
Monte Sky 172
Montero 184
Monteverde Cloud
  Forest Reserve 215
Monteverde M1, B5 208
Montezuma M1, inset
  272
Monumento Nacional
  Guayabo M2, B4 176,
  403
Mora Porras,
  Juan Rafael 407
Moravia del Chirripó
  M2, C5 178
motorbike rental 50
mountain biking 62
  See also cycling
Muelle San Carlos 204
Murciélago Sector 235
Museo de Arte y Diseño
  Contemporaneo 95

Museo de Ciencias
  Naturales 98
Museo de
  Entomología 99
Museo de Jade Fidel
  Tristan 95
Museo de Niños 98
Museo de Oro
  Precolombiano 94
Museo Dr Rafael Angel
  Calderón Guardia 95
Museo Nacional 94
Museo Nacional de
  Ferrocarril 95
Museo Numismática 94

N

Naranjo M2, B2 153
national parks 62, 423
  information sources 25
  For individual national
  parks see under 'Parque
  Nacional'
National System of
  Protected Areas 423
nature tourism 62
newspapers 53
Nicaragua
  border dispute 414
Nicoya M1, C3 261
Nicoya Peninsula 241
Northern region 179
Nosara M1, C3 262

O

Ojo de Agua 147
Ojochal 313
opossums 428
Orosí M2, C3 171
Orosí Valley 170
Orotina 286
Ostional 266

P

Pacuare Nature Reserve
  M2, B5 370
Palmar Norte M3, B2 331
Palmar Sur M3, B2 331
Palmares M2, B2 155
Pan de Azúcar 282
Paquera 269
Paraíso M2, C3 170
páramo 427
Parismina M2, B5 382
Parque Nacional Arenal
  196
Parque Nacional Barbilla
  M2, C5 369
Parque Nacional Barra
  Honda M1, B4 262
Parque Nacional Braulio
  Carrillo M2, B3 162, 182

Parque Nacional Cahuita
  M3, A5 391
Parque Nacional Carara
  M1, C6 287
Parque Nacional Chirripó
  M3, A3 327
Parque Nacional
  Corcovado M3, C3 352
Parque Nacional
  Guanacaste M1, A3 236
Parque Nacional Isla del
  Coco 284
Parque Nacional Juan
  Castro Blanco 152
Parque Nacional La
  Amistad M3, B4 336
Parque Nacional Manuel
  Antonio M3, B1 307
Parque Nacional Marino
  Ballena M3, B2 312
Parque Nacional Mario
  las Baulas de
  Guanacaste M1, B2 249
Parque Nacional Palo
  Verde M1, B4 226
Parque Nacional Piedras
  Blancas M3, C4 332
Parque Nacional Rincón
  de la Vieja M1, A4 230
Parque Nacional Santa
  Rosa M1, A2 233
Parque Nacional
  Tapantí-Macizo de la
  Muerte M3, A2 319
Parque Nacional
  Tenorio 200
Parque Nacional
  Tortuguero M2 376
Parque Nacional Volcán
  Poás 149
Parque Nacional Volcán
  Tenorio M1, B5 225
Parque Nacional Volcán
  Turrialba M2, B4 176
Parque Nacional
  Tapantí-Macizo dela
  Muerte M2, C4 172
Parrita 294
Partido Liberación
  Nacional 411
Paso Canoas M3, C5 334
Paso Real M3, B4 331
Pavones M3, C4 360
Peñas Blancas
  M1, A3 239
Penshurst M3, A5 386
people 417
photography 57
Pital 188
Platanar 204
Playa Bandera 294
Playa Bejuco M2, C2 294
Playa Bonita 374
Playa Brasilito
  M1, B2 250
Playa Cativo M3, C4 359

Playa Chiquita
M3, A6 397

Playa Cocles *M3, A6* 397

Playa Conchal
M1, B2 250

Playa de Cacao
M3, C4 358

Playa del Coco
M1, B3 245

Playa Escondido 307

Playa Esterillo
Centro 293

Playa Esterillo Este 294

Playa Flamingo
M1, B2 250

Playa Grande *M1, B2* 252

Playa Hermosa
M1, B2 248

Playa Hermosa
M2, C1 292

Playa Junquillal
M1, C2 260

Playa Langosto
M1, B2 257

Playa Nancite 235

Playa Naranjo *M1, C5*
235, 269

Playa Negra *M3, A5* 387

Playa Ocotal *M1, B2* 247

Playa Ostional 265

Playa Palma *M2, C2* 294

Playa Pan de Azucar *M1,*
B2 252

Playa Panama
M1, B2 249

Playa Platanares
M3, C4 348

Playa Playitas 307

Playa Potrero *M1, B2* 251

Playa San Josecito
M3, C4 358

Playa Tamarindo
M1, B2 254

Playa Tambor
M1, inset 270

Playa Tárcoles 288

Playa Tortuga 313

Playa Zancudo
M3, C4 359

poliomyelitis 73

politics 413

Portete *M2, B6* 374

post 52

precolumbian history
403

Presa de Cachí 170

primates 427

Pueblo Antiguo 121

Puerto Jiménez
M3, C4 347

Puerto Limón *M2, B6* 370

Puerto Viejo de
Sarapiquí *M2, B3* 185

Puerto Viejo de
Talamanca *M3, A5* 392

Punta Banco *M3, C4* 361

Punta Coral 281

Punta Leona 288

Punta Serrucho 307

Punta Uva *M3, A6* 398

Punta Uvita 313

Puntarenas *M1, C5* 280

Q

Quebrada Grande 232

Quepos *M3, B1* 295

Quizarrá de Pérez
Zeledón 326

R

radio 54

rafting 67

railroad
construction 408

Rain Maker Nature
Reserve 300

Rainforest aerial
tram 163

Rancho La Merced 312

Rancho Las Botijas 326

Rancho Los Tucanes 300

Rancho Redondo
M2, B3 169

reading about
Costa Rica 80

Refugio de Fauna
Silvestre Isla Bolaños
238

Refugio Nacional de
Fauna Silvestre Golfito
M3, C4 358

Refugio Nacional de Vida
Silvestre Caño Negro
M1, A6 197, 205

Refugio Nacional de Vida
Silvestre Curú *M1, C5*
271

Refugio Nacional de Vida
Silvestre Gandoca-
Manzanillo *M3, A6* 396,
399

Refugio Nacional de Vida
Silvestre Ostional *M1,*
C2 265

Refugio Nacional
Silvestre Peñas Blancas
M1, C6 222

Refugio Nacional de Vida
Silvestre Barra del
Colorado *M2, A4* 383

religion 42, 419

reptiles 440

Reserva Biológica
Bosque Nuboso
Monteverde *M1, B6* 206

Reserva Biológica
Durika 330

Reserva Biológica Hitoy
Cerere *M3, A5* 386

Reserva Biológica Isla del
Caño *M3, C2* 346

Reserva Biológica Isla
Guayabo 282

Reserva Biológica Lomas
Barbudal *M1, B4* 227

Reserva Biológica
Tirimbina 187

Reserva Natural Absoluta
Cabo Blanco 272

Reserva Natural Absoluta
Cabo Blanco
M1, inset 275

Reserva Sendero
Tranquilo 218

restaurants 54

Rey Curré *M3, B4* 330

Rincón *M3, C3* 346

Río Tárcoles 287

rip tides 43

road travel 47

road travel to
Costa Rica 37

Roble 285

Rosario de Naranjo 155

Route of the Saints 318

S

Sabalito *M3, C5* 337

Sacramento 160

safety 42

Sámara *M1, C3* 266

Samasati Lodge 392

San Gerardo de Dota
M3, A2 321

San Gerardo de Rivas
M3, A3 326

San Isidro de Coronado
M2, B3 164

San Isidro de El General
M3, B2 322

San José *M2, C3* 18, 83

Amón district 96, 105

Auditorio Nacional 98

bars 113

Centro Commercial El
Pueblo 98

day trips from the city
121

directory 130

eating 109

entertainment 115

festivals 116

history 90

Mercado Central 97

nightclubs 114

Otoya district 96, 105

Palacio Nacional 95

Parque Central 96

Parque Zoológico
Simón Bolívar 96

Paseo Colón 97, 106,
110

Plaza de la Cultura 93

Plaza de la
Democracía 94

sights 92

sleeping 100

shopping 116

Spirogyra 99

sport 119

Teatro Nacional 94

tourist office 89

tour operators 119

transport 86, 123

western suburbs 134

San José de la
Montaña 160

San Juan de Chicúa 169

San Juan de Valverde
Vega 151

San Lorenzo *M3, A1* 319

San Luís 212

San Marcus de Tarrazú
M3, A1 319

San Mateo 286

San Pablo de León
Cortes *M3, A1* 319

San Pedrillo 352,354

San Pedro de Poás *M2,*
B2 150

San Rafael de
Guatuso 203

San Rafael de
Heredia 161

San Ramón *M2, B2* 154

San Vito *M3, C5* 335

Santa Ana 137

Santa Clara *M2, B3* 367

Santa Cruz *M1, B3* 258

Santa Elena Cloud Forest
Reserve 217

Santa Elena *M1, B6* 206

Santa María de Dota *M3,*
A2 318

Santa Teresa *M1,*
inset 276

Santo Domingo
M1, B5 225

Sarchí *M2, B2* 151

security 42

self catering
accommodation 45

Selva Bananito Lodge
M2, C4 385

Selva Verde Lodge 186

sex tourism 42

shopping 55

Sierpe *M3, B3* 342

Siquirres *M2, B4* 369

Sistema Nacional de
Areas de Conservación
(SINAC) 423

Sixaola *M3, A6* 400

sleeping 43

sloths 428

snake bite treatment 78

Southern region 315

Spanish conquest 403

sport 419

stomach bugs 74

student travellers 26

sunburn 78

surfing 64

swimming 43

Tabacón Resort 198
Talamanca
  mountains 337
taxis 51
telecommunications 52
television 54
Tempisque ferry 223
Tenorio volcano 224
Térraba 418
tetanus 73
theatre 420
ticks 77
Tilarán *M1, B5* 202
tipping 41
Tortuguero *M2, A4* 378
toucans 435
tour operators 21
  *See also individual town
  directories*
tourism 416
tourist offices 40
  Costa Rican
  overseas 25
trade war 415
train travel 52
transport 33, 46
travellers' cheques 32
trekking 67
Trinidad 185
tummy bugs 74
Turrialba *M2, C4* 173

turtle watching 62,
  Tortuguero National
  Park 381
turtles 441
Typhoid 72

Ujarrás *M2, C4* 170
United Fruit
  Company 409
University of
  Costa Rica 99
Upala *M1, A5* 203
Uvita *M3, B2* 311

vaccination 31, 72
Valle de Coto Brus *M3,
  B4* 335
Vara Blanca M2, B2 150
Vásquez de Coronado,
  Juan 404
vegetarian restaurants in
  San José 112
Venado Caves 196
Venecia 188
visas 29
Volcán Arenal *M1, B6*
  195
Volcán Barva *M2, B2* 160
Volcán Irazú *M2, B3* 168
Volcán Miravalles M1, B4
  225

volunteer projects 28
  Monteverde 216

Walker, William 406
water 74
Water Land 147
websites 81
whitewater rafting 67,
  224
wildlife 423
wildlife reserves and
  refuges
  *See under 'Refugio' and
  'Reserva Biológica'*
Wilson Botanical
  Gardens *M3, C5* 335,
  337
windsurfing 69
women travellers 26, 43
working in Costa Rica 28

yellow fever 72
yoga 392
youth hostels 45

Zarcero *M2, B2* 153
Zoo Ave 148

Shorts

87 24 hours in the city
44 Accommodation price codes
34 Airlines and internet travel resources
333 ARADIKES
234 Arriving at Playa Nancite – safety in numbers?
115 ¡Bailamos!
93 Churches in San José
418 Costa Rica's provinces
370 Costa Rican bananas, global markets and fair trade
30 Costa Rican embassies abroad
303 Education in Manuel Antonio
329 Fancy a run?
231 Guanacaste Conservation Area awarded UNESCO recognition
378 Independent travelling to Tortuguero
152 Jump off a bridge and fly with the birds
203 La Fortuna or Monteverde?
178 Laguna Angostura – a new Arenal?
112 Modern day Mariachis
81 No romance please
175 Rafting the Reventazón and Pacuare
400 Raptor Watch – an aerial freeway
398 Riptides rumble Russian rouser
68 River ratings

322 Surviving the Talamanca Mountains
56 The fabulous four
89 The fine art of umbrella dipping
253 The Plight of the Baulas
202 The power of wind
373 The rebirth of Puerto Limón
222 Things to do in Guanacaste
368 Things to do in the Caribbean lowlands
282 Things to do in the Central Pacific
244 Things to do in the Nicoya Peninsula
182 Things to do in the northern region
344 Things to do in the Osa Peninsula
320 Things to do in the southern region
321 To the Pacific Coast – direct
20 Top 10 national parks (according to international visitors)
40 Touching down
395 Tough times in the Talamancas
28 UK-based organizations specializing in work abroad
168 Visiting Volcán Irazú
410 Walker Affair, the
214 What a waste
211 What is cloudforest?

Map index

144	Alajuela	**261**	Nicoya
388	Cahuita	**264**	Nosara
166	Cartago	**183**	Parque Nacional Braulio Carrillo
333	Ciudad Nelly		& Puerot Viejo loop
189	Ciudad Quesada	**328**	Parque Nacional Chirripó
46	Domestic flight destinations	**353**	Parque Nacional Corcovado
191	Fortuna	**377**	Parque Nacional Tortuguero
354	Golfito	**245**	Playa del Coco
356	Golfito detail	**413**	Provinces & provincial capitals
232	Guanacaste Conservation Area	**349**	Puerto Jiménez
156	Heredia	**372**	Puerto Limón
418	Indigenous reserves	**394**	Puerto Viejo de Talamanca
290	Jacó	**282**	Puntarenas
228	Liberia	**296**	Quepos
303	Manuel Antonio	**267**	Sámara
208	Monteverde & Santa Elena	**323**	San Isidro de El General
215	Monteverde Cloud Forest	**88, 90, 102**	San José
	Reserve Trails	**65**	Surf sites
273	Montezuma	**256**	Tamarindo
424	National parks	**173**	Turrialba
		195	Volcán Arenal

Advertisers

61	Amerispan, USA
68	Aventuras Naturales, Costa Rica
304	Casa Lydia, Costa Rica
299	Centro de Idiomas Del Pacifico, Costa Rica
24	Condor Journeys & Adventures, UK
34	Exodus Travels, UK
133	Intercultura Language & Cultural Center, Costa Rica
36	Journey Latin America, UK
22	Ladatco, USA
22	Last Frontiers, UK
351	Luna Lodge, Costa Rica
23	Mila Tours, USA
37	Reef & Rainforest Tours, UK
24	Sunvil, UK

Sales & distribution

Footprint Handbooks
6 Riverside Court
Lower Bristol Road
Bath BA2 3DZ England
F 01225 469141
F 01225 469461
discover
@footprintbooks.com

Africa sub-Sahara
IMA
14 York Rise
London, NW5 1ST
T 020 7267 8054
F 020 7485 8462

Australia & New Zealand
Woodslane
Unit 7/5 Vuko Place
Warriewood
NSW 2102
T 02 9970 5111
F 02 9970 5002

Austria
Freytag-Berndt u. Artaria KG
Brunnerstrasse 69
A-1231 Wien
T 01 869 9090-18
F 01 869 8855

Belgium
Craenen BVBA
Mechelsesteenweg 633
B-3020 Herent
T 016 23 90 90
F 016 23 97 11

Canada
Ulysses Travel Publications
4176 rue Saint-Denis
Montréal
Québec H2W 2M5
T 514 843 9882
F 514 843 9448

Denmark
Nordisk Korthandel
Studiestraede 26-30 B
DK-1455 Copenhagen K
T 3338 2638
F 3338 2648

Scanvik Books
Esplanaden 8B
DK-1263 Copenhagen K
T 3312 7766
F 3391 2882

Europe
Bill Bailey
16 Devon Square
Newton Abbott
Devon TQ12 2HR. UK
T 01626 331079
F 01626 331080

France
Guides Gallimard
5 rue Sébastian-Bottin
F-75007 Paris

Germany
GeoCenter ILH
Schockenriedstrasse 44
D-70565 Stuttgart
T 0711 781 94610
F 0711 781 94654

Greece
GC Eleftheroudakis
17 Panepistemiou
Athens 105 64
T 01 331 4180-83
F 01 323 9821

India
India Book Distributors
1007/ 1008 Arcadia
Nariman Point
Mumbai 400 021
T 022 282 4646
F 022 287 2531

Israel
EcoTrip Books & Maps
20a Ben Yehuda Street
Tel Aviv 63802
T 03 528 2811
F 03 528 8269

For a fuller list, see www.footprintbooks.com

Italy
Librimport
Via Biondelli 9
I-20141 Milano
T 02 8950 1422
F 02 8950 2811

Middle East
Peter Ward Book Exports
Unit 3 Taylors Yard
67 Alderbrook Road
London, SW12 8AD, UK
T 020 8772 3300
F 020 8772 3309

Netherlands
Nilsson & Lamm bv
Postbus 195
Pampuslaan 212
N-1380 AD Weesp
T 0294 494949
F 0294 494455

Norway
Schibsted Internasjonale Bøker AS
Apotekergt 12
PB 6972 St Olavs Plass
N-0130 Oslo
T 24 14 69 30

Pakistan
Say Publishing Pvt Ltd
SA 1-3 Shehnaz Arcade
Shaheed e Millat Road
Karachi
T 021 494 5541
F 021 583 4777

South Africa
Faradawn CC
PO Box 1903
Saxonwold 2132
T 011 885 1787
F 011 885 1829

South America
Humphrys Roberts Associates
Caixa Postal 801-0
Ag. Jardim da Gloria
06700-970 Cotia SP
Brazil
T 011 4702 4496
F 011 4702 6896

Southeast Asia
STP Distributors (Books) Pte Ltd
30 Old Toh Tuck Road #05-02
Sembawang Kimtrans Logistics Centre
Singapore 597654
T 6462 3112
F 6462 5761

Spain
Altaïr
Gran Via 616
08007 Barcelona
T 93 342 7170
F 93 342 7178

Sweden
Platypus Dyk & Reseböcker
Inspektorsgatan 4
S-252 27 Helsingborg
T 042 327590
F 042 129941

Switzerland
Office du Livre OLF
ZI3, Corminboeuf
CH-1701 Fribourg
T 026 467 5111
F 026 467 5666

Buchzentrum AG
Postfach
CH-4601 Olten
T 062 209 2525
F 062 209 2627

Tanzania
A Novel Idea
The Slipway
PO Box 76513
Dar es Salaam
T/F 022 2601088

USA
Publishers Group West
1700 Fourth Street
Berkeley, California 94710
T 510 528 1444
F 510 528 9555

Footprint travel list

Footprint publish travel guides to over 120 countries worldwide. Each guide is packed with practical, concise and colourful information for everybody from first-time travellers to travel aficionados. The list is growing fast and current titles are noted below. For further information check out the website **www.footprintbooks.com**

Andalucía Handbook
Argentina Handbook
Bali & the Eastern Isles Hbk
Bangkok & the Beaches Hbk
Barcelona Handbook
Bolivia Handbook
Brazil Handbook
Cambodia Handbook
Caribbean Islands Handbook
Central America & Mexico Hbk
Chile Handbook
Colombia Handbook
Costa Rica Handbook
Cuba Handbook
Cusco & the Sacred Valley Hbk
Dominican Republic Handbook
Dublin Handbook
East Africa Handbook
Ecuador & Galápagos Handbook
Edinburgh Handbook
Egypt Handbook
Goa Handbook
Guatemala Handbook
India Handbook
Indian Himalaya Handbook
Indonesia Handbook
Ireland Handbook
Israel Handbook
Jordan Handbook
Laos Handbook
Libya Handbook
London Handbook
Malaysia Handbook
Marrakech & the High Atlas Hbk
Myanmar Handbook
Mexico Handbook
Morocco Handbook

Namibia Handbook
Nepal Handbook
New Zealand Handbook
Nicaragua Handbook
Pakistan Handbook
Peru Handbook
Rajasthan & Gujarat Handbook
Rio de Janeiro Handbook
Scotland Handbook
Scotland Highlands & Islands Hbk
Singapore Handbook
South Africa Handbook
South American Handbook
South India Handbook
Sri Lanka Handbook
Sumatra Handbook
Syria & Lebanon Handbook
Thailand Handbook
Tibet Handbook
Tunisia Handbook
Turkey Handbook
Venezuela Handbook
Vietnam Handbook

Also available from Footprint
Traveller's Handbook
Traveller's Healthbook

Available at all good bookshops

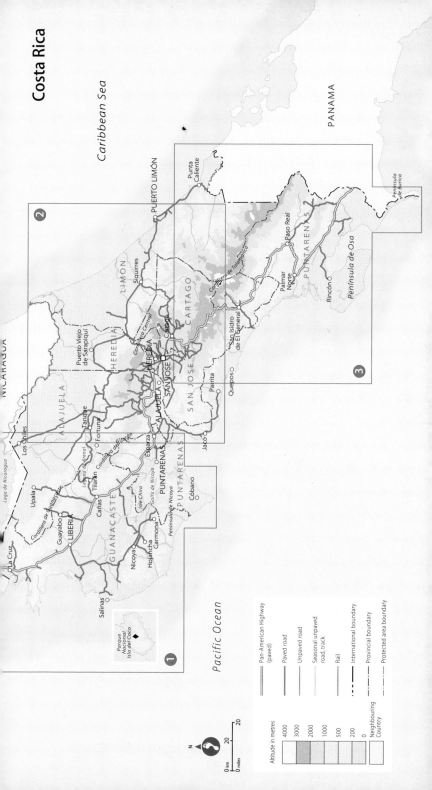

Costa Rica

Caribbean Sea

Pacific Ocean

NICARAGUA

PANAMA

Lago de Nicaragua

La Cruz
Salinas
Upala
Guayabo
LIBERIA
Los Chiles
GUANACASTE
Cañas
Tilarán
Cordillera de Guanacaste
Laguna de Arenal
Cordillera de Tilarán
Fortuna
Tanque
ALAJUELA
Puerto Viejo de Sarapiquí
HEREDIA
Cordillera Central
LIMÓN
Siquirres
PUERTO LIMÓN
Punta Caliente
Nicoya
Hojancha
Carmona
Isla Chira
Peninsula de Nicoya
Golfo de Nicoya
PUNTARENAS
Esparza
PUNTARENAS
HEREDIA
ALAJUELA
SAN JOSÉ
Cartago
CARTAGO
Cordillera de Talamanca
Cóbano
Jacó
Parrita
SAN JOSÉ
Quepos
San Isidro de El General
Palmar Norte
Paso Real
Rincón
Peninsula de Osa
PUNTARENAS
Peninsula de Burica

Parque Nacional Isla del Coco

1 **2** **3**

N

0 km   20
0 miles   20

Altitude in metres

4000
3000
2000
1000
500
0

Pan-American Highway (paved)
Paved road
Unpaved road
Seasonal unpaved road, track
Rail
International boundary
Provincial boundary
Protected area boundary

Neighbouring Country

Map 1

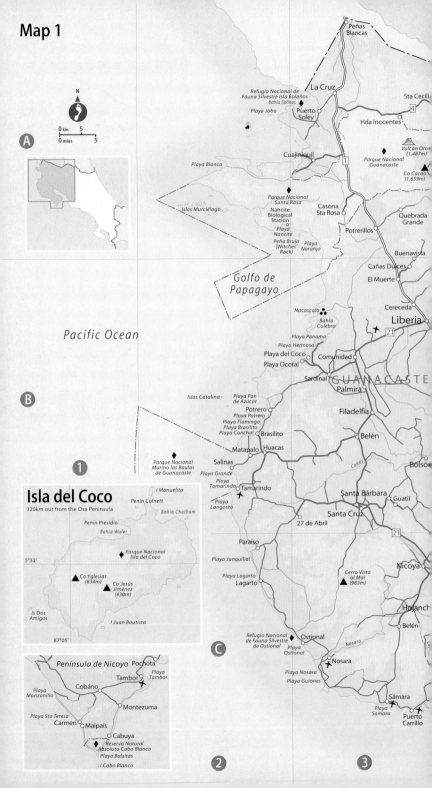

A

N

0 km 5
0 miles 5

Pacific Ocean

B

Peñas Blancas

La Cruz

Sta Cecilia

Refugio Nacional de Fauna Silvestre Isla Bolaños
Bahía Salinas
Playa Jobo
Puerto Soley

Hda Inocentes

4

Cuajiniquil

Volcán Oros (1,487m)

Parque Nacional Guanacaste

1

Co Cacao (1,659m)

Playa Blanca

Parque Nacional Santa Rosa
Nancite Biological Station
Playa Nancite
Peña Bruja (Witches' Rock)
Playa Naranjo

Casona Sta Rosa

Potrerillos

Quebrada Grande

Buenavista

Cañas Dulces

El Muerte

Islas Murciélago

Golfo de Papagayo

Cereceda

Liberia

Nacascolo
Bahía Culebra
Playa Panama
Playa Hermosa
Playa del Coco
Playa Ocotal

21

Comunidad

Sardinal

Palmira

GUANACASTE

Islas Catalina
Playa Pan de Azúcar
Potrero
Playa Potrero
Playa Flamingo
Playa Brasilito
Playa Conchal
Brasilito

Filadelfia

Belén

Matapalo
Huacas

Bolsó

Cañas

1

Parque Nacional Marino las Baulas de Guanacaste

Salinas
Playa Grande
Playa Tamarindo
Tamarindo
Playa Langosta

Santa Bárbara

Guatil

Isla del Coco

320km out from the Osa Peninsula

I Manuelita
Penin Colnett
Bahía Chatham
Penin Presidio
Bahía Wafer
Penin Colnett

5°32'

Parque Nacional Isla del Coco

Co Yglesias (634m)
Co Jesús Jiménez (430m)

Is Dos Amigos

I Juan Bautista

87°05'

27 de Abril

Santa Cruz

21

Paraíso

Nicoya

Playa Junquillal

Cerro Vista al Mar (983m)

Hojanch

Playa Lagarto
Lagarto

Belén

C

Refugio Nacional de Fauna Silvestre de Ostional
Playa Ostional

Ostional

Nosara

Península de Nicoya

Pochota

Playa Nosara
Playa Guiones

Playa Manzanillo
Cobáno
Tambor
Playa Tambor

Playa Sta Teresa
Carmen
Montezuma
Malpaís
Cabuya
Reserva Natural Absoluto Cabo Blanco
Playa Balsitas
I Cabo Blanco

Sámara
Playa Samara
Puerto Carrillo

2

3

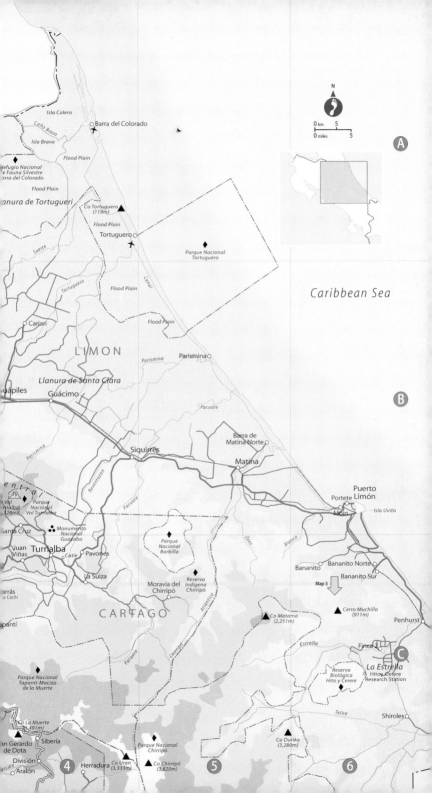

N

0 km 5
0 miles 5

A

Isla Calero

Barra del Colorado

Caño Bravo

Isla Brava

Refugio Nacional *e Fauna Silvestre* *arra del Colorado*

Flood Plain

Flood Plain

lanura de Tortugueri

Co Tortuguero (119m)

Flood Plain

Tortuguero

Parque Nacional Tortuguero

Caribbean Sea

Suerte

Tortuguero

Flood Plain

Canal

Cariari

Flood Plain

L I M O N

Parismina

Parismina

Llanura de Santa Clara

uápiles

Guácimo

Pacuare

B

Reventazón

Siquirres

Barra de Matina Norte

Pacuare

Matina

Puerto Limón

entral

Vol urrialba 28m)

Parque Nacional Vol Turrialba

Portete

Moín

Isla Uvita

anta Cruz

Monumento Nacional Guayabo

Juan Viñas

Turrialba

Catie

Pavones

La Suiza

Parque Nacional Barbilla

Zent

Blanco

Bananito

Bananito Norte

Bananito Sur

Map 3

Moravia del Chirripó

Reserva Indígena Chirripó

Cerro Muchilla (911m)

Penhurst

arrás o Cachí

C A R T A G O

Co Matama (2,251m)

Atlántico

Chirripó

Finca J

Penhurst

C

pantí

Estrella

La Estrella

Hitoy Cerere Research Station

Parque Nacional Tapantí-Macizo de la Muerte

Pacuare

Reserva Biológica Hito y Cerere

La Muerte 491m)

an Gerardo de Dota

Siberia

Teliré

Shiroles

División

Aralón

4

Herradura

Co Uran (3,333m)

Parque Nacional Chirripó

Co Chirripó (3,820m)

5

Co Durika (3,280m)

6

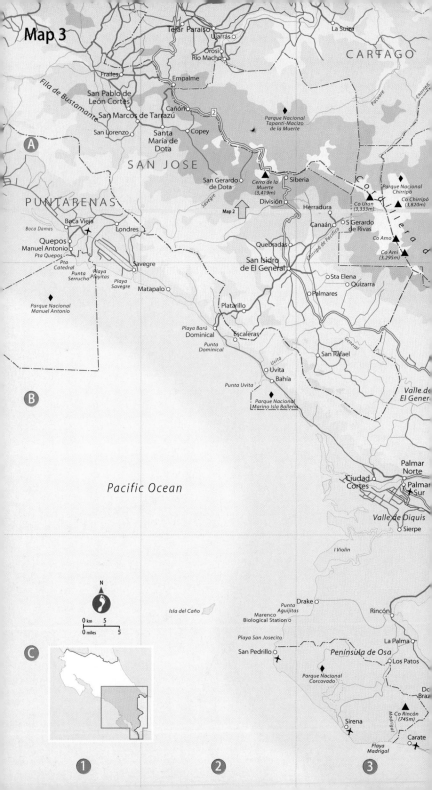

www.footprintbooks.com
A new place to visit

Acknowledgements

There's a lot of tourism in Costa Rica and a lot of ground to cover when trying to write a travel guide to the country. Many, many people have been involved in the creation and production of this guide from inception to bookshelf.

What you hold in your hands is the result of hard work, dedication and unrequited generosity on the part of more people than there is space to mention here. Naturally those thanks are extended to you if not stated here.

Firstly many thanks are due to the Instituto Costarricense de Turismo for their generous assistance and useful contacts throughout the country and in particular to the warm smiles and friendly assistance of Emilia Gonzalez, Susana Orozco, Gerardo Mendez and Rodrigo Herrera "Perkins" Rodriguez.

Secondly a long list of thanks to individuals who assisted and contributed in varying degrees. Many thanks to Dr Caroline Harcourt for her timely return from Ecuador to write the wildlife section and her patience in dealing with my endless meddling.

Purni Morell was a welcome British face in San Isidro de El General with whom to share a supposed sarcastic wit over a few beers. She also covered ground that I could not reach either through time or weather limitations.

Andre Vltchek was vital in filling some of the missing links that invariably appear once you've left a country. His dogged persistence also got some little snippets that I would have given up on a lot earlier.

Many thanks also to Katie Box and Ross Mackenzie who together provided a steady stream of reliable information when visiting the country.

In Costa Rica a few specialist have provided invaluable assistance. Patricia Bliss heads the Costa Rica B&B group with over 200 members throughout the country. Simon Ellis kindly contributed a section on bird watching, Jerry Ruhlow generously provided information on inland and ocean fishing. Fernando Esquivel of Rios Tropicales provided help with the whitewater rafting information and was essential in converting another novice to the excitement of his sport, as was Victor Gallo of Tropical Bungee.

Candyce Speck provided information on Pavones as weather defeated my attempts to get that far south, and Peter Disch-Lauxmann shared his passion for the distant and exclusive Cocos Island. Surfing information came from my good friend Phil Miller, surfer, videographer and all round jolly nice chap, www.dreamingfish.co.uk

More distant assistance came from Phil Withers Green in many ways, not least through his friendship with Allan Templeton which was beneficial to me while staying in Manuel Antonio.

Last of the specific mentions are to Tricolor and Europcar rentals who provided vehicles for different sections of the tour round this wonderful country. I guess I should also thank the crowd of guys at La Alondra on the north shore of Lake Arenal who interrupted a wedding to break in to my car saving me an expensive and rather embarrasing phone call to the rental company.

The great thing about writing a guide book is that you have the chance to stick your nose in where ever you think there may be something of interest. Thanks to all those friendly *Ticos* who tolerated my endless and occasionally bizarre questions.

Closer to home, the Footprint family deserve many thanks for their support and collectively responding to impatient requests with impressive immediacy. In particular thanks to Rachel Fielding for the challenging opportunity to write a guide on Costa Rica and her patience, to Sarah Thorowgood for having the painful task of editing such a book and to whoever it was that got me home from the Christmas party. As ever, thanks to Ben Box, who should be partially blamed for my interest in this part of the world and Footprint.

Thanks to my family who for reasons beyond me tolerate my interest in travel with a patience bordering on sainthood, and to Tessa who I love dearly.

Despite all the work of many individuals in putting together this book it should come together as one piece and will hopefully prove invaluable in helping you plan your trip to Costa Rica and help you enjoy your trip while you are in Costa Rica. Wishing you safe travels.

I've said it before and doubtless will say it again – can I come out now.